MIRROR ON

1941

Cover photo: Soldiers stand around the wreckage of Rudolph Hess's Messerschmitt ME-110 plane from which he had bailed out over Scotland, 10th May 1941.

ISBN: 978-1-9993652-8-8

INDEX

INDEX - 3

INDEX - 4

Daily Mirror

JAN 1

No. 11,563   ONE PENNY
Registered at the G.P.O. as a Newspaper.

BE of good courage, and let us behave ourselves valiantly for our people, and for the cities of our God . . . .

Help everyone his neighbour . . . .

Stand fast in faith . . . . Be strong.

From the Old and New Testaments.

NINETEEN FORTITUDE HOPES, FEARS

THE NEW YEAR WILL BRING DECISIVE EVENTS IN THE WAR AGAINST HITLER AND HIS PUPPET MUSSOLINI.

Official spokesmen yesterday were confident in their predictions of R.A.F. expansion to a smashing force never yet seen, of a Victory Army finally equipped for action anywhere. But there were three notes of caution.

Bombs.—Yesterday the Government agreed on the principle of compulsion for A.R.P. Fire-watching is to be compulsory for all businesses and factories, large and small.

The principle may be extended to other forms of Civil Defence. Details are being worked out.

Mr. Herbert Morrison, Minister of Home Security, announcing this made a radio call to all citizens to man homes, offices, shops and factories against the fire-bomb menace. (See col. 1, this page.)

It is revealed that only bad weather stopped the second wave of the fire-blitz on London early on Sunday night.

Spring will remove that obstacle and Britain may expect bigger raids than any yet.

Invasion.—An R.A.F. spokesman said: "Invasion must be regarded for a long time as a standing dish on the Hitler menu.

"We can have no doubt that Hitler has laid on a thorough detailed plan for the invasion of this country as soon as conditions may be favourable in the early spring.

"Hitler has got to go on thrusting. He wants to get the war over as quickly as possible. I think he has got to come at us one way or another and keep on coming with all he knows."

Official surveys of Britain's war effort on land and sea and in the air declared that—

A great expansion of R.A.F. striking power in men and machines will grow like a rolling snowball 1941 will be the R.A.F.'s great year.

More and more support will be given to the Navy

Italy may lose Libya, Eritrea, Somaliland and Abyssinia.

Britain's Mediterranean Fleet has been used in an offensive which has completely changed the situation in Eastern Europe—if not in the world.

Food.—Lord Woolton, Food Minister, warned the nation that the danger to our food supplies is much worse than in the last war. (See page 11.)

"DAY RAID ON GERMANY"

Four R.A.F. planes over Germany yesterday afternoon, says Official German News Agency. Two, agency claims, shot down by A.A. fire. Others "dropped bombs in fields."—Reuter.

GOVT. TO CONSCRIPT FOR A.R.P.

MR. HERBERT MORRISON, Minister of Home Security, announcing that the Government is to introduce conscription for A.R.P., broadcast to all citizens last night a call to organise fire-watching parties everywhere—immediately.

The Government does not at present envisage general conscription for service or training. It does, however, intend to use its powers as soon as necessary to enforce men and women to train for fire, ambulance and rescue service wherever these services need strengthening.

All Included

Saying the principle of compulsion was yesterday affirmed by the Government, Mr. Morrison indicated that compulsory part-time service applied not only to fire-fighting, "but possibly to other aspects of civil defence as well."

He went on:

"Details are now being worked out and will be made known as soon as possible. Compulsion will apply to everyone of every grade—managers and office workers, as well as manual workers—as the needs of the situation may require.

"Factories and businesses of all kinds, large and small, will be subject to severe penalties for any neglect of their obligations.

"But don't wait for all that. There isn't the time. Tackle the job at once. Not one single house or build-
Continued on Back Page, Col. 4

★

Hitler Has the Same Idea

"**S**OLDIERS of the National Socialist Army of the great German Reich, the year 1941 will bring the completion of the great victory in our history."

That is what Hitler told his soldiers yesterday.

His New Year's Order of the Day to the German Army speaks of "glorious victories of singular greatness" on land, at sea and in the air. Then he declares: I know every one of you will do your duty.

God Almighty will not desert those who, threatened by a world, are determined to help themselves with bold hearts. (See page 2.)

★

REVELS IN CRYPT

BY A SPECIAL CORRESPONDENT

DEEP in the crypt below St. Martin - in - the - Fields 500 men and women civilians, soldiers, sailors and W.A.A.F.s danced the Old Year out beneath festoons and coloured lights last night.

Then, as the church clock chimed out the last stroke of midnight, the whole gathering knelt on the stone flags and sang the hymn, "O God our help in ages past."

The curate, the Rev. A. Motley, stood among them and recited two short prayers—one of thanks that they had been spared the horrors of air-raids in the last hours of the Old Year; the other a prayer for victory in the New Year.

Tears welled in the eyes of many of the women, nearly all of whom were regular shelterers in the crypt.

Comrades of War

Some slipped away to pray before the crib in an adjoining shelter.

After the prayers 500 people, including some children, stood with hands linked and sang "Auld Lang Syne."

Soldiers and their sweethearts passing in Trafalgar-square heard the singing and went below to join in.

The dance, which was free, had been organised out of the church shelter fund. For four hours before midnight old and young had danced in the strange surroundings.

Men of the Fighting Services took the floor and gave an impromptu cabaret

Hundreds of people greeted the New Year from the steps of St. Paul's amid the blackened ruins of Sunday's fire-blitz.

Miss Noreen Helen Rosemary Bailey, youngest daughter of the late Sir Abe Bailey, millionaire sportsman, became engaged yesterday to Flight-Lieutenant Peter A. Simmons, who won the D.F.C. last July. Mr. Simmons' father was a Rhodesian.

Passenger Train Cuts for Coal

Some temporary reductions in certain railway passenger services may be necessary in London and the provinces.

The reason, the Ministry of Transport announces, is the heavy movement of coal supplies and the greatly increased freight traffic as a result of the nation's war effort.

Notice will be given locally of services affected.

FAILED IN WAR JOBS —HONOURED

BY A SPECIAL CORRESPONDENT

THREE failures are consoled for their lack of success in vital wartime jobs by high awards in the New Year's Honours List.

Lord Camrose is made a viscount. In September, 1939, he was appointed chief assistant to Lord Macmillan, Minister of Information and Controller of Press Relations. Five weeks later he gave up his job.

Field-Marshal Sir Edmund Ironside becomes a baron. Known as the Army's tough guy, Sir Edmund was Inspector-General of the Overseas Forces when war broke out, but was immediately made Chief of the Imperial General Staff. On May 26 he left that job for another of less importance.

Sir Kenneth Lee is given a baronetcy "for public services."

Sir Kenneth, a Lancashire cotton chief, was Director of Radio Relations and Communications in the early days of the Ministry of Information.

In November, 1939, he was made honorary Director-General. In August, 1940, he resigned and returned to Lancashire.

Mr. Duff Cooper, Minister of Information, said: "I asked him to remain as Director-General and subsequently I came to the conclusion that a change was desirable. His resignation was received on August 7."

King's Cousin a D.S.O.

But the list which includes one viscount, four barons, three baronets, two privy councillors, one Knight of the Garter and twenty nine knights, is not made up of failures. Many of the names are of men and women with a high record of service and achievement.

Lord Louis Mountbatten, cousin of the King, is awarded the D.S.O.

He brought his ship, H.M.S. Kelly safely to port after she had been crippled by a German torpedo off the enemy coast, defying air attacks and onslaughts by surface craft.

Lord Louis is one of five naval officers awarded the decoration.

The list includes foremen and workers in war factories, and the citizen heroes who man the home front.

Knighthoods go to men who guide our war production, to men of science and art.

Professor William Bragg, Cavendish
Continued on Back Page, Col. 1

AIR WAR LULL

The Luftwaffe were quiet again up to a late hour last night—grounded the other side of the cloud and fog in the Channel.

For several hours after darkness fell there were no raids in any part of Britain. Activity during the day was confined to a few isolated attacks by single aircraft in Kent and Essex, making a raid free night due to bad weather.

One raider, after dropping nine small calibre high explosives on an East Anglian town in the afternoon, flew low and machine-gunned the streets. There were no casualties.

Daily Mirror

JAN 6

No. 11,567 — ONE PENNY
Registered at the G.P.O. as a Newspaper.

BARDIA IS OURS

WITH SIX GENERALS AND 25,000 MEN

BARDIA has fallen. Six Italian generals, including the Commander of the Bardia forces, and more than 25,000 troops are our prisoners.

At midnight last night British G.H.Q. at Cairo issued this dramatic communique:

"All resistance at Bardia ceased at 1.30 p.m. today. The town, with total forces defending it, and all stores and equipment, are now in our hands.

"General Bergonzoli, commanding the Italian forces at Bardia, another corps commander, and four senior generals are prisoners of war.

"It is not yet possible to make a full count, but prisoners so far captured exceed 25,000. Amongst other booty captured or destroyed are forty-five light and five medium tanks."

Messages from the front last night revealed that the defences of Mussolini's "impregnable" Libyan stronghold were virtually smashed in thirty-six hours under one of the most brilliant assaults in military history.

Australian infantry, fighting in perfect co-operation with British mechanised units, R.A.F. fighter-bombers, and the big ships of the Navy, burst through Bardia's iron ring and carved up the Italian defence forces.

By 6 p.m. on Saturday, 15,000 prisoners had been taken, and most of

★ ★ ★

French Cut Road

A detachment of Free French Marines took a very active part in the British attack on Bardia. Now this force, patrolling behind the positions still held by the Italians, has cut the road from Bardia to Tobruk.

★ ★ ★

the points of resistance mopped up.

The final act came with the surrender of the remainder of the Italian garrison.

The Italian flag was hauled down from the mast over Government House inside the town.

Richard Dimbleby, the B.B.C. observer, who was with the first of the British troops to enter Bardia, told how one of our officers, accompanied by seven men, their rifles slung over their shoulders, approached the mouth of a cave which they had decided to search.

The officer went to the cave and shouted, "Come out!"—and 2,000 officers and men, fully armed, walked out and handed themselves over!

They then walked five miles down the road—under the guard of a solitary infantryman!

Amazing Speed

The attacks were delivered with amazing speed and precision.

The Australians, backed up by British armoured forces, dashed through Bardia like an express train. They carried out to the split second the timetable of operations drawn up by their commanders at advance headquarters near the Libyan frontier.

One deep ravine named Wadi Gerfan cuts almost clear across the circle of defences westwards from Bardia, forming a natural barrier against tanks. But it was no barrier to the Australians. They simply charged across it, pouring bullets from their guns.

A combination of coolness and dash had taken them through the enemy barbed-wire positions.

Australian sappers advanced and cut the barbed wire. Australian infantry followed and kept the Italian first line busy while the sappers coolly blew up the sides of tank traps, filled them in with earth, and smashed a strong double apron of fencing.

Through the gaps swept British mechanised units, led by a famous

Continued on Back Page, Col. 5

BEAT FIRE RAID

HUNDREDS of incendiary bombs which were dropped on a London district last night were put out before they could start a single fire.

There seemed to be as many fire watchers as there were bombs. Men, women and boys rivalled each other in the speed with which they dealt with them.

The bombs were dropped by two waves of raiders.

Having put every one of them out, the watchers stood in their doorways and in the streets singing, "We want some more!"

They had not long to wait. A third wave of bombers came over shortly afterwards and dropped more incendiaries. These were dealt with just as speedily as the others.

100 Bombs—3 Fires

"I feel I must tell you how marvellous all these people have been," an onlooker told the Daily Mirror.

"It really was an amazing sight," he said. "When the incendiaries began to fall, scores of people rushed to tackle them. Everyone joined in, sharing stirrup pumps and sand, and the bombs were soon put out."

In another London district fire-watchers nearly equalled this achievement.

About a hundred incendiaries came down on houses and in the roads, but only three fires were started.

These, however, were soon got under control by the fire brigade.

London was the main target of the raiders last night, but the raid

Continued on Back Page, Col. 3

CITY WATCHERS WERE READY

The City of London had a fairly quiet time last night. The smell of burning still hung in the air of empty streets. There was the usual drone of the adventurous low-flyer, the pounding of the guns, the momentary flashes in the sky.

But there was a difference. If the German fire raiders had chosen last night for their mass attacks on the City's square mile, there would have been a very different story to tell.

The fire-bomb fighters were up on roofs of their workplaces as soon as darkness fell.

The great difference was that these watchers now have clear and definite instructions. They are determined to prevent another devastating fire-blitz.

At the sound of guns they ran to their posts.

You couldn't see them, but you could hear them shouting to each other over the rooftops. They were ready. No doubts about what to do should it come again.

The men who did it—General Sir Archibald Wavell, brains behind the Western Desert campaign, and a typical Aussie, one of the shock troops who went through Bardia "like an express train."

STALIN CALLS 4 ENVOYS

Soviet Ambassadors to Bulgaria, Hungary, Yugoslavia and Rumania are reported to be hurrying to Moscow for conferences with Stalin about Germany's increasing flow of troops into the Balkans.

Soviet quarters in Belgrade said that the trip was in connection with "new military developments in Rumania and Hungary and the German troop movements towards Dobrudja."

It is reported in Budapest that Bulgaria has been asked to allow the passage of German troops, and threatened with invasion if she refuses.

The Bulgarian Communist Party distributed leaflets in Sofia at the week-end stating that "Soviet Russia will not allow a single German soldier to set foot in Bulgaria."

From Bukarest it is reported that eight hotels in the Rumanian capital had been occupied exclusively by German staff officers, and a German establishment called "Expeditionary Force Headquarters" has been set up there.

Dinner Was Out of Joint

MANY families in and around London sat down to dinner yesterday without the traditional Sunday joint. For thousands it was the firs meatless Sunday of the war.

Some bought sausages—but they were soon sold out—some had rabbit pie, some managed to get fish, some families pooled what food they could buy and had a communal meal.

As for the rest of the meatless ones, they used their "iron ration"—tins of food they stored before the war.

The Mixed Grill

In a south-eastern suburb, two families pooled their food. One of them had some kidneys and liver, the other sausages and bacon. So they sat down to mixed grill for dinner!

A Ministry of Food official said yesterday:—

"No district was without meat though supplies had to be cut.

"If all of the butchers had measured out their supplies properly there would have been enough for everyone."

Butchers disagreed. A Woking (Surrey) butcher told the Daily Mirror:—

"To try to keep my customers satisfied I closed my shop on Friday afternoon, although I still had some meat left. I thought that I might get some more supplies through for Saturday.

Shops Crowded

"They did not arrive. I opened on Saturday as usual, but within two or three hours all the meat had gone.

"We all had the same trouble here."

Rabbit pie and sausage toad-in-the-hole were the Sunday dinners for practically all East London families. The few available joints—frozen mutton—were sold to the first of the Saturday morning customers.

Many lined up at butchers' shops two hours before they were due to open. The queues became so large at some East Ham and Barking shops that police had to take control.

In Ilford hundreds of housewives rushed for sausages, and quickly "No Sausages" notices appeared in the grocers' windows.

At Leyton rabbits were plentiful. Few butchers were able to supply full ration, but some managed a 1s. 8d. ration to the Saturday morning customers. Most butchers had an afternoon delivery, but the meat was sold as fast as it could be cut up.

At Islington, London, N., some shops were closed at 2.30 p.m.

Daily Mirror

JAN 7

No. 11,568   ONE PENNY
Registered at the G.P.O. as a Newspaper.

With increasing forces in the Balkans, Hitler, according to German rumours, is planning an attack on Greece by moving troops through Rumania and Bulgaria. The map shows the new danger zone.

HITLER'S RUMOUR ATTACK

THE Nazis flooded every news channel in the world yesterday with reports that Bulgaria had accepted an ultimatum to allow German troops across her territory. The National Broadcasting Company of New York said that tomorrow was believed to be the day when Hitler's forces would move into Bulgaria, and that he had already sent 2,500 planes.

Hitler was aiming a mysterious "rumour offensive" at the Balkans.

News agencies and the U.S. radio reported that Dr. Filoff, Bulgaria's Premier, had received the German ultimatum on Saturday and had been forced to agree.

From Nazi propaganda centres in the Balkans came similar statements.

German official quarters in Belgrade went further. They put out reports that the Soviet Union had agreed that the Germans should enter and take over Bulgarian territory, and that in return Germany had "agreed" that Russia should take over Finland and Rumanian Moldavia.

Bulgaria would be rewarded, said these sources, with a slice of Rumania —Northern Dobrudja. In fact, Rumania would be completely carved up, Hungary getting all Transylvania, with the German Army ruling what remained.

Later additions from this quarter said that the Germans would move into Bulgaria when the Danube froze up, but would not "enter" Greece unless Britain showed signs of making Greece the starting point for a drive northwards.

The first of these Belgrade reports held the implication that Stalin's foreign policy depends on Hitler's "agreement." They looked like kite-flying to test out Soviet reaction.

Moscow denied any knowledge of the alleged Nazi ultimatum to Bulgaria.

Turkey Ready

One explanation of the mystery may be that Hitler is trying to bolster the sagging Axis prestige in South-East Europe by scaring the Balkan States.

Hitler, by means of veiled threats and rumours, may be trying to make up the diplomatic ground lost by his partner Mussolini.

This does not rule out the possibility that Hitler is determined to strike at Greece through Bulgaria and repair the tottering fortunes of the Italians.

He presumably cannot allow Mussolini to stagger indefinitely from disaster to disaster.

Turkish authorities realise this. They stated in Istanbul last night that they consider a German occupation of Bulgaria an ever-present danger, and that if it materialises, Turkey will fight.

TAKES BOMBED FAMILY OF 11

Mr. Mitchell Hepburn, Prime Minister of Ontario, Canada, has taken under his wing a family of thirteen who were bombed out of their home in London.

He calls his act "an experiment in practical Christianity."

The family are Mr. and Mrs. Cyril Cooke and their eleven children, who reached Canada by way of Trinidad. They have been established on the largest of Mr. Hepburn's tenant farms in South Yarmouth, a township of Ontario.

Their storage bins are well filled with potatoes, onions, carrots and other vegetables, and there are stocks of sugar and flour.—Exchange.

BRITISH GO ON TO TOBRUK

WITH the R.A.F. battering a path for them, advanced British troops are approaching Tobruk, Mussolini's next port along the Libyan coast, which has a strong garrison and from which the only counter-move by General Graziani could be made after the fall of Bardia.

The continued British and Imperial advance was made evident in a British communiqué issued yesterday at G.H.Q., Cairo, Egypt. It said:

"While clearance of the battlefield at Bardia is progressing, advanced elements of our forces are now approaching the Tobruk area.

"Prisoners counted at Bardia number over 30,000, with quantities of tanks, guns, equipment and stores of all sorts."

This communiqué may be taken as an indication that the next objective may be Tobruk.

How our airmen are paving the way for the land forces was shown in an R.A.F. Middle East communiqué yesterday. It said:—

Tripoli Bombed

"With increasing enemy air activity over Eastern Libya yesterday, fighter aircraft of the R.A.F. were engaged in several combats. As a result eleven enemy aircraft (seven CR.42s and four S.79s) were destroyed.

"Bombing activity throughout yesterday and the previous night was concentrated on Tobruk.

"One very large fire was started and was visible from Bardia.

It was also announced last night that Tripoli was heavily raided by bomber aircraft of the R.A.F. during the night of January 4-5.

"Several tons of bombs were dropped on the target, which included the power station, Customs buildings, five wharves and shipping in the harbour," says an R.A.F. communiqué.

"Large fires were started near the power station and among the Customs buildings. They were clearly visible thirty miles out to sea and continued burning fiercely.

"Other bombs straddled merchant vessels and naval units in the harbour.

Continued on Back Page, Col. 3

SOUTH AMERICAN COUNTRIES FIGHT HALF-HOUR BATTLE

A half-hour's battle has been fought by forces of Ecuador and Peru on their frontier, it was reported by the U.S. radio last night.

Ecuador accuses Peru of aggression. It was stated in Quito, Ecuador's capital, that three Peruvian planes flew over Ecuadorian territory and that a Peruvian patrol violated the Ecuadorian frontier.

Ecuador, on the north-west coast of South America, has a population of about 3,000,000. Peru, which lies south, is about twice as large as Ecuador, and has about 6,500,000 people.

MADE A KNIGHT AT WORK

A MAN knelt on one knee before the King in a Sheffield factory yesterday, while hundreds of workmen looked on.

The King touched the kneeling man on each shoulder with a sword handed to him by his equerry.

It was the first time the accolade of knighthood had ever been conferred beneath a factory roof.

The new knight was Sir Allan Grant, managing director of the Sheffield works of Thomas Firth and John Brown, Ltd., where the ceremony took place. Sir Allan's name was in the New Year's Honours List.

When Mr. Grant's name appeared in the Honours List, and it was learned that the King and Queen were to visit Sheffield, a special request, the Daily Mirror was told, was made that he might receive the knighthood in his own works before his own workmen.

The King readily granted the request, and a dais was erected in a workshop in readiness for the ceremony.

It was kept a secret from Sir Allan till he arrived at the works yesterday morning.

"When I got to the works," Sir Allan told the Daily Mirror, "I was told that someone had made a suggestion that the ceremony should be performed before my own workpeople, and that it was the King's wish that the knighthood should be conferred as suggested.

Three-Hours' Tour

"Of course, I was delighted, and readily agreed, and I think our workmen were delighted, too.

"The King congratulated me on my work for Sheffield's industry and expressed satisfaction with what Sheffield is doing for the war effort."

The King and Queen were making a tour of the bomb-damaged city in fulfilment of a promise made after the savage German raid on December 12.

For three hours the King and Queen walked through the damaged streets talking with the men and women who had shown such resolute spirit on that terrible night.

The Queen talked to the wives and mothers—many of whom had lost their homes—with sympathy and understanding.

TOWN BURNED DOWN

The town of Cordial, in the Spanish province of Castelone, has been destroyed by fire, says Rome radio.

WAR OFFICE 'WARNED OFF'

BY A SPECIAL CORRESPONDENT

ON the door of a weekly newspaper office at 4, Old Mitrecourt, off Fleet-street, London, is fixed

IMPORTANT NOTICE

Instructions are hereby given to all concerned that in the event of any War Office staff officer again entering my premises after business hours and removing property, without my authority, the police are to be notified immediately.

Signed, W. R. Hipwell, Founder and Editor.

The office is that of "Reveille," weekly newspaper for the Forces.

The notice is printed on a sheet of the journal's notepaper, which bears on the top the name of Mr. Winston Churchill as chief patron of "Reveille."

The posting of the notice is the culmination of events which followed the publication in last Friday's Daily Mirror of the news that, in their current issue "Reveille" had revealed cases of abuse of leave privileges by soldiers.

On Friday morning a War Office official rang the offices of "Reveille" and asked for four copies of that day's issue to be sent immediately to Whitehall.

"I was given this message when I reached the office," Mr. Hipwell told the "Daily Mirror" yesterday. "I did not comply with the request.

"For one thing, there were at that time no copies of the paper in the

Continued on Back Page, Col. 3

AMY IS FEARED KILLED

FAMOUS airwoman Amy Johnson is feared to have been drowned when her plane crashed in the Thames Estuary on Sunday.

The story was revealed yesterday by an eye-witness who said he watched the plane glide down into the water and sink before help could reach it.

A seaman from a balloon ship dived into the icy waters to try to save one person in the aircraft. He is now lingering between life and death, unable to say whether the survivor he clutched by the collar for a few moments before the waves parted them was Miss Johnson or another occupant of the plane.

The eye-witness, who was a passenger on a ship, said that suddenly an aircraft was seen flying at about 750ft.

"It started to climb," he said, "and suddenly it turned and started a long glide downwards, coming at right angles to the path of the ship.

"Something white fluttered out and dropped into the sea. It might have been a parachute. If it was, it was a desperate jump, for the plane was less than 200ft. above the water.

"Then it hit a wave, hung suspended for a moment, and nosed over.

Amy Johnson.

Later a speedboat went out to search for Miss Johnson, but she could not be found, although the flight authorisation papers from her machine were discovered.

Miss Johnson was employed as a ferry pilot for Air Transport Auxiliary.

Amy Johnson's name was on everybody's lips when, in 1930, she flew solo to Australia—the first woman to do so.

In 1933 she and Jim Mollison flew non-stop to America in thirty-nine hours.

Amy and Jim were married in 1932, but the marriage was dissolved in 1938.

Daily Mirror

JAN 8

No. 11,569 — ONE PENNY
Registered at the G.P.O. as a Newspaper.

ITALIAN C.O.s QUIT

THREE Blackshirt commanders deserted their troops during the battle for Bardia, leaving the regular commanders to fight on.

This was announced last night in a special communiqué issued from G.H.Q., Cairo.

Tripoli and Tobruk were given another bashing by the R.A.F.

A Middle East communiqué last night said:

"Tripoli was again raided heavily by bomber aircraft of the R.A.F. on the night of January 6-7. Several tons of bombs were dropped among motor vessels in the centre of the harbour causing a series of explosions and clouds of smoke.

"One direct hit was registered amidships on a large motor vessel and was followed by explosions. Several smaller cargo ships were probably hit.

"Fires were caused among Customs

GREEK WARSHIPS SHELL VALONA

Greek destroyers, sailing unmolested into the Adriatic, Mussolini's "home waters," bombarded the Albanian port of Valona.

This was announced by the Greek Admiralty last night.

Sixty shells were fired before the destroyers withdrew.

A Greek spokesman stated that Italy's vast losses in Albania included 35,000 sick and wounded evacuated from Valona.—Reuter and Associated Press.

buildings and wharves. The power station was bombarded and much damage caused. All our aircraft returned safely.

"A further raid was carried out on Tobruk by our heavy bombers. Widespread fires were caused, which were visible from thirty miles away, among barracks, stores, sheds and motor transport concentrations. Our aircraft returned without loss to their bases."

British mechanised forces which swept on to the outer defences of Tobruk found the Italian aerodrome, El Adem, deserted.

They captured forty Italian aircraft which had been put out of action by R.A.F. bombing.

El Adem, air base for Tobruk, is fifteen miles south of the town and sixty miles west of Bardia.

The push on Tobruk means that General Wavell's troops are giving the enemy no rest.

Since December 9, when our offensive action began, we have taken fully 70,000 prisoners. It is estimated that, including these, we have put 94,000 Italian troops out of action.

ITALY LOSES 500 PLANES

More than 500 Italian planes have been shot down in Africa since Italy's entry into the war, it was stated in Cairo last night. British losses are about eighty machines.

American planes are now operating with the R.A.F. in Egypt.—Reuter.

Cancelled by Cash

HIS BREATH SAVED HER

BY A SPECIAL CORRESPONDENT

A GIRL in danger of suffocating under a pile of wreckage cried to her fiancé, "I want to die quickly."

Instead, he took gulps of air and breathed into her mouth, squeezing her ribs to make her breathe. In this way he kept her alive for eight hours until rescued.

Philip Henry Mellor, of Buxton, thirty, a bank clerk, and Molly Beadle, twenty-two, of Taunton, have worked in the same bank at Bristol for five years.

Miss Beadle is still in hospital, and Mellor is staying in Bristol until he can take her home.

She told me yesterday of the amazing courage and devotion of the man she loves.

"There is no doubt whatever that Harry saved my life," she said.

His Promise

"A woman a foot away from me died from suffocation an hour after the building was hit, and of the six other people who were standing in a hall with us only one, a girl next to Harry was dug out alive.

We had only just got engaged and it was really not official.

"We have only told our families so far as we had not meant to get married for six to eight months. But now I hope we shall be able to have our wedding very soon.

"Harry came up to tea with me at a hostel and was caught there by the blitz.

"He had always promised me that he would never leave me in a blitz and that he would protect me, but he offered at first to go outside and put out incendiary bombs.

"Harry and I were standing close

Continued on Back Page, Col. 1

LORD WOOLTON, Food Minister, warned Britain again yesterday: "The position of meat supplies is immediately difficult.... If we find we can't live up to the 1s. 6d. ration we shall reduce it."

But if you have money you can say, "To hell with rations," laugh at food coupons—and eat as much **RATIONED FOOD** as you wish.

The Cabinet, fully aware of this national scandal, has neglected to tackle it.

Now they must act. It is a problem easily solved. Introduce coupons for all restaurant meals and see that nobody gets more than his share.

The nation demands it.

Below Cassandra reveals how easy it is to gorge without coupons.

U.S. ARMS BIG FOUR

PRESIDENT ROOSEVELT has established a supreme directorate of four men to speed up arms production.

A statement signed by all four members of the new defence directorate says their task is "not only of critical importance, but of surpassing urgency."

Mr. William S. Knudsen is director-general, with Mr. Sydney Hillman, the Labour leader, as associate director-general.

The other members are Mr. Henry L. Stimson, Secretary for War, and Colonel Frank Knox, the Secretary for the Navy.—Associated Press and Reuter.

LORD REITH MAKES HIS REPORT TO CABINET

Lord Reith, Minister of Works and Buildings, has submitted his report on methods and machinery of post-war reconstruction to the Cabinet.

A statement will shortly be made on this report, when details will be given of how the recommendations which Lord Reith has made are to be carried out, and what his powers will be.

STOP THIS FOOD SCANDAL

By CASSANDRA

WITHIN five days I have eaten at least seven times my weekly meat ration, five times my bacon ration, nearly half a pound of butter, and have had so much sugar that I couldn't eat it all.

Not content with this debauch, I have swallowed saddle-of-hare in wine sauce, lobster thermidor, the inevitable (if you live that way!) caviare, Hungarian pork goulash, quails-in-aspic and truffled goose livers.

In addition, I have climbed outside two dozen oysters and a considerable quantity of fish, ranging from smoked salmon, by way of tunny, sardines and anchovies, to an enormous Dover sole.

This Everest of Food has been obtained without the loss of a single food coupon.

"Le Steak"

My stomach is stunned.

Without regard to the cost, it has fought in the grill rooms, in the restaurants, in the dives, in the butteries and in the buffets.

From the Savoy Hotel, where they still prefer to call it "Le Steak and Kidney Pudding," to the coffee-stall outside Marylebone Station, where you can eat pounds of delicious hot meat-pies, provided you have the money, I have ranged and ravaged the larder of Britain.

Money Does It!

I have neither deserved nor desired this food. The only consolation in this gutskrieg was that I entertained a London fireman and a war reserve policeman who—even if they didn't desire all the food—probably deserved the greater part of it.

The only quality (?) that has distinguished me from a housewife struggling to feed a husband and two children on six bob's worth of meat for seven days, has been that I borrowed a big fistful of money from the people who employ me on this paper.

I have been in a Corner House where, by paying my bill, going outside the front door and immediately

Continued on Back Page, Col. 2

Daily Mirror

JAN 9

No. 11,570   ONE PENNY
Registered at the G.P.O. as a Newspaper.

FOOD SCANDAL DODGED

BELATEDLY, half-heartedly, the Minister of Food is bestirring himself about people who make pigs of themselves in public eating places.

He is going to make them move from trough to trough if they still want to feed as though Britain were at peace.

Instead of being able to eat to their heart's content in any one place, a new Order will make them spread out their guzzling over different establishments.

Yesterday, the "Daily Mirror" demanded that the Minister, Lord Woolton, should stop this food scandal—restaurant gluttony.

During the day he met representatives of the catering trade. There was a "frank" discussion about luxury eating.

Soon, as a result, only one basic dish may be obtained in any one meal bought in an hotel, restaurant or cafe.

✦ ✦ ✦

The customer must choose between fish, meat, poultry, cheese or egg in the shell.

But the really determined food hog could soon nose his way round this little difficulty—by eating fish at one cafe, meat at another, and rounding off with a crumb of cheese at a third.

Breach of the Order will be a punishable offence, but, unless Lord Woolton is to have an army of food detectives following people as they leave restaurants, it is difficult to see how check can be kept on those indulging in "piggish pilgrimages."

News of the Order coincides with an announcement of still further cuts in the meat ration.

✦ ✦ ✦

The Food Ministry announced last night that, owing to the diversion of shipping for war purposes to the Middle East, during the next few months it will be necessary to vary the meat ration at short notice

And Meat Is Cut Again

within the range of 1s. to 1s. 6d.

For the current week the ration will be 1s. 2d. A weekly announcement will be made.

Lord Woolton, talking of last week's failure to meet the meat ration, asked yesterday: "Would you rather have a little less meat for a week or two, or would you rather have Bardia?"

TOBRUK NOW CUT OFF

BRITISH forces surrounded Tobruk, Italian desert stronghold, last night—three days after the fall of Bardia, seventy-five miles away.

Our troops were on the west of the port. Italian forces could neither leave nor enter it.

Small patrols might get out, but the general garrison could not get away without putting up a fight.

Reinforcements cannot reach the town. Italian soldiers inside face the same fate as their countrymen in Bardia less than a week ago—to surrender or die.

Britain's lightning war is giving the demoralised Italians neither chance to counter-attack nor to run quickly enough to avoid capture.

General Antonelli, commanding the First Blackshirt Division, and a number of high staff officers were captured north of Bardia after it fell.

They had tried to "do a bunk." Two other Blackshirt commanders and their staffs are still missing.

One is General (Electric Whiskers) Bergonzoli.

"It is possible they may have decamped by motor-boat reserved for the purpose," a Cairo communique stated last night.

"The search is continuing."

As the five Italian planes which arrived near Bardia to rescue General Bergonzoli and other officers were destroyed on the ground by the R.A.F., escape by the sea was their alternative.

Hungry, Exhausted

Among the Italians still being rounded up there are many who appear before British detachments hungry and exhausted after several days of wandering in the desert, demanding to be taken prisoner.

In some cases such demands proved embarrassing to units charged with work other than that of rounding up prisoners

The readiness with which thousands surrendered made it difficult to draw a line between prisoners and deserters

But Gayda, Mussolini's spokesman, attempting to bolster Italian morale, declared:

"If the defenders of Bardia suffered heavy losses, the same heavy losses were suffered by the enemy. Thousands of dead and wounded from the British Imperial Army can be counted."

Passengers arriving at Boston from African ports in the liner City of New York reported yesterday that 100,000 British troops were waiting on the Kenya-Abyssinian border for the end of the rainy season before invading Abyssinia.

This statement was not confirmed in London.—Reuter, British United Press and Associated Press.

WARN SOVIET WARSHIPS

NINE Soviet warships were warned yesterday by Rumanian naval vessels to keep out of Rumanian territorial waters.

High naval circles in Constanza (Rumania) believed that the Russian vessels were crossing from Odessa, the Soviet Black Sea port.

They were stated to have steamed to within a short distance of Sulina, the Rumanian port at the mouth of the Danube, where it seemed they were going to drop anchor.

Rumanian warships intervened, says British United Press, and, according to eye-witnesses, the Russians withdrew and have not been sighted since.

Rumanian envoys have left for Odessa to confer with Russia, according to the Swiss radio yesterday.

Repatriation of more Bessarabians from Rumania to Russia and return of Rumanians still living in Bessarabia will probably be discussed, it was stated.

It was stated in London that reports that civil war has broken out in Rumania are exaggerated.

EIRE IS TO PUT BAN ON SIGNPOSTS

Eire is to ban signposts

This is the effect of an emergency Government order which comes into effect on February 1. It will be an offence to display anywhere outside urban areas a sign which furnishes indication, name, situation, direction or distance to any place.

The order also prohibits the display within urban areas of signs indicating direction or distance to any place.

A sign is deemed "displayed" if it can be seen from a road, a train, or a low-flying plane.

Valona Is Tottering

The Italians are evacuating civilians from Valona in readiness for the final defence of the town.

Thirty-five thousand more Italian troops have embarked from Valona, according to the Greek radio.

"This shows how desperate is the situation of the Italian forces in Albania," said the announcer.

The Greeks continue their gains in both the coastal region in the direction of Valona and further east.

Latest figures issued by the Red Cross show that the Greeks have taken more than 14,000 prisoners since the beginning of the war.

The R.A.F. raided Elbasan, the Northern Albanian town still held by the Italians, causing considerable damage to military stores and buildings.

86,000 OFF THE DOLE

BETWEEN November and December last there was a total reduction in the unemployment figures of approximately 86,000.

The total of unemployed on the registers at December 9 last of 705,279 is the lowest figure ever since records were first kept in 1921.

These facts were stated by the Ministry of Labour yesterday.

The wholly unemployed figure dropped by something over 61,000; the temporarily stopped by over 21,000; and those in casual employment by just over 3,000.

The Ministry of Labour has set up a panel to review unemployed women on the registers

About 500,000 more women will be needed in munitions work very soon this year.

CATHEDRAL BOMB DAMAGE

Westminster Cathedral and Westminster City Hall were damaged in recent air raids, and further damage was caused to the Temple.

U.S. FLEET TO BE MANNED FOR WAR

ROOSEVELT has authorised an increase of about 40,000 in the man-power of the United States fleet, it was announced yesterday by Colonel Frank Knox, Secretary of the Navy.

He has also ordered a far-reaching shake-up in the Fleet's command and organisation.

Every warship is to be manned at full war strength, instead of at 85 per cent. strength, as at present. The nation's warships are being reorganised into three fleets — the Atlantic, Pacific and Asiatic—ready to go into action at a moment's notice.

Even ships under construction will be provided with full crews.

The active enlisted strength of the Navy will go up from 192,000 to 230,000.

"I don't think any more destroyers can be detached from our Fleet without seriously impairing its efficiency," Colonel Knox told Press representatives yesterday, but added that the decision whether to send more destroyers to Britain did not rest with him.

He disclosed that the Navy plans shortly to ask Congress for authority to build 200 auxiliary vessels.

"Gradually Enlarging"

"We have been gradually enlarging our Atlantic Fleet, and it has assumed a dignity which warrants its establishment as a separate fleet," said Colonel Knox.

"No change in the size of this fleet, which numbers about 125 ships, is contemplated at present."

The reorganisation comes into effect on February 1, when the new commanders take over their posts.

Major-General E. B. Gregory, U.S. Quartermaster - General, at Detroit yesterday urged the automobile industry to produce within twelve months 150,000 of the world's finest military vehicles in which "to do some blitzkrieging ourselves if the occasion demands."

The Army now has 40,000 motor vehicles in service.—Associated Press, Reuter and Exchange.

Roosevelt's £2,500,000,000 Aid for Britain Plan—page 3.

OCEAN-GOING SUBMARINE LOST

AN Admiralty communique last night announced that the submarine Regulus (Lieutenant-Commander F. B. Currie, R.N.) is overdue, and must be considered lost.

The next of kin have been informed.

The Regulus was completed by Vickers-Armstrongs in 1939, and was one of the Rainbow class of ocean-going submarines.

She had a normal complement of fifty. She was 290ft. long and had a surface displacement of 1,475 tons. Her armament was one 4in. gun, two machine-guns and eight 21in. torpedo tubes.

SUBS IN GUN DUEL

H.M. submarine Tuna, commanded by a D.S.O., fought a running gun duel with a U-boat by night on the surface of enemy waters, the Admiralty announced last night.

Immediately she sighted the U-boat the U-boat made off at high speed, firing her after-gun. Tuna gave chase, and opened fire with her four-inch gun.

The U-boat was certainly hit by one shell on the conning tower. But this was not vital damage.

The Tuna chased the enemy for nearly an hour and broke off the engagement only when forced to dive by the appearance of escort vessels which came to the rescue of the damaged U-boat.

The Tuna had previously sunk an armed tug by gunfire. In neither encounter did she sustain any damage or casualties.

She is commanded by Lieutenant-Commander M. K. Cavanagh-Mainwaring, D.S.O.

Sank Supply Ship

At the end of last September the submarine Tuna reported the destruction of a large supply vessel screened by two enemy destroyers. She was then in command of Lieutenant-Commander Cavanagh-Mainwaring.

Lieutenant - Commander Cavanagh-Mainwaring was given the D.S.O. in November for good services in H.M. submarines in recent successful patrols and operations against the enemy.

On Friday the Admiralty announced that the Thunderbolt (formerly the Thetis) had sunk an Italian U-boat which was proceeding under escort to a base in enemy-occupied territory.

Daily Mirror

(JAN 11)

No 11,572   ONE PENNY
Registered at the G.P.O. as a Newspaper.

LUPESCU, CAROL IN BID TO DIE

U.S. TO AID NAVY

THE United States may repair British warships damaged in battle when President Roosevelt's "Aid Britain" Bill is passed.

Congress leaders, in a statement they issued yesterday, said:

"The Bill could conceivably mean that the British battle cruiser Renown could be repaired in Brooklyn Navy yard if the President considered it in the interest of our national defence to do so.

"It is broad enough to permit the use of any of our military, naval or air bases to fit out or repair weapons of countries whose defence is vital to the defence of the United States."

Senator Bennet Champ Clark (Democrat, Missouri) described the Bill as "simply authorising the President to declare war."

The Bill, which was introduced into Congress in Washington yesterday, **Continued on Back Page, Col. 3**

NIGHT RAID ON SOUTH COAST

"DROVES" of German planes raided a south coast district last night. Fire bombs and high-explosives rained down, after flares had been dropped.

An observer describes the raid as severe.

Elsewhere in the country there was little activity.

Planes were reported over Liverpool and Merseyside but neither guns nor bombs were heard.

London had no night alert.

Mexico May Ban Axis Oil

The United States expects to persuade Mexico to ban all oil exports to the Axis (says John Walters, "Daily Mirror" New York correspondent).

Thus, Germany, which imports large quantities of Mexican oil through Japan and Siberia may soon be cut off from one of the most important sources

In order that Mexico shall not suffer from the ban, the United States is willing to buy Mexican oil

(Mexican President's brother to see Duke of Windsor—page 11.)

FROM JOHN WALTERS

NEW YORK, Friday.

EX-KING Carol of Rumania, imprisoned in his hotel at Seville, Spain, has made three attempts to kill himself, and the plan of Carol and his sweetheart, Mme. Lupescu, to end their lives together has been thwarted. Carol made an attempt to hurl himself from the fifth floor window of the hotel, according to reports brought to America by one of Lupescu's relatives who was a member of Carol's entourage in Spain.

Guards rushed in and grabbed Carol as he lunged towards the open window.

He was later removed to the first floor and kept under a twenty-four-hour guard which included watchers disguised as male nurses and doctors.

A short time later Carol attempted to strangle himself with his braces.

Guards then cleared the room of any objects with which he might harm himself.

Poison Ring

A third effort to end his life was revealed when guards wrested from him a large ring containing poison, apparently smuggled into the hotel.

When it was learned that Carol and Lupescu planned to end their lives together, the guards parted them. Now they can communicate by letter only.

Several attempts have been made in Washington by influential Rumanians to obtain visas for Lupescu to enter this country. The State Department granted Carol a visa but barred Lupescu because she lacked documentary evidence to the claim that he married her in London in 1929.

ITALIAN FLEET IS POUNDED

and R.A.F. Mass Raid by Day

★ Terence Brian Holmes, a Wembley boy, died by Nazi murder when the evacuation ship City of Benares was torpedoed. With the bodies of two other children he was found in a drifting lifeboat by a British destroyer on Atlantic patrol. Back page story

Salute Three Children

tells how the Navy paused a little time from its mission of war to honour the three children.

The R.A.F. have delivered new " Taranto " blows against Mussolini's fleet. And yesterday they delivered their first daylight mass raid—against Hitler's " invasion " targets.

Now the Axis is beginning to feel the fierce 1941 power of the R.A.F.—day and night.

ITALIAN battleships and cruisers, driven off the seas by our Mediterranean Fleet, have been pounded by British bombers in the naval bases of Messina, Sicily and Naples.

The Messina attack was launched on Thursday night—as bombers from Britain were smashing German targets on the Ruhr.

Tons of bombs were dropped on warships in Messina harbour, on wharves, docks and oil plants.

One stick of bombs landed across cruisers in the south part of the harbour. The warships belched out a smoke screen to hide the damage.

Another stick of bombs straddled the Army marshalling yards and oil tanks to the south of the harbour. There were fires and explosions.

Not one of the British machines were lost in this new blow to Mussolini's already crippled sea power.

Italian battleships and merchant shipping were the targets in the heavy raid on Naples, which took place the night before.

It was revealed last night that bombs fell on or very near the stern of a battleship of the Littorio class, causing a dull red glow. Other bombs caused an outbreak of fire among large motor vessels.

Severe damage was done to shipping in raids on Palermo and Benghazi.

At least twelve Italian planes were left blazing on the ground in a raid on Benina Aerodrome.

"TORNADO" HITS NAZIS

CHEERING crowds in a south-east coast town yesterday saw British bombers roaring out over the Channel to deliver the R.A.F.'s first daylight mass raid.

People who last autumn had to watch Goering's massed squadrons flying over the English coast in their disastrous attempt to crack R.A.F. resistance, now saw close formations of Britain's twin-engined bombers bound for "invasion" targets.

Our bombers were closely escorted by 100 fighters.

The last machines were still in sight of the watchers on the English coast when the crump of bombs from the leading formations could be heard over the Channel.

As the fighters kept guard against any interception the bombers dived to dump high explosives on Nazi aerodromes.

German planes were caught on the ground in the Forest of Guines, near Calais, and heavily attacked. The woods were set ablaze.

A nearby railway station was bombed with high explosive and incendiaries, and was left hidden in a cloud of white smoke.

The bombers and their escorts **Continued on Back Page, Col. 2**

Greek Victory Joy

FROM DAVID WALKER

ATHENS, Friday.

TEN minutes after the release in Athens today of the news of the Greek capture of Klisura, strategic Albanian town on the main road to Valona, the streets of the Greek capital were thronged with huge crowds and playing bands.

Valona, Mussolini's naval base, commands the Albanian side of the Strait of Otranto and guards the sea approach to the "heel" of Italy.

It was officially stated today that Greek troops entered Klisura on Thursday morning. Athens military circles think the Italians will now be forced to abandon Tepelini, their left flank having been exposed.

In Athens the joyous ringing of every church bell announced the latest Greek victory. Huge crowds appeared like magic outside the offices of the General Staff, every house hauled up the Union Jack and the Greek flag, and streets were packed with laughing, singing and cheering crowds.

Klisura has been practically untenable for several days owing to the incredible accuracy of Greek artillery.

In Disorder

The enemy are reported to be retreating in disorder, with the Greeks advancing a few miles from Klisura towards Berati.

Klisura is important not only as a great step towards Valona, but as a base from which the Greeks may advance northwards to the key town and junction of Elbasan.

The capture of Elbasan, now within sight of probability, would mean that the Italian forces would have to evacuate Albania—if they could get away.

The Italians are now faced with the problem of defending Elbasan and Valona or beating a retreat to the Albanian coast.

THIS FOOD COSTS LESS THAN PRE-WAR!

The 5-star food-drink helps housewives make ends meet this winter

IT'S amazing, but it's true, that this food is actually *down* in price! It's Cadburys famous Bournville Cocoa—always a favourite standby in every kitchen cupboard, and now a big new help to proper feeding at an economical cost. Down in price to 5d per quarter-pound, and a natural food in itself. Suppose you mix with milk —a cup of Bournville Cocoa gives you the nourishment of two whole fresh eggs and costs you less than a quarter as much. Bournville makes meals go further!

★ EXTRA FOOD VALUE. *Bournville Cocoa is rich in body-building - proteins, natural cocoa butter and carbohydrates to give you energy. So remember, a cup of Bournville—the 5-Star Cocoa—is a cup of food.*

★ IRON—THE BLOOD ENRICHER. *The rich iron content of Bournville Cocoa tones up the corpuscles in your bloodstream, makes you feel stronger.*

★ PHOSPHATES — FOR HEALTHY GROWTH. *Bournville Cocoa is rich in the various phosphates and calcium. These build up bone and muscle, strengthen teeth.*

★ AID TO DIGESTION. *Bournville Cocoa is particularly digestible, helps digestion of other foods and so makes every meal go further.*

★ VITAMINS — VITAL TO HEALTH. *Remember that every tin of Bournville Cocoa retains the natural sunshine Vitamin D, specially necessary for kiddies' healthy teeth and straight, strong bones.*

BOURNVILLE
THE 5-STAR
COCOA

QUALITY UNALTERED

DOWN TO

5ᴅ PER QTR. LB.

Daily Mirror

JAN 13

No. 11,573   ONE PENNY
Registered at the G.P.O. as a Newspaper.

BOMBED SUBWAY

MR. WILLKIE TO FLY HERE

WENDELL Willkie, virtual Opposition leader in the United States, is to fly to Britain soon to get first-hand facts about the war.

He announced that last night as he threw the weight of a vast section of the Republican Party behind President Roosevelt's lease-loan programme of aid for Britain.

He hopes to see Mr. Churchill and other Ministers and tour the provinces.

Willkie, Roosevelt's unsuccessful rival for the Presidency, said he approved the Aid for Britain Bill—"with modifications."

This might, he said, be the setting of a time-limit to the powers granted to the President.

"I refute the statement that our national security is not involved in a British defeat," Willkie went on.

"The difference between a British defeat or victory is not only military, but economic.

"The U.S. is not a belligerent, and we hope we shall not be.

"Our problem, however, is not alone to keep America out of war, but to keep war out of America.

"It is the history of democracy that, under dire circumstances, extraordinary powers must be granted to the elected executive.

"Democracy cannot hope to defend itself in any other way."

Mr. Willkie said he expected to stay in England two or three weeks, says Associated Press.

His endorsement of the Bill came at a time when many Republicans were uncertain whether to vote for it.

Mr. Willkie said Congress, "representing the people," must "retain in its own hands the fundamental power to declare war."

The Bill comes before Foreign Affairs Committee of the House of Representatives today.

1s. 2d. of Meat for Adults— 7d. Children

The weekly meat ration from to-day and until further notice will be 1s. 2d. per person for adults and 7d. for children, it is officially announced.

The Food Ministry warns traders that the Rabbits (Maximum Prices) Order applies to "tame" as well as wild rabbits. Some traders were reported to have evaded the Order by saying that the rabbits they were selling were "tame" ones.

U.S. RAID FEAR

The U.S. Army yesterday asked engineers for help in plans to protect civilians from air raids and other perils in the event of war.

Mr. Henry Stimson, War Secretary, announced the creation of a committee of seven to study A.R.P.

LONDON HAD A WEEK-END BLITZ — OF INCENDIARIES AND HIGH EXPLOSIVES.

There were terrible scenes when a high explosive bomb fell on a London subway, plunging through the surface and bringing the ruins crashing down on people who had taken temporary refuge there. Many were killed.

It was impossible yesterday to estimate the number of people who might still be trapped, but the bodies of a woman and two men were recovered. Rescue workers continued their search.

The bomb dropped in the centre of a roadway which collapsed, and concrete slabs, a tarmac road surface and iron standards trapped those beneath.

Men, women and children staggered through the debris and were dragged out of the crater by helpers. One child who had lost her mother was crying and repeatedly asking for "mummy."

A small fire which broke out just beneath the surface was quickly put out, but high explosives and incendiaries were still falling as the rescuers hacked their way through by the light of torches to get out the wounded.

The caretaker of a building opposite said:

"Girl ambulance drivers sat in their driving seats waiting to take the wounded to hospital. They had no protection from bombs or shrapnel."

R.A.F. GUN GERMANS AT DRILL

ROYAL Air Force, continuing their devastating daylight attacks on enemy-occupied territory, machine-gunned German troops drilling in Holland.

Planes swooped down on the barracks square at Domburg, near Flushing. Their guns blazed at the soldiers.

At Zeebrugge

This raid was carried out on Saturday during Bomber Command attacks on targets on or near the Dutch and Belgian coasts.

Two hits were scored on the mole at Zeebrugge, scene of the British naval triumph in April, 1918.

Barges on a canal at Middelharnis were damaged, said an Air Ministry communique yesterday.

During the night R.A.F. bombers struck at Germany and Italy. A small force flew across the Alps

Continued on Back Page

Daily Mirror

JAN 14

No. 11,574   ONE PENNY
Registered at the G.P.O. as a Newspaper.

RAF NOW TAKES OFFENSIVE IN EUROPE

THE R.A.F. is now a match for the German Air Force at its own kind of attack, and can carry an air offensive into Germany's own territories by daylight as well as at night—and hit hard and often.

This is the considered opinion of aviation experts, and it means that the battles of Britain will become the battles of the Continent.

While this summing-up of the new shift of power in the air was expressed yesterday there was news of the fourth successive daylight air onslaught on enemy-occupied territory—during which German troops were machine-gunned in their trenches— and of new night blows aimed with deadly accuracy by the R.A.F. All this happened within twenty-four hours and spread over five countries from Norway to Italy.

BAND BEAT THE BLITZ

WHILE a raid on a coastal town in south-west England was at its peak last night, people taking cover in the main thoroughfare were surprised to hear a brass band.

At first it was thought that someone had turned a wireless on to the full to drown the roar of the barrage.

But as the music grew louder people stepped out of doorways to see where it was coming from.

Then to their amazement round the corner came a military brass band playing a march. And behind swept a company of infantry in full pack. Metal was falling all round.

The roll of drums and the blare of brass drowned the noise of the barrage. The soldiers sang as they looked up laughing, and saw the shells bursting. Their way lay towards the railway station.

The raid was in force, and lasted for about three hours. It was the town's worst of many raids.

The female ward of one hospital received a direct hit, and another hospital was damaged.

There were direct hits on two surface shelters and a Congregational church. It is thought that the casualty list may be heavy.

Incendiaries fell in showers— thousands of them—and onlookers described the spectacle as "like a grotesque fairyland."

Next came waves of heavy bombers, but civilians and A.R.P. services had worked manfully.

Raiders were also reported over Liverpool, a West of England town and a South Wales town.

DUCHESS OF KENT ON AIR

The Duchess of Kent is to broadcast in the Home Service programme at 5.40 p.m. next Monday.

She will give her personal experiences of the Women's Royal Naval Service, of which she is commandant.

It was announced last night that four types of American bomber are being, or will be, flown across the Atlantic.

They are Lockheed Hudson long-range reconnaissance bomber for Coastal Command;

Boeing B.17 four-engined bomber (The Flying Fortress);

Consolidated two-engined flying boat;

Lockheed Vega Ventura bomber, which is a larger and faster version of the Hudson.

There are, including these four, more than thirty types of U.S. aircraft supplementing the output of factories in Great Britain, Canada and Australia.

In addition, as the R.A.F. has revealed, we now have new "super" aircraft.

Continued on Back Page

DUCE FIRES 6th CHIEF OVER GREECE

MUSSOLINI, in desperate straits in Albania, has sacked General Ubaldo Soddu, his commander there, and appointed the Italian Army Chief of Staff to take over Soddu's command, it was announced in Rome yesterday.

The new commander, General Cavallero, aged sixty, will remain Italian Chief of Staff.

Soddu is the sixth Italian commander to be dismissed since the invasion of Greece.

Soddu, whose "resignation" is said in Rome to be due to "ill health," was appointed to his command of the troops in Albania only on November 19.

The immediate cause of Soddu's resignation is the Greek capture of Klisura, a defeat that puts the Italian army in grave danger of being trapped or forced to evacuate Albania by sea (if they can get away).

The Greeks yesterday reported gains beyond Klisura, the occupation of which has initiated the biggest Greek offensive of the war and on the northern sector.

" **B**RITAIN, a f t e r the war, will not tolerate in her midst the tragic spectacle of abject poverty, nor the existence of that problem of industry which in the past has not been solved — the scourge of unemployment."

Mr. Arthur Greenwood, Minister without Portfolio, a member of the War Cabinet, stated this in a broadcast in the overseas service of the B.B.C. yesterday:

"IT WILL, I BELIEVE, BE THE PRIDE OF THE NATION TO SUCCOUR ITS CITIZENS WHO, DURING THE WAR OR AFTERWARDS, FALL ON EVIL DAYS, THROUGH BEREAVEMENT, DISABILITY, DISEASE, OR OLD AGE," HE SAID.

"We shall look forward to developing our educational system and social services. We are planning to get rid of ugliness in our towns to build a fairer Britain, and to replace the hovels that remain by worthy homes."

✦   ✦   ✦

These are fine promises, Mr. Greenwood, but they must be more than promises.

After the 1914-18 war we had a similar political promise—"a land fit for heroes to live in."

It was broken as soon as it was made, and there followed years of terrible unemployment, strikes, poverty, bitterness.

Britain became a land of shattered hopes.

Remember!

Now Mr. Greenwood, on behalf of the Government, has made 'his splendid new pledge to Britain.

✦   ✦   ✦

CUT OUT MR. GREENWOOD'S WORDS, KEEP THEM, REMEMBER THEM—AND SEE THEY ARE FULFILLED.

MARMALADE

Maximum prices of marmalade have now been fixed at the level ruling on December 2. This new order announced last night comes into force at once.

It is proposed to make a further order soon fixing specific maximum prices for marmalade according to defined standards of quality.

TINNED FISH

New order also fixes prices of canned fish (other than canned salmon) at the level in force on December 2. The Canned Salmon (Provisional Maximum Prices) Order, 1939, remains in force, and the maximum prices are unaltered.

We Cut Off Another Italian Force

Graziani.

ITALIAN forces holding Giarabub Oasis, 150 miles south of Tobruk, are cut off and besieged, it was learned in a Cairo message from Reuter late last night.

Marshal Graziani had concentrated the force there for a drive into Egypt by way of the Siwa Oasis, which commands a difficult road through the heart of the Western Desert to the Nile Valley.

The retreat of the Italians from Bardia placed them in danger.

A few days ago the R.A.F. bombed Italian convoys northwest of Giarabub, but whether these were withdrawing from the oasis or attempting to relieve the troops there was not stated.

The strength of the besieged forces is not known.

Meanwhile the desert is resounding to the roar of gunfire as British artillery continues to pound the perimeter defences of Tobruk preparatory to the final onslaught on the town.

There is still no indication of the full strength of the Tobruk garrison, but it is believed to be considerably smaller than that at Bardia.

The Italians' position is more difficult than at Bardia, as their outer perimeter defences straddle a broader area.

R.A.F.'s Advance

British and Australian fighter and bomber squadrons have eliminated Italian air bases for a distance of seventy miles beyond Tobruk.

The army in Libya has advanced from Bardia to the environs of Tobruk without encountering any other opposition than attempts at ground strafing by the enemy's planes.

According to an Associated Press message from Cairo the R.A.F. now completely dominates the eastern half of Italy's North African colony as far as Benghazi, 280 miles from the Egyptian border, and about 160 miles west of Tobruk.

U.S. MESSAGE TO ITALY?

A special message from President Roosevelt to King Victor Emmanuel, say diplomatic circles in Rome, is borne by Mr. W. B. Phillips, U.S. Ambassador, who has arrived in Genoa on his way to Rome.

Some reports say the message raises the possibility of Italy and the United States refraining from hostilities if there is war between Germany and the United States.—British United Press

THIS PLEDGE MUST BE KEPT

NAVY LETS FRENCH SHIP GO

THE French steamer Mendoza (8,199 tons), caught by a British warship trying to run the blockade, has been allowed to go, it was announced last night.

She left Buenos Aires on Friday for Marseilles with a cargo of meat, wool, and 500 barrels of oil.

The Mendoza had no navicert for her cargo, so she was chased by a British warship. She dashed into Maldanado Bay, Uruguay.

Last night the French Minister in Montevideo stated that the warship caught her, but after verifying the cargo allowed her to continue her voyage to France.

Four other French ships are reported to be preparing to leave the Argentine with food cargoes for France.—British United Press

ITALY PRESSES VICHY

According to Columbia Radio, New York, negotiations are to open soon between Italy and Vichy on Italy's demand to use the naval base of Toulon and the island of Corsica.

If Vichy refuses, says the report, Mussolini (with Hitler's permission) will take military action.

The Night There Will Be No 6 o'clock News

The "six o'clock news" will be broadcast at half-past five next Monday, January 20. Time-signal will be given at 5.30 p.m. and the news will follow.

This rearrangement is to enable British listeners to hear the inauguration of Mr. Roosevelt as President of the United States.

The ceremony will be broadcast from 5.55 p.m. till 7 p.m.

It is believed that this will be the first occasion on which the B.B.C. has broken its six o'clock custom.

Daily Mirror

JAN 16

No. 11,576   ONE PENNY
Registered at the G.P.O. as a Newspaper.

FIRE RAID ON LONDON AS MINISTER GIVES—

FIGHT FIRES ORDER TO ALL 16-60

ALL persons between the ages of sixteen and sixty must Register for fire watching. They will each do forty-eight hours a month.

The Minister of Home Security, Mr. Herbert Morrison, last night signed an Order to that effect.

This is the first time the Government has adopted compulsory measures for the civil population.

At first men only will be affected.

Women will have to register, but will only be called out for duty in extreme cases.

FIFTY PLANES ATTACK WARSHIP

THE bomb - blasted aircraft-carrier Illustrious, attacked for seven hours by forty to fifty German dive-bombers, reached a Mediterranean port under her own power.

It was the heaviest attack upon a single British warship of this war.

The Germans flung torpedoes at the sides of Illustrious—and a hundred 1,000lb. bombs at her flight deck—in a desperate and unsuccessful attempt to put her under water.

German pilots, diving head-on, faced the most terrific wall of withering gunfire I have ever seen, writes an Associated Press special. correspondent aboard the Illustrious.

Hours of Hell

The Germans splattered the decks with machine - gun bullets, and dropped scores of bombs on both port and starboard sides, shaking the huge vessel like a cat would a rat.

The seven-hour hell ended with darkness.

The ship came into port with the British ensign flying high on her mast, the spirit of her officers and crew undaunted by a series of the most brutal and punishing attacks ever handed to any warship.

After thrice narrowly escaping death from bombs and splinters, I saw the Illustrious write a new chapter in the history of the war more glorious than her name, and unparalleled acts of British heroism amid a steady rain of destruction.

Like Hailstones

For part of those seven hellish hours I saw German pilots flying so low that the swastika could easily be seen on their big Junker planes, drop bombs all around the ship.

Some of that time I spent digging my nose into the floor of the bridge, or into the deck, flat upon my stomach, my hands folded across my head, while splinters flew about

Continued on Back Page, Col. 1

Soldiers' Buffets on Trains

CANTEENS serving hot drinks and food to soldiers will be run as an experiment on two L.M.S. trains between London and Glasgow next week.

If they are a success about 400 others will be run on other lines.

The canteens, which will serve troops going on leave or moving about the country for military purposes, will be converted railway carriages staffed by voluntary workers.

One other point about the new train canteens—they will serve food and hot drinks, but not beer.

For men on short leave, who cannot get home, there will soon be comfortably furnished hostels. These will be in empty houses requisitioned by the authorities and run by voluntary workers.

A good deal of money has already been spent on radio for the troops, but nearly 5,000 more sets are now being sent to units.

Troops will be helped to arrange their own concert parties. Existing amateur and official shows, welcome as they are, do not meet a fraction of the demand.

The idea is that every man shall have the opportunity of going to some sort of show once a week. The Army has on order also a large number of film projectors. Until these are available projectors will continue to be hired.

LESS MEAT IN SAUSAGES

FROM next Monday no sausages containing more than 45 per cent. of meat will be sold.

This is the effect of a Ministry of Food order announced last night.

All sausages and sausage meat will be Grade C—containing 30-45 per cent. of meat.

The maximum retail prices remain unchanged as follows:—

Beef sausages, 7d. lb.; pork sausages, 11d.; kosher beef sausages, 10d.; beef sausage meat, 9d.; pork sausage meat, 10d.; kosher sausage meat, 8d.

CUT IN WORK HOURS

LONDON FIRE-RAIDED

INCENDIARIES were again showered on London during a raid last night, but again the quickness of the fire-bomb squads prevented serious outbreaks.

One of the bombs fell on a church, narrowly missing the spire, but a small army of boys, armed with sandbags grabbed from the foot of lampposts and with buckets, appeared from nowhere. Soon the fire, which had threatened to spread to timber work, was out.

The church had been fired in a previous raid.

R.A.F. night fighters engaged the bombers over the London area early today.

Night fighters were heard also over an East England town.

A large number of planes appeared over a West Midlands town. High explosives were dropped.

No casualties are reported, but surrounding property was damaged by blast and debris.

Enemy planes were believed to be near Liverpool, an East Midlands town, and two towns in East Anglia.

WORKING hours in munition factories must now be reduced, before the health of the workers is affected.

The Select Committee on National Expenditure urge this in their third report, issued yesterday.

Any reduction must be nationwide to prevent workers moving from job to job in search of overtime rates.

Last July the Ministry of Labour recommended an immediate reduction of hours to an average of sixty a week, with the aim of a further reduction to fifty-five or fifty-six.

Local Control

It is not proposed to apply the order generally to all parts of the country.

Local authorities will call upon those registered to take their duty in the area according to age groups.

Exempt in the Order are men in the Fighting Services, police and Civil Servants, men physically unfitted for the task and others engaged on specially important work.

Bus drivers carrying on in the blitz will probably be excused.

Local appeal tribunals will consist of three people.

Exemption will be strictly limited.

Wealthy people will not be allowed to hire others to do their watch.

Directors of firms will not be granted automatic exemption.

Separate personal applications for exemption will have to be made by those seeking it.

Double Duty

Many people will be called upon to protect both their homes and their places of work.

The varying sizes of industrial and commercial premises, the smallest of which have insufficient personnel for an independent fire-fighting organisation, have raised other difficulties.

Troublesome points have to be settled arising out of the imposition of compulsory service, outside normal working hours, upon staffs working an agreed number of hours for agreed pay.

Since the great fire which did so much damage to the City of London on the last Sunday night of 1940, the Government has urged the imperative need for a guard against incendiaries.

It is these hours that the Committee recommend should be adopted as soon as possible.

"The three-shift system is the ideal," continues the report.

"For patriotic or money reasons, workers have been prepared to work seven days a week, but experience in the last war showed that fatigue led to reduced efficiency, absenteeism and a rise in the sickness and accident rates.

"These symptoms are beginning to show themselves again."

The Minister of Labour should make greater use of his compulsory powers to move workers to places where production is hampered by lack of suitable labour.

GUNNER BROKE AN ORDER— WON M.M.

Gunner A. E. Bennett was left with another gunner at an A.A. gun. Orders are that a gun cannot be fired without the order of an officer.

But while Gunner Bennett stood there, a Nazi plane came over low.

"I can't let the chance go," said Bennett.

"Bang" went the gun.

Down came the enemy plane.

So Gunner Bennett was led to a court of inquiry over the firing of the gun without orders.

The General Officer Commanding said: No punishment. Gunner Bennett to be awarded the Military Medal.

(See full story on middle pages.)

BLOCKADE— REDS WARNED

Britain is determined to prevent Soviet Russia evading the blockade with cargoes of war materials destined for Germany.

Indirect aid for the Axis from U.S. firms—through Russia—is also alarming Britain.

This problem is to be raised by British representatives at Washington.

News of Russia's plans to smash the British blockade came from Buenos Aires yesterday.

Two hundred merchant ships are being mobilised there to carry produce from the Americas for re-export to the Axis.

An official of the Ministry of Economic Warfare, while not confirming the report, stated:—

"The position is causing some uneasiness.

"The Ministry is carefully watching developments with a view to taking counter-measures necessary to forestalling any major leak in the blockade."

NO ENGLISH COAL FOR EIRE

SHIPMENT of coal to Eire from England, but not from Scotland and Wales, is forbidden from Monday next except under export licence.

Cumberland is affected severely. During the winter Cumberland pits sent 100,000 tons of coal to Eire, and there are not the railway wagons available for its carriage inland.

The order, however, arouses no concern in Lancashire and Yorkshire collieries, which supplied the bulk of Eire's two and a half million tons of coal imports.

Daily Mirror

JAN 30

No. 11,538

ONE PENNY

Registered at the G.P.O. as a Newspaper.

JOB CALL-UP FOR GIRLS OF 20

Air and Land Blows at Duce

VILLAGE IS SAVED BY DONKEYS

TWO boys climbed into a motor-van determined to take bread to a foodless village isolated by huge snowdrifts. With five miles to go the van was trapped in a drift.

But the boys got through on donkeys.

They had left the van and had started a hopeless struggle through the snow with a basket of loaves on each arm when they saw the donkeys standing in a field.

Later that day the villagers of Legsby (Lincolnshire), without food for two days, saw donkeys slowly plodding toward them.

The relief of Legsby had begun.

The boys were Dennis Burn, aged seventeen, son of a Market Rasen baker, and Geoffrey Dent, his young assistant. They got through at first with forty loaves.

Then, almost all the rest of the day, Dennis and Geoffrey, helped by a farm boy, guided the donkeys back and forward between the stranded van and the village.

All the bread was delivered to Legsby.

The village—it has 200 people—was isolated by the district's worst blizzard in living memory.

Not even the mails got through when the donkeys came to the rescue.

A.R.P. AIDS GAOL BREAK

A PRISONER who escaped from Pentonville Gaol, London, yesterday afternoon got a clear start because a warder was unable to blow his whistle and the prison bell could not be sounded.

The prisoner, Bernard Silver, twenty-three, walked off dressed in white overalls. He was one of a working party busy near warders' cottages in Wheelwright street, Pentonville.

The men were under the supervision of a warder.

But the warder is forbidden to blow his whistle because the sound may be mistaken for an incendiary bomb warning.

The warder had to return to the prison with the rest of the working party before he could give the alarm.

No warning was sounded at the prison. The warning before the war was the ringing of a bell. That would now be taken for an invasion signal.

A strong body of warders and police searched the district.

IAN HAY GIVES UP WAR OFFICE POST

Major-General Beith (Ian Hay, the famous author) has resigned his appointment as Director of Public Relations at the War Office.

Colonel Walter Elliot, who succeeds takes up his appointment today.

WOMEN are to be called up for war work, just as men are now called up for the fighting forces. Date of the industrial registration is not announced, but the call-up is expected to begin about the end of March.

The biggest demand will be for women of twenty years of age. It is not expected that younger women will be wanted, but there will be a demand for older women.

In fact the women who will be required will be largely those who do not now go to work. They will be reached, when the time comes, by a general registration by age groups. The rate of call-up will depend upon the national needs.

This was stated yesterday after the Minister of Labour, with four other Ministers, had met the leaders of the T.U.C. and the Employers' Federation to discuss the problems of man—and woman—power.

Orders for the industrial registration of men and women are to be drawn up in consultation with the T.U.C. and the employers. A committee is to get to work at once.

The Minister desires that employers should give facilities and assurances for the re-instatement of employees who go to other work.

IF REGISTRATION IS APPLIED THERE IS A GENERAL WISH THAT IT MUST BE DONE ON A UNIFORM AND EQUAL BASIS, AND THAT THERE MUST BE NO CLASS DISTINCTIONS OF ANY KIND

Allowances

He is anxious, however, to get as many volunteers as possible before compulsion starts, and he is to issue at once appeals to various classes of workers.

Women will, it is believed, be given a first day allowance of 10s., and will receive 24s. to pay for their first week's lodgings.

But they will be set to work as near to their homes 'as humanly possible, and registration will be on a regional basis.

Industrial firms are being asked to put forward schemes which will indicate their minimum of key men, and if the Minister approves, these will be "protected."

THE OPINION WAS AUTHORITATIVELY GIVEN YESTERDAY THAT BEFORE BRITAIN IS THROUGH WITH THIS WAR, NO MAN WILL BE ALLOWED TO STAY IN A JOB WHICH A WOMAN CAN DO.

SHE'S U.S. "CINDERS"

FROM JOHN WALTERS
NEW YORK, Wednesday.

LITTLE Anna Skleplovich, daughter of a poor Polish immigrant, was hailed as the American Cinderella today after she had joked and laughed with the President while diplomats and politicians waited at the White House

And tomorrow night, clad in a new silk dress, Anna, who is thirteen, will be an honoured guest at the President's magnificent birthday ball.

A week ago, in a miserable little shack home in Gary, West Virginia, where her father is a coal-mine mechanic, Anna picked up a newspaper and discovered that the President's birthday is on the same date as her own—January 30. So, on a grubby scrap of paper, she wrote to the President, telling him this and wishing him happy returns.

Brother's "Joke"

In reply, a polite official acknowledgment from the White House Secretary arrived at Anna's home. It was first opened by Anna's brother, who for a joke added the postscript. "We would like Anna to come to the White House and see the President."

Believing the postscript genuine, Anna's parents spent all their money in taking Anna to Washington, where they called at the White House last night.

On presenting the letter, they were told the invitation was not genuine.

Then Mrs. Roosevelt heard of Anna's call and told the President.

They sent officials searching Washington for the girl from Gary, West Virginia, and late last night Anna was found.

HITLER SPEAKS TODAY

Hitler is to speak to the German people today, the eighth anniversary of the Nazis' rise to power.—Associated Press.

Identity Tags for U.S. Army

Four and a half million tags are being printed for the American Army to identify men killed or wounded in battle, wires John Walters from New York.

The tags are of cloth, to be pinned on the breasts of the dead or wounded. In spaces on the tag would be written the victim's name, death, cause or nature of wounds.

The order for the tags has caused a sensation. Army officials say it is simply in line with the American policy of being prepared for anything.

FAMINE WARNING TO EIRE

A GRIM warning of famine was given by Mr. de Valera in a radio address to Eire last night.

"We have not a moment to lose in preparing for the worst," he said.

He announced rationing of tea, and said there was insufficient coal and wheat, and only enough petrol for doctors and essential transport services.

After warning the people that the danger of invasion still persisted, Mr. de Valera said: "Another danger has now presented itself. It is an economic one.

"The belligerents are blockading each other and in doing so are blockading us.

"It is not worth considering whether the blockade of Eire is deliberate or not.

"Even to supply ourselves with enough bread, we must put 350,000 more acres under wheat at once, making 650,000 in all.

"Even then our reserve of wheat will hardly see us through and we must rely on the potato to carry us through the danger months of July and August."

The tea ration was announced as two ounces a week for each adult and one ounce for each child to take effect at once.

There will be no petrol for cars, except those engaged on work of national importance, and there will be fewer buses.

MEN—18 AND 40

This opinion coincided with the announcement of plans to extend the call-up of men to youths of eighteen and men of forty.

Under a new proclamation, youths of eighteen and nineteen, and men of thirty-seven to forty, are to register for military service.

The first to register—on February 22—will be the nineteen-year-olds. Last of all will be the "eighteens."

There will be changes in the schedule of reserved occupations. These will not only raise the age of reservation in some cases, but will make reservation depend on an increasing extent on the nature of the job and

Continued on Back Page

MORE heavy blows by land and air against the Italians were reported last night.

First came the British Cairo H.Q. communiqué. It said briefly: "Our pressure on enemy forces in the Derna area is increasing."

With the air resounding to the thunder of artillery, the British troops drawn up round Derna are sending out patrol after patrol to probe the defence positions of the Italians.

The Italian Air Force has at last come to life. Bombers, escorted by fighters, attacked the British patrols. But Hurricanes roared up and one promptly shot down three enemy machines. Another Italian was destroyed a few moments later.

While General Wavell was thus squeezing Mussolini's next-on-the-list Libyan seaport, the R.A.F. Middle East communiqué revealed last night that our airmen were bombing Italian troops retreating along the 120-mile road from Derna to Barce.

British forces advancing towards Benghazi, farther along the coast, have met some resistance at an Italian post.

The resistance is not serious and it is believed in London that the post will fall within a few days.

Pursuit Goes On

The R.A.F. communiqué also reported a heavy raid on Capodichino (Naples) Aerodrome.

This raid took place on the night of Monday-Tuesday.

Bombs fired a big building and started blazes on the aerodrome. Fierce fires and a violent explosion occurred in the central rail junction and marshalling yards.

On the same night Catania Aerodrome (Sicily) was raided, bombs bursting on the main runway and among buildings on the south side of the aerodrome. Fires were caused.

In Eritrea too, the British push went on.

The Cairo communiqué stated: "Operations in the Agordat-Barentu sector are developing. Our close pursuit of the enemy withdrawal from Umm Hagar is continuing and a further seventy-three prisoners have been captured."

A communiqué from Nairobi, capital of Kenya, last night said: "Strong patrols have crossed the frontiers of Italian Somaliland at many points."

NEW PREMIER WAS A CLERK

GREECE'S hero, General Metaxas, who died yesterday following a throat operation, is succeeded as Premier by a man who began his career as a bank clerk.

Sixty-one-year-old Alexander Korizis, former head of the Greek National Bank, entered politics only at the call of General Metaxas. He is determined to carry on the General's crusade against Europe's bullies.

The Chief-Physician of the British Fleet had flown to Athens from Cairo to help the Greek doctors operating on the General.

The Hero of Europe—See page 7.

Daily Mirror

FEB 6

No. 11,594   ONE PENNY
Registered at the G.P.O. as a Newspaper.

RECORD RUN BY WOPS

TICKLING THE TROOPS

Soldiers, issued with long combination-style woollen pants, are cutting the legs off because they don't like 'em—and in some camps are being fined 3s. 6d. as a punishment.

Pant parade has become the order of the week.

Why do "drawers-woollen"—that's the official title—annoy the troops?

"They tickle," said one soldier.

Another declared they hurt his pride and made him look silly. "Why, I'm shy to let my wife see me in them," he said.

Others said long pants were uncomfortable, made the back of their legs sore and restricted movement.

Military office staff complained they are too hot to wear indoors.

A War Office official said the pants are valued at 7s. 6d. a pair.

"Drawers-cellular, summer wear issue, are short," he added. "Drawers - woollen are always long."

A soldier explained that they could not wear the summer ones in winter; they were too cold. So they cut the legs off the woollens.

"This pays in the end," he said. "After all, you can't buy a new pair of short woollen pants for 3s. 6d."

ITALIAN troops are retreating at the rate of thirty miles a day in Libya, Eritrea and Abyssinia, using all available roads in a "flat out" race for the rear.

Advance of British troops on these fronts has shown a marked speeding-up, the military spokesman in Cairo stated last night.

Concentrated bombing by the R.A.F. is causing heavy casualties among Italians retreating towards Benghazi.

With the troops are hundreds of Italian settlers who arrived in this region with their families only three years ago.

British troops, following close behind the Italians along two parallel roads running west from Cyrene to Benghazi, are meeting with little opposition.

Barce, which is the Eastern terminus of the Benghazi railway, is presumably the next British objective.

It is premature to assume that the enemy is abandoning all Cyrenaica.

But it is problematical whether he will be able to make a stand at Benghazi, which is not provided with permanent defences as at Tobruk.

Town Abandoned

Though Appollonia, near Cyrene, has not been mentioned in the British communiques, it can be assumed that the Italians have abandoned it.

In Eritrea, the Italian withdrawal towards the south-east from Barentu has degenerated into a rout, with 1,500 prisoners out of the race.

The fleeing Italians are abandoning supplies of all sorts in their haste to reach the main Asmara-Addis Ababa road.

In Abyssinia the British pursuit of the Italian column retreating towards Gondar, north of Lake Tanana, is stated to be continuing in spite of the enemy's delaying tactics.

Twenty-three Italian aeroplanes were captured, shot down, or destroyed on the ground on Tuesday, R.A.F. headquarters in Cairo announced yesterday.

One CA 133 and two CR 42s in an unserviceable condition due to air attack were captured at Barentu.

In Southern Abyssinia one fighter of the South African Air Force alone shot down three Italian planes.

"Enemy aircraft raided Malta, but were intercepted by our fighters and at least three Junkers 88s were shot down, while others were severely damaged," adds the R.A.F. communique. "Slight damage was caused to buildings.

"From all operations our aircraft returned safely with the exception of one bomber and one fighter aircraft."

FIRE BOMB RAID AGAIN

RAIDERS over the London area again last night dropped incendiaries and high explosives in a number of districts on the outskirts. Houses were demolished and there were some casualties.

The Alert was sounded some time after dark, after aeroplane engines and heavy gunfire had been heard, but the raid was over before midnight.

Heavy A.A. barrage was put up by the guns in East Anglia as raiders approached London. The planes were forced to fly at a high altitude, and one appeared to be damaged, its engine fluttering.

Fell in Fields

Incendiary bombs were dropped by two planes on the outskirts of the London area. Most of them fell harmlessly in fields, and soldiers helped to extinguish those which endangered houses. Only one fire was started, and this was soon put out.

In an adjoining district two high explosives were dropped and one struck a house. It is believed several people were buried under the debris.

High explosives were dropped in one district of East Anglia. Most of the houses in which they fell were unoccupied, and no casualties were reported.

Previously there had been a shower of incendiaries, but householders rushed out with bags and buckets of sand.

Twenty fire bombs which followed flares in a south-east coastal district fell near a hospital, but were quickly put out.

STOCKING GIRLS FOR ARMS

Midlands hosiery centres, it is understood, are to provide over 20,000 women workers for the armaments industry in the next few months.

The workers will be transferred under a voluntary quota scheme agreed by the Ministry of Labour, manufacturers, and trade union leaders.

War Job for 1,000 CATS

A thousand kittens are to be recruited to help win the war.

So many cats have been destroyed or evacuated from London that rats and mice are multiplying everywhere.

That's why, in the situations vacant column, this "want ad." appeared in London newspapers yesterday: "Wanted, 1,000 male kittens."

Mr. Palmer, owner of a pets' store at Parkway, Camden Town, N.W., has been asked by big firms, warehouse-men and householders for kittens that can be trained to destroy vermin.

"We want them as quickly as possible," he told the "Daily Mirror." "Male kittens are the best for this work."

Darlan Premier: New Plan

ADMIRAL DARLAN leaves for Paris this morning carrying to the Nazis a compromise plan by which Petain will remain head of the State, but not head of the Government, says the British United Press from Vichy.

Darlan would be Premier and Foreign Minister, and Laval Vice-Premier and Minister of the Interior.

Laval, backed by the Nazis, has been demanding to be made Premier.

Laval lost his post in the Petain Cabinet last December because he had completed negotiations with the Germans for them to have the use of the French Fleet and occupy the French naval base at Bizerta, according to information received from Europe in Washington.

Nazis Threaten

On Laval's return to the Cabinet Berlin is demanding the fulfilment of the agreement, but Marshal Petain is unwilling to agree.

German anger against Petain's refusal to give way rose to boiling point last night.

"Remember there is only an armistice between Germany and France, and peace has not been established," was the warning given in French by the German radio.

General Huntziger, Vichy War Minister, yesterday conferred with General Studt, chairman of the Wiesbaden Armistice Commission.—British United Press, Associated Press and Reuter.

RAF DAY RAID ON AIR BASES

STRONG forces of R.A.F. bombers and fighters flew back in formation after swooping in daylight on invasion and blockade bases on the snow-bound French coast yesterday.

The aerodrome at St. Omer was successfully attacked, the Air Ministry announced last night. Two enemy aircraft were shot down. Five of our fighters are missing.

The daylight raid followed heavy night attacks by our bombers on invasion targets from Ostend to Bordeaux. In Germany, the centre of industrial Dusseldorf was left on fire.

Watchers on the Channel coast saw clouds of black smoke roll up into the sky between Calais and Dover while the R.A.F. attacked in the afternoon.

Dull thuds of explosions were heard. When our bombers set out they were protected by layers of fighters. They flew at 5,000ft. in close formation, wing-tips almost touching.

While they were crossing the Channel a squadron of Spitfires patrolled the English coast watching for German fighters.

Invasion Ports Hit

From Ostend to Bordeaux, almost from one end of the German occupied coast to the other, aircraft of the Bomber Command attacked docks and German naval units on Tuesday night and early yesterday.

One of the most persistent raids of the night was made on the naval base at Brest.

The weather was favourable and the whole plan of the docks were clearly visible from the air.

At the height of this attack an oil fire broke out on the docks and was vividly described by one of the many pilots who saw it.

"As we were vertically over the dock," the pilot said, "there was an explosion that almost blinded us.

"For a moment it was really quite alarming because it all happened so suddenly. There seemed to be three separate dashes going off at the same moment. It was as though their light was coming straight at us."

At Bordeaux, from which submarines are sent out to attack shipping in the Atlantic, bombs were seen to fall on one of the principal basins.

At Bordeaux the Germans also use the Merignac Aerodrome as another base from which to attempt a blockade of this country.

For over an hour attacks were made on this landing ground of the large four - engined Folke - Wulf bombers which raid our convoys.

A force of bombers attacked Dussel-

Continued on Back Page

ILLUSTRIOUS SAILED ON

Colonel Frank Knox, U.S. Navy Secretary, said yesterday that the British aircraft-carrier Illustrious was recently able to reach Malta, then Alexandria, under her own power, after receiving a direct hit from a 1,000lb. German bomb.

He disclosed to his Press conference that the German hit killed about eighty men and destroyed twenty bombers—yet it failed even to affect the carrier's navigability.—Associated Press.

CRASH IN EIRE

A German aeroplane crashed and was wrecked near Schull, Co. Cork, yesterday. It is officially announced in Dublin.

Six men were on board. Five were killed and one seriously injured.

Repel it with

GENASPRIN

At the first sign of 'flu (sneeze, sniff or headache), kill it with two tablets of 'Genasprin'. Take two more before you go to bed. If you have acted in time, you'll be well again in the morning. If you have not, keep warm and persevere with 'Genasprin'. It's amazing how it brings your temperature down, soothes your nerves and keeps the germs at bay. Doctors recommend 'Genasprin'. Only chemists sell it. Buy some to-day.

3½d, 7d, 1/5, 2/3, 3/11
(Prices including Purchase Tax)

GENASPRIN

The SAFE Brand of Aspirin

KILLS 'FLU QUICKLY—TIME IT

The word "GENASPRIN" is the registered trade mark of Genatosan Ltd., Loughborough, Leicestershire.

Daily Mirror

FEB 10

No. 11,597   ONE PENNY
Registered at the G.P.O. as a Newspaper.

NAVY BATTERS GENOA WITH 300 TONS OF SHELLS

Premier Tells Reason

GENOA was shelled and shattered by the Navy yesterday because a Nazi German expedition might sail from there to attack General Weygand in the French colonies of Algeria and Tunisia.

Mr. Churchill revealed this last night in a broadcast which was heard throughout Britain and the United States.

"It is right that the Italian people should be made to feel the sorry plight into which they have been led by Mussolini," the Premier said.

"If the cannonade of Genoa, rolling along the coast, reverberating in the mountains, has reached the ears of our French comrades in their grief and misery, it may cheer them with a feeling that friends, active friends, are near and that Britannia rules the waves."

During the winter Germany had the power to drop four tons upon us to our one on them.

"We are arranging so that presently this will be rather the other way round, but meanwhile London and our big cities have had to stand their pounding."

They remind me of the British squares at Waterloo. They are not squares of soldiers, they do not wear scarlet coats: they are just ordinary English, Scottish and Welsh folk, men, women and children standing steadfastly together.

"But their spirit is the same, their glory is the same, and in the end their victory will be greater than famous Waterloo."

Referring to Italy's invasion of Greece, the Premier described Mussolini as "the crafty, cold-blooded black-hearted Italian, who had sought to gain an empire on the cheap." His forces were ignominiously hurled back while Generals Wavell and Wilson had received vast reinforcements in Egypt.

Then came our victory at Sidi Barrani—Wavell saw his chance.

"At that time I ventured to draw

Continued on Back Page. Col. 1

SPEECH WILL HASTEN U.S. AID

Moved by Churchill's plea, "Give us the tools and we will finish the job," Administration leaders in Washington last night predicted that the British Aid Bill will be made law on March 1, leading to the release of an enormous flood of war materials to Britain.

"Churchill's message is superb," said Mr. Sol Bloom, chairman of the Foreign Affairs Committee of the House of Representatives. "It is a complete assurance that democracy is still more than a match for the dictators."—British United Press and Associated Press.

WARSHIPS of the British Mediterranean Fleet battered the Italian naval base of Genoa at dawn yesterday, hurling 300 tons of shells on docks, factories, ships, railways and oil plants.

Two of our most powerful ships, the 32,000-ton battle cruiser Renown and the 31,000-ton battleship Malaya, led the attack.

Between them they carry fourteen 15-inch guns, each throwing a shell weighing 1,920lb. These were in action.

The aircraft carrier Ark Royal was there, too. Her planes bombed as the big guns plastered their targets.

And our total casualties were one Swordfish aircraft and her crew, reported missing.

The action was as glorious a feat as that performed by Drake in 1587, when he sailed into Cadiz and singed the King of Spain's beard.

For in shelling the Duce's chief seaport yesterday, the Fleet sailed deep into waters which Mussolini has exclusively regarded as his own.

By this attack the Navy proved its ability to operate successfully in the seas all around Italy.

The Admiralty stated last night that the bombardment and bombing were more successful than at first thought. The communique stated:

"Our forces, under the command of Vice-Admiral Sir James Somer-

★ ★

175 Miles Onward

ARMY of the Nile has advanced 175 miles along the Libyan coast from Benghazi. General "Electric Whiskers" Berganzoli, second only to Graziani, is one of seven generals captured with Benghazi. (See Back Page.)

★ ★

ville, consisted of Renown, Malaya, Ark Royal and the 9,100-ton cruiser Sheffield, with light forces in company.

"Military targets in and around the port of Genoa were subjected to a bombardment in which over 300 tons of shells were fired.

"The following results were observed: The Ansaldo electric works and the Ansaldo boiler works were heavily hit and large fires started.

"The main power station of the port which also supplies power for the railways was severely damaged and set on fire.

"Many hits were made on the dry docks and on warehouses and harbour works surrounding the inner harbour. Here too considerable fires broke out.

"The main oil fuel installation and oil tanks were repeatedly hit, as were a number of supply ships and the main goods yard of the railway.

"Several tons of bombs and a large number of incendiaries were dropped by naval aircraft on the oil refinery of the A.N.I.C. at Leghorn, and other targets in the vicinity.

"Other naval aircraft attacked Pisa, where the aerodrome and railway junction were hit. This railway junction is the intersection of the main west coast railway from Genoa to Rome and the south, and one of

Continued on Back Page. Col. 5

MASTER OF THE "MED."

Admiral Sir Andrew B. Cunningham ("A.B.C." to the Navy), Commander of the Mediterranean Fleet.

Last week he swept the Italian seas for Musso's fleet—and couldn't find it.

So he sent his ships, under command of Vice Admiral Sir James Somerville, to Genoa, big port of Italy, and bombarded it.

Daily Mirror

FEB 11

No. 11,598   ONE PENNY
Registered at the G.P.O. as a Newspaper.

Lambeth Walk in Desert

THE full story of the rout of the Italians at Benghazi, General (Electric - Whiskers) Berganzoli's attempted escape among a crowd of refugees, and how Costermonger Joe from Lambeth-walk led the desert dash in a Bren gun-carrier, reached London early to-day.

The all-Cockney crew of the gun carrier were the first to reach the Mediterranean after a record-breaking dash through the desert from Mechili.

I met them (writes a British United Press special correspondent) when they were cruising round the mud hut village of Ghemines, near the Gulf of Sirte.

"We got position across the main road from Benghazi to Tripoli only two hours before the enemy columns turned up."

One of this crew was from Islington, another was Costermonger Joe, from Lambeth-walk, who lives in the L.C.C. block of flats called Arne House.

"Costermonger Joe" and his pals looked like anything but British soldiers. They wore red neckerchiefs given to them by Arabs over Italian

Continued on Back Page

Wife of Earl's Heir Is Held

A new portrait of Lady Howard of Effingham, wife of the heir to the Earl of Effingham, who has been detained under Defence Regulation 18B.

When asked last night about his daughter-in-law's detention, the Earl said: "It is news to m e. I'll do nothing about the matter."

He added: "I know very little about her.

(See Back Page.)

BRITAIN BREAKS WITH RUMANIA

BRITAIN has freed her hands in the Balkans. She has broken off diplomatic relations with Nazi-controlled Rumania, now a German military base for plans of action through Bulgaria. A formal British declaration of war on Rumania may follow soon, according to U.S. authorised sources.

The German High Command, it was authoritatively stated in London last night, is building up in Rumania all the elements of an expeditionary force.

Duce's Son in Cyrenaica

Prisoners who fell into British hands at the fall of Barce, Cyrenaica, declared that Bruno Mussolini, the son of the Duce, was in the town a few days before its capture.

A feature of the brilliant campaign in Cyrenaica has been the stamina of the British Forces.

For hundred miles after hundred miles they have brushed aside all difficulties, across the desert and over mountains, marching under the tropical sun, under shell fire and in rain.—Exchange.

At strategical points are massed large quantities of munitions and fuel oil. Not by a single word is the Rumanian Government objecting.

The position of the British Legation in Bukarest has become impossible. The British Minister, Sir Reginald Hoare, his staff and Consular officials are being withdrawn.

City Blacked-Out

Sir Reginald handed a Note to General Antonescu in Bukarest yesterday and asked for his passports.

"The British Note explained clearly why action was taken," said a spokesman at the British Legation.

"It is simple. Rumania has become a base for German military operations.

"Since the Germans came as instructors, their numbers have increased enormously, and there are all the elements of an extensive German force here."

Sir Reginald and his staff will be out of Rumania in a few days. A special ship is waiting at the Black Sea port of Constanza to take them to Turkey.

New York radio reported last night that Bukarest has been

Continued on Back Page

A glance at the map of the Balkans shows how quickly German troops now in Rumania could thrust at Greece through Bulgaria.

THE first enemy province to be captured in this war now has a British Military Governor—and he is General Sir Henry Wilson, Commander of the British Army of the Nile and Sir Archibald Wavell's right-hand man in the Libyan campaign against Mussolini.

The appointment of Sir Henry Wilson was announced last night.

He is Military Governor and General Officer Commanding-in-Chief of Cyrenaica, the Italian province which has been conquered in the British sweep in Libya.

He has relinquished command of the troops in Egypt. His successor is likely to be announced in a few days.

New Administration

General Wilson led the British, Imperial and Free French forces which began the attack on the Italians in Egypt. He is fifty-nine.

General Wilson will be responsible for law and order in Cyrenaica, for the safeguarding of property and the maintenance of essential administrative, judicial and technical services.

A proclamation in which he will call on the inhabitants of the conquered province to obey the orders of the military authorities is to be issued.

Where possible, Libyan mayors will remain in office and the people continue to pay the same taxes.

A political branch has been set up at General Headquarters, Cairo, to deal with all questions affecting occupied enemy territory and its administration.

It is pointed out in Cairo that military occupation has no bearing on the subsequent disposal of territory, which can only be decided at a peace conference.

FRANCO IS IN ITALY

GENERAL FRANCO is in Italy to meet Mussolini and Ciano, Italian Foreign Minister, today, and discuss "all the questions arising out of General Wavell's advance in Northern Africa."

This is reported by New York National broadcasting system which said Franco crossed the French-Italian frontier at Ventimille.

It is learned in Vichy Petain is leaving soon for a short stay at his wife's Riviera estate and might happen to meet Franco and Suner, Spanish Foreign Minister, in the vicinity, says Associated Press.

Franco and Suner might discuss with Mussolini and Ciano the possibility of an Italian-Spanish bloc as an auxiliary to the Axis, but there was no suggestion that France would be included, or that Petain's possible encounter with Franco would be made with this objective.

DARLAN APPOINTED PETAIN'S 'SUCCESSOR'

Admiral Darlan has been appointed Marshal Petain's successor as France's Chief of State and head of the Government "should the latter be prevented from carrying out his functions."

Darlan was only on Sunday nominated Vice-Premier and Foreign Minister, as well as retaining his post of Minister of the Navy.

Latest indications in Vichy were that the changes in the French Cabinet were not expected to take place before Thursday.

General Wilson to Rule in Libya

General Sir H. M. Wilson—the Military Governor and General Officer Commanding-in-Chief for Cyrenaica, the Eastern part of Libya, now in British hands !

NEW BLOW IN ERITREA

ITALIAN defenders in Eritrea appear to be faced with a new threat with the occupation by the British of Mersa Taclai and Karora, announced in yesterday's British G.H.Q. communique issued in Cairo.

Mersa Taclai is a village forty miles down the Red Sea coast from the border between the Sudan and Eritrea. Karora is a small town lying just inside the same border fifty miles inland.

This is the first mention of any British movement from the north.

Abyssinia Advance

Its development, in conjunction with our drive into Eritrea from the east, would threaten the envelopment of the Italian forces now based on Keren and Asmara, capital of the Province.

The Italians in the meantime are being allowed no rest in the other parts of the East African war area. This is shown by the British communique, which states that South African troops have advanced fifty miles into Southern Abyssinia, while intensive patrol activity continues in Italian Somaliland.

Daily Mirror

(FEB 15)

No. 11,602   ONE PENNY
Registered at the G.P.O. as a Newspaper.

BRITISH CHUTISTS FOUGHT SAYS ROME

A DETAILED story of a daring and determined "wrecking raid" on Southern Italy by British parachute troops armed with tommy-guns, grenades and dynamite was given by the official Italian news agency last night.

This sensational development in Britain's Mediterranean war was alleged first by the Italian High Command communique.

It said the parachutists were dropped on Monday night with the aim of wrecking communications and hydro-electric power stations, and claimed that the raiders were all captured "before they did serious damage."

The Italian news agency said that British parachutists were dropped between 10.30 p.m. and 2 a.m. in the Lucania district of Calabria (the "toe" of Italy).

"Having landed in a clearing surrounded by forests, the parachutists occupied some farms and immobilised the peasants," said the agency.

"The parachutists deceived the peasants by shouting 'Duce,' and so inducing them to open their doors.

"After leaving one companion who had broken his leg, the British made their way to the springs which feed the irrigation system, guiding themselves by means of maps.

"Air Force Caps"

"Their scheme failed. Eleven were seized in one place, seven others were arrested a mile or two away.

"The latter attempted to put up a resistance, turning a tommy gun on the patrol consisting of one guard, one police-constable and a shepherd.

"Shots from the British officer's

Continued on Back Page

SEA RAIDER SINKS SIX

SIX ships in a British convoy steaming northwards between Madeira and the Azores are believed to have been sunk following an attack by a German surface raider, apparently a pocket battleship, says Reuter.

More than 100 survivors were landed at Punchal, Madeira, and four were taken to hospital.

The raider hurled salvos of shells into the convoy for about half an hour, then disappeared over the horizon.

All the ships in the convoy returned her fire.

When the action was over those ships which had not been hit dispersed and picked up survivors from the others.

Germany's version of the action claimed that thirteen ships, totalling 82,000 tons, in the convoy were sunk.

RUMANIA MAY BE BOMBED

RUMANIA, now regarded by Britain as enemy-occupied territory, is in the same position as Belgium and Holland and concentrations of German troops there are liable to be bombed.

The British Government's decision that they must regard Rumania as territory under enemy occupation was revealed last night.

From today Rumania will be regarded as an enemy destination for contraband purposes, and all goods of Rumanian origin or ownership will be liable to seizure.

Hitler yesterday received the Yugoslav Premier and the Foreign Minister at his Berchtesgaden retreat.

It was hinted in Berlin that the object of the talk was to "determine Yugoslavia's attitude towards current movements in the Balkans."

The talk lasted three hours, with a short break for tea. Ribbentrop was present.

David Walker cabled from Belgrade last night:

Rumania has been seized by the jitters.

The authorities have asked the German High Command to move their troops from Bukarest so that the capital could be declared an open city. The request was refused.

Royal Farewell

Two special trains carrying the British Legation staff, a few business men, a half-dozen governesses and three English jockeys well known in Rumania, have already left Bukarest.

The American, Chinese and Turkish Ministers saw the party off at the station. Many grey-haired Englishmen toured around the city by taxi to take a last look at Bukarest.

One of those who waved goodbye to the party at the station was Princess Bibesco, daughter of Lord Asquith, who married into Rumanian nobility.

I am able to reveal that Queen Mother Helen asked Lady Hoare, wife of the British Minister, to visit her before going. The two women spent the day together in great friendliness. Then Lady Hoare bade farewell to Rumania.

It was reported that the Greek Government, apparently fearing a German invasion through Bulgaria and Yugoslavia, had called up many additional classes of reservists.

GREEKS' BIG PUSH

THE Greeks have opened an offensive along the entire Albanian front and obtained all their objectives according to plan, Radio Athens stated last night.

At one point, 7,900 prisoners, including many officers, were taken.

Greek troops opened the offensive after Italian counter-attacks of the past days had been beaten back.

They captured a stronghold after the defending Italians had been heavily pounded by artillery.

KEREN ADVANCE IN HARD COUNTRY

Operations for the capture of Keren, in Eritrea, are proceeding, while our troops continue their progress in the difficult country towards Arreza, said yesterday's G.H.Q. communique from Cairo.

It was stated in London that hard fighting around Keren continues and no spectacular results should be expected.—Reuter.

EGGS THREEPENCE DOWN

The Ministry of Food, under an Order to come into force on Monday, is reducing by half-crown per 120, or 3d. per dozen, the maximum prices for all categories of home-produced hen and duck eggs.

FIRE BOMBS BEATEN

Fire-watchers quickly disposed of incendiary bombs which fell in the London area last night. High-explosives also were dropped.

Hundreds of incendiaries fell in several London districts.

Organised squads of fire-watchers covered street after street and prevented any of the bombs causing fires.

Raiders were reported over East Anglia, East Midlands, and towns in East and North-West England besides London.

The Alert in the London area was sounded soon after dark and bombs fell shortly afterwards. The Raiders Passed, however, was sounded before midnight.

Night Fighters Up

Windows of a municipal maternity hospital were shattered when a bomb fell in one London area. There were no casualties, and none of the mothers or babies were any the worse for their experience.

A church in one part of London escaped serious damage when a bomb fell in the road outside the gates, but five people were killed.

Windows in the church vestry and the west door were damaged, and there was a heap of debris inside.

Five people were killed by a bomb which damaged an office building in a square in the London area.

In a residential district A.R.P. workers and men and women fire watchers knocked down fences in their zeal to deal with the fire bombs.

British night fighters were in operation against raiders in an eastern area, A.A. guns were also in action at one time in the same area.

Over East Anglia bombs were dropped in sparsely populated areas. Flares were used.

Daily Mirror

FEB 17

No. 11,603
ONE PENNY
Registered at the G.P.O. as a Newspaper.

No. 11,603 — ONE PENNY — Registered at the G.P.O. as a Newspaper.

Surprise Wedding of King's Cousin

The wedding of Lady Iris Mountbatten, cousin of the King and daughter of the Marquis of Carisbrooke, to Captain Hamilton O'Malley, of the Irish Guards, came as a surprise . . it was thought that Lady Iris would be married towards the end of the month at Brompton Oratory.

♦ ♦ ♦

Picture shows bride and bridegroom leaving St. Paul's Roman Catholic Church, Haywards Heath.

10,000 MILES TAKEN

WITH the capture of Kismayu, third biggest port, British troops now control 10,000 square miles of Italian Somaliland, an area bigger than Wales.

Yesterday's official communique from Nairobi stated:

"The whole of the south-west portion of Italian Somaliland, up to the line of the River Juba, has now been overrun by our troops.

"In this operation units of the Royal Navy are co-operating by the bombardment of enemy concentrations on the coast.

"Numerous friendly natives welcomed the advancing troops. The natives complained of bad treatment, such as forcible removal of their wives, children and stock by the Italians."

Kismayu has 5,000 inhabitants.

Though they had to abandon much material, the Italians fired the oil storage tanks before the British entered. A scuttled ship and three damaged vessels were in the harbour.

"Operations continue for the development of our success at Kismayu," said our Cairo communique yesterday

Reorganising Army

In Eritrea the concentration of troops about Keren is proceeding satisfactorily.

General Wavell's army, from the Egyptian frontier to Benghazi, is being reorganised.

A district which the Italians never colonised extends to within less than 100 miles of Tripoli. This explains the slow and difficult operations now going on.

Nevertheless, mechanised patrols move westward steadily.

ALIENS NOT "HALF-STARVED"

Nazi accusations that Germans interned in Great Britain are being "half starved" were emphatically denied during the week-end by the Earl of Lytton, chairman of the Advisory Council on Aliens.

FEED BRITAIN U.S. CALL TO F.D.R.

ONE hundred prominent Americans are urging President Roosevelt to guarantee Britain's food supplies against the U-boat menace. "Make the United States the larder as well as the arsenal of democracy," they state in a nation-wide appeal.

Britons, the appeal points out, cannot fight victoriously if starvation threatens their homes.

"It is within our power to see that such a threat does not materialise."

The appeal, made in a letter, states:—

"Dear Mr. President,—You have said that, in order to keep war away from America, we must give full aid to the nations who are resisting the onslaught of Axis aggression.

"You have said that we must make ourselves into the arsenal of democracy—that we must supply ships and planes and tanks and guns to those who are defending not only their own homes but the cause of civilisation

Food Is Vital

You have said this and the American people overwhelmingly agree with you. The legislation you have proposed to this end will, we trust, become law within a few days. This should make possible our becoming an effective arsenal

"But the gallant garrisons of democracy may need more than arms, Mr. President. They may need food.

"Hitler boasts that the submarine sinkings to date are only a foretaste of what is to come—soon.

"Men, no matter how brave in order to fight victoriously on land and sea and in the air must know that starvation cannot threaten the homes they are defending. It is within our power to see that such a threat does not materialise.

"We cannot directly help the conquered peoples whose food is being stolen from them to feed the German armies of occupation — they can be helped only by being freed from the yoke of the oppressor.

"But we can see to it that their only hope of liberation is not destroyed—as it would be if the British Isles should be reduced through starvation.

"We ask you, Mr. President, to take such steps as may be necessary to make us not only the arsenal but the larder of democracy

"We ask you to make it possible for us, not merely to put arms into the hands of the beleaguered garrisons, but to ensure food for those who sleep underground—who in their waking moments work and fight and die in order that democracy may live.

"We ask this, Mr. President, for the sake of the heroic peoples whom you have already determined to aid —Reuter.

SIGNOR 'WOE WOE' SILENT

"Signor [Woe Woe] Ansaldo will not broadcast today," said Rome radio yesterday.

BRITAIN IS SURE TO WIN —U.S. ENVOY

I DON'T think Hitler can lick the British, said Mr. Harry Hopkins, President Roosevelt's representative, when he returned from England to New York by Clipper seaplane yesterday

Mr. Hopkins added:

"The English are as tough a crowd as I think there is. With the help of this country there is no question that England will win the war. AND IT WON'T BE A STALEMATED WAR."

He said his opinions were based on observation of England's military and naval strength.

"The British need our help desperately, and I am sure they are going to get it," Mr. Hopkins added.

"I saw their Navy Air Force and Army.

"Their people are determined to win, and can do it without more men, but they've got to have material

"I was sent over on a specific mission, and I have completed it."

Asked if it were only a mission of observation, Mr. Hopkins replied: "It was more than that."

"The British believe that an invasion will be attempted soon," he added. "But I got a clear-cut impression that they are suffering no qualms on that score, being confident in their ability to repulse it."

Associated Press and British United Press

AID FOR BRITAIN DEBATE TODAY

The U.S. Senate begins today its debate on President Roosevelt's sweeping Lease-Lend Bill to aid Britain up to the hilt. The Bill will be passed in a fortnight.

Mr. Roosevelt will probably request £250,000,000 in appropriations and contract authority to build planes, ships, tanks, guns and munitions.—Reuter and Associated Press.

HALF CONVOY SHIPS ESCAPE

NINE ships of the British convoy attacked by a German warship between Madeira and the Azores escaped, and nine others were sunk, according to survivors' stories cabled from Funchal, Madeira.

The raider, according to these reports, suddenly charged into the midst of the convoy and began firing in all directions.

Three ships are reported to have escaped towards the Azores.

The convoy, according to these reports, was composed of eighteen vessels. Some of them were Greek.

The raider escaped after half an hour and after the convoy ships had tried to encircle her.—British United Press.

U.S. SENDS HOSPITAL

A giant mobile hospital, a gift from American friends of Britain, was shipped overseas from New York on Saturday by the British War Relief Society (cables John Walters from New York).

It is the largest field hospital ever constructed in the United States and has beds for a hundred patients.

French Fleet Sails—Says U.S.

All seaworthy vessels of the French Fleet were reported in Lisbon yesterday to have left the naval base at Toulon for Casablanca, French Morocco, according to the "New York News."

"This move, coupled with the rapid fall of the franc, is believed to preface a major crisis between Hitler and Petain," the paper added.

We Mine Gate to Malaya

BRITAIN has laid a minefield as a barrier against shipping approaching Singapore naval base on a direct route from Japan, Thailand, China and French Indo-China.

That move, announced in London yesterday, comes at a time when Japan intends to try to grab the Dutch East Indies, according to Columbia Radio, New York.

The mined area covers a large stretch of sea off the south-eastern tip of the Malay Peninsula.

Meanwhile British women and children in Thailand (Siam) have been advised by the British Legation to leave the country

British subjects were advised also to leave Japanese-occupied China and told: "It will almost certainly be impossible to provide special facilities for departure at short notice."

The Thai Government thought it necessary to issue a radio denial that Japan has asked them for naval bases.

Hong Kong Ringed

The official Chinese Central News Agency said that the Japanese had concentrated ten divisions at various strategic spots round Hong Kong.

Six Japanese divisions were now stationed in Canton, Hainan Island and the Spratly Islands, the agency said.

Sir Robert Craigie, British Ambassador to Japan, has called on Mr. Yosuke Matsuoka, Japanese Foreign Minister.

He is believed to have cautioned Japan concerning her activities in the Pacific.

Mr. W. M. Hughes, Australian Attorney-General and Navy Minister, broadcast: "Although the situation is grave, I see nothing that need alarm or even seriously disturb a resolute people."— Reuter, British United Press and Associated Press.

ALFONSO: FAMILY SUMMONED

Ex-King Alfonso of Spain, who has had a second heart attack within three days, is in a serious condition, according to a Rome message.

Several members of the family have been summoned to the bedside.

Alfonso has been in exile since his abdication in April, 1931, after elections which put Republicans in power. For several years he has lived in Rome. He is nearly fifty-five.—Associated Press and Reuter.

> **15s. To Be Your Food Ration?**
> (Page 3)

Daily Mirror

FEB 20

No. 11,606   ONE PENNY
Registered at the G.P.O. as a Newspaper.

WE MASS PLANES IN EAST

SKY ARMY ALL ACES

Nazis Bomb Greece

From DAVID WALKER

SOFIA, Wednesday.

GERMAN planes, violating Bulgarian neutrality, flew over Greek territory yesterday and dropped bombs. They were fired on.

Their mission appeared to be frontier reconnaissance besides the now open plan to intimidate the Greeks into making peace with the miserably defeated Italian troops in Albania.

Bulgaria has already mobilised two of her three armies and mobilisation is continuing, it was learned from a Yugoslavian source.

Further classes have been called up quietly in Bulgaria for military training. Many German "instructors" in civil clothes have been shifted in the last few days into villages where there are no Bulgarian troops for instruction.

These villages, however, lie in the direct southern route to the Greek frontier.

Massed on Frontier

It was reported recently that Bulgarian troops were massed on the frontier of Thrace (Greece).

Bulgaria's Army at full strength numbers 650,000 men.

A Bulgar - Yugoslav declaration, similar to that signed by Turkey and Bulgaria, is expected to be announced in a few days, it was stated in Sofia last night, says British United Press.

A broadcast by Ankara Radio last night said:

"The Turkish-Bulgarian pact has rendered a German attack on Greece through Bulgaria impossible. As Greece need not fear new aggression, Britain will not have to accord new help to this country.

"Germany will realise it is impossible to invade the Balkans."

A Swiss report says that no official statement is obtainable in Berlin concerning a report of a German ultimatum to Greece demanding immediate cessation of hostilities against Italy.

ITALIAN LOSSES PILE UP

"THE Greek offensive in Albania continues according to plan. Four or five elevated fortified posts have been captured in the central front," says a Greek statement.

"At two points the Italians tried to resist, but they were unsuccessful and sustained heavy losses. Several other counter-attacks were repulsed.

"The Italian Command seems to be indifferent to the loss of Italian lives.

"On the Northern Front the Italians launched an offensive on a wider scale and with larger forces than usual. They were trying to recapture important positions, but were repulsed with heavy losses before they could advance.

"In this action 300 prisoners were taken."

POWERFUL British air forces are ready for action at vital points in the Far East. And the U.S. is to develop Pacific naval and air bases in "total disregard of any Japanese protests."

As Japan's latest manœuvre—the sending of a special mediation offer to the British Government—was revealed yesterday in the Commons, British G.H.Q., Singapore, announced:

"The Royal Air Force in the Far East has received powerful reinforcements of modern bombers and twin and single-engined fighters which are now stationed in various areas of strategic importance."

The U.S. House of Representatives made vital Pacific defence decisions last night.

They approved the development of Guam—U.S. island nearest to Japan, a strategic keypoint—and Samoa, as naval and aviation outposts.

Before the decision, the House heard a letter from Admiral Stark, U.S. Chief of Naval Operations, telling them any Japanese protests would be "unwarranted and should be totally disregarded."

Jap Squeals

Earlier in the day, Mr. Sumner Welles, U.S. Under-Secretary of State, told Japan bluntly: "We are more interested in the deeds of other nations than in the statements of some of their spokesmen."

According to Moscow radio, Japanese are now leaving the U.S.-owned Philippines.

Yesterday the spokesman of the Japanese forces in China squealed at

Continued on Back Page

BLIND BOY'S £600 DAY

A BLIND boy, Jonathan Fisher, who lives with his father at Grange Farm, Ivegill, near Carlisle, Cumberland, has collected £611 in one day for the local War Weapons Week.

Led by his sheepdog, Jonathan set out on a bitterly cold day to collect money.

Jonathan and his dog hiked over hills and dales, calling upon farmers, labourers in the fields and cottagers' wives.

Returning home he added up his money and made out a neat account in Braille. Next morning he presented the £611 to Mrs. Bryson, village schoolmistress, who is treasurer of the Savings Fund.

TRIAL OF DE GAULLE MEN

A big secret trial of officers who have joined General de Gaulle's movement is to begin on Tuesday in the Court of Justice at Gannat, ten miles west of Vichy, states a Vichy dispatch to the Official German News Agency, quoted by Reuter.

The case is presumably being heard in their absence.

Princess's Radio Voice Surprised

Radio listeners heard last night the perfect woman broadcaster. She spoke in clear, ringing tones, with faultless enunciation and accent.

And she wasn't an Englishwoman.

She was Princess Tsahi, daughter of the Emperor of Abyssinia.

She told a moving story of her exile. She described the last days in Addis Ababa five years ago as the Italian invaders steadily closed in and the final order from her father that they must all flee.

Since then she has been in England, learning nursing.

"I have come to know England, and that means to love it. But duty calls me to my own country, and I hope to join an ambulance unit that will soon leave for Abyssinia," she said.

It is probable that the Emperor heard his daughter's voice when the speech was rebroadcast in the overseas programmes.

RAF MEN TRAIN IN U.S.

FIFTEEN R.A.F. officers, from pilot officers to squadron leaders, are being taught to operate the four-engine "flying fortress" bombers at Marchfield (Los Angeles) under the supervision of the United States Army.

A British spokesman declared these ferry pilots were the vanguard of larger contingents.

Detachments of Canadian navigators are expected at Marchfield soon for similar instruction.

A plane output of 18,000 may be expected this year. Mr. William Knudson, U.S. defence production chief, told a Press conference in Washington yesterday.

He added that during January 1,036 planes were delivered by United States manufacturers, of which 957 went to the U.S. Army and Navy and Great Britain.—Exchange and Associated Press.

SEVEN LUNATICS BREAK GAOL

Seven convicts, inmates of the criminal lunatic department of Perth Prison, broke gaol late last night.

A police cordon was flung round Perth, and a watch kept on the railway station and all road traffic.

To escape the prisoners had to scale a wall which is over 30ft. high in places. Police believe the men split up and scattered themselves over the thickly wooded countryside in the black-out.

MORE RAID INJURY PAY?

The Minister of Pensions stated yesterday in the House that an increase in the 14s. a week air-raid injury allowance for women was among matters under consideration.

BY A SPECIAL CORRESPONDENT

MEN drawn from all branches of the Army make up Britain's parachute troops. The county regiments, the Tank Corps and the Pioneer Corps are all represented.

They received intensive preparation for the job. During the first months they did not go up in a plane —they were given lecture after lecture on every detail of the required strategy.

Then came the physical training. Week after week they marched in full kit. They practised swimming in uniform. They did rock-climbing.

At this stage many were weeded out because they did not come up to the necessary standard of endurance.

Only the very fittest, mentally and physically, would do for this new Army.

There have been thousands of volunteers.

You'll Recognise Them

You will be able to recognise Britain's paratroops whenever you meet them.

They will be wearing a special badge on the arm. It shows a white parachute with blue wings—similar to those of the R.A.F.—on either side.

Last night I met the man who taught the paratroops who jumped in Italy. He made his first parachute jump himself only six months ago.

But tall, slimly-built Squadron-Leader L. A. Strange, D.S.O., D.S.C., M.C., who began his flying in 1906 has always demanded action.

He soldiered during the last war as a major with the Dorsetshire Regiment. Later he was transferred to the R.F.C., became a wing-commander. Before the outbreak of the present war he was closely associated with Whitney Straight, the racing motorist and aeroplane enthusiast.

Sqdn. Ldr. Strange

He took up his Service career again in this war as a pilot-officer, but, in the words of a colleague: "We got so fed up with the way things were moving that he went to the Air Ministry. They said, 'Right, we'll give you a job.' And they did."

Squadron-Leader Strange took to his new job of training parachute troops with zest.

"There's nothing in parachuting," Squadron-Leader Strange told me.

"The parachute is opened automatically and the men leave the troop-carrying plane according to a set drill.

"The real job before parachute troops awaits them when they get on the ground."

NAZI GENERAL KILLED

General Roettig, a German officer, has been killed during a clash between Polish armed bands and German police.

There has been serious fighting with armed bands of Polish soldiers in hiding, says Deutsche Rundschau.

This Boy Was Lowered Down Well

Albert White, Stepney evacuee, who was left dangling down a well and thrashed with a dog-whip, according to evidence given at Penzance yesterday.
(Story on page 11.)

Daily Mirror

FEB 21

No. 11,607 — ONE PENNY
Registered at the G.P.O. as a Newspaper.

Don't Kill Your Canary

DON'T kill your canary, budgerigar or parrot because of the Food Ministry's announcement that there will be no grain for pet birds.

There is a substitute for nearly every kind of bird food, the R.S.P.C.A. told the "Daily Mirror" last night.

An official said many people had applied to have their pets destroyed within a few hours of the Ministry's announcement.

Your parrot will be quite content with all kinds of household scraps, including potato peelings, another expert said.

Budgerigars are more fastidious. But with coaxing and patience they will take to root vegetables, carrots, turnips and swedes, mixed with dried breadcrumbs, preferably brown bread.

Talking the food problem over.

Canaries are partial to dried breakfast foods, rolled oats, or even porridge. The porridge has to be cooked first, then dried.

Birds should be broken-in gently to their new diet. In many cases it will be found that the change of food is beneficial rather than detrimental.

"Many fanciers are growing their own seeds, and this should be encouraged," the Editor of "Cage Birds," Mr. E. R. W. Lincoln, said.

"Now the spring is coming, people should collect wild grass seeds for their pet birds. As a soft food substitute, crushed dog biscuits are excellent."

Enlist Your Pigeons

Here's a chance to enlist your racing pigeons in the fighting services. A limited increase in the membership of the National Pigeon Service has been authorised, and owners who wish to join should apply to the Secretary, National Pigeon Service, 22, Clarence-street, Gloucester.

GATE-CRASHED QUEEN'S ROOMS

BY A SPECIAL CORRESPONDENT

MUCH stricter examination of men and women employed casually in and about the homes of the King and Queen has been enforced as a result of an amazing incident at one of the royal homes in the country.

A young soldier told the "Daily Mirror" that he found his way to the Queen's apartments, entered after knocking on the door, and asked her to help him to join the A.F.S.

The Queen was astounded at the ease with which the man was able to wander about the rooms.

Immediately orders were given for a tightening of the regulations concerning the employment of servants in the royal homes.

Papers of all workers in the royal residences will be so carefully scrutinised that it will never again be possible for an intruder to get past the gatekeepers.

Here is the story as the soldier told it: "After deserting and starving for some weeks, I went to the Labour Exchange in a district where the King and Queen live. I got a job as a fitter's mate in the royal household.

"I found out where the Queen's rooms were and made up my mind to see her and ask for her help. I strolled boldly to her room and knocked at the door.

"A voice asked: 'Who's there?'

"I answered and walked in. The Queen seemed surprised to see me, and asked why I had come.

"I said something, and she then asked me to tell her my story. She smiled and was nice to me.

"After I had told her why I had come to see her, she shook my hand.

Continued on Back Page

LIFE FOR HIS LOVE

BY A SPECIAL CORRESPONDENT

MARY was the only sweetheart Roger had ever had. They were to be married in June.

In the little things of life—like helping her on to pavements and off buses—he was chivalrous.

In the moment of danger he did not forget his chivalry. It cost him his life.

He was helping her on to a pavement in the black-out. A car came towards them.

Roger threw himself in front of his sweetheart. The car hit him.

The chivalrous lover was Roger Denis Greener, aged twenty-five, of Grange-road, Erdington, Birmingham.

Engaged a Year

He had been engaged to Mary Rigney, aged twenty-five, of Arthur-road Erdington, for a year.

Last week he was home on leave—he was a Royal Artillery gunner.

Miss Rigney, who is a secretary, is now at home recovering from slight injuries and severe shock.

She told me last night: "Roger was always a most chivalrous boy.

"Just before we crossed the road, he had been walking on the outside of me, as he always did. He remained there until we reached the other kerb.

"It was while he was walking round me, so that he could be on the outside again, and was helping me on to the path, that the car suddenly came on us.

"He threw himself in front of me and received the full force. I was thrown on to the pathway.

"Roger will remain in my memory for ever."

To Save Mother

Mr Greener said that his son had come home unexpectedly on leave. "My wife was in Harlech when he came home," he said.

"He went to see her but returned home a day earlier to be with Mary and me. That night he was killed.

"I have never known a more chivalrous boy.

"Some time ago, while he was out with his mother, he jumped in front of her when he thought a car was going to hit them.

"Mary was the only girl he had ever had. During his leave they had been talking about their wedding."

Mary Rigney, the girl Roger Greener (left) died for.

Use 'Power of Thought' Says M.P.

Sir W. Davison, M.P., is to suggest to the Premier that, "in view of the power of concentrated thought," he should ask all Britons to unite for a moment nightly in some such thought as the virility of the Empire, and the need of its maintenance for peace and freedom.

Eden Flies to Cairo

MR. ANTHONY EDEN, Foreign Secretary, and General Sir John Dill, Chief of the Imperial General Staff, are in Cairo, Reuter reported last night.

They left Britain by air several days ago. It is expected they will have discussions in Cairo for a fortnight.

Commenting on their visit, a spokesman of the British Embassy said:—

"The time is clearly ripe for a full review of the political and military situation in the Middle East and Africa as the outcome of the brilliant victory of the Army of the Nile.

"There is no doubt that there will be full consultations with the military leaders in the Middle East and other authorities."

Road to Addis Won

As Secretary for War, Mr. Eden was in Egypt at the end of last year —a visit which preceded the annihilation of the Italian armies in the Western Desert.

His new visit coincides with the news that British troops have again struck successfully on two fronts at the same time.

Mega, Italian garrison post in Southern Abyssinia, 6,500ft. above sea level, surrendered to South African troops.

This victory gives Britain command of another key road into Addis Ababa, the capital.

Violent attacks carried our troops across the River Juba, in Italian Somaliland.

Lieutenant-General A. G. Cunningham, G.O.C., the East African Imperial Force, in his order of the day on the eve of the successful Jubaland operations, told his troops:—

"Hit them, hit them hard and hit them again!"

NAZIS ACROSS DANUBE

GERMANS were reported last night to be moving from Rumania into Bulgaria over pontoon bridges thrown across the River Danube earlier in the day.

This report was broadcast by Columbia Radio, New York.

Messages from Belgrade and Sofia said the Germans were testing pontoons by crossing in loaded lorries into Bulgaria.

All shipping on the river below the Iron Gate was stopped while the Nazis made their preparations for the pontoons. It was reported in Budapest.

Food Stores Ready

David Walker, *Daily Mirror* Balkans correspondent, cabled from Sofia:—

Behind smoke screens of Balkan good fellowship, Germany is quietly going ahead with plans against Greece.

At Nikopol and other points of the Danube, German detachments have actually thrown over their pontoons and coolly tested them for heavy traffic.

Food which has been collected at nine strategic points is now nearly ready, and the Struma Valley bridges tested again.

During the past forty-eight hours there has been a sharp rise in "tourist" arrivals. February 25 may or may not be the appointed day but the stage is certainly set.

One more "pact of friendship" and the Nazis will probably march in.

Fire Blitz on Welsh Town

RAIDERS heavily attacked South Wales last night with one town as the chief target.

Despite intense A.A. fire they dropped large numbers of fire-bombs. Some heavy bombs were also dropped.

London had a short Alert.

A fierce fight took place in a daylight snowstorm over the Straits of Dover. A patrol of Spitfires intercepted a formation of Germans.

Two Spitfires crashed in flames. Both pilots made parachute leaps.

One of the Spitfires crashed on cliffs west of Dover. The other fell behind St. Margaret's Bay. There was no report of any German planes being destroyed.

(Swansea cinemagoers sing when bombed—page 2.)

GIFT TO FIGHT PNEUMONIA

The Duchess of Kent has accepted, on behalf of the Greek nation, a gift of 1,000,000 anti-pneumonia tablets to combat the disease, prevalent in Greece.

The tablets are valued at £5,000 and 20,000 have already been sent by air mail.

NAVY THANKED FOR SINKING

A German-controlled Norwegian ship of about 1,500 tons has been destroyed by the British submarine Sealion near the Norwegian coast.

The vessel was stopped and H.M.S. Sealion made a signal instructing the master to abandon ship. He replied, "Thank you."

H.M.S. Sealion waited for fifteen minutes while the crew abandoned ship into the lifeboats. The ship was then destroyed by gunfire.

Daily Mirror

FEB 22

No. 11,698   ONE PENNY
Registered at the G.P.O. as a Newspaper.

HUN TROOPS MOVE INTO SPAIN

NO MORE HOKEY-POKEY

Schools to Help Farmers

BY A SPECIAL CORRESPONDENT

SCHOOL holidays are to be arranged to coincide with the times when farmers need help.

An Education Board official told the "Daily Mirror" that last night.

He was explaining an Order issued by the Board.

This empowers local education authorities to close schools at short notice to release children for seasonal farm work.

It does not mean that children will get more holidays, or that they will have to work on a farm if their school is closed.

"Many children gave invaluable help to farmers last year by working during their holidays," said the official.

Willing Volunteers

"The Government is anxious that this willing source of help should be interfered with as little as possible.

"If a farmer needs help he can apply through his county War Agricultural Committee for schoolchildren to be released.

"A census will be taken of children willing to help and, if the farmer's demands can be met from one school, only that school will be closed.

"It is not expected that there will be any lack of volunteers—especially at fruit-picking time."

The Board of Education makes it clear that the Order will be operated with due regard to maintenance of the health and education of the children.

SECRETLY WED FOR 16 YEARS

BY A SPECIAL CORRESPONDENT

MR. Harry Gordon Selfridge, jun., son of the famous London store founder, was secretly married sixteen years ago it was revealed yesterday.

He has generally been regarded as a bachelor, but he told the "Daily Mirror": "Yes, I'm married, and have four children."

Mr. Selfridge returned to America just before the war with his wife and children the eldest of whom is a boy of fifteen.

They are now living at Darien, Connecticut.

Though he was born in the U.S. and is an American citizen, Mr. Selfridge has passed most of his life in England.

Mr. Selfridge resigned from the boards of Selfridge and Co., Ltd., William Whiteley, Ltd., and Selfridge Provincial Stores, Ltd., before he returned to America.

GERMAN troops have filtered from Occupied France into Spain, where they are to help in the reconstruction of Santander, on the northern coast, which was badly damaged by fire during a hurricane at the week-end.

They consist of five detachments described in a report from Madrid yesterday as "small."

A motorised column, sappers, field kitchens and ambulances made up the "repair squads."

Damage estimated at £6,000,000 was done by the Santander fire. Thirty thousand people were homeless.

Meanwhile, the general staff of Hitler's Balkan Army moved from Bukarest to Craiova, forty miles north of the Danube across which the Germans are throwing pontoon bridges.

Columns of Nazi motorised troops, miles long, rolled south through Rumania towards the Danube frontier with Bulgaria.

These reports reached Belgrade in "military messages" and were quoted by Associated Press.

According to a Belgrade report, says Reuter, German troops had been crossing into Bulgaria since Thursday afternoon.

The Yugoslav Cabinet called an emergency meeting. They discussed their attitude to the fast-moving events.

Messages from the Bulgarian port of Ruse, on the Danube facing the

Infiltration

Infiltration of troops into neutral countries is a trick in which Germany is expert. Thousands of German "tourists" are already in Bulgaria and other Balkan countries. This is the first time the Nazis have disguised their troops as firemen and salvage parties.

But there is no truth in the report that they are coming to London to repair air-raid damage!

Continued on Back Page

Big Raid on Welsh Town

WAVES of raiders heavily attacked a South Wales coastal town last night.

Considerable damage was done to property, which included a market, shops and a chapel. There were casualties.

Flares were dropped followed by fire-bombs, which were scattered indiscriminately.

Fires were started. But fire-watchers and the fire services controlled them.

Women and children smothered incendiaries.

Soon afterwards other raiders, flying high, dropped high explosives. The attack was still going on after some hours.

EDEN MEETS ARMY CHIEFS

Mr. Eden, the Foreign Secretary, spent a busy day in Cairo yesterday in consultations with military chiefs. He saw General Catroux, the Free French leader, and dined with General Wavell.

It is possible he may shortly visit Cyrenaica, scene of the triumph of General Wavell's Army.—Associated Press.

MORE woe! More woe for the Italians! On top of their daily doses of defeat in Africa and Albania comes yet another national disaster:—

No more ice-cream after March 1.

Sidi Barrani, Tobruk, Derna, Benghazi—these losses chilled the Duce's men and women of blood and steel.

Now they have lost Hokey-Pokey it leaves them cold.

Organ-grinders wept when news of the death of Wopdom's No. 1 industry was broken yesterday by Signor Gayda, Mussolini's mouth-organ.

"The Government's policy is sincere and serious," he said. "It does not wish to promise what it cannot give."

Didn't the Duce promise a new Empire? A new Italy riding high in a new order?

Britain teaches Musso a lesson. Musso, good boy, learns it. More woe!

But no more promises.

NO MORE HOKEY-POKEY!

MINISTER'S TOUR IS OFF

Because of unforeseen circumstances, the Minister of Labour will be unable to fulfil engagements arranged for this week-end in the north-east.

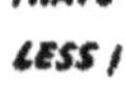

My nerves are steadier now I have a cup of Bournville Cocoa last thing at night—

AND IT'S ONE FOOD THAT'S COSTING LESS!

WHAT'S THIS? A food that's *lower* in price? Yes, madam, Bournville Cocoa costs you less than it did before the war. *It has been reduced to 5d. per quarter-pound.* Housewives now find their old friend Bournville Cocoa to be a big new help in keeping the bills down. And don't forget that it's a natural food and it helps your nerves!

★ **EXTRA FOOD VALUE**
★ **IRON—THE BLOOD ENRICHER**
★ **PHOSPHATES—FOR HEALTHY GROWTH**
★ **AID TO DIGESTION**
★ **VITAMIN D—VITAL TO HEALTH**

BOURNVILLE
THE 5-STAR
COCOA

QUALITY UNALTERED

DOWN TO 5d PER QTR LB

Save Money: Buy the ½ lb tin 9½d or the big family 1 lb tin 1'6

Second Officer John Sargent and Joan Sargent—father and daughter, hero and heroine.

PROUD OF EACH OTHER

FATHER: I am more proud about my daughter's commendation than I am about my medal.

DAUGHTER: I am more proud about my father's medal than I am about my commendation.

FATHER is Second Officer John Chasne Sargent, aged forty-four of the Tottenham Fire Brigade, awarded the medal of the Civil Division of the O.B.E. for courage.

Daughter is Miss Joan Ethel Sargent, nineteen-year-old telephonist who receives a commendation—a certificate for bravery—it was announced last night.

Father showed complete disregard of great danger when fighting oil fires during heavy bombing.

Daughter was eighteen when, in September, a heavy bomb exploded near the station where she was working part-time as an A.F.S. volunteer.

Fire fighters were evacuated, but Joan and another girl, Miss Hilda Ivy Griffith, who is also commended, remained at their post.

Later a fire-bomb set a nearby dump ablaze. Joan and Hilda remained on duty, keeping in touch with the head office.

Certificates for bravery have also been awarded to Mr. Joseph G. Griffiths, Mr. Ernest W. Harris auxiliary fireman, and Mr. R. J. Hubbard, Section Officer, all of Tottenham.

Died with Blitz Victim in Arms

AN A.F.S. man was found in a wreckage-filled room with his arms round the woman he had climbed in to save.

He had been killed as he was carrying her through the doorway to safety.

That story lies behind the formal announcement last night that the King has commended Auxiliary Fireman W. G. Perry of Bristol, for his services.

People standing round a blazing house told Perry a woman was trapped inside. He smashed a window on the ground floor and climbed through.

Suddenly the whole house crashed. His mates trained their hoses on the flaming debris, but could not fight their way inside.

Daily Mirror

FEB 25

No. 11,610   ONE PENNY
Registered at the G.P.O. as a Newspaper.

JAPS WARN WHITES TO QUIT THE PACIFIC

Girl Found Job to Forget

Barracks for Arms Workers

MARRIED quarters may be built for armament workers.

In some of the areas where new munition factories have been established, men who were transferred from towns in the London area found they had little accommodation for themselves and families.

Some had to store their furniture and live in one room.

The position is now so acute that the authorities are considering providing barracks for them.

These would be built as near as possible to the men's place of employment so as to avoid long travelling to and from work.

"Overcrowding"

An official of the Transport and General Workers' Union said yesterday:—

"Many of our members left London to go to the new areas, and we have received complaints from them about the poor accommodation.

"Some were buying their own houses when they were transferred, and they are now living in one room.

"In some areas we hear of definite overcrowding and it is time something was done."

In one area negotiations are taking place to provide houses for transferred families.

WORKERS TO TELL WORLD

WORKERS from British war factories will take their place at the microphone of the B.B.C. in future major overseas broadcasts on Britain's war effort in place of the professors and so-called experts.

This is the result of representations being made by Sir Walter Citrine to the British Government.

Sir Walter has prepared a memorandum to the B.B.C. in which he gives evidence of the United States abhorrence of what they consider a super-varsity patronising accent.

America's plea is to hear the honest unaffected voices of the men and women of Britain who are doing their job.

RAIN SLOWS UP GREEKS

Heavy rain and mist impeded operations on the Albanian front, which still continue slowly, the Greek Press Ministry stated in a broadcast from Athens last night.

Mountain villages, passes and areas recently captured are being systematically cleaned up.

More prisoners were taken, two enemy tanks destroyed in successful local operations. Two enemy planes were shot down by Greek anti-aircraft guns.—British United Press.

Mr. Matsuoka.

AS Mr. Matsuoka, Japanese Foreign Minister, told the House of Representatives in Tokio yesterday that the white race "must cede Oceania (the entire South Pacific) to the Asiatics," Mr. Churchill saw the Japanese Ambassador, Mr. Shigemitsu, in London.

The French Far Eastern Fleet was reported to be cruising in the Gulf of Siam. All Army leave was cancelled in French Indo-China.

Britain's attitude to Japanese expansionist moves in the Far East was made clear by Mr. Churchill in a written reply to inquiries made by Mr. Matsuoka.

Well-informed Japanese in London stated last night that the interview was fruitful and should greatly contribute to dissipate certain misunderstandings that have arisen between the two countries.

The Premier gave the replies to Mr. Shigemitsu in one of three important conferences with foreign envoys. THE TWO OTHER TALKS WERE WITH THE TURKISH AND THE GREEK AMBASSADORS.

Mr. Churchill is likely to describe these talks to the House of Commons soon.

Sir Robert Craigie, British Ambassador in Tokio, saw Japanese statesmen yesterday, and told them of Britain's firm stand.

"Natural Right"

Japan's desire to oust the white race from Oceania was made clear by Mr. Matsuoka in the House of Representatives.

Japan's conception of Oceania, it was thought by U.S. observers, extends to the entire South Pacific, including the Dutch East Indies, the Philippines and possibly Australasia.

This was based on Mr. Matsuoka's reference to the number of people that could be supported in such an area:—

"This region has sufficient natural resources to support between 600,000,000 and 800,000,000 people. I believe we have a natural right to migrate there.

"While it is difficult to conduct political affairs according to advocated ideals, I believe that the white race must cede Oceania to the Asiatics."

The Japanese Press yesterday advised Britain and U.S.A. to call a halt in their defensive measures in the Pacific.

These were described as "an unwarrantable challenge" to Japan.

Sir Archibald Clark Kerr, British Ambassador to China, is leaving Chungking for Hong Kong today by air.

A more hopeful feeling has been inspired in Bangkok by the renewal of the Thailand-Indo-China truce.

Foreign messages from British United Press and Reuter.

HITLER WAS SILENT ON 4 POINTS

HITLER made a speech yesterday in the Munich beer cellar where the Nazi Party was founded twenty-one years ago.

But he forgot to mention four things:—

The invasion of Britain;
American aid for Britain;
The Balkans; and
Japan and Russia.

SAYS U-BOAT WAR BEGINS NOW

"Our new U-boats are beginning to arrive—now our sea war can begin in earnest," Hitler declared.

"Numerous British warships are tied up in the Mediterranean, numerous British planes are tied up in North Africa, numerous British land forces are also tied up," he said. "It is only now that our sea warfare will start.

"We have been waiting to complete the training of the crews in the new U-boats which are now coming from the shipyards.

Fantastic Claim

"Two hours ago I received reports that German surface warships and U-boats had sunk 215,000 tons of shipping in two days. But in March and April a naval warfare will start such as the enemy has never expected.

It was learned in London last night that there is no truth whatever in the fantastic claim that 215,000 tons of **Continued on Back Page**

Continued on Back Page

BY A SPECIAL CORRESPONDENT

SOON after her airman-husband was killed at Narvik, a grief-stricken girl left England for her native land, Australia.

But she returned, said to an officer of the Mechanised Transport Corps: "Please give me plenty of work to help me to forget."

And Mrs. Mollie Orton became an ambulance driver. She worked hard and was one of twelve volunteers for service in Greece.

But when the Duchess of Kent inspected the Greek unit last Tuesday, Mrs. Orton was not there.

It was not until later that the corps learned that she had been killed by a bomb the night before. She was twenty-six.

With her died two of her friends—Lady Moore, widow of Sir John Moore, Director of the Army Veterinary Service in the last war, and Lady Moore's youngest daughter, Mrs. Patricia Parley.

DARLAN PICKS HIS MEN

A NEW Cabinet sworn to collaborate with Germany, with Admiral Darlan in four key posts, was announced in Vichy yesterday.

Admiral Darlan chose the Cabinet, which consists of only five Ministers. There are also eight Secretaries of State.

One is a Secretariat of State for Economy, charged with Franco-German economic collaboration. M. Barnand takes this post.

Darlan is Vice-Premier, Foreign Minister, Minister of the Interior and Minister of the Navy.

"The new Cabinet has firmly decided to follow a policy of Franco-German collaboration," an official spokesman stated in Vichy.

Laval: Minor Post?

Laval, it was suggested, might be offered a directive post in a secretariat of state for home affairs.

Marshal Petain remains head of the State. Other Ministers in the new Cabinet are:—

National Defence, General Huntziger; Justice, M. Jose H. Barthelemy; Finance, M. Bouthillier; Agriculture, M. Caziot.—British United Press and Associated Press.

BEACH EXPLOSION KILLS 2

An object which exploded on a beach in the north of Scotland killed sixteen-year-old Magnus Houston and injured his father, Malcolm Houston, a farmer, so seriously that he died the same night.

The boy found the object at the water edge, carried it up the beach and fetched his father.

They Don't Pan Out Today

If we had a lemon and some sugar to spare we'd have pancakes —if we had the eggs.

Today is Pancake Day—but this year few crisp and tasty pancakes will be tossed from the frying pan.

That's another kick we owe Hitler.

Keen and Courageous

Their deaths were announced yesterday. Lady Moore's housekeeper, Mrs. Rebecca Henry, was also killed in the house, which was demolished by the bomb.

"Mrs. Orton had a cheerful personality and was popular with her unit," Miss Alison Tennant, Lady Oxford's niece, who is in charge of the Greek unit, told me.

Mrs. Mollie Orton.

"She was keen on her work and was a courageous woman. Her husband's death was a great blow to her, but she did not brood over it.

"She was quite willing to talk about it.

"Her death was a shock to her unit. All the members attended her funeral."

Lady Moore was on a brief visit to the house. The owner, an R.A.M.C. officer, was called out on duty shortly before the bomb fell.

A man confined to bed with 'flu in an upper room escaped.

Mrs. Parley was an ambulance driver too.

HUSBAND NAZI, SO ASKS DIVORCE

FROM JOHN WALTERS

NEW YORK, Monday.

NEW YORK Supreme Court was asked to decide today whether a husband's concealment of his German citizenship warranted a divorce by his wife, who detests the Nazis.

The Court was asked to grant a divorce to Mrs. Nome Laage, whose husband is now in a Canadian concentration camp. She testified she married Laage in 1938, believing him to be a naturalised American.

She discovered, however, that he was really a German agent. He was finally caught by the Canadians when he was trying to buy ships in 1940. He once escaped from a concentration camp, but was recaptured.

The Judge reserved his decision, but said Mrs. Laage's view was not unreasonable.

MR. MENZIES AT CABINET

Mr. R. G. Menzies, Prime Minister of Australia, will attend the meetings of the War Cabinet during his visit to this country, it is officially announced.

Daily Mirror

FEB 27

No. 11,612   ONE PENNY
Registered at the G.P.O. as a Newspaper.

FIERCE FIRE RAIDS HIT 2 AREAS

GERMAN bombers made fierce attacks last night on two towns—one in South Wales and one in a Thames Estuary district. Other areas were attacked in the most widespread raid experienced in recent weeks.

Explosive incendiaries were among the bombs used on the blitzed towns.

Showers of flares and fire bombs ringed the South Wales town and district. The attack started early in the evening with the dropping of parachute flares. Machine-gunners shot most of them down but more quickly followed.

Wave after wave of raiders scattered incendiary bombs.

Swiftly the town became lit up by a greenish glow.

From a distant vantage point it was possible to read a newspaper.

As the raiders roared over, the screech of H.E.s mingled with the terrific clatter of the A.A. barrage and the frequent rat-tat of machine-gun fire from British fighters who seemed to be all over the town.

Fires were started but were quickly extinguished. Men and women rushed out to tackle the incendiaries.

A children's home was hit by in-

★

Terrific flashes came from the invasion ports on the other side of the Straits of Dover last night.

Searchlights and bursting A.A. shells added to the scene. The flashes were particularly extensive in the direction of Boulogne.

R.A.F. Masters of Channel.—Back page.

★

cendiaries and part of the building caught fire. The fire was quickly put out.

Among buildings which received direct hits from high explosive bombs were a church, a girls' hostel and a public-house. In the hostel were six girl students, two of whom were injured.

Over the Estuary town the raiders went back to their old tactics of dropping incendiaries first and then high explosives. Few fires were started and they were all extinguished.

The raiders were met by one of the heaviest A.A. barrages. In the lulls British night fighters could be heard.

London's Two Alerts

People were trapped in their homes when one stick of high explosives wrecked houses.

Considerable damage was done to house property and public buildings.

Other areas raided included London, the Home Counties, a south-west town and a south coast town.

London had two Alerts. The first was over well before midnight, and the second—a brief one—was sounded a few minutes after the Raiders Passed.

Bombs fell in several London districts.

Heavy bombs falling within a short distance of each other in one London district demolished some houses.

There were casualties.

Church halls and schools were opened to accommodate homeless.

One raider, caught in the beams of two searchlights on the outskirts of London, is believed to have been brought down. It was seen to dive steeply after A.A. shells had burst near it.

Toffee Carrots Now!

"Toffee carrots, please," children of Shepherd's Bush (London) call out in the sweetshop of Mr. Harold Carter, Eronwald-street. Sweeter than apples—and cheaper—toffee carrots are taking the place of the absent sweets.

Behind his shop, Mr. Carter spends his time busily dipping home-grown carrots in a saucepan of toffee. He is usually sold out before the toffee has hardened on them.

"There are very few sweets these days," he told the "Daily Mirror," "and they are pretty dear to buy with pennies. But carrots are cheap, and Lord Woolton urges us to eat them, so I decided to make sweets of 'Woolton's Wonders.'"

On short sticks, Mr. Carter's toffee carrots sell at halfpenny or penny according to size.

★

MEATLESS DAYS SOON

MEATLESS days soon in restaurants because of acute meat shortage were considered probable by Mr. S. Gordon Scott, catering section chairman, at yesterday's annual meeting of Birmingham Master Bakers' Association.

Coffee, too, is likely to become scarce, he added.

Further details are now available of the order coming into force on March 10 limiting the consumption in catering establishments, residential establishments and institutions of fish, meat, poultry and game, eggs and cheese.

Under the Order a person may be served at a single meal with only one main dish and one subsidiary dish, or two subsidiary dishes.

A main dish contains meat, poultry or game, or one-third or more of its weight in fish, eggs or cheese.

Soup is not regarded as a main dish unless it contains more than 5 per cent. by weight of solid meat, poultry or game.

Oysters Not Included

A subsidiary contains less than one-third of its weight in fish, eggs or cheese.

Generally, not more than one egg may be served as part of any single meal, although this cannot apply to an omelette or to scrambled eggs.

Oysters, whitebait and smoked salmon are not included in fish as they are consumed almost entirely in restaurants. Poultry and game include rabbits, hares and any kind of bird used for human food.

WE CAPTURE ITALIAN ISLE

British forces have occupied the small Italian island of Castellorizo, in the Eastern Mediterranean, one of the Dodecanese group and only four miles from the Turkish coast.

The island has a seaplane base which was used by Imperial Airways before the war. It has a population of 2,238.

It is sixty miles east of the island of Rhodes, which has a naval base, and about 170 miles north-west of Cyprus.

By the Treaty of Sevres after the last war Turkey renounced all rights to the island, and Italy has since numbered it among her Dodecanese possessions.

A communique from the Admiralty and War Office last night said the occupation was carried out on Tuesday.

More U.S. Destroyers?

Admiral Stark, chief of U.S. naval operations, told the Appropriations Committee of the House of Representatives th.: the United States might transfer more destroyers to Britain.

While the transfer of more destroyers on the scale Mr. Wendell Willkie suggested would not be advisable "at the moment," said Admiral Stark, the Government's hands should not be tied.

6 KILLED IN DUTCH CLASHES

SIX civilians had been killed and a number injured, in the course of clashes between police and "disturbers of the peace," it was officially announced in Nazi-occupied Amsterdam last night.

German military administration was set up in the province of North Holland yesterday following strikes

The strikers have been ordered to return to work today.

Marching, meetings, demonstrations and assembling in the streets are forbidden, and political parties of all the Netherlands are banned from activity in the province. Wearing of uniforms and insignias of any kind is forbidden.

Civil violations are punishable by imprisonment up to fifteen years, while offences against the German Army are punishable by death.

German Plot

BY OUR DIPLOMATIC CORRESPONDENT

Germany is trying to induce Bulgaria to attack Greece simultaneously with an attack by Germany. She has offered to equip the Bulgarian Army with modern weapons and to co-ordinate it with the German Army.

Pro-German revisionist elements among the Bulgarian General Staff favour acceptance, as they see in this offer an opportunity for Bulgaria to seize the Ægean ports of Kavala and Dedeagach.

But the present Bulgarian Government are opposed to such a move. They are reconciled to their country being used as a German base against Greece, but still hope to keep Bulgaria out of the war.

WE PLAN GREEK ANSWER

AN Anglo-Greek agreement that neither country will make a separate peace was discussed in Ankara yesterday by Mr. Anthony Eden, Britain's Foreign Secretary, and Greece's Minister to Turkey, according to reports reaching Sofia.

The reports (quoted by Associated Press) said the move was the answer—in advance—to any Nazi attempt to make Greece sign an armistice with Italy under threat of a German attack through Bulgaria.

Following his conversation yesterday with the Greek Minister, Mr. Eden expects to have discussions at Ankara with both the Bulgarian and Yugoslav Ministers to Turkey.

Mr. Eden paid courtesy visits to the Turkish Premier, Refik Saydam, and Foreign Minister, Mr. SaraJoglu. He conferred separately with Mr. John Van MacMurray, the U.S. Ambassador, and the Greek Minister.

SOFIA CABINET CRISIS SESSION

THE Bulgarian Cabinet met in an emergency session last night after a conference between the Chief of Staff, General Nicola Petkoff, and the Premier and Foreign Minister, MM. Filoff and Popoff.

The German Minister, von Richthofen, was reported to have conferred with Popoff in the late afternoon.

Earlier in the day New York radio, in a relay from Belgrade, reported that 12,000 German mechanised troops had crossed the Danube from Rumania into Bulgaria. The report was denied in Berlin.

During the day Berlin officials accused "British agents" of organising disturbances and sabotage in Sofia, the Bulgarian capital.

This, presumably, was an excuse in preparation for possible German "intervention to preserve order."

Later the story grew. Berlin radio said that "fiZ: agents of the British Secret Service and British Embassy" had been arrested.

In a cable from Sofia, DAVID WALKER says that powerful contingents of German naval men have arrived in Vienna and other Danube towns in Austria.

Daily Mirror

MAR 4

No. 11,616 — ONE PENNY
Registered at the G.P.O. as a Newspaper.

Nation Takes Over Huge Docks

BY A SPECIAL CORRESPONDENT

THE great Clyde docks are to be completely reorganised and expanded, and the dock labour controlled, in a drastic scheme to speed up this vital section of the war effort.

The Government is taking complete control of an industry starting with the employers' end first.

It has conscripted the ships which enter the port by means of charters

It is taking over the entire docks through the Ministry of Transport, and has appointed a Regional Port Director, who has set up a Transport Executive.

This comprises representatives of the port authority, Ministries of Food, Supply and Shipping, and railway, cartage and storage companies.

These executives will be a daily working body, knowing what ships and cargoes are expected in the ports.

They will make all the arrangements for rapid discharge and loading of ships and the quick removal of the cargoes from the docks to their destinations.

This new control is expected to give an enormous increase in production.

The dockers, who have been reluctant to give up old methods of payment, will now get a weekly guaranteed wage, plus piecework and bonus rates.

This will end the system under which some of them have earned as much as £22 in eight days.

NAZIS' NEW FLARE

"CHANDELIER flares"—a new type—were used by the Germans in a raid over an East Anglia area last night.

The main flare was an orange colour, and remained almost stationary for about 15 minutes. From it a tail of small white lights was suspended, and a similar string of lights going upwards, the latter remaining almost perpendicular for several seconds. These had a brilliant effect on the area.

Searchlights played on one of the flares; then came the crash of gunfire, and the flare burst into thousands of smaller lights.

Changed Tactics

The Germans appear to have changed their own raid tactics, if only temporarily, it was stated in London last night.

They have apparently abandoned their terror raids on London and other great centres of civilian population, and are concentrating their attacks on ports.

This is probably a contribution to the spring submarine campaign

Fire bombs were scattered like raindrops on a South Wales town last night in a severe raid.

Many fires were started early in the raid. A shopping centre in the town was bombarded by high explosives, and among the places hit were a large hospital, churches and a blind institution. Casualties were comparatively few, but some were fatal. Nurses at a hospital took patients to shelters as soon the raid started

Raider Down

The official German News Agency announced last night that the Luftwaffe had attacked war-important objectives along the North-East Coast of Britain earlier in the evening. Details were lacking.

Several small formations of Messerschmitts flew high, appeared over the south-east coast early last night. They stayed for only a short time before turning back to the French coast.

One raider is reported to have been brought down over Dungeness.

High explosive and incendiary bombs were dropped on a town in South-East Scotland — the raiders' first visit to that area this year.

The Alert was sounded in London and incendiaries were dropped. Fire watchers dealt with them quickly.

Their Ports Bombed

Roaring across the Straits of Dover in pale moonlight soon after nightfall last night, R.A.F. bombers heavily attacked the invasion ports on the French coast.

Terrific flashes lit up the sky above Calais and Boulogne, and scores of searchlights were in action along twenty miles of French coast.

German ground defences offered lively resistance, spraying the sky with star-shells and streams of flaming onions. Flares dropped by the raiders gleamed brightly above the attacked ports during the raid

Mrs. Bessie Angell and her Alsatian, Danny.

Hints Salvage Compulsion

Housewives, caretakers, charwomen, cleaners and others must keep waste paper, metal and bones separately, and place them where they are told to place them. Otherwise they may be compelled to do so.

Mr. Harold G. Judd, Controller of Salvage to the Ministry of Supply, said this to the "Daily Mirror" yesterday. "We shall have to apply a compulsory direction to them if they won't do their bit." he said.

NAZIS SAIL ATLANTIC

The German ship Leck (Captain Frederick Brinkman) reached Rio de Janeiro yesterday from Bordeaux after taking thirty-one days to cross the Atlantic, says Reuter.

There is no steamer Leck in Lloyd's Register, but there is the 3,290-ton Lech, registered at Bremen.

DONOVAN, OBSERVER FOR F.D.R., HERE AGAIN

Colonel W. J. Donovan, United States "unofficial observer" for President Roosevelt, who in the last few months has visited nearly a dozen capitals, arrived in London yesterday. He was here last August and again in December.

"I am afraid not." he replied when asked if he could say anything of the object of his new visit, his plans, or his recent visits to European capitals.

"I do not expect to be here more than a week." he said.

Colonel Donovan hopes to visit other British cities.

BLITZED— BUT BESSIE CARRIES ON

BY A SPECIAL CORRESPONDENT

MRS. BESSIE ANGELL is a British woman who won't be beaten by Nazi bombs. Her invincible spirit in the face of cruel misfortune is an inspiration to the women—and men—of Britain.

It has won the admiration of Mr. Winston Churchill, the Prime Minister, who has sent her a letter expressing his sympathy.

Her husband, Mr. Robert Herbert Angell, landlord of the Pound Tree Inn, Southampton, was killed by a bomb which fell outside the inn. Mrs. Angell bravely decided to carry on The day after her husband's funeral she reopened the bomb-damaged inn.

That night the Luftwaffe struck again. The inn was hit by incendiary bombs and destroyed. Danny her pet Alsatian, perished in the fire

Still in Business

The premises under which she had taken refuge were demolished by a bomb.

But she is still in business—at the bomb-damaged Osborne Hotel, Shirley.

"When I lost my husband, my home and business," she told the Daily Mirror yesterday, "I almost decided to join my sister in America. It was a fine broadcast speech by the Prime Minister that decided me to stay put.

"I was so impressed by his words that I wrote to him

And this is the reply Mr Churchill sent through his secretary:—

"The Prime Minister has asked me to tell you how very deeply he appreciated your kind letter. He feels it especially encouraging to receive such a tribute from one who has suffered so much at the hands of the enemy. He sends you all his sympathy in your great misfortune."

REDS RAP BULGARIA

SOVIET Russia bluntly told the Bulgarian Government last night that she could not approve of the Bulgar capitulation to Hitler.

At the same time German troops, planes and naval units were concentrating for the battle of the Mediterranean.

The Soviet rebuke to the Bulgarians was broadcast over Moscow Radio. It was in the form of a statement by Vishinsky, deputy to Molotov, Soviet Foreign Minister.

The announcement was also broadcast in Bulgarian and German.

Vishinsky in a reply to Kameneff, Bulgarian Minister in Moscow, said that the Soviet Government could not accept the Bulgarian statement that the move to allow German troops to enter Bulgaria was made in the interests of peace.

On the contrary the Soviet Government thought the war would spread and Bulgaria would be involved in it.

"The Soviet Government, faithful to her policy of peace, is not in a position to support Bulgaria in carrying out her present policy, particularly as the Bulgarian Press is still unhindered in spreading rumours which are presenting the Soviet policy in an entirely false manner," added the statement.

It was announced earlier that Sir Stafford Cripps, the British Ambassador to Moscow who is at present at Istanbul plans to fly to Moscow today or tomorrow for an immediate conference with Soviet chiefs.

Sofia Open City?

Preparations to declare Sofia an open city are now being made, according to a Sofia report.

The Bulgarian War Office is being moved to the suburbs, nine miles from the capital and preparations are under way to move the military school and all barracks outside the city.

By last night, about 40,000 German troops were in Bulgaria, said the Nazi radio. Advance units are reported to have reached four points on the Greek border.

A thousand German motorised units are concentrating on the Bulgarian-

Continued on Back Page, Col. 1

NAZI CRASHES IN EIRE

A four-engined German bomber crashed yesterday near Rosslare, on the coast of County Wexford. An officer was taken from the plane dead. Four other members of the crew were interned.

At an inquest later a verdict was returned that the officer's death was due to a bullet wound and severe burns

GERMANS IN U.S. WARNED

The German Diplomatic and Consular Corps in the United States has received instructions to be ready to leave the country at three days' notice (cables John Walters).

All staff members and employees have been given an ultimatum to sign agreements that they will return to Germany when the signal comes from Berlin or quit their jobs.

Berlin apparently fears that war with the United States might come after the Aid Britain Bill is passed.

Go to your STOCKBROKER or BANK-MANAGER

IF you wish to invest so as to help the war effort, yet need a higher income than 2½% or 3%, buy Orthodox Investment Units. The yield improves 5½%, and a fifth of each Unit is composed of the new War Loans. An investment in these Units should remain trouble-free for your lifetime. One reason is that your capital is spread over up to 200 strong securities. All your "eggs" are not in one "basket." Another reason is that these 200 securities are not all of one class or type. The investment is "balanced" over all the chief types— Gilt-Edged, Debentures, Preference Shares, Bank and Insurance Shares, Gold Shares, and nine categories of Industrial Shares, That is the classic way to obtain great Stability of Capital. These policies have made Orthodox Investment Units well-nigh the most reliable medium of investing in Stock Exchange securities. First issued at 7/- in April 1919, the Units are 7/3 now. You may buy Oft sell at 7/3, free of commission & stamp.

ORTHODOX INVESTMENT 'UNITS'

5½%

Particulars from any bank or stockbroker

Orthodox Unit Trust, 17, Gray's Inn, London, E.C.4.

Daily Mirror

No. 11,617   ONE PENNY
Registered at the G.P.O. as a Newspaper.

MAR 5

NAVY RAID ISLAND OFF NORWAY

According to the official German news agency, light British naval forces carried out a raid on an "unfortified" island in the Northern Norwegian Skerries yesterday morning.

"After a short bombardment, which destroyed several fishing boats," the agency says, "soldiers were landed and took prisoner some German and Norwegian fishermen."

The British vessels are stated to have left Norwegian waters after a short stay.—Reuter.

STATE TRANSFER 750,000 TO WAR JOBS

BY OUR POLITICAL CORRESPONDENT

A SCHEME to close most of the factories in ninety non-essential industries and to transfer 750,000 of their workers to war jobs was announced yesterday by the President of the Board of Trade in the House of Commons.

Non-war production will be concentrated into a smaller number of factories working full time.

Lancashire, the Potteries and the Midlands will be mainly affected.

Closed factories will be kept ready to start after the war.

The State will keep a record of transferred workers so they will be able to resume their old jobs.

M.P.s were surprised by the announcement of the scheme.

One said: "I don't see why we should fight Fascism in Italy to establish it here."

Many questions were being asked in the lobbies. Here they are with the answers.

What does the scheme mean, in a sentence?

To free labour, factories and plant for war production, one firm will sometimes do the work of two or three others, crediting their accounts with the results and preserving their trade marks on their quota of goods.

How will the interest of firms that are closed down be safeguarded after the war?

To Retain Goodwill

Records of all shut factories will be kept at the Board of Trade and the Government will do everything to see that they retain their goodwill and restart in good condition.

Restrictions will therefore be put upon the springing up of new firms of the same kind after the war when an unprecedented world demand for goods of every description is anticipated.

How many industries will be affected and how many men and women will be freed from them for war work?

Between seventy and ninety industries are involved—precisely how many depends on the way you sub-divide them.

It was originally estimated that about a hundred thousand men would be released for war work, but for the plan announced yesterday one estimate

Continued on Back Page, Col. 3

52 KILLED FOR 10,000 PRISONERS

SINCE the campaign against Italian Somaliland opened we have taken thousands of square miles of territory, 10,000 prisoners —and our losses have been only fifty-two dead.

In the sixty-two days of the Libyan campaign we took 133,295 prisoners — compared with the 130,476 Germans we captured in sixty-three days in the last months of the last war.

The guns captured from the Italians in Cyrenaica total well over 1,200.

These facts were announced at Nairobi and Cairo yesterday.

"The Somaliland advance continues," said Nairobi. "Isica and Baidoa (fifty miles east of the Juba River) and Bulbo Burti have been occupied."

The number of prisoners captured, adds the communique, and the destruction of enemy formations on the River Juba "give the lie to a statement by the Italians that Italian Somaliland was evacuated voluntarily."

Fort Bombed

A Middle East communique says subsidiary operations are continuing towards the South-East frontiers of Abyssinia, where a further 1,000 prisoners were taken on Saturday.

The fort of Burye has been heavily bombed and enemy positions machine-gunned.

German troops have again clashed with British forces in Libya and taken prisoners, Berlin radio claimed.

The Germans claimed that on February 25, British tanks were destroyed and prisoners taken on the Tripoli-Benghazi road. The truth is that British armoured units met and dispersed enemy units.—British United Press and Reuter.

General Sir Archibald Wavell.

King Honours Victors

THE men in the Army, Navy and Air Force who smashed Mussolini's Empire were honoured by the King last night.

General Sir Archibald Wavell, Commander-in-Chief, Middle East, Admiral Sir Andrew Cunningham, Commander-in-Chief of the Mediterranean, and Air Chief Marshal, Sir Arthur Murray Longmore, Air Officer in Chief, Middle East Command, become Knights Grand Cross Order of the Bath (G.C.B.).

Wavell's right-hand man, Major-General Richard Nugent O'Connor, G.O.C. Army of the Nile, becomes Knight Commander Order of the Bath (K.C.B.).

Lieutenant-General Henry Maitland Wilson becomes Knight Grand Cross Order of the British Empire (G.B.E.).

Air-Commodore Raymond Collishaw, O.C. Bomber Group, Middle East, becomes a Companion of the Order of the Bath (C.B.).

Major-General Noel Monson de la Peer Beresford-Peirse, Major-General Michael O'Moore Creagh and Major-General Iven Giffard Mackay become Knights Commanders of the British Empire (K.B.E.).

Major-General Mackay is G.O.C. of the Australian troops in the Middle East

Admiral Sir Andrew Cunningham.

SYRIA TIGHTENS FRONTIER GUARD

FRONTIER garrisons and defence works in Syria have been reinforced, following events in the Balkans.

Stricter control over foreigners has also been instituted as a precautionary measure.

Nationals of various countries without permits to stay in the country have been arrested in the last few days, and twenty-five suspected persons will be expelled.—Reuter.

'GROOM IS SHOT AS 100 WAIT IN CHURCH

BY A SPECIAL CORRESPONDENT

WHILE a hundred wedding guests were waiting, a happy, excited bridegroom, ready to leave for the church, accidentally shot himself with his Army revolver.

Everyone expected him to recover—otherwise there might have been a wedding ceremony at his bedside—but he died.

The bridegroom was Captain Peter Watkinson, aged twenty-seven, of the Loyal Regiment, only son of Dr. Watkinson, until recently of Tudor House, Hall-lane, Walton-on-the-Naze, Essex.

He was to have married Miss Esme MacKenzie, daughter of Mrs. Moore and stepdaughter of Major Arthur Leslie Moore, of the Old Vicarage, Ticehurst, Sussex, on Saturday.

Twenty-year-old Miss MacKenzie was leaving for the church when news of the accident was phoned to her.

She raced to her bridegroom's side, still wearing her bridal clothes. She was with him when he died at the Kent and Sussex Hospital, Tunbridge Wells.

The flowers which were intended for his wedding will be placed over his grave at his funeral.

Captain Watkinson, who was on special leave, was showing a revolver to his host, Lieutenant-Colonel M. W. Halford, of Skinners Farm, Wadhurst, Sussex.

"He was excited and happy," Colonel Halford told me.

"We were ready to go to the church and Peter was handling the revolver and discussing its mechanism when it went off. He collapsed."

"We got him to hospital and phoned Miss MacKenzie's home."

The vicar, the Rev. O. A. S.

Continued on Back Page, Col. 5

BRITISH-BULGAR BREAK

—Berlin Report

DIPLOMATIC relations between Britain and Bulgaria were broken off yesterday, Berlin Radio stated last night.

"Mr. Rendel (the British Minister in Sofia) will leave Bulgaria as soon as he has made the final arrangements for his departure," the announcer added.

No confirmation of this report was available in London, but it was stated it had been left to Mr. Rendel to make the break when he considered the moment appropriate.

Field-Marshal Chakmak, Chief of the Turkish General Staff, attended a meeting of the Turkish Cabinet which was called yesterday to consider a special message which Hitler sent by plane to President Inonu.

The message contained an assurance that Hitler has no intention of attacking Turkey.

It was presented by Von Papen, German Ambassador, who went to the President immediately the plane bringing Hitler's courier landed at Ankara.

The Turkish Premier, Dr. Saydam, is likely to broadcast his reply within twenty-four hours.

The official Turkish radio last night warned Yugoslavia that she might as well be dead as sign up with the Axis, and said the present moves in the Balkans only showed Germany had not the courage to attack Britain directly.

Soviet Protest Rejected

Germany announced yesterday that the march into Bulgaria continued "without holdups or interruptions" as Berlin officials rejected the Soviet declaration that Bulgaria's pro-Axis policy will spread the war.

The Bulgarian Foreign Minister, M. Popoff, is expected to resign.

Some British nationals from Bulgaria succeeded in reaching Yugoslavia yesterday, but all who tried to go to Turkey were turned back.

All these British people already had their luggage packed when the closing of the Bulgarian frontier was officially announced on Monday, adds the message.—British United Press, Associated Press and Reuter.

CAT REVEALS MURDER

A cat mewing and scratching obstinately at a window led to the discovery of a woman battered to death in a cottage at Cambridge-lane West, Plymouth, yesterday.

It is believed that the woman—Mrs. Elizabeth (Lylie) Darby—was murdered.

Don't buy your toothbrush in a daze

It's not being at all clear to ask for a *nylon* toothbrush. No clearer, in fact, than asking for a *bristle* toothbrush!

You see, *nylon* is the name of an extraordinary new material that stands up to the hardest scrubbing and doesn't go soggy with soaking. And just as Halex have always made the best *bristle* brush, so Halex now also make the best *nylon* brush.

The important thing is the name—Halex. Then the *sort* of Halex—with bristles or with *nylon* instead of bristles.

HALEX

Whichever shape of toothbrush you prefer, there's Halex to suit you, either with bristle (from 1/- upwards) or with nylon instead of bristle (from 1/6 plus tax). Six different coloured handles.

Daily Mirror

MAR 8

No. 11,620   ONE PENNY
Registered at the G.P.O. as a Newspaper.

CAPTURED A SWASTIKA

Above are two of the party which raided the Lofoten Islands, back with their souvenirs. They brought a swastika flag as well, as you see below. Other pictures on back page.

WE SINK AND CAPTURE 12 ENEMY SHIPS

How Our Tanks Went to It

SEE PAGE 4

ADMIRALTY and R.A.F. communiques yesterday recorded the sinking or capture of twelve enemy ships totalling well over 50,000 tons.

The Axis lost eleven of them when we captured Kismayu, important port in Italian Somaliland.

The twelfth was a German supply ship of about 2,500 tons, sunk yesterday off the Dutch coast by a Coastal Command plane.

A Canadian sergeant, one of the first batch to arrive in this country under the Empire air training scheme, got this ship with a direct bomb hit on the stern.

He was flying as navigator and bomb aimer in one of a number of day reconnaissance bombers. They spotted the German close in to the coast. Shore batteries opened heavy fire at them and the ships bow gun was also in action.

Five In Our Hands

The Canadian used only one heavy bomb. It caused a great explosion and clouds of smoke and steam rolled over the ship, which sank rapidly.

Two Messerschmitt 109's came up as if to attack the bombers, but sheered off.

The Admiralty communique recording the Kismayu success stated:

Five Italian merchant ships totalling 28,153 tons fell into our hands at Kismayu.

"These ships are Adria (3,809 tons), Savoia (5,490 tons), Erminia Mazzetia (5,742 tons), Manon (5,597 tons), and Leonardo da Vinci (7,515 tons).

"Four other ships scuttled themselves in Kismayu harbour. One of these is known to be the Italian Marghera, of 4,531 tons

Scuttle Bid Fails

"Losses were also inflicted upon the German mercantile marine.

"The German Uckermark (7,021 tons) attempted to escape. She was intercepted by our forces and tried to scuttle herself. This attempt was frustrated, but the Uckermark subsequently sank while in tow.

"The German Askari (590 tons) was driven ashore."

The Air Ministry said our aircraft yesterday bombed the naval harbour at Den Helder and the enemy-occupied aerodrome at Ockenburg. None of our aircraft is missing from this operation

The plane which sank the supply vessel was one of those which flew on to Den Helder.

At Ockenburg a salvo of bombs hit the main hangar. It was soon enveloped in dense smoke.

16 NAZIS DOWN AT MALTA

FLINGING more than 100 planes into a single attempt to crush Malta's air defences, the Germans lost sixteen machines, including at least four dive-bombers.

R.A.F. fighters shot seven out of the sky. Nine more were blasted by Malta's anti-aircraft gunners.

The German raid was even more costly than this, as several other planes were badly damaged and were unlikely to get back to their base.

The Germans did some damage to buildings, but there were no casualties to R.A.F. personnel. Only one of our planes was shot down.

NEW LIVES—NEW NEEDS

Commercial Traveller
is Copper now

"Well, blow me down! There's a chap in that car I used to know " on the road ". But he's mad at being held up. Well, I wouldn't mind being back in HIS seat." So soliloquizes a W.R. Policeman, one of the many new arms in the law to-day — doing harder work than many people know. Carry on, Coppers!

On the Home Front, battles are being won every day — big little victories over tiredness, irritability, nervous strain. Nature's own tonic, sound natural sleep (whenever you can get it) is the best thing ever for your new wartime lives. A warming cup of Bournvita, still at the old peacetime price, will help you to get your essential ration of body-and-mind-restoring SLEEP. Bourn-vita is a night food-drink with special nerve-soothing properties that bring sleep very quickly.

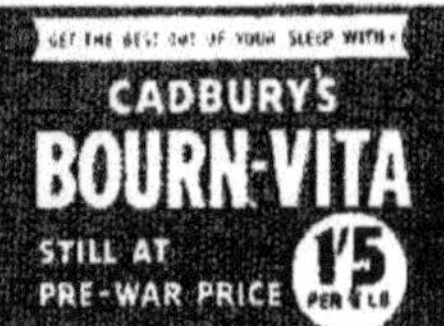

GET THE BEST OUT OF YOUR SLEEP WITH

CADBURY'S
BOURN-VITA

STILL AT PRE-WAR PRICE

1/5 PER LB

HUN GUNS CHILD IN CLASS

A HUN raider dived on an East Anglian village yesterday, fixed his gunsights on a little school, and sent bullets crashing through the roof and into the room where eighteen children were sitting.

Six-year-old Joan Easter was wounded in the thigh. But as the bullets ripped round them, not one of the children panicked. They remained steadily in their places until their schoolmistress made sure that the raider was gone.

"The children were really wonderful," said the schoolmistress last night.

"The bullets also smashed through the backdoor of the school. My house, nearby, was gunned too."

Joan's wound was slight.

Single German planes, using cloud cover, were over most parts of England in daylight yesterday, obviously on reconnaissance. Not only were gun attacks made, but some dropped bombs.

A number of people were killed and injured when a single raider bombed industrial premises in an East Anglian town.

Two raiders were destroyed.

A Dornier bomber was shot down by machine-gun fire off the coast at Gorleston, Norfolk, and a Heinkel 111 which attacked a convoy in the North Sea was shot down in flames by H.M.S. Guillemo.

WE LOSE A DESTROYER

The Admiralty announced last night that H.M. destroyer Dainty (Commander M. S. Thomas, D.S.O., R.N.), has been sunk.

The next-of-kin of casualties have been informed.

circled the village, then started machine-gunning over some fields. Later it came again and dropped bombs."

During two raids on a North Midlands town bombs were dropped and people in the streets machine-gunned. One person was killed and some injured.

Several people were taken to hospital when two houses were demolished at an East Anglian coast town. The German circled the town before diving to release his bombs.

A single plane was the cause of London's short morning Alert. It turned back. There were no reports of bombs.

2 P.C.s SHOT: MAN CHARGED

SHOTS were fired and two policemen were wounded while they were investigating a case of suspected housebreaking at Boundary - road, Carshalton, Surrey, yesterday afternoon.

The wounded men are Police-Constable Frederick Lee, forty, and Police-Constable Sidney Collyer, forty-two. Lee has a leg wound and Collyer was wounded in the stomach.

Although Collyer's injury is serious, both he and Lee were reported this morning to be out of danger.

A man was later taken into custody.

BACON UP ON MONDAY

Bacon is going up, but on the existing ration the rise will make a difference of only a halfpenny a person each week.

As already announced, the price of uncooked bacon will be increased on Monday by from a penny to twopence a lb. reverting to about the price at the beginning of February last year.

People Shot Dead

While rescuers and doctors were at work, the plane appeared out of the clouds for a second time and dropped another heavy bomb. But the rescue work went on. Women ambulance drivers waited coolly at their post.

Another single raider swooped down out of the clouds and dropped a number of bombs and machine-gunned people in a village in the north-west. There were a number of casualties, some of them fatal, and some damage was caused to property.

"The plane seemed to skim the housetops," said an eyewitness. "It

Turks Say No to Nazi Film

An invitation by Von Papen, German Ambassador to Turkey, to attend the showing of the German war film, "Victory in the West," has been declined by the Turkish Cabinet, it is learned in Ankara.

"Victory in the West" is the German version of their victory in France and Flanders. It has been shown in all the countries which Germany has undertaken to "protect."

Daily Mirror

MAR 13

No. 11,624 — ONE PENNY
Registered at the G.P.O. as a Newspaper.

U.S. Farmer to See Churchill

Mr. Tom D. Campbell, friend of President Roosevelt and one of the largest wheat growers in the United States, is in London, "because I like the British people, and want to be of some help, if I can."

He wants to see Mr. Churchill. "I have a surprise for him, if I do," he said. "I mean to carry out the Montana tradition that if you want to show anyone you like them very much you must give them something that belongs to yourself."

£513,000,000 ON U.S. PLANES FOR US

PRESIDENT ROOSEVELT yesterday asked Congress for £1,750,000,000 to carry out the "fixed policy of this Government to make for the democracies every gun, plane and munition of war that we possibly can."

His letter requesting the grant of this vast sum to finance the aid - Britain programme was virtually a command to the United States to "Go to it."

"I strongly urge that this should go through immediately," he told the House of Representatives.

Here is the wide range of armaments and other war materials on which the £1,750,000,000 is to be spent:—

£513,500,000 FOR AIRCRAFT AND AERONAUTICAL MATERIAL, INCLUDING ENGINES, SPARE PARTS AND ACCESSORIES.

£335,750,000 for ordnance, ordnance stores, supplies, spare parts and materials, including armour and ammunition.

£337,500,000 for agricultural, industrial and other commodities.

Tanks, Armoured Cars

£90,500,000 for tanks, armoured cars, motor-cars, lorries and other mechanical equipment, with spare parts and accessories.

£157,250,000 for vessels, ships, boats and other craft, with equipment.

£85,000,000 for miscellaneous military equipment.

£188,000,000 for facilities and equipment for the manufacture of

Continued on Back Page

---

2 DAYS— 120 MILES

THE British African column which conquered Italian Somaliland and is now advancing on the Harar region, sped 120 miles northward in the last forty-eight hours, taking Dagha Bur, Abyssinia, 600 miles north of Mogadishu.

The column is now ninety miles south of Jigjiga with no important enemy forces between it and that point

At Jigjiga the road turns westward for fifty miles to Harar, and thirty miles after that is Diredawa, on the Djibouti-Addis Ababa railway.

The South African Air Force, in addition to giving the troops air protection, again bombed and machine-gunned enemy concentrations in the Jigjiga-Harar region

The Italians have at least 10,000 troops massed for the defence of the

13 Enemy Planes Down

Destruction of thirteen enemy planes is recorded in an R.A.F. communiqué last night.

British fighters have shot down five enemy planes in Albania and severely damaged others.

Five enemy aircraft, it is now known, were destroyed in the raid on an enemy aerodrome in Tripolitania.

An Italian bomber was destroyed at an aerodrome by South African aircraft in Abyssinia. Two enemy planes fell during an attack on Malta.

Jigjiga-Harar region and are reported to be working feverishly on new fortifications there

They are embarrassed by the fact that the existing fortifications face the other way—they envisaged the possibility of attack from Djibouti, but never thought that the invading army would come from Italian Somaliland.

This advance, undertaken by South Africans and black troops from East and West Africa, has proved the most successful of any of the seven boring operations into Mussolini's East African Empire.

Enemy losses in casualties and prisoners since the column crossed the Juba River less than a month ago are now estimated at 31,000.

The remainder of the Italian forces in Somaliland are split and dispersed.

NEW JOB FOR SHIPS CHIEF?

Mr Ronald Cross, Minister of Shipping, may be appointed British High Commissioner in Australia, an Associated Press message from New York stated yesterday

If Mr. Cross does go to Australia, Lord Beaverbrook, Minister of Aircraft Production, is suggested as the new Minister of Shipping, while Colonel Moore-Brabazon, Minister of Transport, might go to Aircraft Production.

Priestley to Quit Radio?

"I AM walking on a tight-rope every Sunday evening," said Mr. J. B. Priestley yesterday, telling the National Trade Union Club in London of his broadcasting experiences.

"I doubt if it will be possible to continue, because you people give me no assistance.

"There is supposed to be a thing called a political truce and a thing called national unity which I am supposed to disturb every Sunday evening.

"Intrigue"

"This is all nonsense. There is supposed to be a bargain, which is kept by the Labour members, but there is not the slightest intention of keeping it by the others.

"It is an intrigue that is going on. I have not the slightest idea how long I shall continue.

"I have had to fight the whole time to put my point of view because I know it is the point of view of the people.

"I have had attacks from the Right, but I have not had the slightest assistance from the Left, and not one word from the Labour or trade union movements."

Mr. J. B. Priestley . . . "I am on a tightrope."

The Lord Privy Seal said on Tuesday in the House of Commons that the Government would look into the B.B.C. ban on people because of their political views. It was the Government's view, he said, that there should be no discrimination.

The B.B.C., as reported on page 6, is now reconsidering its judgment, and is expected to change its mind.

DUCE STARTS BIG ATTACK

ITALIAN troops, directed personally by Mussolini, have begun a general offensive against the Greeks in Albania.

"The Italian counter-attacks of the last three days have developed since dawn yesterday into a general offensive on a twelve-mile front," said a Greek statement last night.

"Not an inch of ground has been lost by the Greeks," it added.

"On the contrary, the Italians have been repulsed everywhere with terrific losses."

Blackshirt youths, whom Mussolini used to glorify with his Fascist "hymn" Giovanezza, have been flung without proper training into the fighting and have been mercilessly cut down.

Blackshirt battalions, counter-attacking to regain vital lost heights, found themselves between the murderous Greek machine-gun fire and their own artillery barrage. Unable to retreat, they were wiped out.

In a six-day battle 3,000 Italians have been taken prisoners.

These men estimate that Italian losses in Albania now total 130,000.—Reuter.

Bomb Blew Back the Laundry

A woman in a North-West town takes her family washing once a week to a small laundry on the opposite side of the street. The bundle is always wrapped up in one of father's shirts.

On Tuesday the bundle went across as usual. The same night the laundry was struck by a bomb.

Yesterday the woman found her week's washing in her backyard—blown back by the bomb, but still wrapped up in father's shirt.

3,000 IN U.S. TRY FOR R.A.F.

FROM JOHN WALTERS
NEW YORK, Wednesday.

More than 525 Americans—each with a minimum of 300 hours' experience—have been accepted in the Air Forces of Britain and Canada since mid-July last, it was revealed here to-day.

Three thousand more Americans also have applied to join the British or Canadian Air Force.

Four Raiders Down in Night Fights

See Back Page

NEW NOTE TO SLAVS

HITLER was reported last night to have sent Yugoslavia another Note calling for "active assistance" to the Axis.

He warns the Slavs that they must agree if they want the "place reserved for them in the New Order" (according to Reuter).

Associated Press cites Hitler's five main demands:

1. The demobilisation of the Yugoslav Army.

2. Complete German control of economy, transport and communications.

3. Right to ship war materials through Yugoslavia.

4. Right to pass troops through Yugoslavia if necessary.

5. Yugoslav signature to Axis pact.

Decision Soon

David Walker, *Daily Mirror* Balkans correspondent, cabled from Belgrade last night:—

Through driving snow, Yugoslav peasants in their curved shoes, with gaily coloured bags containing their belongings over their shoulders, are converging in groups to the mobilisation centres, while their statesmen sit in conclave making the country's supreme decision.

It is felt in responsible circles here that this decision most probably will be made during the coming forty-eight hours. Belgrade seethes with the wildest rumours.

All day long the country's leaders have been driving through the great iron gates of the Prince Regent's Palace, where endless consultations are being held.

Daily Mirror

MAR 17

No. 11,627   ONE PENNY
Registered at the G.P.O. as a Newspaper.

MEN (41-45) GIRLS (20-21) SIGN IN APRIL

Countess Ciano.

110 Axis Planes Smashed in a Week

Loves A Blind Hero

REGISTRATION of men and women for war work is to begin next month. Men between forty-one and forty-five and girls aged twenty and twenty-one are affected.

The first registration will be on April 5. It will apply to men of forty-one and forty-two not employed in certain industries.

On April 19 there will be a national registration of girls aged twenty. Twenty-ones will follow soon after.

These and other far-reaching plans to fill the gaps in war industries were announced by the Minister of Labour in a broadcast yesterday.

He warned girls: "When you take on a job, either in the Services or industry, you must stick to it. It will be hard work."

There are 800,000 girls aged twenty and twenty-one in England, Scotland and Wales.

The Minister said: "From now on there will be a tremendous call on man power for the Forces and Civil Defence. Simultaneously the demands of war industry must be met.

Volunteer Now

"First we are reviewing the reserved occupations, involving a great deal of de-reservation, so that the duty to serve in the Forces and Civil Defence is spread fairly."

There was an urgent demand for the shipbuilding and marine engineering industries.

"Then we have to get a large number of men who have not been in productive industry.

"We want trained men, semi-skilled men, and some who do not need training but who could pick up the work quickly in the factories.

"We want many to volunteer for work or training right away. Do not wait for registration."

Proper Wages

Referring to the registration of men, the Minister said.

"We shall be able to find out who is on essential work and who is not, and be able to advise and direct you to the place where you can give the greatest service

"We have had difficulties in the past about pay. The present arrangements will continue up to March 31

"But after that we are going to make a big change-over and people in training under the Government scheme will be paid proper wages.

"There is a special obligation on men in low medical grades. The Ser-
Continued on Back Page, Col. 4

★ Duce's Daughter Escapes ★ Sea Attack, Say Italians

Pictured above is Countess Edda Ciano, daughter of Mussolini and wife of his Foreign Secretary, who was in a ship torpedoed by two British planes off Albania, according to the official Italian news agency last night. She escaped.

It is alleged that the vessel was a hospital ship and that the Duce's daughter was acting as a volunteer nurse.

The agency asserts: "The hospital ship Po sighted two British torpedo-carrying planes swooping silently down over Valona. The planes struck the ship with two torpedoes."

The ship sank rapidly. Several were killed aboard her.—Reuter.

WE'RE IN IS U.S. VIEW

FIRST American reaction yesterday to Roosevelt's speech pledging his nation's determination to see Hitler smashed was: "Well, that's that—we're in the war."

Officials in Washington declared the broadcast to be an irrevocable commitment of the strength of the United States to the defeat of the Axis.

A tremendous speed-up of the dispatch of war material to Britain is forecast by members of the Cabinet.

It is significant that Mr. Wendell Willkie, the Republican leader has indicated his willingness to follow Roosevelt's leadership.

Mr. Roosevelt's repeated use of "we" and "our" in speaking of the war effort was taken by Canadians as including the United States in the war without a formal declaration.

"How will Hitler react?" most people asked

Ignored By Hitler

Hitler, speaking yesterday (his speech is on page 3), made no reply to Roosevelt, contenting himself with a sneer about America's "goldbag."

First Nazi comment was made on the German radio.

"There is nothing new in Roosevelt's speech for the German people, who are firmly determined to defeat England, and finally to destroy her, because Germany wants peace for the world," the announcer declared. "No help whatever given to England can affect the issue of the war."

Roosevelt's speech—page eleven.

STRIPES FOR GOOD ATS

If they are good girls for two years members of the A.T.S. will be given good conduct stripes similar to those awarded in the Army

Some of the girls have already qualified since service in the Waacs in the last war is counted. The decoration is to be worn at interval chevrons at the bottom of the sleeve. Additional stripes will be given for longer service.

IT is estimated that the Luftwaffe lost 170 men in raids on Britain last week.

Forty-two German machines were destroyed, thirty-five during night raids.

Allowing for planes damaged and unlikely to reach their base, losses in personnel might be considerably over 170

Two other enemy machines were destroyed by the Navy, six were brought down over enemy territory and the Channel, and sixty were destroyed in the Middle East, making a total of 110

Our losses were extremely low, only twenty-two failing to return to their bases. A number of our pilots were saved

Enemy losses thus more than doubled those of the previous week, when the R.A.F. destroyed fifty planes at a cost of sixteen to themselves.

KIND THOUGHT—BY HITLER

Hitler has ordered "dignified graveyards ALL OVER GERMANY" for German soldiers killed in the present war, said the German radio last night.

A special Architect-General will be appointed to conduct the artistic work

Miss Ashdown visiting her fiance. Flying Officer Cooper

BY A SPECIAL CORRESPONDENT

"SOMETIMES I wish I were dead," said blinded Flying Officer Charles W. W. Cooper in a ward at St. Dunstan's Hospital, Church Stretton, Shropshire.

"You should not say that," replied Lady Lou Fraser, wife of the famous blind V.C.

"You have the most beautiful girl in the world coming to see you. My husband says he has the most beautiful wife in the world and he has never seen me."

"Most beautiful girl in the world for Flying Officer Cooper is Miss Margaret Ashdown, of Bovingdon, Herts.

As her blind lover lay seriously ill in his bed, she guided his hand to her own so that he could slip an engagement ring on her finger.

During the week-end the heroic officer air-gunner—who was blinded on the ground by an enemy bomb after shooting down enemy machines—invited his mother and me to a little party to celebrate the birthday of his sweetheart.

Proudly he gave the toast: "Here's health and happiness to Margaret the bravest girl in the world"

"We were engaged on February 13, thirteen days after he was blinded," Margaret said. "Thirteen is our lucky number."

"My aircraft was number 1313," said Flying-Officer Cooper. "I shot down my first Jerry from the cockpit of that machine"

TARANTO VICTOR PROMOTED

Rear-Admiral A. L. St. G. Lyster, who was in command of the aircraft-carriers and planes which crippled the Italian fleet at Taranto, has been promoted.

He has been appointed a Lord Commissioner of the Admiralty and Chief of Naval Air Services. He is to go to Australia as first naval member of the Commonwealth Naval Board.

PRIESTLEY SALUTES SEAMEN

MR. J. B. PRIESTLEY, broadcasting last night, called for a "square deal" for the men of the Merchant Navy—men who "sign on for a voyage and find themselves in roaring hell."

He spoke of reading documents, copies of formal statements by masters on what happened to their ships.

"Somehow," he said, "it made everything else in this war—even the two-mile high combats above the Channel, the bombing of London, the evacuation of Dunkirk, or the desert thunderbolt of Wavell's army—seem like tuppence.

"I don't know why, unless it was because these men have to meet dangers trying to do their ordinary jobs without any uniforms or training.

"One phrase occurs throughout. The behaviour of the officers and crew was excellent." Just that.

Ships Murdered

"Imagine the sudden anxiety of feeling the ship reeling and shuddering before taking its last plunge, for ships are more like people than things

"Our officers and those of the enemy merely lump these half-living creatures of the sea together and call it so much tonnage—50,000 last week 50,000 tons last week.

"But to the men of the sea, ships with names, with familiar tricks
Continued on Back Page, Col. 1

More Details Today

Fuller details of the registration of men over the present military age and the registration of women for war work are likely to be given by the Minister of Labour today.

Men now engaged on what have been defined as essential services can be transferred to other areas.

Some have already been notified that they must make the transfer.

There will be drastic changes in the Schedule of Reserved Occupations, to be announced at the end of this month.

The response to the call to women to volunteer for war work has not been as good as had been anticipated.

The first registration will immediately affect "young ladies of leisure" and those released or displaced from non-essential trades.

and so is

HOOVER SERVICE

In war-time Hoover Limited, formerly manufacturers of the World's Best Cleaner, has other things to do! But for the benefit of our well-over-a-million users Hoover Service can still maintain your Hoover at top-notch efficiency. Today you need its help more than ever, so have it inspected regularly. For inspection or any service 'phone the nearest Hoover office or write address below.

HOOVER

Daily Mirror

MAR 19

No. 11,629   ONE PENNY
Registered at the G.P.O. as a Newspaper.

GIRL WAR WORKERS

HAVE STARTED

BURIED 3 DAYS—LIVES

Ten-months-old Irene Marriott was buried for three days under the wreckage of her home—destroyed in a Merseyside raid—and survived.

Her parents were killed and it was the body of her father which protected the baby from some of the debris.

The picture below shows Irene in hospital. Her arm is in splints. Her head, which was badly cut, is bandaged. But her cheeks are still rosy.

" According to ordinary medical standards she should be dead," say the doctors. " Her survival is a miracle."

When Irene gets well an aunt will adopt her.

Band and Dances in Factory

A JAZZ band plays nightly for dancing from midnight to 1 a.m. in a Midlands war factory.

The idea is to be taken up in another factory, where already they have two mid-day concerts a week.

The nightly dance in the one factory was revealed at Coventry Chamber of Commerce yesterday, when a member suggested that it might affect the output.

But the welfare officer in one of the biggest munition factories in the Midlands told the " Daily Mirror " that they had proved that music for the workers encouraged a bigger output. " We are trying to arrange dancing for our workers."

Classical Music

" At present we have concerts each week from 12.50 to 1.25 p.m. On one day E.N.S.A. give a concert and on the other the concert is given by our workers.

" Many of the workers prefer classical music in between their work.

" Recently many of the younger workers asked for a band, so that they can have dances, and I have recommended to our directors that they should have it."

17's MAY JOIN WAAF

" SWEET Seventeens " may now join the Women's Auxiliary Air Force. The lower age limit for recruits, it was announced last night, has been reduced from eighteen to seventeen and a half years in nearly all trades.

Some of the duties for which girls of seventeen and a half may volunteer are: Radio operator, teleprinter operator, clerk, fabric worker, equipment assistant morse slip reader, cook, sparking plug tester, telephone operator, wireless operator instrument mechanic.

FARR ROBBED OF £3,000 JEWELLERY

Jewellery worth more than £3,000, belonging to Tommy Farr, the boxer, was stolen during the black-out on Monday night from Lady Natalie Ricketts's house at Surrenden-crescent, on the outskirts of Brighton, which Farr is renting.

The chief piece of jewellery was his platinum ring set with a single diamond valued at £2,000.

Mr. Chamberlain's £84,013

Mr. Neville Chamberlain, it was revealed last night, left £84,013, with net personalty £74,203.

He left a settled legacy of £3,000 to Miss Valerie Cole, his niece, and the remainder to his widow for life.

WOMEN who responded to the appeal of the Minister of Labour for war workers are already at the bench.

Others will start work at the week-end.

Most of the volunteers are married, but many girls of twenty have registered before the compulsion date.

The Ipswich, Suffolk, employment exchange told the *Daily Mirror* that 185 women, most of them married, had responded to the appeal.

" Some of the women are already at work today," an official said, " and many more will be within the next day or two.

" By far the greatest number of applicants were housewives whose husbands are on active service or engaged in other forms of war work."

Ipswich is not alone. Girls of twenty and twenty-one who registered before they need have already been given jobs.

A hundred girls queued up outside a South London employment exchange.

Hundreds of girls, those who have never gone out to work before and others from " dead " luxury trades, were among those who registered.

Official registration date for the 20 to 21 class is April 19.

This Week-End

Most of the Midland women who registered yesterday will be at work by this week-end.

The manager of one of Birmingham's biggest Labour Exchanges said: " We have had a wonderful response. Most women in the Midlands who have had factory experience have already returned to the bench.

" During next week there will be a big new recruiting campaign for workers in Midland towns.

" When the debate on the registration of women for war work takes place in the House of Commons, the Government is likely to agree not to compel girls under twenty to go away from home.

However, providing the conditions were suitable and the parents willing, such girls would not be debarred from working in distant towns.

PUBLIC SCHOOL girls train for war work—page 6.

U.S. WARSHIPS VISIT AUSTRALIA

A U.S. naval squadron will reach Sydney tomorrow and stay two days, it was announced in Canberra yesterday by Mr. A. W. Fadden, Acting Prime Minister.

The squadron comprises the cruisers Chicago and Portland and the destroyers Clark, Cassin, Conyngham, Downes and Reid.

The visit is described as a training cruise, and the Australian Government regards it as an extraordinarily significant development in the Pacific situation.

Cheering crowds greeted the ships when they called at Auckland, New Zealand, yesterday.—British United Press.

U.S. Search for U-boats Is On—Page 3.

STOLE WAR OFFICE 32-SEATER COACH

Black-out thieves in one night stole a War Department camouflaged thirty-two-seater motor coach in the City of London; forty-three half chests (about forty pounds each) of tea, valued at £350, from a warehouse at Campion's, Green-street, Shenley;

NIGHT FLYER'S D.F.C.

Squadron Leader Michael Frederic Anderson, of the Auxiliary Air Force, No. 604 Squadron, whose father lives at Hitchin, Herts, has been awarded the D.F.C. During the last four months, says the announcement, he has carried out numerous night operational flights, destroying a Heinkel 111 and probably a Junkers 88, and has destroyed another enemy plane by day.

THREE MORE U-BOATS SUNK, SAYS PREMIER

" I have just received news of the certain destruction of three U-boats. Not since October 13, 1939, have I been cheered by news of such a delectable triple event."

Mr. Churchill said this in London yesterday.

He was proposing the health, at a Pilgrims' luncheon, of the new U.S. Ambassador, Mr. J. G. Winant, whose speech is reported in page 6.

Sinks Nazi Supply Ship

A 5,000-ton German supply ship, heavily laden, was torpedoed and sunk by a bomber of the Coastal Command in moonlight early yesterday.

A heavy explosion was followed by flames, debris was flung into the air and the ship sank rapidly by the bows.

1,000 DIE IN RAIDS

A THOUSAND people were killed and 1,300 seriously injured in last week's raids on Merseyside and Clydeside. Each area was raided twice on successive nights—Merseyside on Wednesday and Thursday and the Clyde area on Thursday and Friday.

An Air Ministry and Ministry of Home Security communiqué issued last night says latest reports indicate that on Merseyside 500 people were killed and 500 seriously injured, while in the Clyde area about 500 were killed and 800 seriously injured.

Activity on Clydeside is now getting back to normal.

Women and children have been taken to safe areas. Some workers are sleeping in shelters to be near their work.

Although many homes in one town were damaged, hundreds of them will be made habitable in ten days.

" First-aid " repairs are being made to the least damaged houses and soldiers are demolishing dangerous buildings.

ALL TO BEAT INVASION

STAND firm. Carry on. Beat the invader." With this slogan the Minister of Home Security ended a broadcast last night.

He said that the Government leaflet of advice about invasion would be distributed soon and families should sit around the fire and study it point by point.

" It is not called, ' How to look after your wife, your family or yourself in an invasion,' said the Minister, " It is called, ' Beating the Invader.' If the Germans land here the only thing that matters is to beat them before they can do serious harm. It lies with the civil population.

" If you are doing anything important for the war effort, you will get to your work and do it for all you're worth, every day and all day. The cows have to be milked, Hitler or no Hitler.

" I want to say one special word to the men and women of the civil defence service. If the time comes when it is the duty of other people to get into their houses and stop there, you know that there is no lying low for you."

Daily Mirror

MAR 20

No. 11,630
ONE PENNY
Registered at the G.P.O. as a Newspaper.

4 HOSPITALS IN LONDON ARE HIT

HITLER SWUNG HIS AIR ATTACK BACK TO LONDON LAST NIGHT AND THE CAPITAL HAD THE LONGEST AND NOISIEST RAID OF THIS YEAR.

FOUR HOSPITALS WERE DAMAGED. MORE THAN 100 OF THE 1,200 PATIENTS WERE QUICKLY EVACUATED FROM ONE HOSPITAL ON THE OUTSKIRTS AFTER IT HAD BEEN DAMAGED BY A SHOWER OF BOMBS. MANY MORE WERE STILL BEING EVACUATED EARLY TODAY.

Nearly all the windows of a large portion of the hospital were blown out. It was from these parts that the patients were evacuated. Nurses and doctors went immediately to the aid of the patients in the wards affected, but there were only a few minor casualties.

In a second hospital a bomb wrecked the maternity ward which was being used as a temporary first-aid post. A number of men and V.A.D. nurses were slightly injured by flying glass and debris.

They had remarkable escapes from more serious injury. There were no injuries among patients, who were in other parts of the hospital.

The nurses' sleeping quarters were damaged.

Drove Through Craters

No casualties are reported from the other two hospitals.

It was the worst night London has known since September, apart from the big fire night.

The fire services magnificently met the challenge. Not even craters in the roads prevented their getting quickly to the job.

IN ONE DISTRICT A CRATER COMPLETELY BLOCKED THE ROAD, BUT THE FIRE ENGINES AND TRAILERS CHARGED A FOOT-HIGH PAVEMENT AND BOUNCED THROUGH A SUBSIDIARY CRATER TO AVOID MAKING A WIDE DETOUR.

So eager were the drivers to get through that a policeman had to mar-

Continued on Back Page

Continued on Back Page

We Storm New Peaks at Keren

British and Indian shock troops battling for Keren have driven the Italians from more important mountain positions.

Enemy counter-attacks in an attempt to halt the advance have been smashed. It was stated last night.

And as our forces closed their grip on the key to Eritrea, it was announced that South African forces striking into Eastern Abyssinia had captured the important town of Jijiga, only fifty miles from Harar.

The Italian commander having concentrated his forces in Addis Ababa, now finds that the speed of the South African advance is trapping his men.

The Imperial troops are sweeping across the enemy's lines of retreat, and only one road to the coast is now left to them.

Patriots advancing on Addis Ababa from the north-west are now putting pressure on Debra Marcos, 130 miles from the capital.

The complete surrender of all Abyssinia is appreciably nearer.

Meanwhile the biggest battle of the East Africa campaign rages round Keren.

A crack Midlands regiment and famous Highland infantry, as well as Indian troops, European and Colonial Free French and Palestinians, are attacking 25,000 Italians.

In the first great assault, launched under a smokescreen with the support of artillery and air bombardment, the British and Indian troops stormed up mountainsides and took first line enemy positions at the bayonet point.

HER NOTE IN EARL'S GRAVE
COURT STORY

SIR DELVES BROUGHTON, who is accused of the murder of the Earl of Erroll in Kenya, said that his wife and the Earl were in love, according to a statement which the police allege he made.

Sir Delves, added the police, said that his wife told him later that Lord Erroll and she loved one another.

Sir Delves and his wife had made a pact, continued the statement, that if either fell in love with someone else they would release one another.

He realised that nothing could be done. He had been accustomed to racing all his life and to cutting his losses.

He told his wife that there was nothing to worry about, that he would go away to Ceylon and that she could have the house at Karen.

Sir Delves Broughton said he became quite reconciled to the new state of affairs.

He denied all knowledge of Lord Erroll's death.

Other evidence given yesterday concerned a huge bonfire which Sir Delves Broughton was stated to have started in his garden the day after the tragedy.—Reuter and British United Press

Sir Delves, added the police, said that his wife gave him a farewell note which she wished to be dropped into Lord Erroll's grave, and he dropped it on to the coffin after the mourners had gone.

Three alleged statements by Sir Delves were read at Nairobi, Kenya, yesterday, at the preliminary inquiry into the earl's death.

According to one of the alleged statements, Sir Delves received three anonymous letters suggesting that there was a liaison between Lady Broughton and Lord Erroll, who had met almost every day.

The first letter, early in January, read: "You were like a cat on hot bricks last night. What about the eternal triangle. What are you doing about it?"

The second: Do you know your wife and Lord Erroll have been staying at Carberry's house at Nyeri together?

The third read: "There is no fool like an old fool. What are you going to do about it?"

The second letter was stated to have been received three or four days before the tragedy and the third perhaps the day before.

Wife Confessed Love

GIRLS PREFER A "CHATTERBREAK"

Many girl workers in war factories prefer a half hour's chat to wireless entertainment or concerts during the lunch break.

Dr. Winifred M. Burbury, honorary psychiatrist at Salford Royal Hospital, thinks this freedom to talk is better than other forms of entertainment for some girls.

Dr. Burbury is quoted in the monthly journal of the Industrial Welfare Society.

More from Newfoundland

Another Newfoundland artillery contingent arrived at a west coast port yesterday.

ONE of the first of W.A.A.F. recruits under the new age limit—seventeen and a half, instead of eighteen years of age—to be accepted yesterday was Betty Curtis—on the right. She enlisted in London.

With her at the recruiting office were her mother and her sister-in-law, both intent on joining up. And while she signed her last forms, her brother, John, was applying for a job in the R.A.F. The family live at Woodlands-road, Guildford.

"I had set my heart on getting into the W.A.A.F.s, and it's wonderful to know I'm in," said Betty Curtis to the "Daily Mirror." "You see, my boy friend, Jean, is serving with the Free Belgians, and expects to get a transfer to their flying force."

Betty and her sister-in-law set off with a contingent of new recruits to their depot yesterday. Mother and John watched them go with a sigh

One of First 17½-Year-Olds

SLAVS EXILE PRO-NAZI

THE pro-Nazi Dr. Stoyadinovitch, former Premier of Yugoslavia, was reported in Belgrade yesterday to be on his way to Greece, under police escort.

Stoyadinovitch had been interned since June last year in the Yugoslav village of Ilidze.

It is understood that a stipulation that Stoyadinovitch must not go into any country within the German sphere of influence has been imposed.

The German Minister in Belgrade, Von Heeren, conferred yesterday for ninety minutes with M. Cincar Markovich, the Yugoslav Foreign Minister, on German-Yugoslav relations.

Mr. Eden, British Foreign Secretary, met M. Sarajoglu, Turkish Foreign Minister, in Cyprus yesterday, and afterwards an official communique was issued in Cairo

It said the two statesmen "re-emphasised the complete identity of views which exists between their two Governments"—Reuter, British United Press, Associated Press

CIVILIAN LEADERS FOR HOME GUARD

FOUR civilians are appointed to the rank of Lieutenant-Colonel and Battalion Commander in the first list of Home Guard appointments published since the new order giving Army ranks to Home Guard personnel came into effect.

They are P L Richardson, Donald Whiteley H L Allsopp and W B Newcombe

General Sir Hubert Gough, who last year resigned from his post as "B" Zone commander of the Home Guard because he was above the age limit—he is seventy-one—resumes the status of a zone commander, with the rank of colonel.

Went for Drink—Fined £10

John Hoyle, of Brown-street, Beswick, Manchester, a process worker on defence work, left the job for an hour and a half and returned under the influence of drink. He was fined £10 at Manchester yesterday.

THE VANISHING HALF-DOZEN

The chief of a fire-watching group in Bognor Regis sent out two girls to watch a certain road, telling them to report back when they came back.

The two girls didn't come back to report.

Somewhat annoyed, he sent out another two girls after the others.

The couple of girls who went after the first couple of girls didn't come back either.

Somewhat worried, the fire watch chief sent out two men.

The two men who followed the girls who followed the first couple of girls also didn't come back.

Terribly worried, the fire-watch chief told the police.

So the police followed the men who followed the girls who followed the first couple of girls. And the police couldn't find any one of them

So they asked the military if they had seen two men and four girls.

"Sure," said the military. "We've been holding them all because not one is carrying an identity card." So the identity cards were produced

Moral: Carry yours

Nazi-Greek "Change"

Swiss radio yesterday quoted Turkish sources for the statement that Berlin no longer considers relations with Greece normal, and that the German Minister in Athens had received "appropriate" orders from Berlin.—Associated Press

Fire Parties' Steel Hats

Free issue of protective helmets for street fire-fighting parties has started in the London area

---

RAID 'FLYING SQUADS' OFF

THREE "flying squads" of the Ministry of Works' mobile corps of house repairers are to help the Clydeside's raided areas.

The Secretary of State for Scotland appealed to the Minister on Tuesday night, and by midday yesterday the first squad of twenty-four was on its way. Another fifty left last night and a third of fifty follows early today.

"These men are some of the 5,000 released by the Army to enable us to repair raid damaged houses, and they are all fully qualified members of the building trades," a Ministry of Works official said last night.

Their headquarters are at the Ministry of Works in London, and we send them out according to local needs. They work in flying squads of about 100 men.

"We have about 2,000 working in London, more than 1,000 in various raided provincial cities, and the remainder of the 5,000 are in Coventry."

The war organisation of the Red Cross and St. John yesterday sent large bales of blankets and towels for Glasgow air raid victims. Similar emergency help was given to the other bombed towns.

TABLE MANNERS WASTE YOUR JAM

FORGET your table manners and make your jam or marmalade rations go further

Good table manners are losing hundreds of pounds of preserves a year, so when you help yourself to marmalade this morning take it straight from the pot to your slice of toast, instead of first putting it on the side of your bread plate

Another tip to help that 1lb. of jam go further is not to transfer it from its pot to the pretty table jar

It won't look as nice, but you'll be saving yourself an extra spoonful.

Daily Mirror

MAR 25

No. 11,634   ONE PENNY
Registered at the G.P.O. as a Newspaper.

RUSSIANS TURKS IN NEW PACT

Turkey has signed a declaration confirming her non-aggression pact with Russia.

Large concentrations of German troops are reported to be moving through Bulgaria towards Greece.

Yugoslavia's Cabinet has decided to make a deal with Hitler. Britain has warned them.

THOSE were last night's developments in the Balkan situation, complicated by intensified fears of a revolt in Yugoslavia.

Last night David Walker wired from Belgrade, capital of troubled Yugoslavia, whose Government have decided to sign an Axis pact:—

"Excited phone calls told me today of tanks, lorries and artillery pouring relentlessly nearer yet another small nation which has not done Germany any harm."

The Huns have been advancing rapidly southwards down the Struma Valley, in Bulgaria, only direct approach to Salonika, since Sunday afternoon, said Reuter's Belgrade correspondent.

Berlin's communique announced: "In Bulgaria movements of troops are continuing according to plan."

Military commentators, knowing Hitler's liking for dramatic coincidences, see significance in the fact that today is the anniversary of Greek independence.

TURKS GET FREE HAND

TURKEY announced officially last night that she had signed a declaration confirming her 1925 Non-Aggression Pact with Russia.

This leaves the Turks a free hand to deal with any German threats. Diplomats in Turkey suggested that if Turkey fights she will get some sort of help from Russia, probably war materials.

"This pact shows that Russia is taking a new diplomatic stand against Germany, declared Ankara radio.

Germany tried to delay the publication of the pact in case it stiffened Yugoslav resistance.

Meanwhile, the Turkish newspapers are preparing the nation for the worst, saying that "any day now we may have to take up arms."

The Turkish communique, issued in Istanbul, stated that the Soviet Government had informed Turkey that—

"In case Turkey should resist aggression and should find herself forced into war for the defence of her territory, Turkey could then, in accordance with the non-aggression pact existing between her and the U.S.S.R., count on the complete understanding and neutrality of the U.S.S.R.

"Should the U.S.S.R. find itself in a similar situation, it could count on the complete understanding and neutrality of Turkey." — British United Press and Associated Press.

SLAVS SET OFF FOR VIENNA

From DAVID WALKER

BELGRADE, Monday.

YUGOSLAVIA'S Premier and Foreign Minister left here tonight for Germany to sign some sort of pact with the Axis.

When this is generally known
Continued on Back Page, Col. 9

'Heavies' Crash on Berlin

OVER 10,000 incendiary bombs were dropped on Berlin on Sunday night as well as a number of heavy high-explosive bombs and a great load of medium H.E.s.

Our "heavies" have had effects comparable to the heavy bombs dropped on us, it was revealed in London yesterday.

New four-engine planes were employed, according to New York radio.

Crossing and recrossing the sky above Berlin in the teeth of an intense box-barrage with superb daring, some of our bombers flew along the famous Unter den Linden to set their course to aim the bombs, which started fire after fire.

Factories and goods yards were attacked, and the glare of the flames glowing through the mist provided a giant beacon for succeeding waves of bombers.

Fires in Kiel

At Hanover, which was also attacked in force, fires were seen in every stage, from the white lights of the first outbreak to the sullen red which showed they had spread to every part of the buildings hit.

In one district our pilots watched nine small fires thrust out their tentacles among factory buildings until the flames merged and became three immense conflagrations.

Squadrons of bombers attacked docks and shipyards in the great naval base of Kiel.

From high explosive bombs which burst in the shipyard seven strong fires took hold.

Bremen, Emden, Calais and Den Helder also felt our bombs.

After bombing the docks at Cherbourg yesterday a Coastal Command Blenheim dived to 100ft. and found the main street of Barfleur, near Cherbourg, occupied by German troops on pre-breakfast parade outside their barrack blocks. They were heavily machine-gunned.

We lost three planes in all our operations. The Germans admitted the loss of six.

£1,750,000,000 IN HALF HOUR

UNITED States Senate last night passed the Bill authorising an appropriation of £1,750,000,000 to make effective the Lease-and-Lend Act for aiding the democracies.

The Bill is being flown immediately by seaplane for President Roosevelt's signature. He is now on a holiday cruise.

The Senate passed the Bill by sixty-seven votes to nine after only half an hour's unexciting debate. They thus shattered all records for the passage of legislation.

No change was made in the Bill. As the debate opened, a number of Senators, led by Senator Adams, including Senator Vandenberg, who had vigorously opposed the Lease-Lend Act, announced their intention of supporting the measure.—Reuter.

U.S. Ports for Our Shipping—Back Page.

DO YOU KNOW THIS BABY?

If you can identify this baby write to us. The photograph is tattered and creased. It was found tightly clasped in a hand of a beautiful young woman who lay dying in the wreckage of a West End club.

Reached by torchlight by a young soldier who kneeled down to her, she managed to gasp out: "Give this to my husband . . . country . . . here." Then she died.

The soldier is now trying to locate the husband and baby. To help he has asked the "Daily Mirror" to print the picture.

U.S. SHIP AS A TRANSPORT

THE U.S. War Department yesterday chartered the 24,289-ton American passenger liner Washington as an auxiliary transport.

Company officials refused to say if the second largest American liner would be leased or loaned to Britain.

As a troopship, the Washington could carry 5,000 men.

NIGHT RAID LULL

The air raid lull continued last night. Up to a late hour no bombers were reported to have crossed Britain's coasts after dark. For London it was the fourth successive night without an Alert.

Another Nazi plane, a bomber, brought down near Redruth, Cornwall, late yesterday afternoon made the day's bag two "certains" and one "probable."

Nazis Execute Norwegians

Germany has warned Norwegians against espionage.

"On various occasions recently," it is stated, "the Norwegians have been deceived by aiding and abetting the British.

"These offences were of such a nature that the German court-martial passed the death sentence in ten cases."—Reuter.

MEN born between January 1, 1903, and December 31, 1903, are to register on April 12.

Some of the thirty-sevens "are likely to be called SOON for the civil defence services, or for special requirements of the Army," it was officially stated.

Men not needed for civil defence or for special requirements " may not be called up for a few months so far as can at present be foreseen."

♦ ♦ ♦

All wishing to be considered for the Police War Reserve, the Auxiliary Fire Service, and first-aid parties of the civil defence services should notify the clerk when they register.

Those accepted may be required to serve in an area away from their homes.

Married men, or single men with similar responsibilities, who have to maintain a home in the area

STALIN SEES MR. MATSUOKA

STALIN was present when Mr. Matsuoka, the Japanese Foreign Minister, had a two hours' conversation with M. Molotov, the Soviet Premier, yesterday.

Previously Mr. Matsuoka had sent gifts to M. Stalin and M. Molotov, through the Commissariat of Foreign Affairs.

Mr. Matsuoka had lunched earlier with the German Ambassador, Schulenberg, at the German Embassy.

Before he had visited the Kremlin for talks, Mr. Matsuoka saw Cripps and Labonne, the British and French Ambassadors.

It is believed these visits to the Ambassadors were official, said Japanese newspapers, which reported them yesterday.

The official German News Agency denied that Sir Stafford Cripps had visited Matsuoka.

Last night Mr. Matsuoka left Moscow for Berlin.

The formation of a totalitarian bloc extending from the North Sea to the Pacific will be Germany's aim in the talks with Matsuoka in Berlin, according to a well-informed Chinese source.

"Matsuoka will insist on the importance of stopping Soviet aid to China," says this source, "but it is considered improbable that he will succeed in altering the Soviet attitude on this point.—Reuter.

State Insures Your Suit

Almost everyone in Britain will be affected by the War Damage Bill, which is expected to receive Royal assent this week.

The Chancellor of the Exchequer is to explain its provisions — it covers everything from a coster's barrow to a Sunday suit—in a broadcast tomorrow.

37s to Go Soon

from which they are transferred will be eligible to receive an additional allowance.

Men may apply to join these services, but they must still register. If a man is accepted for duty after registering, the facts should be reported immediately, as he may otherwise receive an enlistment notice for one of the armed Forces, which cannot be cancelled.

♦ ♦ ♦

Men after reaching the age of forty-one will not be required to register at present. The call-up limit under the Act is forty-one, and it has been officially announced that there is no present intention of altering that limit.

TOAST TO BABY OF HIS RIVAL

—*Court Story*

A TOAST by Sir Delves Broughton, wishing happiness to his wife, Lord Erroll, " and their future child," was alleged at Nairobi, Kenya, yesterday.

Sir Delves is charged with the murder of Lord Erroll, who was found shot in a car near Nairobi on January 24.

Lord Erroll and Lady Broughton were on close terms of friendship, it has been stated.

Lady Carbery who gave evidence yesterday about the alleged toast, said she gave a dinner party on the night before the tragedy, at which Sir Delves, Lord Erroll and Lady Broughton were present.

Counsel asked whether anything was said about an heir.

Lady Carbery replied that something was said about a future heir, and a toast was drunk to the
Continued on Back Page, Col. 5

Daily Mirror

MAR 26

No. 11,635
ONE PENNY
Registered at the G.P.O. as a Newspaper.

Britain's After-the-War Plans

WE'LL KEEP ARMED TO MAINTAIN PEACE

AFTER the war is over, and until we can be satisfied of Germany's co-operation, the nations resolved to preserve both peace and freedom must retain sufficient armed strength to make their will effective.

Lord Halifax, British Ambassador to U.S., stated this when outlining for the first time Britain's war aims in a speech at the Pilgrims' Dinner in New York last night.

The achievement of victory, Lord Halifax said, would be a Dead Sea fruit unless we could also achieve that which must be the greatest peace aim of securing the world, so far as it is within human power to do so, against a repetition of this tragedy.

Past experience taught that a stable international order must admit of ordered change in the relations between States.

"Just as the liberty of the individual must have regard to the needs of the community, so must every nation in future accept its obligations to the general family of nations," Lord Halifax said.

"We for our part are prepared to join hands with any State which genuinely seeks the peace and prosperity of the world by loyally observing its engagements and by ensuring individual liberty within its borders."

The British Commonwealth which by the quality of its resolution was the bastion of world defence today might well by its geographical dispersion become the bridge of greater world unity tomorrow.

"When, therefore, victory has been won it must be our aim to promote the common interest in the greatest possible interchange of goods.

Common Action

Problems involving common needs can only be solved by common action. We see the urgent need for economic co-operation and we are ready to take part in plans to promote it on a world-wide scale.

"Our aim will be prosperity justly shared.

This business of rebuilding after the war will be a task far beyond the strength of any single country.

"Great Britain is resolved to do her utmost, but it is clear that if the world is to be brought back to health after so devastating a sickness it will only be by the united action of all men and all nations of goodwill.

"It will not be easy for we may be very sure that the upheaval now convulsing nations will not leave things as they were. The new world is being born of bitter suffering and the men

Continued on Back Page, Col. 4

SERBS RALLY TO ALLIES

YOUNG Serbs stormed the British and Greek Legations in Belgrade demanding uniforms and transport to the Albanian front last night after the betrayal of Yugoslavia to Hitler.

Hundreds of arrests were made in provincial cities as police tried to check serious trouble.

A detachment of soldiers and their officers joined a demonstration in the Serbian town of Knjazevac, near the Bulgarian frontier.

The crowd marched to the local military headquarters and demanded to be sent to the front.

Wild anti-Axis demonstrations were staged by Serb peasants, Communists, students and "Comitaji" (rebels), in many towns.

The grey-haired "Comitaji" leader, Kosta Pecanac, was reported to have left Belgrade for southern Serbia to recruit the sons of old war comrades for a new fight for Serb independence.

Curse Regent

Pecanac is famous as hero of the Salonika campaign during which he dropped from a plane into occupied Serbia and organised the revolt.

People in the streets of Belgrade cursed Prince Regent Paul and the Government and wept with indignation as they read the news.

Police and riot squads arrested several hundred schoolboys and students who left their classrooms and paraded, singing and shouting, "Down with Hitler, down with Mussolini."

A patriotic leaflet said: "Adolf Hit-
Continued on Back Page, Col. 2

PRINCESSES GROW FOOD

PRINCESS ELIZABETH and Princess Margaret, who are evacuated to the country, have converted their flower beds into vegetable gardens, and are now growing onions and carrots.

This is in response to the King's appeal to everyone connected with the royal household to grow as much food as possible.

The King has given plots of ground in the royal gardens at Windsor Castle to every lodgekeeper on the estate.

Enough ground is being allotted to each lodgekeeper to grow enough vegetables the whole year through for his family.

In a notice circulated to employees the King stresses the importance of growing every possible ounce of vegetables.

Gave Life for Sailor

Commander Charles F. Hallaran, R.N., former Irish Rugby international, has died on active service in attempting to rescue a sailor who had fallen into the sea. It was disclosed last night.

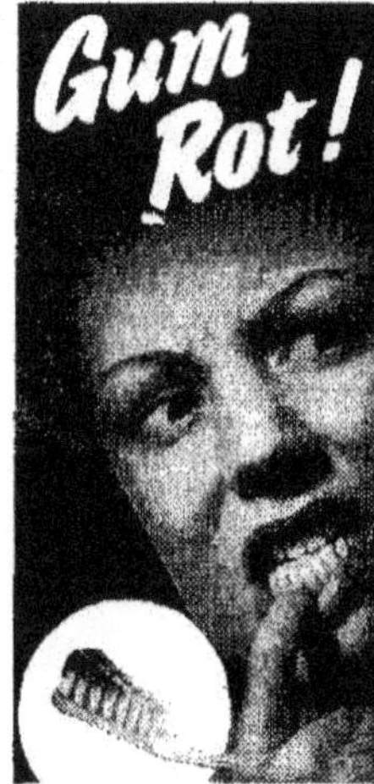

Thurston

Gaol Break by Car, Pony, Bike

SCOTLAND Yard men last night watched London night haunts for the man no prison can hold, Stanley Hilton Thurston, who at dawn had made a spectacular escape from Dartmoor by horse, bicycle and motor-car.

Warders and police in cars, on horseback and on foot, aided by a huntsman and his pack, searched the moor as news flashed to the underworld that the "Houdini" of the Gaols" was free again.

But last night it was believed that Thurston was nearer London than Dartmoor.

Using the black-out to cloak his activities, he may try to steal a service uniform to get lifts to London without arousing suspicion.

The combination of luck and cunning which favoured Thurston in his six months' freedom after his clever escape from Lewes Gaol in 1939 served him well yesterday.

Again he is believed to have used a key.

A bicycle was left unattended at Princetown.

Soon after Thurston's escape this was reported stolen.

Robin Hood Deeds

A few miles away, at Merrivale, a car stood outside an inn.

More good fortune—Thurston is a good mechanic and driver.

He was also seen riding a stolen horse near Tavistock.

This was a ruse to foil pursuers. The car was still in his possession.

The owner yesterday found the stolen bicycle in place of his car, a red and black Austin saloon BND 829.

Thurston 5ft 9in., medium build, blue eyes, clean shaven was wearing grey prison clothes.

Thurston believes he is a Robin Hood, lived like one after his Lewes escape.

Posing as a wealthy son of a baronet
Continued on Back Page, Col. 1

PRICE RULES TO END RAMP

BILL to control prices of goods other than food, now being framed by the Cabinet, will limit profits in the wholesale and retail trades and kill the middleman ramp.

The President of the Board of Trade stated in Parliament yesterday that conditions had changed greatly since the passing of the Price of Goods Act. That Act had worked satisfactorily up to the present in limiting prices to reasonable levels in relation to costs.

"But," he added, "I am satisfied that a further measure of price-regulation is needed and the new legislation will also effect a number of improvements in the system of price regulation.

"In particular I propose to ask for powers to fix maximum prices for specified goods and maximum wholesale and retail percentage margins.

"There will also be power to deal with other charges made for services such as the storage of furniture.

"Provision will be made to prevent increases in the prices of articles which are controlled under the limitation of supplies orders owing to commission transactions between registered persons and others or to the intervention of unnecessary intermediaries in such transactions.

Duchess Radios to Greece

The Duchess of Kent, broadcasting to Greece last night on its 21st Independence Day, said: "To the Greek nation and my friends in the country of my birth, I send my hearty greetings and the confidence that we shall see a victorious peace and the return of happier days."

Loud-speakers among the Greek forces in Albania broadcast singing from Athens Cathedral above the roar of artillery.

ENEMY SHIP SUNK, ANOTHER CAUGHT

An enemy vessel was sunk when R.A.F. bombers attacked shipping off the Dutch coast, the Air Ministry announced last night. One of our planes is missing.

The German cargo ship Ober 8,518 tons has been intercepted by a naval sloop while trying to escape from Massawa, principal port of Eritrea.

Ships Dive-Bombed

Three planes dive-bombed ships off the south-east coast, but there was no apparent damage, and two Spitfires drove the raiders away. Bombs were dropped on a south coast town and at a place in the West of England, but no one was injured.

Priestley Again Off Air

MR. J. B. PRIESTLEY'S postscripts to the Sunday night news are ending.

Sunday's postscript will be by Mr. A. P. Herbert, who has attacked Priestley as a member of the "Something-Must-Be-Said" party.

The B.B.C. say they have not fired Mr. Priestley, but that they are merely giving the other side a hearing.

Mr. Priestley, it is added, has given eight postscripts, instead of the six first suggested, and he will be asked to return after an interval of six or eight weeks.

"There is no question of any difficulty or trouble whatever," an official said.

'Walking on Tight Rope'

Mr. Priestley has broadcast eight postscripts since he returned to the Sunday programmes and he was preparing more.

He recently warned that the "Nothing-Must-Be-Said" influences were working against him.

He told the National Trade Union Club:

"I am walking on a tight rope every Sunday evening. I doubt if it will be possible for me to continue, because you people give me no assistance.

"There is supposed to be a thing called a political truce, and a thing called national unity, which I am supposed to disturb every Sunday evening.

BOYS OF 14 PAY INCOME TAX

BY A SPECIAL CORRESPONDENT

HUNDREDS of boys aged fourteen are now paying income tax.

Many of them, not long out of school, are being paid at the rate of 1s. 3d. per hour by contractors. With overtime they are earning nearly £5 a week.

Inland Revenue authorities are faced with a problem.

If the tax is not stopped at the source they cannot take action against those who fail to pay tax.

Being minors, such boys can only be sued through their parents or guardian.

Everyone, even an infant in arms, is liable for income tax," an income tax authority told the Daily Mirror yesterday. "Age does not matter. It all depends on the amount of earned or unearned income."

Milk Bottle Crime

Future prosecutions by the Food Ministry will include people who keep their milk bottles to use for other purposes, or who do not take proper care that they are returned to the distributors.

Daily Mirror

MAR 31

No. 11,639   ONE PENNY
Registered at the G.P.O. as a Newspaper.

MUSSOLINI'S ITALY IS REELING TODAY UNDER TWO MORE CRUSHING BLOWS FROM OUR MAGNIFICENT FIGHTING FORCES.

Three Italian cruisers and two destroyers have been sunk in the Mediterranean action.

Italy's Navy has failed, not only because of material losses, but because its nerve is clearly broken.

And Mussolini's African empire is virtually gone. His men have quit Abyssinia's key rail town, Diredawa.

Hitler now sees that Italy's Navy is broken, her colonial armies shattered, her empire lost. The German dictator's Balkan plan halts —for his indecision over Yugoslavia still awaits any other explanation.

The Zara, 10,000 tons, crew 765. Built in 1930, the sinking of Zara leaves one more of this class to go.

The destroyer Maestrale, 1,449 tons, crew 153. Completed 1934 —laid to rest March, 1941.

WE SINK FIVE IN SMASHING SEA VICTORY

BIGGEST NAVAL VICTORY OF THE WAR IS ADMIRAL SIR ANDREW CUNNINGHAM'S SMASHING DEFEAT OF THE ITALIAN NAVY, ANNOUNCED LAST NIGHT. AND IN WINNING IT THE BRITISH NAVY SUFFERED NEITHER CASUALTY NOR DAMAGE.

Three of the Duce's biggest crack cruisers, all 10,000-tonners mounting eight 8in. guns; one big destroyer of nearly 2,000 tons, and one smaller destroyer were sunk.

These sinkings are confirmed by the Admiralty. Other ships are probably damaged, including one of the enemy's newest battleships, while a Greek report suggests that a third destroyer is sunk.

To add to their humiliation, the Italians had to call in the German Air Force in a vain effort to shake off the relentless British forces.

We Had No Casualties

Last night's Admiralty communique says:—

"The Commander-in-Chief, Mediterranean, reports that no casualties or damage were suffered by H.M. ships throughout the recent operations. Two of our aircraft, however, are not yet accounted for.

"So far it is confirmed that the following Italian warships have been sunk: The 8in. gun cruisers Fiume, Pola and Zara, the large destroyer Vincenzo Gioberti and the destroyer Maestrale.

"Further details are awaited."

Indications of further damage or loss which may be revealed by late reports are the First Lord of the Admiralty's statement on Saturday that one of the powerful Littorio class battleships was believed severely damaged, and a Greek report last night that survivors have been picked up from the flotilla leader Alfieri.

The Vittorio Alfieri is in the same class as the Vincenzo Gioberti.

Excellent staff work and co-operation contributed to the British vic-

Continued on Back Page, Col. 1

Admiral Sir Andrew Cunningham

FRENCH GUN AND BOMB OUR SHIPS

THE French near Gibraltar yesterday shelled and bombed British light naval forces ordered to inspect a French convoy carrying war material for Germany.

In the interests of humanity, said the Admiralty communique issued last night, our ships, though fully justified, did not fire on the French vessels, which entered the port of Nemours, Algeria.

The Admiralty stated that the French ships passed through the Straits within Spanish territorial waters, and when our forces called on them to stop on leaving territorial water, French shore batteries fired.

Our ships were compelled to reply in their own defence and hits were observed on the shore batteries.

When our ships were returning to Gibraltar, French bombers twice unsuccessfully attacked them.

Vichy issued its own version later, through the French official news agency.

This said that a British cruiser and five destroyers attacked the convoy in French territorial waters. The convoy took shelter in Nemours, under the protection of its one escorting destroyer, naval shore batteries and aircraft, "which replied to the fire of the aggressors and drove them off."

It was stated that the cargo consisted of food supplies for the

Continued on Back Page, Col. 3

ITALIANS QUIT KEY TOWN

WITHOUT waiting to put up any sort of a fight against the South African forces striking toward Diredawa, Mussolini's men have quit this key town on the Addis Ababa-Jibuti railway.

Mussolini yesterday admitted that Diredawa had been evacuated. Later, our Cairo H.Q. stated that the South African troops advancing from Harar were "well on the way" to Diredawa.

The retreat from Diredawa, enabling our forces to get astride the rail line from Addis Ababa to the coast, means that Mussolini's remaining forces in Abyssinia are cut off

Nearly a Rout

The South African Air Force did not allow the Italians to get out of Diredawa easily. They bombed and machine-gunned lorries and killed many troops.

In Eritrea, the Italian retreat towards Asmara from Keren is now "an extremely rapid retirement, if not a rout," said a British military spokesman yesterday.

The R.A.F. at the week-end, harried the Italians as they retreated toward Asmara—and bombed Asmara into the bargain.

Already we have captured 3,775 prisoners, including sixty-eight officers, together with a number of guns.

Military sources put Italian casualties in the Keren battle at between 5,000 and 6,000.

British casualties, considering the nature of the operations at Keren, were called "amazingly slight."

U.S. SEIZE LINER, 31 OTHER AXIS SHIPS

UNITED STATES coastguards yesterday boarded and seized twenty-eight Italian ships in American waters and took the crews into custody, cables John Walters from New York.

In addition to the ships seized in U.S. ports was the 23,255-ton liner Conte Biancamano, which was in Panama Harbour. U.S. troops leaped from three lorries and swarmed on the liner. A U.S. destroyer drew up alongside and 500 of the crew were removed.

"Ours Now"

Also included was the 4,733-ton Italian tanker Colorado, at San Juan, Porto Rico.

Seizure of these ships, on the ground that Italians were sabotaging them, will, it is predicted, result in their being used for transporting American arms to Britain.

The only three German vessels in American waters were also boarded. Coastguards with revolvers and sub-machine-guns ran up gangways of Italian vessels in sixteen ports, lined officers and crews on deck and told them the U.S. Government was now in possession.

The crew of the Italian motorship Leme, at Portland, Maine, threw up their hands in fear when forty-five Americans boarded her.

A British United Press Washington message stated last night that crews of five Italian ships had been sent to Ellis Island.

These five vessels, it was added, had been methodically wrecked. One member of a boarding party said the crews "must have spent at least a week smashing the machinery."

The seized Italian ships, apart from the liner, totalled 175,000 tons, their crews numbering more than 1,000 men.

TWO JAP DESTROYERS CONVOY GERMAN SHIP

Two Japanese destroyers were reported to have met the German merchantman Rameses when she slipped out of Shanghai after lying in the Whangpoo River since September, 1939, says Associated Press.

The Rameses was believed to be headed for Kobe to load supplies for Nazi raiders.

Daily Mirror

APL 1

No. 11,640   ONE PENNY
Registered at the G.P.O. as a Newspaper.

What Is Left

MUSSO'S SHRINKING NAVY.—The black ship behind represents the size of the Italian Navy at the time of Musso's entrance into the war. The white ship is the proportionate size today, following the Battle of the Mediterranean. Bombings and pummellings by British air and sea forces have reduced Musso's fleet to two-thirds of its former self.

FLIRT SHIP LURED WOPS

A FOUR-HOUR FLIRTATION LURED THE ITALIAN WARSHIPS TO THEIR DOOM IN THE EASTERN MEDITERRANEAN BATTLE, IT WAS REVEALED LAST NIGHT. ORION, SISTER OF THE BRITISH CRUISERS AJAX AND ACHILLES, OF GRAF SPEE FAME, WAS THE FLIRT.

She spotted the Italian warships, including the crack new battleship Vittorio Veneto at fifteen miles range and sailed in offering herself as a target. She looked a tempting prey and the Italians gave chase.

She lured them seventy miles off their homeward course—seventy miles nearer the British battle fleet which was racing up from 120 miles away in the hope of bringing the Italians to battle.

Vice-Admiral H. D. Pridham-Wippell was in Orion, which spent anxious moments dodging long-range shelling by the Vittorio Veneto as well as from the cruisers.

"Some 15in. bricks fell close," said the Admiral, "but the Orion, like the rest of the British ships, didn't even have her paint scratched."

That was only the beginning of a 200-mile chase lasting twelve hours in which the Italians were—

Battered and slowed down by pursuing planes;

Blasted nearly out of the water by broadsides from battleships only two miles away, but invisible in the dark; and

Sunk by destroyers that dashed in to complete the destruction.

For Admiral Sir Andrew Cunningham and his boys it was triumph of brilliant strategy, tactics combining air power with supreme naval skill. Surprise was an essential element.

It was the first time in the long history of sea warfare that a fleeing enemy has been overtaken by aircraft, battered and slowed down to give the guns of the pursuing warships a chance.

It was the first time since Jutland

Continued on Back Page, Col. 3

The cruiser Orion . . . lured the Italians to their doom.

Admiral Pridham-Wippell.

★ His First Command

Lieutenant G. R. G. Watkins, thirty, was the commander of the destroyer Havock who radioed Admiral Cunningham: "I am hanging on to the tail of the cruiser Pola. Shall I board her or blow her stern off with depth charges!"

Havock is his first command and he has held it exactly three weeks.

But the spirit of the sea was bred in him. He is the only son of Admiral G. R. S. Watkins, D.S.O. His mother was a Rooke —descendant of the illustrious Admiral Sir George Rooke who captured Gibraltar for the British in 1704.

7 Shells Hit Italian Cruiser—It Vanished

Admiral Cunningham revealed last night that in the Mediterranean battle one Italian 8in. gun cruiser was struck by at least seven 15in. shells simultaneously, and completely disintegrated in one burst of flame.

"Not a pleasant spectacle," commented the Admiral.

This cruiser, he said, was struck in practically all her vital parts, and disappeared in one terrific explosion. It is not known whether there are any survivors.—British United Press.

CRISIS CALL TO SLAVS

A DRAMATIC broadcast proclamation from their Premier last night told the Yugoslav people that the country's armed forces were ready, and called on them to "stay put," even if it meant dying on their own doorsteps.

In this answer to Hitler's fierce "nerve war," the Premier, General Simovitch, declared:—

"The Army, the Air Force and the Navy are ready to do their duty. All State and local authorities and clergy should remain at their posts no matter what happens.

"Any evacuation is forbidden. There is no reason for this, and it might cause bad consequences. The interests of the State demand that everybody should stick to his home, and if necessary die at the door of his home for the good of the country, the King and the people."

Simovitch fought against Fifth Column alarmists by urging the people not to heed "foreign agents," and to remain calm.

When some of Belgrade's inhabitants began to leave for the country he enforced his evacuation ban by placing armed police at the rail stations.

As Hitler was still getting ready last night to tell Yugoslavia that his patience was exhausted, Mr. Anthony Eden had already acted.

The Greek Government revealed that Britain's Foreign Secretary and General Sir John Dill, Chief of the Imperial General Staff, were back in Athens and had resumed their consultations with the Greek leaders.

At the same time it was reported

Continued on Back Page, Col. 5

INCOME BEATS BUDGET FIGURE

BRITAIN spent the record amount of £3,867,245,670 in the financial year, which ended last night.

That was total ordinary expenditure. Against it total ordinary revenue was £1,408,867,097, leaving a "deficit" of £2,458,378,573.

Revenue is greater by nearly £49,000,000 than the Chancellor expected, largely due to the success of the new taxes.

Expenditure was £116,000,000 less than estimated.

Despite the war there was a net increase in total ordinary revenue of £359,678,404 over last year.

Income tax more than came up to expectations. Sir Kingsley expected £510,540,000, but received £523,949,000.

Excess profits tax also did well with £72,103,000 — more than £3,000,000 over estimate.

ITALIANS LOSE 4,000 MEN

MORE than 3,000 Italian officers and men were killed in the Mediterranean battle with the British Fleet, according to estimates in Alexandria yesterday.

Another 1,000 officers and men were taken prisoner. Among them were thirty-five Germans, imported to pep up the Italian crews.

✦ ✦ ✦

This is what the battle cost Italy in ships: Cruisers Fiume, Pola and Zara (each 10,000 tons and confirmed as sunk); cruiser Giovanni Delle Bande Nere (5,069 tons—damaged, possibly sunk); destroyers Vincenzo Gioberti and Maestrale (confirmed as sunk) and Vittorio Alfieri (probably sunk).

Also the powerful new 35,000-ton battleship Vittorio Veneto, which was hit at least three times and severely damaged.

✦ ✦ ✦

In the Vittorio Veneto was Admiral Arturo Riccardi, who was only recently appointed Commander-in-Chief of the Italian Navy.

So if ever Musso's navy was to be reckoned with as a fighting force, it isn't now. More than one-third of his original fleet has been put out of action since the war began.

✦ ✦ ✦

Admiral Cunningham, delighted over the latest big smash-up of Mussolini's Fleet, said last night that he hopes to "speed up" the job of wiping enemy warcraft from the Mediterranean. "We are going to do our best," he said, "to finish off the Italian Navy before the end of the year."

SILENT NAZI BOMBER GOT ARMS SHIP

HUGE four-engined German bombers, equipped with silencers, have been daily preying on British shipping in the Atlantic.

This is reported by passengers aboard the Holland-American liner-freighter Bloomersdijk, which has reached Hoboken, New Jersey, from Liverpool.

They said that on March 19 a German bomb struck an east-bound freighter laden with munitions. The vessel burst into flames and sank within five minutes.

Apparently all hands were lost.

Night Fighters Active

Aerial activity was greater over Eastern England last night than for some time past. Shortly after dark enemy planes were crossing the coast but met with a hot reception from our fighters.

Daily Mirror

APL 2

No. 11,641 — ONE PENNY
Registered at the G.P.O. as a Newspaper.

DEMAND BY AXIS TO U.S.A.

AS many Axis ships blazed in South American ports yesterday—set on fire by their crews—Germany and Italy demanded the release of their vessels and crews seized by the U.S.A.

Notes sent by the Axis to Washington were said to be angry and threatening.

"The seizure of Axis shipping in American ports is an absolute violation of human rights," declared officials in Berlin.

But America is not worried. Mr. Cordell Hull, Secretary of State, said the protests were receiving scant consideration, and would have no effect on U.S. policy.

The idea of Germany, the world's most notorious breaker of international law, accusing the U.S.A. caused amusement in Washington.

Meanwhile the Attorney-General, Mr. Jackson, ordered prosecutions to begin in sabotage charges against Axis seamen.

A Mexican Navy Ministry official announced last night that marines had been ordered to place twelve German and Italian ships under protective custody.

Planes Seized

Peruvian troops yesterday took over the airport at Tambo, Lima, Peru, and prevented a German-controlled aeroplane from taking off.

They are also reported to have taken over two Junkers 30-seater planes in which Nazi employees of German shipping firms were trying to leave the country.

Swiss radio said last night that eighteen Italian ships were scuttled off the Philippines.

The Peruvian destroyers Almirante Guise and Almirante Villar and war planes have been sent by the naval authorities at Callao to chase two German ships which left the port unexpectedly.

British United Press, Reuter Associated Press and Exchange.

5 BOMBERS DOWNED

THE Nazis lost five bombers in attacks on Britain yesterday. One was brought down in Suffolk, two off the Welsh coast, one in Shropshire, and the other crashed in Co. Waterford.

Night-raiders were over a south-west area, but up to a late hour London's lull continued. It was London's twelfth raid-free night.

Single raiders dropped bombs at points near the south and east coasts. At two points on the south coast damage and casualties—some fatal—were caused.

A squadron leader who was taken prisoner by the Germans when he was shot down over Dunkirk in May last year, destroyed the plane, a

Continued on Back Page, Col. 4

Lieutenant Edward Dees.

BRITON SHOT BY HUN SENTRY

THE shooting of a British officer prisoner by a German sentry was explained last night by the officer's father.

The officer was sketching from a window when the sentry, who thought he was breaking the rules by leaning out, challenged him and, receiving no reply, shot him.

The prisoner was Lieutenant Edward Dees, twenty-six, of the 6th Battalion of the Durham Light Infantry, held in a prison camp known as Oflag Seven C/H.

"Edward was captured near Dunkirk last May," his father, Mr. Edward Dees, of Besconsfield-avenue, Low Fell, told the Daily Mirror.

"We heard of his death through a letter written to his widow from a fellow officer."

This letter stated:—

"He was killed on Saturday, January 25, while standing at a window sketching as he had been doing for two days previously.

"Apparently one of the sentries thought he was leaning out of the window and this would be a serious infringement of camp rules, so after shouting the sentry fired.

NURSES' PAY TO BE RAISED

The War Minister announced yesterday that he is reviewing conditions in the nursing services and hopes very shortly to announce increases in nurses' pay.

---

8 MPs KILL SUNDAY THEATRES

THE House of Commons last night killed the Defence Order permitting theatres and music halls to open on Sunday. The voting was 144 to 136—a majority of eight.

Result was announced by Mr. Thomas Magnay, who slapped his thigh, waved his order paper, and shouted "Hurrah!" to cheering M.P.s.

The House was packed just before the division, but more than 100 M.P.s did not vote.

The Government will not try to overrule the decision of the House—arrived at on a free vote—or to bring the matter up again unless there is such a demand from the country that it could not be ignored.

The Home Secretary was one of the first of many to shake hands with Mr. Magnay, who led the opposition to his Order.

Mr. Magnay, National Liberal member for Gateshead, took the stage first with an attack on crooners and London ("playground of the idle rich").

The opposing "leading man" was Mr. A. P. Herbert, who said that, as Independent M.P. for Oxford University, he represented more Church of England clergymen than any other member.

He had not received a protest from a single clergyman.

The Bible Readers

Points from speeches:—

Mr. MAGNAY.—Today, in literature, every man is a cad and every woman a vamp. You hear crooners breaking their hearts every night. If they broke their necks I shouldn't be sorry.

Mr. CROWDER (Con., Finchley)—I recall the Premier's statement that Yugoslavia has found her soul. Do not let us do anything to lose our own.

Mr. WEDGWOOD (Soc., Newcastle-under-Lyme).—This is still a Bible-reading people. There are many whose enthusiasm behind the Government will be injured if we pass this Order.

Mr. BEVERLEY BAXTER (Con., Sutton, Plymouth).—Girls prefer to go to the pictures and be able to hold hands—to the glare of the music hall.

HOME SECRETARY. — Sunday theatres would help in keeping members of the Forces and war workers cheerful and happy—important in the prosecution of the war.

NAVY PRAY FOR MORE VICTORIES

Thousands of officers and naval ratings of the Mediterranean Fleet bared their heads yesterday and thanked God for victory over the Italians.

Standing on the quarter-decks of battleships, cruisers, destroyers and anti-aircraft carriers, before the muzzles of the big guns, they joined in a few minutes' thanksgiving service.

Captain Arthur Latouche Bisset, of the aircraft-carrier Formidable, told an American reporter: "There is a fifty-fifty chance that we sank the battleship Vittorio Veneto."

An R.A.F. flight-lieutenant said: "The enemy fleet zig-zagged violently. Now and then one would get in another's way. Our bombs added to the confusion."

Story of the Battle—Page Ten.

YOUNGEST SQUADRON LEADER PRISONER

Squadron Leader E. H. Lynch-Blosse, aged twenty-four, youngest squadron leader, reported missing last month after a big raid on Berlin, is a prisoner. His uncle, Squadron Leader P. W. Lynch-Blosse, is one of the oldest bomber pilots.

BBC BANS 2 NAUGHTY STARS

THE B.B.C. has started a new purity drive. Two famous comedians, Douglas Byng and Sydney Howard, have been barred from the air for telling naughty stories.

Douglas has three months suspension, Sydney six months.

Douglas told the one which begins with the secretary asking her boss what he thinks of the Greek position. Sydney told a story about a soldier.

Several producers have also been on the carpet.

Director - General Ogilvy has ordered every show to be watched. If anyone spins a blue joke, he must immediately be cut off the air.

Sydney Howard laughed heartily when the Daily Mirror told him of his "sentence."

"It's news to me," he said. "But I think I know what has caused the trouble. It was when I broadcast in Jack Payne's Guest Night a few weeks ago and had to gag to fill in a gap the censor had cut out.

"I only knew about the cut at the last minute and had to think up something quickly. The offence was a joke about a soldier home on leave. It just slipped out.

"But, after all, it was pretty harmless—and at that time of night all children should be in bed!"

Douglas Byng said: "I'm so accustomed to hearing that I've been banned for this or that I'm not surprised. But why the B.B.C. should ban me I can't think. They read every word of my scripts and I never deviate from their version.

"Often their revised version seems ruder to me than my original.

"It all seems very strange to me."

ASMARA FALLS

ASMARA, capital and seat of government of Italian East Africa, has been captured, it was announced last night from British G.H.Q., Cairo.

This leaves the way open for the British drive towards Massawa, Italy's last Red Sea port.

Despite blocked roads caused by Italians blowing up mountainsides and country as difficult as that through which they had fought for two months, the British forces advanced seventy miles in the five days following the fall of Keren.

One of Asmara's strongholds, Fort Baldissera, built on a hill to the south-west of the town, has always been proclaimed as impregnable.

Shortly before news of the fall of Asmara was received, it was reported that hundreds more prisoners had been taken, including a brigade commander, and much material.

A Bersaglieri officer who was taken prisoner told a war correspondent, "It will be over soon."

From Abyssinia comes news that our advance from Diredawa, astride the railway and road to Addis Ababa, is also making rapid progress.

A Nairobi communique states:

"Our leading troops advancing in Diredawa found the Italian population being injured by a large armed band, consisting mostly of deserters from their own forces.

"Our troops restored order."—British United Press and Reuter.

SHOT EARL IN HONOURS LIST

THE Earl of Erroll, who was Second Lieutenant (Acting Captain) in the Kenya Regiment, is among those mentioned for distinguished services in the Middle East in last night's "London Gazette."

Lord Erroll was found shot dead at the wheel of his car while on leave in Kenya. Sir Delves Broughton has been accused of his murder.

Among others mentioned in the list for distinguished services is Lady Sidney Farrar, a captain of the Women's Transport Service. She is sister of the Earl of Buckinghamshire.

An O.B.E. (Military Division) goes to Sister (Acting Matron) Helen Gwladys Lawford, of Queen Alexandra's Imperial Military Nursing Service.

Boot Girls Reserved

All women workers in the boot and shoe industry are "reserved," it was announced yesterday by Mr. George Chester, general secretary of the National Union of Boot and Shoe Operatives.

Daily Mirror

APL 7

No. 11,645   ONE PENNY
Registered at the G.P.O. as a Newspaper.

BRITISH ARMY IS FIGHTING BALKAN INVADERS

Europe's New Battlefield

The frontiers of Yugoslavia, which now become Europe's latest battlefield.

Belgrade, Yugoslavia's capital, had its first air-raids yesterday, and German troops are attacking Greece from Bulgaria.

They are making a determined drive down the Struma Valley in an attempt to reach Salonika, which, with its quays and good anchorages, and its important railway position, is a key to the Middle East.

BRITISH troops in considerable force—Belgrade estimated 150,000—and a greatly strengthened R.A.F. last night defended key points in Greece against German invaders who marched against Greece and Yugoslavia at dawn yesterday.

As Berlin admitted that German troops were meeting with tenacious resistance, especially in the Struma Valley, Athens officially stated that the Greek advance forces were holding their own everywhere on the eastern front.

Ten German tanks were destroyed, five planes shot down, and some prisoners taken. The German forces left bodies piled high before the Greek defenders without being able to advance, said a Greek Government spokesman.

"One of the greatest epics of Greek history has been written today by our soldiers," he declared.

In Ankara it was reported that the Greeks had occupied a village in Bulgaria and that the Yugoslavs were standing firm against the main thrust.

The Greek communique stated:

"Powerful German forces, equipped with the most modern war machines and supported by tanks, abundant heavy artillery and numerous aircraft, this morning suddenly and repeatedly attacked our positions defended only by small Greek forces.

"A violent struggle occurred all day in the main zone of the Bulgarian frontier area, particularly in the district of Beli and the Struma Valley.

"Our fortifications, despite heavy shelling by artillery and dive-bombing, have resisted except one, which fell after a particularly strong enemy attack.

"Some areas of national territory were evacuated in time by our
Continued on Back Page, Col. 4

Speedy U.S. Aid for Yugoslavia

The United States Government is proceeding, as speedily as possible, to send military and other supplies to Yugoslavia.

Mr. Cordell Hull, U.S. Secretary of State, announced this last night after consultation with President Roosevelt.

Mr. Hull said this action was in line with his Government's "policy of helping those who are defending themselves against their would-be conquerors.

"This barbaric invasion of Yugoslavia, and the attempt to annihilate that country by brute force, is but another chapter in the present planned movement of attempted world conquest and domination," he added.

"The American people have the greatest sympathy for a nation which has been thus so outrageously attacked, and we will follow closely the valiant struggle the Yugoslav people are making to protect their homes and preserve their liberty."—Associated Press.

BELGRADE BOMBED

SOUNDING of Belgrade's air-raid sirens at 3.25 a.m. yesterday was Yugoslavia's first indication that the nation was at war.

Axis warplanes attacked Belgrade and other open Yugoslav towns.

Three raids were made on Belgrade, in spite of Yugoslavia's announcement that in the event of war Belgrade, Zagreb and Ljubljana—capitals of the three component States of Yugoslavia—would be declared open towns.

Waves of dive-bombers, escorted by fighters, made the raids on Belgrade, where they encountered heavy anti-aircraft fire, it was stated in Berlin.

It was claimed that the railway station was set on fire, the radio station destroyed, successful attacks made on barracks and aerodromes, and forty-four Yugoslav planes destroyed on the ground. The loss of four bombers was admitted.

Berlin declared last night that the Yugoslav Government had withdrawn from Belgrade.

German bombers during the day attacked Salonika, where one was destroyed, and Athens had two Alerts.—British United Press and Exchange.

PREMIER SEES TURKISH ENVOY

The Turkish Ambassador in London called on Mr. Churchill yesterday and had a long conversation.

In Ankara, the Turkish Foreign Minister received the British Ambassador and the Yugoslav envoy.

A Government spokesman said Turkey had anticipated the Yugoslav situation and added, "There is nothing to get excited about."

Air Vice-Marshal Elmhirst and Lieutenant-General Sir James Marshall Cornwall arrived at Istanbul (Turkey) on the way to Thrace, after leaving the Anglo-Turkish staff talks at Ankara. The talks are continuing in their absence.—Associated Press.

Naval Yacht Sunk

An Admiralty communique last night said that H.M. yacht Wilna (Temporary Lieutenant L. W. Cleverly, R.N.R.), has been sunk. There were no casualties.

Addis Ababa Ours

IT was officially announced last night that British Imperial Forces had entered Addis Ababa, capital of Abyssinia.

The city was apparently handed over by the Italians, the garrison walking out at the last moment.

A Free French patrol has penetrated to within eight miles of the Red Sea port of Massawa, which is expected to fall in two or three days.

South African troops now at Addis Ababa have covered 700 miles from the time they crossed the border into Abyssinia on March 7, which is exactly four weeks.

50 Miles a Day

In the last two days they have advanced more than 100 miles against strong enemy forces and over roads blasted by the Italians in their retreat.

The R.A.F. has played a big part, too. It was announced last night that Addis Ababa was heavily raided by the R.A.F. on Friday. Heavy bombs hit hangars, aerodrome buildings and barracks, and Italian planes on the ground were destroyed.

Before the entry of the Imperial troops into Addis Ababa the Italian envoy gave to Lieutenant-General A. G. Cunningham, East Africa G.O.C., a message from the Duke of Aosta.

It expressed the Duke's appreciation of the measures taken by the British Forces for the protection of women and children in Addis Ababa.

SOVIET SORRY FOR SLAVS

HOUR after hour last night Moscow radio proclaimed its friendship for Yugoslavia and condemned the aggression of Germany. It was as if the Hitler-Stalin Pact had been torn up, or never existed.

When Moscow radio spoke of the new pact with Yugoslavia (reported on page 2) the commentator, speaking very slowly, said, "In spite of this Hitler ordered his armies at dawn to march against Yugoslavia."

The text of the treaty was published prominently by the newspapers and was given first place in broadcasts in foreign languages. No mention was made of the air and land attacks on Yugoslavia.

The German communique was omitted for the first time, and no reference was made to Hitler's proclamation.

Investia said: "The efforts of the new Yugoslav Government to preserve peace could not fail to arouse Soviet sympathy, primarily because any act directed towards the strengthening of peace coincides with the fundamental, undeviating aims of Soviet policy."

The Turkish radio said: "In consequence of the friendship pact signed by Soviet Russia and Yugoslavia, the good relations between Turkey and Yugoslavia have certainly been strengthened."—Reuter and British United Press.

Moscow Raid Test

Important military manoeuvres, with the main theme of defence against air attack, took place on Saturday in twenty-five towns and villages in the Moscow area, according to a Moscow message to the Vichy News Agency.

An alarm was given and a black-out ordered at 5 p.m.—Reuter.

The Bribe They Refused

Yugoslavia was to have got Salonika in return for signing the Axis Pact, says an Italian Government communique quoted by the official (Stefani) news agency.—British United Press.

'200,000 FOR LIBYA'

COMMENTING on German movements in Libya, the Turkish radio pointed out last night that General Wavell had given priority to political considerations when he decided not to continue the offensive towards Tripoli.

Had Wavell chosen to continue the advance, it would have been impossible for him to give assistance to Greece and now to Yugoslavia.

"We do not believe," said the announcer, "that the Benghazi withdrawal will be extended all over Cyrenaica. At least 200,000 men operating in East Africa will soon be available for Libya."

Cairo opinion is that Wavell will hand to Hitler the first Nazi land defeat.

Attacks from Many Points

GERMAN troops were yesterday attacking the Yugoslavs from many points trying to divide the army into two.

The Yugoslavs are withdrawing to the south of the Danube, where they have good, prepared defences.

Three German divisions are advancing from Rumania in the general direction of Belgrade.

Another two divisions and one armoured division are operating from Szigeth (Hungary), also in the general direction of Belgrade. Twelve to fifteen German divisions operating from Austria are advancing to Zagreb (Croatia).

Parachute troops are operating in the Struma Valley.

An attack is being made at two points on the Greek frontier.

The German communique declared that "In view of the penetration towards the northern Greek frontiers by British troops which landed in Greece, and after joining up of these troops with the mobilised Yugoslav troops became known, units of the German Army counter-attacked."

17th Bombless Night

Up to a late hour there was no Alert in London last night—the seventeenth night in succession that the capital has had no bombs.

What appeared to be slight coastal activity by enemy aircraft was reported from south-west England and from east and north-east Scotland last night, but there were no reports of bombs falling anywhere in Britain.

15,000 Strikers Return

Over 15,000 men in the West Wales tinplate industry will resume work today after being on strike for two weeks because of the suspension of a clerk.

You can buy Oxydol everywhere, 1/-, 6d. & 3½d. Remember, Oxydol is triple-tested.

THOMAS HEDLEY AND COMPANY LIMITED, NEWCASTLE-ON-TYNE.

Daily Mirror

No. 11,646   **ONE PENNY**
Registered at the G.P.O. as a Newspaper.

APL 8

Cost of Living

The cost of living is not to be allowed to rise any higher, the Chancellor of the Exchequer told Parliament.

The Exchequer, already paying £100,000,000 a year to keep down the price of food, is to subsidise essential goods and services.

Cost of living index will remain as now.

RAF RAID SOFIA: SLAVS FIGHTING IN ALBANIA

THE R.A.F., quickly avenging raids on Belgrade, has struck fiercely at German military concentrations in Sofia, capital of Bulgaria. Britain has not declared war on Bulgaria—she recalled her Minister three weeks ago—but the Bulgars have allowed their country to become a Hitler war base.

A Yugoslav army, after artillery preparation, is attacking the Italians in North Albania. Late last night it had won considerable successes, according to Ankara (Turkish) radio.

The Greek High Command announced that, " to avoid unnecessary sacrifice, Western Thrace is being evacuated according to plan by our few advanced elements."

Elsewhere, the Greeks held their ground yesterday in spite of violent German attacks.

Two forts in the Struma Valley were captured by the enemy. Another fort was captured but was retaken by the Greeks.

Many German tanks were destroyed Athens claimed.

Last night's Greek communique said:—

" German troops penetrated into the fort of Teritori. After a struggle inside the fort all the German attackers were decimated and fort is again in Greek hands."

On the Albanian front the Greeks made a strong offensive. They took 500 prisoners.

Berlin claimed that German troops had penetrated the Yugoslav and Greek frontiers to a depth of between twenty and twenty-five miles. Shock troops, after a stiff fight, were said to have seized a bridgehead over a river near the Yugoslav frontier and prevented the defenders from blowing up the bridge.

Sofia Station Bombed

News of the R.A.F. raid on Sofia, carried out on Sunday night, was announced in Cairo as Britain broke off relations with Hungary because she had become a base for operations against the Allies.

Sofia's main railway station and marshalling yards, the railway junction, warehouses, motor transport shops, and a large factory were heavily bombed.

Many explosions occurred. One large fire and several smaller fires broke out. Trucks were hurled into the air.

After carrying out their attack, aircraft dived and machine-gunned objectives and motor transport on the roads in the Struma Valley, only practical military route from Bulgaria into Greece.

Considerable damage was caused. All our planes returned.

Earlier a small force of R.A.F. Hurricanes, with no loss to themselves, shot down five Messerschmitt 109s and severely damaged others in a battle over the Rupel Pass bottleneck in the Struma Valley.

German planes bombed Belgrade again yesterday, Berlin radio claimed. Ankara reported that the Yugoslav Government had left Belgrade for an unknown destination.

Athens radio said that German parachute troops had been captured in Macedonia. Nazi leaflets dropped from air addressed the Greeks as comrades.

(British United Press, Associated Press and Reuter.)

"Ship from U.S. Held"

Nazi radio said yesterday that a French steamer on her way to France from the United States was captured by the British and taken to an English port.

For Troops in Greece

The new 3d. air mail postcard service to H.M. Forces in the Middle East is also available to the troops in Greece, as forming part of the Middle East forces.

First Civilian Pigeon Post Starts Today

Britain's first civilian pigeon post will be launched today when a flight of pigeons will leave Fort Dunlop, Birmingham, for Wardington, near Banbury, Oxford.

One pigeon will carry a message from the workers at Fort Dunlop to the chairman of their company, and another will carry a film the size of a postage stamp.

" The flight will take about an hour and a half," Mr. Eley, of Fort Dunlop, told the " Daily Mirror."

" In the event of invasion, our telephone lines may be cut, but the pigeons will take our messages and allow us to carry on."

YOU SAVE AS YOU PAY BIGGER TAX

Compulsory saving;
Two million more people to pay income tax;

Standard rate of income tax 10s. in the £;
Tax allowances cut.

THESE are the pay points in the new Budget, introduced in the House of Commons yesterday by the Chancellor of the Exchequer.

Compulsory saving, the chief feature, is disguised as increased taxation, which will go to the credit of the taxpayer in the Post Office Savings Bank—after the war.

All but those with the lowest incomes are affected. A single man with £2 5s. a week will have to save 2s. a week, and a childless married couple with £3 a week will have to save 1s.

The saving works as an offset to the cuts in personal allowances and earned income allowance. The extra tax imposed by the cutting of these reliefs will be credited to the taxpayer as savings.

Lowering of tax exemption level to £110 a year instead of £120 for single people and cuts in allowances will make 2,000,000 more people pay income tax.

And the tax goes up to 10s. in the £, standard rate. The tax on the first £165 of taxable income will be 8s. 6d. instead of 5s. This means that the lower incomes bear the full 1s. 6d. increase.

At present one-sixth of earned income is tax free. In future only one-tenth will be tax free—up to a maximum of £150.

Personal allowances will be cut to £140 instead of £170 for married men

★ No Change ★

These tax items remain unchanged:—
Cigarettes and tobacco;
Beer and spirits;
Children's allowances in income tax reliefs;
Purchase tax, which has produced £26,000,000;
Excess profits tax remains at 100 per cent., but there will be a 20 per cent. rebate after the war to help industrial reconstruction.

★ ★ ★

and £80 instead of £100 for unmarried.

The new Income Tax rates will begin to operate in November. Income tax changes will mean an addition of £250,000,000 in a full year and £150,000,000 in the current year.

Another tax change in the Budget is the abolition of duties on patent medicines, though the purchase tax, which is levied on many of them, remains.

Total Budget expenditure is estimated at £4,206,957,000, compared with last April's estimate of £2,566,790,000 — an addition of £1,540,167,000. Estimated revenue is £1,786,360,000 — an addition of £551,969,000.

Estimated expenditure over revenue is £2,420,597,000—£988,198,000 more than last year.

D.S.O., 2nd Bar to D.F.C.

Conspicuous gallantry and initiative in hunting and attacking enemy raiders, often in bad weather, has won a second Bar to the D.F.C. for a pilot of twenty-four who also holds the D.S.O.

Acting Squadron-Leader Roland Robert Stanford Tuck, No. 257 Squadron, who has brought down twenty-two of the enemy, won the D.F.C. last June, a Bar in October, and the D.S.O. in December.

What You Pay to Win

SINGLE MAN			
Earned Income	New Tax	Rebate after war	1940
£120	£7 10s.	£7 10s.	—
£200	£32 10s.	£10 16s.	£18 13s.
£400	£111 2s.	£23 6s.	£70 6s.
£1,000	£381 2s.	£43 6s.	£282 18s.

MARRIED (NO CHILDREN)			
Earned Income	New Tax	Rebate after war	1940
£160	£1 6s.	£1 6s.	—
£225	£20 6s.	£14 12s.	£4 7s.
£400	£81 2s.	£28 0s.	£40 18s.
£600	£171 2s.	£35 0s.	£111 7s.
£1,000	£351 2s.	£48 6s.	£253 0s.

MARRIED (ONE CHILD)			
£220	£2 12s.	£2 12s.	—
£300	£26 0s.	£16 5s.	£7 10s.
£400	£66 2s.	£19 5s.	£28 4s.
£600	£146 2s.	£35 0s.	£90 2s.
£1,000	£326 2s.	£48 6s.	£231 15s.

MARRIED (TWO CHILDREN)			
£270	£1 19s.	—	—
£350	£24 7s.	£17 6s.	£5 8s.
£400	£60 2s.	£19 5s.	£18 17s.
£1,000	£301 2s.	£48 6s.	£210 19s.

MARRIED (THREE CHILDREN)			
£325	16s.	16s.	—
£400	£46 2s.	£18 8s.	£3 6s.
£600	£298 2s.	£35 0s.	£47 12s.
£1,000	£276 2s.	£48 6s.	£189 5s.

HOW PLAN WORKS

THIS is how the Chancellor of the Exchequer explained his " Save As You Pay " plan:

The extra tax you pay by reason of the reduction in the personal and earned income allowance will be offset after the war by the credit which will then be given in your favour in the Post Office Savings Bank.

A single man with 45s. a week paid no income tax last year. He will now pay 2s. a week, the whole of which will be treated as a credit.

The married man with two children and an earned income of £350 paid £5 8s. 4d. last year. Now he will pay £24 7s. 6d., but of this increase of about £19, £17 6s. 8d. will be credited to him.

£125,000,000 Credit

The maximum amount to be treated as credit in respect of tax paid in 1941-42 will be £85.

These alterations in the allowances will produce £125,000,000 in a full year and £54,000,000 in the current year. Total income tax changes will bring in £250,000,000, more in the full year, of which one-half will fall to be treated as credit.

The taxpayer cannot claim or use his credit while war continues.

An official of the Income Tax Payers' Society told the Daily Mirror last night: " It appears certain that the credits will not be repaid all at once after the war.

" The intention may be to pay back so much every year in the case of the larger sums, but the small sums credited may be paid without delay."

MILKMAIDS WILL WORK "ORDINARY" SUMMER TIME

When the extra hour of Summer Time is introduced on Sunday, May 4, special provision will be made to ease the situation in agriculture.

Milking will be ruled by " ordinary " Summer Time, and milk trains will be re-timed accordingly. The extra hour will last until August 10.

Saved Four Times More

A White Paper, first of its kind, published yesterday estimates gross personal savings last year at £608,000,000, or more than four times the 1938 figure.

LOOKED LIKE A CONVICT

(and Was One)

WALTER BEMAN, who escaped from Dartmoor Prison on Thursday, was captured in Plymouth last night.

He was challenged by an astute policeman and tried to bluff his way out. But finally cornered, he admitted: " It's all right, it's me."

Police-Constable Riggs, off duty and in plain clothes, was standing at a store's snack counter when Beman, wearing a brown suit and trilby hat, asked for a cup of tea.

Riggs challenged him. Beman replied: " Do you think I look like a convict?" The officer said: " I do. Let's have a look at your identity card."

Beman could not produce one. Asked where he lived, he said, " Dockroad." There is no Dock-road in Plymouth.

He told the officer he was working for a transport firm and had to meet a pal. They went to the supposed rendezvous, but no pal turned up.

He was taken back to Dartmoor. Beman had served all but five months of his sentence of four years' penal servitude.

Stanley Thurston, who also escaped from Dartmoor, is still free. He has been at liberty twelve days.

Queen Visits A.A. Men

The Queen yesterday motored along cart tracks and walked across rough fields to visit A.A. batteries and searchlight stations in isolated parts of the Home Counties. She had many informal chats with the troops.

Daily Mirror
(APL 10)

No. 11,648 — ONE PENNY
Registered at the G.P.O. as a Newspaper.

GERMANS CLAIM 5 BIG ADVANCES

Massawa's Fall Frees Our Forces

WHILE our troops occupied the capitulated Massawa, Eritrea, whose fall was announced by the Premier yesterday, mobile columns continued their advance south and southwest along the Dessie and Gondar road.

Here the Duce's broken armies, await their inescapable doom.

With the fall of the important port, the last Italian resistance in Northern Eritrea has been overcome.

Warships Trapped

Massawa gives us a port from which our forces can be shipped to areas where the need is greatest.

There must still be several naval units and Italian and German merchant vessels at Massawa.

In Addis Ababa, the Nairobi communique reports, we captured a large number of prisoners, including two complete Blackshirt battalions, more than sixty pilots and '00 Air Force ground personnel.

Indian troops took part in the capture, in addition to the South, East and West African troops previously reported to have participated," the communique adds says Associated Press.

GERMAN SHIPS SUNK OFF LIBYA

Two big ships rushing supplies to the Germans in Libya are believed sunk by a British submarine.

An Admiralty communique issued last night says: One of our submarines in the Central Mediterranean has carried out a successful attack on a south-bound convoy of heavily-laden transports and supply ships.

A ship of about 12,000 tons was hit by two torpedoes and another ship of about 6,000 tons was also hit by a torpedo

FIVE victories besides the capture of Salonika were claimed by the German High Command last night— but the R.A.F. equalling its finest exploits in the Battle of France last year, smashed Nazi tanks and convoys, in Greece and Yugoslavia, and caused thousands of casualties. The German claims were:—

1.—The Greek Army, trapped east of the Vardar Valley leading to Salonika, have " offered their capitulation and laid down their arms."

[The Greek High Command said: " Our troops in East Macedonia held their lines intact in spite of the fall of Salonika."]

2.—German troops have broken through the Rupel Pass bottleneck in the Struma Valley, " stubbornly and fiercely defended by the Greeks."

3.—On the Greek frontier, German mountain divisions, supported by dive-bombers, have broken through the Metaxas Line, " a modern fortification in the mountains."

4.—German shock troops and armoured units have captured Nish and Maribor in Yugoslavia. They have taken 20,000 Yugoslav prisoners, including six generals.

5. — After occupying Skoplje (capital of Serbia) and Veles, in Yugoslavia, German troops crossed the Vardar Valley, took Tetova and Prilep, and reached the Albanian frontier.

All day the German radio kept up a running commentary

Every half-hour a special announcement was broadcast. The news must have been known for several hours in Berlin, but to increase tension it was divided into several bulletins.

To Spare Belgrade?

But late last night the Berlin announcer declared: " The German people must remember that our troops still have a difficult task to carry out before they reach their goal."

The Panzer divisions have yet to meet the B.E.F., reported in Turkey to be massed in and around Katerini, south-west of Salonika and near Mount Olympus.

Mr. Churchill, who announced the loss of Salonika in Parliament, said: " The British and Imperial troops in the Balkans have not been engaged up to the present."

Late last night a London statement repeated Mr. Churchill's and added: " No British or Imperial troops were east of the Vardar."

Vichy reported that—" as a result of foreign diplomatic intervention" —the Germans seem to have agreed

Continued on Back Page, Col. 4

Field - Marshal List, Nazi Balkan commander. He has been ordered to cut through to the hard-pressed Italians at any cost.

SAY SIX BRITISH GENERALS TAKEN

SIX Generals, two Colonels acting as Generals and more than 2,000 men were captured by the Germans and Italians when they took El Mekili, about fifty miles south-east of Derna, Libya, according to a claim broadcast by Berlin radio last night.

The announcement was from the German High Command. It added: " The booty and war material is not yet counted."

The German and Italian forces are now outside Tobruk, according to Rome.

Tobruk, the stronghold captured from Mussolini, is sixty-five miles along the coast road into Italian territory.

" Our tanks and reinforcements are now returning," said Lord Moyne, Leader of the House of Lords, yesterday.

" By means of our sea power they have established themselves in force in the strong fortifications of Tobruk," he added.

Yesterday's Cairo communique said: " Libya: Yesterday our rearguard, whose role it was to delay the enemy advance while our main concentrations were being completed, were heavily engaged all day by numerically superior forces"

In his statement, Lord Moyne said: " We hope that with the complete liquidation of Italian bases in the Red Sea, President Roosevelt would soon strike off the Red Sea from the list of combat zones.

" It would be invaluable to us if the generous help of America and the Lease-and-Lend Bill could be shipped straight by the Red Sea route to the Near East. The avoidance of transhipment in Britain would save very much shipping and time."

FIRST VICTORY —THEN DEATH

A FIGHTER pilot-officer, Peter Ferris, of Alton, Hants, after his first battle wired his operational centre: " I've shot down a Heinkel. Its crew and machine in flames.'

Peter spoke again.

" I'm hit," he said.

Nothing more was heard of Peter, and he was reported missing.

His body has now been washed up on the Channel coast.

Peter was twenty-five and engaged to be married.

NAZI WOMEN FLEE WARSAW

EVACUATION of German women and children from Warsaw for unexplained reasons, reported in Helsinki, has roused speculation on Soviet-Nazi relations, says Associated Press.

The Soviet Legation in Budapest has issued visas to the British Minister in Hungary, Mr. Owen O'Malley, and members of the Legation staff, allowing them to enter the Soviet Union.

The Belgian and Netherlands diplomats have also received visas to enter the U.S.S.R.

The British Minister in Hungary was instructed to withdraw his mission because Hungary has become a base for operations against the Allies.

We're Ready in Pacific

" If the balloon goes up in the Pacific we will get powerful naval reinforcements and get them quickly, whether the U.S. comes in or not," said Vice-Admiral Sir Geoffrey Layton, Commander-in-Chief, China Station, yesterday.—Reuter.

HALIFAX TO BE THEIR GUARDIAN

The Government are to introduce a Bill appointing an official guardian for British children sent to America and Canada under official evacuation

This guardian is expected to be Lord Halifax, Ambassador to Washington.

An urgent operation for appendicitis might be necessary, but under State Law in America a doctor cannot operate without the consent of the child's parent.

In wartime the consent of parents across the Atlantic could not be got quickly enough.

More Marmalade Pulp

Despite shipping difficulties, 500 tons of orange and grape fruit pulp for making marmalade have been sent to Britain from the West Indies.

15 DOWN— SWEEP BY FIGHTERS

THIRTEEN German raiders have been shot down so far in the moonlight battle over Britain—six during Monday night and seven on Tuesday night.

Two additional ones were shot down yesterday by our fighters which swept over the enemy-occupied coast. One of our fighters is missing.

A.A. gunners got one on each night —the one on Tuesday was their 500th victim, shot down near the Isle of Wight. The rest were destroyed by our night fighters.

The two enemy bombers shot down by Hurricanes yesterday morning were caught in the act of bombing shipping off the west coast. These made a total of nine enemy bombers within twelve hours.

One German plane was shot down yesterday by the destroyer Valorous and another by the combined fire of the destroyer Avon Vale and the trawler Kingston Beryl.

There was another raid on the West Midlands last night. Incendiary and

Continued on Back Page Col. 1

Children's Teeth in War-Time

Even in war time a child's diet *must* contain a proportion of sweet things for nourishment and energy. But sweet things cause acid-mouth which encourages the germs which attack and decay the teeth. To protect the teeth a child's toothpaste should contain plenty of 'Milk of Magnesia,' the most effective neutralizer of mouth acid known. Only in one toothpaste is 'Milk Magnesia' brand antacid to be found and that is Phillips' Dental Magnesia which contains 75%.

Children who use this pleasant tasting toothpaste regularly, always have the whitest teeth and are practically free from decay with its distressing toothache and disfiguring gaps. Get a tube today.

Sold everywhere, 7½d., 1/1 and 1/10½d.

(Including Purchase Tax).

PHILLIPS' DENTAL MAGNESIA

Coventry nurses are still smiling, despite another savage raid by Goering's bombers on Tuesday night. Story on back page.

Daily Mirror

APL 15

No. 11,651 — ONE PENNY
Registered at the G.P.O. as a Newspaper.

GERMAN TANKS BEATEN IN FIGHT AT TOBRUK

A GERMAN tank attack on Tobruk, in Cyrenaica, has been beaten off, with great loss, by the British garrison. This was revealed in a War Office communique last night.

The communique said: " This morning enemy infantry supported by tanks launched an attack on Tobruk.

" At one point about twenty tanks crossed the outer defences. An immediate counter-attack was launched by our tanks as a result of which the enemy were ejected after sustaining very severe losses both in tanks and personnel.

" The situation has been completely restored."

Berlin radio claimed last night that " The British forces concentrated at Tobruk represent the last remnants of the British Expeditionary Force in North Africa."

" They are defending themselves fearlessly in preparation for re-embarkation," said the announcer.

" Out of fourteen British tanks which attempted a local counter-attack, eight were destoyed by German anti-tank guns."

The German High Command yesterday claimed the capture of Sollum, on the Egyptian frontier, but the War Office communique made it clear that the town was still in our hands.

The communique said:—

" Our troops are in contact with, and have inflicted considerable casualties on, advanced enemy detachments in the vicinity of Sollum."

R.A.F. Attacks

The R.A.F. Middle East communique last night said:

" In Cyrenaica yesterday both bomber and fighter aircraft of the R.A.F. were employed in dispersing enemy concentrations in various areas

" Successful bomb and machine-gun attacks were made on enemy motor transport convoys on the roads between Msus and Sollum.

" Tripoli harbour was raided during the night, and one large vessel was seen to be burning fiercely. Bombs straddled the Customs house power station

According to New York radio two to four German armoured divisions and ten Italian divisions, 80,000 men, are employed in the Libyan-Egyptian drive.

The New York National Broadcasting Company says the British plan in North Africa is to withdraw as far as Mersa

Cont. on Back Page, Col. 5

BRITISH CHILDREN AT F.D.R.'S PARTY

Thousands of children, including 130 from all parts of Britain, were guests of President Roosevelt in the White House yesterday at an Easter tea party.

The British children, all evacuees, joined in a gigantic game of egg rolling as bands played.

In the White House itself the children had ice cream, cake and a cinema show.

U.S. MAY ARM SHIPS

The U.S. Navy is preparing for the arming of privately-owned vessels in case of necessity, says the *Journal American.* —Reuter.

Egyptian M.P.s Discuss Defence

A secret session of the Egyptian Chamber of Deputies last night discussed steps the Government propose to take in view of the presence of hostile forces on the Egyptian border.

The session was called by the Premier, Hussein Serry Pasha, who said he wished to make a statement on the situation.

Earlier General Sir Archibald Wavell called on the Egyptian Premier.

The Egyptian Minister for Defence was present at the interview, which was followed by a full Cabinet meeting.—Associated Press.

ONLY 21 HG CHIEFS 'MR.'

OF a total of 319 men appointed as officers in the Home Guard, only twenty-one are plain " misters."

Peers, baronets, knights and brigadier-generals are among those newly appointed.

Captain the Hon. Michael Claude Hamilton Bowes-Lyon, an elder brother of the Queen, is made a battalion commander.

Brigadier - General Maurice Lilburn MacEwen, who is appointed battalion commander with the rank of lieutenant-colonel, was seventy-two last Sunday.

Major-General Edward Bailey Ashmore, who receives a similar appointment, is sixty-nine.

Viscount Cowdray is possibly the youngest of the new battalion commanders. He is thirty-one. He had his left arm amputated after being wounded in Flanders last June.

NEW SECRET DEFENCE DEVICES ARE SUCCESS

In the last British invasion manoeuvres completely new means of detecting enemy forces were extremely successful.

The existence of new British secret means of defence in case of invasion was reported in the B.B.C. broadcast for the German forces.

NAZIS HAVE 'VACANCIES'

Germans of the 1923 class are urgently required to volunteer for the Nazi Motorised Corps, said the Berlin radio yesterday.

Fire Raid on North Towns

HIGH flying German planes dropped incendiary bombs on two north-east coast towns last night. The raiders were driven off by heavy anti-aircraft fire.

At one town several hundred incendiaries fell. and these set fire to a school and houses.

Private houses were also damaged by fire bombs in another town, The fires were quickly subdued.

London was without an Alert for the fourth successive night.

During the afternoon a big German bomber swooped down to within a few hundred feet of the ground to make a surprise raid on the outskirts of a north-west of England town.

The raider had apparently glided down with its engines switched off.

Making use of heavy cloud formations it caught holidaymakers unawares and they scattered hurriedly for shelter.

A small number of bombs—apparently not of heavy calibre —was dropped in the town. The damage was not severe. A.A. guns roared out and it is believed the raider was hit.

BIGGER JAP NAVY CALL

The Japanese Navy must make a considerable increase in its personnel equipment and establishments, the Japanese Navy Minister said yesterday.

This was due to the " ominous. complicated and delicate" situation.—Reuter.

When it's
NO SMOKING
by Order

A man-size job ahead—no chance of a smoke. In times like these, keep Rowntree's Fruit Clear Gums handy. Those varied fruit flavours help the job along. (In 2d. tubes).

ROWNTREE'S
Fruit Clear Gums
soothe and refresh

★ If Gums and Pastilles are out of stock—don't blame the shopkeeper. He does his best to get them, and we do our best to keep a fair supply all over the country with the materials available.

Man on motorcycle above is the Grenadier Guardsman we knew in the old days as the fine figure in red tunic and huge busby. Now he's mechanised with a motorcycle on which is mounted a tommy-gun.

GREEK FRONT IS 'STRONG'

A CONFIDENT review of the position on the Balkan front was given last night by a Greek War Ministry bulletin.

The Nazis' failure to break through in the first days of their attack, together with the new reinforcements of British troops, confirm that a strong front has been established from the Adriatic to the Ægean, the bulletin said.

The positions occupied by the Greek and British troops are naturally suitable for defence.

Some days ago the Germans were attacked by the Greeks with the bayonet, and this had the same disastrous effect on them as it had on the Italians

Describing the Yugoslav situation, the announcer said it seems certain that the great bulk of the Yugoslav Army is intact and has retired to the mountains. They have taken up positions which constitute a serious and permanent threat to the Nazis.

Yugoslav forces advancing from the Kachnik Pass are now threatening to join forces with the British and Greek troops in that region.

The Yugoslavs are also operating successfully in Albania.

SOFIA RAID, SAY BULGARS

Sofia, capital of Bulgaria, was raided on Sunday night by British and Serb planes, says a Bulgarian communique.

WE WITHDRAW, HOLD UP HUNS

BRITISH forces in Greece have withdrawn to new positions, but have inflicted heavy losses on the Germans, whose persistent attacks failed.

Announcing the withdrawal, a War Office communique said last night:

" During the night of April 12-13 our forces withdrew to new positions. Our covering troops inflicted severe casualties on the enemy, who maintained continuous pressure on our eastern sector during this withdrawal.

" Marked activity on the right of our lines but no serious clashes

" In the centre of our sector persistent German attacks failed, largely owing to our vigorous artillery fire.

" Weather extremely cold, with snow.'

Many R.A.F. Sorties

A large number of sorties were made by our bombers against enemy columns on the roads

Direct hits were obtained by most of our planes.

Enemy bombers, escorted by fighters, were intercepted by our fighters in the Koritza area, one being destroyed and others damaged

The Adolf Hitler Division—fully motorised S.S. troops and the Fuehrer's pride—is now known to have been the Nazi Force repulsed by British troops at bayonet point

All these Huns have passed stringent inquiries for racial purity as well as arduous physical tests. But, according to Athens radio yesterday, " they were afraid of the British."

German mechanised columns, hampered by mud and snow in Macedonia, yesterday failed to push forward against the strengthening British-Greek front extending from the Albanian passes to the Gulf of Salonika

Fresh troops, including additional Greek reservists, sped to their positions while Allied patrols clashed at several

Continued on Back Page, Top of Column Five

PILOT RAN FOR LIFE

A HURRICANE pilot, a D.F.C., forced down in No-Man's-Land between the German and Anglo-Greek lines. saw another R.A.F. plane circling above him, intending to land to pick him up

He waved it away. He knew a German patrol was hunting him

" Then I sprinted as hard as I could " said the pilot yesterday

He ran three miles across rough ground with the Germans after him " the pilot added.

" I must have been running about fifteen minutes and was just about dead beat when an Australian patrol found me and exchanged shots with the Germans "

TWO BOMBERS SHOT DOWN INTO THE SEA

An He 111 was shot down early yesterday by H.M. trawler Kingston Amber (Skipper J. Plett, R.N.R.).

No damage or casualty was sustained by the trawler.

On Saturday a Junkers 88 was shot down into the sea when it attacked a Free French submarine chaser on patrol duty.

Daily Mirror

(APL 18)

No. 11,654   ONE PENNY
Registered at the G.P.O. as a Newspaper.

GREEKS' ALBANIA RETREAT

A GREEK retreat in Albania was admitted in last night's Greek communique, which said that Klisura and Ersek had been evacuated.

Informed quarters in Cairo described the situation in Albania as "serious," and said that the Greek Army might have to withdraw completely from Albania.

This might have repercussions on the British and Imperial Forces in Greece.

Despite the Greek retreat, the Allied line remains intact. Bitter fighting raged last night on the heights round Mount Olympus. Wave after wave of German infantry was hurled back by British and Imperial Forces.

In Yugoslavia, the Germans say, resistance has ceased. Berlin said last night that the Yugoslav army had surrendered. The official German News Agency said: "All the Yugoslav armed forces which had not been disarmed before laid down their arms unconditionally at nine o'clock tonight. The capitulation comes into force at twelve noon tomorrow."

Heavy German Casualties

Against the British line—forming the right flank in Northern Greece—the Germans have been thrown in regardless of losses and their casualties have been enormous.

Australians, holding a part of the line, have been particularly heavily engaged. The famous Olympus Pass itself is held by New Zealanders.

An officer of a well-known mechanised regiment said: "Tank for tank, we are better than the Germans. Not one of our tanks has yet been put out of action by gunfire. Our shells go through the German tanks like cheese.

"But in numbers they have the upper hand.

Backing up the German Army is a powerful air fleet. Mount Olympus resounds to the thunder of German dive-bombers.

Athens radio said at midnight: "Our army and our ally are resisting stubbornly —defending the national soil inch by inch. Fierce battles are taking place everywhere."

One British armoured unit has brought down five Stukas with Bren guns.

An observer who had returned from the front said: "The Germans are strafing the roads from planes, but they are catching hell from the R.A.F."

CHEESE FROM CANADA

Supplies of cheese from Canada are assured for Britain this year. At least 112,000,000lb of high quality cheese will be sent.—Reuter.

Duty Done

He was a London fireman who, in London's greatest air raid early yesterday morning, gave his life for his country.

He saw his duty clearly and followed it unflinchingly to the end. For him the fire and fury have passed. He is at peace and none will doubt that "the path to duty was the way to glory."

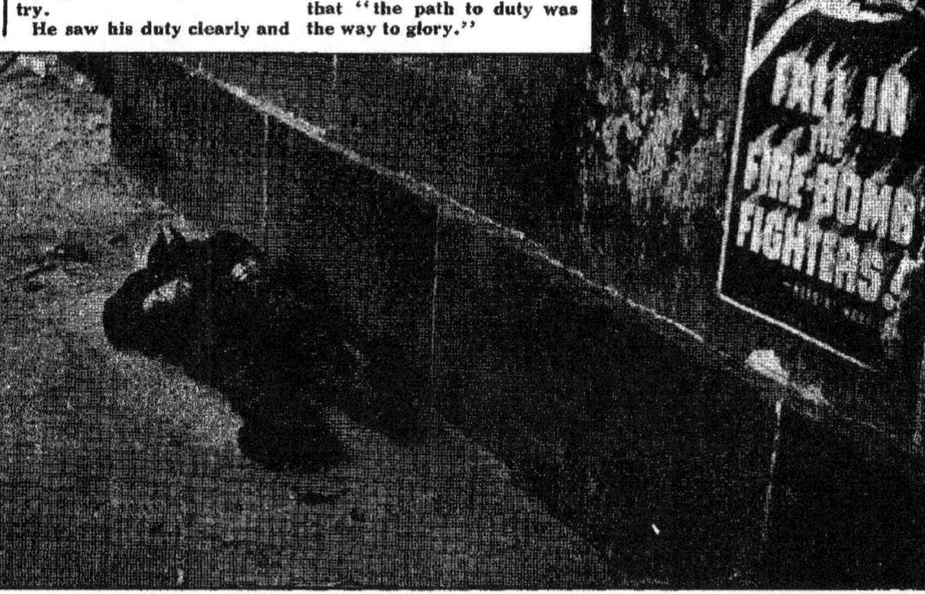

Plane Watchers for U.S.

A NATIONAL Warplane Warning Service, enrolling 500,000 civilian volunteers co-operating with the Army Air Corps, is to be formed in the U.S.A., it was announced by the War Department in Washington last night.

The War Department termed the move "another step in real preparedness for a possible emergency"

The Service will be similar to Britain's Observer Corps.

Preparations are being made to provide adequate A.R.P. organisation in all large Japanese cities.

The Government plans include schemes for large scale evacuation of town dwellers, the rapid restoration of damaged cities to normal, the designation of special air defence areas, and the protection of factories and traffic systems.—Associated Press and Reuter.

CASH GRANTS TO RAID SUFFERERS

The Assistance Board will provide cash grants to people who suffer in raids, without prejudice to any claims they may subsequently make, Lord Rushcliffe, chairman of the board, said yesterday.

The grants are to cover loss of clothes, furniture and craftsmen's tools. Every claim will be dealt with promptly and sympathetically, he said.

Squadron Got Two, Score Is Now 101

When a Spitfire squadron shot down two ME 110's yesterday it raised its bag of enemy aircraft to 101.

The squadron leader, who brought one down, made his sixteenth confirmed kill.

The R.A.F. is believed to have made another heavy attack on German aerodromes in Northern France yesterday. It was the third time in twenty-four hours that heavy explosions have been heard from the French coast.

RAID SEEN 40 MILES

FLARES dropped by German planes in a heavy raid on the South Coast last night could be seen forty miles away.

Watchers far inland could see the flashes as heavy bombs followed.

A German bomber crashed in flames and blew up in a country district.

Raiders which crossed the East Coast scattered bombs in rural districts.

Night fighters were up, and it is believed that a number of raiders jettisoned their bombs in their haste to avoid destruction by the R.A.F.

Enemy planes were also reported over a north-east town.

London had a brief Alert early today.

REPORTING TO MOSCOW

The Turkish radio last night reported that the Russian Minister to Turkey is leaving for Moscow.

2 BLOWS AT LIBYA HUNS

BRITISH warships and warplanes have struck heavy blows at Panzer units in Libya, destroying tanks, motor vehicles, aircraft and causing many casualties among troops.

Fort Capuzzo in the Bardia area, was blasted twice—from sea and air. The damage was described in last night's communiques.

Our Navy shelling the fort, hit a concentration of 100 enemy tanks and motor transport with a large number of salvoes

The warships also successfully bombarded the aerodrome at El Gazala and its supply dumps

At least two Junkers 88 dive-bombers were shot down by naval gunners. Others were damaged

The Navy, the Admiralty added, suffered no damage or casualties in these operations

Capuzzo Again

The R.A.F.'s part in strafing the Axis drive on Egypt was described in the Middle East communique

Bomber and fighter aircraft maintained punishing attacks throughout Wednesday and the previous night on enemy mechanised units, troops and landing grounds in Cyrenaica.

Near Capuzzo, a motorised column was attacked and a number of vehicles destroyed Casualties were caused among troops

Meanwhile the British troops at Tobruk are making daring sorties outside their defences.

One of their patrols pene-

Cont. on Back Page, Col. 2

FRENCH WARSHIPS OFF GIB.

Three French submarines and one destroyer have been seen in the Straits of Gibraltar. They were apparently heading westward, presumably for Casablanca.—Reuter.

"THROW ME A BOMB"

SOLDIERS found an unexploded mortar bomb.

"Throw it to me," one of them said to a friend There was an explosion, and Private James Henry Cook, twenty-two, of New Cottages, Hindhead, Surrey, died.

This was the story told at the Folkestone inquest yesterday In adjourning it, the coroner suggested proceedings might be taken elsewhere.

HE NAMED HIS FASCIST KILLERS

Italian anti-Fascist newspaper proprietor John Arena named his assassins a few hours before being executed by Fascist secret police in Chicago, cables John Walters from New York.

He told the Dies Committee investigator that his death had been ordered by a prominent New York business man who is he "Tsar" of the Fascist spy system in U.S.A.

A stand-up meal

for a non-stop worker

Fry's Sandwich Chocolate

Rationing of raw materials and heavy Service demands may cause a shortage of Fry's Chocolate in the shops. We are doing all we can to ensure even distribution.

Daily Mirror

APL 24

No. 11,659   ONE PENNY
Registered at the G.P.O. as a Newspaper.

ALLIED STAND BEFORE ATHENS

IT'S NOT ALL BLACK

Libya Lead Is Ours Again

BRITISH forces have now assumed the initiative in local offensive actions in the Sollum and Tobruk areas.

The sorties from Tobruk on the night of Monday-Tuesday are described as very satisfactory, and an indication that we are certainly not sitting down on the defensive.

It is learned that the enemy bombed a party of 400 prisoners—their own men—who were being brought into Tobruk after this operation.

This is the latest of several sorties which have produced about 1,500 prisoners, mostly Italians.

The attacks were carried out by Australians, who captured seventeen Italian officers and 430 other ranks. Our casualties were slight.

One enemy field gun was destroyed in the Sollum area. Our patrols and artillery are continuing offensive activities

Guns Spiked

The British landing party put ashore at Bardia last Saturday night, it can now be revealed, destroyed an important bridge and a dump of stores and put four coast defence guns out of action

The Italians claimed to have captured the whole party. This is untrue. Most of them returned safely to base, but about sixty members failed to re-embark.

Yesterday's R.A.F. Middle East communique said a large force of enemy aircraft was intercepted over Tobruk on Tuesday by R.A.F. fighters

Although greatly outnumbered, our aircraft shot down one Ju 87, two Me 109s and one G 50.

The communique adds that in Greece ground defences brought down four dive-bombers (Ju 87s) and one Dornier.

In all the operations the enemy lost seventeen planes for two of ours

BABIES TO GET FRUIT

The next shipload of oranges to arrive in this country will probably be distributed to mothers with young babies.

The Ministry of Food is considering a scheme to make this possible.

But many babies will soon be drinking blackcurrant pulp instead of their morning orange juice.

Experts have been experimenting with pulp made from last year's crop.

Blackcurrants contain a higher percentage of Vitamin C than lemons

BOMB EXPERT BLIND

THE man who designed the "beautiful" new bomb with which the R.A.F. are blasting Germany lost his sight during last Wednesday's blitz on London.

He is Air Commodore Patrick Huskinson, one of the Air Minister's "boys in the back room."

He was blinded when he left his bed and went to his window to watch the effect of explosions.

There is some prospect of his sight being restored soon, though "it will be days before this can be known definitely," it was stated at the Ministry of Aircraft Production last night.

Air Commodore Huskinson was last month appointed Director of Armament Development

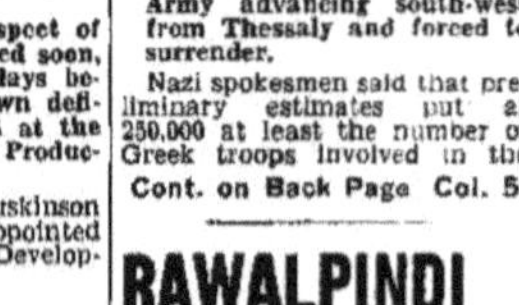

Air-Com. Huskinson.

POTATO SUBSIDY

Prices of new potatoes will be controlled from May 17 states the Food Ministry. Maximum wholesale and retail prices will be announced later.

Potato growers will receive on May 1 the seasonal increase of 10s. per ton provided in the price schedules, but a subsidy is to be paid to prevent this increase being passed on.

Maximum prices will be stabilised at the existing figures

THE British Army in Greece, its men and guns ready in the new defence positions guarding the way to Athens, yesterday awaited the storm expected to burst upon it at any hour.

German Panzer divisions were massing for the full-scale attack which will be their final effort to smash through our lines

Over almost the whole front there was a lull in the enemy drive.

But all day advance German units, supported unceasingly by dive bombers, attacked at one point—the Pass of Thermopylae, famous for the Greek stand against Persian invaders 2,000 years ago.

Last night the main Greek Army and our Empire troops were still standing firm, their line intact, their spirit superb.

The Greek Army of the Epirus surrendered yesterday to the Italian 11th Army.

It was a bitter defeat, for the Greeks had fought gloriously in Albania against this same Italian army — the "cowardly eleventh"—which refused to fight until the Germans went and forced them to do so.

Forced to Surrender

King George of Greece, now in Crete with his Cabinet—a Crete occupied and fortified by Empire troops—said that the Epirus Army had signed an armistice without our knowledge."

The Epirus Army had been retreating from Albania and were cut off by the German Army advancing south-west from Thessaly and forced to surrender.

Nazi spokesmen said that preliminary estimates put at 250,000 at least the number of Greek troops involved in the
Cont. on Back Page Col. 5

RAWALPINDI SISTER SUNK

The Admiralty announced last night that the armed merchant cruiser H.M.S Rajputana (Captain F. H. Taylor D.S.C. R.N.), had been torpedoed and sunk.

The Rajputana (16,644 tons) was a sister ship of the Rawalpindi, which earned undying fame as an auxiliary cruiser early in the war when she fought the German battleship Deutschland until the auxiliary cruiser sank in flames.

A famous P. and O. liner, the Rajputana was one of the most popular ships plying between India and Britain

Captain F. H. Taylor, who retired in 1936 after thirty-four years' service, spent most of his naval career with submarines.

His home is at Lower Bourne, Farnham, Surrey.

NO 2d. CHOCOLATE

There will be no more 2d. bars of chocolate soon. The price is to be 2½d., but the bars will be bigger. Block chocolate now selling at 2½d., 3d., 5d., 6d. and 1s. will be reduced in weight.

LOOK at this photograph —the King and Queen, the cop, the kids, the crowd—and not a gloomy face among them. The picture was taken yesterday when the King and Queen were in the bombed areas of London's East End; everyone in it has known the horror of Nazi hate raids, but knows, too, that though the war news is grave, IT'S NOT ALL BLACK.

+ + +

Britain's second new 35,000 - ton battleship, Prince of Wales, sister ship of King George V, is now in commission.

WE retake the lead in Libya (as told in column 1).

HUGE supplies from America include:— One thousand assembled aircraft already handed to the R.A.F. (see col. 5). Submarine chasers able to do 60 m.p.h. are ready to hand over (back page).

+ + +

TRIPOLI'S bombardment was the biggest in history — our naval guns were still hot twelve hours afterwards (see page 3).

PERFECT WARDEN —ONE BOMB FELL

In a south-west coast town district where Mr. T. R. A. Windeatt was chief warden they said there was nothing he didn't know about A.R.P.

His organisation was perfect. He kept his helpers on their toes even while there was little to do.

Till Tuesday night. Then a lone raider dived low, dropped one bomb, scored a direct hit on the Windeatts' home.

The A.R.P. squad were at work at once, well trained for such a job.

It took two hours to rescue Tom Windeatt and his wife. But in the ruins their daughter, 6, and son, 14, lay dead.

U.S. TO R.A.F. IN 7½ HOURS

A BIG fast bomber built in the U.S. for the R.A.F. roared across the Atlantic in seven and a half hours.

And this is only one of nearly 1,000 warplanes built in the U.S. and Canada which have been delivered to the R.A.F., the Minister of Aircraft Production told the Lords yesterday.

The seven - and - a - half-hour flight was "from coast to coast," probably from Newfoundland to Britain — 2,400 miles.

Another plane flew from the Canadian mainland to Britain in nine hours.

The only previous record with which these flights can be compared is a crossing from Botwood (Newfoundland) to Foynes (Ireland) in 10 hours 33 minutes by the flying-boat Cambria in 1937.

Only one plane had been lost in course of delivery by air from across the Atlantic.

Plan for Fighters

Direct delivery of warplanes across the Atlantic by air was likely to be extended.

It was hoped that soon we would be able to fly fighters across "over a somewhat different route" (presumably with a refuelling stop, perhaps at Greenland).

The Minister revealed that one consignment which arrived by sea a few days ago comprised ninety - five aircraft—
Cont. on Back Page, Col. 3

The Minister of Aircraft Production told this story yesterday to illustrate the keenness with which our bomb experts get on with their job—

The expert, Squadron-Leader R. H. Garner, made a bomb test reported at the Air Ministry, and left at 4 p.m. for an airfield. There he loaded his big bomb into a bomber, flew to Emden, unloaded the bomb and watched its effect.

At nine o'clock next morning he was back at the Air Ministry. At ten o'clock he was calmly reporting on his bomb in technical terms.

LAST NIGHT I WAS OUT OF SORTS

TO-DAY I FEEL FINE!

Beechams pills are the ideal remedy for a disordered stomach or liverishness, the sure preventive of constipation and all its kindred ills, the happy solution to the problem of sound and regular healthy sleep.

Purely vegetable

Beechams Pills

BRAND

Sold Everywhere

Boxes 1/5 & 3/5 (Including Purchase Tax)
Also obtainable in PENNYWORTHS

Worth a Guinea a Box

44

Daily Mirror

APL 28

o. 11,662
ONE PENNY
'egistered at the G.P.O. as a Newspaper.

U.S. TURN SEA WAR IN FAVOUR OF BRITAIN

Soviet Mass on Frontier

Mr. Churchill's reference to Germany's possible moves in the Ukraine and Spain were the result of dramatic news which reached London last week, writes Bill Greig.

On Thursday normal traffic on the Russian railways between Bessarabia and Odessa—the port of the Ukraine—was suddenly reduced, and crowded troop trains passed to the Ukraine frontier.

The Russians thus face in strength the twenty-eight German divisions which I revealed earlier this month to be in Moldavia without apparent reason.

★

Germany has already demanded from Turkey a free passage for ships through the Dardanelles and several ships which have already entered the Black Sea are believed to constitute a direct threat to the vital port of Odessa.

★

Berlin radio said that British troops landed on the Persian Gulf.

Fought Way to Port

AS Hitler's High Command announced yesterday that the German army had captured Athens, crossed the Gulf of Corinth, and pushed into the southern tip of Greece, Vichy radio reported that British troops had re-embarked forty-eight hours earlier.

Against odds worse than Dunkirk, the British Army fought a slow retreat to the southernmost Greek embarkation port, wires a correspondent who has just left the country.

Greek infantry, with no chance of escaping from the country, fought to cover the British flank.

Feats of heroism by the British and Greeks saved the forces on the Olympus line from encirclement.

'quipment Lost

But for this heroism it might ave been impossible to evacuate more than a small fraction the Australian and New Zealand divisions and British dements.

A large amount of mechanised equipment, guns, munitions and stores necessarily may have to be written off as a loss.

"The Greek Air Force will fight on against the Axis, and he whole of the Greek merchant fleet, running into millions of tons, is at the disposal of the British Government," M. Dimitri Capsalis, the Greek Minister to Egypt, told a British United Press correspondent in Cairo.

GREEKS IN RE-SHUFFLE

Greece's Prime Minister, M. Tsouderos, becomes Acting War Minister by royal decree, nd M. Maniadakis, Minister of he Interior and of Public Security, becomes Minister of Food upplies.

General Ivison Papagos is laced on the retired list, and Pericles Argyropoulos, former oreign Minister, is appointed overnor-General of the Ægean slands.

The Greek King and his overnment are now in Crete.

ROCKEFELLER'S APPEAL

Mr. John D. Rockefeller, jun., ead of the Rockefeller family nd one of the richest men in he world, in a letter to the New ork Times yesterday, said that he American people "should and by the British Empire to he limit, and at any cost."—ssociated Press.

TURKS' CRISIS

HITLER is reported to be in the Yugoslav town of Maribor after a visit yesterday to Klagenfurt, capital of Austrian Carinthia, and Von Papen, his Ambassador to Turkey, has left Berlin to meet him.

Inonu, Turkey's President, has left Ankara.

One Ankara report says his destination is Smyrna, on the coast of the Turkish mainland.

Another is that he is going to the Thrace region.

Causing Concern

This was the diplomatic situation yesterday as Hitler considered his next move in relation to Turkey.

Berlin diplomatic circles said "Most important political developments " are pending.

The ease and speed with which the Germans have captured Greek islands controlling the approaches to the Dardanelles are causing concern in Turkey.

The occupation of Lemnos and Lesbos would enable the Germans to ship military supplies to Greece and the Dodecanese from Rumania and Bulgaria via the Dardanelles.

Two German vessels are reported to have already passed through.

TWO BOMBERS BROUGHT DOWN

Two German bombers are believed to have been brought down during raids last night.

London had no Alert up to a late hour, but heavy bombs and a large number of incendiaries fell on a South Coast town.

Bombs were also dropped by an enemy raider which was over the coast of North-East Scotland.

GRAB OIL COMPANY

Rome radio stated last night that all activities of the "Anglo-Yugoslavian Oil Company" have been transferred to the Italian National Petrol Company as far as the Slovene parts of Yugoslavia are concerned.

He Made The Typhoon

This is Mr. Sydney Camm, the designer of Typhoon—Britain's newest fighter plane. Experts describe it as " a great aircraft of the future." It can climb like a rocket, going almost straight up into the air with its full load, is a single-seater with a speed well over 400 m.p.h. This Sabre-engined super fighter is faster, better armoured and has a longer range than any planes now in use by the R.A.F.

NIGHT PILOTS FROM CANADA

THE largest single contingent of Empire airmen has arrived at a British port.

They include Canadians, Australians, New Zealanders and men of our own R.A.F. who have completed their training in Canada and America. The Americans in the party will be mainly employed ferrying machines from factories to air fields.

They have all had experience in night flying, sometimes in temperatures as low as 35 degrees below zero.

The most interesting American personality is P. Clark, a Californian, who, in a thrill-packed life, has fought in China against Japan and helped the Republicans against General Franco.

REAL BATTLE TO COME, SAY RUSSIANS

The real battle of the second Imperialist war is still to come, asserts the May issue of the Journal of the Soviet Communist Party.

"The great disproportion of military strength following the defeat of France has decreased and continues to decrease, first because of the mighty support of the United States towards England and the growing mobilisation of the resources of the British Empire," it declares.

Egypt's Frontier Pierced

TWO enemy motorised columns, advancing eastward south of the escarpment which runs to the sea at Sollum have entered Egyptian territory at several points, according to a British communique from Cairo.

They are being harassed by British light mobile troops, it is stated.

The advance is believed to extend no more than fifteen to twenty miles south from the sea, and there is no indication of a sweep to the south. The columns are stated to be largely composed of Italians.

Light Detachments

It is pointed out in Cairo that enemy forces have been active in the Sollum and Fort Capuzzo for the last fortnight. Their tactics have consisted of sending out light mobile detachments in much the same way as last September.

There has been a screen of light British mobile forces facing the enemy, but what lies behind this screen remains for the enemy to find out.

The Axis objective may be Sidi Barrani, but it is not thought that their forces are as heavy as those used by the Italians last September.

Anzac's Part

R. CHURCHILL, in one of his greatest speeches of the war, warned Britain in his broadcast last night to expect the war in the Mediterranean to become very fierce and wide-spread.

The Battle of the Atlantic was in a more grim yet more favourable phase.

" It was with indescribable relief that I learned of the tremendous decision lately taken by the President and people of the United States," Mr. Churchill said. "The American Fleet and flying boats have been ordered to patrol the wide waters of the western hemisphere and to warn the peaceful shipping of all nations outside the combat zone of the presence of lurking U-boats or raiding cruisers belonging to the two aggressor nations.

'We British will, therefore, be able to concentrate our protecting forces far more upon the routes nearer home, and to take a far heavier toll of the U-boats there."

Other vital points from a brilliant review of the war were:—

1.—The war may spread to Spain, Morocco, Turkey, and Russia. Germany may strike at the Ukraine, for wheat, or the Caucasus, for oil.

2.—Britain will conquer or die—but Britain will not be conquered—except by invasion or the loss of our ocean life lines with the U.S.

3.—Wavell never had more than two divisions — 30,000 men—available for his Libyan victories.

4.—Comparing German strength with that of the British Empire and the United States, we had unchallengeable command of the ocean, would soon have decisive air superiority, and had technical resources greater than the rest of the world put together.

Britain was honour bound, Mr. Churchill said to go to the aid of Greece

Greece declared she would fight on alone if necessary. We could not allow that. It would be fatal to the honour of the British Empire.

"The Governments of Australia and New Zealand felt the same as Britain, and an important part of the mobile portion of the Army of the Nile was sent to Greece.

" It happened that the divisions available and best suited to the task were from New Zealand and Australia, and that only about half the troops who took part in this

Continued on Back Page

RAID VICTIMS HEAR PREMIER

Plymouth people, bombed out of their homes and temporarily housed in rest centres, were among the most enthusiastic listeners to Mr. Churchill's broadcast last night.

Wireless sets were specially installed at ten centres, which included a church crypt and a labourers' hall.

It was thought that mothers might be concerned about the radio keeping the children awake, but there was a chorus of " We want Winnie." A vote was taken, and there was a unanimous vote to hear the Prime Minister.

FRANCE HAS TWO VOICES

While the Vichy Government is displaying a more hostile attitude toward Britain, the people of Dieppe have been punished for anti-Axis sympathies.

A fine of 1,000,000 francs has been imposed by the Germans on Dieppe because a cinema audience cried out " Down with Hitler ! " " Down with Mussolini ! "

Vichy's stronger line towards Britain was shown yesterday by the announcement that "authoritative French quarters" that if British troops, or troops in the service of Britain, should land in Syria or seek refuge there, they would be interned.

Hitler Fixes Treachery's Price.—Page 3.

PHOSFERINE

gives excellent results

especially in times of extra work and strain
—says Mrs. M. W.

"I have found that Phosferine gives excellent results as a tonic, especially in times of strain when things seem to get on top of one. A few days' treatment will completely reverse the position I have recently taken Phosferine to ward off the colds, etc., that often occur at this time of year, and have kept very fit."

10 DROPS WILL LESSEN THE STRAIN

Within 15 minutes you begin to derive benefit. Each succeeding dose will put back into you what work or worry have taken out of you—energy, strength, vitality. Ask your chemist for a bottle of this really great tonic today.

PHOSFERINE, Tablets or Liquid, 1/3, 3/6 & 5/6 (including Purchase Tax).

Two Tablets equal ten drops of Liquid.

PHOSFERINE
Brand

THE GREATEST OF ALL TONICS FOR

Depression   Neuralgia   Sciatica
Headache   Sleeplessness   Anaemia
Indigestion   Influenza   Debility
Brain Fag   Rheumatism   Neurasthenia

WARNING. THE PUBLIC IS WARNED AGAINST PURCHASING WORTHLESS IMITATIONS.

Daily Mirror

APL 29

No. 11,663   ONE PENNY

Registered at the G.P.O. as a Newspaper.

Wins D.F.C. in Popeye Plane

"Popeye has always brought me luck. I have him drawn on the fuselage of my Spitfire," said Squadron-Leader Barrie Heath, 24, of the Auxiliary Air Force, last night, when the "Daily Mirror" told him he had been awarded the D.F.C.

His wife, Mrs. Joy Heath, who is a company commander in the A.T.S., was so excited when she heard the news at their home at Wood End, Teddington, Gloucestershire, that she dropped the telephone receiver and rushed to her husband, who is home on leave.

"For the past two months I have been flying a Spitfire that my father, Mr. George Heath, gave to the R.A.F." Squadron-Leader Heath said. "I am home on a week's leave, and it is a coincidence that my wife is home on a week's sick leave. We shall have a party tonight."

BRITISH WARSHIPS BLOCK JIBUTI

BOYS DIE IN TRAIN

Two Sons of a Premier

TWO sons of the Belgian Prime Minister were among the six schoolboys killed when they jumped from a blazing coach at the rear of the mid-day London-Newcastle express yesterday near Claypole, Lincs.

A third son is one of the seven boys injured.

M Pierlot, the Belgian Premier, had seven children—four sons and three daughters The dead boys were Louis, aged 16 and Jean, aged 14

The injured son, Gerard, 13, is in Newark Hospital

The news was broken to M. Pierlot at his Surrey home by the Charge d'Affaires Vicomte de Lantsheere.

They were members of a party of sixty-four boys in a special coach going from London to Ampleforth, the Roman Catholic public school, near York

They were in charge of one of the masters, 'he Rev H. Dunstan Pozzi.

The six other boys suffering from burns and injuries are:—David Winstanley, 16, of Hampstead; Joseph P Patron, 15, of Haslemere, Surrey; Michael Harar, 14, of Gloucester - place, London; John Reid, 17, of Petworth, Sussex, whose parents 're in Egypt; Eustace Maunsell, 16, of Ridgeway, Farnham, Surrey; and Roger Burrows, 16, of Guildford.

Jean Pierlot.

The L.N.E.R. stated in an official account of the tragedy last night:—

"The coach next to the rear brake van of the 12.50 p.m. King's Cross to Newcastle express caught fire between Hangham and Claypole yesterday.

"The train was stopped and every effort was made by the train cr w to extinguish the fire, but the coach immediately in front and the brake van behind caught fire before the train could be uncoupled and cleared of the blazing vehicle

Ambulance Train

"The coach in which the fire started was reserved for sixty-four Ampleforth College boys, and a number of them jumped from the train before it could be brought to a standstill.

"It is understood that six were killed and seven injured.

"A special locomotive brought doctors from Newark, where the injured are now in hospital

"The cause of the fire is under inquiry."

M. Hubert Pierlot escaped to England from Belgium in October last and was joined by his wife and seven children in January They had flown from Lisbon

CANADA WARNED

Mr. Mackenzie King, Canadian Premier, warned the Dominion House of Commons yesterday that there would be more reverses on land and sea, but "as long as Britain stands no reverse will be decisive."—Reuter.

Giant Plane Hit Hun

ONE of our new giant Stirling bombers made a daring and successful attack on Emden, in north-west Germany, in daylight yesterday.

It came down to a low altitude, dropped a heavy load of bombs and then opened machine-gun fire from 1,500ft.

Blenheims of the Coastal Command yesterday morning sighted two enemy destroyers escorting supply ships off the Dutch coast

Defying a heavy storm of anti-aircraft fire, the bombers pressed home their attack from a low altitude, and their bombs were seen to strike home.

Later one of the enemy warships was seen spouting a great volume of smoke and came to a standstill

Four of our aircraft are missin from this gallant attack, but, according to the German News Agency last night, some members of the crews were rescued by German seamen

Ships to Rescue

Other shipping was also attacked yesterday at several points off the coast of France and Holland, vessels of 2,000 and 1,500 tons being hit and believed sunk

Bombs were dropped on a factory and railway goods yards at Meppel, near the Zuydee Zee. One aircraft of the Bomber Command is missing.

Fighter Command aircraft destroyed an enemy bomber off the Dutch coast One of our fighters is missing

HITLER'S GIB PLOT READY

HITLER is expected to put final pressure on Admiral Darlan for the handing over of the French Fleet as soon as Nazi divisions now being assembled are ready to march through Spain to attack Gibraltar.

If Darlan agrees, Britain would be fully justified in bombing any port—whether in Occupied or Unoccupied France — from which the ships may sail, and also military objectives in Paris, writes a diplomatic correspondent.

At present, the French Fleet is based at Toulon, Marseilles and Dakar in French West Africa.

Thousands of Portuguese gathered in Lisbon yesterday to offer their birthday greetings to the Premier, Dr. Salazar, heard him say: "National dignity, liberty, independence and territorial integrity are values to which everything else ought to be sacrificed."

Gib. at Bay Again—Page 3.

KEYNES OFF TO WASHINGTON

Mr. J M. Keynes, the economist, is visiting Washington at the request of the Chancellor of the Exchequer to confer with the United States administration

WANT 'VEG.' PRICE CONTROL

A National Market Traders' Federation deputation is to ask the Ministry of Food for price control of all greengroceries and vegetables

BRITISH warships have appeared off Jibuti, capital of French Somaliland, completely blockading the port, according to a Vichy statement last night.

This move has completely trapped the Duke of Aosta's 35,000 men, driven from Dessie by the British. Jibuti was the only port from which they could have escaped.

The Vichy statement added that the warships did not open fire.

Meanwhile, Free French forces, supported by British motorised units, are massed on the southern frontier of French Somaliland, near the Jibuti-Addis Ababa railway, according to a dispatch to Vichy

Another report stated that de Gaulle's men had already attacked.

Other Free French forces, it is stated, have landed at Zeila, in British Somaliland

Vichy Fears

Marshal Petain's Government is understood in Vichy to be seriously considering a plan for the reconquest of the French colonies in Africa controlled by General de Gaulle.

The French Government is reported to fear that the French colonies may be drawn into the war if the Axis forces seriously penetrate Africa, and will be absorbed by the Axis

British capture Dessie—Page 5

THEY GAVE 'EM HELL

ITALO GERMAN forces which crossed the Egyptian border on Saturday took possession of Sollum, Cairo military sources stated yesterday.

After an initial move across the frontier line into the coastal region of the Western Desert, the Axis forces' advance petered out as a result of harassing tactics by a well-known British armoured division.

Australian forces in Tobruk are giving the besieging Italians "merry hell." Two Australian fighting patrols in a single day's work outside the Tobruk defences charged enemy artillery with bayonets, killed over 200 Italians, captured eighteen officers and 437 other ranks, and destroyed eight Breda guns, three anti-aircraft guns

Whenever the Australians go out they make things hot for the enemy. One patrol fought a force five times stronger than itself for five hours

A youthful Australian formerly a salesman in Victoria, told of one raid 'itting huddled

Cont. on Back Page, Col. 2

SPECIAL WAR ZONE COURTS

War zone Courts, to operate in any area invaded or heavily bombed, have now been formally established throughout England and Wales.

The Minister of Home Security made the order last night High Court Judges are to be appointed to act as presidents of these Courts, which cannot function until an area is declared a war zone

Only cases of crime calling for speed will be dealt with

BRITISH ENVOY INTERNED

United States Minister to Yugoslavia, Mr. Arthur B. Lane, on arrival in Budapest yesterday, said he believed the British Minister to Yugoslavia, Mr. Ronald Campbell, with his staff and other British subjects had been interned by the Italians near Dubrovnik, the Yugoslav port on the Adriatic.—British United Press

MINISTER'S POSTSCRIPT

The Minister of Information will give the B.B.C. postscript on Sunday, May 11. The last postscript by Mr. A. P. Herbert is next Sunday.

Giant Plane Hit Hun

3 RAIDERS SHOT DOWN

AT least three German bombers are believed to have been shot down during last night's raids.

The bombers split their attack. While a South-West Coast town was being heavily raided, another raiding party dropped bombs on a town in East Anglia.

Heavy bombs fell in residential areas of the south-west town, causing casualties.

Fires started in the early stages of the attack were quickly controlled. The absence of searchlights round the area helped to confuse the raiders, whose numbers increased with each succeeding attack.

These are the eyes offered to a hero.

OFFERS EYE TO HERO

A BURLY British workman went last night to the London hospital where Air Commodore Patrick Huskinson—designer of the R.A.F.'s new big bomb—lies with the threat of blindness over him.

"If it will save him from blindness, let him have one of my eyes," he said.

There was a smile on Albert Fairclough's face as he said it. Ever since war broke out he has been trying his utmost to do his bit by joining one of the Services

"My Chance"

"When I read about this man being in danger of losing his eyesight, I thought, 'Well, here's another chance to have a go at doing my bit," he told the Daily Mirror.

"So I came straight up to the hospital to offer one of my eyes

"I can do my job with one, and this chap is needed to beat Hitler. Good luck to him if he does it with one of my eyes.

"I don't mind losing time and wages while they do the job."

Fairey, as his mates call him, lives in Ingrave-street, Battersea, and is a camouflage traveller and painter.

"I told my wife I was going

Contd. on Back Page, Col. 5

London Meat Strike Threat to Rations

See Back Page

Louis Pierlot, who with his brother, perished in the blaze

The bombers were seen to strike home.

Daily Mirror

MAY 3

No. 11,667   ONE PENNY
Registered at the G.P.O. as a Newspaper.

WAR IN IRAQ: 'DROME FIGHT

All-Out Order to U.S.

NEW "FIGHT FIRE" ARMY

ALL Britain's fire-fighters — A.F.S. men and regulars—are being reorganised into an "army" on a national service basis, with control in the hands of Whitehall.

Every month as they are conscripted, 1,000 men will be drafted to the service. Any control either by police forces or by local councils, as now exists in the provinces, will disappear.

Already the London County Council, whose fire brigade under Major F. W. Jackson is the finest in the world, has agreed in principle to the taking over by the State, but the Council awaits the final Government scheme before announcing its decision.

Men who are conscripted to the service will be spread out over the country for preliminary training in drill and hose-work, and then they will be transferred to London or some other area for practical experience. They will receive fire service rates of pay and work the "48 hours on, 24 hours off" shifts.

Here comes the sna Experienced firemen are anxious
Contd. on Back Page, Col. 5

N.Z. DEAD UNDER 200

THE New Zealand division's losses in Greece were between 100 and 200 killed, between 500 and 600 wounded, and 800 missing, Mr. Frazer, N.Z. Premier, announced last night.

These figures for a division which was in the thickest of the fighting indicate that our losses in dead are much lower than was at first feared.

Australia's Army Minister announced that the number evacuated may yet be increased.

Final figures of the Empire troops got off will, it is thought, be between 41,000 and 45,000.

Casualties at sea are not likely to exceed 500. It is believed.

Berlin claimed the capture of 200 prisoners in the Peloponnesus, mostly Anzacs.

Call to Axis

Penelope Durrell, 10 months, youngest Briton to be evacuated from Greece, seen here with her mother.

PENELOPE LEFT WITH THE BOYS

PENELOPE DURRELL, 10 months, was the youngest Briton to be evacuated from Greece.

She had had many hardships before her parents got her on a ship which carried a number of civilians, mainly Britons, who were being evacuated with the British Forces.

The soldiers christened Penelope Pinkie. She and her parents had spent three days and nights in a small open boat dodging Germans. She was not seasick or afraid.

Even when the battleship's guns spat A.A. shells at raiders she went on sucking her thumbs.

Penelope is the daughter of Mr. and Mrs. Laurence George Durrell. The father is a novelist and has lived in Greece for the past five years. Mrs. Durrell was formerly Miss Nancy Myers, of Gainsborough, Lincs.

Tommies, Aussies and New Zealanders helped her and other babies on board. One Tommy became "O.C. babies' bottles."

A Scot dried nappies in the boiler-room, handing them to a cockney private who carried them to the nurses.

No Sugar for Cafes

FROM the beginning of June the sugar allowance to catering establishments for hot beverages is to be withdrawn.

This means that customers will have to take their own sugar for tea and coffee or make the best of saccharin which may be provided.

The prices of gooseberries, strawberries, raspberries, loganberries, blackcurrants, redcurrants and whitecurrants are to be controlled.

TOO MEATY SAUSAGES

For putting too much meat in "sausage meat," Leonard Thirkettle, of Thorpe, near Norwich, was fined 10s. at Norwich yesterday.

CAROL, LUPESCU SAIL FROM LISBON

King Carol and Mme. Lupescu sailed from Lisbon yesterday aboard the American steamer Excambion.

Rumanian sources thought they were on their way to Cuba and would halt at Bermuda.—Associated Press

THE war in the Middle East spread rapidly yesterday to Iraq, where after days of tension native troops attacked British forces at the vital air base of Habbiniyah, sixty miles from Basra.

British troops returned the fire, and last night fighting, which began at dawn, was still going on.

Rashid Ali, the pro-German Iraq Premier, according to information reaching London, applied to Berlin for assistance.

The people of Iraq were warned in a B.B.C. Arabic broadcast yesterday of the misery they will experience if the war is extended to Iraq. The text of the appeal was:—

"**People of Iraq. Disown Rashid Ali and those few military leaders who for the sake of their own gain have sought a quarrel with Great Britain and betrayed the interest of your country.**

"**Rashid Ali has overthrown the Iraq constitution and threatened the life of the lawful Regent whom he has driven from the country.**

"**He is ready to extend the war to Iraq at the bidding of the Axis and will bring untold misery on your country unless he is quickly repudiated.**

"**You desire to live in peace. Overthrow these mercenary intriguers and let law and order reign.**"

The fighting was announced officially in London soon after news agency messages had told of how the native forces were advancing towards the British troops.

Threatened Us

The German radio claimed that Iraqi troops had occupied aerodromes, strategic road junctions and oilfields, and that Iraqi garrisons had been reinforced.

There was no official confirmation of these reports in Berlin.

"It is stated in Bagdad," said the radio, "that the British Minister has been informed that should new British forces endeavour to land at Basra, they would be prevented by force.

"At the same time the Minister was requested to see that Indian troops which landed on April 30 should leave at once for Palestine."

His True Colours

Britain is estimated to have 20,000 troops in Iraq. The Iraq Army and police force total some 40,000 officers and men.

Trouble began a month ago when the pro-German, Rashid Ali, supported by certain high army leaders, seized power.

When Britain notified its wish to open the line of communications through Iraq for British forces, in accordance with arrangements made with the Iraqi Government a year ago, he agreed to this action. Troops
Contd. on Back Page, Col. 3

MERSEY RAID: 1 DOWN EARLY

A GERMAN bomber crashed in a wooded area during raids on England last night.

One of the crew was taken prisoner. Search is being made for others.

Approaching in waves, enemy planes launched an attack on Merseyside. British night-fighters were in action. It appeared that a big-scale attack was developing.

North - east coast defences were in action. Bombs were dropped in one coast area.

PLANE HAD NO 'PROPS'

FIGHTING off the attacks of five Messerschmitt fighters over Holland, an R.A.F. bomber set course for home with oil pouring from the port engine.

The engine stopped—and the propeller fell off.

Out over the North Sea, on one engine, flew the bomber. The English coast was crossed —and then the second airscrew, also damaged dropped away.

But the pilot brought his machine down to a safe landing in a field.

He had attacked oil storage tanks near Rotterdam in daylight.

A shell burst through the nose of the aircraft, and then the five Messerschmitt 109s attacked.

For twenty minutes the fight went on. Our gunner was wounded and the mechanism of his gun carriage put out of action, but he fought on, turning his guns with the hand control.

One by one the Messerschmitts broke off the fight.

PUT CLOCKS ON AN HOUR

You will put your clock forward another hour tonight. Tomorrow Summer Time will be two hours in advance of Greenwich Mean Time.

Tomorrow morning, too, the black-out will end forty-five minutes before sunrise and begin forty-five minutes after sunset in Wales and every county in England except Northumberland, Durham and Cumberland.

Present Summer Time (one hour in advance of G.M.T.) applies to all farmers and farm workers, unless they mutually agree to work to the double Summer Time clock.

NOTED CRICKETER MISSING

R. J. Crisp, the Springbok and Worcestershire cricketer, is reported missing following the evacuation from Greece, says Reuter.

Crisp distinguished himself for South Africa as a fast bowler. He spent several years in England.

ROOSEVELT yesterday ordered his war production chiefs to put defence machines and machine tools on a 24-hour day and seven-day week.

"America," he said, "is confronted with a critical situation."

This was his order:—
Mobilise every useful machine in the nation.

Use these machines and tools where they are most needed.

Re - canvass the entire nation, including the armed forces, for skilled workers to obtain maximum output.

Roosevelt revealed that U.S. motor manufacturers have for months been producing parts for fighter and bomber planes. Twenty-five of the fifty oil tankers promised by the U.S. to Britain will be delivered at once.

More than twenty of America's latest transport planes will be sent in a few days.

PREMIER SPEAKS TONIGHT

Mr. Churchill is to broadcast in English to Poland tonight at nine o'clock in the Home and Forces programmes. His talk will last for five minutes.

Hosiery worker *goes over to munitions*

She is one of the fine-spirited girls who volunteered to leave her silk stocking factory, to help in the armaments drive. A real key worker at last, she's glad to know that even tho' the job is hard at times, she's putting her weight in the war effort.

On the Home Front, battles are being won every day — big little victories over tiredness, irritability, nervous strain. Nature's own tonic, sound, *natural* sleep (whenever you can get it) is the best thing ever for your new wartime lives. A warming cup of Bourn-vita, *still at the old peacetime price*, will help you to get your essential ration of body-and-mind-restoring Sleep. Bourn-vita is a night food-drink with special nerve - soothing properties that bring sleep very quickly.

...FOR THE BEST OUT OF YOUR SLEEP WITH...

CADBURY'S BOURN-VITA

STILL AT PRE-WAR PRICE

1'8 PER ½ lb.

Daily Mirror

MAY 5

No. 11,668   ONE PENNY
Registered at the G.P.O. as a Newspaper.

R.A.F. Halve Iraq Air Force

THE R.A.F., taking drastic action against hostile Iraqis, yesterday halved the Iraqi air force and—

Smashed up the enemy's main air base in two raids;
Bombed the railway line, turning an armoured train back;
Plastered gun positions, mechanised units, and troop concentrations outside our aerodrome at Habbaniyah all day.

Iraq's air force is estimated at fifty planes, half of which were put out of action at or over their base, Moascar Raschid, outside Bagdad.

One of our planes made a forced landing, but the crew was rescued by another R.A.F. machine.

Our first raid severely damaged aerodrome buildings and workshops, and at least twenty-two Iraqi planes were put out of action, said a Cairo communique last night.

Sheds and the aircraft depot got direct hits on the second raid. One plane was destroyed on the ground.

Our Drome Shelled

Two Iraqi fighters which tried to intercept our bombers were shot down. Our planes returned safely to their base.

Iraqi guns resumed their shelling of Habbaniyah yesterday morning. There were non-combatant casualties.

R.A.F. bomb and machine-gun attacks reduced the shelling.

German radio broadcast a claim that Iraqi planes bombed the British military camp on Habbaniyah Aerodrome.

Raschid Ali, pro-Nazi Premier, announced that he has suspended work on the British-owned Iraq Petroleum Company's concession, which produces 5,000,000 tons of oil a year.

The flow of oil through the pipeline to Haifa has been stopped, said Raschid Ali.

Earlier yesterday the British War Office announced that our Forces have seized control at

Continued on Back Page

TURK TALK ON IRAQ

THE Turkish Foreign Minister has received the Ministers of Iran, Iraq and Afghanistan—countries with which Turkey signed the 1937 Saadabad Pact of non-aggression.

The Pact can be denounced by any of the signatories should one of them become an aggressor.

Sir Hughe Knatchbull-Hugessen, the British Ambassador, also saw the Turkish Foreign Minister, probably to tell him of the latest developments in Iraq.

HITLER, ranting over the air last night through 140 radio transmitters, tried to convince the world that the war was all the fault of one man—not himself but Mr. Churchill.

In terms of venom, hatred and the coarsest abuse he singled out the Premier as his great foe—and thereby showed his fear.

Churchill was "diseased," "a madman," said Hitler, and—

"We are prepared to drop 100 bombs for each British bomb until the British people get rid of Churchill."

"The appeal of this fool Churchill to the German people on May 1 to leave me can only be explained by a paralytical illness.

"Churchill is a paralytic, diseased and drunken raving madman.

"This man has been running about throughout Europe for years like a fool looking for something which could be set on fire."

Editor's Note.—Hitler gains nothing by his guttersnipe references to Mr. Churchill. He is insulting, not the individual, but the leader of the British nation. The loyalty and courage of the British people can, in no circumstances, be shaken by anything Hitler says—or does. His petulant corner-boy anger is a confession of weakness—and of fear.

Hitler's Speech—page 3.

FLY WOMEN TO SAFETY

THE R.A.F. evacuated thousands of men, women and soldiers from Greece, using bombers, flying-boats and even captured enemy warplanes in their gallant work.

The order for the withdrawal set the R.A.F. their greatest task of the campaign it was revealed yesterday.

All day and all night, aircraft, packed to capacity with troops and civilians, flew to safety and returned for more.

For more than a week the men who formed the brain-centre of the evacuation from Greece hid in a Greek graveyard while low - flying Nazi reconnaissance planes tried in vain to find them.

Khaki desert Army uniforms draped with olive leaves were their camouflage.

The instant dusk had fallen, these naval experts shed khaki, put on blue and went into action.

By radio or flashlight signals and by barked orders they guided British and Allied craft of every conceivable description into hidden coves, tiny harbours and obscure fishing ports, where, between dusk and dawn, tens of thousands of lives were being saved.

WARMER IN THE STRAITS

The month-old cold spell in the Straits of Dover broke last night.

The wind left the north-east and veered to the south. After a day of brilliant sunshine the weather was fine, and the sea smooth under a cloudless sky.

HITLER'S BLAH BLAH BLAH

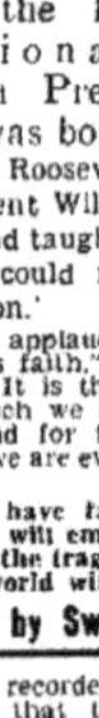

A close-up of Hitler speaking . . . he said a mouthful!

16 Night Bombers Down

BRITAIN'S night defenders took record toll of the Luftwaffe's moon raiders on Saturday night. They wiped out at least sixteen of them.

Thirteen of the raiders were shot down by night fighters — two over Northern France as they returned to their bases—and two by A.A. fire. The other fell to the balloon barrage.

Squadron-Leader John (Cat's Eyes) Cunningham, D.S.O., increased his "bag" to eleven by bringing down a raider.

While the Luftwaffe was suffering these heavy losses the R.A.F. was bombing Cologne in equally bright moonlight. It did not lose one machine. (See page 2.)

LIVERPOOL RAIDED 4th NIGHT RUNNING

LIVERPOOL and Merseyside were attacked by German bombers last night for the fourth night in succession.

Thus, within twenty-four hours of Liverpool's worst - ever blitz (reported on page 3), the Luftwaffe resumed its work of destruction.

Raiders were over other parts of Britain and an East Anglian town was bombed.

London had an Alert for the second night in succession after a lull of some days. It was sounded shortly before midnight. No gunfire was heard for a long time.

Hurricanes destroyed one of a flight of Messerschmitt 109's which crossed the Kent coast at dusk yesterday. It burst into flames as it passed over Margate and crashed into the sea.

A formation of twenty-four raiders flew over the south-east coast area. They were met by heavy fire from the ground.

As they crossed the coast and swooped low to attack. Spitfires and Hurricanes got in among them and drove them off.

Two R.A.F. fighters were lost during yesterday's patrols. Both pilots are safe.

WANT TO PAY MORE TAXES

Taxpayers in Bradford Woods, Pennsylvania, U.S.A., have done the strangest thing ever—asked to pay more.

They told the local council they were in favour of paying about £400 a year extra for three years for road repairs.

BOMB HITS ON ENEMY CONVOY

A convoy of enemy merchant vessels, escorted by destroyers, was attacked in the Mediterranean by R.A.F. bombers, a communique from R.A.F. headquarters, Middle East, stated last night.

Direct hits were made on the destroyers and on three merchant vessels of 12,000, 8,000 and 4,000 tons.

Other activity by the R.A.F. was also reported in the communique. In Cyrenaica bomber aircraft continued to harass the enemy throughout Friday and Saturday.

Two Junkers 52 troop-carriers were destroyed by bombs and machine-gun fire and many others were severely damaged.

All our aircraft returned safely from all these operations.

AMERICA IS READY TO FIGHT: FDR

"THE American people have fought before, and they are ever ready to fight again for the existence of democracy."

President Roosevelt said this in a speech at Stanton, Virginia, yesterday. He was dedicating the house as a national shrine in which President Wilson was born.

Mr. Roosevelt said that President Wilson in the last war had taught that "democracy could not survive in isolation."

"We applaud his judgment and his faith," said the President. "It is the kind of faith for which we have fought before and for the existence of which we are ever ready to fight again.

"I have faith that democracy will emerge triumphant from the tragic conflict which the world witnesses today."

Perish by Sword

"All recorded history bears witness that the human race has made a true advancement only as it has appreciated spiritual values.

"Those unhappy peoples who have placed their sole reliance on the sword have inevitably perished by the sword.

"Physical strength can never permanently withstand the impact of spiritual force.

"In the conflict which the world witnesses today, and which threatens everything we have most loved as a free people, we see more clearly than ever before the unyielding strength of things of the spirit."

U.S. aid for Britain increased one-third in March, according to the first report on arms shipments since the Lease and Lend Act was passed.

U.S. Aid Jump

America shipped £12,300,000 worth of war supplies to the British Commonwealth of Nations during March, compared with £8,000,000 worth in February.

Materials sent to Britain included:—

Warplanes worth £5,430,000; automatic rifles, £542,000; ammunition, £1,434,000; grenades, bombs and mines, £654,000; aeroplane parts, £370,000; and aero engines £3,360,000.

Even greater supplies will soon be sent, Colonel Frank Knox, U.S. Secretary of the Navy, stated at the week-end.

"In ninety days' time," he said, "the United States will be producing more fighting equipment than any other country in the world, including Germany."

Mr. Wendell Willkie informed President Roosevelt that his advisers all favoured the outright use of U.S. convoys rather than the present neutrality patrol system.

Vital Decision

Leading American Navy and Army experts have expressed the opinion to Mr. Roosevelt that Britain is unlikely to win a complete victory over Germany unless U.S. armed forces play a more active part in the war, writes John Walters from New York.

During the next few days, it is predicted, Mr. Roosevelt and his advisers will ponder a decision which would have a vital effect on the war's future.

ARMED LINER FEARED LOST

The armed merchant cruiser Voltaire, 13,301 tons, formerly a Lamport and Holt liner (Acting Captain J. A. P. Blackburn) is overdue and must be considered lost.

Daily Mirror

MAY 6

No. 11,669
ONE PENNY
Registered at the G.P.O. as a Newspaper.

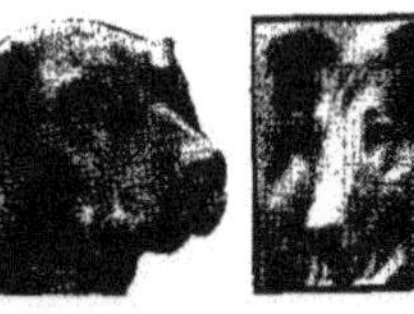

Dogs as Soldiers

TURKS OFFER TO MEDIATE IN IRAQ WAR

DOUBLE AIR AID from U.S.A.

U.S. aeroplane output now equals that of Germany.

This was revealed in Washington last night, where it was learned that 1,493 machines were turned out in April.

[Last week it was estimated by our experts that Britain had passed German aeroplane production.]

It was also learned in Washington last night that 414 aeroplanes were sent from the U.S. to Britain in March.

This compares with 258 planes in February.

But despite the big increase in output, President Roosevelt last night called for still more big bombers.

30,000 Next Year

He instructed Mr. Stimson, Secretary for War, to get on with a "substantial increase in heavy bomber production."

He gave Mr. Stimson a figure but this was kept secret. He said he knew it would be a big strain on U.S. production efforts but command of the air by the Democracies must be made absolute.

Aircraft engines sent to Britain in March totalled 983. There were only 2ss in February.

The export figures for aircraft in the first quarter of the year reached the record level of £31,000,000.

The production figures bear out the forecast made in Washington by Mr. James Jouett, President of the Aeronautical Chamber of Commerce, that the monthly output was nearing that of Britain and Germany, which figure he put at 1,500.

He estimated then that the United States would produce 18,000 machines this year and 30,000 in 1942.

ANOTHER PLEA FOR CONVOYS

Mr. Carl Vinson, chairman of the Naval Affairs Committee of the U.S. House of Representatives, said yesterday that he was in favour of U.S. convoys to Britain immediately.—British United Press.

THE WORLD'S BIGGEST

Eighty-two tons of flying war is this Douglas plane, B.19—the biggest bomber in the world. And this the first picture of it complete, after it had been wheeled out at Santa Monica.

What can it do? Well if you put eighteen tons of bombs in it, making a flying weight of 100 tons, it could fly from U.S. to Berlin, drop its bombs and fly back to U.S. WITHOUT STOPPING at nearly 300 miles an hour.

HITLER'S VOICE IS OFF U.S. RADIO

American radio audiences will no longer hear Hitler's voice over the major networks, it was disclosed yesterday by the *New York Daily News*.

Broadcasters rate Hitler as having "insufficient listening interest" to warrant carrying his speeches over their networks. Only summaries are to be put on the air.

Asked why Mr. Churchill gets full radio coverage, the invariable reply was "Hitler speaks German and needs translating, while Churchill is a swell orator."

IF your dog "joins" the Army in response to their appeal for such "recruits," it will be trained for routine duties similar to those dogs performed in the last war. Some also will be trained for "secret" duties.

Airedales, Collies, cross-breeds, lurchers and retrievers are particularly needed, but intelligence and natural ability will be the deciding factors.

Dog-owners are asked to lend their pets for the duration of the war. Dogs will be given an intensive course of training at Willems Barracks, Aldershot, to which offers should be made by letter.

Those which do not pass the test will be immediately returned.

Give Full Details

"Owners should send full particulars of age and breed, abilities and its prize records, if any," an official told the "Daily Mirror."

"The dogs will first be given a preliminary test of their powers of observation, temperament and obedience.

"After the preliminary test they will start the course for which they are best suited."

Many of the dogs will do guard duty with soldiers in isolated posts.

V.C. IS ALLIED C.-IN-C. IN CRETE

Major-General B. C. Freyburg, V.C., Commander-in-Chief of the New Zealand Expeditionary Force, has been appointed Commander-in-Chief of the Allied Forces in Crete.

This is announced in an Order of the Day to all officers and ranks in Crete by M. Tsouderos, the Greek Prime Minister and War Minister.

YOUR INSURANCE QUESTION

GOVERNMENT scheme for the insurance of household furniture against bomb damage is troubling insurance companies and brokers.

Here are the answers to some of the questions, collected from insurance companies and Lloyd's brokers yesterday.

Do I have to insure? No; not private property. But if you don't insure you won't get compensation beyond the limit of free compensation. If you want to insure you must do it before May 30 or you will not be covered.

What is the extent of free compensation?—A householder who is single is covered to the extent of the first £200. A married householder can claim up to an additional £110 for his wife and £25 for each child under sixteen. Non-householders have free insurance up to £50.

My family is evacuated, my furniture is in store, I'm in digs. What do I do to get cover for all my effects? Property is covered wherever it is, and if the total value of your goods is not more than £350, you are covered against bomb damage of either your furniture or your family's personal effects. If they are worth more, you must insure at the rate of £1 for every £100 worth.

When do I receive compensation? After the war—plus 2½ per cent. interest. But immediate compensation will be paid in cases of real hardship. You would almost certainly be paid money to buy new beds but not a piano.

Must I make out an inventory? Generally speaking, no. But it is as well to make a note of any valuable items, with evidence of their value, to avoid dispute should you have to make a claim.

Is my house included? It is not included in this scheme. You don't have to worry about it at all just now. The Inland Revenue will write to you after July 1 to tell you how much you must pay. If you hold it on mortgage, the premium will be shared by the Building Society or other mortgagee. If you rent, the entire responsibility is on the owner, unless you hold it on more than a seven years' lease, when the premium is split.

Where do I insure? Go to your usual insurance agent, or any assurance company.

Shelter as Arms Works

ONE of the largest underground shelters in a London borough is to be converted into an engineering workshop as part of the nation's arms drive.

Several hundred girls are to be drafted into the district to train as engineering workers, and instructions will also be given to Army technicians.

Occupants of the shelters are protesting against their eviction and have approached the Mayor. But they will have to find other accommodation in the borough, as armament production takes priority.

Over 300 people have used the shelter since the beginning of the war.

BRITAIN has demanded the withdrawal of Iraqi troops from around the R.A.F. aerodrome at Habbaniya before entering into any negotiations with Raschid Ali's Government. This was confirmed in London this morning after an offer by the Turkish Government to mediate.

But the British Government greatly appreciate the friendly motives of the Turkish Government in putting forward their offer.

Turkish radio and newspapers pointed out that Iraq has nothing to fear from Britain as she is fighting for the independence of small nations. The Axis Powers, however, have obviously robbed small nations of their independence.

Meanwhile, the Egyptian Government, after a long meeting, has appealed to Iraqi leaders to stop fighting and seek a peaceful settlement.

Iraq's Quisling Premier, Raschid Ali, has lost the greater part of his Air Force of 120 planes within four days of the start of his anti-British rising.

It fell a victim to the R.A.F. either while trying to attack British camps or during our air attacks on its bases, according to British G.H.Q. in Cairo.

Iraqi forces occupied Rutba after attacking an unarmed British bridge construction party, consisting of three or four officers, a few sappers and local labourers.

Airport Gunned

The R.A.F. machine-gunned Bagdad airport and dropped 24,000 leaflets in Arabic over the capital.

Reports from various Axis sources said:—

1.—British warships, including a heavy cruiser, have arrived at Basra, now under British control.

2.—Demonstrations in favour of the Iraqi Government took place in several unspecified Syrian towns yesterday. (This was a Vichy report quoted by German radio.)

3.—Iraqi troops, after firing British oil dumps, have occupied the aerodrome at Sil El Deban (West Iraq).

Associated Press, Reuter, British United Press, Exchange.

NAVY SINKS NAZI SHIP IN ANTARCTIC

BRITISH naval forces have blown up a Norwegian whaler repair ship in the Antarctic to prevent it being used by Germans, according to members of Admiral Byrd's expedition, which returned to U.S. yesterday.

The expedition also brought back reports of the presence of Germans and Japanese in the far south.

8 Down in a Night

SEVEN raiders were destroyed—six by fighters and one by A.A. fire—on Sunday night during attacks on Britain.

An eighth enemy bomber was bagged by a destroyer.

The week-end "bag" of enemy aircraft is now twenty-four, of which nineteen were destroyed by R.A.F. fighters.

Sunday night's eighth victim had attacked H.M. destroyer Southdown (Commander G. N. Loriston-Clarke) with bombs. The Southdown's A.A. guns sent it crashing into the sea.

His Gun Practice

A MESSERSCHMITT 109 was shot down into the Channel yesterday afternoon by a pilot who was merely out to test his guns.

He said later: "I took a long shot with my cannon and fired for only two or three seconds. One Me. went straight into the sea. It was a most satisfactory practice." This was one of two day raiders destroyed yesterday.

Daily Mirror

MAY 7

No. 11,670 ONE PENNY
Registered at the G.P.O. as a Newspaper.

U.S. READY FOR ANY RISK—JOINS BATTLE OF ATLANTIC

AMERICA APPEARED LAST NIGHT TO BE ON THE VERGE OF WAR.

The evidence piled up as official action and public clamour swung to a climax on the road to outright intervention on the side of Britain.

1.—Mr. Henry Stimson, U.S. Secretary for War, declared "America must immediately use her Navy, AT WHATEVER RISK, to ensure that war supplies reach Britain."

2.—It was revealed that Roosevelt is to send four naval cutters to Greenland—now under U.S. protection—to prevent Axis activity. U.S. will send no more arms machinery to Russia.

3.—President Roosevelt called his War Cabinet to plan greatly increased bomber production and received a report from his Navy and Army Air chiefs on British needs.

"THE United States will be in deadly combat with the forces of Germany and Italy within a week or ten days, this capital believes tonight," wrote a Washington correspondent last night.

"At nightfall Washington drums of war had reached a crescendo and spokesmen were calling for outright use of the armed forces of the nation."

Meanwhile, Colonel Frank Knox, U.S. Secretary for the Navy, told the Naval Committee of the House of Representatives:—

It is critically important now for the Navy to have a landing force ready for co-operation with the Fleet.

President Roosevelt's War Cabinet, meeting at the White House last night, received a special report from Major-General Arnold, Chief of the U.S. Army Air Force, who had just returned from England, on Britain's aircraft needs.

An hour after the Cabinet met Rear Admiral J. H. Towers, Chief of the Bureau of Aeronautics of the Navy Department, was called in.

Nazi Agents in U.S

Mr. Stimson's speech was broadcast to the American nation. He said:—

"Unless we are ready for sacrifice, and if need be to die for the conviction that the freedom of America must be saved, it will not be saved."

"Germany's advance agents are already busy in South America, building strategic air lines and creeping towards the Panama Canal.

Its armed forces are threatening West Africa, looking towards a jumping-off place within easy reach of Brazil. Its propagandists already are active in our own population.

"Hitler and his associates now arrogantly confront the world.

Continued Back Page. Col. 2

An isolationist amendment to defeat the Bill to transfer Axis ships in U.S. ports to Britain was defeated in the U.S. Senate last night.

Senator Claude Pepper, in the debate, said: "The American people are willing to spill their blood to crush Germany.

British Soldiers

ESCAPED BY 1,200 MILE HIKE

Mr. Stimson, U.S. War Minister—NO ROSE-COLOURED SPECTACLES FOR HIM.

TWO British soldiers, captured in Northern France, lay in a ditch a few miles beyond an East Prussian prison camp and plotted by the stars a course to liberty. Then they shook hands and went stealthily into the night.

Week afterwards they shook hands again, two men who had dared all—and won through.

Their escape, revealed in the House of Commons yesterday, had taken them nearly 1,200 miles, from Prussia into Poland, into Hungary, Czechoslovakia, into Yugoslavia, into Greece, and so to safety.

All the time as they travelled southwards a great silence was round them, for the Foreign Secretary told M.P.s they could not speak one word of the language of any of the countries through which they passed.

The sun and the stars alone had any message for them, and that message kept them going.

Imagine their hardships as warm days and nights of autumn went and the mists and snowstorms came

Every Day Harder

Every day for two wearied men the journey was harder; some days they must have made only a few miles, sometimes, no doubt, they crept under the tarpaulins of goods trucks and waited for the wheels to start up their staccato freedom song.

They "won" their food where they could as they went through war-torn, starving Poland; through a Hungary waiting the bidding of Hitler; through Yugoslavia still held undecided by the dictates of her Regent Prince.

They drank from streams; they snatched sleep, but they never knew rest.

Mile after mile, and every one of them hard-won. At the end of 1,200 miles they were in Athens.

So two men gained freedom. Now they are again fighting on its side

They have rejoined their units in the Western Desert.

Cheaper Fish

FISH of all kinds will be cheaper from June 1. Reason is that the trade has agreed on a voluntary system of price control—only alternative to compulsory control threatened by the Minister of Food.

Dockside options, which are blamed for excessive prices, will go.

Following a meeting at Leeds yesterday, Mr. Jack Vincent, of Grimsby, chairman of the price control committee, told the *Daily Mirror*: "There will be a maximum price for each variety of fish. It will show a considerable reduction on present prices."

Mrs. E. Chapman, a Leeds merchant, said, "My only fear is that when the price is controlled fish will be scarcer than ever."

Less Petrol

A CUT will be made in supplementary petrol allowances for the next rationing period (June and July).

Greatly increased requirements of the fighting forces necessitate further economies in the civilian use of petrol, says the Secretary for Petroleum.

Motorists also warned that a recent announcement about the permanent immobilisation of motor vehicles in the event of invasion does not relieve them from their existing obligation to put a vehicle out of action before leaving it unattended.

Tobacco Plan

MR. A. H. MAXWELL, the Tobacco Controller, who has recently returned from the United States, where he went to arrange tobacco supplies, said last night that he will make a statement in a day or two about the tobacco situation.

He revealed that tobacco is to come from America under the Lease and Lend Act

---

The 1,200-mile escape route

No Eire Bases —so Men Drown

EVERY month we have to watch hundreds of thousands of tons of our shipping sunk, and thousands of British sailors drowned—because we cannot obtain the use of Irish ports.

Mr. H. B. Lees-Smith, M.P. for Keighley, said this in the House of Commons war debate.

Mr. Lees-Smith said the chief theatre of war is still the Atlantic, and described our position because of the lack of Irish ports as "fantastic."

"The position in the Mediterranean," said Mr. Lees-Smith, "is becoming urgent.

"If we could obtain ports on the west coast of Ireland—there in our own dominion—Berehaven and Lough Swilly, the naval war would be transformed in a night, and we could send ships down to the Mediterranean.

Saved by Navy

If it were not for the British Navy, southern Ireland would be in the same position as Poland, Denmark or Holland."

Public attention in the U.S should be drawn to this position, and representations from that country would have more influence with Southern Ireland than from any other country in the world.

Hitler had taken enormous risks in Africa, and we had the opportunity of turning those risks against him. If that were done, he would suffer the most resounding defeat since the Battle of Britain.

He hoped there would be no kid glove methods over any German infiltration into Syria.

He criticised our Secret Service for being taken by surprise by events in Iraq, and asked

Contd. on Back Page. Col. 1

PANZERS, NOT PANSIES: M.P.

"The Government is not ruthless enough. What we want is a Panzer Government, not a pansy Government," said Mr. M. Petherick (Cons., Penryn and Falmouth) in the House of Commons yesterday.

"There are in the Government a number of those we once called 'Glamour boys.'" he added.

He described the Ministry of Information as "an elderly aunt of Left Wing tendencies, married to a retired Anglo-Indian major-general living in Matlock making busts for pin money which nobody buys.

"I would not like any Cabinet Minister to go further abroad than the Isle of Man," he said, when criticising Mr. Eden, and saying he could not see in his career much on which they could place confidence.

Stalin Takes Over

STALIN, Soviet Communist Party leader, became Premier of the U.S.S.R. last night.

Molotov, who was Premier and Foreign Minister, remains as Foreign Minister.

This was announced by the Moscow Radio.

Molotov, Premier for eleven years, has been relieved of the post at his own request as he has too much work.

---

201 NIGHT NAZIS DOWN THIS YEAR

The ninth enemy bomber brought down on Monday night brought the total of night raiders destroyed this year to 201. Night raiding has thus cost the Germans more than 800 airmen in four months.

The total night raiders brought down in the whole of last year was 130.

Marshal of the Royal Air Force Sir Edward Ellington said yesterday at Manchester that it was becoming increasingly difficult to find aerodrome sites in "this small island."

He foresaw the end of the Nazi night raider.

Daily Mirror

MAY 9

No. 11,672   ONE PENNY
Registered at the G.P.O. as a Newspaper.

Lieutenant F. J. Owen will be remembered as one of Britain's bravest sailors. When H.M.S. Patia, bombed, was sinking, it was necessary, in order to save trapped seamen, for someone to go below decks—he went himself, and died. Nearly 100 men escaped.

An orphan boy, he always wanted to be "a brave sailor."

39 DOWN IN 24 HOURS

Germans Lose 300 Airmen in a Week

German bombers shot down in raids on Britain during the seven days of this month now total seventy-five.

The Germans can stand the loss of planes, but the loss of men is a big blow. It means 300 trained German airmen lost in a week.

And during that same period we lost only a score of men in night raids—five planes.

Wednesday night's weather was ideal. That helped. But the success was no fluke. An analysis of night fighter successes shows a steady and persistent improvement. Last month's figure was ninety.

'WHIPPET'S' 1,200 MILES

"OLD NASTY hadn't enough wire to keep us in. We had a tough time, but we got through all right."

This is all Sapper Evelyn Sidney White, of the Royal Engineers, told his wife about his escape from a German prison camp and his 1,200-mile hitch-hike across Europe from East Prussia to Athens.

He and another soldier walked through Poland, Hungary, Yugoslavia and Greece. Sapper White, 31, is so small that at home he was known as The Whippet. He was so fond of hiking that he became a postman.

His wife, who lives in Abbey-road, Aylesbury, Bucks, has received a telegram from him from Athens: "Am O.K. Are you still well?"

Mr. A. R. White, his father, of Monarch-road Northampton, said yesterday: "We always called him The Whippet because he was so small and wiry.

"I wouldn't be surprised if the other soldier is one of his pals, an Aylesbury postman."

Sapper White.

SUEZ BOMBED FOR 2 HOURS

Enemy aircraft raided the Suez Canal zone for two hours during the night, says a communique issued in Cairo yesterday.

Some damage was done to Egyptian State Railway property, but there were no casualties.—Associated Press.

THIRTY-NINE German planes down in twenty-four hours was the score up to late last night when the destruction of one of last night's raiders was announced.

The other thirty-eight comprised twenty-four bombers shot down in Wednesday night's raids, thirteen fighters shot down in daylight, and another bomber shortly before dark.

The night figure is a record and so is the night fighters' performance in shooting down twenty of the bombers. The day figure of fourteen, too, is the best so far this year. Our losses in the same twenty-four hours were two bombers and one fighter.

And the latest tribute to the R.A.F. comes from the Germans themselves over the Berlin radio. In an account of an attack by British bombers on German minesweepers, a German fighter pilot broadcast:

"They are monstrous, these new bombers. They are magnificent, deadly machines. One must get down first to save one's own skin."

In another broadcast telling of a clash between a night bomber and a British fighter a German pilot said:

"He gives us a burst and disappears before our gunners can reply. He is an excellent pilot."

Many Damaged

That German bomber got away, but "with only one motor working, with our landing gear smashed and with 107 holes in our fuselage," said the German. Fighters got twenty. A.A. guns three and the balloon barrage one.

The Under-Secretary for Air told the Commons yesterday:—

"A considerable number also were damaged. I cannot give the exact number possibly brought down, but the 'pick-up' looks like being double figures."

Daylight successes yesterday were mostly by fighters, which got ten Me. 109s and a bomber. A.A. guns got two more Me.s.

CALLING UP ALL SEAMEN

ALL men between the ages of 18 and 60 who have served at sea since January 1, 1936, and have since got other jobs, must go back to sea to help us win the Battle of the Atlantic.

They will have to register at employment exchanges in the week starting May 26.

The scheme, announced yesterday by the Ministers of Shipping and Labour, is similar to those which have brought back many skilled men to shipbuilding, engineering and other industries.

Seafaring men called up will supplement a Merchant Navy Reserve Pool.

No Choice of Ship

The pool will consist of all officers and men who, on May 26, are serving on ships on agreements opened in this country unless when those agreements end they sign on again for employment with the same company. All officers and men who have been discharged from their ships since April 28 automatically enter the pool.

"Seamen can no longer have the freedom of the choice of ship," says the Shipping Minister.

"While we are fighting the Battle of the Atlantic the only cargoes that may come to this country are those needed for the war effort."

The new National Maritime Board agreements which bulked largely in the new arrangement will ensure continuity of employment, longer leave on pay, and payment while awaiting appointment to a ship.

GRANT FOR THE CITY

To keep the City of London's rates low, the Common Council of the City appealed to the Government for a grant, it was revealed at a meeting of the Common Council yesterday.

The Council made a rate of 6s. 4d., an increase of 4d. But for the grant it would have been necessary to increase rates by 3s. 4d.

FRANCO SEES LISBON ENVOY

Senor Nicolas Franco, Spanish Ambassador to Portugal, arrived in Madrid by air yesterday. He is a brother of General Franco.

The Woman and the Hun

HE was a Nazi rear-gunner who had baled out from a blazing plane and landed in a garden.

SHE was a Polish Jewess, wife of an Austrian doctor, who had suffered Himmler's persecution and been hounded from Vienna by the Gestapo. Welcomed by friends in England, she is today caring for the baby daughter of people who gave her sanctuary.

✦ ✦ ✦

Just before dawn broke they met for the first time in the drawing-room of a villa "somewhere in England."

Carried into the villa by a fire watcher to whom he meekly surrendered his revolver, the airman stared at the careworn face of the woman from Vienna.

She spoke in German. The Nazi shuddered.

Then he held out a photograph humbly to the woman his nation had caused so much pain.

It was a picture of his wife, and in a perambulator his child.

The woman did not take the photograph.

"No—I knew what was passing through that man's mind," she told the "Daily Mirror."

He Was Afraid

"I could see he was afraid what might become of him.

"Then all the horror of the past months came surging over me. I was possessed by terrible fury.

"He put his hand to his head, explaining that he had hurt himself in his fall.

"Somehow I managed to overcome the impulse to tell him that he and his kind were fit for nothing but to be thrown to the dogs.

"Then quietly I said I was sorry he was hurt and told him of the other men's wives and babies massacred by German bombs."

✦ ✦ ✦

The airman hugged his shoulders.

NAVAL YACHT SUNK

The naval yacht Fiona (Commander A. H. H. Griffiths, R.N.R.) has been sunk, it was announced last night.

RASCHID ALI, the pro-German Premier of the rebel Iraqi Government, has left Bagdad, his capital, in a hurry after a public demonstration against his Government. This was reported from Cairo late last night.

It was added that Tewfik Suweidi Bey, who was Foreign Minister in the Cabinet that Raschid Ali overthrew, left Bagdad by air for Amman (Trans-jordan) to meet the deposed Regent, Amir Abdul Illah.

The Regent has been reported leading a loyalist force into Iraq to fight Raschid Ali.

A few hours before the flight of Raschid Il, the Iraqi rebel army command had admitted that the railway stations at Bagdad were bombed at ten o'clock yesterday morning.

The Vichy News Agency said that the raid was "extremely severe."

The R.A.F. Middle East communique yesterday said: "Bagdad airport was bombed yesterday and some damage was caused to buildings.

"Violent explosions occurred when direct hits were obtained on a magazine at Washash, near Bagdad."

Iraqi Retreat

Admission of a withdrawal by Iraqi troops was made in yesterday's rebel communique issued by the German News Agency.

The communique says: "The enemy undertook a surprise action against our troops which were besieging the aerodrome of Senn el Debanne. Our troops were forced to take up new positions seeing that further resistance after heavy fighting appeared to be useless."

Nazis "Ask" Syria

General Dentz, Syrian High Commissioner, has received a demand from Germany for permission to land forces in Syria for a drive on Suez, the Berne correspondent of the New York Times stated yesterday.

Germany, he said, is threatening to land parachute troops on the coast of Syria, declaring that "if resistance is encountered Syria will be considered as having taken up arms."

The correspondent believed that there is a connection between this demand and the German concession to Vichy.

All telegraphic links between Iraq and Syria have been cut off, says the Vichy News Agency.

AIR BASES FOR NAZIS

GERMANY will gain the use of French air bases in Morocco and Syria under the agreement made with the Nazis by Admiral Darlan, according to the Free French radio at Brazzaville, Equatorial Africa.

Despite Admiral Darlan's return to Vichy, Franco-German conversations are continuing in Paris.

The Vichy spokesman yesterday said:

"The results so far obtained constitute the first lap. Certain sections of the armistice must be modified in a spirit of mutual understanding."

Columbia radio stated yesterday that the French Government is to build cargo ships and tankers for Germany.

FRENCH CONVOYS PASS GIB.

Two French convoys escorted by French naval units have passed through the Straits of Gibraltar—one into the Mediterranean and one into the Atlantic, says the Vichy News Agency.

TRAITOR TO DIE

AFTER a trial which lasted just over a day and was held in camera, George Johnson Armstrong, 38, engineer, was sentenced to death at the Old Bailey yesterday for an offence under the Treachery Act.

The court was cleared except for officials, essential witnesses, police, jury, and counsel. Doors were locked and screened.

This is the fifth sentence of death passed under the Treachery Act, 1940.

The first—passed upon Mrs. Dorothy Pamela O'Grady, of Sandown, Isle of Wight—was quashed on appeal, and reduced to a sentence of fourteen years' penal servitude for offences under the Official Secrets Act.

Three spies, posing as refugees, were hanged last December.

'MY CARD'

Landing by parachute in a potato patch, a Nazi airman who had leaped from his blazing plane, clicked his heels as ex-Serviceman Ted Ashdown came up—then presented his visiting card.

"How was your plane brought down?" Ted asked the immaculate blond young giant.

"Fighter. Spitfire," replied the airman, smiling.

"One minute we were flying through the moonlight. Suddenly came a burst of gunfire.

"We did not wait. We baled out at 20,000ft. Our plane was in flames as we floated down."

NIGHT RAID IN FORCE

A plane flying at a great height, was brought down last night following anti-aircraft fire. Raiders crossed the East Anglian coast in force, they were reported in the Midlands and North-West and London had an Alert.

Daily Mirror

No. 11,675
ONE PENNY
Registered at the G.P.O. as a Newspaper.

HESS, HITLER'S DEPUTY, LANDS IN BRITAIN

THIS IS HESS

HESS, the man who was Hitler's confidant, his adoring friend, companion of his unsuccessful days, is 44.

This may not be the first visit Hess has made to this country since crisis came to Europe. It is confidently believed by some that the mysterious visitor who landed at Croydon from a German plane a few days before war broke out was Hess.

Handsome, dark, strongly built, he is the idol of millions of German women. If he hadn't been a Nazi leader he might easily have been a film star.

Hitler's right-hand man since the days of the Munich beer cellar putsch, he still carries the scar of a beer jug thrown while he was Hitler's bodyguard in one of the early Nazi riots.

Thrown into prison with Hitler when the Munich putsch failed, he helped him write Mein Kampf.

He was the one man in Germany allowed to see the Fuehrer without appointment.

Whenever Hitler had one of his fits, it was said in Germany, he allowed none to come near him except Hess.

Hess, son of a wealthy Ger-

The wreckage of the plane from which Hess landed.

man merchant, was born in Egypt. He went to an English school in Alexandria and speaks perfect English.

He would have been prepared, it is thought, to negotiate rather than go to war.

He has left behind him in Germany his wife and little boy, 4.

How highly he was regarded by Hitler was evident in the speech Hitler made to the Reichstag on the day he invaded Poland.

Hitler then named Goering as his successor in war, with Hess the man to follow Goering.

RUDOLF HESS, Hitler's deputy, the man who knows Germany's every secret, has landed in Scotland, having flown from Germany in defiance of Hitler's desperate efforts to stop him.

How He Arrived

This is the story of how Hess reached this country, as telephoned on Sunday by a "Daily Mirror" reporter who was near the spot at the time.

A GERMAN airman who says he stole his plane has landed in a lonely part of Scotland. He baled out just before the plane crashed and landed in the fields of a farm near Glasgow. It was moonlight.

Overhead had seen the plane circle for some minutes. It came down low. We thought it was searching for a landing place. It crashed.

A ploughman heard the noise and ran from his cottage. He saw the wrecked plane. Not far away was the pilot. He limped. It was obvious he had injured one of his legs.

Tea in a Cottage

The German offered no resistance. The ploughman told me that as he approached the pilot, "a man about fifty," smiled and appeared glad he had landed in Britain.

The plane carried no bombs. Those who spoke to him told me this mystery pilot speaks good English. His first inquiry was: "Where am I?"

Then, to a few Scottish countrymen, he told how he had stolen the plane and flown it to this country.

The ploughman took his captive to his home and offered him a cup of tea. All he would drink was a cup of water. He remained in the cottage until Army officers arrived and took him to a military camp.

This announcement was made to the Pressmen of the world at the Ministry of Information a few minutes before midnight last night.

The following statement was issued from 10, Downing-street, 11.20 p.m. last night:

"Rudolf Hess, the deputy Fuehrer of Germany and Party Leader of the National Socialist Party, has landed in Scotland in the following circumstances:

"On the night of Saturday the 10th inst. a Messerschmitt 110 was reported by our patrols to have crossed the coast of Scotland and to be flying in the direction of Glasgow.

Guns Unloaded

"Since a Messerschmitt 110 would not have the fuel to return to Germany this report was at first disbelieved. However, later on a Messerschmitt 110 crashed near Glasgow with its guns unloaded.

"Shortly afterwards a German officer who had baled out was found with his parachute in the neighbourhood suffering from a broken ankle.

"He was taken to hospital in Glasgow where he first gave his name as Horn, but later on declared that he was Rudolf Hess.

"He brought with him various photographs of himself at different ages apparently in order to establish his identity.

"These photographs were deemed to be photographs of Hess by several people who knew him personally.

"Accordingly an officer of the Foreign Office who was closely acquainted with Hess before the war has been sent up by aeroplane to see him in hospital."

The first news of Hess's flight

Continued on Back Page

VOICE OF THE GERMANS

Nominally Hitler's deputy, Hess was much more. He wielded tremendous influence over the Fuehrer, wrote his speeches, worked out policy with him, and more than Goering was the power behind the scenes.

In recent years he has become more and more the voice of the German people, and there was a large section of the Nazi Party as well as of the ordinary people who thought Hess should have been appointed to succeed Hitler instead of coming after Goering.

SUEZ RAIDED AGAIN

Enemy aircraft raided the Suez Canal zone for the third successive night,

The Scots ploughman who found Hess.

U.S. PINS VICHY

AMERICA wants to know what Count de Brinon, French representative in Paris, meant by the threat that if the U.S. tried to occupy Dakar it would have to be by force.

To obtain an explanation, Admiral W. D. Leahy, United States Ambassador to Vichy, has asked for an interview with Marshal Petain, says the British United Press.

Marshal Petain arrived in Vichy yesterday from Antibes and was to consider reports made by Admiral Darlan, French Vice-Premier, on his conversations with the Germans.

Darlan left Paris on Friday night and was reported in Vichy to have negotiated with "high German personalities"

ONE DAY AT WHIT FOR NON-VITAL WORKERS

There will be no official Whitsun holiday this year.

But workers in non-essential trades and arms workers who can be spared will get one day.

"We hope factory chiefs will be able to arrange a day's holiday for workers," said the Ministry of Aircraft Production yesterday. "But men and women on vital jobs cannot be spared."

PANIC AT WAR RUMOUR

Tokio (Japan) stock market dropped sharply as the result of a persistent rumour that America is ready to enter the war.

Daily Mirror

MAY 14

No. 11,676   ONE PENNY
Registered at the G.P.O. as a Newspaper.

Roosevelt's Speech Delayed by Flight

Hess's arrival in Britain was one reason for the cancellation of the important speech which Roosevelt planned to make today, it was stated in Washington yesterday.

The President felt that with the world's attention focused on the Hess mystery his message might not be sufficiently studied. There is also the possibility that Hess might make revelations important enough to attend Anglo-American plans.

Roosevelt was privately informed of Hess's landing in Scotland hours before it was announced to the world.

Rudolf Hess's flight to Britain has staggered America no less than the rest of the world. "A great blow to morale of German people," was the opinion in Washington.

Americans believe the British are alive to the possibility of an audacious trap and will be wary in using any information he offers.

"The first rat to leave the ship," was one comment in Cairo on Hess's flight.

Otto Strasser, leader of the anti-Nazi Black Front, declared yesterday that Hess's escape seemed to indicate that the German army chiefs and Goering were seeking to overthrow the Nazi Party.

CHURCHILL MAY SEE HESS IN SECRET PRISON

WITHIN the next two days Mr. Winston Churchill may see Rudolf Hess at his secret place of detention.

Hess was last night in a military hospital "Somewhere in England," having been moved from Glasgow. He was accompanied by a doctor, a Foreign Office official, and a Special Branch officer from Scotland Yard. He spent most of the day writing.

His Wife in Turkey

Hess's wife, child and mother arrived in Ankara yesterday.

They arrived, says a *New York Times* correspondent, in the same plane as Von Papen and his family.

He is dressed in the plain Army pyjamas issued to officers in hospital—his own clothes still bear Nazi decorations. An officer is guarding him, and outside the bedroom door stand armed soldiers.

Treated with formal kindness by nurses and doctors, but by no means pampered, he is recovering rapidly from the slight injury he received when he baled out from the plane in which he escaped from Nazi Germany.

I am told that but for slight pain in one of his ankles he is otherwise "quite well."

In the hospital to which Hess was taken were other German airmen who "failed to return" after Clydeside raids.

Seen by Specialists

When he came to his new hospital he was given ordinary issue of tooth brush, tooth paste and other toilet requirements.

He is quiet and cheerful. Between his writing and his resting he exchanges a few words with his nurses. He is eating well—just the usual simple but wholesome hospital diet. For one meal yesterday he was given chicken and rice.

Writing seems to have developed into a kind of compelling passion with him.

And what he is writing, judging by his absorption in the task and the deliberation with which he writes every word, may well be one of the most important documents in history.

No Government official is yet prepared, however, to indicate the nature of the documents he

DON'T MAKE A HERO OF HIM

Don't make a hero out of Hess, warns *Die Zeitung*, the German anti-Nazi journal published in London, in a leading article this morning. It says:

"There is one thing we must earnestly warn against—that easy sentimentality of some British people which, in the gossip columns, tends to convey the impression that this Hess is 'not so bad,' and pour out moving tales of his shyness, his pleasant smile and his affection for his wife and child.

"Make no mistake about it: he is as bad as the worst of them. His hands are stained with the blood of thousands of innocent people. His fanaticism and ruthlessness match that of a Himmler and Streicher. His flight is ground for grim satisfaction, not for softhearted pardon."

GOVT. CONTROL OF FIRE SERVICE

THE Government is to take over all the fire brigades in the country and put them under a unified control.

They will no longer be in the hands of local authorities, but under the general control of the Home Secretary and the Secretary for Scotland.

Local authorities, however, will still have to contribute to their upkeep on a basis of a regular fire service. The Exchequer will find the rest of the money.

75 per cent. of the yearly cost of the yearly cost of a regular fire service. The Exchequer will find the rest of the money.

These proposals were announced in the House of Commons yesterday by the Home Secretary.

He said the plan was to regroup all fire-fighting resources into larger units for purposes of administration and control, to constitute mobile fire fighting units for reinforcing purposes or other special duties.

Drastic Change

Many lessons had been learned in the hard school of the past eight months' experience.

"Now, with intensified attack, a drastic change of organisation must be made," said the Home Secretary. "In spite of all that has been done to develop and improve the emergency fire services, a fundamental difficulty remains, and springs from the fact that the fire service is a local service."

It was no reflection on local authorities that the task had grown beyond local resources.

Some of the preliminary measures could be carried out under existing powers, but for other purposes the Government would submit to Parliament as soon as practicable a Bill to confer any necessary additional powers on the Secretaries of State.

It is understood that Mr William Mabane, one of the Parliamentary Secretaries to the Ministry of Home Security, will take principal charge of the new force.

WAR COURT FOR LONDON

The Home Secretary has constituted as a War Zone Court district the Metropolitan Police District, including the City of London, with Mr. M. Nops, clerk to the Central Criminal Court, as clerk.

HORSEFLESH WITH BEEF

A certain admixture of horseflesh with beef is, to some extent, taking place in various articles of popular consumption, the Minister of Health stated in a written reply.

Petain Warned

THE U.S. Ambassador to France, Admiral William D. Leahy, warned Marshal Petain when he saw him in Vichy last night that any gesture of military solidarity with Germany would be interpreted by the U.S. as abandonment of neutrality.

Rumours that the Germans have asked for freedom of action in French ports and in Morocco and Dakar were circulating in Vichy last night.

Admiral Darlan's close associates are insisting that the time has arrived for France to choose collaboration with Germany.

Admiral Leahy's warning was given when he discussed with Petain the meaning of Darlan's conferences with Hitler.—British United Press.

BOMBS DESTROYED LETTERS TO M.P.s

Scores of letters to M.P.s from their constituents and others have been destroyed in the bombing of the old House of Commons.

Invitations to meetings and dinners may also have been lost, so that the organisers of the functions are now wondering who will and who will not turn up.

INDIAN WARSHIP LOST

The loss of an Indian warship was announced yesterday—H.M.I.S. Parvati.

One warrant officer and fifteen ratings are missing, believed killed, and the commanding officer, a warrant officer and twelve ratings are wounded.—British United Press.

Earl Killed by a Bomb

The Earl of Suffolk and Berkshire, thirty-five-year-old scientist who has been killed by a bomb, is seen here with his wife (formerly Mimi Crawford, musical comedy actress), his six-year-old heir and a younger son.

He had been a Guards officer, went round the world as a sailor, worked as a farm labourer in Australia, and at thirty-two gained his B.Sc. with honours at Edinburgh University.

VON PAPEN AS THE DOVE

AS Von Papen arrived back in Ankara posing as a "dove of peace," German military circles in Budapest were spreading reports that Hun troops are preparing to smash through Turkey on their way to Egypt.

So began yesterday what appeared to be a new Nazi war of nerves against the Turks.

The second spring offensive will start about June 1, Budapest informants told a *New York Times* correspondent.

German troops were said to be pouring into Greek ports through Thrace and Bulgaria ready for an assault on Turkey to begin simultaneously with an offensive along the North African coast.

This is what Von Papen said on arrival by air in Ankara:

"I arrive as a dove of peace bearing an olive branch, and I can assure you that you may spend all the summer at the seaside."

PREMIER WITH THE KING

The Prime Minister had audience of the King yesterday.

Hitler Worried

Hitler called all his Gauleiters (Nazi local "dictators") to a meeting yesterday. Berlin radio said last night that the Fuehrer made a speech, and all the Gauleiters "expressed their will to victory."

It is obvious, however, that Hess was the subject of the conference. Said the Deutschlandsender commentator: "There is no German who has not been shocked by Hess's flight."

Another significant statement broadcast in Germany yesterday was:—

"The war will go on until British rulers are finished OR READY TO NEGOTIATE PEACE WITH GERMANY."

is penning. When he tires of writing he relaxes for half an hour or so with a novel or an English geography book.

One thing is certain—Hess is perfectly sane. That has been established beyond all doubt by specialists.

Hess brought with him no peace terms or overtures. The motive for his flight was escape, and he came to Britain because he knew that in a neutral country. Nazi agents would have reached him.

Several Washington officials

Continued on Back Page

Don't get your toothbrush the wrong way round

You don't go into a tobacconist and ask for 'ten cigarettes'. You ask — if you're a man and married — for the brand your wife prefers!

'...and when you buy a toothbrush it's just as important to get things the right way round. The name first ...Halex. Then the *kind* of Halex — either with bristles or with *nylon* instead of bristles (*nylon* is the wonderful new material that keeps springy and firm in spite of soaking).

By remembering to say Halex first, you get the finest toothbrush that ever went away for a weekend, and you avoid that freezing silence from behind the counter that warns you of having said the wrong thing.

HALEX

Regd. Trade Mark

Whichever shape of toothbrush you prefer, there is a Halex to suit you, either with bristles (from 1/- plus tax) or with *nylon* instead of bristles (from 1/6 plus tax). Six different coloured handles.

Convoys May Not Be Only U.S. Move

THE whole of America is waiting for the word to go forward, Colonel Knox, U.S. Navy Secretary, said yesterday.

"We cannot half-...ht this battle," he said. "Our choice is to oppose the aggressor with enough force to scare him off or to defeat him.

"It is possible," he added, "that convoys will not be the answer after all. Perhaps we may have to develop a new defence to ensure the arrival of our goods on the other side."

Rear Admiral E. King, Commander-in-Chief of the United States Atlantic Fleet, saw Roosevelt in Washington yesterday.

"President Roosevelt's speech included an announcement that on May 1 800 ships, totalling 5,055,400 tons, were under contract or being constructed.—Associated Press and Reuter.

ing-point of the war," declared "Merry Go Round," the Washington political column, yesterday.

"The die is now cast," the writer asserted. "The President has made up his mind to use convoys and all that goes with them."

News of progress in the U.S. defence programme yesterday included an announcement that on May 1 800 ships, totalling 5,055,400 tons, were under contract or being constructed.—Associated Press and Reuter.

Daily Mirror

MAY 15

No. 11,677   ♦   ONE PENNY
Registered at the G.P.O. as a Newspaper.

VICHY GIVES IN TO REGAIN PARIS

The Perfect Raid

THE perfect raid has been achieved by the R.A.F.— a daylight assault on Heligoland which went "according to plan" down to the last detail.

Our bombers attacked in line abreast at 150ft.

Before the defences could open up our pilots were bearing down on their targets. They covered the fortified area of the island with sticks of high explosives.

Columns of smoke, mixed with the dust and wreckage of shattered buildings, rose immediately and spread.

"It was the perfect theoretical raid carried out in practice," said the pilot who led the attack. "We came in at exactly the right spot after more than two hours' flying and started many fires.

"It was a punch in the face for Heligoland—we left our knuckle marks right across the island."

Front and rear gunners poured bullets into streets and naval barracks.

WORKERS TO TALK TO U.S.

British working men are to tell America how they and their trades are affected by the war.

A series of broadcasts has been arranged by Mr. George Gibson, Trades Union Congress chairman, in which a farm worker, a dock labourer, a bus conductor, and other workers will tell their stories.

No ban is placed on a worker airing a legitimate grouse.

Broadcasts have already been given by Mr. Gibson and a school teacher. The next talk is to be given by Mr. Charles Jarman, of the Seamen's Union.

ONE MORE DOWN

One enemy bomber was shot down on Tuesday night, bringing the total of night raiders destroyed during May to 138.

FRANCE is to get back Paris and 250,000 of the 2,000,000 French prisoners held by the Huns.

The price she must pay is:

1.—French industry to help in re-armouring German tanks;

2.—France to help the Nazis with submarine repair work.

These are expected to be the main clauses in the collaboration agreement which the Vichy Government is now prepared to sign with Hitler.

Yesterday the terms were unanimously approved by Petain's Cabinet.

Unanimous Approval

Petain presided over the Cabinet meeting, which opened with an account by Admiral Darlan, the Vice-Premier, of his recent talks with Hitler at Berchtesgaden and with high German officials in Paris.

The text of the communique issued afterwards said:

"The Cabinet unanimously approved the terms. The effect of these negotiations will soon be felt."

Vichy considered the communique to be a warning to the United States that France is committed to collaboration. It is hoped this policy will prevent America's entry into the war.

According to the Independent French Agency, Hitler attaches

Continued on Back Page

CALL UP MAY SHUT CINEMAS

UNLESS the Ministry of Labour modify their call-up plans, 75 per cent. of the cinemas in this country may be closed by autumn and complete closure of all cinemas by the end of the year is a possibility.

In June, cinema operators, previously reserved at twenty-five, become de-reserved under thirty-five.

More than 75 per cent. of operators are under thirty-five, and according to Mr. Tom O'Brien, general secretary of the National Association of Theatrical and Kine Employees, there is no possibility of substitute labour.

"Doing National Work"

"There aren't any men that can be trained in the time," Mr. O'Brien told the "Daily Mirror."

"It is doubtful if women could do many of the jobs involved in operating.

"It is odd that while leading members of the Cabinet have, as individuals, praised the part played by the cinemas in organising entertainment, providing relaxation for war workers and helping to keep up public morale, the Government as a whole should not have recognised that the industry was thereby doing useful, national work."

U.S. COULD FEED ENGLAND BY AIR

Speaking at Schenectady, Mr. Kenneth Farrell, the food chemist, said that if shipping was unable to reach Britain it would be possible for the U.S. dried food industry to supply enough supplies by plane to feed every man, woman and child in Britain.

He calculated that 300 bombers could supply one day's food.—Exchange.

DEATH RIDDLE IN RICH MAN'S HOUSE

A doctor called to a house in The Avenue, Branksome Park, Poole (Dorset), yesterday found Mr. Thomas Leadbitter Boardman, 52, of independent means, dead, apparently from poison.

While the doctor was there it is understood that Mrs. Edith Mary Isobel Gregorson, 52, was taken ill and died.

Branksome Park is a well-to-do suburb of Poole.

BURN DIDN'T FIRE-WATCH

Fulham Council last night dismissed Mr. E. C. Burn, one of their clerks, for refusing to do fire-watching at the town hall on the ground that he considered organised fire-watching to be non-combatant service "designed primarily with a view to the more effective prosecution of the war."

★ A London street yesterday. The line across the entrance OUGHT to be red tape.

The Queen's Sticking-Plaster

When the Queen went with the King yesterday to inspect the damage done to Westminster Abbey, she was walking with a slight limp; and the instep of her left foot bore a piece of sticking-plaster.

PRICE LIST FOR LETS?

A TARIFF of charges for furnished lettings may have to be drawn up by the Ministry of Health.

Local authorities, anxious to bring proceedings against people demanding extortionate rents, are being urged to take legal action by the Department.

But some of them are dubious about the rent that must be demanded before it can be described as "extortionate" or "exorbitant."

"If we could have some guidance from the Ministry, we should have something on which to base our cases," a council clerk told the Daily Mirror yesterday.

"It might be possible to give rough classifications, based on furniture and property values, to indicate a reasonable charge."

30,000 ITALIAN BODIES FOUND

Bodies of 30,000 Italian soldiers, apparently from sunken Italian troop transports, have been washed ashore in Tunis, North Africa, states Columbia Broadcasting System, New York.

U.S. SHIPS WILL BE LIT

Despite the Nazi threat to sink U.S. ships in the Red Sea, the ships, expected soon, will not sail stealthily, but as neutral craft brightly lit and with big American flags painted on their sides.—Associated Press.

COULDN'T JOIN US—DIED

Rudolf Landmann, 19, of Toronto, Canada, a German, tried to join the Canadian Air Force, was refused and committed suicide under a goods train.—British United Press.

Hess's damaged ankle is yielding to treatment, and the slight abrasions to his arm also received in his parachute jump are healing rapidly.

He is stated to be in excellent spirits, quite happy, and apparently enjoys the light diet of chicken, fish and eggs.

It is understood that he may be sufficiently rested in a few days to leave the hospital where, of course, his room is UNOSTENTATIOUSLY under military guard.

He hears the B.B.C. bulletins daily—[this is a privilege absolutely banned to other enemy prisoners] — and converses freely with the officer

---

WHAT HESS WRITES

RUDOLF HESS has written out a complete statement on events which led to his decision to leave Germany. It was revealed yesterday.

It was also stated that Hess may broadcast to the German people.

While no official statement has yet been made concerning the reasons for his flight to Britain, it can now be said that Hess did not leave Germany unaided.

The Foreign Secretary in a speech yesterday said:

"When you have the spectacle of a small group of men possessed of immense military power, you are certain to see, in times of stress and strain, evidence among them, not only of tension, but of dissension. In this you may well find in part at least, an explanation of the parachute descent that electrified the world last week-end."

While the German radio yesterday was still trying to convince the world that Hess was

---

"Landed on Duke of Hamilton's Estate"

Columbia radio, New York, stated in its foreign languages news bulletin that Hess landed in the grounds of the Duke of Hamilton's state.

★ ★ ★

suffering from a "mental collapse," the B.B.C. European Service was giving to German listeners a dull and long explanation of the implications of Hess's flight.

"But," it was stated, "nothing precise will be known till Mr. Churchill divulges as much as he thinks fit of what Hess has been saying and writing in the hospital where he now lies."

Major Vyvyan Adams (Cons., W. Leeds) is to ask the Minister of Information—

"Why, since Rudolf Hess, the deputy of the enemy dictator, descended in Scotland at some moment during the night of May 10 and 11, he did not take steps to anticipate the German broadcast, alleging Hess's insanity, by an announcement of our own anterior to midnight, May 12 and 13."

---

2 PLANES LAND— FRIENDS OF HESS?

Ankara radio yesterday quoted reports from Stockholm that two German planes had made a forced landing in southern Sweden, having exhausted their petrol. It is not disclosed who were in the planes.

You'll Be So Glad

on guard and the nurses.

★ ★ ★

This report was issued by the Press Association yesterday.

Hess is apparently being treated as if he were a royal invalid, a dear and valued friend. And so that his feelings —feelings that have sent thousands to their deaths—should not be in the least hurt, his room is "of course unostentatiously" guarded.

What will the thousands who have been bombed out, whose homes are ruins, whose relatives are killed, think of the treatment given to this Hun murderer?

Hess may have disagreed with the Nazi chiefs, but he still wants to see Germany crush Britain.

Daily Mirror

MAY 16

No. 11,678   ONE PENNY
Registered at the G.P.O. as a Newspaper.

WE'RE ALL WITH YOU, ERNIE

HESS IS A KILLER: HIS FLIGHT A NAZI RUSE

MR. ERNEST BEVIN, Minister of Labour, revealed both Herr Hess, Hitler's Deputy, and his flight to Britain in their true light yesterday. He said in London:

" From my point of view Herr Hess is a murderer. He is no man I would ever negotiate with, and I DO NOT CHANGE, EVEN FOR DIPLOMATIC REASONS.

" Nazism is Nazism to me.

" I do not believe that Hitler did not know Hess was coming to England.

"GERMAN STUNT"

" For a good many years I have had to deal with these totalitarian gentlemen and Communists, and I have seen this kind of stunt over and over again.

" I think they are very much like burglars. When a burglar is successful he never changes his tactics.

" I am not going to be deceived by any of them, but I am anxious London shall give its answer.

"SMASHED UNIONS"

" You can understand my feeling about Hess when I tell you he was the man who collected every index card of every trade union leader in Germany and the Social Democrats, and when the time came they were either sent to concentration camps or murdered."

Keep This Man in a Gaol

BEVIN'S warning is timely.

Hess must be treated as the murderous blackguard he is and allowed no contact whatever with any of the rich fools who were appeasers until the very outbreak of the war. The Fascists are still among us, planning a Fascist Britain under a German overlord

He Has Not Changed

They have not changed any more than Hess has. Given any latitude, the Nazi, schooled in intrigue and corruption, will be organising a fifth column to destroy our Victory Government and replace it by men prepared to accept negotiated peace.

There is only one way to prevent this happening.

PUT HESS IN A CONCENTRATION CAMP, KEEP HIM THERE — AND ALLOW HIM NO VISITORS.

Duke of Hamilton Sees Hess: Back page.

U.S. SENDING FOOD TO US

Farm supplies worth £22,500,000 have already been sent to port for Britain. Mr. Carl Robbins, president of the Commodity Credit Corporation, told a meeting of the Banking Committee of the House of Representatives yesterday.

"Some of the emergency needs of the British," he said, "have arisen for supplies that could only be met by the surplus marketing agency.—Reuter

THE TOOLS—AND THE JOB

A new twelve-gauge shotgun is in the post for David McLean of Scotland from David McLean of Denver, Colorado, U.S.A. With it is the message: "I can't get over myself, but I can see that a McLean has something better than a pitchfork with which to fight the Hun."

HUNS LAND IN IRAQ

THERE were two vitally important developments in the Iraq situation yesterday:—

1. Britain announced her intention to bomb German aircraft using aerodromes in Vichy-controlled Syria for flights to Iraq.

2. British G.H.Q. in Cairo reported that " a certain number " of German planes have arrived in Iraq carrying Axis specialists.

And last night the German official news agency in Berlin declared that the first group of Syrian volunteers had left for Iraq.

The German planes, said the Cairo communique, arrived in Iraq in response to the urgent appeal of Rashid Ali to his Axis partners. Propagandist agitators are included among the specialists they carried.

American sources reported that high German officers, including two generals, were in the planes.

A neutral source in Vichy yesterday said the British had already attacked one Syrian aerodrome, but the French Foreign Office declared they " knew nothing of Syrian events."

The German planes passing across Syria numbered about thirty, and, according to the Free French Agency, were escorted by French fighters. They had no German markings and

Continued on Back Page

Daily Mirror

MAY 28

11,686   ONE PENNY

gistered at the G.P.O. as a Newspaper.

AVENGED
LAST HOURS OF THE BISMARCK

Finished Bismarck

It was H.M. cruiser Dorsetshire which sank the Bismarck. Her torpedoes finally avenged H.M.S. Hood.

Dorsetshire is of 9,975 tons, has 850 crew, carries thirty-six guns, eight torpedo tubes, and a catapult plane—that's her in the picture below.

"SINK THE BISMARCK WITH TORPEDOES."
The cruiser Dorsetshire received this order at a few minutes to eleven yesterday morning.
At 11.01 the Bismarck sank.
H.M.S. Hood was avenged.

So ended the 1,750-mile chase in which the mighty German battleship had fled from Arctic seas to within 400 miles of her base, shadowed night and day for eighty hours with never a hope of escape from the relentless hunters of Britain's Navy and Air Force.

No hope of escape, for Britain took no chances.

From the moment Bismarck left Bergen last Thursday (as the Prime Minister revealed in Parliament yesterday) she was doomed.

Her sinking of H.M.S. Hood made her destruction doubly sure

How Lucozade brings desperately needed energy

500 PLANES IN RAID ON FLEET

FIVE hundred German planes attacked the British Fleet off Crete, incessantly bombing our warships in the greatest sea and air battle.

It was fought after the destruction of the German troop convoy bound for Crete.

Scores of enemy planes were clawed out of the sky by the Navy's A.A. gunners who faced without flinching the intense fury of a bombardment that lasted all day.

And the German pilots machine-gunned British sailors—survivors from the six warships which were sunk—as they struggled in the water. And the six warships—without exception—were sunk by the bombers.

A correspondent on board a British battleship in this battle described the Luftwaffe's attack as the most sustained ever carried out by the Germans against the British Fleet.

Streams of German bombers and dive bombers took part. The air was filled with the scream of bombs and the roar of planes as the Germans came swooping from the skies to drop their bombs.

Swam for Lives

They scored hits on one destroyer and a cruiser, forcing our men in the water to swim for their lives.

Then the Germans deliberately turned their attack upon them, bombing and machine-gunning them as they tried to reach the nearby coast of Crete.

The battle reached its peak on Thursday in the Kithera Straits, between the western end of Crete and Greece, when 100 bombers of all descriptions attacked incessantly from 5.30 a.m. until 8.15 p.m.

It began when the Battle was pushing its way through the Kithera Straits to help the cruisers which had broken up the attempted German landing from the sea.

Two cruisers had been damaged by bombs during the attack, but the German planes

Contd. on Back Page, Col. 1

Navy 'Boy' Sank Her

CAPTAIN B. C. S. Martin, of H.M.S. Dorsetshire—the man who sank the Bismarck—began his career in the Navy in 1907 as a bluejacket boy.

He is only the second ranker officer to reach the rank of captain since commissioned rank was opened to the lower deck in 1912.

In the Battle of Jutland he served in H.M.S. Malaya as a warrant officer.

He was awarded his commission in the first lower deck promotion list after the battle.

Captain Martin's wife told the *Daily Mirror* at her Havant home last night:

"It is the most thrilling news I have ever had. It makes up for the fact that I haven't seen him for over a year."

Tall, fair-haired, with steel-blue eyes, Captain Martin looks a typical Navy officer.

He has four children. Kenneth, 21, is training in the R.A.F. A second son, 17, is at school.

One of his daughters Vivienne, 15, was named after her father's destroyer command, H.M.S. Vivienne, at the time she was born.

Captain B. C. S. Martin, of H.M.S. Dorsetshire.

WINANT IS GOING BACK TO REPORT

The United States Ambassador in London, Mr. J. G. Winant, is to return to the U.S. this week-end to report.

This is his first trip home since his appointment three months ago.—Associated Press.

Spotted—the Hunt Begins

As soon as aircraft reported that she had put out from Bergen, the skies and the seas were quartered by our ships and planes as a dog will quarter a field on the scent of a hare

Planes picked her up first. Then the Navy took up the hunt. The cruisers Norfolk and Suffolk were ordered to take up their positions in the Denmark Straits to lie in wait for her.

And they didn't have long to wait.

On May 23, look-outs on the Norfolk spotted the Bismarck speeding on a south-west course through storms of snow and sleet with drifting mist bringing visibility down to a mile.

Now the real hunt had begun. All through that night they dogged her, and in the morning a Sunderland flying-boat sighted her, too.

All the time mighty ships of Britain's Fleet were racing to join action with the Bismarck and cruiser Prince Eugen that was escorting her.

Shadowed by Planes

H.M.S. Hood and H.M.S. Prince of Wales came within action distance.

Then came the shell that struck Hood and sank her. Prince of Wales was also damaged. And Bismarck, damaged, too, started her dash for safety.

But still on her trail were the Norfolk and Suffolk. Aided now by reports from Catalina flying boats which reported every trick and device of the Nazi to evade action. Nothing could shake them off.

The flying boats were hopping from cloud to cloud, seeing, but themselves mostly unseen.

When they did come into clear sky Bismarck put up a terrific barrage of shells.

One Catalina was hit, her hull holed in several places, but with such a prize beneath her she did not turn back.

Cont. on Back Page, Col. 4

WHEN patients are too weak and ill to take ordinary sustenance the effect of giving LUCOZADE is little short of miraculous. LUCOZADE is unique. It is a palatable drink containing glucose, the source of bodily energy. Absorbed directly into the bloodstream without needing question, LUCOZADE brings prompt vital strength and builds up reserves of energy. Soon the patient is strong enough to take other food and is then well on the road to recovery. Doctors and nurses say when other food is rejected patients have no difficulty in keeping LUCOZADE down. Keep a bottle at home. You will find many occasions to use it

—BENEFIT FROM—
Lucozade

—TONIC
—FOOD
—BEVERAGE

At all Chemists and Stores 2/3 per bottle including purchase tax.

U.S. FORCES IN STRATEGIC POSITIONS: ROOSEVELT'S SPEECH, BACK PAGE

Daily Mirror

JUNE 2

No. 11,692 — ONE PENNY
Registered at the G.P.O. as a Newspaper.

Rations Set Style

EXTRAVAGANT dress fashions — and white weddings— will be off until after the war with the new clothes rationing order, which came into force yesterday.

Coupon clothes will be bought to last, and hopes that "date" will be shunned by the careful shopper.

These are among forecasts which resulted from conferences of heads of clothing firms who met yesterday to consider the effects of the scheme, explained fully in the official announcement on page 4.

IRAQ'S KING SAFE

FEISAL, boy-King of Iraq, is reported to be safe in Bagdad, where all is quiet following the armistice under which Britain promises full aid in re-establishing the legal Go rnment.

British troops are to be allowed right of transit, and Germans and Italians are to be interned.

The Regent entered the capital yesterday morning.

A Cairo report says all fighting in Iraq ceased at 8 a.m. yesterday.

It is stated that the Iraqi Governor of the Mosul area, where the chief oilfields are situated, is an opponent of Raschid Ali, and it is considered that the Iraq trouble is virtually at an end.

The Swiss radio says the oil wells are intact.

In Syria, however, there are signs that Germany, with Vichy's approval, is preparing to land troops.

NIGHT HUNS— RECORD BAG

FIVE week-end night raiders were brought down over Britain—three on Saturday and two on Friday, bringing the May toll of night bombers to 156—a record.

London completed three weeks without bombs—longest period since heavy raids began in August, but in Merseyside some damage was done on Saturday night, and there were a number of casualties.

London last night had an Alert, which was followed by gunfire.

Raiders were also reported over the North Midlands and North-West England.

Footwear may be dearer. Obviously sales will be affected, Mr. E. J. Ward, a director of boot firms, said yesterday, but overheads will not decrease.

Families with incomes up to £5 will barely be affected, but higher wage earners and their families will have to do without many things to which they have been used

Run on Shops Stopped

The danger of a widespread run on clothing shops was one reason for the introduction of rationing, and it has come just in time or there would have been little left to ration. This was stated yesterday by an official of the Board of Trade.

Three women — a business girl, a housewife and an experienced buyer—and five men of varying ages and tastes, all experts in trade administration —advised the Board of Trade.

Dress designers prophesy a

Contd. on Back Page. Col. 4

NEW CAIRO AIR C-IN-C

APPOINTMENTS of a new Air Commander-in-Chief for the Middle East and an air marshal for "special duty" were announced last night.

Acting Air Marshal A. W. Tedder, Middle East Deputy Chief, is the new Commander-in-Chief and is promoted to Temporary Air Marshal. He succeeds Sir Arthur Longmore, who becomes Inspector-General of the R.A.F.

Sir Arthur has been advising from this country since the beginning of May, having been recalled for consultation.

Air Marshal Tedder is a Scot, aged 50. He was flying in the last war, has held several commands, and was at the Ministry of Aircraft Production before going to the Middle East as Sir Arthur Longmore's deputy last November.

Air Vice-Marshal A. T. Harris is seconded for special duty and becomes Acting Air Marshal.

Air Vice-Marshal N. H. Bottomley becomes Deputy Chief of Air Staff, and Air Vice-Marshal R. M. Drummond becomes Deputy Air Commander-in-Chief Middle East.

Temp. Air Marshal Tedder.

The margarine page in your ration book should be intact with twenty-six coupons on it. Some of them may have been cancelled, but they are valid for buying clothes.

If you have deposited your ration book or the page with your margarine retailer, get it back from him.

If any of the coupons have been detached by your retailer (this should not have been done), go to your local food office, who will see that you get them back.

All over the country men and women — especially women—are raising their own rationing problems. Here are answers to some:—

CLOTHES QUERIES—

CAN A HOUSEWIFE POOL FAMILY COUPONS?
Yes.

CAN I GET WOOL FOR KNITTING TROOP COMFORTS?
Yes, through W.V.S. and other voluntary organisations who have the wool ration free.

UNTIL CLOTHING CARDS ARE ISSUED TO SERVICE OFFICERS CAN THEY BUY REGULATION UNDERWEAR?
Yes, but they must sign a slip to say they are going to use it personally.

WILL RANKERS BE GIVEN EXTRA COUPONS FOR LEAVE CLOTHES?
No, they will be expected to wear uniform or the civvies they had before rationing.

WILL WOMEN IN UNIFORM BE GIVEN COUPONS FOR DANCE FROCKS, STOCKINGS, SHOES ETC.?
Probably, but this is a matter which must be decided between the Army and the woman. Commanding officers will have the final say.

WILL CIVILIANS IN UNIFORM HAVE TO GIVE COUPONS FOR UNIFORM?
The Board of Trade is thrashing this out. Clippies and London Transport workers will have to provide coupons. "But," said a London Transport official, " our workers will have to have suits or frocks and coats for off duty, and how can they get them if their coupons are used up?"

Local authorities can supply clothes without coupons, so the A.F.S. and A.R.P. workers will probably be given uniform. The position of postmen and policemen has yet to be discussed.

★

DOES UNRATIONED LACE AND NET INCLUDE FINE MUSLINS?
No, muslins are classified as cotton piece goods and rationed according to width. You can make a white lace wedding dress without coupons . . . but will have to give them up for the slip to go underneath!

ARE THIN OILSKIN "POCKET" MACS RATIONED?
Yes.

CAN I BUY UNRATIONED TABLECLOTHS, COLOURED SHEETS OR BLANKETS AND MAKE THEM INTO FROCKS AND JACKETS?
Yes, if you're that clever with your needle.

HOW ARE FURNISHING FABRICS DISTINGUISHED FROM CLOTHING FABRICS?
They aren't. If you buy them in the piece they will cost you coupons. But the shopkeeper can make them up into curtains or upholster your furniture without coupons.

★

WILL GLAMOUR GIRLS, DANCERS, NIGHT CLUB HOSTESSES WHO ARE BOMBED-OUT GET EXTRA ALLOWANCES?
Yes. Account will be taken of their jobs. People will be given enough clothes to enable them to carry on their business.

WHAT ARE THE PENALTIES FOR ILLEGAL TRAFFIC IN COUPONS?
An offence would be against the Defence Regulations and punishable on conviction by a term not exceeding three months, or a fine of £100, or both; and on conviction on indictment to a term not exceeding two years' imprisonment or a fine of £500, or both.

CAN I BUY THE BOY FRIEND A BIRTHDAY TIE?
Only if you take his ration book along with you.

ARE COLLARS ATTACHED TO SHIRTS RECKONED SEPARATELY FOR COUPONS?
No. A sports shirt with attached collar will require five coupons, eight if made of wool. A shirt with the usual two separate collars will take seven of your coupons, each separate collar costing a coupon.

IF I AM OUTSIZE, WILL I BE ALLOWED EXTRA MATERIAL FOR DRESSMAKING?
No.

WILL EXPECTANT MOTHERS RECEIVE EXTRA COUPONS TO KNIT FOR THEIR BABIES?
No. They will have to use their own clothing coupons.

We'll Tell You—

See Page 7

RAF GUARD 15,000 OUT OF CRETE

BRITISH fighter planes on defensive patrols guarded British ships in the Mediterranean as our troops were being evacuated from Crete. Yesterday, according to the R.A.F. Middle East communique, in battles over the sea they destroyed five Ju. 88 bombers and two Italian bombers, and damaged other Ju. 88's so severely that several are unlikely to have got back.

German radio stated last night that many of the British troops left the island in sailing boats and fishing boats and other small craft.

Earlier yesterday the War Office announced our withdrawal from Crete—but did not say whether it was complete—"after 12 days of what was undoubtedly the fiercest fighting of this war."

FIFTEEN THOUSAND OF OUR TROOPS HAVE BEEN WITHDRAWN TO EGYPT. IT WAS ADDED THAT OUR LOSSES IN CRETE HAVE BEEN SEVERE.

The decision to evacuate Crete was taken on Thursday, and by Saturday night 10,000 men had arrived in Egypt.

Local air superiority, due to strategic advantages, was the deciding factor in Germany's favour.

Used 1,000 Planes

Germany, with bases in Greece, was able to throw 1,000 planes, including troop-carriers, into the battle. Many of these were dive-bombers and the dive-bombing was the worst of the war.

It was impossible to maintain fighter aerodromes in Crete, and we had to rely on the slower long-range fighter

Contd. on Back Page. Col. 5

SUSPECT 'KEY' SPY

Suspected as being a leading Nazi spy, Paul Huissel, 39, is being questioned by G-men in New York (cabled John Walters last night).

When Huissel was arrested he tried to destroy a list of Nazi agents throughout the world.

Children's Teeth in War-Time

A.R.P. PAY INCREASES

WHOLE-TIME members of civil defence services holding certain intermediate ranks are to receive higher pay than the basic rate of the rank and file, which is £3 10s. a week for men and £2 7s. a week for women.

The increase will date from June 1.

Generally, the increase will be 2s. 6d. for the first rank above the rank and file, such as the leader of a first-aid party, or senior warden, and a further 2s. 6d. for such ranks as post or head warden, or ambulance service section leader in charge of four or more ambulances.

Such ranks as first-aid party supervisor will receive a further 2s. 6d. or 5s. according to the number of parties under control, as will section leaders in the ambulance service.

SFAX BOMBED AGAIN

At Sfax in Tunisia, the Italian ship previously attacked on May 30 was again bombed and machine-gunned. Three direct hits on the ship were followed by clouds of black smoke.

Even in war-time a child's diet must contain a proportion of sweet things for nourishment and energy. But sweet things cause acid-mouth which encourages the germs which attack and decay the teeth. To protect the teeth a child's toothpaste should contain plenty of 'Milk of Magnesia,' the most effective neutralizer of mouth acid known. Only in one toothpaste is 'Milk of Magnesia' brand antacid to be found and that is Phillips' Dental Magnesia which contains 75%.

Children who use this pleasant tasting toothpaste regularly, always have the whitest teeth and are practically free from decay with its distressing toothache and disfiguring gaps. Get a tube today.

Sold everywhere
7¼d., 1/1 and 1/10½d.
(Including Purchase Tax).

PHILLIPS' DENTAL MAGNESIA

'Milk of Magnesia' is the trade mark of Phillips' preparation of Magnesia

Daily Mirror

JUNE 3

No. 11,693   ONE PENNY
Registered at the G.P.O. as a Newspaper.

One Frock for Six Girls—

Don't panic. You don't all wear it at once. You form a clothes club, pool your coupons, buy one or two good "occasion" dresses and take it in turns to wear them.

And before you decide that such a scheme couldn't possibly work take a look at Page 7 where "Daily Mirror" experts give you full details of this plan to overcome the rationing difficulties, and answer the questions you have already raised.

It's up to you to look as attractive now as ever you did. With care and thought and patience, you can.

Which means—don't rush off to spend your money and your coupons now. You'll gain by waiting.

★

AXIS PREPARES FOR ANOTHER BIG PUSH

THE AXIS IS ALREADY AT WORK ON ITS NEXT STEP IN THE BATTLE FOR CONTROL OF THE MEDITERRANEAN.

Hitler and Mussolini met in the Brenner Pass yesterday to discuss Hitler's next move.

It may be made in Spain, for Franco yesterday was preparing to let German troops through to attack Gibraltar and Petain was getting ready to keep his troops out of the way by withdrawing them sixteen miles back from the northern frontier of Spain.

At the same time General Weygand, boss of Vichy French North Africa, rushed by air to Vichy for a talk with Petain. And General Dentz, Vichy French High Commissioner of Syria, declared a state of siege in Eastern Syria—the Syria-Iraq frontier—and tightened frontier control.

HITLER and Mussolini were accompanied by their Foreign Ministers and Army Chiefs-of-Staff — Ribbentrop and Keitel, Ciano and Caballero.

They found plenty to talk about. The talks lasted five hours, with Hitler doing most of the talking and official announcements afterwards made the usual claim that they took place "in a spirit of friendship and ended in complete agreement."

It was the tenth meeting of Hitler and Mussolini, and the sixth since the war started.

One topic discussed was the possibility of further action by the United States involving French West Africa, the Azores and other Atlantic islands.

Vichy's decision to withdraw French troops from the Spanish border is one of the concessions made by Darlan in his recent talk with Hitler.

Hitler's Guarantee

In exchange the demarcation line between the occupied and unoccupied zones in France is to be moved an average of twenty-two miles to the north.

It is also reported that Hitler told Admiral Darlan that in exchange for more intimate collaboration he would guarantee the territorial integrity of Metropolitan France.

Hitler agreed to guarantee the French African possessions if they were really controlled by Vichy.

This statement by Hitler decided Admiral Darlan to take energetic action against General de Gaulle.

It is understood that Italian objection to Hitler's guarantee ing French territory demanded by Italy from France is holding up the campaign against General de Gaulle.

DAY RAIDER HITS SCHOOL

Diving out of clouds, a hit-and-run raider dropped bombs near a large private house used as a senior mixed school on the North-East coast of England in daylight yesterday.

The building was badly damaged. But it was empty.

Two enemy planes were destroyed by our fighters yesterday evening, one of the new high-flying Messerschmitts over the Channel and a bomber off the north-east coast.

Cyprus Is Ready

Cyprus, believing it may be next on Hitler's list, is speeding completion of its defence plans.

Old people and children have been moved to the hills, and some English women and children have left for the mainland.

Defence regulations announce penalties for looting and spreading alarmist rumours. They also give the authorities wide powers of commandeering.

The "Cyprus Post" says:—"We are nearest our own air bases and aerodromes on the mainland, as were the Germans in Crete. The British Fleet is only a few hours from the island. And within the island itself we have a body of defenders as resolute and determined as those who fought so magnificently in Crete.

"All the factors make a German attempt against Cyprus an extremely hazardous venture.

"Cyprus now stands between the enemy and his grandiose Middle East ambitions."—Reuter.

NO COUPON TIME LIMIT

IF you have not spent all your 66 clothes coupons by May 31, 1942, it is probable you will still be able to use them, the Board of Trade told the "Daily Mirror" last night.

"We do not want to penalise people for failing to use coupons they do not really need," said an official, "so there will probably be an extension."

There is no compulsion to use the twenty-six "wearable margarine" coupons in your food book before August, when the 40-coupon clothing book should be ready.

You need not apply for it until the end of May, 1942. So if you don't want to buy any clothes before Friday, May 29, 1942, you could spend twenty-six coupons on that day, change your book, and spend the other forty all at once.

Towards the end of the week the Board of Trade will issue a slightly longer list of rationed and coupon-free articles to remove any doubts about the present list.

It will be more specific with such items as "other garments, including corsets," because there are doubts whether certain articles come within the rationing scheme.

An official said: "Without coupons it will be impossible to buy materials such as cretonne, which are to be made up into curtains, even though the shop actually makes the curtains.

"But household textile goods already made up do not require coupons."

Army's Clo' Cards

SOLDIERS are to have some form of clothing ration cards. The number of coupons has not yet been decided.

Other ranks will receive fewer coupons than officers, who have to buy all their clothes, while the men have a free issue of uniform, underclothing, socks and boots.

Until their cards are issued soldiers can buy such items as handkerchiefs, which are not an Army issue, on production of a document signed by them stating that the articles are for their own personal use. The order must be countersigned by the C.O. and bear the orderly-room stamp of his unit.

Officers also can buy from retailers before their cards are issued by certifying on the shop bill that the goods are for their personal use

If the Laundry—

THE Board of Trade is to set up a special committee to deal with cases of people who lose their clothes otherwise than due to the wear.

Should your laundry lose your clothes or have them destroyed through accident, fire, or are stolen, you will be given coupons to make up for the loss.

You will have to apply to the Board of Trade and produce evidence.

★   ★   ★

WEST END stores think women will be buying "all Contd. on Back Page, Col. 4

He Didn't Have a Day Off

TEN million workers in Britain had a day off yesterday. But not Hitler. He was meeting Mussolini on the Brenner Pass to prepare another blow at this country, as you see in Column 4.

We want more weapons, more tanks, more planes, more ships. But yesterday factories on war production were either stopped or working on short time. Shops and offices were closed.

Whitehall, nerve centre of the Empire, was ticking over on only one cylinder. Keymen of Government departments and war material factories all over the country had taken the day off.

But cinemas, theatres, restaurants, amusement parks, flower shops and public-houses were not closed. They were doing a roaring trade.

One Pub—300 Cars

Outside one public-house, a few miles from a provincial city, there were 300 cars at lunch time.

There were long queues outside places of amusement, and even restaurants. Food stocks ran out at some restaurants and they had to close early.

Greyhound racing and football attracted bumper crowds.

In blitzed towns heaps of rubble and twisted metal which once were buildings had a special fascination for thousands who apparently had no better way of spending Bank Holiday. They came from outlying districts, many of them bringing their children, to see the bomb wreckage.

But they hindered no one. There was no one to hinder. Most demolition workers, too, were off for the day.

Many of London's buildings Contd. on Back Page, Col. 2

Picture is of Tommy Maloney, typical 3-year-old Londoner.

It stands on the mantelpiece of Mrs. President Roosevelt's room in the White House, Washington, U.S.A.

Because Mrs. Roosevelt has adopted Tommy under the Foster-Parents' Plan for War Children. She sends £2 16s. for his keep every month.

So from his bombed London home in Sutton-street, Shadwell, E.1, Tommy has gone to Mrs. J. B. Priestley's home in Herefordshire. Every detail of Tommy has been sent to Mrs. Roosevelt, and she writes letters to him and sends him presents from America.

The Cockney Picture in Roosevelt Home

LEFT BEHIND, FED BY R.A.F.

R.A.F. planes have made heavy attacks on Crete, dropped supplies to isolated parties of our troops on the island, and continued to guard ships engaged in the evacuation.

The story of this three-fold task was told in this R.A.F. Middle East communique last night.

"Large formations of fighter aircraft of the R.A.F. and the South African Air Force continued their protective patrols throughout yesterday over H.M. ships and merchant vessels engaged in the evacuation from Crete.

"Enemy aircraft were repeatedly intercepted and many were attacked. Several others, including four Ju 87's and three Ju. 88's, were compelled to retire before they had time to make an attack.

"On the previous day a Cant 1007 and a Me. 110 were destroyed by our patrols while on similar duty. These are in addition to the seven enemy aircraft claimed in yesterday's communique.

"During the night of Saturday-Sunday our heavy bombers attacked aerodromes at Maleme and Candia (Heraklion).

"Several fires were started Contd. on Back Page, Col. 1

MAY CONTROL BOOT REPAIR PRICES

A hint that the Government is to control boot repair prices was given by Mr. Harry H. Payne at a Boot Trades' Federation conference at Leicester.

He denied that repairers were guilty of overcharging.

People who bought shoddy boots and shoes might need all their coupons to keep them in footwear, said Mr. H. Treadwell, and Mr. A. P. Watts, secretary of the federation, said there should be a law preventing such footwear.

GONDAR ROAD CUT

Abyssinian Patriots have cut the road from Debra Tabor to Gondar.

Daily Mirror

JUNE 11

No. 11,700 — ONE PENNY
Registered at the G.P.O. as a Newspaper.

Government to Take Your Eggs

IF you keep more than twelve chickens the Government is to take all your eggs.

This was announced last night by the Food Ministry, which is to form a national company to buy the eggs from packing stations.

Every poultry-keeper, except those with twelve birds or less on one holding or selling eggs for hatching, will soon have to register with the packing station or a licensed dealer or collector—who will be known as "approved buyers."

Producers should complete arrangements with packing stations or approved buyers not later than Saturday week.

VICHY OFFERS FULL AID TO THE GERMANS

ADMIRAL DARLAN announced last night that Vichy is not going to oppose Germany any more, and will allow nothing to stand in the way of collaboration leading to a separate peace without waiting for the end of the war.

He made his announcement, admission of complete subservience to Hitler, in a broadcast appeal to the people of France to follow the leadership of Vichy "on the path of salvation."

He did not mention Britain or Syria in his speech over Vichy radio.

"The armistice does not mean peace yet for France. It is yet only an armistice, and that means that France has recognised in Germany the victor.

"Therefore France has submitted to Germany and entered a new line of national development.

"Germany wants to rebuild the whole of Europe in a new way under her supervision. We have the choice of collaboration or death.

Way of Salvation

"The Government of France has chosen the way of salvation, and that means not to oppose any more the hereditary enemy of France.

"You have the choice and you can go with the Government or not. But you should know what it means not to follow our leadership

"Under the orders of Marshal Petain we can rebuild France in collaboration with Germany. That is the first task of the Government.

"The second is to prepare for peace in so far as the vanquished can, creating a favourable atmosphere for a peace convenient for France

"The French Government will not allow anything to stand in the way of such an atmosphere.

"The situation is unprecedented. We have to negotiate with a nation at war with another country.

"The third task of the Government is to gain for France an honourable place in the new Europe."

'WARNED' BY CHURCHILL

MR. CHURCHILL astonished the House of Commons yesterday by warning it—and the people of Britain —that it would be a mistake to get into the habit of calling for explanations of any particular reverse. He was replying to the debate on Crete.

No full explanation could possibly be given without revealing valuable information to the enemy.

"I have not heard," said Mr. Churchill, "that Herr Hitler had to attend the Reichstag and say why he sent the Bismarck on her disastrous cruise without waiting a few weeks for her to be accompanied by the Tirpitz.

"I have not heard any announcement that Signor Mussolini has made a statement on the reasons why the greater part of his African empire and 200,000 of his soldiers are in our hands

Only One Part

"I think it would be better if I were permitted on behalf of the Government to choose the occasions for making statements about the war, which I am anxious to do."

Then he dealt with questions about the defeat in Crete.

Why were there not enough guns provided for the two serviceable airfields?

No one could judge without an intimate knowledge of our resources.

"A man must be a perfect fool," said the Premier, "who thinks that we have large quantities of anti-aircraft guns and aircraft lying about unused at the present time.

"Lamentable"

"Our position is very different from that of the enemy. Mr. Hore-Belisha made today a thoughtful contribution to the debate, but he used a very different mood and tone in the speech recently delivered in the country.

"That, at any rate, makes it necessary for me to say that the state in which our Army was left when he completed his two years and seven months' tenure of the War Office during the greater part of which he was also responsible for production and supply was lamentable.

"We were assured that every essential, more particularly that very class of weapons—A.A. guns anti-tank guns and tanks

Continued on Back Page

THE BEER EFFORT

It is in the public interest that the production of light beers should continue at the present amount, the Food Minister said in the Lords yesterday.

OUR WAR DEAD 90,000

British war dead—excluding civilians—total 90,000.

At least 85,000 of these were from the Mother Country, Mr. Churchill told the House yesterday, repudiating German propaganda.

In Crete, in killed, wounded, missing and prisoners we lost 15,000 men, excluding Greeks or Cretans.

These British units fought in Crete: The Rangers, Black Watch, Argyll and Sutherland Highlanders, Leicestershire Regiment, Welch Regiment,

York and Lancaster Regiment, Royal Artillery, Royal Engineers and Royal Marines, "who formed that very gallant rearguard."

Of 2,000 Royal Marines landed in Crete, 1,500 became casualties or prisoners. Naval loss of life alone in these operations exceeded 500 officers and men. At the same time we also lost 1,500 men in Hood.

"I believe that about 5,000 Germans were drowned in trying to cross the sea and at least 12,000 were killed or

wounded on Crete itself," Mr. Churchill continued.

"In addition the German Air Force lost more than 180 fighter and bomber aircraft, and at least 250 troop-carrying aeroplanes at a time when our air strength is overtaking the enemy."

The Air Minister said aircraft lost or destroyed in the air on all fronts in the first four months of this year, according to British official communiques, totalled 360 British, 494 German and 637 Italian.

No Rationing of Fuel Yet

RATIONING of coal, gas and electricity has again been under consideration, but "there is no reason to think that fuel will be rationed in the immediate future," the Under-Secretary for Mines, told the Daily Mirror last night.

"The point when rationing is necessary has not yet been reached, but the utmost economy in all forms of fuel is needed," he said.

Should rationing of coal, gas and electricity come a Ministry of Fuel will be established.

Children's Teeth in War-Time

Even in war-time a child's diet *must* contain a proportion of sweet things for nourishment and energy. But sweet things cause acid-mouth which encourages the germs which attack and decay the teeth. To protect the teeth a child's toothpaste should contain plenty of 'Milk of Magnesia, the most effective neutralizer of mouth acid known. Only in one toothpaste is 'Milk of Magnesia' brand antacid to be found and that is Phillips' Dental Magnesia which contains 75%.

Children who use this pleasant tasting toothpaste regularly always have the whitest teeth and are practically free from decay with its distressing toothache and disfiguring gaps. Get a tube today.

Sold everywhere
7½d., 1/1 and 1/10½d.
(Including Purchase Tax).

PHILLIPS' DENTAL MAGNESIA

'Milk of Magnesia' is the trade mark of Phillips' preparation of Magnesia.

AIR ARM FOR ARMY

THE Army is to have an "air arm" incorporating the features the Germans have "carried to such extraordinary perfection."

This was promised by the Premier in the Commons yesterday.

"I think it is of the utmost consequence that every division, especially every armoured division, should have a chance to live its daily life and training in close and precise relationship with a particular number of aircraft that it knows and can call up at will and need," he said.

"Under its own command?" asked an M.P.

Mr. Churchill: Certainly, for the purpose of everything that is a tactical operation.

He pointed out that it was not possible last year to provide this on a large scale without encroaching on other domains more vital to our safety but added:

"It is our intention to go forward on that path immediately and to provide the Army with a considerably larger number of aeroplanes suited entirely to the work they have to do and, above all, with the development of that wireless connection between ground forces, the air and the military which the Germans have carried to such extraordinary perfection."

NAZI PLANE CRASHES IN FLAMES IN EIRE

A German plane crashed in flames near Churchtown, Carnsore Point, Co. Wexford, yesterday morning and all five occupants were killed.

French Retreat in Syria

VICHY last night admitted a retreat in Syria, where British and Free French troops, said to number several divisions, are advancing on Beirut and Damascus.

Between the Jebel Druse and the Hermon mountains, it was stated, the advanced posts of Quinetra and Sheikh-Miskine have retreated after fighting a delaying action and causing severe casualties.

Vichy admitted also that British forces had gained a foothold near the River Litani, north of Tyre. This naval landing was made to prevent the blowing up of a bridge according to Cairo.

Our troops are now on the outskirts of Damascus.

British warships are shelling positions along the coast. Villages have been razed.

On Turkish Frontier

Ankara reported that British troops, advancing across Syria from Iraq, have reached the Turkish frontier near Kamechlie, gaining control of the Turkey-Iraq railway.

The R.A.F. communique from Cairo said patrols were carried out from warships. Five enemy aircraft were shot into the sea.

Night bombers heavily raided the island of Rhodes, where German air troops await orders.

Hostile aircraft raided Haifa, Palestine. Casualties and damage were slight. A.A. fire downed one plane, damaged others.

Before the last raider had returned to the German controlled base at Aleppo, British aircraft were over the aerodrome, bombing aircraft on the ground and the flare path along which planes were landing.

PECKED BY A PEACOCK

Pecked on the face by a peacock in a Dunfermline park yesterday, Albert Dexfield, 4, was treated in hospital.

WOMEN WIN SMOKE RIGHT

WOMEN are to have equal tobacco rights with men.

Proposals now under discussion to ban the sale of cigarettes to women, the refusal of many tobacconists to serve them during the present shortage, have caused resentment, and the proposals will be dropped.

The Rev. Albert D. Belden, B.D., a psychologist pointed out the harm that might arise from such a measure.

"Nerve Sedative"

"It is profoundly unjust," he said. "Also smoking is a nerve sedative, and where there is a need for this it is possible that some other more harmful habit—such as alcoholism — might be formed."

Dr. Maude Royden, woman preacher, said:—

"If there really is a shortage of cigarettes, then I think they should be rationed equally between men and women serving in the Forces or doing work of national importance."

1900s Sign June 21

ALL men born in the year 1900, whatever their occupation or employment, must register on June 21, unless they have already done so under the Registration for Employment Order.

Those born between January 1 and June 30, 1900, both dates inclusive, will be registered under that order.

Those born between July 1, 1900, and December 30, 1900, both dates inclusive, will be registered under the National Service Acts.

This means that the 40 age group — excepting those already 41—will be called up for military service.

This exhausts the existing Royal Proclamation, and another will be needed if it is necessary to extend the age limit.

Men born between January 1, 1922, and June 30, 1922, both dates inclusive, must register on July 12 under the National Service Acts.

Daily Mirror

JUNE 14

No. 11,703 — ONE PENNY
Registered at the G.P.O. as a Newspaper.

R.A.F. TORPEDO BATTLESHIP ON RAID BID

AXIS RAID FOR VICHY, LOSE 7

YOUR NEW RATION

BUTTER rations are to be reduced, but cheese and preserves will be increased. Milk will be rationed in the autumn or early winter.

Details of these food changes, announced yesterday, are:

At the end of this month butter allowances will be halved (4oz. to 2oz.), but cheese rations will be doubled (1oz. to 2oz.).

In August, the ration of preserves — jam, syrup and marmalade — will be doubled, becoming 1lb. per month instead of 8oz.

The Ministry of Food emphasised yesterday that the total fats ration of 8oz. will remain unchanged.

It will be possible to obtain 2oz. butter, 4oz. margarine and 2oz. cooking fats, or, alternatively, 2oz. butter and 6oz. margarine.

Heavy Workers Unaffected

The special cheese ration of 8oz. per week for underground miners, agricultural workers and vegetarians will be unchanged.

Plans are being made for a milk rationing scheme to be introduced in the autumn or early winter.

There is no likelihood of any shortage during the summer.

Today is the last day for registering for eggs.

ENEMIES IN OUR MIDST

OUR food position is secure. But there are enemies in our midst—the cheats and the racketeers.

The Food Minister said that in a broadcast last night, adding:—

"We must root them out. That is the job of the public as well as the Food Ministry."

He appealed to shoppers to supply evidence of infringements of regulations.

"We shall chase the racketeer relentlessly," he said. "Do not leave it entirely to us. Give us the evidence. These people are public enemies."

He mentioned the coming increases in the cheese and jam rations. Cheese was important to many, and he was buying larger quantities of cheese from the Dominions.

Less butter would be shipped. That was why the public would have to take 6oz. of their fat ration in margarine.

BIG manufacturers of sweets and chocolates yesterday decided to control all prices immediately and ensure fairer distribution. The plan will not mean more sweets.

Restrictions are to be placed on the small manufacturers who have come into the market since the shortage.

It is hoped that the plan, approved by the Food Ministry, will stamp out—

Racketeers, who have been flooding the market with inferior goods at top prices; and

Profiteers, who have been breaking up block chocolate and selling at more than double the makers' retail price.

RAID BID

THE R.A.F., striking another crippling blow to Hitler's dwindling Navy, scored at least one hit on a pocket battleship with a half-ton torpedo yesterday.

The battleship, either the Lutzow (ex-Deutschland) or the Admiral Scheer, was brought to a standstill off Mandal, most southern tip of Norway.

Later, she was sighted being nursed towards the Skagerrak by her escort of five destroyers, sailing at greatly reduced speed.

The enemy force was first found by the pilot of a Blenheim. They were heading north, starting out on a raid on shipping or a land station—possibly attempting the task the Bismarck failed to do.

Patrolling off the Norwegian coast, he sighted a Heinkel seaplane, which disappeared into the clouds. He followed.

A few minutes later he emerged into a clearer patch. Directly below him he saw the enemy warships. He reported to his base and a force of bombers was sent to the attack.

One Beaufort scored a direct hit amidships. A mass of smoke billowed from the battleship.

Another Beaufort launched its torpedo into the smoke.

The Beaufort which attacked first was piloted by a flight-sergeant from Coventry, and the navigator was a sergeant from Saskatchewan (Canada).

Less Than 100ft. Up

"The enemy force was in a clear patch of weather," said the pilot last night. "The pocket battleship was in the middle with one destroyer immediately ahead and two others on either side.

"They formed a pretty effective screen from torpedo attack. It was fairly light—you could see for several miles—and we flew in at right angles across the stern of the battleship.

"Then we made a rightabout turn and came back at her broadside, less than 100ft. up.

"I had to skid the aircraft round the stern of one of the destroyers to get into position to drop the torpedo. The destroyer was very close. We could see its camouflage in detail.

"I let the torpedo go just after we had passed the des-

Continued on Back Page

REDS DENY HUN MOVE

SOVIET Russia, broadcasting in many languages last night, officially denied "senseless" rumours that—

Hitler has made demands on the Soviet;

Negotiations for a new pact have taken place; and

Russia is preparing for war with Germany.

Moscow radio branded the rumours as "clumsily concocted propaganda by forces hostile to Germany and the U.S.S.R."

FINNS' BAN ON FOREIGNERS

Finland has restricted travel by foreigners in northern and border areas. Similar restrictions were imposed during the war with the Soviet Union, and before transit of German troops last autumn.—Associated Press.

THE Axis air forces lost at least seven bombers yesterday, the first day they tried to help Vichy against the Allied troops in Syria.

Four Junkers 88s bearing Italian marks were destroyed by Australian fighters while attacking a British naval squadron off the port of Sidon.

Australian planes shot down three Nazi planes, also Junkers 88s, and damaged others in other operations.

Damascus is practically surrounded by Allied forces. But because of negotiations being carried on in an effort to avoid bloodshed, the entry of our forces has been delayed.

A Free French division holds the city's strong outer defences.

Continued on Back Page

Navy Bag Dozens of U-Boats

The Navy has sunk dozens of U-boats which suddenly appeared in the Atlantic.

The day is not far distant when we will be equally safe at night from bombing attacks as we are during daytime.

THESE statements were made by the Minister of Labour at Leicester last night.

"We have made night fighting expensive to the enemy," he said. "Scientists, engineers, skilled craftsmen and craftswomen are building up armour for night defence.

"I shall be the last to hold out false hopes, but the day is not far distant when you will be equally safe at night in your beds as you are now during the daytime."

Sir Ronald Cross, on his way to Australia as new High Commissioner, said in New York:

"The ratio of loss of war materials in the Battle of the Atlantic is probably less than that of raw materials and foodstuffs, which are less vital to Britain."

F.D.R. PLEDGE TO THE KING

In a birthday message to King George, President Roosevelt yesterday declared:—

"The United States has pledged full material assistance to Britain and her Allies in this struggle, and I assure your Majesty of the determination of the Government and people to carry out that pledge.

"I do not need to emphasise my sympathy and the sympathy of the whole American nation in the great cause of freedom and justice which the peoples of the British Empire are now so valiantly defending."

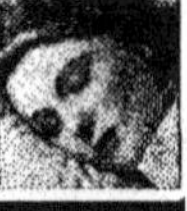

Boy Aged Six Saves Sister from Canal

Charlie Crosby, 6, with his sister Eileen, 3, whom he rescued from a canal. A brother was drowned. Story on page 3.

Daily Mirror

JUNE 18

No. 11,706 — ONE PENNY

Registered at the G.P.O. as a Newspaper.

Get In on the Ground Floor

Radiolocation, Britain's secret weapon, is more than a war weapon. Its devices will be of tremendous importance to air and sea navigation in peacetime.

It can help to guide home ships and planes as easily as it now detects and locates the enemy.

Radio technicians who answer the appeal for men to handle this weapon will be "getting in on the ground floor" of one of the most remarkable developments of modern times, says Sir Philip Joubert.

200 PLANES BLITZ NAZIS' INVASION PORTS BY DAY

BRITAIN launched her anti-invasion air offensive last night.

In full daylight an R.A.F. armada, estimated at 200 planes, carried out an hour upon hour raid on the French coast around Boulogne, loosing hundreds of tons of bombs on stores and equipment which Germany had been building up for the assault on England.

Crowds cheered on the English cliffs as the R.A.F. forces swept back victoriously.

Thirteen enemy fighters were shot down it was stated in London last night, We lost ten. The Germans claimed that twenty British planes were shot down, with the loss of only one of their machines.

For an hour and a half people watched from the cliffs at one south-east coast town while our warplanes swept up and down the Channel.

Once three Me. 109s were seen flying very high but as a squadron of our planes approached they hurriedly retreated to France.

As our bombers came home, people noticed that they were flying at only a few thousand feet, and that they had retained their formation.

The planes roared over the coast, and small groups of people at this point waved to the returning pilots.

Explosions

Explosions on the French coast were so heavy that some of our latest bombs were believed to have been unloaded in salvoes.

Visibility was good. The French cliffs between Boulogne and Calais could be seen through the evening haze.

"It was a cheering and grand sight," an eye-witness said in describing the return of our air armada.

Other fighter squadrons also took part in the operations, some patrolling over the Channel at a great height, acting as a screen.

Others swept up and down the Straits only a short distance off the French coast.

Time after time these planes, often less than 500ft. above the water, flew within easy reach of the French coast.

BRITAIN HAS SECRET AIR WEAPON

BRITAIN'S big secret weapon, best-kept secret of the war, is radiolocation, which finds enemy raiders in dark, fog or daylight, Air Marshal Sir Philip Joubert revealed last night.

With the revelation came a call throughout the Empire for at least 7,000 men and 3,000 women technicians —radio-'tecs — to operate and maintain this new weapon, now in use all over the country.

It was on a spring morning in 1935 that a group of young scientists gathered around a mass of complicated apparatus on a lorry near Daventry found that at last their long research had triumphed.

Radiolocation was born.

Now, no enemy ship or plane can approach our shores without its presence being indicated by radiolocation.

It keeps ceaseless, silent watch over these islands—and many parts of the Empire as well.

Making the first official announcement of this, until now, secret weapon, Air Marshal Joubert described it as one of the most important factors in our war organisation.

In Battle of Britain

It has played an invaluable part in the detection of night bombers and led to their destruction by our fighters, he said.

Details of radiolocation are still secret, but this much can be said: It is a system of sending out far beyond our shores other waves which are unaffected by fog, darkness or cloud.

Any solid object crossing the path of these waves sends back a reflection to the detecting station.

The men chiefly responsible for perfecting radiolocation are Mr. Robert Alexander Watson Watt, former Scientific Adviser on Tele-communications, and now Scientific Adviser to the Ministry of Air

Continued on Back Page

Sollum—Huns in Danger

WAVELL'S armoured forces thrusting into Libya, now fighting one of the heaviest tank battles of the war, have reached Capuzzo and threaten to cut off the enemy troops in Sollum.

This was stated in Cairo early today.

It was added that our troops had not yet occupied the fort at Capuzzo.

Fierce fighting is continuing in the triangle formed by Sollum, Capuzzo and the Halfaya (Hellfire) Pass, where the British took up the offensive three days ago.

Big Tank Battle

Most of the fighting has been taking place on top of the Sollum Escarpment, but so far it has consisted almost entirely of encounters between mechanised units, with no hand-to-hand fighting.

German and Italians are taking part. Both sides are jockeying for a position in the Sollum - Capuzzo - Halfaya Pass area, which could be used as a good jumping-off place.

Reports reaching Cairo last night said one of the biggest encounters with tanks took place on Sunday on the escarpment near Halfaya Pass.

CLIMATE WORRIES THEM

A Nazi soldier in a report from the North African front broadcast over the Deutschlandsender said:—

"The immense sandy wastes before us are full of hidden danger. From behind any rock an Australian soldier may shoot us. The heat is terrific, our eyes are red with sleeplessness and swollen by sandstorms."

RATION YOUR SMOKING

HELP to solve the tobacco problem by rationing yourself. That appeal is made to you by tobacconists.

The question of issuing an official appeal to the public to cut down their consumption was discussed by a meeting of tobacco wholesalers and retailers in London last night.

There is no hope of production catching up with consumption," said the secretary of the National Union of Retail Tobacconists yesterday.

"There is only one other way to meet the situation—by self-rationing."

Tobacco comes into this country at the cost of lives and ships, at the cost of food and the munitions of war.

IS A SMOKE REALLY WORTH ALL THAT?

RAIDERS OVER NORTH EAST

Enemy aircraft were active over the north-east coast early today.

Mr. Robert Alexander Watson Watt, who played a big part in perfecting the new anti-aircraft device. He is Scientific Adviser on Tele-Communications at the Ministry of Aircraft Production.

He is a Scot, 49, and lives quietly with his wife in a detached house near the gates of Richmond Park, Surrey.

U.S. TO HOLD NAZIS

TO ensure that Roosevelt's order freezing Axis funds is not evaded, Germans in the U.S. have been forbidden to leave the country.

Berlin yesterday protested against the decision to expel German Consular officials. Washington will not be surprised if the Nazis withdraw their entire Embassy staff.

Several Central and South American countries may soon follow the example of the United States and expel all Nazi Consular officials. Mexico and Cuba are reported to be about to do so.

Heavy guards of police surrounded the German Consulate at New York, where Nazi officials were burning documents in preparation for their departure.

G-men said that the departure of German Consular officials would be the end of a huge espionage ring which has been sending detailed reports of arms sent to Britain.

("Daily Mirror," British United Press and Associated Press messages.)

NEW G.O.C. FOR NORTHERN IRELAND

Major-General V. H. B. Majendie has been appointed G.O.C. Northern Ireland District.

He is 55. In the Great War he was a temporary lieutenant-colonel at the age of thirty.

GREECE D.S.O.

Commander Kenneth Michell, M.V.O., D.S.C., R.N. (retired), is awarded the D.S.O. for distinguished services during the withdrawal from Greece.

Offensive by French in Syria

"**W**E are no longer on the defensive but have taken the offensive on all fronts to drive the enemy from Syria," reported Vichy's General Dentz last night.

Ankara reports said the Vichy Air Force in Syria had been heavily reinforced, and that yesterday it used for the first time Nazi dive-bombers with French colours.

Ankara radio declared that a brilliant strategical move had taken the Allied forces by surprise, and that supply columns behind Damascus had been cut. Despite this, however, pressure on Beirut continued.

A heavy detachment of the French Fleet has been sighted

Continued on Back Page

War Derby Today

Bouverie's tip for today's war Derby (2.0, Newmarket) is given on page 3.

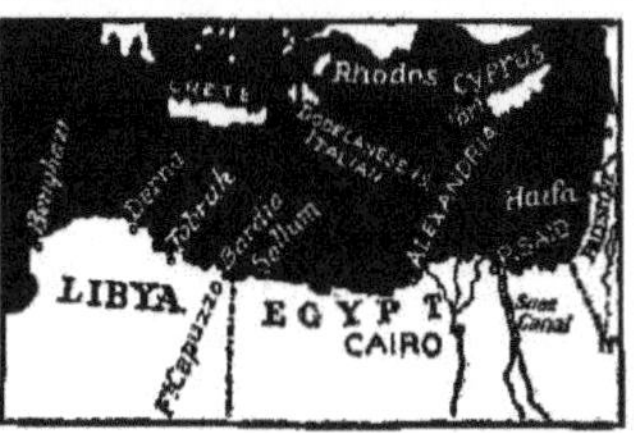

Today's high spot of the war, Fort Capuzzo, towards which Gen. Wavell has made a penetration. Germans have had to rush reinforcements from Tobruk;

Miss Mary Owen, family nurse, was relief steward in the bombed steamer St. Patrick. When the ship was sinking her chief thought was for the captain's twenty-year-old son, whom she had tended from birth. But she went to the aid of the passengers and saved a girl who had lost her lifebelt.

Full story on page 3.

Daily Mirror

JUNE 19

No. 11,707   ONE PENNY

Registered at the G.P.O. as a Newspaper.

HITLER-TURK PACT

GERMANY and Turkey signed a ten years' "pact of friendship" in Ankara last night.

Von Papen, German Ambassador to Turkey, and M. Sarajoglu, Turkish Foreign Minister, initialled the agreement at 9 p.m. Chief points in the pact are:—

1. The signatories agree to respect each other's territorial integrity.

2. Both countries will in future discuss in a friendly manner all questions of common interest.

Germany and Turkey have also signed a declaration extending and speeding up trade relations.

They will both stop Press and radio propaganda hostile to each other.

The Pact carries the proviso that it is signed "without prejudice to the present obligations of both countries."

This presumably includes the Turkish Pact of friendship with Britain.

Although the terms of the Pact may not appear to be of great advantage to Germany, Berlin began to exploit its propaganda value as soon as it had been signed.

A German spokesman said that the Pact meant that Turkey was staying out of the war.

Britain Kept Informed

Just as the Wilhelmstrasse at the beginning of the war came to terms with Russia, thereby removing the possibility of Poland's neighbour causing trouble, so now the German Army can pursue operations in the Near East without fearing Turkish opposition, the spokesman said.

M. Sarajoglu, in a statement to the Press, said:—

"It is with great pleasure that I notify the signature of this Treaty of friendship, and I consider it to be my duty to make special reference to the very special efforts that my friend, Herr Von Papen, who knows my country well, has made to bring about this result."

It is suggested in London that Turkey resisted the full German demands, and countered with modifications which the Germans have accepted. Turkey kept Britain aware of the progress of all stages of the negotiations.

Honour to Unseen Hero

THE people of a tiny Yorkshire village are going to raise an everlasting memorial to a brave R.A.F. pilot they have never seen.

He is the pilot who, fearing his disabled plane would crash on the village, stayed at the controls and guided the machine over some fields.

It was too late to bale out then, and he was killed. But the villagers and their children still lived.

The airman hero was Sergeant-Pilot Bruce William Smeaton, R.A.F.V.R., 22. The village was Cutsyke, near Pontefract.

The villagers have collected £19 for the memorial to their unseen hero. Part of the money may go to provide a "Bruce Smeaton Shield" for good attendance at Cutsyke School, and part towards some trophy at Smeaton's own school.

Smeaton's parents live at Carshalton Beeches, Surrey.

"Bruce came home on leave recently," Mrs. Smeaton told the *Daily Mirror* yesterday. "While he was with us he had a photograph taken because he had just been given his air gunner and the gunner's wife

◆ Continued on Back Page

J. B. PRIESTLEY, referring to a statement in one of A. P. Herbert's radio postscripts, said yesterday:

"My friend Alan Herbert says that there is no Act of Parliament granting us the right of free speech. There is no Act of Parliament granting me the right to light my pipe. I never heard such nonsense.

"We are half way to Nazism when we begin to ask for Acts of Parliament to tell us what to do in our ordinary life."

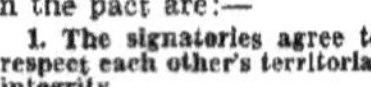

TO

Stating that the B.B.C. was controlled by the Ministry of Information, which in turn was controlled by the War Cabinet, he added: "I make no reference to the series of history lessons with which we are being entertained on Sunday evenings." Mr. Priestley said he had learned that "exalted circles" considered him one of the most disliked people in Britain. But all he had suggested was that the war could not be fought on a negative basis.

"We'll never get people to fight the Gestapo by asking them to do so for the Eton and Harrow match, Ascot and the Boat Race," he declared.

"One of the chief horrors of this war is the gobbets of blah and guff we have to hear and listen to day after day."

Our Subs. Destroy 8 Vessels

BRITISH submarines operating in the Ægean and the Mediterranean have sunk eight enemy vessels, including one carrying troops.

These feats were announced by the Admiralty last night.

The Italian tanker Giuseppina Gherardi (3,319 tons) was torpedoed and sunk in the Ægean.

Also destroyed there were three Greek sailing ships and an Italian schooner.

The sailing ships were on their way to one of the German-occupied islands in the Ægean. One of them was laden with German personnel and stores, and another was laden with drums of oil.

The schooner was carrying troops, ammunition and stores.

In the Central Mediterranean an enemy supply ship of about 4,000 tons was sunk. Another supply ship of about 2,500 tons and a 500-ton auxiliary sailing ship were also sunk.

R.A.F. WIN CHANNEL FIGHTS 9-4

NINE enemy aircraft were destroyed yesterday when the R.A.F. again made extensive sweeps of the Channel and Northern France. Four of our fighters were lost.

A military camp was one of the objectives which was heavily bombed.

This was the R.A.F.'s second day of mass raids on the invasion ports (see page 3), and large forces of warplanes were again engaged.

One formation of fighters which crossed the S.E. coast on its way numbered several squadron

Waves of Fighters

A heavy bombardment was heard along the Kent coast shortly after the bombers and fighters had been seen flying out across the mist enshrouded Straits.

Explosions of salvos of bombs and a cannonade from the Nazi A.A. defences along the invasion coast indicated that a big attack had been launched.

Later in the evening waves of fighters crossed and recrossed the coast, disappearing in the direction of Boulogne and Calais.

A German supply ship of 1,500 tons was bombed and hit by a Coastal Command aircraft off Brest yesterday.

OLD SCHOOL TIE —SECOND HAND

The old school tie in future may be second-hand. One school, Worksop College, is to open a second-hand clothes shop.

The headmaster, announcing this at yesterday's Special Day, said Sunday suits would no longer be compulsory.

VAN OF FOOD LOOTED

More than £200 worth of rationed foodstuffs, including sugar, bacon and meat, was stolen from a provision merchant's van owned by R. Gunner, Ltd., of Lever-street, E.C.

WE DEMAND SURRENDER OF DAMASCUS

DAMASCUS, capital of Syria, had till 5.30 this morning to surrender.

A message from General Sir Henry Maitland Wilson, Allied G.O.C., was broadcast late last night calling on General Dentz, Vichy High Commissioner, to withdraw his troops from Damascus to save it from attack.

An answer was demanded by 5.30 a.m. today. If no answer arrived, or if Dentz rejected the demand, we would take military action immediately, said General Wilson's message.

More British troops have been landed in Syria, it was revealed in Cairo last night.

While strong Allied forces were closing in on Damascus last night fresh troops were being landed ready to back them up.

Earlier messages from Jerusalem said that Free French troops had reached the western suburbs of the Syrian capital.

The Free French, with Colonel Collet and the Circassians, closed in attacking infantry and artillery.

Vichy artillery was shelling the road to delay the fall of the city, but Allied forces were steadily closing in ready for the final assault.

Until Last Bullet

Kuneitra, cross-roads village of strategic importance, was held by a small body of Allied troops who had to yield it after a terrific fight against vastly superior numbers.

But it was won back again inside 150 minutes with the help of reinforcements.

The big fight in which we temporarily lost it is a story of heroic defence by a famous London regiment of the line —one that won fourteen V.C.s in the last war.

From dawn on Tuesday they held off for twelve hours a Vichy force which outnumbered them by five to one.

They were a company against a battalion, but it was a story of the sublime sacrifice of infantrymen who fought until their last bullet was expended.

"I have seen German and French infantry in action, but I have never seen a finer lot of men," said a Free French officer, referring to the Britons.

"Surrounded on all sides, they maintained their fire and handled grenades with the greatest efficiency, inflicting terrible losses on the enemy."

SAYS WIFE LOVED EARL

Sir Delves Broughton, on his fourth day in the witness-box stated yesterday that his wife was madly in love with the Earl of Erroll.

Sir Delves is charged at Nairobi, Kenya, with murdering the Earl.

Asked by counsel for the prosecution whether Lord Erroll's death was not a satisfactory solution to his domestic troubles, Sir Delves replied: "No, I don't think the average man would have resumed married life with one who had been madly in love with another and was still."—Associated Press.

ALEXANDRIA BOMBED

Alexandria was raided for an hour early yesterday. The Egyptian Home Office said: "Few bombs were dropped. There is only one casualty.

'Ultimatum to Russia'

Reports were current in Ankara last night that Rumania has dispatched an ultimatum to Russia demanding the return of Bessarabia and that the German attack on Russia started some hours ago at fifteen points.

"We know that these rumours are not true," a Columbia broadcast from Ankara stated, "but it is significant that they are being spread tonight."

We Bar Finn Port.—Back page.

ACTED LIKE A MIRACLE

A MARVEL HOW IT MOVES INDIGESTION

Dear Sirs,   *Wolverhampton.*

I have given MACLEAN BRAND Stomach Powder a trial and feel it my duty to let everyone else know of the great relief I have obtained from it.

The first dose I took acted like a miracle on my stomach. It has removed all pain since I have taken it regularly after each meal, and I think all stomach sufferers should give it a trial. I shall always recommend it to sufferers of stomach trouble and indigestion as I think it a genuine cure if taken as directed.

My next-door neighbour has been suffering from indigestion this past week. He has purchased a bottle and tells me it is a marvel how it moves indigestion. So here you have a good recommendation from two sufferers and you are at liberty to make use of this letter if you wish to do so.

Yours faithfully (Mr.) G. H. A.

MACLEAN BRAND Stomach Powder is the speediest and most successful remedy for Pain, Flatulence, Heartburn, Nausea, and the proved safeguard against those dread complications Gastritis and Stomach Ulcer.

Remember, this remarkable remedial combination, used in hospitals, and approved by doctors and nurses alike, is the one that really does bring instant relief and ends the trouble entirely.

MACLEAN BRAND Stomach Powder is obtainable from all chemists. Price 1/5, 2/3, 3/7½. Also in Tablet Form in 7d. boxes or bottles at 1/5 and 2/3 (including Purchase Tax). Only genuine if the signature ALEX C. MACLEAN appears on the package.—(Advt.)

VAST NEW TECHNICAL ARMY

BRITAIN is to have a vast Civilian Technical Corps, in which men from abroad will be enrolled for service in the repair and maintenance establishments of the Navy, Army and R.A.F.

This was announced by the Secretary for Air in the House of Commons yesterday.

A great number of skilled technicians will be required. The R.A.F. alone, it is learned, will need 25,000 men.

Meanwhile, under a Ministry of Labour scheme, boys and girls of sixteen are to be trained as radiotees—to work with Britain's new weapon against enemy raiders.

It was stated in Ottawa last night that 2,500 Canadians are studying radio mechanics in Canadian universities in preparation for service here as radiotees. They will be ready for overseas about September.

A call for an American civil expeditionary force of from 15,000 to 30,000 men to help man Britain's secret detectors was made in Washington last

night by the British Embassy's Air Attache.

The appeal was made with the full consent of the U.S. Government, and a recruiting station will be opened at once in New York.

The Americans will be stationed in various outposts throughout the British Isles. They will sail from Canada in heavily-convoyed liners.

The British Civilian Technical  Continued on Back Page

Daily Mirror

JUNE 21

No. 11,709   ONE PENNY
Registered at the G.P.O. as a Newspaper.

Wife Defies Hitler

Frau Thomsen, wife of Dr. Hans Thomsen, German Minister in Washington, has told him she will never return to Hitler's Germany even if he is recalled.

★ This split between Hitler's chief representative in the United States and his wife caused a sensation in diplomatic circles last night.

Friends of Frau Thomsen, famed for her outspokenness, said her decision is the result of six years' of strain to which she has been subjected as a prominent figure in a diplomatic organisation teeming with intrigue and ambitious wives. ★

War Minister's Daughter Is Red Delegate

Miss Janet Margesson.

"DAILY MIRROR" EXCLUSIVE

THE People's Convention, led by extreme Leftist Mr. D. N. Pritt, K.C., M.P., and chiefly organised by the Communist Party, has been asked by the American Youth Congress to send a delegate to its meeting in Philadelphia. It has chosen—

Miss Janet Margesson, 23, debutante daughter of wealthy Captain the Right Hon. David Margesson, M.C., M.P., His Majesty's Secretary of State for War in the Government which the People's Convention seeks urgently to replace.

Miss Margesson, presented at Court in 1936, is flaxen-haired and blue-eyed, a student at Newnham College, Cambridge, and a declared Socialist.

The People's Convention has applied to the Home Secretary for an exit permit to enable Miss Margesson to fly by Clipper to America.

Communists Active

The American Youth Congress has many young Communist groups associated with it, and Mrs. Roosevelt had described its stand against conscription as "claptrap."

Originally a supporter of the youth movement, she finally broke with it "because its opposition to conscription and short-of-war aid to Britain is contrary to the best interests of democracy."

In an exclusive interview with the *Daily Mirror*, Miss Margesson said:—

"We are not defeatists. We want to see the Nazis crushed.

"But I hope to give the American people a new angle on the conditions in Britain.

"I'm excited about my trip, and I shall do my best to live

Continued on Back Page

DEATH LEAP TO SWINGTIME

Playboy Richard Johnson, 24, engaged two swing musicians in Chicago yesterday and ordered them to play "Music, Maestro, Please," on the roof of his hotel.

While they played, Johnson threw himself into a gay swing dance, stepping and twirling towards the edge of the roof.

Suddenly he threw up his hands like a diver and plunged to his death to the street seventeen storeys below.

NAZIS GIVE US NOTICE—F.D.R.

PRESIDENT ROOSEVELT last night described the sinking of the Robin Moor as ruthless and the act of "an international outlaw," and declared that the United States did not propose to yield the use of the high seas to Germany.

Reaction in Washington was that American merchantmen will soon be armed.

The President made his pronouncement in a special Message to Congress, which permitted him to use stronger language than would have been required by a formal diplomatic note.

WAR WORK 'SHORTAGE'

MR. JACK TANNER, president of the Amalgamated Engineering Union, yesterday replied to a statement issued by the National Union of Manufacturers describing as "fundamentally untrue and mischievous" his charges of inefficiency and delay in war production.

He told the A.E.U. Conference at Llandudno yesterday that he had reports on a questionnaire sent out to thirty-one firms engaged on aircraft production—some big firms, some small, some doing sub-contract work.

The reports indicated that there is a shortage of work in 22 cases. Three state that there is a temporary shortage or shortage in particular departments.

Shortage of Material

Only six say there is no shortage of work. Shortage of work means that skilled and other grades of workers are idle or are not working to capacity.

Reasons given are shortage of material, metals, tools and machinery, delays in renewing contracts, changes in design, and so on.

"Our members claim that much of this is due to bad management and lack of organisation, planning and preparation," said Mr. Tanner.

TURKS CUT OUR NEWS

Ankara radio, for the first time last night, failed to broadcast the British war communiques.—British United Press.

Commenting on the Turkish-German friendship pact, German radio said last night: "There was little difference between the English broadcasts from Ankara and the B.B.C.—this will, of course, now cease."

Wintringham Resigns From H.G.

TOM WINTRINGHAM, expert in modern warfare and military correspondent of the *Daily Mirror*, has resigned from his post of lecturer and adviser to the Home Guard Training School, because he feels that the War Office cannot develop the Home Guard to the full strength that possible and necessary."

The present policy of the War Office, he declares in his letter announcing his resignation, "starves the Home Guard of manpower and materials and treats as relatively unimportant all those ideas of modern training tactics that I have been advocating."

Strong Language

The President had apparently particularly chosen to make his pronouncement a special message to the Congress of the American people so that his protest might be couched in the most forceful language at his command.

"This Government can only assume that the Government of the German Reich hopes, through the commission of acts of cruelty to helpless and innocent men, women and children, to intimidate the United States and other nations into a course of non-resistance to German plans for universal conquest.

"The Government of the German Reich may, however, be assured that the United States will neither be intimidated nor will it acquiesce in the plans for world domination.

"The Government of the United States holds Germany responsible for the outrageous and indefensible sinking of the Robin Moor. Full reparation for the losses and damages suffered by American nationals will be expected from the German Government."

Tom Wintringham

Here are the reasons for his resignation which Wintringham gives in his letter to the War Office.

The failure of the War Office properly to use two of his associates, Hugh Slater, military strategist, who helped Wintringham to found the first Home Guard school at Osterley, and Roland Penrose, camouflage lecturer to the Home Guard.

The decision of the War Office, despite the lesson of Crete, to close down recruiting for the Home Guard.

The lack of a strong framework of full-time officers and

Continued on Back Page

SOVIET GO TO HITLER

THE Soviet Ambassador in Berlin is to be received by Hitler. He has already visited Ribbentrop, Nazi Foreign Minister, many times and had conversations lasting two hours.

This was reported from Sweden yesterday as warnings were given in Britain and the U.S. that Axis-inspired rumours of war on Russia might be intended to mask some other move by Hitler—perhaps an invasion of Britain.

"I cannot avoid the opinion that the mobilisation of large numbers of German troops on the Russian border would be precedent to any German invasion of England," said Senator Walter P. George, chairman of the Foreign Affairs Committee of the U.S. Senate.

Moscow radio said tens of thousands of schoolchildren are being sent from all over the country to Ural and other Asiatic mountain regions "to enable them to spend a vacation in open country."

Finns Called Up

The German radio in its English propaganda transmission was deliberately obscure. It said: "The reason for the slighter activity of the German Luftwaffe over Britain may soon become apparent to a surprised world."

Meanwhile, the Finns called upon all age classes from 1897 to report.

As in reply to all this, the Moscow radio said yesterday that the lessons of the Russo-Finnish War and of the German campaign in the west are being applied in military exercises now taking place.

THREAT TO TRADE WAR

British economic warfare against Germany appears to be threatened with difficulties because of the Turco-German pact.

A new German trade drive launched yesterday aims to secure chrome and copper ores on which British buyers have options but are unable to take out of the country owing to scarcity of transport.

Nazi circles claim that the Turkish Government can hardly continue to assist the British monopoly over vital Turkish raw materials.

Assurances that Turkey would never permit passage of German troops or war materials across her territory were given to the British Ambassador, Sir Hughe Knatchbull-Hugessen, in Ankara yesterday.

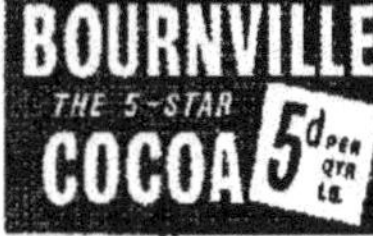

EXTRA daylight—extra night work—mean that, literally, night and day you're making more calls on your strength than ever before. Last thing at night take a drink; but make it a drink that puts strength into you. Bournville Cocoa does that in these five ways.

It gives you :
★ EXTRA FOOD VALUE
★ IRON — THE BLOOD ENRICHER
★ PHOSPHATES—FOR HEALTHY GROWTH
★ AID TO DIGESTION
★ VITAMIN D—VITAL TO HEALTH

BOURNVILLE
THE 5-STAR
COCOA 5d per qtr lb

LESS THAN PRE-WAR PRICE

100,000 WANTED IN SIX MONTHS

"IT is vital that we should get, in the next six months, 100,000 women for the A.T.S. and very nearly as many for the W.A.A.F.

"The need for the A.T.S. is the more pressing just at the moment."

That appeal was made last night by the Parliamentary Secretary to the Ministry of Labour.

He continued: "It is thought in some quarters that the A.T.S. are not allowed to take off their tunics when on duty in hot weather, or wear engagement rings, or use make-up.

"None of these things is true, and although they must sound trivial the sooner the truth is known the better."

He added that to release men it was essential that no job should continue to be done by a fit, strong man, if it were possible for that job to be done by a woman.

Daily Mirror

JUNE 23

No. 11,710 — ONE PENNY

Registered at the G.P.O. as a Newspaper.

RED BOMBERS HIT BACK AT HUN INVASION

All Our Aid to Russia

─ Daily Mirror ─

Geraldine House, Fetter-lane, E.C.4. Holborn 4321.

'WAR ON TWO FRONTS'

WE begin with a warning—Hitler's attack upon Russia must not "for a day, for an hour, for a moment," be used as an excuse for any weakening of our attack upon Hitler.

On the contrary, this latest and largest of Nazi wars is a signal to us, a call, an incentive to renewed and intensified effort.

Through the R.A.F., and with every other means in our power we must continue to smash at Germany in the West, as, in the East, Hitler begins his enormous gamble on the other front. "The war on two fronts." It is for us, and for the U.S.A. to see to it that Hitler faces what he has always proclaimed that he would never face.

Don't Heed the Dope!

We must not relax. We must not suppose that Germany cannot attack us too. We must not heed the two dope-opinions that have so often spoiled our chances in the past.

The first dose of dope was already being administered yesterday—mainly from American sources.

There was cheery talk in Washington about our having "gained time." The U.S.A. would have time "to meet all commitments." Hitler would now not invade Britain. The position in the Pacific would be "eased"—this from Mr. Hoover. "Put on the nightcap and take a snooze." No, put on the gas-mask and be ready.

"Bulwark Against Bolshevism"

The second bottle of dope *may* be swilled by the lurking appeasement crowd everywhere—including our own country. In Vichy-land, in Spain, in certain Catholic circles, will it be possible for Hitler, after all his lies, to raise again the spectre of Bolshevism?

Evidently he intends to try!

His ravings revert to the old cries of "Mein Kampf." Jewish-Bolshevism, the Communist doctrine of international Jewry the appeal to God against godless Russia —all the hoary cant streams anew from the mouth of the man who has simply no convictions whatever about any social, political or religious doctrine—except the one doctrine that he is predestined to rule the world.

The doctrine of power at any price! With or without God—though preferably without Him, except as Hitler's gauleiter. The real God is Hitler himself. The Deity may come in useful as a sop for noodles.

The War Has "Spread"

That said, we can at least rejoice in this answer to one of our wealthy leftists' absurdly naïve question: "Must the war spread?" It must. It has. Even Stalin cannot avoid it. Japan, Spain, Sweden, the U.S.A. may now be forced to assist in the spreading of Hitler's world war. Presently the only country against which Hitler will not have declared or made war will be Germany.

The Germany that hurls its masses hither and thither as cannon-fodder at the Nazi command. The Germany that hears its Fuehrer eat his own words and reverse his declared aims. The Germany that swallows all lies, believes all that it is told and can utter no word of protest or even of perplexity. It is for us by swift action so to batter this politically imbecile Germany that Hitler may have to make his last war in holding its stupid snout to the grinding machine of his wild ambition.   W. M.

GERMANY, aided by Italy, Finland and Rumania, let loose her mighty forces against Russia at 4 a.m. yesterday, attacking in five powerful spearheads on a 1,500-mile front stretching from Finland in the north to the Black Sea in the south.

Stalin swiftly hit back. Russian bombers raided towns in East Prussia soon after German, Rumanian and Finnish troops had crossed the frontiers at several points and huge forces of German planes had bombed Russian-occupied Esthonia and the towns of Shitomir, Kiev and Sebastopol.

German and Finnish troops are making a joint attack from Finnish territory on the Karelian isthmus, and are striking in the direction of Leningrad, close to the Russian frontier with Finland, according to the Helsinki correspondent of the Stockholm newspaper. "Allehanda."

"Prisoners Taken"

Up to a late hour last night all news of the fighting came from Axis sources. One German correspondent said that the Nazis "took prisoners in the first few minutes," that there was "no black-out on the Russian side of the frontier," and that the Russian airmen were completely inexperienced and behaved like children.

The official German News Agency last night claimed that Nazi planes had been attacking aerodromes, airfields and A.A. positions. "Their attacks appear to have achieved considerable success," said the Agency with unexpected caution.

So far this news does not take one beyond the opening stages of the new war.

A Helsinki report received via Washington admitted that Russian planes had "bombed the Finnish port of Alskar and had attempted to bomb" two warships.

Before hostilities began the Russian Army withdrew from the marshy eastern plain of Bessarabia according to Ankara.

The Russians are said to have

Continued on Back Page

ITALY, TOO

Italy considers herself at war with Russia since 5 a.m. yesterday. Count Ciano, Italian Foreign Minister, is reported by Rome Radio to have informed the Russian Ambassador — British United Press

Scene of the fighting between Germany and Russia . . . the thick black line marks the 1,500-mile frontier stretching from as far north as Finland, down to the Black Sea. The shaded territory west of the frontier is under Nazi command; east, is the vast country of Soviet Russia.

BRITAIN is to give full aid to Russia. Mr. Churchill gave this assurance in a broadcast to the world last night.

"We shall give whatever help we can to Russia and to the Russian people," he said.

"We shall appeal to all our friends and Allies in every part of the world to take the same course and pursue it as we shall steadfastly to the end.

"WE HAVE OFFERED TO THE GOVERNMENT OF SOVIET RUSSIA ANY TECHNICAL AND ECONOMIC ASSISTANCE WHICH IS IN OUR POWER AND WHICH IS

Continued on Back Page

27—1 R.A.F. BAG

Twenty - seven more Me 109's were destroyed by Hurricane and Spitfire pilots over France yesterday afternoon. We lost one plane.

The R.A.F. was continuing its offensive sweeps over the northern coast of France, in co-operation with small forces of bombers.

Yesterday's score follows a bag of twenty-eight Me 109's on Saturday.

As the British fighters approached the French coast, scores of German fighters were sent up in an attempt to stop them.

The operation was carried out to schedule and the Messerschmitts brushed aside as squadron after squadron swept on its way

Daily Mirror

JUNE 27

No. 11,714 — ONE PENNY
Registered at the G.P.O. as a Newspaper.

FIGHT HUN NOW CALL TO U.S.A.

PRESIDENT ROOSEVELT'S Home Secretary, Mr. Harold Ickes, last night called to the United States to enter the war IMMEDIATELY.

" The American people must, not tomorrow, but now, make the supreme choice," he declared. "Britain needs all-out aid.

" We must offer in full measure the blood, sweat and tears which the heroic British are yielding at the call of Churchill."

Meanwhile the Soviet Ambassador to U.S.A., M. Oumansky, was visiting the State Department (Foreign Office) for his first conference with Mr. Sumner Welles, Under-Secretary, since Germany attacked Russia.

Mr. Ickes was speaking for the Committee to Defend America by Aiding the Allies, at Hartford, Connecticut.

" We are living too long on borrowed time," he said.

" We must decide now whether we are willing to buy a craven's truce, as Lindbergh urges, or to work and sacrifice, fight, and die if need be, for liberty, in the inspiration of Washington, Lincoln and Churchill.

WREN'S BANNS ON WARSHIP

A LEADING Wren has made naval history by being the first in her service to have her marriage banns called on board a vessel afloat.

She is Daphne Dorothy Briand, 23, cook on H.M.S. Eaglet, anchored in a Liverpool dock, where officers attached to the naval base eat and sleep.

When the senior chaplain called her banns she was described as " Spinster, of his Majesty's Ship Eaglet."

Leading Wren Briand, who works a twenty - four hour watch and sleeps on board when on duty, is to marry A/C1 Fitter Ronald Float, 25, next week-end. The wedding is to take place in the village of Outwood, near Redhill, Surrey.

The couple have known one another for two years.

Leading Wren Briand intends to return to duty after her wedding.

" I have been in uniform for eighteen months now and I think the service is grand," she told the Daily Mirror.

Wrens' living quarters ashore are referred to as " ships," and have galleys, cabins and mess rooms, but not until recently have Wrens been allowed to sleep on real ships.

This was permitted after the blitzes on Liverpool.

SPAIN GIVES US A PROMISE

The Spanish Government has undertaken to give full satisfaction regarding the anti-British demonstration outside our Embassy in Madrid, with assurances against repetition.

DOUBLE SUGAR ISSUE

HERE'S news from the Food (and Drink) Front.

Your sugar ration is to be doubled for each of the four weeks, June 30 to July 27.

This extra 2lb. is your allowance for preserving stone fruit. You must keep it until the fruit is available.

★

The meat ration for the week beginning next Monday will remain at 1s., the Ministry of Food stated last night, adding: "A statement on the future meat ration will be made within the next few days."

This announcement followed "certain statements that have been made."

Earlier it had been unofficially reported that the meat ration will soon be increased, possibly by an extra 6d. per head.

★

Sunday hours of opening may soon be introduced in public houses throughout the country unless brewers get a bigger and fairer distribution of raw materials.

Present output of beer is only slightly less than before the war. Yet "Closed—No Beer" notices are now frequent.

In badly blitzed areas there is no shortage.

Brewers are to ask the Ministry of Food for a more equitable distribution of materials so that breweries supplying reception, military and industrial areas will get part of the supplies now going to the "thinned-out" districts.

"Where there are big troop concentrations, soldiers go from pub to pub drinking them dry and giving the local 'regulars' no chance." said one brewer.

★

Babies are now being guaranteed half an orange each day at Greenwich infant welfare centres.

Fruit brokers and greengrocers are reserving weekly quotas for the centres.

Help to prevent rickets.

Lewisham and Woolwich are issuing to mothers tickets which may be traded for oranges at greengrocery shops.

LUTZOW AT KIEL

It is believed that the German pocket battleship Lutzow, which was hit by a torpedo from a Coastal Command plane off Norway on the night of June 12, may be lying at Kiel.

Since the night of the torpedo attack Kiel has been raided four times. Three other German warships are bottled up at Brest.

FRENCH SHIP CAPTURED

A British cruiser has captured the French steamer Indo-Chinois in the South Atlantic after thwarting the crew's attempt to scuttle the vessel, according to a New York report. —Associated Press.

Hun Road to Dakar

EIGHT thousand refugees, rounded up in Marseilles by the Gestapo and packed into French merchant ships, have been landed at Algiers and other North African ports to speed up work on Hitler's road across the Sahara to Dakar, French West Africa.

Refugees arriving at Gibraltar yesterday said that hundreds of Poles, Czechs and Frenchmen were arrested in their homes or in food queues.

They were given two hours to pack under police supervision and then marched in small groups to the docks, writes the "Daily Mirror" Gibraltar correspondent.

Officials in Marseilles state frankly that they were ordered to supply sufficient refugee labour to guarantee completion of the road before autumn.

Among the thousands of recent chain-gang arrests were a large number of intellectuals.

Marshal Badoglio has arrived in Spain. Technically "on holiday" he has been constantly hopping to and from North Africa.

The Italians are believed to have charge of the construction of this road, but owing to the slowness of the work appealed to Germany to supply extra labour.

There is no doubt that Hitler is planning to occupy North and West African ports, for which the Sahara road to Dakar is vital.

The Golden Chance

"The Russo - German war does not provide a breathing spell, but needs greater effort.

"This is the psychological moment to strike hard and fast. Such a golden opportunity cannot be expected to recur.

"Britain cannot be expected to continue indefinitely while waiting for us to do our part more adequately and effectively.

"The Battle of Britain and the Atlantic are, in very truth, the Battle for America. Let's stop fooling ourselves.

"If it is not to be America next, we must leave nothing undone to help Britain to repel Hitler's hordes.

"If America does not go quickly all out for Britain, she may find herself all in without Britain."

Japan was reported last night to be on the eve of invading Russia in the Far East, while Italy, Spain and Vichy France were completing plans to send troops to aid Germany on the Soviet's Western front.

There was still no official news of the Russo-German war in London yesterday. The only information came from the biased claims made by both sides.

Russia

THE German Air Force carried out no particular activities yesterday. The enemy fighter force put up only a slight resistance to our bombers.

Fierce tank battles raged in the Minsk and Luck sectors (Russian-occupied Poland).

In the latter there was obvious advantage to the Russian troops.

Russian troops successfully frustrated enemy attempts to force the River Prut in the Cernauti sector (Rumania).

On the Bessarabian front Russian troops have firmly maintained their positions and are holding the enemy at the frontier.

The enemy, who tried to advance from Kulent, was driven back to the western bank of the river with heavy losses.

The Russian Air Force bombed Bukarest, Ploesti and Constanza (Rumania).

Two U-boats were sunk in the Baltic.

A powerful Russian counter-offensive has recaptured Przemysl, on the Russo-German demarcation line in Poland.

Germany

PROGRESSIVE and powerful damage to the Soviet Air Force has given the Luftwaffe supremacy over the fighting zone and thrown the Soviet airmen on the defensive.

German troops driving against the Baltic States captured town after town.

Operations continue according to plan, after a number of fights on the frontier had been settled. Large-scale operational successes are being gained.

The port of Turku (Aabo), in south-west Finland, was heavily attacked by the Soviet Air Force yesterday. Many fires broke out and the castle was hit by a bomb.

Two Nazi E-boats sank a Soviet submarine in the Baltic.

The commander of the submarine was unable to submerge his vessel in time and had to go into action with his guns.

German bombers have raided Leningrad again.

Russian bombers did considerable damage to Hungarian towns of Rhovo and Kaschau yesterday.

CONTINUOUS PERFORMANCE

DAILY Over France   NIGHTLY Over Germany

THE R.A.F. non-stop blitz over Northern France continued yesterday with great intensity. A big formation of bombers, protected in force by fighters, crossed the Kent coast and penetrated well inland on the other side of the Channel. Vichy radio said the attack was on the Calais region.

Of the enemy fighters which tried to intervene, nine were shot down. Only three of our fighters are missing.

As our planes swept in over the French coast they met A.A. fire, but the ground defences appeared taken by surprise as the R.A.F. pilots altered course so that the sun made detection difficult.

As on previous days, nothing was seen of the Luftwaffe over the south-east coast or Channel. They have even stopped sending small formations of high-flying Messerschmitts on tip-and-run raids.

15th Night

During Wednesday night our bombers raided Germany for the fifteenth consecutive night. Boulogne docks, too, were bombed—by the Fleet Air Arm.

Germany was being hit left and right for while our night bombers were raiding in the West, Russian bombers were attacking in the East.

Our air communique stated:

" The naval base of Kiel and the port of Bremen were attacked by Bomber Command last night, and a number of large fires were started.

" One aircraft of Bomber Command is missing."

The German radio said yesterday: " Some of the bombs dropped exploded on prisoner-of-war camps.

" Russian planes last night attacked frontier districts in the east with small forces. Bombs caused little damage."

NEW SALVAGE ARMY STARTS

A new salvage army of volunteers will soon go into action following meetings of voluntary organisations in country districts which 475 rural district councils have been asked to hold this week and next.

Mr. H. G. Judd, Controller of Salvage, stated yesterday that there are many districts not covered by a regular refuse collection who are urgently requiring reinforcements.

To increase the collection of valuable waste materials—paper, rags, metal, bones and kitchen waste—volunteers will be enlisted to operate under salvage wardens.

These wardens will be appointed for each parish, or hamlet, or street.

Heroine, but Must Wash Up

A.R.P. ambulance girls, even if they are heroines, have to obey orders to wash the dishes.

A girl who was stated "to have been out in the blitz and funked nothing," but who refused to do canteen work, was summoned at Birmingham yesterday for disobeying this order.

She was Miss Sylvia Margaret Durham, of Carlisle-road, Edgbaston, Birmingham. Two summonses against her were dismissed on payment of one guinea costs.

It was stated for the defence that as an ambulance girl in the blitz she had " performed in a grand manner," and " all she had done" in refusing canteen work was "to make some men make their own tea and wash their own dishes."

The magistrate (Lord Ilkeston) said that it was a lawful order and not an unreasonable one in present circumstances

WODEHOUSE ON GERMAN RADIO

MR. P. G. WODEHOUSE, English author freed by the Germans from a civilian internment camp and now living in a Berlin hotel, is to broadcast his experiences to the United States once a week.

" General chats, entirely non-political," he explained in an interview.

" I'm quite unable to work up any kind of belligerent feeling—really. Just as I'm about to feel belligerent about some country I meet a decent sort of chap. We go out together and lose any fighting thoughts or feelings."—British United Press.

MOSCOW CLOSED CITY

Everyone not normally resident in Moscow has been forbidden to enter the city unless on an official mission.—Reuter.

Daily Mirror

JUNE 28

No. 11,715   ONE PENNY

Registered at the G.P.O. as a Newspaper.

P. G. Wodehouse..

P. G. WODEHOUSE has cracked his worst joke. And the laugh is against his own country. IT'S BITTER LAUGHTER.

Freed from a German internment camp he has agreed to thank the Nazis by broadcasting once a week to America. They have given him freedom within Germany, and all they asked was that he should pay for that freedom. How?

P. G. Wodehouse has paid. He lived luxuriously because Britain laughed with him, but when the laughter was out of his country's heart, Wodehouse was not ready to share her suffering. He hadn't the guts (or was it that he hadn't the wish?) even to stick it out in the internment camp.

What's his explanation? That the broadcasts (the first was made early yesterday) will be non-political, just general chats about his experiences.

Maybe, but no one needs to tell you, Wodehouse, what propaganda value those general chats will have to the Nazis. THEY MAY HAVE GIVEN YOU THE FREEDOM OF GERMANY, BUT BY GOD THEY WON'T GIVE YOU THE FREEDOM OF THE MICROPHONE.

Take one phrase you used in your broadcast. It was "whether England wins or not." That's a doubt true Britons do not share with you.

You must have known the price you had to pay, you're not the first one who has paid it.

You told interviewers, "I never was really interested in politics. I'm quite unable to work up any kind of belligerent feeling. Just as I'm about to feel belligerent about some country I meet a decent sort of chap. We go out together and lose any fighting thoughts or feelings."

The "decent sort of chap" this time seems to have been Baron von Barnikow. You met him during your internment, made a friend of him, knew him by the nickname of The Raven, a title he won when he fought and killed your countrymen in the last war.

FOR A TIME YOU'VE LOST YOUR FRIEND, FOR THE RAVEN HAS FLOWN. STILL A BLACK-HEARTED HUN, TO FIGHT AGAIN AND, IF HE CAN, TO KILL, WITH THE NAZIS IN THE EAST.

You say you can't work up any belligerent feeling; that, again, is where you are different from the ordinary Briton. But he just calls it hate, AND ONE OF THE THINGS HE HATES MOST, WODEHOUSE, IS A MAN WHO LETS DOWN HIS OWN COUNTRY.

THE PRICE IS ?

BRITISH MISSION IN USSR

BRITAIN'S military mission, sent to help Russia in her war with Germany, are in Moscow.

They include Lieutenant-General F. N. Mason Macfarlane, our greatest authority on tanks and German military tactics.

The mission accompanied Sir Stafford Cripps, Ambassador to Russia, who returned to his post as secretly as he arrived in London just over a fortnight ago for consultations with the Government.

Yesterday, Sir Stafford Cripps presented the mission to M. Molotov, Soviet Foreign Minister. With General Mason Macfarlane were:—

Rear-Admiral G. J. A. Miles, 51, commander of H.M. battleship Nelson from July, 1939, till June 14 this year;

Air Vice-Marshal Alfred Conrad Collier, 46, member of the British mission to Moscow during the 1939 negotiations with the Soviet Government; and

Acting Colonel K. G. Exham, 38, Far East expert, with a good knowledge of Poland and the Baltic States; and a second class Russian interpreter.

"Invisible Man"

General Macfarlane, 51, tall, big stooping shoulders, with a grim eye and a bulldog chin, has been described as the "Invisible man" of the British Army.

He was military attaché in Berlin while Hitler was preparing for war.

It was he who conveyed to Prague Hitler's "final terms" for a peaceful settlement during the Munich crisis of 1938.

Gen. Mason Macfarlane

With the outbreak of war he went to France with the B.E.F. as Director of Military Intelligence and was personally responsible for the safety of the King during his tour of the battlefront.

He was the man who held the gap near Arras with a scratch force formed on May 17, 1940, and disbanded eleven days later. It was called the Mac Force.

Last August he was appointed second in command at Gibraltar.

Rear-Admiral Miles is a specialist in navigation.

During most of his command of the Nelson he was flag captain to the Commander-in-Chief, Home Fleet.

Air Vice-Marshal Collier was the first British Air Attaché to be appointed to Moscow, serving from 1934 until 1937.

He has been Director of Intelligence (Security) since March. He was air adviser to the Estonian Army in 1928.

R.A.F. Hit Big Ships in Convoy

Aircraft of the R.A.F. and Fleet Air Arm attacked convoy consisting of a number of merchant vessels, each of 5,000 tons, off the south coast of Italy.

At least two ships were hit by torpedoes and one was hit amidships by a heavy bomb. Further results were not observed owing to darkness, states yesterday's Cairo communiqué.

TURK AID TO VICHY

Vichy France has nearly reached the end of the rope in Syria. — British spokesman in Jerusalem.

THE Turkish Government last night granted permission for Vichy troops fleeing from Allied forces in Syria to escape through Turkey.

They will travel as unarmed civilians.

The Vichy Embassy in Ankara hope to evacuate 20,000 "refugees."

But an Ankara spokesman stated that only a fraction of General Dentz's Army could leave Syria owing to lack of transport.

Most of the Vichy officers are expected to escape.

British naval units yesterday morning bombarded the Syrian coast north of Sidon, according to Vichy.

British forces are gradually closing in on the strongly fortified pipe-line town of Palmyra.

Twenty-three enemy planes were destroyed in Syria and Cyrenaica, and a number of others damaged, states an R.A.F. Middle East communiqué. Five R.A.F. planes are missing.—British United Press.

8,000 GROUND CREWS

The Canadian Air Minister said yesterday that Canada is sending 8,000 ground crew men of the Royal Canadian Air Force to man new squadrons already in Britain.—Exchange.

ONE EGG— PERHAPS!

One egg per person per week—perhaps!

That's going to be your ration under the Ministry of Food egg control scheme during July.

"Until the Ministry has obtained experience of the number of home-produced eggs and has observed the distributive machinery in operation," it was cautiously explained last night, "it is not possible to state precisely the number of eggs that will be available for consumers.

"There is, however, every reason to hope that each domestic consumer will be able to obtain during July at least four eggs from the retailer with whom he has registered.

"But it should be understood that no guarantee can be given that this number will be available for every consumer."

The first allocation of eggs is being made next week.

MEAT 1s. 2d.

THE meat ration will be increased to 1s. 2d for adults and 7d. for children from Monday, July 7, the Ministry of Food announced last night.

These increases of 2d. and 1d. have been made possible by the exceptionally large quantities of frozen meat which have arrived from the Southern Hemisphere in the last few weeks.

It is expected the ration will be maintained on the new level for some time without any reduction of our reserves.

There will be no increased issue of meat to catering establishments.

THE SOLUTION

A Cannock (Staffs) trader has found a solution to the queue problem by posting up in his window the following notice: "The first six in queue will not be served."

NAVAL SLOOP SUNK

The naval sloop Grimsby (Commander K. J. D'Arcy, R.N.) has been sunk, the Admiralty announced last night.

Puppets Fight Russia

ALL Hitler's puppet States in the Nazi New Order are lining up in the German war against Russia.

Hungary and Croatia are the latest to declare war on the Soviet.

Hungary gave as her excuse the alleged Soviet bombing of open towns in Hungary on Thursday.

The Spanish Falangist (Fascist) Party opened a recruiting office in Madrid to enrol a volunteer legion to fight Russia.

Latest claims are:—

Russia

SOVIET troops left for new positions and new battles after heavily defeating the enemy in the direction of Siauliao (Lithuania), Vilna and Baranavichi (about 120 miles south-west of Minsk).

Russian planes relentlessly bombed tank formations in the Vilna, Baranavichi and Brody areas.

The bombing of military objectives in Bukarest and Ploesti has caused great damage. The port of Constanza was also severely damaged.

Germany

THE first five days of operations have proved that the Soviet forces were prepared for an attack on Central Europe. Our troops found Soviet forces massed for attack.

German troops have won decisive issues on all fronts. Their announcement is imminent.

The High Command: A full statement on the situation for Thursday, was again postponed till Sunday at the latest.

The German Official News Agency claimed that German troops, led by Panzer divisions, drove deep into the Russian defence lines—but didn't say where.

"How Soviet Russia Can Stop Hun"—by Tom Wintringham. See back page.

PRINCE PAUL IN KENYA

Prince Paul of Yugoslavia and his wife are in Kenya.—Associated Press.

GNEISENAU IS A RUIN

GERMAN battlecruiser Gneisenau may have to be rebuilt, so badly was she damaged by one of Britain's big new bombs in an R.A.F. raid on Brest.

This is disclosed in authentic uncensored messages reaching New York from Nazi-occupied France, says British United Press.

It is stated that 128 of the crew were killed when a bomb struck the Gneisenau amidships. The fuel tanks exploded, causing further explosions and a fire.

Stern Under Water

The Gneisenau, slightly damaged in an earlier raid, had been put into dry dock.

The first bomb dropped by a Blenheim on a German supply ship in the Channel yesterday struck her plumb on the stern, and as our force of Blenheims—out with a strong escort of fighters on a sweep—turned for home the stern of the ship was already under water and the sea washing over her decks.

Three ships were seen about ten miles off Dunkirk, the formation dive-bombed the middle one, a vessel of about 3,000 tons.

Two Polish fighter squadrons led by a Canadian swept over Northern France yesterday and, unable to contact enemy fighters,

Continued on Back Page

R.A.F. PLASTERS FRANCE AGAIN

A LARGE force of R.A.F. bombers carried out a half-hour attack on the other side of the Channel shortly before dusk last night.

Bomb explosions shook the South-East Coast.

A heavy barrage from the German A.A. batteries met the striking force.

R.A.F. fighters were active over the Channel during the raid, but there was no enemy opposition.

Daily Mirror

JULY 2

No. 11,718   ONE PENNY
Registered at the G.P.O. as a Newspaper.

LUCK AND RIGA FALL SAY HUNS

General Wavell's successor as G.O.C. Middle East—General Sir O. J. E. Auchinleck.

GERMANY claimed last night important successes on three fronts—

Northern.—Capture of Riga, capital of Latvia.

Central.—Spearhead of drive on Moscow cut the River Beresina, sixty miles east of Minsk on the road to the Russian capital.

Southern.—Capture of Luck, in Southern Poland, on the route of the Nazi drive for Kiev, capital of Ukraine.

Russia claimed that after a night long battle in the direction of Minsk, German attempts to advance were beaten back.

Here are the rival claims.

Germany Says :

LUCK was captured by three German tanks which crossed a burning bridge just before it collapsed and defeated six Russian tanks.

The Fuehrer's H.Q. reports that between the Carpathians and the Pripet marshes formations of the German Army and Slovak troops are pressing forward in pursuit of the defeated enemy on both sides of Lwow (Poland)

The Soviet armies encircled between Bialystok and Minsk made desperate but vain efforts throughout the day to break through.

German and Finnish troops on the Salla front advanced right across Karelia to Kandalaksha, on the White Sea, and cut off the Russian forces on the Murmansk peninsula from the south

Russia Says :

OUR troops carried out stubborn battles in the directions of Murmansk, Kexholm, Dvinsk, Minsk and Luck yesterday.

In the Murmansk direction our troops by fierce fighting are stemming the advance of the numerically superior enemy forces.

In the Kexholm direction the enemy launched an offensive at several points. By vigorous counter attacks our troops repulsed the enemy's attacks, inflicting heavy losses.

In the Dvinsk direction our troops are frustrating the enemy's attempts to penetrate towards the crossing over the Western Dvina.

In the Minsk direction our troops are counter-attacking and holding back the advance of enemy tank units.

Our troops, retreating according to plan and in accordance with orders, left Lwow.

'NON-STOP' BLITZ

FOR the second day in succession the R.A.F. struck twice at Germany in daylight yesterday. They were also twice over Northern France, the second time on a large scale.

So many planes were used in the second attack on France that it took 20 minutes for them to pass over a south-east town.

And last evening many squadrons of our fighters swept Northern France without getting a fight. The Germans were nowhere to be seen.

In the raids on Germany, Oldenburg, railway yards south of the town, and the seaplane base at Borkum, in the Friesian Islands, were attacked at a cost of two Blenheims and a heavy bomber.

One Messerschmitt was shot down and several damaged.

One of our bombers was unsuccessfully engaged by six fighters, and one beat off an attack after the rear gunner had been wounded.

Fighters Over France

British fighters carried out offensive patrols over France during the early afternoon

In the evening a large number of bombers, with a heavy fighter escort, continued the non-stop blitz

The sky over the Channel was filled hour after hour with the drone of warplanes

As the leading formations passed out of sight eastward, Kent coastal towns shook with the crash of bombs

A YEAR LATE FOR WEDDING

A *marriage has been arranged, and will take place at the Cathedral Church of St. Mary, Palmerston-place, Edinburgh, on Friday, May 24, 1940, at four o'clock, between Captain Ronald Edward Warlow, the Gordon Highlanders, and Eda, daughter of the late Mr. J. E. and of Mrs. J. E. Hedin, of Rufalo New York, U.S.A.*

THE wedding has not taken place and this is why. Miss Hedin sailed from New York on April 27, 1940. On May 8 she landed in France, planning to fly to London.

But two days later the Nazis invaded the Low Countries. She was kept a prisoner. Later she went to live with friends in France.

In March this year she reached Portugal. For three months she tried to get to England. Then she caught the Clipper to New York where she arrived yesterday.

"I have been told there is no chance of my being able to get from here to England as an ordinary passenger," she said. "So I am going to Canada to enlist as a nurse for active service in England."

SOVIET SEEKS U.S. AID

Mr. Sumner Welles, U.S. Under Secretary of State, disclosed last night that the Soviet Ambassador had asked for war supplies. The orders will be "strictly business transactions," and will be carried in Soviet ships.—Reuter.

PATROL SHIP SUNK

H.M.S. Pintail (Lieutenant J L. S. McClintock, R.N.), a 580-ton patrol craft, has been sunk. Next-of-kin of casualties have been informed.

What Does It Mean ?

IS it demotion promotion? —or just a rest? That question naturally arises from the announcement that Wavell has been moved.

He is reputed to be the best general we have, the only one who so far has shown the brilliance of the German commanders.

Why, then, move him ? Is there any truth in the rumour of his disagreement with the politicians over the Greece and Crete campaigns ?

He has had a tremendously arduous job—Abyssinia, Somaliland, Libya, Iraq Greece, Crete and Syria all came within his command.

And besides the purely military responsibilities which were his as Commander-in-Chief he has had also to shoulder the political work involved

Lyttelton's appointment means that at least the new G.O.C. will be free of those political worries

There's plenty of work for Wavell to do in India. Whether it is the work for Britain's best soldier, even when "resting," is, however, another matter.

And about it there will be some uneasiness

WAVELL IS MOVED: INDIA C.O. SUCCEEDS

GENERAL Sir C. J. E. Auchinleck has succeeded General Sir Archibald Wavell as General Officer Commanding in Chief in the Middle East.

Wavell takes over Auchinleck's place as Commander-in-Chief in India.

Captain Oliver Lyttelton, former President of the Board of Trade, becomes Minister of State and a member of the War Cabinet.

He goes to the Middle East "to concert on behalf of the War Cabinet measures necessary for the promotion of the war in that theatre other than military."

He will thus be a Middle East "viceroy," relieving General Auchinleck of extra work.

These sensational changes were announced from No 10. Downing-street this morning, when it was stated that the duration of the military appointments would depend on the war situation.

Generals Wavell and Auchinleck met at Basra, in Iraq, a few weeks ago. It was assumed that they discussed Middle East operations from the angle of the defence of India

General Sir Claud Auchinleck, 57, is first and last an Indian Army man. He joined the Punjabis in 1903, and except for brief spells has spent the whole of his Army life in India and the East.

Captured Narvik

In this war he commanded the Allied forces at Narvik. General Sir Archibald Wavell is regarded as the military genius of the war—the most vigorous personality in the British Army in the field

His campaign in Libya which swept Mussolini's legions from their strongly-fortified positions and made 100,000 of them prisoners

Continued on Back Page

2 Bodies in Garden

WHEN Mrs Phyllis Watson 28, pushed her 18-month-old baby Eileen down their street she had a smile for everyone. The Watsons of Goringway, Greenford, Middlesex were known as "a perfect married couple."

Then one day about three weeks ago neighbours missed Mrs. Watson's smile. They heard she had been evacuated and were all sorry

On Monday night her body and that of her baby were found buried in the back garden of her home.

Police had been called in following complaints from neighbours, and the body of the baby was found wrapped in a pillow slip lying beside her mother 2ft. beneath the earth.

"Mr and Mrs. Watson were one of the best young couples I have ever met," a neighbour told the *Daily Mirror*. "We were sorry when we heard that Mrs. Watson had been evacuated to Scotland

"The last time we saw Mr. Watson was on Sunday, when he came home to clean the windows"

A man has been detained at Greenford, and will appear at Ealing today

(Picture in Back Page)

Daily Mirror

JULY 3

No. 11,719   ONE PENNY
Registered at the G.P.O. as a Newspaper.

RUSSIA DENIES HUNS CAPTURE KEY TOWNS

'THEY MIGHT MIX WITH MEN'

"THE ballroom area is rather small. Frequently officers, N.C.Os and men have to share the same table. In some dances they also dance with the same partner, and an officer might have to take his partner back to a table where N.C.O.s and other ranks may be sitting.

This was the excuse offered yesterday by the Southern Command headquarters, for having placed Bournemouth Municipal ballroom out of bounds to officers.

The Command's statement added:

"While no cases suggesting any kind of friction have ever arisen, it is obviously undesirable that these conditions should be allowed to continue, since there is a possibility they might lay the groundwork for contention.

Why Not?

"It has always been the Army policy to avoid any possibility of this, and it was therefore thought desirable to allow only N.C.O.s and men to use the ballroom in the future."

Bournemouth people are laughing—and some of them are annoyed at the excuse.

The municipal ballroom can comfortably accommodate about 900 dancers on the floor, and there is seating and table space for 700.

Bournemouth people are wondering why officers should not be allowed to come into contact with N.C.O.s and men in this ballroom any more than in any other public ballroom, or, for that matter, on the Corporation's transport vehicles.

---

18 to 10

R.A.F. Eagles—the squadron formed by U.S. pilots—scored their first successes yesterday. They bagged three of the eighteen German planes destroyed in our sweep over North France.

We lost eight fighters—two of which crashed after colliding—and two bombers.

The Nazis sent up more fighters than usual to check an R.A.F. sweep on objectives at Lille. "It was just like the old Dunkirk days," said a pilot.

About sixty Me. 109s, flying in fours, went up against the fighters protecting our bombers. Running fights continued all the way to the French coast.

A Spitfire pilot destroyed two planes with one burst of fire. The Eagle Squadron's leader got one, and the youngest member of the squadron scored a hit, although his own plane had been damaged.

MOSCOW made two claims last night which suggested that Germany's campaign is not going according to plan. They are:—

1.—The two vital towns of Minsk, at the start of the road to Moscow, and Riga, capital of Latvia, claimed by Germany, are still in Russian hands.

2.—The Russian Army is battering the German tanks which thrust a spearhead in the direction of Minsk. Many are cut off from supply lines.

Germany issued yet another special communique from Hitler's headquarters making colossal claims of Russian losses in warplanes, tanks and men between June 22 and July 1.

A Vichy report said that the Russians had launched powerful counter-attacks on all fronts. These were slowing up the German push.

Latest successes claimed by both sides in land and sea battles on the three fronts include:

NORTHERN. — German troops captured Windau, port in Latvia.

CENTRAL.—Nazis captured 100,000 prisoners, 400 tanks and 300 guns in "final destruction of a large part of the Soviet Army surrounded east of Bialystok, in Poland.

SOUTHERN.—Cossacks attacked in one unnamed town, swinging sabres and shouting fierce cries as they galloped in front of infantry. Russian naval squadron destroyed German naval base at Constanza.

Here are the rival statements:

Russia Says:

GERMAN claims to have taken Minsk and Riga are untrue.

The Russian Army, attacking the German tank spearhead near Minsk, concentrated on wiping out the advanced armoured forces which had penetrated their lines.

Leading German machines

Continued on Back Page

R.A.F. Stop German Works

THE FIRST SINCE CROMWELL

THE R.A.F.'s raids on Western Germany have brought industry to a standstill, declared a cable yesterday from the Zurich correspondent of the *New York Post.*

Scores of plants in the Mannerheim district have been destroyed and thousands of workers are either standing idle or have been drafted into demolition squads.

Similar conditions are reported in the shipping centres of Bremen, Hamburg and Kiel.

The R.A.F. is also believed responsible for the slackening in the drug exports from Germany to Lisbon: first by damaging production centres, and secondly by making the Germans themselves use more sedatives.

The R.A.F. kept up their after-dark raids on Tuesday.

Our bombers attacked the naval base at Brest, where three enemy warships—the battleships Gneisenau and Scharnhorst and the cruiser Prinz Eugen—are still lying.

Bombs straddled the dry dock in which one of the battleships is berthed, according to the Air Ministry.

Two aircraft are missing from these attacks.

General Sir Robert Haining.

THE War Office has gone back to Cromwell for a title for its latest appointment.

This is the post of Intendant-General, and it is a Middle East appointment created for General Sir Robert H. Haining—the man who planned the Greek evacuation from Whitehall.

The rank of Intendant-General is a standard rank in the French Army and its holder deals with administrative matters. It is believed that there has been no such appointment in the British Army since the days of Cromwell.

NEW BRITISH LANDING AT BASRA, SAY NAZIS

Berlin radio broadcast the following last night:—

"According to reports from Ankara, British reinforcements have been landed at Basra (Iraq) and on the Bahrein Islands (in the Persian Gulf)."

Red Cross Ship Held

THE Italian hospital ship Ramb IV, intercepted off Aden, has been detained for British use.

The British Government made this decision following enemy violations of The Hague Convention.

A declaration by the British Government states that they made a protest to the German Government, through the United States, against thirty-one deliberate and flagrant attacks upon British hospital ships and carriers.

Many of these ships were severely damaged and three, the Maid of Kent, Brighton and Paris were sunk.

All these sinkings, and at least half the other attacks, took place in broad daylight.

The Ramb IV will be retained for at least six months. If in the meantime the Government are satisfied that the enemy not only firmly intended to stop further attacks on British hospital ships, but has also the power to ensure that these intentions are carried into effect, the return of the Ramb IV will be considered.

WANTS TO TOUR HESS IN A CAGE

The American midget impresario, Billy Rose, yesterday wired Lord Halifax asking that Rudolf Hess be turned over to him for a United States tour in a cage in aid of British war charities.

NEW FORCE ENTERS SYRIA

A new strong British motorised column from Iraq is advancing along the Euphrates Valley, said last night's Vichy communique on Syria.

The column has made contact with advanced Vichy elements in the vicinity of Deir el Zor.

British forces have intensified their action in several sectors the communique added.

British troops have recaptured a position overlooking Palmyra which had been temporarily lost as a result of a Vichy counter-attack.

About two-thirds of the Vichy tanks engaged in the unsuccessful counter-attack on Nebek, in the Damascus sector, were destroyed.

BELGIAN TROOPS ARRIVE

A detachment of Belgian troops has arrived in this country. They were trained in Canada and will join the Belgian forces here.

HE SOLD PARDONS TO CONVICTS

From JOHN WALTERS

New York, Wednesday.

ACTIVITIES of ex-Governor Rivers, of Georgia, are being investigated because of the suspicion that he has been selling pardons to hundreds of dangerous convicts in his state for from £5 to £20 apiece.

Among his salesmen who are alleged to have toured prisons using high-pressure methods in selling pardons is his former negro chauffeur, Albert Chandler who was arrested today.

Chandler with a bundle of blank pardons said to be signed by the Governor would wave the sheaves before the convicts.

Twenty-two murderers were among those immediately released after, it is alleged, paying Chandler for pardon.

During his term of office Governor Rivers pardoned 2,000 convicts.

CAN'T BUY PRAMS

In six leading London stores yesterday there were only two prams for sale.

Reason for the shortage is the wait for the production of the standardised "national pram."

Ban on Tobacco Shops

AS the result of information placed before the Tobacco Trade Association by the Tobacco Controller, disciplinary action has been taken against six more tobacco firms.

Maldistribution, and in one case hoarding, were the subjects of the complaints.

In one case, a London wholesaler-retailer has had his wholesale business closed and his retail business reduced by two-thirds.

In another case, a London wholesaler-retailer has had his retail business closed.

In a third case, a London retailer has had his business curtailed so that it must not exceed his 1940 figures.

Severe warnings have been given by the Tobacco Trade Association to three retail firms in the provinces against whom complaints were lodged.

Secret Buyer Uproar

Uproar broke out when 5,000 salvaged cigarettes were knocked down at 75s. a thousand—equivalent to the retail price of 9d. for ten—at an auction in London yesterday.

"Who bought them?" demanded the crowd. The auctioneer refused to tell.

No action is planned to prevent further auctions, the *Daily Mirror* was told last night.

"Actually only a small number of cigarettes were involved in the sale today," said an official of the Tobacco Controller.

"The auction is merely another method of getting cigarettes into the market. Should any abuse occur the Tobacco Controller's office would act."

HOARDED FOOD —FINED £50

Fined £50 at Glasgow Sheriff Court yesterday for hoarding a ton of food for a household of three, James Garrett, The Granary, Weybridge, Surrey, and Mirrilees-drive, Kelvinside, Glasgow, was said to have stored tea, cocoa, sugar, cereals, chocolate, biscuits, jam and tinned fruit, meat and vegetables.

For Garrett it was said that he was ignorant of the Order.

WATCH ON RABBIT PRICES

The high price of rabbits is under consideration by the Food Ministry, the Parliamentary Secretary stated yesterday.

PRINCE BERNHARD BACK

Prince Bernhard of the Netherlands has returned from Canada to England in a bomber.

Daily Mirror

No. 11,729 — ONE PENNY
Registered at the G.P.O. as a Newspaper.

MR. CHURCH-ILL'S SMILE AS HE TALKED ABOUT THE BOMBS WE ARE NOW DROPPING ON THE ENEMY.

NAVY, RAF HIT 13 AXIS SHIPS

"IN the last few weeks alone we have thrown upon Germany about half the tonnage of bombs thrown by the Germans upon our cities during the whole course of the war. This is only the beginning…"

Mr. Churchill said this yesterday afternoon.

Speech Reported on Page 3

BOMBS AND THIS IS HOW

BRITAIN'S battering of Axis supply lines on land and sea continues with calculated ferocity.

Eight more enemy ships have been destroyed by our planes and submarines, it was officially announced yesterday. Two others were listed as "damaged and probably sunk," and the more suffered direct hits by bombs.

At the same time our bombers maintained their onslaught on docks, railways, locomotive sheds and factories in enemy - occupied territory.

Eight of the thirteen Axis ships hit by British bombs and torpedoes were attacked in the Mediterranean area of operations. The Navy's share of the "bag" was five.

PEACE PLAN— U.S. WARNED

NEW York's Mayor, La Guardia, told visiting South Americans yesterday that Hitler, "through " his agents, is trying to exploit well-meaning people in this country as tools to try to get across a peace proposal."

A few days ago, he said, at Washington, "a representative of the German Government disclosed the proposal to representatives of a peace movement in this country, with the instruction to try it out and prepare a foundation for its acceptance."

Lindbergh a Danger

A warning against Lindbergh as a Nazi tool was given by Mr. Ickes, U.S. Secretary for the Interior, last night.

Lindbergh had offered the Nazi Party line to the United States.

"No one," Mr. Ickes continued, "has ever heard Lindbergh utter a word of horror at the bloody career the Nazis are following, nor a word of pity for the innocent men, women and children deliberately murdered by the Nazis in practically every country of Europe."—Associated Press.

GERMAN-TURK TRADE PACT

An American correspondent stated this morning in a broadcast from Ankara that a new trade agreement between Germany and Turkey is being negotiated now.

"Reich Can Stand a Million Casualties"

Rome - radio, commenting on a Moscow report that 1,000,000 German soldiers had been put out of action, said:—

"This figure is not far from the real number of German casualties, but Germany can stand this."

German correspondents early today told of the terrific Russian resistance.

"The ground in the Stalin line must be won foot by foot," said one. "Murderous fire pours from the Russian forts and all buildings. When driven out of the forts the Russians fight to the death—street by street."

COLONEL'S BAT(H)MAN

Scene : Minehead (Somerset) bathing pool.

A LARGE Army lorry pulls up at the entrance with curtains drawn across the back. Jumping from his seat, a private soldier pulls them on one side, and then stands stiffly to attention.

Out clamber a Colonel, an elderly woman and two girls in A.T.S. uniform. Collecting their bathing dresses, the Private follows the four into the pool.

After a suitable interval, he returns with a pile of wet bathing gear and escorts the party back into the Army lorry, pulling the curtains together behind them with another salute.

Then, with its precious but hidden cargo, the lorry sets out to return to its base miles away

The War Office has issued stringent orders to the Army about economy in petrol.

SPAIN GENERAL IN BERLIN

General Grande, leader of the Spanish volunteers going to fight against Russia, flew to Berlin yesterday, accompanied by officers.

Submarine Uses Gun

Here is the Admiralty communique, issued last night:—

"The Commander - in - Chief, Mediterranean, has reported further successes by submarines under his command.

"The Italian tanker Strombo (5,232 tons), which had put into Istanbul seriously damaged by a torpedo from one of our submarines, has now been sunk while on her way back to Italy to undergo repairs.

"A heavily-laden supply ship of about 5,500 tons sailing in convoy and escorted by an armed merchant cruiser and a destroyer has also been sunk.

"A large sailing vessel transporting enemy troops and military stores has been sunk in the Ægean.

"Another submarine, finding

Continued on Back Page'

GERMAN'S SABOTAGE CALL TO GERMANS

Over Moscow radio last night Michel Niederkirchner, who in peace time had a job in a Berlin steel factory, broadcast to Berlin steelworkers a call to sabotage Nazi war production.

"Remember, friends," he said, "each cartridge which does not explode is a shot into the heart of Hitler."

SOME of the R.A.F. bombers now penetrating night after night deep into the heart of Germany are carrying three times the load that our planes took over a year ago.

In addition, while the raiders we sent over twelve months ago could be numbered by the score, they can now be numbered by the hundred.

With our latest monsters like the Halifax, the Short Stirling and the Avro Manchester it would be possible to send fewer planes than we sent last year and yet do more damage. As it is, while the Whitleys, Wellingtons and other stock bombers are going over in ever-increasing numbers they are frequently accompanied by the new devastating types.

Ports Attacked

A month's survey of the R.A.F. offensive shows the terrific battering the Germans are getting.

Stopping traffic from seaports is one of the main objects of our plan. During the last month we have made sixty-nine raids on seaports in German and German-occupied territory, and thirty-seven attacks on coastal shipping.

Behind the ports we have made twenty-seven attacks on railway centres and goods yards. There have been nine successful raids on power stations, seven on specific munition works, seven on oil plants, and seventy-three on industrial targets.

Hundreds a Day

Our losses, naturally, have been heavier, but it must be taken into account that we are now on the offensive. In daytime our sweeps over the French coast often involve hundreds of planes being used a day.

But never yet have we lost anything like so many planes as the Luftwaffe lost in the Battle of Britain.

Here are the month's losses: German losses over Britain, 56; R.A.F. losses over Britain, 1 (pilot safe). German losses over Europe, 314. R.A.F. losses over Europe, 268.

The mere fact that the Air Ministry is prepared to lose 268 planes in a month indicates the terrific proportions which the R.A.F. have reached in both planes and personnel — and more and heavier stuff is on the way.

GEN. WEYGAND TRIES TO ROAR

General Weygand, in a petulant speech to a Morocco crowd yesterday, declared: "Britain today is France's enemy."

He sounded as if he were trying to make himself angry, but was half-hearted about everything.

"Britain," he said, "has betrayed France. The future is not with Britain, but with France has a future."

He Roars—But He'll Never Fight—Page 2.

MOSCOW 2 a.m. CLAIM

GERMANS MAULED

EARLY today a Russian communique stated that in the terrific battles raging on the three great fronts, repeated Red Army counter-attacks had savagely mauled the Germans.

"Our troops opposed the enemy offensive of tanks and motorised units, and in repeated counter-attacks inflicted heavy losses," said the communique.

"In the central sector our troops and Air Force destroyed about 100 tanks and a great number of enemy cars.

"In the south-western sector our troops defeated a large enemy unit of about 3,000 men.

15 Ships Sunk

Russian warships, planes and coast guns have sunk two German destroyers, thirteen transports and a barge loaded with tanks. In addition, thirteen other transports and one destroyer were heavily damaged and left in flames, said the Russian communique.

We captured a great number of guns, machine-guns, cars and ammunition.

"In the night of Sunday and during Monday our Air Force attacked enemy aircraft on their aerodromes and struck powerful blows against enemy troops, tanks and motorised units.

Continued on Back Page

Daily Mirror

JULY 19

No. 11,733 — ONE PENNY
Registered at the G.P.O. as a Newspaper.

GO-SLOW BOSSES TO GET SACK

Smolensk Is Hun Claim

THIS special ann ucement "from the Fuehrer's headquarter." was broadcast by all German stations last night:—

"After breaking through the strongly-fortified Stalin Line between Mogilev and Vitebsk, German forces reached Smolensk. The town was occupied in spite of stubborn resistance on Wednesday. All enemy attempts to recapture Smolensk have been frustrated."

The German official news agency last night said: "German troops continued their drive towards Leningrad."

Bayonet Fighting

Dispatches to the newspaper *Izvestia* said new battle conditions had arisen with the Russians digging individual trenches to escape German artillery and aeroplanes.

One Soviet battalion was reported to have repulsed eight successive German assaults with these tactics, another to have withstood attacks for twenty hours

Berlin officials claimed yesterday that German troops had smashed more than sixty-two miles beyond the Stalin Line at some points.

The Soviet communique, issued this morning, did not admit the fall of Smolensk but merely said:

"Heavy fighting took place on Friday in the sectors of Pskov - Porhov, Polotsk - Nevel and Smolensk. Both sides suffered heavy losses."

Nevel is sixty-five miles northeast of Polotsk, and about the same distance due north of Vitebsk.

NEW JAPAN MOVE HINT

Movements of Japanese troops towards the Soviet sphere of influence in Outer Mongolia were hinted at in a Peiping message last night.

It was reported that the crack Peiping-Fusan express has been temporarily suspended. No reason was given, but it is believed to be due to military requirements.

Trains are being collected for the transport of Japanese troops brought back from the Shansi region—some say to Manchuria, others to Kalgan, Inner Mongolia, which is considered more likely.

Halifax Warns Japan—page 3

STRONG war measures, giving the State powers to punish shareholders, employers and workers who obstruct production, are announced today.

An Order in Council issued under Defence Regulations authorises the Government to:—

1.—Remove and replace managers who obstruct controllers appointed to any undertaking;

2.—Acquire any company's shares and transfer them to Treasury nominees at a fair price.

A person removed from one office will not be allowed to hold another in the same company without permission.

If he pretends to be retaining his office he will be liable to penalty under the Defence Regulations.

An amendment to the Essential Work (General Provisions) Order, announced by the Ministry of Labour—

Restores the right of employers to suspend a worker without pay up to a limit of three days.

Power to Suspend

The Order did not interfere directly with an employer's power to suspend a worker, but the guaranteed minimum wage had the effect of entitling a worker to wages in respect of the whole of "prescribed period" (a week or a day), even though he might have been suspended.

Continued on Back Page

Make Sunday V-Day

" JULY 20 is the date of Europe's mobilisation against the Germans. Tomorrow the V Army —Europe's invisible army of many millions—will come into being."

Colonel Britton, mystery leader of the Victory-V campaign which has been going on for a week, said this when he broadcast to Europe from the B.B.C. early this morning.

Members of the V-army were asked to do two things — to take a vow to continue faithfully the fight in the best way they can

To take every opportunity tomorrow to demonstrate the mobilisation of the V-army, by putting V.s on walls and everywhere they can, and by beating out the V sound

"The Germans will not drown the knocking of fate however loud they beat," he declared.

"You know, of course, that the number 5 is a V. I advise you to read in the Book of Daniel, Chapter 5, Verse 5.

" *In the same hour came forth fingers of a man's hand, and wrote . . .*

" *Then the king's countenance was changed, and his thoughts troubled him, so that the joints of his loins were loosed and his knees smote one against another.*"

Victim of the Garden Grave

" Daily Mirror " picture of Phyllis Elizabeth Crocker, 32, whose body and that of her eighteen-month-old daughter, Eileen, were found buried under the path flagstones in the garden of the house in which they lived at Goringway, Greenford, Middlesex.

Lionel Rupert Nathan Watson, 31, bakelite moulder with whom the woman and child lived, has been remanded on a charge of murdering them. It was stated that traces of cyanide were found in both bodies.

NEW MENACE TO TURKS

MOSCOW radio last night reported that eighteen to twenty German divisions are concentrated on Bulgaro-Turkish frontier, ready to strike in the direction of the Dardanelles.

The German "Africa Corps," led by General Rommel, is being hurriedly transferred to Bulgaria and also sent to the Turkish frontier the announcer said.

"As all German attempts to force Bulgaria to a war against Russia have been frustrated by the Bulgarian War Minister, who declared that his army will never fight Russia," he added. "Germany prepares an attack on the Straits with Bulgarian help."

An Istanbul message said vast military preparations under the direction of the German General Staff are in progress in Bulgaria.

EXTRA daylight—extra night-work—mean that, literally, night and day you're making more calls on your strength than ever before. Last thing at night take a drink; but make it a drink that puts strength into you. Bournville Cocoa does that in these five ways.

It gives you:

★ EXTRA FOOD VALUE
★ IRON — THE BLOOD ENRICHER
★ PHOSPHATES—FOR HEALTHY GROWTH
★ AID TO DIGESTION
★ VITAMIN D — VITAL TO HEALTH

LESS THAN PRE-WAR PRICE

★ He's a Gallant Father ★

Police-Constable W. Hanlon, Manchester, outside Buckingham Palace holding his second set of twins (three months)—the first set were born eleven years ago. He had just received the medal of the Order of the British Empire for air-raid bravery.

POLES' PACT HOPE

GENERAL SIKORSKI, Premier of Poland, has declared that he sincerely desires an understanding with Russia.

"As for Germany," the General said, " I flatly and resolutely reject, in the name of the Polish Government, the ostensible favours which Hitler's bloody executioners are seeking to offer us today."

The General who was speaking at a Polish Air Force ceremony added.

"I sincerely desire an understanding with Russia, despite the wrongs Russia has recently done to Poland, despite the 150 years of profound dispute.

"But it must be a genuine agreement, and not one which would violate the frontiers and sovereignty of the Polish State and which would throw doubt on the sincerity of the Allies' intentions in their struggle for the most sacred principles of right and Christianity."

R.A.F. PUT NAZI SHIP AGROUND

An enemy supply ship of about 6,000 tons, escorted by patrol vessels and fighters, was attacked by the R.A.F. off Dunkirk yesterday. Later, reconnaissance showed that a similar ship was aground

Fighters escorting our bombers shot down one of the enemy fighters. Two of our bombers and one fighter are missing

Two Nazi bombers were shot down by our fighters off the south coast yesterday.

U.S. BIGGER BLACK LIST

THE United States is to extend her export control measures and add to her black list practically all countries outside the British Empire.

Mr. Dean Acheson, U.S. Assistant Secretary of State, said last night that lists were being prepared of firms and individuals in countries other than Latin America deemed to be helping Germany and Italy.

These included, he added, virtually all countries outside the British Empire, such as Japan, Spain, Portugal and Sweden.

He declined to indicate how soon the new black list would be published, says Associated Press.

SALAD ONIONS SCARCE

The Food Minister has fixed 7½d. a lb. as the maximum price for green or salad onions from Monday.

This Order has been made to discourage the premature lifting of the main onion crop. Consequently there will be a shortage.

Daily Mirror

JULY 23

No. 11,736 — ONE PENNY
Registered at the G.P.O. as a Newspaper.

JAPS ASK VICHY FOR BASES TO HELP HITLER

RUSSIANS FIGHT TO STEM BIG NEW PUSH

U.S. WANTS HOTTER NEWS

"WE want our war news hot," is the urgent plea of American journalists in this country.

They complain that Germany gets in first with the news, and by the time America receives Britain's version it has gone stale.

Miss Dorothy Thompson, famous U.S. journalist, expressed the American woman's point of view forcibly when she arrived in this country yesterday.

"American women are realists, but they are women," she said. "They don't want to lose their menfolk, and if they live in, say, Kansas City, it's mighty difficult to convince them that this war is any concern of theirs.

"You don't help any. Your propaganda . . . ." Miss Thompson paused and raised her eyes as though seeking help.

"Well," she added, " we can stand a lot more information.

German Pictures

"We have no British pictures and plenty of German ones. We use these in our papers, but we don't use them because they are German, but because they are very good pictures."

Mr. J. F. Evans, vice-president of the Association of American Journalists in London, said yesterday.

"We want news when it is news, not after Germany has had the chance of putting her coloured interpretation before the American public, and ours, instead of appearing on the first page, gets on page 17 two or three days later."

(Hitler fears this woman—page 2.

6 WAAFS DIE IN AIR CRASH

Ten people, including six Waafs, were killed in an air crash in Northern Ireland.

A Hudson bomber collided with a telegraph pole and then crashed into a N.A.A.F.I. canteen.

RUSSIA'S WAR AIM

Moscow radio, in a war aims statement last night, said: " No one in the Soviet Union wants to export revolution. Britain and the Soviet Union are fighting for the freedom of all countries against their enemy—Hitler."

SPAIN : 'IMPORTANT STEPS'

The Spanish Cabinet will meet shortly to take important steps, states Rome radio.

All military commanders have been told to fly to Madrid.

Now You Know

revealed yesterday—the writing clerks but by schoolchildren.

By working in school hours, the cost of extra clerical labour, books out to 45,000,000 people on time, and did a grand job for Britain.

"Without this help it is doubtful if books could ever have been got out," said a Ministry of Food official.

"We arranged the scheme with the Board of Education.

The local food officer of a district where six schools handled 80,000 books told the " Daily Mirror ": "The children saved the day for us here. They took great pains to be neat and accurate.

Did you think the handwriting on the front cover of your new ration books was schoolboyish ?

The explanation was revealed yesterday—the writing was done not by Government, they saved local food offices, helped to get the new double

HITLER'S RACE FACTORY

UNCENSORED letters arriving from Occupied France by a new "underground post" tell of the Nazis' latest move in their effort to "Germanise" Europe.

Pioneer units of Rassenmutters—race-mothers—are now at work in girls' schools preaching their foul doctrine.

"Moral Duty"

Of pleasing appearance and cultured voice, with a thorough knowledge of midwifery and child care they address groups between 15 and 18 years old.

They begin with a message from " the glorious Fuehrer, who loves you so well and has your welfare so sincerely at heart that he wishes you to have children of his own pure blood."

Then they subtly develop their theme, which is the " moral duty " of every girl to bear children by German officers and soldiers.

NOW THEY FEEL FINE

Call to Lieutenant Hornemann, of the 372nd German Infantry Regiment, was broadcast by Moscow last night.

Hornemann was told by no means to worry about fifteen of his soldiers, whom he had sent on patrol.

"The whole patrol has deserted to us and we are authorised to inform you that they feel fine," said the announcer.

EAST COAST BOMBS

Raiders were over an East Coast district last night and a few bombs have been dropped.

Duke's Sister Had RAF Petrol

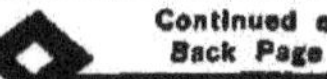

Lady Rachel Stuart.

LADY RACHEL STUART is the wife of the Government Whip and the sister of the Duke of Devonshire.

From such should be expected good example if not leadership. Yesterday at Salisbury she was fined

£10

FOR POSSESSING PETROL BELONGING TO THE R.A.F.

Why only £10?

The maximum penalty is £20 —low enough, surely—and that is what she should have got.

Petrol is brought to this country at the risk of men's lives. To the R.A.F. petrol is precious beyond price, for on it England's safety depends.

R.A.F. petrol is not for civilians, however nobly born and influential they may be.

Mr. W. Ireland prosecuting, said a gardener revealed that some petrol had been brought to Lady Rachel's home at Springfield, Downton, Wilts. When interviewed, she told the police she put some in the tank of her shooting brake and stored the rest.

A sample taken after other petrol had been put in the tank was found on analysis to contain R.A.F. petrol not exceeding 2¼ per cent.

"A person in Lady Rachel's position should set a better example than that." said Mr. Ireland

Received It Openly

Mr. G. L. Lush, defending, said the petrol was brought to Lady Rachel by a friend in September last year. Thinking it might be useful in her work as an A.R.P. volunteer driver, she accepted it, but had no idea it was R.A.F. petrol.

She received the petrol openly in front of her house, and when questioned gave a full explanation.

The chairman (Mr J M

Continued on Back Page

LONDON FOOT-BALL REVOLT

London football clubs have refused to accept the Football League fixtures for next season and have withdrawn from the competition.

Instead, they will run their own tournament—London War Football League. Eleven London clubs and five others are expected to take part in the contest.

Aldershot and Reading have already been elected. Three more places have to be filled.

These may go to Watford, Luton and Southend.

A committee, consisting of G. F. Allison (Arsenal), C. W. Fielding (Q.P.R.), G. Wagstaffe Simmons (Spurs), F. A. Davies (Brentford) and another to be co-opted, has been appointed to manage the new League.

LOWER HEELS IN NEW FOOTWEAR

The new national footwear is not expected before the autumn. it was stated in Leicester yesterday.

"Very high heels will not be obtainable in the proposed national ranges," a leading manufacturer said.

The national scheme will, it is hoped, help distribution problems.

Widow of 10 days, speaks for 1st husband in murder trial.—See page 5.

VICHY and Japan are negotiating over French Indo-China, where the Japs want bases from which to threaten British and U.S. possessions.

The news of the talks came last night from authorised circles in Vichy soon after the British Singapore radio had issued a blunt warning about Japanese moves in Indo-China.

And President Roosevelt stated in Washington yesterday that he had just learned that the Japanese Government had imposed a complete censorship on wireless and cable communications.

The President said that he regarded this move as " significant."

The Singapore statement, read in English and French, referred to

" Rumours circulated to pave the way for action by Japan."

These rumours were to the effect that Britain was contemplating action in Indo-China.

The Singapore radio added: ' An attempt may be made to justify new Japanese demands in Indo-China by the bogy of British intervention.

" It is realised that strong pressure is being brought to bear on Admiral Decoux from Vichy, and it is hoped that he wl! e able to resist it."

[On the collapse of France last year, Decoux, who was Commander - in - Chief of France's Far-Eastern Fleet, was appointed Governor-General of French Indo-China in place of General Catroux. Later, General Catroux joined the Free French.]

Japan aims at securing air and sea bases in Indo-China from which Singapore and the Philippine Islands (U.S.) could be threatened

4 BEAUTIES —£500,000

FOUR ex-Follies girls share the entire estate of the late William Guggenheim, American dollar-millionaire philanthropist.

This was learned yesterday when the will was filed for probate.

It makes no provision for the widow, Mrs. Aimee Steinbergen Guggenheim, or for son William. "I have made ample provision for them during my lifetime," states a clause in the will.

Guggenheim was heir to a huge copper fortune.

The show girls, who share his £500,000 estate equally, are Mildred Borst and Lilyan Andras, Mary Alice Rice and Florence Sullivan.

Famed for their beauty, all have at one time been the toast of New York society

BANK HOLIDAY— BUT GO TO IT

August Bank Holiday will not be cancelled, unless there are " unforeseen circumstances."

The Government view is that many people on urgent production or services should work. Others should not extend the holiday into Tuesday except in cases where Bank Holiday happens to form part of their arranged summer holiday.

Everyone is asked by the Government to avoid travel wherever possible.

WHILE Moscow was being raided again last night the Germans were making a new triple offensive against Leningrad, Moscow and Kiev.

All-day battles raged in the Smolensk wedge, where the Nazis are said to be attempting a gigantic encircling movement to trap the Soviet troops in the elbow of the Dnieper River.

Moscow's latest communique indicates that in the Ukraine the Russians have withdrawn from Novograd-Volinsk, near the 1938 frontier, to Shitomir, about eighty-five miles west of Kiev.

There was also heavy fighting in the direction of Porkhov, Smolensk and Petrozkvodsk on Lake Ladoga.

The communique reported that eighty - seven German planes were shot down during

Continued on Back Page

Daily Mirror

JULY 25

No. 11,738   ONE PENNY
Registered at the G.P.O. as a Newspaper.

First Raid by U.S. Air Forts

AMERICAN-BUILT flying fortresses went into action for the first time yesterday—in an R.A.F. daylight raid on the German battleship Gneisenau at Brest.

They scored seven direct hits. Simultaneously, other heavy bombers hit Gneisenau's sister ship Scharnhorst, found to have been moved from Brest to the port of La Pallice, near La Rochelle, 240 miles to the south.

Twenty-four of the German fighters which tried to stop the raid were destroyed. We lost fifteen bombers and seven fighters.

Other R.A.F. news last night included a three-minute V-blitz by daylight on French railway yards, destruction of a convoy of four merchant ships in the Mediterranean, and hits on two ships off Norway.

Reconnaissance planes spotted the Scharnhorst at La Pallice on Wednesday.

Before darkness fell Stirling heavy bombers had attacked the Scharnhorst as she lay alongside the breakwater.

Heavy armour - piercing bombs were dropped. A direct hit was seen.

At 2 p.m. yesterday a very strong force of heavy bombers made simultaneous attacks upon the Gneisenau at Brest and the Scharnhorst at La Pallice.

Direct Hits

It was the heaviest daylight attack which the R.A.F. has yet made.

The spearhead was a formation of "flying fortresses," which arrived over Brest at a great height, scarcely visible to anyone on the ground.

Thousands of feet below the flying fortresses their crews saw a tight formation of many Hampdens sweeping in over the target, and they could also see a star cluster of flames where bombs from the Hampdens had ringed the German warships.

The Hampdens had come with a guard of fighters and after they had finished their

Continued on Back Page

U.S.A. WARNS JAPS

THE U.S. Government last night strongly denounced Japan as an aggressor in Indo-China, and declared that any Japanese move there would menace American security and endanger American territory and interests in the Far East.

The U.S. Under-Secretary of State, Mr. Sumner Welles, issued a formal statement asserting that Japan's action in Indo-China was primarily in preparation for further "movements" of conquest in adjacent areas.

The statement was considered in Washington to be the first public move in the anticipated joint Anglo-American counteraction to Japanese occupation of Indo-China.

"Would Have Had War"

President Roosevelt admitted at the White House yesterday that the United States had been allowing Japan to obtain oil as a measure of appeasement in order to prevent the Japanese from invading the Dutch East Indies. "You would have had war," he added.

An embargo on oil shipments to Japan was urged in San Francisco last night by Mr. Wendell Willkie.

Unconfirmed reports in Shanghai yesterday said that Russian and Japanese troops had clashed on the Manchukuo-Siberian border.

MOSCOW OFF THE AIR

MOSCOW radio shut down last night just as the usual news bulletin was about to be read at 7 p.m. (B.S.T.).

The announcer said: "We are about to give you the latest news."

Then, after a few seconds' silence, he added: "Our radio stations are closing down."

The Red Army held on grimly yesterday in the battle in the direction of Smolensk.

A Soviet communique yesterday said:

"There was intense fighting throughout the night in the directions of Porkhov, Polozkhevel, Smolensk and Zhitomir.

For the third night in succession German bombers raided Moscow.

SHE WAITS A SECOND TIME . . .

DAY followed day, and no news came to young Mrs. Benson of her husband, reported missing fighting with the Rifle Brigade near Amiens.

Her baby boy was born was christened Ronald. He was six months old when at last his mother learned that her husband had been taken prisoner by the Germans.

Her man came safely home to her when the war was over —twenty-two years ago

★

Mrs. Benson, grey - haired, middle-aged now, sits in her home in Mayfield-road Swathling, Southampton waiting again for news.

Her son Ronald fought with the Royal Marines in the gallant rearguard action of Crete. He was one of the 2,000 who stayed to the end; he is posted missing.

And as she waits Mrs. Benson prays one day he will come home from the war as his father came home

HE'S DONE IT AGAIN

SENATOR Burton K. Wheeler, chief U.S. Isolationist, has been trying to sabotage the war effort again.

U.S. War Secretary, Mr. Henry Stimson, revealed last night that Wheeler had mailed a million cards to officers and men urging them to oppose America's entry into the war.

Mr. Stimson said: "This comes near the line of subversive activities, if not of treason."

Wheeler admitted mailing the cards, but denied they were directed primarily to officers and men.—Associated Press.

DANGEROUS DRUGS LOST

Seven phials of dangerous drugs in an unaddressed white envelope were lost in Westminster or Holborn yesterday. An appeal was broadcast asking the finder to communicate with Scotland Yard.

3,000,000 TO SIGN UP FOR WAR JOBS

MORE than 3,000,000 men and women—the men up to the age of 45—are to register for war work in the next five months, it was announced by the Ministry of Labour and National Service last night.

Registration is likely to carry straight on for women up to 40 and men up to 50.

The dates and ages of registrations are:—

WOMEN

Date	Class
August 2	1916
August 30	1915
September 27	1914
October 25	1913
November 8	1912
November 22	1911
December 6	1910

MEN

Date	Class
August 16	1897
September 13	1896
October 11	1895

Nearly 595,000 men have been registered in the 1898, 1899 and 1900 classes.

About 100,000 have so far been selected for interview.

About 40,000 have been found to be already engaged on work of national importance or not to be available for transfer.

At June 28, 11,500 had already been placed on the national work register or transferred to other work.

Inadequate Results

These results are inadequate. Much more drastic action may be necessary.

Employers will have to be prepared to substitute women for men.

The country can no longer afford that men should be doing jobs that can be done by women.

Girls in the 1920 to 1917 classes have already been registered. They total nearly 1,233,000.

Of these 800,000 not already

Continued on Back Page

NAVY ATTACKS ENEMY CONVOY

Light naval forces operating during the night of Wednesday-Thursday in the Straits of Dover encountered a heavily-escorted enemy convoy, the Admiralty stated last night.

During the engagement one of the enemy patrol vessels was sunk and others were severely damaged. We had no casualties.

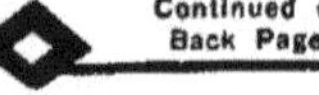

Swimming ashore in full infantry kit, and with rifle, are British soldiers.

They are OUR shock troops, in training for the day when we do a spot of invading enemy countries. The men in the picture are from the Oxford and Bucks Light Infantry, and are training in Northern Ireland.

Daily Mirror

JULY 26

No. 11,739   ONE PENNY
Registered at the G.P.O. as a Newspaper.

In a great sweep across the bare countryside, Russian peasants dig defences to check the onslaught of the German panzer troops. As their homes are threatened the women, whose menfolk are already in the fight, take their places beside the old men and boys left behind, and unite the whole Soviet nation against the savagery of the Nazi attacks.—BRITISH PARAMOUNT NEWS.

THE WOMEN OF RUSSIA

EMPIRE AND U.S. "FREEZE" JAPAN

ALL Japanese gold and other assets are to be frozen in the British Empire and the United States as from this morning.

This move—first simultaneous British-American action of the war—is being made in retaliation for Japan's occupation of Vichy naval and air bases in Indo-China.

The announcement was made in London last night following a statement by President Roosevelt.

He said the United States would take "specific action" but refused to divulge its nature.

Economic Sanctions

Washington observers thought economic sanctions against Japan would be coupled with intensified American aid for China and Russia.

The British Foreign Secretary saw M. Maisky, Russian Ambassador, and Mr. Wellington Koo, Chinese Ambassador, yesterday afternoon.

This followed an important but mysterious statement made in Parliament by the Foreign Secretary.

He said, amid cheers: "The Government regards this [Indo-China] development as a potential threat to our territories and interests in the Far East.

"In anticipation of that, we have been in close communication with the United States Government, the Government of the Netherlands, and, of course, the Dominions.

"Certain defence measures in Malaya have already been

Continued on Back Page

60 ILL AT MINISTRY: POISONING

AN hour after a canteen lunch, sixty members of the staffs of the Ministry of Transport and the Ministry of Economic Warfare were rushed in ambulances to three London hospitals yesterday.

Food poisoning was diagnosed. Fifty-six people were detained, but only one case was regarded as serious.

The hospitals were asked to stand-by for more cases which might take longer to develop.

Several girl typists and men collapsed at their desks.

Doctors were hastily summoned. They sent their patients to Charing Cross, Westminster and St. George's Hospitals.

"It was like a battlefield," a Civil Servant told the *Daily Mirror* last night.

"People, mostly women, were flopping out all around. "Others were running to their aid and carrying them into the corridors and cloakrooms."

About 300 people eat at the Ministry canteen every day. An investigation is being made.

QUIET DAY FOR R.A.F.

Except for the now customary patrol activity by R.A.F. fighters, it was quiet over the Channel and south-east coast yesterday.

NEW TANK FAST AS A TRAIN

A new type of British tank, which "made rings round the Germans" in the Middle East, and can travel as fast as an express train, has been named "Crusader."

A General of the Royal Armoured Corps said yesterday: "The way these machines fired as they raced over the desert surprised the Germans and stupefied the Italians.

Threaten Portugal

By BILL GREIG

PORTUGAL, Britain's oldest ally, has received from Germany what amounts to an ultimatum demanding U-boat and air bases.

Baron Hoyningen, the German Minister, has seen the Portuguese Foreign Minister every day this week in an attempt to press home his point.

In return for the bases Portugal is offered "complete sovereignty" in the New Europe against the limited sovereignty arranged for other nations.

Hoyningen has threatened that if the bases are not given Portugal will be given to Spain in the New Europe. London and Washington are being kept informed of the negotiations.

RUSSIANS TO BUY FROM U.S.

Mr. Sumner Welles, U.S. Acting Secretary of State, announced yesterday that Russia is sending a special mission to the United States to buy war supplies.

The Soviet Ambassador has already discussed the orders Russia wishes to place.—Reuter.

Her Joy Ride in Warplane

(See Back Page)

NAZIS DRIVE NORTH AGAIN

GERMAN forces resumed their drive towards Leningrad yesterday.

This ended the two-day lull in the Germans' second offensive, which had almost slowed to a standstill.

There is again heavy fighting in the Pskov sector of the Leningrad front, it was stated in London yesterday.

Stiff fighting rages around Smolensk, but few details are available, while near Kiev the battle is still indecisive. German forces there are pushing towards the south-east and are trying to encircle the Russian Army in Bessarabia and to "roll up" the Russian lines.

Intensive fighting on four fronts was reported in the second communique issued by the Russians yesterday.

"During last night," it stated, "intensive fighting continued in the direction of Petrozavodsk (on the Finnish front), Porkhov (in the Leningrad sector), Polotsk-Nevel (on the Moscow front) Smolensk and Shitomir (on the Kiev front).

Division Wiped Out

"Our aircraft operated against the enemy in co-operation with land forces."

"Russian troops, standing astride the road to Moscow, annihilated a whole German infantry division in the Smolensk sector, the first Russian communique stated.

The annihilated 5th Infantry was "freshly arrived at the front."

The Germans were unable to claim any big victory.

Still using the well-worn phrase that "operations are continuing according to plan" along the eastern front, the

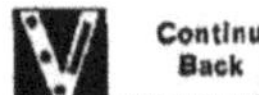

Continued on Back Page

CAMOUFLAGE MAN LENT TO RUSSIA

Britain is to lend one of her camouflage experts to the Russian Government. He is Captain L. M. Glasson, of the Directorate of Camouflage.

Professor W. N. Thomas, Professor of Engineering at the University of Wales, attached to the Department of Research and Experiment of the Ministry of Home Security, has also been loaned to the Soviet. He is an expert on the safety of buildings.

FIVE ITALIAN PLANES BAGGED OVER MALTA

One Fiat bomber, one Savoia reconnaissance plane, and three fighter escorts were shot out of the sky without loss or damage to our own fighters over Malta yesterday.—Associated Press.

CADBURYS PRICES

The following are the present prices of some of the Cadbury favourites:

BLOCK CHOCOLATE

	Small Size	½lb	1lb
Bournville		2½d	5½d	11d
Bournville				
Fruit & Nut	2½d	5½d	—
Ration Chocolate	2½d	5½d	—
Milk				
Whole Nut Milk	2½d	6d	1/-
Almond Dessert	Packet 6d	
Fine Dessert	Packet 6d	

FILLED BLOCKS

Caramello	
Peppermint Creme	2½d each
Creme Pineapple	
Plain Tray Block	3d

ASSORTMENTS

	Per Qtr	½lb	½lb	1lb
	Loose	Box	Box	Box
Vogue	—	—	1/9	3/4
Plain Tray	7½d	8d	1/4	2/8
Roses				
Milk Tray	—	—	1/4	—

FOOD DRINKS

	½lb	½lb	1lb
Bournville Cocoa	5d	9½d	1/6
Bourn-vita	9d	1/5	2/9

All Cadburys prices are based on careful costing and are only changed as cost changes demand

Cadbury Bros.

Daily Mirror

JULY 28

No. 11,740   ONE PENNY
Registered at the G.P.O. as a Newspaper.

It'll Take Our Whole Army to Beat Russia

—Nazis Told

TWO German newspapers yesterday prepared the German public for a hard war against Russia They said:—

1.—The entire German Army must be used to beat Russia.

2.—The war against the Soviet is the most adventurous in history.

General Liebmann, writing in the *Berliner Boerzen Zeitung*, said:—

"The German people must not expect the war in the east to be won in a short time even though our troops have entered on the decisive battle.

"This decisive phase cannot be won by motorised or tank troops

"The Russian resistance makes it necessary to throw into the battle the entire German Army, the majority of which consists of un-motorised infantry and horse-drawn wagons and batteries.

"This battle, which has put a very great strain on our troops, has entered the open battlefield, but this must be considered only as the beginning of the decisive battle."

"Adventurous War"

The *Frankfurter Zeitung*, reviewing the war, stated:—

"The war in the east has developed into quite a different kind of war from that in the west and has become the most adventurous war in history."

"Although it is realised by the tank troops that after breaking the oncoming wave of enemy troops this wave ever and again closes behind them, our troops do not retreat. Everything depends on whether reinforcements arrive in time.

"Lately Russian troops have developed the same tactic of often deeply penetrating our lines.

"Therefore it is difficult today to designate our exact

Continued on Back Page

RUSSIAN SONGS ON RADIO

Under the new scheme by which national songs are being substituted for the national anthems of the Allies, the B.B.C. broadcast last night, before the nine o'clock news, half a dozen Russian national marches and songs.

Champagne of Memories

"Lot 443. One bottle champagne. Vintage 1928." . . . Extract from Red Cross and St. John auction list.

But Lot 443 holds memories. . . .

With the bottle she had never had the heart to open, Mrs. C. F. O. Kelly, of Bristol, sent a letter, saying:

"This was bought as a toast for my first wedding anniversary, but having lost my husband before this arrived I should like it to be given to the great cause."

CAN'T KILL THIS LAMB

WHEN his daughters brought home a lamb purchased from an R.A.F. officer who won it in a raffle, Mr. Bert Tropnell, of Mendip-road, Weston-super-Mare, had pleasant thoughts of "lashings" of roast lamb, mint sauce and green peas.

But when he told the good news to a pal, he learned that livestock could be slaughtered only under licence.

He tried to get a licence, only to learn that he would have to surrender meat coupons to the market value of the lamb.

And so Flossie the lamb is still alive—and earning her keep. She is parading Weston-super-Mare with a box on her back collecting coins for the Red Cross Penny a Week Fund.

Their Lies	We publish on page 5 some of the grimmest pictures of the war. They will hurt you.
Her Tears	
Your Hate	But they will help to make you hate the loathsome monsters responsible for the ghastly crime revealed.

An E-boat travelling at speed.

WREN IN A NAVAL VICTORY

WITH a number of Very Important Brass Hats, Mr. Peter Fraser, Prime Minister of New Zealand, was walking to his car after inspecting a naval station in south-east England.

Behind him he heard a voice crying: "Mr. Fraser, Mr. Fraser!"

The whole party swung round. Breathlessly a Wren — a pretty Scots girl—ran up waving a sheet of paper.

"I'm sorry I haven't got an autograph book, Mr. Fraser," she said, "but would you give me your autograph on this?"

The Very Important Brass Hats were dumbfounded. Some faces registered horror. Had such a thing ever been known tion?

Mr. Fraser, smiling signed his name.

Then the Wren turned to the General Officer Commanding—AND ASKED FOR HIS AUTOGRAPH AS WELL.

There was a moment of terrible suspense in the ranks of the Brass Hats.

But the G.O.C. was smiling too. He signed.

AIR WAR SCORE FOR WEEK: 69 TO 65

AIR losses last week on the Western Front and the Middle East were ninety-five Axis machines and seventy-four British aircraft.

The German High Command claimed to have shot down last week 127 British planes and to have lost only seven of their own in the west.

The actual figures were sixty-nine German and sixty-five British aircraft.

The Luftwaffe had five destroyed over Britain and sixty-four over Germany and occupied territory.

The R.A.F. lost one over Britain and sixty-four (with one pilot saved) in large-scale raids on Germany, occupied ports and shipping.

MALTA SANK 17 TORPEDO RAIDERS

THE enemy lost eight secret torpedo boats, at least nine E-boats and three planes in their attack on Valetta Harbour, Malta, it was announced in London last night.

E-boats appeared off the harbour entrance shortly before 5 a.m. on Saturday. The fixed defences manned by the military garrison swung into action.

One of the E-boats blew up. Four others were destroyed by gunfire.

The E-boats were acting as cover for eight smaller torpedo-carrying craft—on which the Italians claim to have been working in secret for years.

These midget ships tried to break into the harbour They were heavily engaged by gunfire from the shore defences. None of them got into the harbour Each was either blown up or sunk

R.A.F. fighters pursued the remaining E-boats, sank four more of them and damaged others

According to Signor Gayda the men manning torpedoes have little hope of returning.

They are claimed to be able to skip over torpedo nets

The men, wearing bathing suits and cork belts and crash helmets, THEORETICALLY detach themselves from the torpedo and return in a tiny boat with an outboard motor, which is attached to the torpedo on the outward trip.

Our fighters then met enemy aircraft which were trying to support the retreating boats.

Three enemy planes were

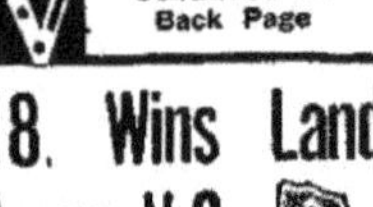

Continued on Back Page

18. Wins Land Army V.C.

Miss A. Eke . . . on her breast the Sustained Courage Badge of the Women's Land Army, presented to her at Maidstone (Kent) yesterday at a W.L.A. rally.

With bombs falling round her, machine-gun bullets and shells whizzing past in the Dover area, this 18-year-old former library assistant day after day went calmly and bravely on with her job. So did six other Land Army girls also awarded the badge.

JAPS GO INTO INDO-CHINA

JAPAN began to occupy Vichy's Indo-China yesterday. Troops disembarked at ports in Cambodia, bordering Thailand (Siam), and containing the important naval base of Koh-Kong.

At the same time, Japanese military lorries entered Saigon, capital of Indo-China. Bombers roared above them.

According to the Chinese National Military Council in Chungking, Japan has also presented demands to Thailand to join the "new order in East Asia."

From Saigon it was reported that Japan will station a powerful force within easy striking distance of Thailand.

"U.S. Navy Is Ready"

In Ottawa, Mr. Mackenzie King, Canadian Premier, announced that Canada has severed trade relations with Japan.

America too had something to say.

Admiral William Standly, former Chief of Naval Operations, declared in a broadcast:

"The United States Navy is ready and adequate to meet defence needs in the Pacific and, at the same time, give the British enough support to win the Battle of the Atlantic."

PLANE HIT HOUSE —TWO KILLED

Two people—a motor-cyclist and a woman passenger—were killed when a British plane, which had collided with another in mid-air, crashed on a house and exploded in Lincoln last night. Parts of the plane struck them.

Other casualties were caused, and property was damaged. Firemen and demolition squads were called out.

The pilots of the planes escaped by parachute.

Daily Mirror

No. 11,742   ONE PENNY
Registered at the G.P.O. as a Newspaper.

Forces on Toes for Sept. 1

BRITAIN'S armed forces have been warned to be at concert pitch by September 1, opening of the invasion season, and to maintain the utmost vigilance meanwhile.

Stating this in his speech in the House of Commons yesterday the Premier said:

"When I look out on the whole tumultuous scene of this ever-widening war I feel it my duty to give a very serious warning to the House and country. We must be on our guard equally against pessimism and optimism. (Cheers.)

"There are no doubt grounds for optimism. It is a fact that the mighty Russian State, so foully and treacherously assaulted, has struck back with magnificent strength and courage and has inflicted prodigious and well-deserved slaughter for the first time on the Nazi Army.

"It is the fact that the Nile valley is much safer now than it was twelve months ago or three months ago.

Worst Not Over

"It is the fact that the German air superiority has been broken, and the air attacks on this country have for the time being almost ceased to be serious.

"It is the fact that the Battle of the Atlantic, although far from being won, has partly through American intervention moved impressively in our favour.

"It is the fact that the United States, the greatest single Power in the world, is giving us aid on a gigantic scale and is advancing in rising wrath and conviction to the very verge of the war.

"But all these massive

Continued on Back Page

NAZI NINE MILE RUN

A SOVIET regiment defeated a big German force in the Ukrainian marshes and chased them nine miles before annihilating them, according to a dispatch from Moscow.

Marshal Budenny, the Russian commander in the southern sector, appeared when the Russians were preparing to attack, and personally assumed command.

"Is it hot, boys?" he asked the troops.

"It is much hotter there," they replied, pointing towards the enemy.

The marshes were filled with German corpses, lorries and guns after the battle.

"Nazi Units Encircled"

The German advance has been generally checked, and Russian tanks have cut into the enemy's rear in many places, forcing leading units to retreat, said M. Lozovsky, the Soviet Information Bureau chief, last night.

The Soviet counter-attacks had hurled the Germans back, M. Lozovsky asserted, and action continued along the front on the flanks in the enemy's rear. Some of the Nazi units, he said, were reported to be encircled.

This morning's communique reports particularly heavy fighting in the Smolensk direction, where the Germans were driven back.

Between Sunday and Monday seventy-four planes were brought down for the loss of fifty-one Russian planes. At least nine German planes were destroyed in an attempt to blitz Moscow.

But You Must Bring Proof...

Expectant mothers are to get an extra fifty clothing coupons to buy wool and other materials for babies' clothes.

Those who can bring proof that twins will be born will get a double allowance.

Proof means a certificate from a doctor or midwife or from the medical officer of an ante-natal clinic.

Until special cards of fifty coupons are issued, about the end of August, emergency vouchers of five will be supplied by public health departments of local child welfare authorities.

DUKE FLIES ATLANTIC

FIRST member of a royal family to fly the Atlantic, the Duke of Kent arrived in Ottawa, Canada, from Britain, yesterday.

He had flown in an American-built four-engine Liberator bomber, which has a range of 3,000 miles and a speed of 330 m.p.h.

Six Weeks' Visit

The Duke, who is to inspect R.A.F. training centres, will visit every province, travelling by air, and intends to stay about six weeks.

Time will not allow a U.S.A. tour, it is stated, nor are there plans for a meeting with the Duke of Windsor.

There had been reports that the Duke of Windsor might visit his ranch in Alberta this summer, and that the visit would be timed for a reunion. —Reuter.

M.P.s NOT YET SATISFIED WITH OUR OUTPUT EFFORT

THE House of Commons remains unconvinced that the Government's war production drive is as good as it could—and should—be.

Chief critic during yesterday's debate was Sir John Wardlaw-Milne, who, as chairman of the Select Committee on National Expenditure, speaks with greater authority than anyone outside the War Cabinet.

He refused to accept the Prime Minister's long and optimistic statement (given on page 2) of the nation's effort, and was supported in his criticisms by other Conservative, Socialist and Liberal M.P.s.

"Reasonable and careful criticism is the duty of the House of Commons." he declared.

"If we are not fighting for free discussion in the House, a free Press and free criticism, for what are we fighting?" he demanded.

Sir John said: "To some of us the Prime Minister has not dealt in the detail expected with criticism made in the previous debate

Still Short

"Before the last debate on production I said we were not working to more than seventy-five per cent. of the possibilities of the nation. I am still convinced that taking our total effort, we are still short.

"A great advantage of these debates will be that the nation is brought to realise that we must get that extra 25 per cent. from them."

Since his 75 per cent. estimate, Sir John said he had had hundreds of contacts and in only one case—and that very guardedly—had he not been confirmed in his estimate. The rest suggested that he was over-optimistic.

He had never suggested that his estimate that war production was at present only seventy-five per cent. of its full capacity was anything more than an estimate. He could only speak his own idea based on such information as he had of the maximum which industry could achieve.

"One of the objects I had in view," he went on, "has been achieved, because it has brought to the notice of the Government the fact that a very large number of the people in this country do not believe

Continued on Back Page

BOY FIRED TO THE END

WHEN his ship was attacked by an enemy submarine, Ordinary - Seaman Stanley Anderson, 16, refused to leave his gun though wounded and was killed by a shell.

Young Anderson will be known as the "Jack Cornwell" of the Merchant Navy. He has been posthumously awarded the Lloyd's War Medal for bravery.

Anderson was on his first voyage, and the story of his deed says that he behaved with "great courage and coolness." He was wounded early in the action. Two other ship's gunners died with him.

Two Hours' Fight

Anderson's third officer, Percy Donald Jones, who was in charge of the gun's crew, gets a similar medal.

He was wounded in the head and chest, but continued to use his gun till it was hit.

The merchantman had a fight of nearly two hours with the submarine. Only when fire was raging in the bridgehouse and holds did the master give orders to abandon ship.

The submarine continued firing till the vessel sank.

R.A.F.'s 34-0

IN one of its most brilliant actions of the war, the R.A.F. on Monday smashed thirty-four planes without loss to us in swoops on four Sicily airfields.

Yesterday's Middle East R.A.F. communique, giving this news, said many other enemy aircraft were damaged and casualties inflicted on ground staffs.

Sir John Wardlaw-Milne —who, as Chairman of the Select Committee on National Expenditure, is watchdog of war costs. It is his job, with twenty-eight other M.P.s, to cut out waste. He is Conservative M.P. for Kidderminster.

OUR NEW BOMBER

Head-on and side views of our latest new big bomber, the Short Stirling. Although it has been in action some time these are the first pictures released. Four-engined, it is one of the world's largest military aircraft. It can carry a very heavy load of bombs, and has a top speed of 250 m.p.h. at 10,000ft., and possesses a very heavy defensive armament.

Daily Mirror

JULY 31

No. 11,743   ♦   ONE PENNY
Registered at the G.P.O. as a Newspaper.

300,000 POLISH ARMY RELEASED TO FIGHT NAZIS

Start of Big Soviet Drive

ALTHOUGH there is no evidence in London that the Russians have launched a major counter - offensive, authoritative quarters believe their latest attacks may be the start of a larger offensive.

The Russians have launched strong counter-attacks, particularly in the Smolensk sector.

Yesterday Russian High Command communique stated:—

"During the night our troops were engaged in stubborn fighting in the Nevel, Smolensk and Shitomir sectors.

BY ENDING A TWENTY YEARS' QUARREL, RUSSIA AND POLAND HAVE PUT ANOTHER ARMY — OF 300,000 FIRST-CLASS SOLDIERS—IN THE FIELD AGAINST HITLER.

The British Foreign Minister announced in the House of Commons last night that a Soviet-Polish agreement had been signed in London during the afternoon and was now in force.

Russia consents to the formation on Soviet territory of a Polish Army under Polish command, to fight under Soviet direction.

Russia also gives the Poles a place on the Red Army supreme command.

There are 300,000 Polish prisoners of war in Russia, and they are all first-class fighting men.

Now they will have weapons such as they lacked when the Germans attacked Poland at the opening of the war.

These Poles surrendered when the Red Army entered Poland to form the protective belt against the Nazis which has proved so useful in the present war on the Eastern Front

Five-Point Pact

Russia and Poland had never been friendly since the war fought between them in 1921.

Now the memory of that war and of 1939 will be wiped out by a common fight and an agreement on territory

The agreement says:—

1. The Government of the U.S.S.R. recognises the Soviet-German treaties of 1939 as to territorial changes in Poland as having lost their validity. The Polish Government declares that Poland is not bound by any agreement with any third

Continued on Back Page

The Duke of Kent (left) stepped into a Liberator bomber a few minutes after this picture was taken. Nine hours later he was in Canada—first member of the Royal Family to fly the Atlantic. He and his party wore electrically heated flying suits to protect them from the cold, "but we couldn't find any place to plug them in," commented the Duke.

RESCUED —THEN RESCUER

WHEN sister and father went to the rescue of a girl who feared she was drowning all three got into difficulties.

The rescuing sister was drowned and the father was saved by the daughter he had gone to rescue.

The story was told at the inquest at Chapelton, North Devon, yesterday on Phyllis Mary Ford, 26, a non-swimmer.

Daisy Irene Ford told how she got into difficulties while swimming in the River Taw, near her home.

"We Went Under"

"I felt as if I had gone into a pit. I called to my mother and father, who were on the banks, and then Phyllis came towards me

"Dad came out as well. We all seemed to struggle very hard for a while, and we went under. I called out to my father: 'I am sorry, I am going; say goodbye to mother.'

"Then I got away a bit. Phyllis floated away from me. I caught hold of my father and tried to pull him out.

"I got a bit further out, still holding my father. I held up his chin and eventually got him to the shallow part unconscious."

Accidental death was the verdict on Phyllis.

'YES TO CONSCRIPT PLAN'

The House of Representatives Military Affairs Committee yesterday approved President Roosevelt's plans to retain conscripts and reservists for service beyond their call-up term. The Senate Military Affairs Committee had already approved

Huns Roasted

"The Russian Air Force, cooperating with the land forces, dealt heavy blows at enemy mechanised and motorised units infantry and artillery.

"A guerrilla unit, having found out that a German tank column had taken refuge in a forest, set the whole forest ablaze.

"More than 600 German soldiers were enclosed in the ring of fire. They perished "

Nazi spokesmen claimed last night that the fighting was "fast approaching important decisions," with pressure increased on Leningrad and on the Russians, said to be encircled east of Smolensk.

In the south, the Germans claimed steady progress, with the Rumanian and German forces controlling all Bessarabia, and said that they had made a thrust to the southeast to within thirty miles of Odessa.

Their Fuse Failed

Leningrad was said to be in a precarious situation because of German successes north and north-west of Lake Peipus.

In one sector, said Moscow radio last night, a weak German force in a wood put microphones beside their machine-guns and hung loud-speakers on trees, so that the amplified noise made the Russians think a strong unit was opposed to them.

Russian patrols discovered the trick and the Nazis were wiped out.

Russian torpedo boats in the Baltic scattered a German convoy yesterday and sank a barge laden with tanks and infantry.

DEMAND RIGHT TO QUIT FARMS

FARM workers are demanding to be allowed to go to other work unless their application for a £3 a week minimum is granted immediately.

They are dissatisfied with the reply given yesterday by the Minister of Agriculture to their protest against the decision of the Central Agricultural Wages Board, which deferred their claim till November.

A deputation of the National Union of Agricultural Workers and the Transport and General Workers' Union will ask the Minister of Labour to remove agricultural workers from the Restriction of Engagements Order.

There is still hope that the Board's decision will be altered. Failing this, the workers contend that it is unfair to ban their changing to other jobs in which they could get higher wages.

COUPONS CAUSE GLUT IN OVERALLS

Women are refusing to give up seven coupons for overalls, and hundreds of thousands of overalls are "frozen" on traders' hands.

Mr. Bernard Ely, of Wimbledon, chairman of the Drapers' Chamber of Trade War Emergency Committee, revealed this at a meeting of the chamber yesterday.

PICTURES FOR NAZI ARMY

The Russians have produced, in German, "The Illustrated Front for the German Soldiers."

The illustrations show the wreckage of Nazi tanks and aeroplanes, of which during the first month, the paper declares, 3,000 and 5,000 respectively were destroyed.

Another illustration shows a long row of German soldiers' graves.

DOGS IN BLONDE HUNT

POLICE dogs were used in a search over wild Hampshire country yesterday for Miss Margaret Sargeaunt, pretty blonde Liverpool clerk, missing from the hamlet of Ashley, near Winchester.

Daughter of Lieutenant-Colonel and Mrs. Sargeaunt, of the Old Rectory, Ashley, she is thought to have left the house for a walk on Sunday morning, but had neither money nor food. Nothing has been seen of her since.

She was wearing dark green trousers and green blouse and was hatless

Her brother, Mr. Tony Sargeaunt, told the Daily Mirror: "My sister had been working in the postal censorship department in Liverpool and went through all the raids. I know that she often went for long periods without sleep.

"When she left to go for a walk she seemed perfectly well and normal. I can only think that she may have been more exhausted than we imagined and that she may be suffering from loss of memory."

JAP BOMBS HIT U.S. GUNBOAT

The American Navy announced yesterday that the United States gunboat Tutuila (370 tons) had been damaged by Japanese bombs during an air raid on Chungking.

She was reported to be anchored in the Yangtze River, where she is employed on patrol, when raiders loosed several bombs, which slightly damaged the stern superstructure.

Navy sources said that the damage was incidental to the general raid.

The British and Soviet Embassies were damaged.—Associated Press, British United Press and Reuter.

SENTRY'S SHOT KILLED OFFICER

A sentry's shot fired at a motor-car after a challenge in a country lane killed Lieutenant John Michael Hugill, an intelligence officer at Cambridge, whose home is at Sanderstead, Surrey.

Lieutenant Hugill was driving his small touring car in the dusk, accompanied by Miss Pamela Florence Humphrey, 17, of Trumpington, Cambridge.

The girl heard the sentry's challenge, but apparently Lieutenant Hugill did not, although it was repeated twice.

As he did not stop the car, the sentry fired. The bullet passed through the car and struck the officer in the region of the heart.

HOMES FOR RAID ORPHANS

Hundreds of offers of homes for children orphaned through air raids have been received by the Ministry of Pensions.

ITALY SAVES CRACK SHIP

Italy's crack 35,000-ton battleship Vittorio Veneto, torpedoed in the Battle of Matapan on March 28, has reached port.

VENISON FOR ALL—IN TINS

Canned venison may soon be available for all classes of the community, the Secretary for Scotland told the Commons yesterday.

Roosevelt to Fix Prices

PRESIDENT ROOSEVELT plans to control prices and rents to prevent inflation.

In a message to Congress yesterday asking for authority to do this, he said that inflationary price increases were threatening "to undermine our defence efforts."

He also asked for authority to purchase materials and commodities when necessary to assure price stability.

He said rents were already soaring, and "this development must be arrested before rent profiteering can develop to increase the cost of living and damage civilian morale."

Congress is sharply divided on the question.—Reuter.

Daily Mirror

AUG. 2

No. 11,745 — ONE PENNY
Registered at the G.P.O. as a Newspaper.

RUSSIAN PUSH ON ALL FRONTS —NAZIS ADMIT

MILLIONAIRE IS SHOT DOWN

A WOMAN who obtained eight rations instead of four, by getting duplicate ration books on a false statement that she had lost the originals, was sent to prison for one month by Sheriff Macdonald at Edinburgh Sheriff Court yesterday.

It was stated that Mrs. Elizabeth Ramsay, staying in lodgings at Grindlay-street, Edinburgh, first said she had lost the ration books of herself and her daughter.

She signed application forms for duplicate ration books, and used them to obtain double rations.

Later she represented that she had lost her husband's and son's ration books and was issued with two more duplicate books. She thus obtained eight rations instead of four.

Double Ration —Gaol

BERLIN OFFICIALS LAST NIGHT ADMITTED THAT THE RUSSIANS WERE COUNTER-ATTACKING HEAVILY ON ALL FRONTS ALONG 2,000 MILES FROM LAKE LADOGA TO THE BLACK SEA.

The German radio admitted that the Finns were meeting strong Russian counter-attacks on the Karelian front.

Hungarian troops fighting with the Germans are also being made to take their part in the slaughter to aid their Nazi allies.

They are facing very strong Russian counter-attacks, the Hungarian communique said.

German tanks designed for "blitz" tactics are being earthed—by the Nazis themselves.

In the Smolensk area, where the Russians are furiously counter-attacking, the Nazis have been forced to sink their tanks into the earth for use as "pillboxes."

Fresh Soviet troops and Russian tanks of a new type are being thrown into the battle.

Airborne Tanks

These tanks are believed to be better than any in the world, it was stated authoritatively in London.

The arrival of the new troops and new tanks, it was added, settles doubts about Russia's armoured resources.

The Nazis tried the idea, worked out by the Russians earlier of landing light tanks by air behind their enemy's lines.

Most of these airborne German tanks were destroyed and the survivors are battling desperately to escape.

Nazi troops were forced to dig trenches in an effort to hold ground against the reseated Russian attacks.

This morning's Russian communique reports that a German regiment had been "completely smashed," and six tanks, two armoured cars, guns and lorries captured.

There was no substantial change in the positions of the troops.

Russian cavalry detach-

Continued on Back Page

Film star Robert Montgomery, who drove an ambulance in France, gets a new job.

DURING an air battle over the Channel yesterday, R.A.F. pilots heard their squadron-leader, millionaire Wing Commander Whitney Straight, M.C., say over their radio:—

"I have been hit. Going to force land in France. I order the squadron to return to base."

Wing Commander Whitney Straight was leading a squadron of Hurricanes in a fighter - escorted bombing attack on enemy shipping.

When diving on to the ships they were met by withering flak. The wing commander was seen to pull out of the dive and level out with white smoke pouring from the engine.

After his radio instruction, the pilots swept the vessels with their fire, levelled out, and flew back to their base as instructed.

Some of them reported that they saw their leader's plane gliding down over the French coast towards the land.

Many Adventures

Straight, who is 28, is the son of an American millionaire, and is a director of twenty-one aviation companies. He was educated in England, and was naturalised in 1936.

He has had many adventures as a pilot and racing driver.

He won the M.C. in Norway, where he was severely wounded. He flew over a frozen lake, surveyed it and directed the layout as a base for Gladiator fighters.

When he was wounded his wife, Lady Daphne Straight, sister of the Earl of Winchilsea, was in America.

Film Star Is Naval Attache

FILM star Robert Montgomery reported for duty yesterday morning at the American Embassy.

He flew the Atlantic and arrived in England on Thursday.

His appointment is that of an assistant naval attache, and he is staying in an hotel a few minutes' walk from the Embassy.

Mr. Montgomery drove an ambulance in France during the German invasion.

R.A.F. READY IN EAST

AS Tokio reports yesterday indicated that Thailand was yielding to Japan's pressure, it was revealed that the R.A.F. in Burma had been "considerably" reinforced and were already in new advanced bases.

And in a Singapore broadcast, Lieutenant-Commander J. C. R. Proud, of the Australian Navy, stated that our land forces had been recently stengthened by mechanised British regiments.

The air reinforcements include American-built Brewster Buffalo multi - gun fighters which have been shipped across the Pacific.

'Dromes in the Jungle

Burma is now equipped not only for defence, but for offensive air action.

Aerodromes made in the jungle midway between the coast and the frontiers of Thailand and China are now complete, and give the R.A.F. advance bases for bomber squadrons.

Latest Japanese threat was revealed in two Tokio announcements that Thailand had recognised Japan's puppet State of

Continued on Back Page

NO U.S. FUEL FOR JAPAN

EXPORTS to Japan of United States motor fuel and oil were cut off by an order issued in Washington last night.

President Roosevelt directed his export control administrator to prohibit exports of motor fuels and oils for the use of aircraft "to destinations outside the Western Hemisphere or the British Empire, or unoccupied territories of countries resisting aggression."

Commenting on the United States decision to send aid to the Soviet via the Pacific, a leading Japanese newspaper declares: "Japan, as signatory to the Tripartite Pact, cannot remain aloof to seeing the Pacific being used for such purposes."

F. R. D. Praises Russia.—Back page.

Offer to Work Free

DOCKERS on strike at Liverpool yesterday offered to go back to work—and to work four-hour shifts for a day without pay—on one condition.

The men's offer was made to prove that they had no desire to impede the war effort.

Their condition was the abolition of the "pen"—a corrugated iron enclosure in which they are supposed to wait until their turn for a job comes along.

Their offer was passed on to the Regional Port Controller, Mr. J. Gibson Jarvie.

Last night Mr. Jarvie met union officials, and today another attempt will be made by the union to persuade the men to return to work.

'Like Concentration Camp'

The Controller gave an assurance yesterday that the pen enclosures are only temporary, and that proper enclosures will be put up

"The pen is roofless, made of salvaged timber and iron sheeting, and reminds us of a concentration camp," the men told Mr. J. Donovan national dock organiser

"We advised the men to return to work while we negotiated the question of the pens, but they were adamant. They refused to work until they are abolished."

Glasgow dock labour dispute was settled yesterday. "The position is as you were," said a trade union official.

"The Ministry of Transport have agreed to withdraw the new labour allocation system and the old system will continue."

BIG ARMS CONVOY ARRIVES

ONE of the biggest convoys ever to cross the Atlantic has reached this country —WITHOUT THE LOSS OF A SINGLE SHIP.

The convoy carried large supplies of ammunition and other war material from Canada and the U.S.A. as well as food and personnel.

A member of the crew of one ship said that the only excitement during the voyage was when escorting warships chased around dropping depth charges.

There were nearly 250 lumberjacks from Nova Scotia who are to join their mates already in Britain, and a party of nurses and doctors from Canada and the United States who have come for hospital and first-aid work.

The Third Canadian Division, commanded by Major-General C. B. Price, has also arrived in Britain. In the same convoy were hundreds of United States technicians.

Arrival of these thousands of fresh troops implements the promise by Mr. Mackenzie King, Canada's Prime Minister — "Every month will see more Canadians in Britain to share in the defence."

Major - General Price, an N.C.O. when he went to France in the last war, was wounded three times and won his commission in the field.

V-MEN FIRED HITLER MOUNTAIN

The explanation of the great petrol fire which recently enveloped in smoke Hitler's mountain retreat at Berchtesgaden was given by Moscow radio last night.

At a meeting of the Communists at Salzburg it was reported that train after train of petrol tanks had gone into the mountain side near Berchtesgaden.

Petrol was being stored in salt mines to keep it safe from air attack.

A small party of men were ordered to destroy the petrol. They succeeded so well that the fire lasted for days.

NEW POWERS FOR DARLAN

Power to order removal from his home of any person whose presence is deemed a danger to national security is given to Admiral Darlan, Vichy Minister of the Interior, by a new law.—Reuter.

JOB FOR CHURCHILL'S SON

Major Randolph Churchill, son of the Premier, has been appointed to the staff of the Minister of State in the Middle East.

FINNS BREAK WITH BRITAIN

Finland took the initiative last night in severing diplomatic relations with Great Britain. M. Gripenburg the Minister in London, called at the Foreign Office, on instructions from Helsinki, to ask for his passport.

Sweden will look after Finland's interests in Britain, and when Mr. George Vereker has taken similar action in Helsinki it is expected that the United States will watch Britain's interests there.

The Finnish Legation may be transferred to Dublin, according to a suggestion made by the Nazis.

It is considered that Finland has been forced by the Nazis into breaking off relations.

It is expected that Britons in Finland will be exchanged for Finns in this country.

"DON'T TRAVEL" PLEA IGNORED

Despite official appeals for a stay-at-home August Bank Holiday, yesterday was one of the busiest pre-holiday Fridays for many years at some London railway stations.

At King's Cross thirteen additional trains were scheduled for Scotland and the north, and at Euston twelve were run.

At Waterloo there was heavy traffic all day for the West. Eighteen additional trains had to be run, and one ran in five parts.

The demand for sleeping accommodation was exceptionally heavy. Last night queues at the booking offices threatened even heavier travelling on the main lines to the north today.

GENERAL'S SPECIAL DUTY

The rank of Acting Major-General has been granted to Colonel (Temporary Brigadier) R. G. Lewis, who is to be specially employed, states the London Gazette. Major-General Lewis has been General Staff Officer at the War Office.

Daily Mirror

AUG. 5

No. 11,747

ONE PENNY

Registered at the G.P.O. as a Newspaper.

HUNS WIN SLIGHT GAINS IN PUSHES ON KIEV

He saved a girl with rod and line

A QUIET morning's fishing over the week-end brought Mr. Southern Dexter, a retired Civil Servant, a catch to beat all fishing stories.

He was baiting up his line on the beach near St. Dogmaels, Cardigan, when a man the other side of the river estuary signalled at an object floating upstream.

The fisherman could not make it all out, but decided to leave nothing to chance.

He cast his line and hooked the object first time.

Swept Away by Tide

His "catch" was Margaret Coushin, a Liverpool evacuee, aged ten, who had been bathing with friends from the other side of the water and swept away by the tide.

Unable to swim, she had the presence of mind to lie still. She floated, and had drifted a mile.

"She was in the water for twenty minutes, and not being able to swim it is a miracle she did not drown," Mrs. A. M. Lloyd Evans, wife of a coastguard to whose bungalow the child was taken after being rescued, said yesterday.

"We kept her with us for the night and her guardians called for her the next day."

Cheap milk to age of 17

TO ensure the health of the youth of Britain, all children up to the age of seventeen years will soon be able to get cheap milk.

This extension of the existing milk scheme will cost £29,000,000.

At the same time the price of milk to the consumer may be increased soon to 11d. a quart.

Doctors Urged Scheme

A scheme to make cheap-milk facilities possible for young people has been submitted by the Ministry of Food to the Milk Marketing Board.

The medical profession has long since pressed for such a scheme, explaining that the most vital stages of growth take place up to the age of seventeen.

Apart from milk at schools, the present milk scheme provides for one pint of milk daily for twopence only to expectant or nursing mothers and children under the age of five.

Certain households can, however, obtain their pint free—if the joint weekly income of the parents is less than 40s. (plus 6s. for each non-earning dependent member of the household); if the income of the only parent or guardian is less than 27s. 6d. (plus 6s. for each non-earning member of the household), or if the head of the household is receiving public assistance.

VICHY 'NO' TO AXIS

A VICHY spokesman indicated last night that the Axis would not be granted military facilities in French North Africa such as Japan was given in Indo-China, even should the Vichy Government consider that its African territory was "menaced."

It was the most official utterance possible at the moment, since Admiral Darlan, the vice-Premier, does not hold Press conferences.

The Vichy spokesman was replying to the statement made by the U.S. Acting Secretary of State, Mr. Sumner Welles, on Saturday, in which he stated that the United States would be governed in its relations with the Vichy Government and French colonies by the effectiveness with which French territories were defended.

RUSSIA WILL BE AT OUR TALKS

Our new Ally, Russia, will be represented at the next Allied war conference which will discuss post-war reconstruction problems — particularly economic.

The meeting will be held in London and will be similar to that held on June 12, when the members pledged mutual assistance against the Axis Powers.

U.S. PLEDGES RUSSIA AID

The United States, in an exchange of notes, has promised all practical economic help to Russia.

VC

Sergeant James Allen Ward

Lord Gort toasts General Franco

Special honours were accorded Lord Gort, Governor of Gibraltar, when he visited Algeciras yesterday.

A guard of honour of the Spanish Legion played the British National Anthem.

At a reception General Ortiz, Military Governor of Algeciras, proposed a toast to King George, and Lord Gort toasted General Franco.

Month's road toll: 618 die

DURING June 618 people died in road accidents in Great Britain, compared with 479 last year.

In addition, 3,592 were seriously and 11,593 slightly injured.

Of the 618 dead, 239 were pedestrians.

Though 139 in excess of those in June last year, the deaths were the lowest in any month of the first half of this year, the totals being:—

	1940	1941
January	629	741
February	418	689
March	496	834
April	451	726
May	449	701
June	479	618

This is the first time since the war began that figures of the numbers injured in road accidents in Great Britain have been issued.

SCHOOL TILL 18 FOR ALL

The Under-Secretary for Scotland said last night: "Compulsory education for all up to the age of eighteen is coming after the war."

BEAT FIRE ON WING

THE Victoria Cross has been awarded to a New Zealand Air Force sergeant, 22, who crawled along the wing of a bomber in flight and smothered a fire near the engine.

He is New Zealand's first V.C. of the war and the seventh airman to win the decoration.

The sergeant, James Allen Ward, fought his way to the engine though the slipstream from the airscrew was like a hurricane and nearly blew him off the wing.

Fire broke out near the starboard engine after the bomber, when flying over the Zuider Zee at 13,000 feet, was hit in an attack by a fighter.

The crew forced a hole in the fuselage and tried in vain to reduce the fire with the extinguishers, and even the coffee in their vacuum flasks.

Hand and Foot Holds

As the last resort Sergeant Ward volunteered to try to smother the fire with an engine cover which was in use as a cushion.

At first he proposed to discard his parachute to reduce wind resistance but was finally persuaded to take it.

Breaking the fabric to make hand and foot holds where necessary, and also taking advantage of existing holds in the fabric, Sergeant Ward descended three feet to the wing.

Lying three feet behind the engine he smothered the fire in the wing fabric. With the navigator's help he made the perilous journey back into the aircraft.

MINESWEEPER SUNK

H.M.S. Snaefell (Lieutenant-Commander F. Brett, R.N.R.), an auxiliary minesweeper, has been sunk.

GERMAN forces advanced for the first time for several days when troops made slight gains of territory in the pincers movement towards Kiev, capital of the Ukraine. This was stated in London yesterday.

The Russian communique issued early today says that fighting continues in the same areas—indicating no big advance has been made.

The communique says: "Yesterday our troops continued fighting the enemy in the directions of Porkhov, Smolensk and Byela-Tserkov (forty-five miles south-west of Kiev).

"Acting in co-operation with the land forces, Russian aircraft dealt blows at enemy mechanised and motorised units, infantry and artillery.

"On Saturday, twenty German planes were shot down for the loss of six Russian machines."

The main German thrust despite the Kiev diversion is still from Smolensk towards Moscow, where the fighting is hard.

Kiev, an important industrial centre, would be of great value to the Germans. There the broad River Dnieper can be crossed easily.

The drive on Kiev is an opportunist move by the Germans to gain some swift local victory to satisfy their people.

30 Panzer Divisions

At the present rate of advance Kiev is not in immediate danger. The Germans are paying high for their limited gain.

The Moscow newspaper Pravda says that when the Germans declared war on Russia they had forces numerically three times as strong as the Russian defenders.

In France, says "Pravda," the Germans had ten panzer divisions, now they have thirty.

In France they had 5,000 first line planes and 7,500 tanks. In the East these figures are almost doubled.

DOG KILLS NEW BABY

A TERRIER dog—the pet of the family—attacked and killed a five-week-old baby in its pram yesterday.

The baby, Graham Clark, was left out in its pram at the back of the parents' home in Bradford-street, Handbridge, Chester. The dog jumped into the pram and savaged the child about the face and head.

The dog was destroyed.

Friends of the family said, "The dog was a real pet and very gentle with the other child. Probably the fuss everyone made over the new baby annoyed the dog."

ITALIAN GENERAL KILLED

General Edoardo Majnardi, in charge of a division in East Africa, has been killed in action. It was announced in Rome last night.—British United Press.

SERBS IN REVOLT

GERMANY last night admitted a serious revolt had broken out in Yugoslavia.

The German radio called it a Serb Communist movement and claimed that it had been crushed, but it is known that it is still going on in many places.

The official German news agency reported from Zagreb that ninety-eight Jews and Communists were executed after the explosion of four bombs yesterday.

Zagreb was regarded as the Nazi stronghold in Yugoslavia.

28 Injured

The bombs were thrown at a detachment of militia. Twenty-eight men were wounded.

The B.B.C., broadcasting in Czech, said there had been a considerable number of revolts all over the Serbian territory.

"There had been heavy fighting in many places, especially smaller towns, and around Belgrade, where German troops are chiefly concentrated and have been reinforced in a hurry from the Turkish-Bulgarian frontier," the announcer said.

Guarded Account

"The revolt seems to be directed by a central command. Many arrests have been made."

The German radio said:

"Thanks to the vigilance of the Croat security authorities, the Serb Communist movement did not achieve any major effect."

Warspite off Siam, report

A British naval squadron, including the 35,000-ton battleship Warspite, has been sighted in the Gulf of Siam, according to an unofficial report in Saigon, quoted by Associated Press.

Australia's Navy Minister, Mr. Hughes, announced at the week-end that Britain is able if necessary to send a fleet to the Pacific. His statement has caused great satisfaction in Singapore.

According to Rome radio, the Soviet Government has given America the use of Vladivostok as a naval and air base.

SO RUN, YOU ——S

In a send-off speech to Italians leaving for the Russian front Mussolini said: "Remember that in battle he who hesitates is lost."

Daily Mirror

AUG. 8

No. 11,750   ♦   ONE PENNY
Registered at the G.P.O. as a Newspaper.

JAPAN REJECTS WARNING

THE Japanese Government yesterday rejected British and American warnings against Japanese action in Thailand (Siam) as "unwarranted and created out of their own conjectures."

According to a Tokio radio commentator, "War may come at any moment."

The British and American Ambassadors in Tokio are understood to have amplified to Japan the "Hands off Thailand" warnings given by Mr. Eden and Mr. Cordell Hull, leaving Tokio with no illusion about the British and American position.

Should the warnings need to be backed up by action, it is emphasised once again in Singapore that Malaya and Burma are ready for any emergency.

British troops in the Far East are being steadily reinforced, and a large proportion have been in Malaya and Burma for a considerable time.

"Just Round the Corner"

They are effectively trained in jungle warfare, whereas the Japanese troops have only just begun to penetrate this type of terrain in south Indo-China.

There are also insistent rumours at Singapore that a sizeable British naval force is already "just round the corner."

British residents have now joined Americans in the exodus from Saigon, Indo-China, although the British Consulate gave no specific warning to leave.

The dispatch of Japanese troops and war material westwards across Indo-China is being speeded.

Thailand is undoubtedly in a position of danger, but opinion in authoritative quarters in London is that she will do her best to resist if attacked.

4 AXIS SHIPS TORPEDOED

Four Axis ships have been torpedoed in the Eastern Mediterranean, say reports in Istanbul —two while trying to reach safe harbour after spending several weeks loading at Istanbul.

These reports said that the Alba Julia (5,700 tons) and Balcik (3,600 tons) were torpedoed near the outlet of the Dardanelles when making a dash for an Italian port after painting out their Rumanian names and colours. One was believed to have been sunk.

In addition an Italian ship, Capo More, and the German vessel Salzburg, were also torpedoed, the Salzburg sinking.—Associated Press.

Non-Union boss 'wrong in wartime'

A COURT of Inquiry into a dispute at a war materials factory, the managing director of which refused to have any dealings with a trade union and claimed that he was entitled to run his works on non-union lines, finds that his attitude is against the national interest in wartime.

"In wartime we think that, however strongly individuals may desire to run their works in their own way, it is their duty to their country to fall into line with the vast majority of other good employers and assist the Government in the accepted methods of conciliation."

The case for the National Union of General and Municipal Workers was that after a meeting had been announced, the managing director and a member of his staff took a union official inside the factory and sent for the police.

"Fifth Columnist"

The managing director said that he "arrested" the official because he thought he was a "Fifth Columnist."

After the dismissal of a woman employee the workers refused to "return without Emily," and left their employment.

The firm, Trent Guns and Cartridges, Ltd., Grimsby, claimed that steps were taken to improve wages, and that the woman was dismissed in the interests of production.

20-SECOND COURTSHIP

Miss Laverne Mayer sat in a semi-darkened cinema on Broadway, New York, yesterday when a young man she'd never seen before fell on his knees crying, "I love you, I love you. Will you marry me."

The love-lorn cries of young Michael Chanker were followed by screams of the girl to whom he was proposing, causing uproar throughout the cinema.

He was seized and handed over to the police. Chanker protested, "I am absolutely sane. While lights were on I saw the girl's face and fell desperately in love with her."

Miss Mayer said: "I cannot accept a proposal after a twenty-second courtship."

★ Dogs have gas masks in Russia

During a gas-mask demonstration in Kiev, capital of Russian Ukraine, people marched through the streets accompanied by their dogs —also wearing gas-masks.

SHE ROWED THROUGH MINEFIELD

STRANDED up-country in Finland when the Germans took control of that country and began their assault on the Russians, Lady Constance Malleson, of Blagdon, Somerset, escaped by rowing in an open boat for twenty-five miles in the mine-infested Gulf of Finland to reach Helsinki.

In Refugee Boat

When she reached the Finnish capital the Finns had just broken off diplomatic relations with Britain, and she was held up six days by the port authorities.

Eventually she was allowed to board a refugee boat which made for Swedish territorial waters and was then convoyed to Stockholm by Swedish warships.

This news, all that has been allowed to pass the censor, was given in a letter from Lady Constance.

Lady Constance went to Finland to help in the administration of relief to the stricken Finns at the time of the Russo-Finnish war.

LONGER U.S. SERVICE VOTE

By a majority of forty-four to twenty-eight, the U.S. Senate last night voted to keep Army selectees, national guardsmen, reservists and enlisted men in uniform eighteen months beyond their present service periods.—Associated Press.

200 Hun tanks trapped

TWO hundred German tanks were destroyed when Russian troops attacked a miles-long column of the 8th Tank Division, according to dispatches from the front reaching Moscow last night.

The Russians allowed the Panzer column to advance several miles along a road, then attacked from three directions from the surrounding woods.

The Russian garrison at Smolensk, which has been besieged for three weeks, was reported in a letter from the front received in Moscow yesterday to be still fighting.

Russia Takes Islands

The letter, from a Russian soldier at Smolensk, said the Germans dropped a large number of parachutists and light tanks in the attack on the town, but never gained a foothold.

The letter was brought out of Smolensk by hand, indicating that the Russians held the road open to the besieged fortress.

Continued stubborn fighting in the Smolensk, Byelaya-Tserkov and the Estonian sectors, with no major operations on other sectors, was reported in the Soviet communique.

Moscow claims the capture of two islands near the base of Hango, Gulf of Finland, by marines.

The Nazi radio war commentator claimed last night that mobile German troops have made further progress "toward the large bend of the Dnieper," in the Ukraine sector.

PREPARE FOR MORE BOMBING

WARNING to expect heavy night bombing of our towns and cities again this winter was given last night by General Sir William Bartholomew, Regional Commissioner, North-Eastern Civil Defence Region.

Sir William, who was broadcasting a war commentary, said. "We are going to intensify our attack.

"Does anyone suppose that the Germans are not going to try to hit back when they can and as hard as they can?

"Don't let us deceive ourselves. So long as Germany has an efficient heavy bombing force we must expect attack on our cities.

PAID OFFICERS FOR NEW FIRE WATCH ARMY

FIRE-WATCHING is to be thoroughly organised as a "front line" civil defence service, with its own paid officers and N.C.O.s and training schemes throughout the country.

This was revealed last night following the announcement that all men between 18 and 60 in vulnerable areas must now register with their local authorities for fire guard duty.

In each local authority area the chief warden will be responsible for fire-guard organisation.

Fire guard staff officers—a new rank—will be paid from £300 to £500 a year, and their assistants from £200 to £350.

Head fire guards will be paid £3 15s. a week, and senior fire guards £3 13s. 6d. Depot superintendents will receive from £4 10s. to £5 a week.

The chief warden will have the assistance of the district or divisional warden.

A newly-appointed fire guard staff officer, with an assistant in the case of large authorities, will act as adjutant for fire prevention to the chief warden.

Junior Officers

District (and divisional) wardens will be assisted for fire prevention by junior officers to be known as head fire guards and senior fire guards.

Head fire guards will be responsible under the district or divisional warden for organising courses of training. Senior fire guards will organise train and supervise the work of fire guard parties.

There will be approximately one senior fire guard to every 600 fire guards—that is one to about seventy-five fire guards actually on duty at any given time.

There will be one head fire guard for approximately eight senior fire guards outside London, and in London one head fire guard for each district warden.

Where circumstances make it necessary, fire guard posts or depots will be set up under depot superintendents, who will be responsible for the preparation of rotas and duties and the mustering and allocation of fire guards, sleeping and feeding arrangements, and equipment.

Local authorities are being

Continued on Back Page

U.S. TANKERS FOR SOVIET

MR. Ickes, U.S. Petroleum administrator, announced yesterday that four American tankers are being transferred to Russia for transport of aviation petrol.

Mr. Ickes told newspapermen that a shortage of aviation petrol in the United States with possible severe effects on military and commercial flying was likely unless the capacity for producing it was increased immediately.

A compulsory plan to conserve petrol on the east coast might not be far ahead.

Despite efforts to influence motorists to curtail their consumption, petrol consumption on the Atlantic seaboard had increased materially during the last fortnight.—Reuter.

→>>> **THE** <<<←

CHOCOLATE CODE

I won't try to buy chocolate in all the shops I pass. I'll ration myself of my own free will.

I won't eat chocolate just for pleasure. I'll leave it for the children. I know that it's an important food for them, and a rare treat as well.

I won't try to get more chocolate than I used to eat in peace-time. I'll make up with other foods not so scarce.

I won't blame the shopkeeper if he can't serve me with chocolate, I know he's doing his best.

I'll only eat chocolate to give me energy for hard work that is helping on the war effort.

ISSUED BY

FRY'S

Makers of Good Chocolate

"The methods of our active defence in finding the enemy at night and destroying him are improving and he will find, if I am not mistaken, that night raids this winter will be a costly business.

"But we have not yet reached the stage where we can stop them, and we must prepare to meet most determined attacks.

"That is an unpleasant thought I know, but if any false sense of security lulled us and we became slack the awakening would be grim indeed.

D.336 22745

Daily Mirror

AUG. 15

No. 11,756   ONE PENNY
Registered at the G.P.O. as a Newspaper.

STALIN CABLED BY CHURCHILL AND F.D.R.

Mr. Churchill and President Roosevelt have sent a joint telegram to Stalin. It is believed to reaffirm the intention of Britain and America to give full support to Russia. Mr. Cordell Hull, U.S. Secretary of State, hinted last night that the Churchill-Roosevelt talks might result in a further announcement about Russia.

IT was no secret that Mr. Churchill and President Roosevelt were meeting in the Atlantic. All the world had known it and discussed it for days.

Only real secret—which was well kept from the enemy — was the actual meeting place, and the United States Press made many guesses at that.

Washington diplomatic circles suggest that Mr. Churchill and President Roosevelt met aboard a United States warship "somewhere off Iceland."

It was stated that a line of U.S. battleships protected the conference ship.

The meeting was prompted by President Roosevelt. He and Mr. Churchill were in close consultation for three days.

First clue seized upon by the U.S. Press was the cancellation of the Premier's speech in the House of Commons on August 5

It is eight days since the New York Herald - Tribune said Roosevelt and Churchill were meeting.

The newspaper added that "only such a melodramatic conference" could have caused the absence from Washington of chiefs of the Army and Navy.

Vichy knew

On Thursday of last week the Vichy radio announced that Churchill and Roosevelt had met aboard the Potomac.

*   *   *

By Saturday there came a cryptic message from the President's yacht: "The ship is anchored in fog. Prospects for fishing appear poor to-day Everything quiet on board; no special news."

U.S. Press comment on that was that Washington seemed to be in the same fog.

Meanwhile, European radio stations, nearly all German controlled, had broadcast the story of the meeting.

BEAVERBROOK IN WASHINGTON

Lord Beaverbrook, accompanied by General Marshall, U.S. Army Chief of Staff, arrived at Washington yesterday afternoon in giant U.S.-built bomber with British markings.

Lord Beaverbrook crossed from Britain in a plane which was accompanying the one that crashed into a hillside, after the take-off on Sunday night, with the loss of twenty-two lives.

The open secret

By W.M.

THERE is nothing half so exciting as a secret that is known to the entire world.

Everybody tells the secret to everybody else. When it becomes as familiar as the tune of the National Anthem there is a melodramatic hush.

The public is told to stand by and listen. There is a short suspension of news. The radio is monopolised. We hold our breath. Then those who think they have been keeping an open secret suddenly announce what everybody has been telling everybody else for the past fortnight.

Thus, in an anti-climax, did good Mr. Attlee yesterday reveal the already celebrated encounter at sea of our Prime Minister with the President of the United States.

It was not his fault—it was the fault of the gossips — that the announcement sounded as though he were admitting that Napoleon had sailed on the Bellerophon to St. Helena

As to the remainder of the news or secrets thus so stalely revealed, it all amounts, briefly, to a new statement of the old war aims which have been tentatively published so long ago as in the far-off age of the extinct Chamberlain Government.

The novelty is, of course, in the fact of a joint declaration between Britain and the U.S.A. of purposes as yet unrealisable. For we have not yet won the war.

Many of us think that it was, or would have been, wiser to stick to Mr. Churchill's original emphasis upon that "point" or aim —to win. Possibly President Roosevelt did not agree.

So we have today our nobly phrased, somewhat Wilsonian declaration. And we can only hope that these aims may in the end be more honestly and successfully realised than poor Woodrow's.

At any rate we know, today, that America is "nearer" than ever our ally.

This Zec cartoon appeared in the "Daily Mirror" on Monday with the caption

SOMETHING BIG?

And now we know what the catch was !

ALL-FRONT BATTLE ON

"FIERCE fighting took place today along the whole front from the White Sea to the Black Sea." said last night's Moscow communique.

The communique admitted that in the southern sector the Soviet troops had evacuated towns of Kirovograd and Pervomaisk (on the River Bug) north-west of Nikolaiev.

The Russians, however, deny the German claim to have encircled Odessa, and declare that the German offensive is being smashed.

Germany's best divisions, says the newspaper Pravda, have either been destroyed or "are losing blood" and "the German Army is throwing into battle new reserves, after taking smashed divisions to the rear, re-forming them and sending them back to the fighting fronts.

"The German Army is still powerful, but the myth of its invincibility is crushed."

Figures are published showing that the Russians have totally destroyed one tank corps, five tank divisions, four infantry divisions, one Black Guards division, one motorised division and twelve regiments.

A German High Command communique reports that: "In advancing down the lower course of the Dnieper, German mobile units took the iron ore district of Krivoirog."

'Objective Reached'

Berlin radio said last night: "The German armies in the Ukraine have reached their objective in the campaign in the south."

The evacuation of Kirovograd suggests that the German Army has made a ninety-five miles thrust to the east from Uman.

(Kirovograd lies about 120 miles north of the Black Sea port of Nikolaiev, and is fifty miles from the bend of the Dnieper River.)

A German report speaks of a "series of violent battles" in the northern sector, where a two-pronged drive is being made on Leningrad.

GERMANS' LOVE RATIONS

Love ration coupons have been found on captured German troops, says Moscow radio. Each coupon entitles the owner to visit one of the divisional "love establishments."—Associated Press.

Freedom for all

DISCLOSING the Roosevelt-Churchill meeting, Mr. C. R. Attlee, Lord Privy Seal and Deputy Prime Minister, in a special broadcast, said:

The President of the United States and the Prime Minister, Mr. Churchill, representing his Majesty's Government in the United Kingdom, have met at sea

They have been accompanied by officials of their two governments, including high ranking officers of their military naval and air services

The whole problem of supply of munitions of war as provided by the Lease and Lend Act, for the armed forces in the United States and for those countries actively engaged in resisting aggression, has been further examined.

Joint Policy Declared

Lord Beaverbrook, Minister of Supply of the British Government, has joined in these conferences. He is going to proceed to Washington to discuss further details with appropriate officials of the U.S. Government.

These conferences will also cover the supply problem of the Soviet Union.

The President and the Prime Minister have had several conferences. They have considered the dangers to world civilisation arising from the policy of military domination by conquest upon which the Hitlerite Government of Germany and other Governments associated therewith have embarked, and have made clear the steps which their countries are respectively taking for their safety in facing those dangers

They have agreed on the following joint declaration:—

"The President of the United States and the Prime Minister, Mr. Churchill, representing his Majesty's Government in the United Kingdom, being met together, deem it right to make known certain common prim-

Continued on Back Page

14-5 IS R.A.F. DAY SCORE

FOURTEEN to five—that was yesterday's score in favour of the R.A.F. in sweeps over Northern France.

British planes were heard crossing the coast again last night and A.A. guns on the French coast were in action. Searchlights ringing Calais threw up a cone of white light.

Three Polish squadrons of the R.A.F. had a great day. Flying as a wing, they went out with a number of other squadrons. They discovered scores of enemy fighters and at once engaged them.

When they returned to their bases the Poles had a story to tell of thirteen Messerschmitts shot down. Their own casualties were three fighters missing.

The fight lasted thirteen minutes with Huns going down one a minute.

One squadron got eight. "We have only once before had a chance of shooting up German fighters," said the squadron leader. "That was last Saturday, when we destroyed two Me's.

"Today we let them have it so fiercely that the enemy formation was broken up and several of them crashed in flames."

Earlier in the afternoon Blenheim bombers, escorted by fighters, attacked Boulogne docks

Bombs were seen to burst on the target. One enemy fighter was destroyed in this engagement and we lost two fighters.

NAZI MASS MURDERS

A FRESH wave of terrorism against the Serbs in Yugoslavia and more acts of revolt against the Germans were reported yesterday.

Americans who have just got out of Yugoslavia tell of thousands of deaths in ruthless shooting, destruction and brutality. In Novisad more than 7,000 Serbs have been killed so far.

In an effort to round up guerrillas, the German commander of occupied Serbia has ordered all officers and men of military age to report to the German occupation authorities.

The official German News Agency said last night that in a mutiny at a "detention camp" in Bosnia twenty-nine of the prisoners were shot. Another forty-one were condemned to death by court-martial and executed.—Reuter.

"Glorious Example of Dunkirk"—Nazis

"The Soviet attempt to copy the glorious example of Dunkirk by an attempt to evacuate the Red forces by sea was prevented by the bombing of Soviet troop transports," said Berlin radio yesterday.

ENVOY WANTS SHIP INTERNED

BRITAIN'S Ambassador in Turkey is asking for the internment of the Italian ship Trevisio, which has arrived at the Dardanelles, according to the National Broadcasting Company's Ankara correspondent.

The Trevisio is listed as a warship, and is on the way to the Black Sea with war supplies.

Daily Mirror

AUG. 19

No. 11,759 — ONE PENNY
Registered at the G.P.O. as a Newspaper.

TWO GIRLS FACE WAR JOB CHARGE

HUNS TAKE TOWN 70 MILES FROM LENINGRAD

MOSCOW this morning admitted the evacuation, after stubborn fighting, of a town seventy miles from Leningrad—Kingisepp, north-east of Lake Peipus.

This indicates that Marshal Voroshilov's Army is falling back on Leningrad's outer defence ring, just inside the old Soviet frontier, which the Nazis have only just crossed.

While the Germans resumed their drive against Leningrad, moving east along the railway in northern Estonia, at the other end of the front a million and a half Germans were locked in the great battle for Odessa.

Marshal Budenny's rearguards last night were fighting bitterly to hold off heavy thrusts towards the wide, fast-flowing Dnieper River that blocks Hitler's path to the wealth of the Don Basin.

Against Budenny's men are opposed forty-five infantry divisions, forty-five panzer divisions and about fifty others.

In Berlin the High Command spokesman claimed that German infantry detachments had already reached the river eighty miles east of Krivoi Rog, threatening Dniepropetrovsk.

This great industrial city, with its iron and steel works served by the world's largest hydro electric plant, sprawls along the banks of the river some 140 miles from the Black Sea.

New Fortifications

The next few days will show whether Budenny is successful in taking his main forces across the River Dnieper.

The Russians are reported in authoritative London quarters to have built powerful new fortifications along the Dnieper, which, it is stated, should form a very strong defence line.

The German radio claimed that in air attacks on the harbour of Odessa, six Soviet transport vessels totalling 15,000 tons were so heavily hit that they can be regarded as total losses, and one cruiser and one torpedo boat received direct hits.

Odessa was stated yesterday to be still in Russian hands, but there was no indication whether or not they intended to make a Tobruk of it.

Heavy fighting by tank units was reported from south-east of Smolensk.

Here, it was stated, two Soviet divisions were destroyed and 10,000 prisoners taken.

Moscow claimed the sinking of a German submarine and two transports in the Baltic. — Reuter.

Jean Fotheringham and Jean Addison after the secret hearing of their case yesterday.

U.S. TO FERRY PLANES FOR MIDDLE EAST

PRESIDENT ROOSEVELT, back in Washington after his meeting with Mr. Churchill, revealed last night that delivery of U.S. planes to the British forces in the Middle East would be speeded up by a ferry service run by Pan-American Airways.

Congress leaders who had a ninety-minute conference with the President yesterday said afterwards that they gained these impressions from the talk:

That no British invasion of the Continent was contemplated at present.

But Britain realised such a move must be made eventually to defeat Germany.

That Russia had a "real chance" of resisting indefinitely against the Nazis.

That Russian resistance would probably forestall any German attempt to invade Britain this year.

President Roosevelt's statement about the planes for the Middle East, said the system would provide "direct and speedy delivery" of aircraft from what the President has called "the arsenal of democracy" to critical points on the front against aggression.

R.A.F. tackle Hun fighters six miles up

SHELL-FIRING R.A.F. fighters, escorting bombers in an attack across the Channel yesterday, shot down at least three enemy fighters in dogfights at 30,000ft.—nearly six miles up.

Two of the enemy, including one of the latest Me.109F's, were claimed by a Belgian squadron and the other by a Czech.

Many fighter squadrons took part in two operations in which bombers were escorted to attack targets in Northern France during the day.

They saw considerable numbers of enemy aircraft, but reported that on the whole the enemy was reluctant to engage. Three of our fighters are missing.

Blenheims bombed and sank three enemy patrol vessels off the Dutch coast.

Other Blenheims, accompanied by strong fighter escorts, bombed an industrial plant at Lille and other targets, and the escorts destroyed three enemy fighters.

More fighters carried out a sweep over the coast of Northern Brittany, attacked an aerodrome and troops with cannon and machine-gun fire.

Keep big army demand

NEVER again must Britain sack her army, as was done in 1918 and after all previous wars, declared the Minister of Labour yesterday.

The Navy was always there; the Air Force could always be expanded, but the Army always had to be built up after a war started and was always smashed up after the victory was won. Defence on the cheap—that was the old outlook.

He hoped that at the end of this war we would have not only social security, but a social obligation.

He still believed in a citizen army and a democratic army. He still believed it was a social obligation of each man to defend his homestead.

The Labour attitude to the problem of defence would have to be re-examined, not for our own country but to maintain international discipline if we got anything like a world order established.

Fixing Wages

He could not believe that industry would ever go back to the methods employed before the war. Picking up labour like an old cloak and then throwing it down again was an inhuman procedure.

He wanted every avenue in industry open to every man and woman. It was a right and the State needed it.

On the subject of wages and prices he said he refused to be a party to the stabilisation of wages till the price policy was settled.

The difference in the situation now was that the Government had decided to stabilise prices. Experience had shown that wages followed prices, but a long way behind.

The Government was considering a fairly wide development of rationing, not merely to control prices, but to get a correct distribution. This was vital.

The Trade Union movement had asked for stabilisation and the Government had given it. They had published a document and it would be found that it left the situation at which most of the unions were aiming.

On the joint Churchill—

Continued on Back Page

OUR ARCTIC PLAN: PARIS

According to German-controlled Paris radio, Britain is preparing to send an expeditionary force to the Russian Arctic ports, to keep communications open between the two countries.

28 "TOO OLD TO FIGHT"

MEN of twenty-eight taken from civil life into the Army are too old to withstand the rigours of modern warfare.

This is the decision of the U.S. military authorities, and President Roosevelt yesterday signed legislation under which men who were twenty-eight on or before July 1 will not be conscripted, cables the *Daily Mirror* New York correspondent.

Those already conscripted must apply for discharge. They will be dismissed "as soon as practical and when such dismissal does not conflict with the interests of national defence."

It is estimated that there are in the U.S. Army 112,000 conscripts of twenty-eight or more. Specialists in this group will be held over, and the rest gradually released.

It is expected that the President will sign a Bill extending Army service by eighteen months to two and a half years.

EMPRESS ON HER WAY TO ABYSSINIA

The Empress of Abyssinia, with her suite, left her Bath home secretly some time ago and is expected in Addis Ababa soon to rejoin the Emperor.

With her has gone her younger daughter, Princess Tsahai, who trained as a nurse in London and who hopes to start a nursing service on English lines in Abyssinia.

BERLIN OFF THE AIR

Berlin wireless went off the air last night—the usual sign of the presence of R.A.F. or Russian planes. — British United Press.

CASE HEARD BEFORE A SECRET COURT

THERE was a secret hearing yesterday before the Ministry of Labour Appeal Court in Birmingham of the case against two Scots mill girls who refused to work in the factory to which the Ministry sent them.

The result of the hearing will not be known for some days, as the tribunal's findings will be first considered by the National Service officer in Birmingham, who will then recommend what should be done.

Didn't Like It

The girls, both aged 20, are Jean Fotheringham, of Cameronian-street, Stirling, and Jean Addison, of Broad-street, Stirling. They volunteered to go to Birmingham on munition work.

Miss Fotheringham told a reporter, after the hearing, that whatever the decision and whatever the consequences, they would not work at the factory to which they were sent.

They complained that they were not sent to the factory they had chosen, but to another.

"We did not like the place," said Miss Fotheringham, "and we said so. We did not like the lodgings, either. We told the Ministry of Labour that we did not intend to start work there.

"Next morning the manager of the factory had us turned out of the lodgings. We went to an aunt of mine and found other work."

"Propeller bombs" scare Germans

"New British bombs fitted with propellers" are terrorising Germans, according to a man who has reached Switzerland.

But Berliners, he says, console themselves with the thought that the British are so short of bombs that they are forced to use up the Navy's torpedoes!

Health Tribute from

NEW ZEALAND TO GREAT BRITAIN

"I Am Very Pleased with Yeast-Vite"

BRAND TONIC

Dannevirke, New Zealand.
April 15th, 1941.

Dear Sirs—I am very pleased with Yeast-Vite tonic tablets. I have been sick with bad headaches and nerves and indigestion for two years. When I was in the garden I felt the ground was coming up to meet me. Two months ago I was riding on my bike towards home and I was so nervous I thought a motor-car was running upside down. When I got home I went right out; I did not know anybody for two hours.

I went to the hospital with indigestion, and when I came home somebody told me to try some tonic as I was getting worse.

I was looking in a paper one morning and saw an advertisement of Yeast-Vite tablets. I read the advertisement and went to the chemist and bought a small bottle. Now I feel 100% better.

Last Wednesday I went up to town to buy some things; the chap in the shop said he had a bad headache. I gave him three Yeast-Vite tablets, and told him they were very good for headache. I must buy a large bottle this morning; they are worth a pound a bottle.

I buy a small bottle to have up town, and one day a chap was talking to me. "How are you feeling to-day?" I asked him. He said he wasn't feeling too good. I gave him half of my bottle of Yeast-Vite. On the following day I saw him again, I said, "How did those tablets do?" He said they were the best tablets he had taken, and put his hand in his pocket to pull out a large bottle, and said, "You saved my life."

That is not the only case; I have told dozens of people about them.

You can let anybody see this letter. (Sgd.) T. H.

Yeast-Vite brand Tablets being quick relief from Headaches, Nerves, Lassitude, Depression, Insomnia, Rheumatism, Indigestion, etc. Sold everywhere at 7d., 1/1; 3/5 and 5/8, including purchase tax.

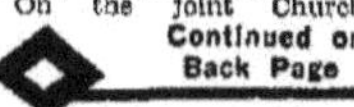

Map shows Kingisepp, seventy miles from Leningrad, which the Russians admitted this morning they have abandoned in face of strong German pressure.

Daily Mirror

AUG. 21

No. 11,761   ONE PENNY
Registered at the G.P.O. as a Newspaper.

Office milk is safe

Milk for your office tea is safe under the new Milk Distribution Scheme which comes into operation on October 1.

Provision will be made for the supply of milk for consumption as a beverage by industrial workers and to holders of special permits for tea.

Purchase of milk under these arrangements will be restricted to holders of special permits to be issued by food executive officers. The holder will be required to nominate his supplier at the time of application.

Industrial undertakings having arrangements for the supply of milk to their workpeople, and holders of special permits for tea, should apply at once to the local food office for the necessary application form stating whether the milk is for industrial workers for consumption as a beverage during working hours or for use in tea.

The completed application form should be returned to the food office, and a permit will be issued in due course.

Co-tenants are asked by the Ministry of Food to register with the same dairyman, to economise on the cost of bringing milk to your doorstep.

BIG NAZI PUSH ON LENINGRAD STARTS

WHILE the battle for Leningrad developed sharply near Novgorod last night, 100 miles to the south, the Germans officially claimed another victory in the Gomel sector.

Gomel, just east of the Pripet Marshes, is 150 miles north-east of Kiev, and 170 miles south-west of Smolensk.

The Germans claimed to have taken "78,000 prisoners, 144 armoured cars, 700 guns of all sizes and two armoured trains."

Whether the German attack in the Gomel sector is ultimately intended as a means of supporting the German troops in the Smolensk area or as a prelude to a drive southwards along the left bank of the Dnieper remains to be seen

It is part of the "all over the place" tactics being tried out by the Germans to prevent any effective concentration of Soviet forces in particular areas and a stabilisation of the front.

Russians' Local Advance

Confidence in the result of the battle for Leningrad was expressed in Moscow since the Novgorod province, covered by forests and dotted with some 1,200 lakes, is well adapted to guerrilla warfare.

A local advance which began four days ago and is still going on was reported in Moscow.

Forces led by General Konev drove the Germans out of three successive defence lines, stated *Red Star*, the Soviet Army newspaper.

Five villages were recaptured. The advance was continuing.

Aircraft, artillery, tanks and infantry combined in the counter-attacks.

The assaults drove the Germans out of their first lines and routed them as they tried to entrench in a second line.

The Soviet units forced the

Continued on Back Page

HUNS SAY SHIPS HIT IN BATTLE

A Mediterranean naval battle is referred to by German radio, claiming that one British cruiser, three destroyers and six smaller war vessels were under repair at Gibraltar.

A tanker and a merchant ship were also being repaired, said the announcer.

Rome radio, quoting Tangier reports, said last night that heavy gunfire had been heard from British warships. Later batteries at Gibraltar joined in the firing.

CADETS FLY INTO SCRAP— GET HUN

ALTHOUGH permission had not been obtained from the Air Ministry, two air cadets went on patrol with men of a Dominion squadron, in a Sunderland flying boat over the Atlantic and approaches to the Channel.

After a time a wireless message came in saying: "Am in action with the enemy." Then there was silence.

The Squadron Commander said, "I will lose my commission over this."

Axis threat to Turkey?

THE Bulgarian Army is almost fully mobilised, and the Press and radio continue their attacks on Turkey.

The Ankara correspondent of an American broadcasting company made this announcement last night, and added:

"All Bulgarian cars are requisitioned by Government decree for September 5.

Another U.S. radio commentator, also speaking from Ankara last night, said:

"German troops have reappeared in Bulgaria for the first time since the start of the German-Russian war, according to reliable reports from diplomatic quarters in Turkey.

"Indications are that at least two divisions will have entered Bulgaria by the end of this month. Units already arrived are said to include a high proportion of elite S.S. troops, and it is inferred that they come not from the Eastern front but from the German interior.

"Further reports from Bulgaria state that many new young German pilots and ground staff have arrived in Sofia during the past ten days.

"For the past two weeks," added the commentator, "there has been a further strengthening of the Italian garrisons in the Grecian islands which form a long cordon around Turkey's western coast."—Reuter.

DAYLIGHT HITS ON NAZI DROME

Blenheims of Bomber Command, with fighter escort, attacked an aerodrome near Alkmaar, Holland, yesterday afternoon.

Bombs burst across the target and one of the hangars received a direct hit. Other Blenheims, searching for shipping, attacked a number of patrol vessels near the Frisian Islands.

Fighters carried out several offensive patrols over the Channel and Northern France.

N.Z. AIR TORPEDO FORCE

A special New Zealand torpedo bombing squadron has been formed.—Reuter.

My planes —and my son

The Air Training Corps Squadron Commander wondered how he should break the news to the boys' parents, when out of the dusk glided down the flying boat.

"We Got 'Em"

The wireless had been shot away. Out of the machine climbed two uproarious cadets with thumbs up, saying, "We got 'em."

This story was told in London yesterday by Air Commodore J. A. Chamier, Commandant of the Air Training Corps.

He added that after this exploit, the town in which the cadets live asked to raise two more squadrons because of the increase in recruiting.

Eric Roe ... missing.

BRITAIN'S first pilot, Sir Alliott Verdon-Roe, founder of Avros, maker of aeroplanes, has given his life to flying.

Last night he learned he may also have given a son.

Squadron Leader Eric Roe, 25, has been posted as missing.

"My son was as keen on flying as I was at his age." Sir Alliott told the *Daily Mirror*: "I am distracted by the news."

"I NEVER, NEVER REALISED THAT HUMANITY WOULD HAVE BEEN SO UTTERLY MAD AS TO USE AIRCRAFT FOR SUCH DESTRUCTIVE PURPOSES.

"I had hoped to see a saner world—a world in which nations settled their differences by arbitration."

Sir Alliott made his historic first flight in a home-made plane at Brooklands track in 1908. Later, as head of A. V. Roe and Co., he was responsible for some of the chief developments in British aviation.

In a foreword to a book on flying in 1936 he wrote: "One cannot help feeling what a tragic farce air warfare is."

A MOTHER'S VENGEANCE

The vengeance of a mother whose son was shot in a small village by German soldiers was told over Moscow radio last night.

The mother buried him, joined a guerrilla group and led the men to the village, which was set on fire.

The German soldiers escaped, but later their hiding place was discovered and one by one they were shot at dawn.

MISSING GIRL IS TRACED BY PHOTO

A *Daily Mirror* photograph traced Sylvia Smilitsky, 15, missing from her home at Prince George's-road, Stoke Newington, N., for nearly three weeks.

Her parents were notified yesterday that she had been found by the police at Pembroke Dock, Wales.

JAP GAOL CAMP FOR AMERICANS AND BRITONS

From JOHN WALTERS
NEW YORK, Wednesday.

JAPAN has built two big concentration camps in China for Britons and Americans, according to information received from Tientsin by a New York business house today

British and American business men in China are being intimidated by Japs, who warn them they will be thrown into the camps if the crisis between Japan and Britain and America grows more serious

One camp at Peitaiho, near Tientsin, was described as a "hospital" while it was being built, but now its real purpose is admitted.

A New Yorker, Mr. W. Nichols, who was in Tientsin last spring, said tonight:—

"I am not surprised to hear about the concentration camps.

"I myself saw a place described as a hospital being built and I was mystified by the fact that all around it were also constructed sentry boxes and machine-gun emplacements"

GOEBBELS PEP TALK IS—FEAR

GOEBBELS has started a new propaganda drive to frighten the German people of the chance of defeat.

He is using this tear campaign in the hope that they will consolidate behind Hitler, Moscow radio said last night.

Leading Nazi newspapers are describing the terrible future which threatens the German nation if it loses the war.

The *Voelkischer Beobachter* cries hysterically that Roosevelt wants to sterilise the whole German male population. *Das Reich* publishes an article with the significant heading, "If Germany Were Defeated."

STOLE MEAT IN TRAFFIC HOLD-UP

During a traffic hold-up at Walton a small car drew up alongside a meat delivery van. Later the driver of the van discovered the loss of six tins of liver weighing 10lb. each and valued at £3.

At Chertsey yesterday Percy Harold Barber was sentenced to six months' imprisonment with hard labour for stealing the meat. He was recognised by the driver as having previously played darts with him.

Drink clubs to be closed

CLUBS that have sprung up recently, near new arms factories, to trap workers into drinking, are hampering the war effort.

They are to be stamped out by police chiefs who have been granted new powers.

Defence Regulation 42 (C), which gave power to police chiefs to close undesirable places, has been amended.

New provisions enable them, on the authority of the Home Secretary, to lay down new opening hours or close a registered club if:—

The club is frequented by people engaged on essential work.

Efficient performance of this work is being interfered with by drunkenness permitted or not prevented at the club.

WARSHIP TAKES SURVIVORS

The Portuguese trawler Maria Leonor has wirelessed that a destroyer has taken on board British survivors from a torpedoed ship that were in the trawler. Five Chinese survivors remain.—Exchange

INDIGESTION

AND FLATULENCE AFTER MEALS

You get burning pain and distressing wind after meals because your stomach is always too acid Food simply can't digest and your stomach is tortured in the attempt. Why endure this mealtime misery when Milk of Magnesia Tablets will stop it this very day? They relieve acidity and sweeten a sour stomach at once. The stomach starts digesting your food right away and finishes its work with perfect ease. You feel nothing—no heartburn, no flatulence, not a twinge of your old stomach pain. If you suffer from acute attacks of gastric pain Milk of Magnesia Tablets will stop them in five minutes. Try them today! Neat flat boxes for the pocket, 7d. and 1/1½d. Also family sizes, 2/3 and 3/11½d. (Including Purchase Tax.) Obtainable everywhere.

'Milk of Magnesia' is the trade mark of 'Phillips' preparation of Magnesia.

Ministry stops onion ramp

FOOD Ministry officials have struck a blow at a new-type onion ramp at Covent Garden.

Onion growers have been sending onions with leaves attached for sale as "green onions," for which there is a higher controlled price.

Ministry of Food officials have been at the market each day this week and have prevented the sale of the onions.

For green, or salad, onions the controlled retail price is 7½d. a pound, and for ordinary onions it is 4½d. Growers would make about a penny a pound more for the salad variety.

Names and addresses of the growers are being taken, and a Ministry official said yesterday: "If it can be proved that growers are trying to sell above maximum prices we shall prosecute."

Daily Mirror

AUG. 26

No. 11,765   ONE PENNY
Registered at the G.P.O. as a Newspaper.

Give more power to war workers

—State Report

BY OUR INDUSTRIAL CORRESPONDENT

COMPLETE endorsement of the engineering shop stewards' demand (reported in yesterday's "Daily Mirror") that industry must take the workers into co-operation to win the Battle of Production came yesterday from a committee of inquiry set up by the Government itself.

In a report on arms output it declares there is room for great improvement, and adds:

Idling is frequently due to bad management or want of supervision;

Some of the worst cases are at factories working on the cost-plus-percentage basis;

Whether a recruit to industry becomes a good or a bad worker depends largely on the way he is handled.

Now these words bear the hall mark of a Select Committee and they were printed by H.M. Stationery Office.

When they are uttered by trade unionists, shop stewards and the workers, as they have been many times during the past year. Whitehall makes excuses.

How are they going to dodge the frank indictment of a Select Committee?

Confide in Workers

It is remarkable that the report should follow the meeting of shop stewards of engineering and allied trades in London on Saturday, when similar criticisms of management and constructive proposals for increasing production of vital war materials were advanced by workers' leaders.

The shop stewards had stated on Saturday what the Select Committee stated yesterday, that: "Managements should take their workpeople more closely into their confidence.

"In particular, when lack of work is unavoidable and temporary transfer is not possible, managements should explain the cause to their workpeople.

"Men should be appointed as charge-hands and foremen for

◆ Continued on
Back Page ◆

Duchess cancels her engagements

THE Duchess of Gloucester will not, for the next few months, be undertaking any further public engagements.

The Duke is now on active service, and the Duchess spends much of her time knitting for the Services and Merchant Navy.

ATTACK BY LAND, AIR AND SEA IN IRAN

IRAN will fight against Britain and the Soviet Union, declared Premier Ali Mansur to the Iranian Parliament last night.

He announced that British forces had attacked Iran by land, sea and air.

The Iranian authorities, he said "have taken all necessary measures to face this attack."

"British forces have attacked Iranian ships in port," he said, "and have bombed and shelled our towns."

Earlier, it was reported that Iranian forces offered resistance when Britain and the Soviet Union made their first joint land war effort yesterday by marching into Iran.

British and Indian mechanised troops, supported by the R.A.F., are taking part in the advance. There are 3,000 Indian troops in Iran under Indian command.

Although it is not known exactly where our troops were resisted, a landing at Bandar Shahpur was opposed. The landing was successful.

The British troops entered Southern Persia at many points.

To Prevent Nazi Coup

The Soviet forces entered Iran from the north-west by way of the Caucasus, the rich oil-bearing part of the U.S.S.R. where Nazi agents from Iran had been planning sabotage.

Soviet troops also entered the country by the southern coast of the Caspian Sea—the Russians have a Caspian flotilla—and by the Soviet frontier in the north-east.

Berlin radio quoted a report from Ankara that clashes had occurred between the Russians and Iran forces on the Caucasian border.

Britain and Russia have entered Iran to prevent a Nazi coup and rid this vital area of a nest of Hitler spies and armed bandits.

General Wavell is in supreme command of the British operations.

The Anglo-Soviet move will lead to contact between British and Red Army soldiers and airmen, and will open the way to a British and U.S. supply channel to the U.S.S.R. and, immediately, to Marshal Budenny's army.

★ ——— ★

TURKS SIDE WITH IRAN

Turkish opinion supports Iran in her dispute with Britain and Russia, the Ankara wireless declared last night.

Turkey is an ally of Great Britain, but she recently signed a peace pact with Germany.

Britain and Russia have told Turkey that they have no territorial designs against Iran.

Saracjoglu, Turkish Premier, is understood to have said Turkey would remain neutral.

RED ARMY YIELD RAIL TOWN

MIDNIGHT Soviet communique stated that Russian troops left Novgorod, important railway junction 100 miles south of Leningrad, after tenacious fighting yesterday.

Heavy rain has been falling on the Russian front for the past twenty-four hours.

If it continues it may have an enormous effect on slowing up the German operations at all or many parts of the front.

Already roads other than the main routes, which are not numerous, are bogged.

Eight successive waves of Russian planes attacked German forces in the central sector, Berlin radio admitted last night.

The Germans claimed that all the raids were driven off.

Warships of the Soviet Baltic Fleet destroyed a German convoy carrying troops, war materials and tanks and part of its escort, a Russian war communique stated yesterday.

Reconnaissance ships discovered four enemy transports escorted by E-boats. They tried to escape.

Transport Blown Up

A sharp battle between Soviet motor-torpedo boats and enemy E-boats followed.

One enemy transport blew up when hit by a torpedo. Another caught fire and sank. The other two beached themselves.

The battle for the great Dnieper Dam at Dniepropetrovsk, at the northern corner of the River Dnieper bend, and for the great industrial city and its valuable hinterland, continued violently throughout the night, the Russian communique added.

Radio ghost talks again

THE ghost voice of the German radio made its appearance again last night at 8.45.

Music was being played at the time, and the speed was immediately quickened and the strength increased, making the voice inaudible in England.

At 9 p.m., when the news bulletin was due, the music was continued while the announcer shouted: "We will now give you the news."

The Germans were taking no risks of there being a gap for the ghost's voice. For a few seconds the music went on, the announcer shouted—and the ghost could be heard in the background.

Then the news was read at terrific speed, the announcer almost screaming the words, at times choking and tumbling over phrases in his anxiety to beat the intruder on the ether.

Deutschlandsender certainly had the jitters.

NURSES ARE WANTED

Women aged twenty-six who have to register for war work on Saturday can, if they wish, express a preference for nursing.

Crook given commission —by post

AN Army commission was offered by post to a man, with nineteen convictions, who had been photographed in a Fascist shirt and was dismissed from a factory for causing disaffection.

The story was told at York yesterday when James Wilson Reid, 38, an engineer, of Wheatlands-grove, York, was sent to gaol for five months on defence charges.

For the Director of Public Prosecutions, Mr. G. F. Mitchell said that Reid, after applying to be placed on the register of the Army Officers Emergency Reserve, gave the name of Mr. C. Christian, a York consulting engineer, as reference.

A letter purporting to come from Mr. Christian was received by the War Office, who were satisfied with the particulars and offered Reid a commission in the R.A.O.C. by letter.

Later they cancelled this offer by telegram.

Faked Notepaper

The letter supposed to have come from Mr. Christian described Reid as the "type of man the country is in need of."

The prosecution alleged that Reid had notepaper printed with the heading "C. Christian," and had the reference typed for him.

Mr. Mitchell added that when the police searched Reid's house they found a Fascist shirt and belt.

Revealing that Reid had served sentences of from two months to two years for false pretences, fraud and bigamy, Police-Superintendent Williams said: "He was dismissed from his employment at an important north of England aircraft factory for causing disaffection among the employees."

FOR A 'DEAD GUERRILLA'

Moscow radio stated last night that the German High Command had offered a reward of 400 marks to any person who will deliver a Russian guerrilla fighter to the German authorities alive. For a dead guerrilla 300 marks is offered.

ONE PLANE FIGHTS FOR CONVOY

FOURTEEN ships in a British convoy, which had been under enemy attack for three days, arrived at Lisbon yesterday and reported how a lone British Catalina seaplane had repulsed repeated assaults by German planes.

At a Press conference attended by a British naval officer, captains said U-boats, at night, sank six merchantmen, the tug Empire Oak, and a corvette.

Berlin had claimed the sinking of twenty-five merchantmen and three naval escort vessels.

The convoy consisted of twenty freighters.

More Planes the Answer

The Luftwaffe, mainly through the efforts of the seaplane, failed to sink one ship.

The naval officer said the only answer to complete convoy protection was more aeroplanes.

"The German planes kept well off because right above a big Catalina flying boat circled," one captain said. "When the Germans came near the Catalina—although outnumbered—drove on them and they scattered, dropping their bombs in the sea."

LONE DAY RAIDER

Slight damage to property was caused by bombs dropped on a north-east of England town by a lone raider yesterday morning.

Map of Iran shows where British troops entered — at Bandar Shahpur, a port with a direct railway line to Teheran, the capital. Russian troops marched over the frontier at a point, not revealed, in the Caucasus, which lie between the Caspian Sea and the Turkish frontier with the Soviet.

Daily Mirror

AUG. 27

No. 11,766   ONE PENNY
Registered at the G.P.O. as a Newspaper.

GHOSTS' LAUGHING CHORUS

THE German "radio ghost" turned up again last night—this time with a band and a laughing chorus.

Every time the Deutschlandsender announcer tried to read the war reports, the ghostly chorus just laughed and laughed and laughed.

Then, when his pals nearly laughed themselves into hysterics, the "Chief Ghost" gave them a rest, and brought his band to the secret microphone.

They began to play some nice music, but it proved too much for Deutschlandsender, which suddenly cut out the war reports and played some rival tunes.

After this competition had gone on for a time, the war reports were resumed—without a word of explanation.

And the "ghosts" laughed and laughed and laughed.

Changed Wavelength

During a later broadcast at 8.45, there were further interruptions.

The news bulletin began at 9.3 and was interrupted fourteen times within nine minutes. Then, with only half the news read, the announcer advised listeners to tune in to the medium wavelength.

The only words distinguishable were at the beginning of the interruptions. The words "German youths," "Roosevelt" and "Hitler" were distinctly heard.

EAST AFRICA IS NEW MILITARY COMMAND

Creation of an East African Command, with Lieutenant-General Platt as G.O.C., was announced yesterday in Simla.

It will include all territories between the southern borders of the Anglo-Egyptian Sudan and the northern frontier of Southern Rhodesia.

HAW-HAW TELLS THE TRUTH

"Unprovoked attacks on small nations will never pay," said Lord Haw-Haw in concluding his last night's talk about Iran.

6,000,000 silk stockings

THREE million pairs of silk stockings will be released to the women of Britain this week

These are stockings which have been "frozen" by the manufacturers since the Board of Trade order last October prohibiting manufacture except for export, and which have been found "unsuitable" for sale overseas.

Arrangements have also been completed for the sale of shop-soiled or damaged goods, either without coupons, or upon the surrender of half the number of coupons required for the equivalent articles when new.

To prevent racketeering in new goods sold as "damaged," the Drapers' Chamber of Trade has fixed a scale of charges at which shop-soiled goods may be sold which makes dishonesty by traders not worth while.

A damaged cotton shirt may be sold at half the coupon rate if the reduced price at which it is sold does not exceed 3s. 4d., or coupon free if it does not exceed 1s. 8d.

Only the stars to guide him

Five hundred miles to land, with only the stars for guide, Chief Officer Horace Thompson navigated a boat full of survivors after his ship was torpedoed. Twenty-seven men owe their lives to him, including the captain of the vessel. Thompson has been awarded the M.B.E. Story on page 4.

NAVY GIVES SPAIN STRONG HINT "KEEP OUT"

POWERFUL units of the Navy, including the aircraft carrier Ark Royal, have returned to Gibraltar after giving a strong "Keep out" hint to Franco, and raiding North Sardinia.

The warships approached within eight miles of the coast of Spain, turned and steamed parallel to the shore at Valencia.

Fifteen fighters roared overhead in full view of the city, their formation making a huge victory V.

Then eighteen bombers, escorted by fighters, flew just outside the three-mile limit, also in V formation.

During the display, which lasted an hour, a submarine surfaced. Planes detached from formation found it to be Spanish.

The unwillingness of Italian warships to engage the British was again shown in this cruise, during which an important cork forest in North Sardinia was set ablaze.

The Italians were not expecting a raid in this quarter as only one A.A. gun went into action and no fighters appeared.

Several hundred 25lb. explosive incendiary bombs were dropped on the forest and a factory on the outskirts of the town of Tempio was set on fire.

Fires raging in sixteen square miles of forest could be seen seventy-five miles away.

The Admiral signalled, "Estimate enough burnt cork to give every Nazi a Hitler moustache."

'Hitler plans Gib. grab'

Moscow radio said last night that Hitler was plotting in Spain to occupy Gibraltar, which should play an important role in his Atlantic plans.

"More than 80,000 Germans are in Spain, and more men are continuously concentrating on the French side of the Spanish border," the announcer said.

Intense German military preparations in Bulgaria were reported last night in an Istanbul message quoted by the Soviet official news agency.

Germany is expected in a few days to demand that Turkey allow German troops through to Iran says the New York Post.

Door-to-door works buses

DOORSTEP to factory special buses will take workers to and from work this winter

Fleets of buses have been converted into "workers' specials." Seats for thirty passengers line the bus sides leaving room for thirty more people to stand.

Regular services of these buses will pick up workers in the residential districts and drop them at their jobs.

"By this means the congestion and discomfort of last winter will be done away with," an official at the Ministry of War Transport told the Daily Mirror.

WE LOSE A DESTROYER

Ex-American destroyer Bath, manned by the Royal Norwegian Navy has been sunk

The Bath is the first ex-American destroyer to be sunk in the Allies' service.

More troops than arms, says Minister

"**W**E want such an output of tanks and anti-tank equipment that we have more than our troops require. At present we are in the unhappy state of having more troops than weapons."

The Minister of Supply who has just returned from U.S. said this yesterday

He also said he would like to see America in the war—but it was the U.S. citizens' own business to decide.

Asked whether he was likely to go to Moscow he replied: "I do not know."

Referring to his "battle for bigger production in Britain," he said:

"I am not at all satisfied with what is being turned out by the supply services

"Failure to keep up to the programme had been due to a number of causes, including mistakes in production, failure in management and lax factory conditions

"But we have to struggle upwards towards the light, always improving the position

Other points made by the Minister were:

Last week's tank production

Continued on Back Page

DNIEPER CITY IS TAKEN

—Say Nazis

OCCUPATION of the great industrial city of Dnepropetrovsk, on the Dnieper, was claimed last night by the Germans in a High Command communique.

The city is a great steel-making centre, powered by the Dnieper dam. A hundred miles to the east are the Don and Donetz basin, the huge industrial area of South Russia.

The Soviet midnight communique made no mention of

Slovaks desert to Russians

Thirty thousand Slovak soldiers have been withdrawn from Germany's army at the front because so many deserted to the Russians, according to Moscow radio.

the city, but merely reported stubborn fighting along the whole front.

Earlier yesterday the Moscow newspaper "Pravda" claimed that a Russian counter-offensive in White Russia had driven the Germans from a big city, which was not named.

The Germans attacked heavily in the direction of Staraya-Russa, south of Lake Ilmen, but the Russians dug in under bombing and artillery preparation, and repulsed the infantry when it attempted to charge through barbed wire in close, unending waves.

Capture of the town of Luga, about ninety miles south of Leningrad is claimed by the Germans. Before troops could enter the town says the German radio they had to destroy 1,000 defensive positions and render harmless 92,000 land mines.

WARDER ATTACKED BY DARTMOOR CONVICT

It was learned last night that a vicious attack was made upon one of the officers of Dartmoor Prison on Friday last.

The officer—whose name is believed to be Curtis—was knocked down by a convict and kicked about the head, and it is reported that he is in hospital in a critical condition.

BRITISH ADVANCE SWIFTLY IN IRAN

IRAN communique last night said British or Russian planes had bombed towns on the Caspian Sea.

Soviet naval units in the Caspian Sea and British units in the Persian Gulf attacked Iran coastal defences, the communique added.

Swift advances are being made by the British and Russian troops, who are meeting with little resistance.

We have landed air-borne troops far into the interior to protect Britons in isolated districts, particularly the families of men working for the Anglo-Iranian Oil Company. These troops were in time to prevent sabotage.

Latest diplomatic move was a meeting between the British and Soviet Ambassadors and the Shah of Iran at the Shah's request. It is understood that he made no protest.

Seven Axis ships, two with their crews on board, have been captured at Bandar Shahpur at the head of the Persian Gulf.

R.A.F. bombers dropped leaflets on Teheran, Iran's capital, and other towns, saying that we have no quarrel with the Iranian people and no designs on their independence.

All Britons in Teheran are safe.

Daily Mirror

AUG. 28

No. 11,767 — ONE PENNY
Registered at the G.P.O. as a Newspaper.

LAVAL SHOT IN TRAITOR PARADE

SOVIET GET 120 MILES OF IRAN

RUSSIAN forces, penetrating 120 miles into Iran, yesterday straightened their line right across from the Turkish frontier to the Caspian Sea.

Moscow, giving this news, says that the advance is continuing swiftly and the Russians are meeting no opposition.

Good news— in fag packet

"I am a prisoner, quite well. Do not write."

THIS pencilled message on a cigarette packet told Mrs. B. Beckett, of Sturdee-avenue, Ipswich, yesterday that her son, Corporal W. A. Beckett, 24, is safe.

He had been missing for four months. The empty carton bears a Corinth postmark and has been stamped by German and British censors.

Mrs. Beckett told the "Daily Mirror" last night: "William fought with his two brothers in Crete. The other two got away, but he was unlucky.

"He was one of the last British soldiers to leave Dunkirk last year."

FOOD ORDER FOR TURKEY

Great Britain is to place orders with Turkey totalling about £4,500,000 mainly for dried fruits, preserved foods and fish, according to an Ankara dispatch to the Vichy News Agency.

Iran's reported peace plea

Iran has offered terms for a peaceful settlement, according to an Associated Press message from Teheran, capital of Iran. The message reached London last night after being delayed the previous day.

It says that the British Minister and the Soviet Ambassador after seeing the Shah transmitted to their Governments an Iranian plea that the invasion cease.

In return the Shah offered a guarantee that all Germans would be expelled from Iran within a week,

Chief town captured by the Russians is Tabriz, second biggest town in Iran and important railhead.

Most of Iran's precious oil-fields and refineries are already safely in our hands and intact. It is revealed by yesterday's British communique from Simla.

Germans Captured

Tempted by German credit terms, the Iranian Government has sold for export nearly the whole of the year's grain harvest as well as stocks of tea and sugar, with complete disregard for the needs of the Iranians.

The communique from Simla names four important towns now completely occupied—Bandar Shahpur, naval port in the Persian Gulf, and the three south-western oil towns.

This puts a big oil area safely into our hands.

We have cleared all the Iranians from Abadan Island, at the head of the Persian Gulf, occupied a naval floating dock and made the river passage

■ Continued on Back Page

Russia counter attacks

RUSSIAN troops have launched counter-attacks "with all their available forces" on the lower Dnieper River battlefront, according to an Hungarian message last night.

The counter-attacks were reported in Moscow to have hurled the Germans back from the approaches to the city "K," driving them far from their objective and the front line.

Nearly half the men in the German 71st Infantry Division have been lost in battles near the town, and one regiment has been almost completely wiped out.

"Opposition Terrific"

Claiming the capture of a town in the Dnieper estuary, a German military observer admitted:—

"The ground had to be wrung from the Russians yard by yard. The opposition was terrific and the fighting incredible. Our soldiers have never experienced anything like it before, and it is doubtful whether they will ever meet it again.

German radio, in a special announcement, claimed that the 22nd Soviet Army had been encircled and destroyed at Velikiye Luki, and the city captured.

Velikiye Luki, about 280 miles west of Moscow, and 170 miles north-west of Smolensk, has an important aerodrome.

The announcement said that Velikiye Luki was taken after a hard fight, and that 30,000 prisoners and 400 guns had been captured.

STEELMEN GIVE UP HOLIDAY

Most U.S. steel workers in the principal producing districts are forgoing Labour Day holiday on Monday and will keep production running full blast.—Reuter.

AS the traitors of France paraded at Versailles yesterday to sign on as soldiers for the Axis against Russia, Pierre Laval, biggest traitor of them all, was shot twice by a man who stepped from the crowd.

Four shots were fired, and Laval, who was sitting on a platform hearing the oath of allegiance of the volunteers, was hit twice—in the body and arm.

Reports of his condition are conflicting. One said his condition was "grave," with a wound in the liver.

Another said he had telephoned his wife from bed, assuring her "I'll recover."

Two other quislings who were with Laval were also shot, but neither was seriously hurt. They were Marcel Deat, editor of the Nazi-controlled Paris newspaper L'Oeuvre, and Major Durvy, member of the French Fascist Party.

The assailant's name is given as Paul Colette, aged about 28, a member of the Communist Youth Organisation. He was caught, manhandled, and dragged off to Versailles Prison.

The shooting occurred in the midst of waves of unrest and sabotage which are sweeping through occupied and unoccupied France.

Trains Derailed

Three trains have been derailed near Paris, Vichy admitted yesterday. In each case bolts had been removed from the rails.

The German and French authorities have been getting together in an effort to crush the "Communist and Jewish elements"—their name for those who favour Britain and De Gaulle.

Over 1,000 Communists were among the 7,000 persons arrested in Paris following the shooting of a German naval officer.

From other countries, too, come reports of unrest.

Five Dutchmen who helped

◎ Continued on Back Page

YOUR NEW HAT MAY HAVE NO LINING

Hat linings may disappear when manufacturers' stocks are finished. The Board of Trade is considering not to allocate further lining material.

"Though the ban is still under consideration it is fairly certain to go through," an official told the Daily Mirror last night.

De Gaulle offers bases to America

AS Vichy announced yesterday that its War Secretary, General Huntziger, was taking over command of French troops in North Africa, General de Gaulle, leader of the Free French, revealed that he had offered African bases to the U.S.

"I've offered the United States lease of the principal ports in Free French Africa as naval bases against Hitler," he said in an interview which appears in the Chicago Daily News.

"I have asked only that the United States make use of these bases to counteract Dakar.

German "Collaborator"

"The ports are Duala, in the Cameroons, Port Gentile, in Gabon, and Pointe Noire, in French Equatorial Africa." General de Gaulle was asked:

"Then you don't believe the United States should attempt to take Dakar by force at any time, but rather that the American Fleet and Air Arm should establish bases to check German advances into French Equatorial Africa?"

De Gaulle replied: "You have grasped it."

Huntziger, Vichy's new North African commander, has been appointed by Darlan. He was one of the delegates, with Admiral Darlan, who signed the armistice with Germany.

BLACK HEART

"THAT French quisling commonly called Laval," as Mr. Churchill denounced him in a recent broadcast, is known in France as "Black Heart."

Politician, lawyer, journalist, several times Cabinet Minister, Foreign Minister and Premier of France, he is feared for his cunning ambition.

He is Hitler's friend. When tragedy overtook France and Petain took over and made him Vice-Premier and Foreign Minister, Laval worked unceasingly to further Germany's ends.

Last December, when Petain dismissed him from office, Laval went to Paris, and since then the Nazis have worked hard to get him back to power, but this is the one thing that Petain has resisted successfully.

Marcel Deat, nicknamed Tom Thumb, has clamoured for support of Laval's plan to get collaboration with Germany. Laval is behind his Fascist organisation, which held its meetings in Paris under Nazi protection.

Planes collide, crash on town

SIX people were killed and sixteen severely injured yesterday when two planes collided over Blackpool and crashed, one of them through the roof of the Central Station's entrance hall.

With its tail torn off, this plane came down in a corkscrew dive, its petrol tank exploding.

People were trapped inside the station entrance hall, which caught fire. Some were carried out with their clothes alight, and soldiers beat out the flames.

The other plane crashed on the house, in Reads-avenue, of Mr. and Mrs. L. H. Franceys.

Two walls and a large part of the roof collapsed, but Mr. and Mrs. Franceys were unhurt.

The pilot of the plane tried to bale out, but was killed. His body, to which was attached an unopened parachute, was found 200 yards from the damaged house.

Daily Mirror

AUG. 29

No. 11,768 — ONE PENNY
Registered at the G.P.O. as a Newspaper.

ALL EX-MINERS MUST RETURN TO PIT JOBS NOW

COMPULSORY powers will be used to bring thousands of ex-miners now in other jobs back to the pits.

Instructions have been given to Ministry of Labour to order men to leave their present work and report at once.

Discussions between the President of the Board of Trade and the Coal Production Council have revealed the urgent need for building up winter coal stocks at once.

Following the recent registration of ex-miners and the appeal to them voluntarily to return to help the drive for more output, only a few thousand have answered the call.

To meet a shortage of miners in the Midlands about 2,000 ex-miners in Wales are to be transferred, while compulsory orders are being sent to thousands of former pit workers in other parts of the country.

At the moment demand for coal is outstripping supply, winter demands are beginning to set in, and it has been belatedly recognised that the industry must get a move on.

GOVT. PAYS TO KEEP RAIL FARES DOWN

AS from January last the Government will pay the four main-line railway companies and the London Passenger Transport Board a total of £43,000,000 a year as compensation for increased costs due to the war.

Agreement to this effect was officially announced last night. The Government has taken this step to stop a threatened rise in fares and freights.

This total is exclusive of payments required to meet interest and redemption charges.

The companies will also continue to receive profits from their road transport investments and the revenue accruing from rail investments in Eife and Northern Ireland.

Minimum Guaranteed

Under the control agreement reached in February, 1940, the four amalgamated railway companies and the L.P.T.B. were jointly guaranteed a minimum net revenue of £40,000,000 a year, compared with £33,800,000 earned in the last accounting periods of the five lines.

All receipts and expenses of the companies were to be pooled.

Any further revenue above this sum up to £3,500,000 which the companies might earn was to accrue entirely to them.

Jap note mystery

JAPAN'S Ambassador to Washington, Admiral Nomura, yesterday handed President Roosevelt a personal message from the Japanese Premier, Prince Konoye.

Admiral Nomura, who saw both the President and the Secretary of State, Mr. Cordell Hull, refused to tell reporters what the message contained.

When asked whether his message related to shipments to Russia, he replied that he "did not think so."

Mr. Cordell Hull said at his Press conference that there might be another, or several more meetings between President Roosevelt and the Japanese Ambassador.

He added that the State Department would not disclose the contents of the message.

PLAGUE THREAT IN U.S.

Medical experts from eleven U.S. States met in Salt Lake City, Utah, yesterday, to discuss a plan of action following several reports of bubonic plague in eastern States.—British United Press.

"Cease fire" in Iran ordered

IRAN'S new Government gave orders, as soon as it was formed yesterday, to the Iranian forces to cease resisting the British and Soviet forces marching into the country, says Reuter.

The new Premier, Ali Furanghi, told Parliament of his Government's decision at an extraordinary meeting, according to the Teheran radio.

This had been done, Ali Furanghi said, "to prevent further bloodshed."

The Allies were advancing rapidly when the Iranians gave in.

Berlin officials, commenting on the news, said: "The British attacked in a gangster-like fashion, without a declaration of war."

A Day's Work

In less than twenty-four hours after entering Iran, British forces

Retook control of the world's largest oil refinery plants at Abadan;

Captured the whole Iranian Navy;

Seized the strategic wireless station at Khorramshahr; and

Entrapped several Axis merchantmen who were in the harbour at Bandar Shahpur.

In addition, some 700 prisoners and some field batteries were captured by our forces driving northwards.

Indians' Bravery

The advance was made in blazing heat and scorching south winds.

Starting from Basra in the early hours of Monday, Lieutenant-General Harvey, of the Indian Army, commanding the attacking forces in Iran, pushed in three lines of attack.

The first was made by Indian Infantry, who sailed down the Tigris in tugs and sloops and made a surprise landing at Abadan.

The second, an Indian Infantry

Continued on Back Page

General—does private's work

Lieutenant-General Edward Pellew Quinan is in command of the British and Indian forces operating in Iran, it was revealed yesterday.

The first three letters of General Quinan's name are pronounced to rhyme with "high." His nickname is Q.

If he sees any detail of organisation or operation which could be improved by the subaltern or N.C.O. in charge he unhesitatingly attends to it himself.

One day, after inspecting forward positions, he spotted a machine-gun section which might have been doing greater damage.

In a flash General Quinan scrambled up a hundred yards of craggy slope, jumped into the machine-gun nest and was firing the gun himself as it should have been fired.

Children get more coupons

EXTRA coupons will be issued in October as a special clothing ration for older children.

These will be available for the family pool if parents have drawn upon their own coupons for their children in the meantime.

Forty extra coupons will be given to children in Classes 1 and 2 below; twenty "extras" to those in Class 3.

1. Children born on or after July 14, 1927, who are 5ft. 3in. or more in height (measured without shoes and stockings), or weigh 7st. 12lb. or more.

2. Children born on or after July 14, 1925, but before July 14, 1927.

3. Children born on or after January 1, 1925, but before July 14, 1925.

"National" corsets are to be plentiful and cheap.

To help out the restricted quota of corsets, certain standard types are soon to be quota free, which means that there will be plenty of them in the shops, at the same coupon value as other types.

VICHY DIPLOMAT'S WIFE INJURED

Mme. de Brinon, wife of Count de Brinon, the Vichy Government's representative in occupied territory, has been seriously injured in a bicycle accident near her home in the Pyrenees. She was found unconscious in the road, with a fractured skull.

CIANO: AN OPERATION

Ciano, the Italian Foreign Minister, has had a successful operation on his throat, says Rome radio.—Reuter.

VILLAGE LIT UP IN BLACK-OUT

RESIDENTS of sleepy Ugborough, a village near Plymouth, are trying to get to the bottom of a mystery.

Ugborough, which is not even on a bus route, and has no village policeman, was the most prominent place in Britain when, between 1.50 a.m. and 3.30 a.m., its seven street lamps were lit up as if Hitler had never been heard of.

Mrs. F. Woodley made the surprising discovery.

"I woke up and saw the street lamps blazing through my window," she told the Daily Mirror yesterday.

"Without stopping to dress, I ran to my brother's house, and he went for the special constable.

"Everybody turned out before long. Some of us thought an armistice had been signed."

The special constable telephoned to the police at Wrangaton, a few miles away, and to the power station which supplies Ugborough with current.

Villagers Took Action

"It is impossible," gasped a bewildered electrician at the other end of the line.

But there it was. Ugborough folk were walking round, mostly in their night clothes, with the village as bright as day.

Finally they took action themselves. Ladders were fetched and men in pyjamas climbed up the standards to unscrew the bulbs. Some were smashed.

With the black-out restored, Ugborough heaved a sigh of relief and went back to bed. Nazi planes were reported over the south-west during the night, and Mr. Jack Moore, Ugborough's warden, thinks fifth columnists might have turned on the lights, but added that an accidental short-circuit might have been responsible.

An official at the power station said it was impossible for anyone to have switched on the lights, which are controlled by a clock which was put out of action when war began.

Huns tell Turks 'Expel Britons'

GERMANY is increasing her pressure on Turkey to allow Nazi troops to pass through her territory to attack the Allies in the Near East.

Boston radio stated last night that Germany will ask Turkey to expel all Britons and Russians.

If Turkey does not obey, Germany will march, giving as an excuse the intervention of Britain and Russia in Iran.

Meanwhile, Von Papen, German Ambassador to Turkey, was received by President Ismet Inonu of Turkey in Ankara yesterday in the presence of M. Sarajoglu, the Turkish Foreign Minister, Ankara radio stated.

A delayed message from Istanbul told of another German demand.

"No More Demands"

Hitler has informed Turkey, it stated, that he may soon need the use of Turkish territorial waters in the Black Sea, but has assured the Turks he has no further demands of them.

The Turks have banned motor and rail traffic to Europe and closed Thrace to foreigners, declares the Hungarian News Bureau.

6 die in bid to aid airmen

SIX men are believed to have died yesterday in an effort to save the crew of an R.A.F. plane which fell into the sea off Rhosneigr, Anglesey, in full view of hundreds of holidaymakers who lined the shore.

Some of the crew baled out, and two succeeded in reaching the shore, a quarter of a mile away, little the worse for their immersion.

A third airman, who was wearing a life-saving jacket, was apparently dead when brought ashore.

Although terrific seas were running at the time, a rowing boat, manned by two soldiers, put out in an effort to reach the plane.

Before the boat got near the plane it capsized, but the soldiers clung to their craft and were washed ashore in an exhausted condition.

Planes Take Part

A larger boat, manned by six soldiers and Police-Constable Arthur, of the Anglesey police, and Mr. Arthur Owen, a Merchant Service officer, then set out.

All went well until they experienced the full fury of the waves, and the boat capsized. All the occupants were flung into the sea and the spectators on shore could see them struggling in the water.

Several succeeded in getting hold of oars, but others had to try to keep themselves afloat without support.

Several planes appeared, and life-saving jackets were dropped from some of them, but heavy seas carried them away from the drowning men.

A third boat put out in an effort to reach the struggling men, but this also was overturned.

One of the rowers from this boat, although fighting for his life, managed to get hold of an oar and reached a drowning

Continued on Back Page

Their kisses won an army

When Rumanians left Bukarest to fight for the Germans on the Eastern front, beautiful women at the railway station rushed to kiss them, apparently out of patriotic fervour.

But later the troops found Soviet leaflets in their pockets and many deserted.

Daily Mirror

SEPT. 9

No. 11,777 — ONE PENNY
Registered at the G.P.O. as a Newspaper.

ARMY RAID ISLE IN ARCTIC: FOIL NAZI PLAN

This remarkable picture shows how a U-boat surrendered. The man standing up on the rubber float is a British naval officer. He is calling on the U-boat crew to give in.

The U-boat had been bombed by a Hudson R.A.F. plane, and put out a white flag. The Hudson kept guard over them until relieved by a Catalina flying-boat, which called up destroyers. A gale was blowing, and the warships could not lower boats for several hours.

It is the first case on record of a submarine being "captured" by an aeroplane. (Another picture on Back Page.)

BRITISH troops are operating in the Arctic, where they have made a bloodless landing at the Norwegian islands of Spitsbergen, and landings have also been made on the coast of Occupied France.

This was announced by the War Office last night.

"Hundreds of big tough British soldiers cross the Channel on speedboats every night," a U.S. bomber ferry pilot told New York reporters.

"They creep up to German officers," he said, "and quietly give them the works. These raiding parties terrorise the Nazis. They wreck airfields or destroy communications."

It was recently decided to send a military force to the Arctic "for various purposes," says the War Office communique, but the landing at Spitzbergen is the only activity disclosed.

The landing was made by a mixed British, Canadian and Norwegian force, under Canadian command to foil a Nazi plan to use the island's coal mines.

The communique says:—

The main purpose of the landing was to prevent the enemy from utilising for their own war purposes Spitzbergen with its rich coal mines.

"Previously a proportion of the Spitsbergen coal had been at the disposal of the population of Northern Norway. But it has become known that the enemy's plan was to seize all coal available, including that from Spitsbergen, which would be used mainly for war transport to the far north.

"This source of fuel has now been denied to the Germans. An immediate result of the Spitsbergen landing is that a considerable number of Norwegian miners with their families have now arrived in Great Britain to play a part in the Allied war effort here.

"Most of them will be joining the Norwegian forces or the Norwegian Merchant Service."

Spitsbergen, a group of Arctic islands, about 500 miles north of Norway, is blocked by ice for

Continued on Back Page

Leningrad push is held

THE German armies under Von Bock yesterday made a big push in an effort to break through the western and southern defences of Leningrad. They failed.

They were held off by Voroshilov's forces, who kept up their repeated counter-attacks.

Nowhere have the Germans been able to penetrate the Russian lines.

A German High Command communique yesterday claimed —as it has claimed before—that Leningrad was now cut off. It was claimed that the Finns had cut the Murmansk railway, completing the encirclement of Leningrad.

Bridgehead Fight

These claims are not confirmed by the Russians and the indications are that the enemy is held.

Berlin radio last night reported repeated counter-attacks by the Russians in the northern sector of the front.

In the central sector, it was claimed, Soviet attempts to recapture a German bridgehead had been repulsed.

Leningrad was active enough on the air yesterday, when the workers broadcast a special programme hurling defiance at Hitler and proclaiming their determination to hold the city whatever the cost.

In the central sector, in the Smolensk and Gomel directions, the great battles of last week seem to have died down with the Nazis remaining on the defensive and the Russians still initiating action at some points.

DUKE TO WASHINGTON

The Duke and Duchess of Windsor will spend twenty-four hours in Washington on September 25-26 en route to their ranch in Alberta, the British Embassy in Washington has announced. They will stay at the Embassy.—Associated Press.

U-boat is captured by plane

FOR the first time in history a submarine has surrendered to an aeroplane, the Air Ministry announces this morning. The U-boat has been safely towed to a British port.

It was an R.A.F. Hudson which made the capture, in the Atlantic. The Hudson had to circle the U-boat for nearly four hours to guard it after the surrender. Other planes had to circle it for ten hours waiting for a warship to take over the prize.

All that time more than twelve hours, the U-boat was held prisoner from the air with no contact, only the threat of machine-guns.

The Hudson first sighted the U-boat, in poor light and bad weather, less than a mile ahead and immediately dived to attack.

The navigator called, "Machine - gun them, let's machine-gun them." The wireless operator dropped to the floor, and rapidly wound down the belly-gun.

Then the plane dived

Continued on Back Page

SPITFIRE BLOWS UP SHIP

A GERMAN flak ship was destroyed off Ostend today by a Spitfire armed with cannon and machine guns.

The Spitfire was on reconnaissance when the pilot saw three flak ships near Ostend.

He dived on them, and, while still firing his first burst, saw one of the ships explode, and the superstructure

disintegrate, throwing pieces all round in the air.

His comment on his return was, "It is highly probable I hit the magazine. I broke off the engagement while I was still 200 yards away."

Flak ships are the equivalent of British A.A. ships and are usually the size of large trawlers.

MAY END BAN ON WOMEN

Shortage of male teachers may cause Swansea Corporation to revoke its ban on married women teachers.

ITALIANS FIRE ON EACH OTHER

ITALIAN destroyers again fired on each other when Fleet Air Arm planes swooped on a convoy of three merchant vessels, each protected by a destroyer, in the Mediterranean.

Two torpedoes from the planes hit a tanker, three hit one of the other merchant ships.

Germans got U.S. bomb sight

Details of the United States' most secret bomb-sight — the Norden—have been given to Germany.

This was the allegation made by Mr. Harold Kennedy, the United States Attorney, at the trial in New York yesterday of sixteen members of a spy-ring said to be working for Germany.

Mr. Kennedy said that one of the accused, whom he did not name, had obtained specifications of the Norden bomb-sight in 1938 and transmitted them to Germany.—British United Press.

CHILD'S HAND FOUND IN RIVER

The discovery of a child's hand in the Avon below the weirs at Bathampton, three miles on the London side of Bath, is being investigated by the police.

The hand, which has been submitted to a medical expert for examination, is that of a very young child,

Daily Mirror

SEPT. 12

No. 11,780   ♦   ONE PENNY

Registered at the G.P.O. as a Newspaper.

GERMANS START BIG THRUST FOR MURMANSK

NAZIS FACE BIG STRIKE IN NORWAY

DEFIANT Norwegian workers' threat of a general strike is expected to result in an extension by the Nazis of the state of civil siege declared in Oslo.

The strike is considered inevitable, according to Swedish reports received by N.B.C. radio, New York.

Oslo and other big towns are surrounded by German troops.

The situation is said to be critical in the towns of Moss, Fredrikstad and Sarpsborg, says Associated Press.

One minute's silence in memory of the Norwegian trade union leaders executed by the Nazis—ten others were given life sentences—was observed by delegates at the Swedish Trades Union Congress, says Reuter.

Gestapo sent secrets to G-men

UNTIL five days ago Gestapo agents in Germany were daily communicating by wireless with G-men in the United States in blissful ignorance of their identity.

They thought they were in touch with Sebold, a former German and now a naturalised American, who, acting as a Nazi spy, was really working for the Federal Bureau of Investigation.

This was revealed when the "spy ring" trial was continued in New York yesterday, says British United Press. Sixteen men and women are accused of spying in the U.S.A. for the Nazis.

A G-man said his department kept touch with the Gestapo through Hamburg station. Several hundred messages were exchanged in code. Bogus information was sent to the Germans.

In return the G-men received instructions from the Gestapo to their spies in the United States.

More than 250 G-men have been dismissed or transferred owing to their hectic associations with glamorous young women who, it is feared, may have obtained vital defence secrets from them, cables the *Da.'y Mirror* New York correspondent

Detectives were yesterday "grilling" these young women, one of whom is Paula von Luckner, 22, who says she is cousin of Count Felix van Luckner, German "seadevil" of the last war.

Went to Gay Parties

Some of the dismissed G-men attended gay parties at Paula's hotel, where she introduced them to a bevy of beautiful girls.

Hearing about the gay goings-on of his G-men in New York and elsewhere, their chief, Hoover, assigned other G-men to spy on them.

2 HEADLIGHTS FOR CARS SOON

The Lighting Restrictions Order is being amended to enable drivers of motor vehicles to use two masked headlamps, each giving as much light as is now permitted for one masked headlamp.

They will also be allowed to show more light from their rear lamps.

The Minister of Home Security reveals this in a written reply.

CALL FOR GREER INQUIRY

A resolution calling for an inquiry into the encounter between the U.S. destroyer Greer and a U-boat was introduced in the United States Senate yesterday.—British United Press.

There's little rent profiteering

After studying reports from all local authorities in England and Wales, the Minister of Health is satisfied that in the greater part of the country there is no evidence of rent profiteering.

Of 1,468 authorities involved, it is understood that 1,047 have reported that they have no evidence of profiteering in their area.

This means that in the greater part of England and Wales no one has complained to the local authority that the rent the landlord is charging is unreasonable.

Some authorities are still investigating complaints and cannot yet give a final report, but 275 state they have successfully dealt with complaints by negotiation with the landlords.

Standard suits in autumn

PRICES have been fixed for standard "utility" clothes for men and boys. The cloth is on the looms, and stocks should reach the shops by the autumn.

A large number of wholesale prices will be issued by the Board of Trade and retailers will be allowed a 33 1-3 per cent. profit.

A man will be able to buy a pair of flannel trousers in a shop for 15s. 6d.; a good made-to-measure suit for 100s.; a tweed suit for 69s.; and an overcoat for 54s. 6d.

There will also be a man's sports jacket at 31s. 6d., gaberdine raincoats (sizes 34-42) at 38s. 10d.; and a 6 to 8-year-old boy's two-piece lined flannel suit for 26s. 5d. These prices may vary slightly.

There will be four types of men's standard suits, two of overcoats and six of trousers.

Prices for women's and girls' "utility" clothes have not yet been fixed.

POPE AND U.S. ENVOY IN TALKS

Great importance is attached in Washington to secret conferences being held in the Vatican between the Pope and Mr. Roosevelt's special envoy, Myron Taylor. They talked for more than an hour yesterday, cables John Walters, from New York.

Washington believes that Mr. Roosevelt and the Pope hope to reach agreement on the postwar world as revealed in the eight points announced after Mr. Churchill's meeting with the President.

JAPS REORGANISE DEFENCE

Creation of a general staff for the defence of Japan proper, Korea, Formosa and Sakhalin was officially announced yesterday. It will be under General Otozo Yamada, Director of Military Education.—Reuter.

GERMANY has started a big attack in the region of Murmansk, Russia's only ice-free port in the Arctic, where British warships last week sank a destroyer and two other ships in a German convoy.

Two hundred miles to the south, just outside the Arctic circle, the Russians have launched an attack in the Lake Topo Sero sector, pushing back the Finns,

In the central sector, the Russian counterthrusts are still making headway.

Latest success on this part of the front is the rout of German forces which were preparing to cross the river Dvina. The Germans made a hasty retreat leaving 700 dead.

From Gomel (also in the central sector) the Germans appear to be making headway in a thrust to the southeast, while the Russians are attacking on a line parallel to this thrust.

The rival attackers are thus behind each others' lines.

In the Kiev region an attack by "major Soviet forces" is referred to by the German radio, which claims, as usual, that the attack was repulsed.

Leaflets on Leningrad

The battle for Leningrad goes on with unabated fury, but no new details are available. The city was heavily bombed again on Wednesday night, says Berlin.

German leaflets were dropped warning civilians that if they took up arms in defence of the city it would "suffer the same fate as Warsaw."

Autumn rains and early frost in the area were reported last night.

The Germans are trying to confuse the issue by their propaganda.

They put out one report yesterday that Leningrad was likely to fall in ten days and another report that isolating Leningrad from the rest of Russia was all Germany intended to do.

Odessa Defiant

At the other end of the front in the Ukraine, Odessa yesterday celebrated a month of successful defence under siege. It sent a message to Stalin vowing to continue the defence of the city, and sent greetings to the defenders of Leningrad and Kiev.

"Odessa is one of the most terrible battlefields' of all time," says the Italian newspaper, "Ambrosiano."

"The ground is covered with the bodies of men and horses, and abandoned lorries, guns and tanks. The cries of the wounded are louder than machine-guns and bombs."

LAUNDRY 1d. in 1s. INCREASE ILLEGAL

The Central Price Regulation Committee has recommended the Board of Trade to make an order providing that the maximum charges for laundry work of articles of domestic or personal use shall be those ruling during the week beginning September 1.

Effect of the order is to make the proposed increase of a penny in the shilling as from September 15 illegal.

Huns fake victory film

★ A COMPLETE German propaganda film entitled "The Fall of Kiev" has been captured by the Russians. It was prepared some time ago in anticipation of a quick victory —but Kiev, capital of the Ukraine, still stands.

More than 30,000 Huns died in a vain attempt to take Kiev, "Pravda" said yesterday.

"Pravda" revealed that between August 5 and 11 the Germans "had their bloody claws" on Kiev, capital of the Ukraine, but were driven back.— Reuter.

DEFENDS AIRCRAFT MINISTER

MR. CHURCHILL defended the Minister of Aircraft Production (Colonel Moore - Brabazon) in the Commons yesterday against the charge that he had expressed the wish to see Germany and Russia annihilate each other.

"I am satisfied," he said, "that, though the phrasing of what he said might be misconstrued, he is in full accord with the policy the Government are earnestly pursuing."

But Mr. Churchill opposed a request for publication of the Minister's actual statements and his admission that the statements were made.

Mr. Gallacher, Communist M.P., asked the Prime Minister whether the remarks in the recent speech of the Minister of Aircraft Production represented the policy of the Government.

Mr. Churchill said the versions of the speech which had been given to the public represented neither the policy of the Government nor the views of the Minister.

"I happen to know what the views of the Minister are, because on the day that Hitler attacked Russia, I told him on the telephone the line I was going to take that night," said Mr Churchill.

"Enthusiastic Assent"

"He wholeheartedly supported that line and he expressed enthusiastic assent.

"I am satisfied that he was, and is, in the fullest accord with the policy of the Government."

Mr. Shinwell asked the Premier if he had read the correspondence which passed between the Minister of Aircraft Production Sir Ernest Simon and Mr. Blackburn, organiser of the A.E.U. who made the complaints.

Mr. Churchill said: "I have read the correspondence, and I was astonished that anyone could have taken the mischievous action of making of this a sensation, which does nothing but harm to Russia and Britain, and leads to suspicion."

Mr. Shinwell: If you now

Continued on Back Page

BRISTOL'S DEBRIS GOES TO NEW YORK

Today in New York I walked among the ruins of Bristol, England, my home town, John Walters cabled last night.

Hundreds of tons of bricks and rubble from blitzed Bristol are being used as foundations for new roads in New York.

The material was brought here as ballast in English freighters.

With her children at their East Grinstead (Sussex) home, Katharine, Lady Stamp, who was a peeress for a moment. Her husband and his father Lord Stamp were killed by the same bomb, which wrecked their home. The House of Lords has ruled that the son lived momentarily after his father and thus became Lord Stamp. The decision means that the children take the title of "Honourable." They are the Hon. Jessica Catherine (on tricycle), the Hon. Nancy Elizabeth (striped frock) and the Hon. Veronica.

D.336 22746

Daily Mirror

SEPT. 15

No. 11,782   ONE PENNY
Registered at the G.P.O. as a Newspaper.

ADMIRAL SWAM FOR IT

U.S. MEN HERE ON WAY TO SOVIET

Bus protest: men's leaders seized

THE president and secretary of a committee set up by Midland workers to protest against new arrangements for conveying them to and from work were arrested yesterday under the Defence Regulations and will appear in court today.

Last week, as reported in the *Daily Mirror*, nearly 2,000 men employed in building a Government factory barricaded the road leading to the site and held a protest parade to which the police were called.

The men complain that until recently they were taken to and from a town where several hundreds of them live to the factory site ten miles away, by bus.

Now trains have been substituted for the buses by the Ministry of War Transport and as a result the men spend hours daily in getting to the station, waiting and travelling.

"10,000 Hours Wasted"

Yesterday they followed up their demonstrations with a meeting which demanded the restoration of the buses.

They claimed that 10,000 hours are wasted every week.

The two officials who have been arrested are Albert Loan, a clerk, and Edwin Endersby, a bricklayer.

At the time of the demonstrations the Transport and General Workers' Union refused to recognise the men's action and the workers declared they would send their grievance to the Premier and the Minister of Labour.

Iran Huns —we force action

UNDER pressure from the British and Soviet authorities the Iran Government are to get the 800 German "tourists" and technicians out of the Nazi Legation at Teheran and concentrate them in barracks.

Later the Germans will be sent to India and Russia.

Delaying tactics by Nazi Legation officials had previously held up the departure of the unwanted Germans.

"Encouraged" by Britain and Russia the Iranian Government has closed down a Teheran newspaper which was the mouthpiece of the Shah, and which declared that Iran's diplomatic relations with the Axis would remain intact in spite of recent events.

Finland has 'good hopes of peace'

M. TANNER, Finnish Minister of Trade, declared in a speech at Helsinki yesterday that Finland had "good hopes of peace in the nearest future."

While denying Finland intended a separate peace with Russia, M. Tanner stressed that she was fighting a purely "defensive war" to secure her frontiers.

"To a great extent this aim has already been achieved," he declared, "but our ultimate frontiers can only be decided at a future peace conference.

"It is obvious that we cannot, while war is raging, let the enemy know whether we intend to stop or advance further, and if so, how far."

NEXT DANCE—AT VICTORY

King Peter of Yugoslavia has made a vow not to dance again until his country's freedom has been restored.

'COULD SPEED ARMS 30 p.c.'

"A 30 per cent. increase could be made in production in the area I cover in a very short time, without any great sacrifice by anyone."

ALDERMAN D. PLINSTON, official connected with Ministry of Labour supply committees, said this at a conference of trade unionists from arms factories in a north-west town yesterday.

The principle of giving workers closer co-operation in management to speed production was endorsed.

Delegates expressed disappointment that only a few instances of idle time had been quoted. An engineering representative said:—

"If people name instances of mismanagement which amount almost to sabotage, their names may get back to the managements."

An N.U.R. delegate quoted a case where the delivery of a bag of bolts to a destination forty miles away took a week.

WEEK'S AIR SCORE: 18-45

Last week's air losses in Western Europe and the Middle East were eighteen Axis aircraft and forty-five of ours.

He refused to put his men in extra peril by going on their overloaded raft. Vice-Admiral L. D. I. MacKinnon swam for it, and was saved.

HE LEFT RAFTS FOR HIS CREW

THE last raft was full. Seven men were all she could take, and the eighth man turned away as the raft pushed off from the stern.

The eighth man—the last man—on a ship in convoy, fast sinking in the Atlantic from a torpedo. And as the waters rose about him he dived and swam.

The last man was Vice-Admiral L. D. I. MacKinnon. Once he flew his flag on H.M.S. Resolution. Now, at fifty-eight, he had come back to serve his country in the battle of the seas. Admiral MacKinnon swam for three hours and, half dead from exposure, was saved.

The last raft he left to his men was lost.

And yesterday, to the *Daily Mirror*, Admiral MacKinnon, of Marl Close, Frampton, Dorset, made light of his bravery.

"Oh, I just swam around on a plank for a time," he said, "and finally was picked up by an escort vessel. Two other officers from my ship were saved about the same time."

What Admiral MacKinnon did not tell was the real story.

When the ship was hit by the submarine torpedo the boats were damaged in the explosion.

The admiral supervised the construction of rafts from any material they could find.

He saw the crew safely off the

Continued on Back Page

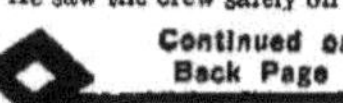

SERVICE WOMEN TO HAVE POLICE

THE W.A.A.F. and the A.T.S. are to have their own women police.

Two W.A.A.F.s—an officer and an N.C.O.—are already assisting the Service police.

At A.T.S. headquarters, an officer told the *Daily Mirror*: "Plans are under way for establishing women police patrols.

"They will be trained to be guide and friend to women members of the Forces, as well as keeping an eye on dress and discipline."

Adding that the correct amount of make-up was encouraged, and that the girl who "plastered it on" was liable to warning, the officer said:—

"Recruits for the women military police will be chosen for their **appearance** as models for the rest of the Force."

In other words, the new women military police are going to have chic, glamour, common sense.

COAST TOWN BOMBED

High explosive bombs were dropped at a north-east England coastal town last night by a single raider. There were some casualties.

50% want fire guard exemption

At many Labour Exchanges yesterday about fifty per cent. of the men registered for compulsory fire guard duties applied for exemption.

The applications were mainly on the ground that those making them were already engaged in civil defence work.

The men registering yesterday were those from eighteen to thirty-five in all local authority areas in which the Fire Prevention (Business Premises) Order is operative.

Fire Guard Rules—Page 3.

MR. AVERELL HARRIMAN, head of the U.S. Mission to Moscow, with other members of the Mission, which includes transport and oil experts, arrived in London last night, after flying the Atlantic.

They were accompanied by M. Oumansky, Soviet Ambassador to the U.S.

A wing of the R.A.F. has arrived in Russia to fight under Russian orders.

British naval warplanes, striking at the enemy's sea supply lines to his troops on the North Russian front, have sunk one ship and damaged others.

These developments were revealed yesterday.

Eight-gun Hurricane and American-built Tomahawks may be included in the R.A.F. wing sent to Russia.

Tomahawks are believed to have been shipped from Britain to Murmansk, Russia's Arctic port, and there assembled.

Hurricanes might have been flown from the Middle East to the Soviet-Iranian frontier by easy stages, to provide fighter support in Southern Russia.

A wing of the R.A.F. is a self-contained unit fully equipped with machines, pilots and ground personnel. The ground staff includes maintenance men.

An Admiralty communiqué issued yesterday said that at dawn on Friday, carrier-borne naval aircraft sank one 2,000-ton enemy supply ship and damaged others in the Bodo area, off the Norwegian coast.

The First Lord of the Admiralty said at Nottingham yesterday: "There are many ways in which naval help can be and is being given to Russia, but I am not going to help the enemy by going into details of what is being done."

Leningrad attack: Nazis lose warships

TWO German destroyers were sunk as the Nazis made their first attempt to enter the sea approaches to Leningrad, the Moscow *Izvestia* reported last night.

The Germans yesterday renewed their desperate efforts to make one spectacular victory—the capture of Leningrad—before the winter campaign begins.

Danger to the city has grown. Yet there was no news that its fall is near.

Day and night artillery duels have turned the battlefield outside Leningrad into an inferno.

A Soviet communiqué received in London this morning said:—

"Fierce fighting continued along the whole front.

"After many days of stubborn fighting our forces evacuated Kremenchug (a Ukraine town on the east bank of the Dnieper).

"On the north-western front one unit of Marshal Voroshilov's army, in the course of repeated battles, destroyed more than 10,000 Germans, 200 tanks and hundreds of motor-cars and guns."

Ankara reports last night said that General Ciuperca and several other Rumanian officers had been shot for refusing to advance beyond the River Dniester, which marks the boundary of Bessarabia, which Rumania ceded to Russia a year ago.

Daily Mirror

SEPT. 16

No. 11,783   ONE PENNY
Registered at the G.P.O. as a Newspaper.

GERMANS ADMIT BIG BLOWS BY LENINGRAD

Towns shirking food duty

ONE hundred and twenty out of 200 odd towns in South - West England have taken no steps to plan emergency feeding.

If invasion or heavy bombing causes temporary dislocation of food supplies the population in these areas will have nothing to fall back on.

"One reason is that local councils are reluctant to enter into competition with restaurants which are probably among the towns' biggest ratepayers," a Food Ministry official stated yesterday.

"They need not be afraid," he added. "So far I have not heard of a single business which has been adversely affected by the setting up of one of our centres."

Bristol Lag

At present thirty-five south-western councils have opened fifty-nine British Restaurants and not one of these has shown a loss.

Plymouth leads the way to the whole country outside London with eighteen restaurants serving 4,000 meals a day.

Even the small Devonshire market town of South Molton has one restaurant serving twenty-eight weekly mid-day meals daily.

Yet Bristol, by far the largest city in the west, with its shopping centre and many restaurants blitzed, has only one British Restaurant to serve its population of nearly half a million in emergency.

NEUTRALITY ACT MAY GO

PRESIDENT ROOSEVELT and legislative leaders of the United States yesterday discussed:

The repeal of the Neutrality Act, which would permit U.S. warships to enter British ports, and merchantmen to be armed, and

A possible censorship of news from the U.S. to the rest of the world.

No conclusions were reached at the conference on the Neutrality Act.

President Roosevelt reported to Congress yesterday that the value of actual war exports of American war supplies to the nations fighting the Axis, under the Lease-Lend programme, totalled £47,500,000 to August 21.

This figure represents expenditure for weapons and other supplies actually sent abroad.

Defence articles transferred, including some awaiting shipment, amount to an additional £14,000,000, while various services, such as repairing naval vessels, came to £19,500,000.

Bases for Britain

The energies of the American Government, the President said, are making available to Soviet Russia urgently needed supplies.

His report discloses that some Lease and Lend funds have been utilised to build naval and military bases for the British.

Administration officials declined to disclose the whereabouts of these bases.

The plan for the censorship of communications between the U.S. and the rest of the world is being worked out jointly by the War and Navy departments.

The Under-Secretary of the Navy, Mr. James V. Forrestal, told the House of Representatives this in Washington yesterday.

AXIS RAIDER OFF PANAMA

An Axis raider operating near the approaches to the Panama Canal is reported in messages from Balboa.

These reports come with the announcement by Colonel Knox that the U.S. Navy has been given its orders to capture or destroy Axis raiders. (His speech is on page 3.)

According to a dispatch to the *New York Times* yesterday, many vessels arriving at Balboa report picking up messages from other ships saying that they were being attacked by a raider. The names of these ships have not been revealed.

Drowning, with fire above him

A R.A.F. pilot, trapped in his sinking bomber, while the half of the plane still above water was on fire, struggled to get his head above the water.

Then he saw a light on top of the water above him. It was the fire in his plane. But he thought it might be the light people are said to imagine when they are drowning.

The pilot's cockpit was about 10ft. under the sea. The bomber, hit and set on fire off Ostend, had come down nose first, and it was sinking vertically. From the navigator's table to the rear turret there was a mass of flame.

"I Gave It Up"

"I struggled to get out of the pilot's escape hatch," the pilot said yesterday, "but I couldn't because half of it had jammed.

"For a moment I gave it up. It didn't seem possible that I could get away. I held my breath for as long as I could and then I began taking in water.

"I was all but drowned when I saw a bright light above me. That must have been the fire. I made for the light.

"I felt the various things go past me—the wireless set, the oxygen bottles, the main spar. I tried for the astro hatch, but I was too weak to open it.

"Then I saw more lights still further up. For a second

Continued on Back Page

NAZIS CLAIM LINER SUNK

Claim that a British passenger liner of between 10,000 and 12,000 tons was sunk off the East Coast on Sunday night by a German bomber was made by Berlin yesterday, says British United Press.

Court at bedside

A COURT sat yesterday at the bedside of Maureen O'Hara, 21, film actress, to hear her claim for annulment of her marriage to George Brown, now a R.A.F. pilot.

Irish-born Maureen is recovering from an appendicitis operation in a Reno hospital, cables the *Daily Mirror* New York correspondent.

She was married to Brown, former director, in Ireland in 1939 and left next day for America. She has not seen him since.

Her action will be on the grounds of "want of understanding."

Maureen made her screen debut playing opposite Charles Laughton in "Jamaica Inn," and it was at his suggestion that she was taken to Hollywood to play with him in "Hunchback of Notre Dame."

RAID TOLL ONE-SIXTH OF YEAR AGO

During August, 169 civilians were killed in air raids or are missing, believed killed, and 136 were detained in hospital.

In August last year, 1,085 were killed and 1,265 seriously injured.

THE German High Command admitted yesterday that the Russians defending Leningrad are making repeated counter-attacks with heavy tanks.

It claimed that the attacks had been broken and that the close encirclement of Leningrad was "irresistibly continuing, in spite of bitter resistance."

German admission of bitter resistance is probably an attempt to excuse in advance their heavy losses. Moscow says 4,000 Germans were killed and 15,000 wounded in three days on the approaches to Leningrad.

A Berlin spokesman said that Von Leeb's army was now attacking Leningrad's inner defence ring in the suburbs, but that bad weather was hampering operations.

In some spots they were within fifteen miles of the centre of the city.

Armour-Plated Defences

Some idea of the strength of the city's defences was given in a German broadcast last night.

A commentator said the outer defences consist of tank traps, barbed wire, and fortifications with steel armour plates—all excellently camouflaged.

This outer ring stretches a hundred miles from the Lake Luga to the city.

Yet these were described as only temporary defence works, built by civilians, including women, "with traditional Russian skill and ingenuity."

The main defences are in the inner ring.

There was a fierce air battle over the approaches to Leningrad yesterday. A hundred planes were in the air and seventeen German bombers were shot down.

The withdrawal of the Russians from Kremenchug, in the Ukraine, implies that the Kiev

Continued on Back Page

DEATH LEAP FROM FIRE

Miss Kathleen Skellan, 32, a Liverpool shorthand-typist, leapt to death yesterday in a desperate attempt to escape from a burning bedroom.

A neighbour who saw her said she was "outlined in flames and appeared to be on fire before she jumped."

NO SPEECHES ORDER TO ARMS MEN

ON condition that neither should address any meeting on a factory site while on bail, Isaac Loan, a clerk, and Edwin Alfred Ted Endersby, a bricklayer, were remanded on bail at a North Midlands town yesterday.

The men were charged with addressing, on September 10, a meeting in a protected place—a Royal Ordnance factory—without having obtained permission of the approved authority, contrary to Regulation 14 of the Emergency Powers Act.

Legal Assistance

Two members of the Workers' Committee told the *Daily Mirror* last night: "We are going to get legal assistance for Loan and Endersby, and the men are going to pay for it out of their small wages. We are also urging the Transport and General Workers' Union to take up their case."

Loan is president of the Workers' Committee, and Endersby secretary. Their arrest stopped a mass meeting of protest, and followed complaints of transport difficulties made by workers, who are employed on a Government factory site.

Their grievance is that to travel by train instead of by bus means leaving home earlier and getting home later.

Harriman: 'Moscow soon as possible'

"We are anxious to get to Moscow as soon as we can," said Mr. Averill Harriman yesterday, following his arrival in London with members of the United States Mission to Moscow.

"We shall have consultations with Lord Beaverbrook, and then I hope we shall get away as soon as possible."

I WAS ASTONISHED

The Improvement in My Health is Really Remarkable

DRAMATIC TRIBUTE TO YEAST-VITE

London, W.C.
August 12th, 1941.

Gentlemen,
Having been troubled with a very acute condition of nervous debility and general run-down condition of the whole system—seeing your advertisements, I was persuaded to try your Yeast-Vite Tablets, and I was astonished. I had come across something that had done me a vast amount of lasting good.

The improvement in my health is really remarkable. If the public only knew the value of your infallible preparation, if it was the last money they could spare, they would never be without it.

With best wishes,
(Sgd) E. M.

About Time I Told You

Cambs.,
August 20th, 1941.

Dear Sirs,
Your Yeast-Vite tablets have not once, but many times, proved their weight in gold in keeping myself and family in really good health. I thought it was about time I told you how much I value them.

(Sgd) Mrs. D.

Yeast-Vite Tonic Tablets bring quick relief from Headaches, Nerves, Lassitude, Depression, Insomnia, Rheumatism, Indigestion, etc. Sold everywhere.

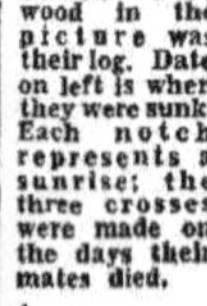

Each notch a day snatched from death

Remember the three men of the U.S. torpedoed ship Sessa, who were saved after nineteen days spent on a raft? The wood in the picture was their log. Date on left is when they were sunk. Each notch represents a sunrise; the three crosses were made on the days their mates died.

Daily Mirror

SEPT. 17

No. 11,784
Registered at the G.P.O. as a Newspaper.

ONE PENNY

The new Shah of Iran, who was Crown Prince to his father. He married a sister of the King of Egypt.

Allies enter Iran capital today

BRITISH and Russian troops, in equal numbers, will enter Teheran, capital of Iran, today.

Last night they were only a few miles from the city, from which the Shah had departed on his abdication earlier in the day.

They are determined to clear up once and for all the situation in Teheran regarding the Germans who were to have been deported, and stop the Axis tricks to delay their departure.

The staff of the German Legation in Teheran, as well as German women and children there, will leave Iran today, the Italian news agency stated last night.

The Allied forces are considerable, and the British are headed by one of the most famous regiments of the Army.

The Shah has gone to exile in Isfahan, 220 miles south of Teheran.

His eldest son, Shahpur Mohammed Riza, 21, has succeeded him.

It was the British Minister in Teheran who advised the Shah to abdicate when the Shah sent secretly for advice.

80 Germans Vanish

Eighty Germans who left Teheran last Saturday for internment have completely disappeared, it was revealed last night.

The Germans left by train for Ahwaz, but on reaching there the train did not stop but went on to Bandar Shahpur, on the Persian Gulf.

But there was no sign of the Germans then, and Iran police and British officials are searching for them.

The cause of the trouble is believed in Teheran to be due to "misdirection of the train due to instructions getting crossed."

The gulf ports are held by the Indian Army. It was at Bandar Shahpur that seven Axis ships were captured.

Another party of Germans attempted to cross the Turkish frontier from Iran in a car, but were captured by a Soviet patrol.

[Tailor's apprentice to ruler page 4.]

SHELLS BREAK 8-DAY QUIET

After a silence of eight days, German long-range guns opened fire across the Straits of Dover last night.

SABOTAGE SWEEPS EUROPE AS HUNS GO EAST

A WAVE of sabotage is sweeping Europe in the wake of Hitler legions recalled to face the Russians in the East.

With yesterday's reports that Germany has withdrawn nearly half a million men from France and the Low Countries alone, and more from the Balkans, came a stream of messages from occupied States telling of shootings, fires, strikes, sabotage and go-slow tactics.

Not all the rigour of the Nazi terror can check it.

Here are last night's reports from countries under Hitler's heel:—

FRANCE

German reprisals in France are met with counter-reprisals. The Germans yesterday shot ten more hostages as a reprisal for the shooting of German soldiers. At the same time loyal Frenchmen shot at two German N.C.O.s in Paris.

It was revealed that the son of Colonel Petreaux, leader of Petain's new official party, was kidnapped a week ago, taken off in a car and that the search for him has been fruitless.

Sabotage has been committed by metal-workers in seventy-four factories; 1,800 trucks of war supplies for Germany have been destroyed in two months, and 194 trains derailed.

CZECHOSLOVAKIA

Several trains have been blown up, including one full of arms from the Skoda works.

More than 250 German troops were killed in one accident.

In Slovakia mass firing of crops at night has destroyed thousands of tons of grain.

YUGOSLAVIA

Serbian guerrillas attacked the Belgrade-Nish railway and tore up the tracks.

Armoured trains now tour the railways hunting the guerrillas and trains are frequently escorted by fighter planes.

The Quisling Government is alarmed for its safety, and threatened yesterday that if any of its members is attacked members of the former Government of King Peter will be executed.

RUMANIA

A chemical factory in Bukarest has been destroyed by fire. Sabotage is admitted to be the cause.

NORWAY

There has been so much sabotage on the railway from Oslo to Sweden that two policemen are now stationed every 200 yards along the line.

The "London Bus" runs regularly taking people from areas where radio sets have been seized to neighbouring towns and villages where they listen to B.B.C. bulletins.

FIRE REGISTRATION DUTY

Men between the ages of 18 and 35 who were unable to register for fire prevention duty last Sunday should do so at the earliest opportunity at the nearest employment exchange and not wait until the next registration day.

BOMB ROME NOW

CAIRO was raided in the early hours of yesterday. Incendiary and explosive bombs were dropped, causing thirty-nine deaths and injuring ninety-three people. Slight damage was done to property.

On April 19 this year the British Government issued a warning from 10, Downing-street, that if Athens or Cairo were raided we would commence systematic bombing of Rome.

"Once this has begun it will continue to the end of the war," added the statement.

"The greatest care will be taken not to bomb the Vatican City and the strictest orders to that effect have been issued."

The "Daily Mirror" expects the Government to be as good as its word.

Sentiment must not deter us from thrusting at the heart of Italian Fascism.

WE MUST BOMB ROME NOW.

Smile all the while

Whatever the day brings we've got to keep smiling. So let's make our smiles worth while. Above all don't take chances with your teeth. Don't risk using tooth-pastes which employ abrasives to secure whiteness. They can't avoid injuring the thin coating of enamel which alone prevents decay. What about the paste you are using now? Grind a little between your front teeth. If there's the least trace of grittiness, change to Odol. All Dentists know that Odol is absolutely safe, yet it makes and keeps your teeth like pearls.

Besides being perfect for natural teeth, Odol Tooth Powder cleans False Teeth and Plates beautifully.

Keep the winning

Girl on the right is Assistant Section Officer George, who has made history as the first woman Assistant Provost Marshal (Assistant Chief of Military Police). The man is R.A.F. Provost Marshal Group-Captain F. G. Stammers. Together they are inspecting a smart sergeant-policewoman of the W.A.A.F.

Women military police have been formed to supervise the well-being and discipline of the W.A.A.F.

Waaf's woman police chief

FLARE-UP IN WESTERN DESERT

Great activity is reported in the Western Desert (says Exchange from Cairo).

Our patrols are in contact with German-Italian armoured units, which in some instances are using British tanks captured some months ago.

The usual communiqués from Cairo General Headquarters and R.A.F. Headquarters in the Middle East had not been received in London up to a late hour last night.

SOVIET WIN BATTLE OF LENINGRAD ISLES

RUSSIAN bayonets have smashed a second German attempt to land troops by sea and air on Oesel. Baltic island off the Estonian coast, and have cleared the enemy out of islands in a river which they hoped to use as a base to attack Leningrad.

The Germans tried for two days to achieve a landing on Oesel.

But Russian bayonets and guns annihilated every landing party as it approached from sea or tried to land from the air, and then, in their own words, "the remnants were thrown in the sea."

Though Germany claimed yesterday that the second ring of Leningrad defences had been broken at a number of points, the Russians told how they had driven the Germans out of strategic positions near Leningrad after bitter hand-to-hand fighting.

Von Leeb's forces had seized a group of small islands in the River "V" with the evident

Continued on Back Page

Families can get extra shelter free

IF you have a big family—too many to get inside together in an Anderson or indoor shelter—you may be supplied with an extra indoor shelter.

This applies to those who have already received "free shelters, and there will be no charge for the extra one.

Many of the Anderson shelters distributed earlier have already been enlarged

Night bombs on the east coast

A raider dropped incendiary bombs at a place on the east coast last night. Enemy aircraft were reported over East Anglia, and single machines were believed over Liverpool and another district in the north-west.

15 KILLED ON MANOEUVRES

Four officers and eleven men of the Eireann Army were killed and sixteen soldiers injured during explosive exercises yesterday in the Wicklow Hills.

A letter to the Premier

MR. T BLACKBURN, the engineering union official who first revealed the statements on Russia made by Colonel Moore-Brabazon at a private meeting in Manchester, has written to the Prime Minister objecting to Mr. Churchill's comments in the Commons.

The letter read as follows:—

"I feel constrained to write you because of your inference that the motives underlying my revelations of the statement made by the Minister of Aircraft Production was mischievous.

"I have no desire to provoke controversy written or verbal. The matter is too grave.

"Neither had I, nor have I, any desire to injure Colonel Moore-Brabazon as an individual.

"Whatever the consequences I felt it my duty to the country, and the workers whom I represent, to reveal and attempt to eradicate the terrible attitude of mind drawn towards our most powerful ally the U.S.S.R.

"My immediate reaction to the speech was that the Minister was not the only man in a high place to have these thoughts, but that there were many others who thought like him.

"I have to remind you that I prosecuted the business in a formal manner.

"At the outset I wrote to Sir Ernest Simon to protest my belief that the words spoken by the Minister implied a flagrant

Continued on Back Page

Daily Mirror

SEPT. 20

No. 11,787
ONE PENNY
Registered at the G.P.O. as a Newspaper.

GERMANS CLAIM THE CAPTURE OF KIEV

"I am on my way to Moscow"

—Beaverbrook

"I AM on my way to Moscow," was the message of Lord Beaverbrook, Minister of Supply, sent last night to the tank builders of Britain.

"I am taking with me your pledge and promise to the soldiers and workers of Russia," the message added.

"I leave you, each one of you, responsible for production results during my absence. And I rely on you to see that the promise I make on your behalf is fulfilled.

"So send me a message on September 30 telling me what you have done, and let me tell the Russians then that in the last days of September you devoted yourselves to their needs, that you built more tanks than ever before in the history of our country."

M. Maisky, Soviet Ambassador, accompanied by members of the Soviet military mission, will visit two big tank factories on Monday and receive the first tanks to be sent to the defenders of Leningrad, Moscow and Odessa.

Monday is the first day of the "Tanks for Russia Week."

THE German High Command claimed last night that Nazi troops had entered Kiev, and that the swastika was flying over its 200-year-old citadel.

The claim was made in a special communique, which added that the troops had broken into the city "after a bold penetration of the defences on the west bank of the Dnieper."

The German claim to have captured Kiev is not admitted in the latest Russian communique, which admits, however, that "particularly serious" fighting is continuing round the city.

It also said that fierce fighting was continuing in the Murmansk area, where heavy losses were inflicted on three S.S. battalions.

Earlier the Soviet admitted that Nazi troops had reached the outskirts of Kiev through a breach in one sector of the outer defence ring.

This was the wording of the German communique:

"In the course of encircling operations announced today, the attack against Kiev, capital of the Ukraine, was begun.

"After a bold penetration through the strong fortifications on the west bank of the Dnieper, our troops have penetrated into the town.

"The Reich flag has been flying from the citadel since this morning."

Just before the communique was broadcast on Berlin radio.

"You're telling us!"

"Today is the day of most important decisions in the fight against Bolshevism," said Deutschlandsender last night.

"Thanks to the military genius of the Fuehrer, we always achieve successes with the smallest possible losses. Of course, we had to suffer losses, and there will be more in future ——"

And the "ghost" interrupted with: "You're telling us!"

a military commentator was saying:

"The encircling action round

Continued on Back Page

He'll still call her 'Mum'

LITTLE George Lambert, a nervous cobbler's apprentice, started his first job at fifteen in a tiny shop in Charlbert-street, St. John's Wood, London.

George never remembered having any parents. He was brought up in an orphanage until he was old enough to go to work.

So it was natural when he called the cobbler's wife, who made him a cup of tea of an afternoon, "Mum."

It was the first time he had known what it was to have a mother, and Mrs. Grace Lowe was all that to him.

Good Apprentice

George turned out to be a good apprentice and—a good son. Mr. and Mrs. Lowe became so fond of him that they adopted him. Since then Mrs. Lowe has never been anything but "Mum" to George.

For forty-two years he worked at the shop. He had rises, not very big ones, but always put his money away on a Saturday. George wasn't one for girls or cinemas. Secretly he was saving to repay "Mum" one day for all her kindnesses.

Then, when Mr. Lowe fell ill, he had to work harder than ever. He had charge of the shop.

Seven months ago the old cobbler died after an illness in which George had helped "Mum" to nurse him.

But now George and "Mum" are smiling happily once more. They are to be married tomorrow.

£1,000 Gift

And George is giving "Mum" his life's savings—£1,000—for a wedding present.

"Mum's the only real sweetheart I've ever had," he said shyly. "I feel a lucky man."

Mrs. Lowe, who is now 71, but looks younger, interrupted.

"I don't know what we'd have done without our George all these years," she said. "If he makes as good a husband as he has son we are going to be happy. Though George is only 57 I don't think the difference in our ages will matter much."

When he went to draw such a large sum from his banking account George was asked what he wanted it for. "Love and Affection" was the reason he gave.

FIXED PRICES FOR RABBITS AND HARES

Maximum retail prices for wild and tame rabbits and hares in force on Monday will be, except in certain large urban areas:—

Wild rabbits: Unskinned, 10d. lb.; skinned, 1s. lb. Tame rabbits: Unskinned, 1s. 2½d. lb.; skinned, 1s. 7d. lb. Brown hares; 4s. each.

A mother's remembrance

The woman in the picture is Mrs Kate Lindmeyer. Each week she places a bunch of flowers at the foot of a little wooden cross at this scene of devastation.

The site is in Tabard-gardens, Southwark, London, called "Blitz-square."

Last winter the Lindmeyer family were in the shelter you see at the bottom of the picture. Mrs. Lindmeyer went back to the house to get a warm coat for her baby. While she was away a bomb fell—killed her two girls, a boy and a tiny grandchild. Her husband, her last son, and herself placed the wooden cross on the site for remembrance—and a weekly pilgrimage.

PRIVATE CARS TO MEET TROOPS AT NIGHT

PRIVATE cars will meet Servicemen and women arriving at railway stations after bus hours in the black-out this winter.

Motorists wishing to volunteer for this service should register with local welfare officers and will get the extra petrol necessary for it.

This is only one of the plans which the Services welfare authorities are making for the comfort of serving men and women.

Another plan is for socks to be darned by volunteers, the wool being supplied by the authorities. This has already been done in many localities.

Officers will have chances of going shooting and will be admitted to social and sporting clubs as honorary members at reduced fees.

The main consideration during the winter months will be entertainment and study.

TEHERAN ENTERED BY BRITISH TROOPS

A British column consisting of several hundred armoured vehicles occupied the inner suburbs of Teheran yesterday. Russian forces which had filtered into the city by mistake on Wednesday withdrew.

STRANGE PLANE OVER EIRE

An unidentified aeroplane flew over the Dublin area yesterday and was fired on by ground defences.

Football sent to Russians

A FOOT-SQUARE plywood box and a letter were handed in at the Soviet Embassy yesterday by an English soldier.

In the box was an ordinary English football—but transfigured and glorified into a symbol of British will to victory and British sportsmanship.

On every inch of the leather, grouped round a painted crest of the Royal Engineers, were the signatures of 215 men.

The letter addressed to M Maisky, Soviet Ambassador, said:—

"Dear Sir,—Will you kindly forward the enclosed football, inscribed with the names of the Warrant Officer Non-Commissioned Officers and men of the —— Field Company, Royal Engineers, to a similar unit of the Red Army Corps of Engineers?

"Will you please let them know on our behalf that we send this small present as an expression of our comradeship in the common war against Hitlerism, and in appreciation of the magnificent fight they are putting up?"

The ball was bought with pennies contributed by the men.

The men have asked for a reply, if possible, from the Red Army unit which receives the ball. M. Maisky is going to write to them.

12 of our ships in U.S.

TWELVE British warships, including the battleship Warspite, are now in U.S. ports for repairs, provisioning or other purposes.

U.S. Navy Department revealed this last night under the new publicity policy.

In addition to these ships, several other British craft are also in U.S. harbours.

The Navy Department said the Warspite is at Bremerton, Washington, and the British aircraft carriers Formidable and Illustrious at Norfolk, Virginia.

The other ships listed by the Department are: Cruisers Delhi and Dido at Brooklyn, New York; cruisers Liverpool and Orion at Mare Island, California; the Asturias, described as a converted cruiser, at Newport News, Virginia; submarine Pandora at Portsmouth, New Hampshire; corvettes Nasturtium and Primrose at Charleston, South Carolina; and a coastal minesweeper at Baltimore.

HOARE COMING HOME

Sir Samuel Hoare, British Ambassador in Madrid, is coming home next week to report.—Reuter.

13 MEN AND A GIRL 6 DAYS IN BOAT

After a six-day voyage in a motor fishing vessel thirteen young men and a girl have landed at an East Scottish harbour from Norway. Their boat flew the Norwegian flag.

Most of the men were sturdily built, wearing grey flannels and woollen jerseys.

The girl was neatly dressed in a grey costume, blue blouse, light stockings and shoes. She had a small handbag.

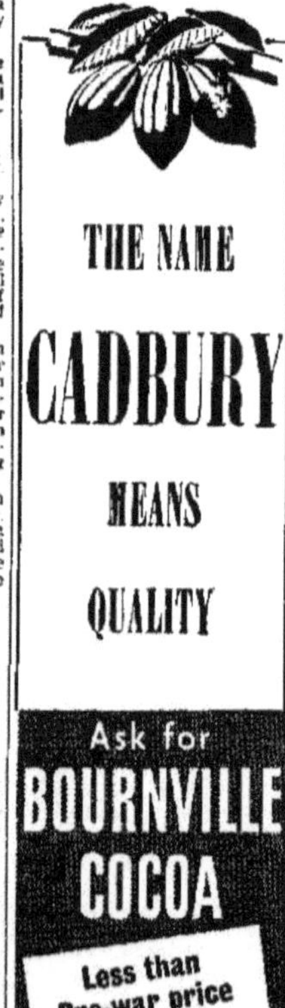

Daily Mirror

(SEPT. 22)

No. 11,788 — ONE PENNY
Registered at the G.P.O. as a Newspaper.

KIEV EVACUATED AFTER FIGHTING IN STREETS

Paddy needs another Hun for his 21st

Flight-Lieutenant Finucane smiling after his bag of three Nazis on Saturday.

FLIGHT - LIEUT. Brendan (Paddy) Finucane, D.F.C. and double Bar, will be 21 within the next few days.

If he shoots down one more Nazi plane in that period he will have destroyed twenty-one planes by the time he is 21.

On Saturday he knocked three Huns out of the sky. And yesterday, during R.A.F. sweeps, he bagged two more.

Twenty-four enemy planes were destroyed by strong formations of fighters escorting bombers in an attack on the power station at Gosnay, near Bethune, and on railways at Lille yesterday afternoon.

Bombs were seen to hit the targets.

Thirteen of our fighters were lost, but no bombers.

Every house a German grave

Moscow radio, dealing with the battle of Kiev, stated last night that the temporary loss of territory was not decisive for them.

Decisive for the outcome of the war was that every house was defended to the utmost, and that every house became the grave of German soldiers.

MOSCOW'S midnight communique stated "Kiev has been evacuated." The people of Kiev, trained as partisan warriors, had defended their city to the last, fighting fiercely side by side with the Red Army even in the streets.

Russian forces are making a mass counter - attack at Poltava, south-west of Kharkov, in the Kiev "battle of the bulge."

This offensive was reported by the German radio, which also said that Marshal Budenny had been recalled "following the loss of Kiev."

After a stubborn and "extremely bloody" battle, the Red Army recaptured thirty-two villages covering a strongly-fortified line on the central front, Moscow stated.

Two Soviet armies, advancing from Yartsevo in the north and Yelnya in the south, appear to have invested the ruined city of Smolensk, an American correspondent stated in broadcast from Moscow.

Big German Claims

Germany made big claims about the progress of her forces. They were:—

NORTHERN FRONT.— Capture of Arensburg, capital of the Estonian island of Oesel, which Soviet bombers raiding Berlin have used as a base.

UKRAINE FRONT.— 150,000 prisoners, 151 tanks and 602 guns taken in big battle of Kiev.

Moscow instead told of a desperate attempt by the enemy to take Odessa, the besieged Russian Black Sea port.

"All enemy attempts to break through have so far failed, and at certain points the enemy has been driven back. The enemy's losses have been particularly heavy in the last few days."

Fascists stone minister after camp rioting

WHEN Mr. Osbert Peake, Under-Secretary for Home Affairs, visited the Internment camp at Peel, Isle of Man, last night to plead with the Fascists there to stop rioting, they stoned him.

One Fascist shouted, "He's a Jew. Don't listen to him."

Mr. Peake did eventually address the internees, and advised them to keep order in their own interests.

The Fascists went to their own quarters without causing any further disturbance.

On Saturday night the guards were forced to stand by with loaded rifles for hours while the rioters pelted them with stones, bottles and rubbish without fear of retaliation.

They were under instructions not to fire unless the men tried to get through the barbed wire. The internees refrained from attempting this, but pelted the guards from 9 p.m. to close on midnight.

The officer in charge of the guard, Captain Curie, was wounded on the hand by a stone. Several members of the guard were also hit.

This was the result of amazing leniency shown by the authorities to the prisoners when they rioted because their demand for the return to the camp of three unrecaptured British internees had been refused.

Caught at Sea

The three men, who are in prison, are Arthur Leonard Mason, 29, of Forest Gate, London; John Barry, 25, of Wealdstone, Middlesex, and Joseph Walker, 30, of Great Nelson-street, Liverpool.

They broke camp last Wednesday and were caught on Saturday in a motor-boat at sea. Seven hundred Fascist internees demanded that the men should be let out of gaol and put back into camp.

As soon as their request was refused, missiles of every sort were thrown at the guard, the guard headquarters and the surrounding area.

The rioting went on for

Continued on Back Page

"Soviet, Japs in clashes"

Persistent border incidents are occurring between Japanese and Russian troops, the Chungking correspondent of the N.B.C. (New York) said yesterday.

Both Russia and Japan are stated to have moved up reinforcements.

No confirmation of this report has so far reached London.

OUR WARSHIPS IN U.S.

The British cruisers Liverpool (9,100 tons) and Orion (7,215 tons) are being repaired at Mare Island Navy Yard, California.

Scene of the attempt by a police party and men of the Home Guard to rescue Lt. Reginald Walter Swain, a Bristol Home Guard company commander who was drowned during manoeuvres yesterday. His wife was among the 5,000 people who saw him go under while swimming across the harbour in full kit.

H.G. drowns as wife watches

A HOME GUARD officer was drowned during manoeuvres yesterday while leading his men, swimming in full kit, across Bristol Harbour to attack a shed on the other side held by the "enemy."

His wife was one of 5,000 spectators who saw him sink. His schoolboy son attempted to rescue him.

The officer was Lieutenant Reginald Walter Swain, 39, of Colston Villa, Horfield-road, St. Michael's, Bristol, commanding No. 1 Platoon, A Company, 9th Gloucester (City of Bristol) Home Guard.

He was a very strong swimmer. He himself had planned the manoeuvre.

A loudspeaker told the public what was happening.

A Daily Mirror reporter saw Lieutenant Swain, tommy-gun slung across his back, lead three other men into the water.

Police Boat Rescue

Half way across Swain sank. Police in boats saved another Home Guard who was in difficulties. The loudspeaker ceased its bright comments.

Suddenly a woman cried, "There's Reg gone." It was Mrs. Swain.

Then the loudspeaker called out: "If Lieutenant Swain is here, will he answer?"

There was no reply.

Shouting "The old man's gone," Paul Swain, 15, a member of his father's platoon, dived

Continued on Back Page

Mrs. Swain.

NAZI WISHFUL THINKING

"Every English prayer should end with the words: 'Oh, God, let us be conquered.'" Deutschlandsender told its listeners yesterday.

"And the English should see to it that it is fulfilled," the announcer added wistfully.—Reuter.

2 GIRLS SHOT— HUNT FOR MAN

HUNDREDS of police in the Midlands were searching last night for a soldier with a wild, glaring look who shot two girls with a rifle in a field in Walsall.

The girls, Miss Kitty Lyons, 18, of Union-street, Walsall, and her friend, Miss Violet Richards, 24, of Tantarra-street, Walsall, were walking across a field near Rushall Church when a soldier appeared and fired point-blank at them.

A bullet went through Miss Lyons's head. She died instantly. Miss Richards was shot in the chest, and is in a serious condition.

The soldier disappeared. He is described as about 23, medium build, inclined to be fair, with blue eyes.

EX-SHAH LOSES PROPERTY

All property of the ex-Shah of Iran has been confiscated by the new Government.

Maisky plea for tanks

M. Maisky, Soviet Ambassador in London, yesterday issued an appeal to the British Government for more and more tanks.

The appeal, which coincides with the opening of "Tanks for Russia" Week today, says:—

"We need tanks, more tanks, and yet more tanks! We produce many tanks ourselves, but our losses in tanks on the 2,000-mile front are great.

"We require your urgent help to reinforce our own efforts.

"Your tanks will not be wasted. They will go out to battle at once.

"The best testimony is the great fight which the Soviet forces and the whole Soviet people have put up during the last three months against the panzer barbarians of Hitlerite Germany.

"The sooner you will send us tanks and the greater their number will be, the earlier will the Nazi hordes be defeated.

"We have with you one common front.

"The slogan of the day is: Tanks, more tanks, and yet more tanks!"

BORIS TO SEE HITLER

King Boris of Bulgaria is believed to be on the way to a conference with Hitler, said National Broadcasting Company's correspondent in Ankara early today.

Daily Mirror

SEPT. 23

No. 11,789   ONE PENNY
Registered at the G.P.O. as a Newspaper.

SUBS SINK 2 LINERS—10,000 AXIS TROOPS DIE

Italian liner Vulcania (24,469 tons) may have been one of the liners sunk by our submarines

ITALY SAYS GIB. IS ATTACKED

THE Italian High Command, in a special communique yesterday, claimed that Italian naval craft had penetrated into Gibraltar harbour and sunk three ships.

The communique read:

"Special craft of the Royal Italian Navy penetrated the roadstead and inner harbour of the fortress of Gibraltar and sank:

"A tanker of 10,000 tons;

"Another tanker of 600 tons; and

"A steamer of 6,000 tons loaded with munitions.

"A steamer of 12,000 tons loaded with war material was hit and seriously damaged.

"This vessel ran aground on the rocks, and can therefore be considered as lost."

At the end of July eight small Italian torpedo-carrying craft unsuccessfully attacked Malta.

All the craft were destroyed, together with nine of the E-boats escorting them.

"Suicide Sailers"

In addition three enemy aircraft were shot down into the sea by British fighters. One R.A.F. machine was lost.

Italian newspapers claimed that a new type of torpedo, piloted by specially trained "suicide sailors," had been used in the attack on Malta.

These torpedoes, it was asserted, can skip over torpedo nets.

Milk: two pints a week

EVERY grown-up is to get two pints of milk a week from October 12, when the rationing scheme begins.

To avoid milkless days, many people may have to cut their rations themselves.

Milkmen said last night that only in the case of large families will they be able to make the traditional daily delivery. For other families costs are likely to rule out more than two deliveries a week.

More for Sick

These will be the rations for children: Up to the age of 6, one pint a day. From 6 to 17, half a pint a day.

The sick and other special cases will get an extra allowance.

An official of a big dairy told the *Daily Mirror*:

"It will be impossible for us to split up the two-pint ration into daily deliveries for many reasons.

"It might be possible to avoid milkless days for large families of adults by supplying a part of the ration for members of the family on alternate days."

"Left in Air"

Mr. William Sharp, a dairyman, of Battle, Sussex, declared: "We milkmen are being left in the air. With rising costs it is almost impossible to pay my way delivering small quantities of milk.

"I run three motor vans, pay good wages, have an expensive sterilising plant, and often have to travel a long way to deliver as little as half a pint. And the average life of a pint milk bottle costing 6d. is only ten deliveries."

Officially, the scheme is known as "equalisation." It will divert large quantities of milk to the industrial north.

CIVIL SERVICE MATERNITY LEAVE

Married women Civil Servants, both permanent and temporary, are to have "maternity leave" by an agreement reached between the Treasury and National Whitley Council.

Women of the permanent staff will receive full pay for a period not exceeding three months. Those of the temporary staff will not be paid, but their absence will not be taken into account when qualifying for increments or other privileges.

King George of Britain greets King George of Greece on his arrival in London yesterday. With the King and Queen were the Duke and Duchess of Kent, Mr. Churchill, the Foreign Secretary, Dominions Secretary, War Minister and General Sir John Dill. The King of Greece had come to this country from Egypt.

Black cat kills five in bus

A BUS passenger handed to the care of the driver a basket containing a black cat and four kittens.

While the bus was on its journey the cat jumped from the basket and fixed her claws in the driver's back. The driver put up both his hands to pull the animal off. The bus swerved; there was a crash. **FIVE PEOPLE WERE KILLED AND THIRTY-THREE INJURED.**

The accident happened in Edinburgh.

The driver of the bus, George Harkess, Mentone-avenue, Edinburgh, was at Edinburgh Sheriff Court yesterday found not guilty on a charge of having driven the bus without due care.

James Miller, a commercial artist, The Anchorage, Port Seton, one of the injured, said that his father, who was killed, had given the care of the cat and kittens to the driver.

Another of the injured, John Johnston, a colliery overseer, of Cardowan-drive, said he saw two black paws come through the edge of the basket and then the head of a cat.

The cat was fierce and wild-looking.

A woman passenger said she saw something black fall on the driver's back.

The driver took his hands right off the wheel before she ducked her head and was rendered unconscious.

A policeman said the kittens were found after the accident, but there was no trace of the cat.

Use oven only once a week

Use your oven only once a week. Never use it for a single dish. Share the cooker with your neighbour. These are points in an appeal by more than 400 electrical companies in Britain and Northern Ireland.

They ask housewives to use as little fuel as possible.

"Economise to the point of inconvenience" is the new slogan. Use your toaster, iron, vacuum cleaner sparingly, and use only one living-room during the winter.

Future accounts will have attached a slip asking for the most rigid economy in the use of gas, electricity, coal, coke, fuel oil and paraffin.

FEW NIGHT BOMBS

Only a few slight casualties were reported as the result of small scale raids on the East and South-East Coasts on Sunday night. Germans say they "bombed the harbour at Margate."

Red army fighting out at Kiev

RUSSIAN forces encircled in the Kiev area are fighting desperately to break through the Nazi lines, the German communique stated yesterday.

"Heavy and bloody casualties were inflicted on the enemy," it added.

The Kiev command is believed to have successfully withdrawn

★ ★ ★ ★ ★

Representatives of the American and British Governments arrived by plane yesterday on Soviet territory, Moscow radio stated last night.

The Prime Minister has asked Sir Charles Wilson, President of the Royal College of Physicians, to join the British Mission to Moscow to advise him on giving medical help to Russia.

★ ★ ★ ★ ★

a large part of its forces safely across the Dnieper.

This was suggested by Moscow reports, and is supported by a Berlin broadcast which said that the Russians had a "mixed force" of thirty-four divisions east of Kiev.

Marshal Budenny, according to a Rome report, is forging a new defence line on the east

Continued on Back Page

ONE KILLED, THREE HURT IN FACTORY EXPLOSION

An operative was killed and three others received minor injuries in an explosion at a Royal Ordnance factory in the north-west yesterday.

Material damage was slight and production will not be affected by the accident, into which an inquiry is to be held, states the Ministry of Supply.

An explosion also occurred yesterday at a Middlesex factory. It caused a serious fire but the large staff escaped without injury.

AT least 10,000 Axis troops were killed, it was stated in London last night, when British submarines sank two 24,000-ton Italian liners in the Central Mediterranean on Thursday.

The enemy also lost much valuable war equipment.

The third liner in the convoy, which was carrying reinforcements to Libya, is believed to have been damaged.

"On Thursday, September 18, submarines of the Mediterranean Fleet on patrol in the Central Mediterranean successfully attacked a fast and heavily-escorted Italian convoy carrying reinforcements to Libya.

"The convoy consisted of three liners. Two have been destroyed. It is probable that the third was damaged.

"One of the liners in this convoy was similar to the Vulcania of 24,469 tons.

"The other two were of approximately same tonnage."

972 Ships Lost

The great havoc inflicted on enemy shipping by the British Navy is revealed in the latest figures issued in London.

Since June 3 last British submarines in the Mediterranean have destroyed liners and supply ships of a total of more than 158,000 tons.

The total enemy shipping losses since war began are:—

German ships, 526—2,320,747 gross tons.

Italian ships, 319—1,533,231 gross tons.

Former neutral ships, 73—153,000 gross tons.

In protective custody, 54 ships—324,000 gross tons.

Total of 972 ships—4,330,978 gross tons.

SHIP BLEW UP — PLANE LOST

A BRITISH warplane was destroyed by the blast when a schooner which it had bombed blew up with terrific force off Tripoli.

Another schooner was bombed and set on fire. The crew abandoned it, an R.A.F. Middle East communique stated yesterday.

A heavily laden merchant ship and a destroyer were also hit.

Benghazi was raided. The central and outer moles were hit.

Two of our planes are missing.

Newlyweds told their first duty

When John Greaves, 20, was charged at Jarrow, yesterday with having failed to obscure a light at his home, his young wife stated they were married the day before and had not had time to put up the black-out in the bedroom.

Greaves was fined 10s., the chairman telling the wife that the first thing they should have done at their new home was make sure about the lights.

VICEROY UNTIL 1943

The Marquis of Linlithgow, Viceroy and Governor-General of India, is to hold office for a further period, until April, 1943, it was announced from Downing-street last night.

Daily Mirror

SEPT. 25

No. 11,791   ONE PENNY
Registered at the G.P.O. as a Newspaper.

Arms lag not works' fault

by Mr. E. C. Gordon England, chairman of the Engineering Industries Association, speaking at a special war production meeting of engineers in London yesterday.

"It is the unpleasant truth," he declared, "that war production in engineering industries, measured by square foot of factory space, or pound weight of product per man hour, has declined.

"Speed up," say women

DISSATISFIED with the speed of production and the waste of woman power, women war workers are to discuss their problems at a conference in London early next month.

This lead for action has come from women shop stewards.

"We are not satisfied that the Government is using the nation's woman-power to anything like its capacity in the national effort," a woman shop steward told the Daily Mirror yesterday.

"We are lined up with the men workers to get the last ounce of production out of British factories," another woman shop steward said.

"Used to long busy hours in shops and domestic service, women are cynically amused at the idleness in some of the factories."

Idle at arms work

MEN are idle for half the time at a filling factory where he is a Government inspector, Councillor G. Farquharson told Erith Urban Council last night.

He told the Daily Mirror:

"The men are supposed to work sixty-six and two-third hours a week, including Sundays, for which they are paid double time. It would be fair to say that only thirty-three hours are actually worked.

"Men are standing about with nothing to do. It is not their fault, but due to lack of material, bad management, and because there is no co-operation between the departments. It is a positive scandal.

"In justice to the girl employees, I must say that they are pulling their weight better than the men. But then they are getting work to do, whereas the men are not."

ASKED WHAT THE MEN DID WITH THEIR SPARE TIME, COUNCILLOR FARQUHAR SAID THEY SLEPT DURING THE AFTERNOON AND FILLED IN THE TIME AS BEST THEY COULD.

CALL for modern business methods in war industry instead of those of the Civil Service was made

"The principal cause is the lack of an adequate plan to use to the full all productive capacity and every available man hour, both managerial and operative.

"Those of us whose business it is to produce the equipment so badly needed by our Fighting Services are frankly disturbed.

Separate Jobs

"It is no secret that the science of production is but little known in the production departments, and it is also true that the Treasury and industry cannot share the same bed.

"Some of the leading production engineers, after a careful study of the problem, have come to the conclusion that the supply Ministries should be primarily concerned with the function of buying and that the responsibility for production should be put on the manufacturers."

This would involve the substitution of modern business methods for Civil Service procedure. By this means we could achieve a standard of war production not yet considered possible

"Lack of Knowledge"

He suggested that the fighting Services showed the same lamentable lack of knowledge of the science of production as the production departments. There was an entirely wrong idea in the fighting Services that constant change in design was a military necessity.

Second D.F.C. bar for pilot

The second bar to his D.F.C. is awarded today to Acting Flight-Lieutenant Brendon Finucane, of the Royal Australian Air Force, who shot down five enemy aircraft over Northern France last week-end, bringing his total to twenty.

Finucane, who is twenty received his D.F.C. in May and the first bar less than three weeks ago.

He is the third airman to win the double bar to the D.F.C. The other two are Flight-Lieutenant A. L. Taylor and Squadron Leader Roland Tuck.

MISSIONS REACH MOSCOW

The British and American delegations to the Moscow conference, which arrived in Russia on Monday, reached Moscow yesterday.—British United Press.

R.A.F. SCORE IN RUSSIA IS 7 TO 1

FIRST official "score" of the R.A.F. fighter squadrons now fighting in Russia is seven to one.

It was revealed yesterday that the seven Nazi planes were destroyed by one R.A.F. squadron in two engagements.

In the first they brought down three Me. 109's with the loss of one plane, the pilot of which was killed, and in the second they bagged four Mes without loss.

A Stockholm dispatch to Vichy last night said "squadrons" of British planes were taking part in the defence of Leningrad, and serious losses had been caused to the Nazis.

The Moscow Red Star said yesterday that the Russians had attacked the positions of the German 136th Infantry Division and after a battle which lasted all day had recaptured point "D" and advanced to a new position.

Nazi counter-attacks had been repulsed and the battlefield strewn with the corpses of Germans.

In the northern part of the central sector, Soviet troops, after a four days' struggle, drove back the Germans from strongly-fortified positions on the eastern bank of the River Western Dvina.

In a tank battle in the Leningrad area twenty German tanks were damaged and sixteen captured intact. In one tank a German general was found dead.

Shows how he shot parents

HERBERT DICK, 6, yesterday showed the Hull coroner how he loaded a rifle, pushed what he called "the knob,' and pulled the trigger.

He was re-enacting what he had done at his home in Danube-road, Hull, when the rifle went off and the bullet killed both his parents.

The father, Herbert Dick, 29, a private in the East Yorks Regiment, was on seven days' leave, and his wife was sitting on his knees in front of the fire, Herbert Dick told the coroner:

"I was in the kitchen with mummy. Daddy came home and put his rifle in a corner of the scullery.

"I went to it and lifted it up.

Daddy gave me five bullets in a clip, and I shared them with Paddy and Kathleen (his stepbrother and step-sister). I put one bullet into the rifle and pushed up the knob."

The boy went on to say he had previously taken the rifle to his father and asked him to open it.

"Daddy opened it," he said, "and gave it back to me, and I put the bullet in and pushed the knob up. I was sitting on the kitchen floor and the barrel of the rifle was pointing upwards.

"I pulled something and there was a bang, and I fell back."

A verdict of Death by misadventure was recorded.

PARIS IN A STATE OF SIEGE— VICHY REPORT

A STATE of siege has been declared in Paris following on new incidents in the city, according to unconfirmed reports which reached Vichy last night.

The Germans in Paris have issued an appeal to the population to surrender all arms to the authorities.

With these reports came others from all over enemy-occupied Europe telling of the ever-increasing wave of sabotage.

Hundreds of imported German workers were killed and 900 were injured in a tremendous explosion at the famous Skoda munitions works at Pilsen, Czechoslovakia.

As German troops immediately surround the works, another great explosion blew up the power station, and ninety German soldiers were injured and taken to hospital.

Several hundred dead are still buried under the debris. Fires from the explosion lasted several days.

The story of the explosion was revealed last night by Moscow radio.

Another explosion, causing several million francs worth of damage, occurred at a Bordeaux alcohol factory producing synthetic petrol.

Wave of Strikes

All the tanks exploded, and part of the factory buildings crashed down.

A big explosion in a warehouse at Nantes, in Occupied France, destroyed tons of food.

There were more reports of sabotage in Belgium—fires in factories and interruptions of telephone and telegraph facilities.

A wave of strikes is sweeping throughout Belgium, particularly in the Borinage area, where 125,000 workers have participated in various strikes.

The miners in Bernage, Belgium, were on strike for eight days.

Fire swept through one-third of the Norwegian island of Kristiansholm, near Bergen, yesterday, causing serious damage.

Twelve thousand Serb guerillas have attacked a town in Serbia, says a Budapest message. The town was not named.

German dive-bombers were rushed to disperse the insurgents, and forces from the army of General Milan Nedich. the Serb Quisling Premier, were sent up and attacked the guerillas. Fighting is still going on.

Fascists treated too kindly

PROTESTS at the mild treatment of Fascist rioters at Peel (I.O.M.) Internment camp will be made in the island's parliament, several members stated last night.

Manxmen are indignant at the British Government's decision to consider the rioting incident closed and to restore the internees' privileges.

"Right to Protection"

The British Government should either control this mob or send them elsewhere, is the general feeling.

Mr. D. J. Peace, senior Member of the House of Keys, told the Daily Mirror last night: "The Home Office may rule the camp, but we have a duty to the people of the island. The people of Peel have a right to be protected."

Peel Town Commissioners have decided to ask the Home Office, through the Manx Government Office, for more protection.

A Daily Mirror reader in Northumberland writes: "I see that because of the amazing leniency of the authorities at an internment camp at Peel,

Continued on Back Page

Gen. Wavell visits London

General Sir Archibald Wavell, Commander - in - Chief, India, has been on a visit to London, where he had consultations with the Imperial General Staff.

He came by air and has now returned.

He had several talks with Mr. Churchill, Sir John Dill, Chief of the Imperial General Staff.

The object of his visit was to discuss problems arising out of the situation in Russia and the Middle East.

U.S. GLIDER PLANES FOR PARACHUTISTS

Moscow radio learns from New York that the United States Government has ordered large glider planes with a maximum load of 5,000lb. for the transport of parachutists.

His big war job— weeding

BRAWNY Stan Burke, Post Office engineer's assistant—a reserved occupation—did a heft job of war work yesterday

He spent a busy day grubbing weeds from a patch of gravel in front of Palmers Green telephone exchange, trundling them round to the back and returning with barrowloads of sand.

To indulge in this landscape gardening, far removed from his normal routine of bells, batteries and cables, Stan has been brought off an important job of laying new lines at Hatfield—by OFFICIAL ORDER.

The reason? Today Palmers Green telephone exchange switches from manual to automatic operation.

To celebrate this commendable—but not unduly remarkable—engineering feat, high executives of the Post Office and telephone services, the local mayor and other worthies will perform an opening ceremony.

Executives in busy factories can wait for the lines and instruments they need. What matter?

Post Office executives mustn't see weeds. Stan has a war job —Priority Plus.

ADVICE ON WHEELS

Lambeth has the first mobile information unit, a loud-speaker van fitted with seats, desk and cupboards, to tour the borough giving information and advice after a raid.

Sausages are nicer served with

95

Daily Mirror

SEPT. 26

No. 11,792   ONE PENNY
Registered at the G.P.O. as a Newspaper.

SHOPGIRLS OF 20-25 MUST DO WAR SERVICE

Bid to end U.S. neutrality

A RESOLUTION to repeal the Neutrality Act was introduced in the U.S. Senate yesterday by Senator McKellar, a supporter of the Administration.

Declaring that the Act was "in direct conflict with our freedom of the seas policy," he told the Senate that the law should be repealed outright.

"We made the mistake of passing a law which has done us no good and has merely cluttered up the situation," Senator McKellar said.

He added that the neutrality law was being observed in the Atlantic and disregarded in the Pacific, apparently referring to the fact that U.S. ships had not been banned from Far East waters because of the Sino-Japanese war.

"By retaining the law we are indirectly consenting to the German claim to control of part of the Atlantic," he said.

Senator Taft (Isolationist Republican) expressed the belief that the repeal of the Act would be "equivalent to a declaration of war."

"Merest Shell"

Representative Wadsworth told the House of Representatives that he hoped the Act would be "wiped off the Statute Books.

"In all our history we have fought for the right to sail the seven seas at will," he said. "In the Neutrality Act we surrendered that right."

Representative Woodruff described the Neutrality Act as "the merest shell of an empty statute."

SWEDISH STEAMER SUNK

Swedish steamer Garm (1,230 tons) has been sunk off Iceland, states the Stefani news agency.

Huns hurled back at Leningrad

THE tide was yesterday apparently turning in favour of the Red Army in the great battle for Leningrad, while in the south four German divisions were preparing to attack in the Crimea.

Failing in their attempts to pierce Soviet positions in the Leningrad sector, the Germans are concentrating on frenzied air attacks, sending over 100 Messerschmitts and Junkers over one area for five hours without stopping, says the "Soviet War News" in London.

The area was described as "N." The German attempts to shake the Russians' morale failed.

Moscow reported an increasing number of counter-attacks in ever greater scope, in various Leningrad sectors.

New German reinforcements were arriving to replace the enormous losses, but the Red Army and the Leningrad guerrillas are forcing the Germans back.

Cluttered with Dead

One Russian counter-attack on the approaches to Leningrad hurled the Germans back six miles. Two villages were recaptured.

Enemy tanks broke through the forward Russian positions in one sector south-east of Leningrad, but Russian tanks counter-attacked, forcing them back to their original positions.

In another sector Russians attacked the German 126th Infantry Division and dug themselves in on new positions.

The battlefield was described as being cluttered with German dead tanks and guns.

A German garrison of 300 men was wiped out when Russian troops recaptured an island, Moscow radio said.

Hand-to-hand fighting, in which bayonets, grenades and other arms were playing a bloody rôle, was taking place at several spots on the outskirts of Leningrad, Berlin stated.

Principal effect of the Finns' success in crossing the River Svir east of Lake Ladoga has been to deprive the Russians of

Continued on Back Page

MAN WHO TRAILED BISMARCK GETS AWARD

The captain of the Catalina flying-boat who spotted and shadowed the Bismarck is among sixteen R.A.F. men in an awards list published today.

But the list does not reveal which of the sixteen he is. He is simply referred to as "one of the recipients, who has made many long patrols and has a total of 700 hours' operational flying to his credit."

Three of the hundreds of heroes and heroines who met at yesterday's reception to George Cross and George Medal holders. They are Lieutenant Newgass, Lieutenant J. Miller and Lieutenant H. Taylor, all George Cross winners.

Nazis' plane admission

GERMANY has not enough planes at the moment to make big attacks upon Britain, admitted a German radio speaker last night.

"But that is not the only reason," he went on. "We are carrying out our policy of dealing with our enemies one by one. Britain knows that she will get her share of bombs.

"We are well aware that with the longer nights we shall get heavier raids by the R.A.F., but we hope for the best and are prepared for the worst."

KIDNAPPER NOT TO DIE

The death sentence passed by a military court in Dublin on John McCaughey, alias John Dunlop, for kidnapping Stephen Hayes has been commuted by the Eire Government to penal servitude for life.

GREATEST GATHERING OF HEROES

THE biggest-ever gathering of heroes and heroines danced to the music of a Guards band in Grosvenor House ballroom, London, yesterday.

On their coats they wore the ribbons of the George Cross or the George Medal in their buttonholes each the red rose of England.

Above them stretched Union Jacks and Empire flags, the hammer and sickle — red flag of Russia—and a great banner with a crimson cross, the banner of St. George.

They were heroes and heroines of the blitz. And they had come from all parts of the country—400 of them—to be the guests of the Royal Society of St. George and to accept honorary membership of the society.

There were nurses and sailors, soldiers and airmen, A.R.P. workers and V.A.D.s, fire fighters, police . . . and just plain civilians who, while death was raining down performed deeds of valour.

From Aldeburgh, in Suffolk, came Mrs. Dorothy Clark, the first George Medallist, and her friend, Mrs. Jane Hepburn, G.M. They walked across a minefield to rescue an injured soldier.

Sister Patricia Marmion, G.M., another guest, was injured while rescuing patients in a London hospital. When a bomb hit another hospital, she scrambled out of her sick bed to save fellow-injured.

But she doesn't like to talk about it. "It was my job," she said.

Corporal Vivian Holloway, R.A.F., was there with his pal, Corporal Paddy Campion. They got their George Crosses for pulling airmen out of burning fully-loaded bombers.

SOVIET PETROL RECORD

Production of petrol in the Grozny region of Russia has risen 180 per cent. in the past three months, reported Moscow radio last night

U.S. to double plane petrol output

Mr. Ickes, U.S. Defence Petroleum Co-ordinator, stated yesterday that plans are being studied to treble U.S. refining capacity for aviation petrol at a cost of £37,500,000.

ALL shop girls aged 20-25 are to be withdrawn from retail distribution, other than food, to do war work.

Employers and trade unions have approved of this order announced last night by the Ministry of Labour.

It is hoped that the girls will volunteer at once for the A.T.S. or for training to fit them for munitions.

Girls cannot be compelled to join any of the Services.

But they can be compelled to do war work.

Girls who refuse to do war work will not get unemployment benefit.

They may go before an Appeals Board. If the Board decides that a girl is unreasonable and she persists in her refusal, she will be prosecuted. The penalties are a fine or imprisonment, or both.

Girls will be ordered to do war jobs if they fail to volunteer for one of the Services, of which they will be given a choice.

"We have full powers to compel selected women to do war work and we shall use them," said a Ministry of Labour official last night.

Key Women

The procedure of the call-up is this. Starting at once, the Ministry will write a letter to each employer—giving him seven days to state his reasons why any of his women staff in this age group should be retained as "key women" while a substitute is trained.

If there is no good reason why a temporary exception should be made, then, a week

Continued on Back Page

NO FRILLS ON "NATIONAL" CHEAP UNDIES

WOMEN'S controlled-price undies and night-clothes are to have no frills and little, if any, lace.

Every garment will have a national monogram—a Government stamp, "CC41."

Garments controlled will be those scheduled under the "utility" quota — underwear within the reach of everyone's pocket.

Luxury underwear with expensive trimmings will still be obtainable, but not controlled and will not be stamped

What They Will Cost

"Prices are being controlled through a fixed margin of profit for the retailer wholesaler and maker-up," a Board of Trade official told the *Daily Mirror* yesterday.

Slips, knickers, panties, vests, cami-knickers, nightdresses and pyjamas are listed as "utility" garments.

Fabrics with which they can be made are rayon locknit—plain, dyed or printed with semi-bright or bright finish; woven rayon; crepe de Chine; crepe satin; spun rayon and winceyette.

Vests will cost 4s. 6d. to 7s. 5d., nightdresses 8s 8d to 18s. 10d., pyjamas 11s 4d to 15s 9d

New Suits for Old

Many women may soon be walking around in men's old suits—and looking smart—if an idea of some East End tailors spreads.

These tailors are giving a discount on men's new suits for the surrender of old ones which they remodel into women's two-piece costumes. These are sold, legally, coupon-free as second-hand clothes.

F.D.R.'s FRIEND SEES PORTUGAL'S PREMIER

Mr. Myron Taylor, Roosevelt's personal envoy to the Pope, has called on Dr. Salazar, Portugal's Premier, in Lisbon.

He declined to make a statement, but Mr. Frederick Hibbard, U.S. Embassy Counsellor, said, "It was a courtesy call and a most cordial one."—Associated Press.

D.336 21744

Daily Mirror

OCT. 9

No. 11,803

Registered at the G.P.O. as a Newspaper.

ONE PENNY

The choice of Mr. Imms

Doctors said that an invalid boy ought to have a serious operation. His father, who dearly loved him, was afraid the operation might kill him.

Should he defy the doctors? Or should he ignore his own judgment founded on experience in the last war?

That was the choice of Mr. Frederick William Imms, of Pontyclun, father of six children.

Mr. Imms defied the doctors. And at Glamorgan Sessions yesterday the jury endorsed his action.

They found him not guilty of neglecting his son, Terence, 6, in a manner likely to cause injury to his health, and failing to provide adequate medical aid.

In July, 1939, Terence went into Glanely Hospital, Cardiff, with a tubercular knee. Doctors and nurses lavished care on him and in fourteen months he was well enough to be discharged.

Last April he was rushed back to hospital much worse. An operation was decided on, but the father withheld permission.

"The Only Hope"

Dr. Alexander Brownlie, the medical superintendent, said it was impossible to save Terence's leg. An operation was the only hope of saving his life.

"I think he will die if it is not done," he said.

The father did not give evidence, but Mr. Carey Evans, his counsel, said his defence was that he had seen many amputations in the last war which proved fatal.

Afterwards the father told the "Daily Mirror": "If I thought my boy would get over the shock I would allow his leg to be amputated. He is only six. I fear it would kill him."

SOVIET CALL FOR BRITISH MOVE IN WEST

FROM Moscow, threatened last night by fresh German advances, came a new call to Britain to strike in the West at once. At the same time:—

1.—The Russians admitted the evacuation of Orel, seventy-five miles south-east of Briansk, after fierce battles.

2.—The Germans claimed they had encircled seven Soviet divisions in a two-way advance in the southern sector.

"Red Fleet," official newspaper of the Russian Navy, declared that Britain should open up a front in the West while the Germans were putting forward their strength in the East.

The Germans, it said, were using 200 divisions on the Russian Front, including all reserves, and had left fewer than twenty-five to thirty divisions in France, while the bulk of the Fleet, including more than 125 submarines, was concentrated in the Baltic and the Barents Sea.

Virtually the whole of the German Air Force and the Army was concentrated on the Russian Front.

THE MOMENT HAD ARRIVED, IT SAID, WHEN THE BRITISH NAVY, AIR FORCE AND ARMY WERE ABLE TO TAKE DECISIVE ACTION IN THE WEST, TO BOTTLE UP GERMANY AND CLOSE THE APPROACHES TO THE NORTH SEA.

"Take the Initiative"

A similar appeal was made in the monthly organ of the Communist Party, "The Bolshevik."

"The British Empire now has a chance to take the initiative in dealing crushing blows to the foe of all mankind, Hitler," it stated.

The Red Army newspaper, Red Star, reported yesterday that the German tactics in the new offensive are to drive a Panzer wedge in the Russian lines and then carry out flank attacks.

Three hundred German tanks which penetrated to the Russian rear were all destroyed.

"Particularly fierce fighting took place in the directions of Vyasma, Briansk and Melitopol," last night's Soviet communique said.

"Our troops evacuated Orel after fierce battles."

A special announcement by

Continued on Back Page

MINERS STAYED AWAY

In the first case of its kind in Scotland, two miners who failed to comply with directions to return to the pits were each fined £5 or thirty days' imprisonment at Edinburgh yesterday.

RESERVATION —INDIVIDUAL TEST SOON

THE end of reservation from military service on the basis of age, trade or profession, and its substitution by individual exemptions was forecast yesterday by the Minister of Labour, when he replied to the man-power debate in the House of Commons.

"Block reservation will have to go," he said, "and individual reservation will have to take its place."

That means working out another very great machine and these great administrative machines are not easily created.

He would have liked to have had the country trained and manned for a double purpose Army such as Germany had.

"I would have liked to have seen an Army where the whole nation was trained for war both for fighting and for production.

"Germany has done it, and one effect of that is seen in the great communications along which she is fighting in Russia."

He answered those critical of our production effort with these pungent words:

"If anybody asks me who is responsible for the mess I say all of us because we refused to face the facts.

"We hoped against hope that the war would not arise and it did. It is best to acknowledge that and then do our damnedest to get out of it."

During the debate Mr. Davidson (Soc. Maryhill) said that men supposed to be on vital war work played cards and crown and anchor because they had nothing better to do.

Men after building a aerodrome were employed by Messrs.

Continued on Back Page

Baby kept her from the Palace

DETERMINATION to see the King decorate her husband with the D.S.M. caused a Glasgow woman to start a train journey of more than 500 miles although she was on the point of giving birth to her first child.

Between Carlisle and Crewe the woman, Mrs. Agnes Wood, of Crossloan-street, Glasgow, was taken ill, and when the train stopped at Crewe she was removed to a maternity home. She gave birth to a fine boy a few hours later.

Recipient of the D.S.M. was Leading Stoker Owen Wood, of the submarine service.

He told the Daily Mirror: "I waited on the platform at Euston for my wife's train.

"Presently a major came up to me and asked if I was Leading Stoker Wood, and told me what had happened."

Mrs. Wood, when seen by a Daily Mirror reporter yesterday, said: "I had looked forward to seeing my husband decorated, but it is a wonderful consolation to have this fine baby boy."

Call-up for A.R.P.

Compulsion for all forms of Civil Defence is under consideration by the Government.

This was revealed in the Commons yesterday by the Lord Privy Seal when he replied to Sir Thomas Moore (Con., Ayr Burghs), who had asked for the introduction of compulsory service.

AUSTRALIAN AIR CHIEF HERE

Air Marshal R. Williams has arrived in England to take up his duties as Air Officer Commanding Royal Australian Air Force Overseas H.Q.

TANK CHIEF IS CRASH VICTIM

MAJOR-GENERAL V. V. POPE, Brigadier H. E. Russell, and Colonel E. S. Unwin, have been killed in a flying accident in the Middle East, it was reported in London last night.

Major-General Pope, who was fifty years of age, was one of the best-known British tank officers, and was First Military Member of the Tank Board.

He served in France, Belgium and Russia from September, 1914, to the end of the Great War.

He won the D.S.O. and the M.C., was mentioned seven times in dispatches, and rose to command a battalion of the North Staffs Regiment.

"IT CAN'T BE DONE"

The Chancellor of the Exchequer told Mr. Mainwaring (Soc., Rhondda, E.) in the Commons yesterday that he could not contemplate the proposal that the State should make up to all members of the Forces the difference between their Service pay and their remuneration prior to enlistment.

Family secrets for income tax men

PERSONAL secrets of their family budgets are being laid bare before Income Tax Inspectors by hundreds of black-coated workers, staggered by the amount of their recently-received assessments.

Pride and reticence have vanished before the alarming liabilities with which they are now faced, many for the first time.

Only non-industrial workers are receiving their assessments now. Having striven to keep up their position in face of increased war-time expenses, their assessments have sent them flocking to their local tax inspectors.

They bring their family budgets with them, noted in detail. Rent, rates, light, heat, insurances—these are ordinary domestic details. But the budgets reveal secrets that have been closely guarded till now.

Mr. Smith's prosperous appearance is belied by his meagre allowance for weekly food and his one cheap suit a year. It is a blow to Mr. Jones to reveal that his piano won't be his for some months yet, and that other hire purchase payments figure largely in his budget.

"Pretty Grim"

Mrs. Brown makes a gallant show on the very small allowance her husband can make her. Outstanding bills are revealed only in the financial urgency of the situation.

"They present their details and helplessly ask, 'How can we pay?'" Mr. A. L. Houghton, General Secretary of the Inland Revenue Staffs Federation, told the "Daily Mirror."

"It is certainly a problem to tell them. They ask if all manner of expenses can be put in for rebate—even down to a dog licence. Of course they can't, and the only advice can be that living expenses must be adjusted to the new situation. It is pretty grim, but Nazi domination would be worse."

U.S. SHIPS— F.D.R. MOVE

President Roosevelt will send a special message to Congress today asking for revision of the Neutrality Act.

Immediately the message has been received Bills will be introduced into the Senate and the House of Representatives.

These will ask for repeal of sections of the Act which prohibit the arming of merchant ships and voyages to Britain.—British United Press.

DEAL, U.S., TO DEAL, ENG.

The Mayor of Deal, Kent, is to receive £1,000 from the Mayor of Deal, New Jersey, to be used for relieving distress caused by bombing.

The money was raised by a carnival held in Deal, Monmouth County New Jersey.

NOT SO BLACK-OUT

A STATEMENT on the proposed relaxation of black-out restrictions in towns and cities is to be made in the House of Commons by the Minister of Home Security.

Better lighting is to be provided almost immediately.

The "master switch" device used by Moscow, whereby all outside lights are switched off at once on the approach of enemy aircraft, is unlikely to be adopted here.

In London alone there is still much gas street lighting which cannot be turned on and off at will. The cost of extra cables and equipment involved in such a scheme has also carried weight against the idea.

Instead, a modified form of black-out lighting, better than last winter's, but not by any means approaching peacetime standards, is likely to be introduced here.

The Government refuses to change road restrictions during the black-out.

This was stated in the House of Commons yesterday by the Parliamentary Secretary to the Ministry of War Transport.

Japs tell Axis —make peace

Domei, the Japanese semi-official news agency, in a special article yesterday urged the Axis to end the war against Russia, to conserve German manpower and equipment for an all-out assault against Britain.

Domei warned that if the war with Russia were prolonged, the Axis might be faced with a sudden dearth of materials, while Britain and the United States would become stronger.

Daily Mirror

OCT. 15

o. 11,808 — ONE PENNY
Registered at the G.P.O. as a Newspaper.

LIGHTERS FOR ALL—6/6

Everybody's cigarette-lighter is on the way. Born of the match famine and meetings between the Board of Trade and the manufacturers of British lighters—it will be mass-produced.

The President of the Board of Trade said yesterday that steps were being taken to facilitate the manufacture of a "simple" lighter.

Two models are under consideration. The first is a metal "tube," but owing to the fact that only 1oz. of metal is allowed to be used for each lighter the petrol capacity is very small indeed.

The second—and the one most likely to be adopted—is the "Nulite," made of plastic material. Its petrol capacity should last a week.

The new lighter, say the Board of Trade, must not cost the public more than 6s. or 6s. 6d.

V.C. stalked and killed 33 Nazi snipers

V.C.s have been awarded to two New Zealand heroes of Crete—Second-Lieutenant Charles Hazlitt Upham and Sergeant Alfred Clive Hulme.

Day after day Hulme went out alone, or with one or two other men, stalking snipers, and himself killed thirty-three of them.

In Galatos village his unit's counter-attack was held up by a strong force of the enemy concealed in a school.

He went forward alone, threw grenades into the school, and so disorganised the defence that the counter-attack was able to proceed successfully.

He also, on his own initiative, penetrated the enemy lines to put a mortar out of action, killing the crew of four.

Wounded severely, he was ordered to the rear, where, under fire, he organised stragglers into units.

Shammed Dead

The official account of Upham's gallantry, which covers eight days, says:—

"When his platoon was ordered to retire he sent it back under the platoon sergeant, and he went back to warn other troops that they were being cut off.

"When he came out himself he was fired on by two Germans.

"He fell, and shammed dead, then crawled into a position, and, having the use of only one arm, rested his rifle in the fork of a tree. As the Germans came forward he killed them both. The second to fall actually hit the muzzle of the rifle as he fell."

Alone, with revolver and grenades, he silenced three machine-guns.

Shot Twenty-Two

On another day, with a Bren gun and two riflemen, he climbed a steep hill overlooking a ravine through which Nazis were advancing.

"By clever tactics," says the report, "he induced the enemy party to expose itself, and then, at a range of 500 yards, shot twenty-two and caused the remainder to disperse in panic."

During these operations he was suffering from wounds in the shoulder and foot, and from dysentery.

4ft. water drowns six in car

SIX people in a car were drowned in four feet of water yesterday when the driver missed a turning in the black-out and ran into a drainage dyke.

The dyke, four feet deep, barely has water in it, except in mid-winter. The victims were:—

Clinton Rose, 28, baker, of Kirkstead (Lincolnshire), who was driving.

George Semper, 28, single, of Woodhall Spa (Lincolnshire).

Mrs. Jack Winter, junior, of Kirkstead.

Miss Winnie Hawkins, 16, Kirkhall, Woodhall Spa.

Mrs. Joan Edith McKenzie, Roughton (Lincolnshire), and her husband, Private J. McKenzie.

Mrs. McKenzie, who was formerly Miss Joan Baxter, had been married only a few weeks.

Rose leaves a widow and two-weeks-old baby. Mrs. Winter's husband is abroad in the Army.

Mile from Home

The six victims had been to a dance at Linton, where Rose, who managed a bakery and haulage business for his widowed mother, had been doing the catering. His passengers had been helping him at the dance.

They had covered sixteen miles of their journey home and had only a mile to go when the car missed a right-angle bend near Kirkstead toll-bridge.

EIRE READY TO SEND 400,000 CATTLE HERE

Following the removal of the nine-month ban on the import of cattle from Ireland, it was stated that Eire should be able to export about 200,000 fat and at least 200,000 store cattle in the coming months, as soon as shipment can be arranged.

R.A.F. MERCY BOATS TO COVER WORLD

The swift, armed motor-boats that skim across the Channel to pick up air crews shot into the sea will soon be speeding on their mercy errands in every part of the world where the R.A.F. operates over coastal areas.

Private owners and others are being asked to place their motor-boats at the disposal of the Air Ministry's new Directorate of Aircraft Safety, which will be in charge of the expanded service.

The success of the boats in saving baled-out flyers, British and German, led to the decision to widen their range.

Our threat to crash Hun radio

THE B.B.C. yesterday threatened Germany that they would broadcast on the Nazis' own wavelength when the R.A.F. have driven the German stations off the air.

They said they would do this as a retaliation for the "ghost" that has been interrupting the B.B.C. programmes.

Meanwhile the B.B.C. have put secret plans in hand to deal with the German.

There was an intruding voice on the B.B.C. Forces programme again last night, but it was much weaker.

During the 9 o'clock news the announcer broke off and said: "Listeners in some parts of the country may be hearing another voice. This is, of course, the voice of the enemy trying to make itself heard."

WOMEN OF 40 TO REGISTER

Women up to the age of 40—perhaps even older—and men up to the age of 50 will, it is believed, have to register for industrial service early in the New Year.

Men of 45 registered last Saturday; women aged 31 are due to be called up on December 6.

There has been no official announcement yet, but it is understood that the Government plans to continue registrations till men of 50 and women of 40 are called to industrial service.

Call-up of women is to be speeded. Those not in jobs will be the first to be called up, and next will be those not engaged on important work.

3 London murders in week

DISCOVERY last night of an elderly widow dead in a house in Holland Park, W., gave London its third murder mystery in less than a week.

Police were already investigating the deaths of John Childs, park-keeper, of Hendon, found shot on Friday in Mote Mount Park, Mill Hill, and Mabel Church, 19, found naked and strangled in a bombed house in Hampstead-road, N.W., on Monday.

The widow was Mrs. Greenhill, 63.

May Have Known Her

There was no sign of the house having been broken into, and the police are working on the theory that Mrs. Greenhill met her death at the hands of someone she knew—someone to whom she had opened the door without suspicion.

"Mrs. Greenhill was a reserved woman," a neighbour told the Daily Mirror last night. "While one could not call her a recluse, she kept to herself and seldom went out."

She lived with one of her own daughters in a ground-floor flat.

In the case of Mabel Church, police yesterday used for the first time in criminal history a new method of taking fingerprint impressions from a dead body.

The girl's body bore clear impressions of finger-prints, but tests pointed to the fact that they were made by the girl herself.

THESE ONIONS MAKE 'EM WEEP

On a train to London yesterday went 2,000lb. of onions grown by a Barnham, Sussex, nurseryman.

Only six miles away was a Bognor Regis greengrocer who had offered to buy all those 2,000lb. of Barnham - grown onions.

When the grower told the National Vegetable Marketing Company that he proposed to sell the onions locally and thus save transport he was told he must send the crop to London.

GERMANS MAKE FRESH GAINS IN BATTLE OF MOSCOW

A NEW threat to Moscow is revealed in the Russian midnight communique, which says fierce fighting is going on 90 miles north-west of Moscow on the railroad to Leningrad.

Scene of this battle is Kalinin. At the same time the communique announces the evacuation of Mariupol, north of the Black Sea, on the extreme southern arm of the German offensive.

It declares that Russian troops on the Central Front are still stubbornly resisting the advancing enemy, who tried to drive a wedge into the Russian lines, ignoring his tremendous losses.

On one part of the front alone, said the communique, the Germans lost 12,000 in dead and wounded.

It was revealed earlier yesterday that German advance units had got to within sixty-five miles of Moscow in their push from the Vyasma region, but had been repulsed.

3,000,000 Prisoners Claim

After a fortnight of the fiercest fighting, the big battle for Moscow is now near crisis point, with the Germans still pouring tremendous forces into the city's approaches.

Berlin radio claimed last night that the number of Russian prisoners taken since the beginning of the campaign was 3,000,000.

Hitler's forces, despite big losses and severe strain, are still in good fighting trim, and his generals, by skilful manoeuvre, are still hurling superior numbers into every push and thrust.

But their plan of encircling and annihilating huge Russian forces has failed, and the Russians, reinforced by well-trained and well-equipped regulars, are stiffening their resistance. One report speaks of "endless columns of reinforcements"

General Yeremenko's forces, after abandoning Briansk, have taken up new positions and are beating back new German attacks in this sector.

Despite the German claims,

Continued on Back Page

F.D.R. snubs the Windsors

From JOHN WALTERS

New York, Tuesday.

Washington was surprised to learn tonight that the Duke and Duchess of Windsor will not lunch with President Roosevelt at the White House on Friday, as had been expected.

It was learned that the President planned to leave Washington on Thursday for his home at Hyde Park, thus absenting himself from the capital during the Windsors' visit there on Friday.

It is recalled that when the Duke and Duchess were in Washington at the start of their holiday, a White House luncheon for them was suddenly cancelled owing to the death of the President's brother-in-law.

INTERNEE DEATH MYSTERY

When an inquest on Charles Barnick, an internee at Peel Detention Camp, Isle of Man, was adjourned for a month for an analysis to be made of certain organs, the coroner, Mr. R. O. Johnson, said he was not satisfied that the man died of apoplexy, as indicated.

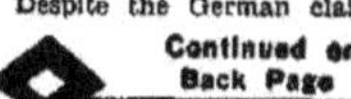

FRY'S

for

Good

Chocolate

+

D.345.35941

Daily Mirror

OCT. 16

No. 11,809 — ONE PENNY
Registered at the G.P.O. as a Newspaper.

GERMANS REACH MOSCOW'S OUTER DEFENCES

Canadians at Archangel?

Reports reaching New York from Ottawa admitting that the Canadian War Office spokesman declined to answer questions as to whether Canadian troops were involved in the reported arrival of British Forces in Archangel recall that Canadians were at Archangel in the last war.

It has been frequently pointed out in recent weeks by military correspondents that Dominion Forces would be best fitted for duty in these wintry regions.

SECRET MUST COME OUT—M.P.

"THIS scandal cannot be kept quiet much longer. It must come out. It ought to have come out some time ago."

Mr. Higgs, Conservative M.P. for West Birmingham, made this declaration in the House of Commons yesterday, when defending the resignation of the Air Services Sub-committee because the Select Committee on National Expenditure refused to present to the House a report setting out instances of waste.

The report was sent to the Premier for his decision as to publication.

Mr. Austin Hopkinson (Nat., Mosley) said the House having set up the committee had proceeded to sterilise it to a large extent.

One by one the House had thrown up the privileges it had fought for through the centuries, and he thought it might consider whether it would be a good thing to revoke that committee.

"Worthless Scheme"

Another case was bound to come up soon in which public money had been spent and thousands of men occupied on a perfectly worthless scheme.

"Are we to have that committee reporting that the steps are unjustified and that steps should be taken to remove the person responsible?" he asked.

"Are we to have the report presented to the Prime Minister for him to say it is not in the public interest for Parliament to know about it?

"What is the House of

Continued on
Back Page

OIL FOR TURKEY

Six thousand, eight hundred barrels of British oil and petrol have arrived in Turkey from Haifa to ease the difficulty caused by the suspension of Rumanian oil deliveries.

Fixed price for women's new clothes

MAXIMUM prices for women's and girls' coats, skirts, costumes and slacks have been fixed under the Board of Trade scheme for the production of general utility clothing.

These prices refer only to garments made from Government stamped cloth. It will be some time before they will be on sale.

Including purchase tax, the maximum retail prices range from 17s. 3d. to 26s. 3d. for skirts, 21s. to 31s. 1d. for slacks, from 63s. to 95s. 2d. for coats and from 65s. 2d. to 86s. 2d. for costumes.

More kettles and saucepans will be available in a few days' time.

LORD GORT'S B.E.F. STORY TOMORROW

Lord Gort's dispatches dealing with the B.E.F. in France and Flanders last year will be published tomorrow.

A complete summary of the thrilling story, with Gort's sensational disclosures and his own views on the lessons of the campaign, will appear in the Daily Mirror.

A short sixpenny book by Ian Hay (Major-General Ian Hay Beith), with maps, describing the campaign, will be on sale at the same time.

GIRLS MAY BE CONSCRIPTS

"DEAR Madam,—Unless . . . the A.T.S. target-for-Christmastime of 100,000 new recruits is reached, drastic action will be taken by the Ministry of Labour."

Women may' be conscripted for the Forces—just as men are today—which will mean the passing of a new law.

At the moment, a woman can do one of two things.

Volunteer, Or—

When she is interviewed after registration she can either volunteer for the women's auxiliary services or she can be compelled to take up work of national importance — as a munition worker, a bus "clippie," a postwoman.

Failing conscription — and the Ministry are reluctant to press for its introduction—it is possible that more and more men may be taken from industry for the Army and the women compelled to fill their places

GERMAN forces have reached the far-off approaches to Moscow.

The Red Army newspaper, "Red Star," admitted this yesterday, while Berlin officials made an astounding claim. They said:

German motorised columns were driving four abreast along the roads to Moscow in the wake of advanced panzer units.

The panzer spearheads were experiencing the only real fighting.

To ease pressure on Moscow, Russian troops counter-attacked strongly with tanks at Leningrad, advanced two miles and killed 10,000 Germans.

The Hungarians officially claimed last night to have reached the River Don, in North Caucasia.

Red Star called for Moscow's immediate defences to be strengthened at once.

Despite huge losses, the Germans have a considerable advantage in the Vyasma sector, in parts of which the balance of forces is unfavourable to the Russians.

The Germans are hurling in fresh forces against Kalinin, 100 miles north-west of Moscow.

Main Line Held

The Russians are still holding their main line of defence and are driving the Germans back.

Small units of Germans broke through to Kalinin's approaches.

The Germans are using parachute troops against Kalinin. All have so far been wiped out.

The Germans have failed to

Continued on
Back Page

Husband "dead" returns

SHE had just finished entertaining the troops last night when she was told that she was wanted outside.

Awaiting her was her husband, an airman, whom she believed to be dead.

Seven days after his wedding, Eddie Rowberry, of Buck-lane, Kingsbury, Middlesex, was ordered abroad.

His wife, Gwen, did her bit by appearing at concerts for the troops.

Eddie was shot down over Bardia and held captive by the Italians.

"I was in their hands," he said, "eating their food and in general being rather an encumbrance.

"I was more than surprised when a number of us were set free to return to the British lines.

"So here I am, having landed yesterday. We intend to make up for lost time now that we are reunited and mean to enjoy every minute of my special leave."

FINLAND OUTLAW NATION, SAYS U.S.

The United States regard Finland as an outlaw nation, and will furnish her with no more credits or food supplies, it was learned in Washington last night.

The Finnish Government has angered Roosevelt by refusing to withdraw from the invasion of Russia, cables John Walters from New York, but there is no question of a diplomatic break.

Actress Gertrude Lawrence has refused a medal offered by the Finnish Government for helping to raise money for their people in 1939-1940.

FOR LONDON ONLY

It is not intended to extend the one-class railway travel system to outside the London area, the Ministry of War Transport Parliamentary Secretary said yesterday.

BULB GROWERS WARNED

Growers who plant the maximum number of bulbs must be careful to plant only those varieties wanted for export, as the yield from unsuitable varieties may be left on their hands.

A bomber's end

Crashing and burning (in the top picture) is an Italian torpedo bomber. And there are ten more of them scattered over the sea. The bombers attempted to sink a large British convoy in the Mediterranean. Planes from the Ark Royal went up. They destroyed eleven of the Italian bombers, and convoy got safely through. In the lower picture is a close-up of the last of the torpedo bomber of the first picture—just blazing oil on the surface of the water; with the Ark Royal in the background.

Died in fire to save child

Returning to her burning house at Parleigh-road, Stoke Newington, N., to try to rescue her niece, 7, yesterday, Mrs. Mary Green, 49, was burned to death.

Her body was found under the child's bed.

The child, Leila Lightstone, was rescued suffering from shock and slight burns. Mrs. Sara Cohen, 60, was taken to hospital suffering from shock and slight injuries.

"Mrs. Green had got out into the street and went back for Leila," said a neighbour. Her sister, Mrs. Lightstone, had brought out her other child."

Daily Mirror

OCT. 17

No. 11,810   ONE PENNY
Registered at the G.P.O. as a Newspaper.

SOVIET DIPLOMATS QUIT MOSCOW FOR NEW CAPITAL

THE Russian Foreign Office, the American Ambassador to the U.S.S.R—Mr. Laurence Steinhardt—and the entire Diplomatic Corps are leaving Moscow for a temporary capital, the whereabouts of which has not been revealed.

German and Rumanian troops have entered the Black Sea port of Odessa, which is in flames, according to reports from Berlin and Bukarest last night.

A Rumanian High Command communique claimed that Rumanian troops marched into the port after the last pockets of resistance had been overcome in street fighting.

Berlin reports say that every Russian man, woman and child capable of bearing arms fought against the invaders to the last.

The Soviet midnight communique said fighting continued along the whole front, and was particularly fierce in the Moscow direction. Both sides sustained heavy losses.

With the enemy almost at its gates, Moscow radio yesterday broadcast a defiant appeal by the German Communist Party to Nazi soldiers, workers and women to "finish Hitler and his gang."

Moscow radio was off the air during the day for some hours, but came on again suddenly with the dramatic appeal.

"Hitler is doomed. He can never win, but you German soldiers, workers, peasants and women — you can finish the bloodshed by finishing Hitler and his gang," the statement said.

"But he won't be able to force a decision, because the material and moral reserves of the Soviet Union are inexhaustible.

"Hitler Is Doomed"

"While hundreds of thousands of German soldiers are dying, Britain gathers a colossal strength in her Empire.

"Hitler is doomed. He can never win, but you German soldiers, workers, peasants and women — you can finish the bloodshed by finishing Hitler and his gang.

"If you won't do that the German army will be completely destroyed, and Ger-

Continued on Back Page

500,000 TONS BEEF

Argentina has agreed to sell Britain 500,000 tons of beef during the next twelve months, and is negotiating for the sale of a further 50,000 tons of preserved meat.—Associated Press.

Jap war lords demand action

JAPAN'S war party has won a big triumph in forcing Prince Konoye's "appeasement" Cabinet to resign. That is the opinion of officials in Washington, cables John Walters from New York.

The Japanese war lords believe the time has come to stab Russia in the back. Russia's Allies are alarmed, as these events show :—

President Roosevelt cancelled the Cabinet scheduled for yesterday and instead conferred for two hours with his military advisers.

Talks between Britain, Australia and America were speeded up to counteract the growing Japanese menace in the Pacific.

The Allied countries are expected to make definite moves if Japan is guilty of aggression.

The situation is so critical that President Roosevelt may have to give a public warning to Japan.

In Congress, Senators Gerald Nye, the North Dakota Isolationist, and Lister Hill, of Alabama, who are usually far apart in their outlook on foreign affairs, agreed that the Japanese Cabinet resignation bore ominous implications for the future of Japanese-American relations.

Canadian Cabinet Meets

Senator Nye said, "We can't tell much until the new Cabinet is appointed, but the resignation of the former one apparently means a complete military set-up in Japan."

The "New York Post" Washington correspondent last night wrote that the Japanese - American tension had "reached a point where war may be considered imminent."

Far East developments are understood to have been responsible for a sudden meeting at Ottawa yesterday of the Canadian Cabinet.

The Canadian Government is maintaining constant communication with Britain.

U.S. gives us 2 submarines

Colonel Frank Knox, U.S. Navy Secretary, announced last night that two recommissioned U.S. submarines would be transferred to Britain under the Lease-Lend Act.

The Navy Department said both submarines, which were operating in the Atlantic, would be manned by British officers and crews before leaving American waters.

EVACUEE NAMES SHIP

Anne England, 9, war guest in Canada and daughter of a Wallington (Surrey) journalist, was co-sponsor with the wife of Lieutenant-Governor Woodward when British Columbia's first 10,000-ton cargo vessel was named.

GORT'S B.E.F. SHOCKER

Tragically ill-equipped the B.E.F. had not up to May 10—last year—the day when Germany invaded Belgium and Holland—been provided with armour-piercing shells for field guns.

Anti-tank regiments were short of guns and there was a shortage of almost every type of ammunition.

R.A.F. forces were at one time reduced to fifty fighters.

Invaluable aid in meeting the enemy could have been gained had the B.E.F. had an armoured division and a complete Army Tank Brigade.

Troop increases promised to Lord Gort never arrived.

Fought Half-Trained

Flung into the three-week battle which preceded Dunkirk were half-trained men taken to France as labour units.

Supplies of technical apparatus for light anti-aircraft requirements, predictors and signal lights and technical and specialised vehicles were deficient.

These are points in the tragic story of neglect and unpreparedness—which were the background of Dunkirk—but could not prevent it from becoming the greatest story of courage and endurance in British military annals.

T. E. A. Healy tells you about it in detail from Lord Gort's own story of the Battle of Flanders on page 2.

ARMY TO HAVE OWN BORSTALS

THE Army's "bad boys" are to have their own "Borstals."

At certain detention barracks separate wings have been set aside for young soldiers, under the age of twenty-one, sentenced to fourteen days or more.

All men under twenty-one who are detained, whether serving in young soldiers' battalions or other units, will, in future, go to these junior detention barracks.

The reason for this is to keep separate the young men from the older ones since, in most cases, reasons for detention are not the same.

The juniors, whose crimes on the whole are less serious, will receive slightly different supervision.

DUKE'S NEW JOB

The Duke of Kent has a new job under the Ministry of Labour—making inspection visits to war-production factories to get first-hand knowledge of wartime conditions.

You are a detective today

YOU are a detective today !

SCOTLAND Yard is anxious to interview a monocled man with a cultured voice in connection with the death of Mrs. Theodora Greenhill, 65, widow, who was found strangled in her flat at Elsham-road, West Kensington.

They appeal to you to help trace him.

He may be in your town or village.

The man frequently describes himself as "Dr. Trevor," "Mr. Marjoribanks," and "Mr. Atkins," and sometimes assumes military rank.

He may seek accommodation at an hotel, boarding or apartment house, and has an extensive knowledge of south coast seaside resorts, the Home Counties, London and Birmingham.

Here is the man's photograph and description:

Aged 64, height 5ft. 11½in., slim build, complexion fresh, hair grey, thin on top, well back from the forehead, fairly thic eyebrows, eyes brown, two small moles on right of face, scar over left eye, scar back of left forefinger.

Speaks with cultured voice. May be wearing grey flannel trousers, grey trilby hat and fawn raincoat.

Have you seen him ?

"Dr. Trevor."

Airmen not to smoke on roads

AIRMEN have been forbidden to smoke within a mile of one operational station near London because their C.O. regards it as "merely a matter of decent behaviour and pride in the Service."

The ban affects not only the main road that runs through the camp, but on roads within approximately a mile radius.

The commanding officer told the *Daily Mirror*:

"No officer would walk about the roads with a cigarette dangling from his lips, and I do not expect an airman to do it.

No Ban in Camp

"There is already much laxity in London you can see men in the Forces mooching along with pipes or cigarettes in their mouths, holding newspapers in front of their faces and ignoring officers

"The men can smoke as much as they like in camp when they are off duty, but not in public places near. I am a smoker, I would not think of doing it.

"All decent R.A.F. camps have similar regulations."

But at other well-known R.A.F. camps, the *Daily Mirror* was told that there was no such regulation. So long as the men were off duty they smoked where and when they liked.

There is no Air Ministry regulation against smoking," it was stated at the Air Ministry.

Three seamen cost country £400 a day

It was stated at Jarrow (Co. Durham) yesterday, when two seamen were summoned for being drunk and incapable of performing their duty on board ship, and another with being absent without leave, that—

The ship was delayed six days, and the cost to the country was estimated at roughly £400 a day.

Each seaman was fined £10.

Daily Mirror

OCT. 18

No. 11,811 — ONE PENNY
Registered at the G.P.O. as a Newspaper.

Disobeyed — won V.C.

WHEN the order to retreat was given to the New Zealand troops in Kalamai, Greece, a sergeant disobeyed it — and won the V.C.

Shouting "To hell with this—who'll come with me!" he dashed to within a few yards of the nearest German gun and hurled two grenades, which wiped out the gun crew.

The sergeant was John Daniel Hinton. His V.C. is the fourth to be awarded to New Zealanders in this war.

After he had killed the gun crew, Sergeant Hinton came on with the bayonet, followed by a crowd of New Zealanders.

The Germans abandoned the first six-inch gun and retreated into two houses. Hinton smashed the window, and then the door of the first house, and dealt with the garrison with the bayonet.

He repeated the performance in the second house. Then he fell with a bullet through the abdomen, and was taken prisoner.

Hinton, who is single, is in the same unit as the V.C.s Upham and Hulme, announced this week. In civilian life he is a motor driver.

RUSSIANS QUIT ODESSA, LEAVE IT IN FLAMES

ODESSA has been evacuated. This was admitted in the Russian midnight communique. The evacuation had been going on for eight days and was carried out in perfect order, the troops being taken off by sea and transferred to other sectors.

Rome radio said that the Russians set fire to Odessa before leaving, and three-quarters of it was destroyed.

The communique says the evacuation was carried out in accordance with the decision of the Soviet High Command strategy and was not due to pressure from the German and Rumanian forces.

The Germans have made no further progress in front of Moscow, though they claim an advance on a flank, but fighting is still extremely fierce and Moscow radio warned last night that it will become even more stubborn.

Women are taking their places in the battle line ready to help in the defence of Moscow. So keen are they that they are queuing up pleading to be given a job in the defence of the capital.

British Embassy Leaves

The situation is serious, and the whole population of Moscow, with the Red Army, is heroically defending the approaches, says "Pravda."

The well-known Russian writer, Glebov, said in a Moscow broadcast yesterday: "Veterans of the last war, veterans of the revolution are ready. People of all ages are learning the use of modern arms. Girls are queueing in front of recruiting offices to enrol for war work of any kind."

Sir Stafford Cripps, the British Ambassador, with his staff and the British Military Mission left Moscow yesterday at the request of the Russian Government as the Germans claimed a fresh advance on the flank and Vichy reported that

Continued on Back Page

New Axis moves bring war crisis to U.S.

AMERICAN relations with the Axis Powers yesterday reached their most critical stage since the beginning of the war.

While Washington was ordering all U.S. merchant ships in Far Eastern waters to speed to the nearest British or American port, the U.S. destroyer Kearny radioed she had been torpedoed in the North Atlantic.

The Kearny was on patrol duty 350 miles south-west of Iceland when she was torpedoed. There were no casualties and the destroyer is proceeding to port under her own power.

Cause of the recall of U.S. ships was the announcement that pro-Nazi General Tojo had been asked to form a new Japanese Cabinet.

This means the militarist group have got control in Japan, and the new Cabinet will be dominated by Generals and Admirals.

Washington consequently fears a serious new threat in the Pacific and a new military adventure—possibly an attack on Siberia.

According to the New York Daily News, "not since 1917, when U.S. severed diplomatic relationships with Germany over submarine warfare, has the Capitol been so tense."

"Soon at War"

In Congress circles last night there were predictions that before long the U.S. would be fully at war with Japan and Germany, according to a cable from John Walters, Daily Mirror New York correspondent.

"Chances of a peaceful settlement with Japan are meagre indeed," said Senator Gillette, of the Foreign Relations Committee, as President Roosevelt anxiously awaited any move by Tokio's new Cabinet.

The President was in constant telephone communication with Secretary of State Cordell Hull, who has been instructed to take a firm, unrelenting attitude toward the Japanese military clique now in power.

President and Cabinet have, it is understood, decided that if Japan makes certain aggressive moves, American economic mea-

Continued on Back Page

RUSSIA £50,000 FROM NUFFIELD

Mrs. Churchill yesterday received a telegram from Lord Nuffield informing her that he will give £50,000 to her Red Cross Aid to Russia Fund.

EX-SHAH ON ISLAND

The ex-Shah of Iran is in Mauritius, Indian Ocean island. It has been found desirable that he should go there owing to the war situation, says an official statement.

Murder on the First Floor Back

London's 4th in a week

SCOTLAND YARD'S murder squad was faced yesterday with a new death mystery—the fourth in seven days—by the discovery of a silent murder in a room on the first floor back of a house at Regent's Park within half a mile of the spot where Maple Church was found strangled on Sunday night.

Latest victim in this strange series of London murders was Mrs. Edith Eleanora Humphries, widow, of Gloucester-crescent, Regent's Park, N.W.

She was found, clad only in her nightdress, shortly after eight o'clock yesterday morning, sprawled across a bed in a back room on the first floor back dying from terrible head wounds.

A black mongrel dog to which Mrs. Humphries was much attached was found locked in a cupboard.

She was rushed to hospital where an eminent brain surgeon, Dr. Guy Rigby Jones, decided on a million-to-one chance operation in an attempt to save her life. The operation failed.

No One Heard

This new murder is remarkable because no one was aware of it until a woman living in rooms above came downstairs and saw Mrs. Humphries lying on the bed.

Mrs. Humphries was the widow of a taxi-driver and owned the big semi-detached house where she lived. She had been working as a cook at an Islington A.F.S. station.

The police have traced the driver of a taxicab which, on Tuesday, took a man with a cabin trunk from outside the flat in Elsham-road, Holland Park, W., where Mrs. Greenhill was strangled.

He has given valuable information.

A trunk and small articles belonging to Mrs. Greenhill have been found in a Birmingham suburb.

Last night, Inspector Salisbury, of Scotland Yard, who has been searching Birmingham for a sixty-four-year-old monocled man, returned to the Yard.

COMPANY WITHOUT CAPITAL

Seeds Import Board has been registered as a company, limited by guarantee, without share capital, state Jordan and Sons. "To act on behalf of the Minister of Agriculture in the supply and distribution of seeds imported from the United States under the Lease-Lend Act."

BROTHERS DIE IN BATH

A FOURTEEN-YEAR-OLD boy, Joseph Burton, dived into the Stoke-on-Trent swimming bath yesterday and saw the bodies of two boys on the bottom.

The boys were taken from the bath, but artificial respiration failed to revive them.

The boys were Eric Cornes, 9, and his brother Frederick, 7. They seemed to be all right when they were seen by the attendant in the water, shortly before Burton found them.

Nobel peace prize has been cancelled

The Swedish Government has decided that the Nobel Prizes usually awarded annually for outstanding work in the interests of physics, chemistry, medicine and physiology, literature and peace, shall not be given this year.

PRICES FIXED FOR BREAKFAST CEREALS

Maximum retail prices for twenty-five specified cereal breakfast foods, to come into force on Monday, have been fixed.

The prices of breakfast foods not specified remain controlled at the level ruling on December 2, 1940.

CORVETTE SUNK

The corvette Fleur de Lys (Lieutenant A. Collins, R.N.R.) has been sunk. Next-of-kin of casualties have been informed.

Baby born to music

A baby was born in Chicago yesterday to Mrs. Pauline Siegal, by a Caesarean operation while she listened to Tchaikovski's Concerto in B Flat minor, and hummed the accompaniment.

Mrs. Siegal had an anaesthetic, which left her conscious, and she listened all the time to the programme broadcast especially for the birth for one and a half hours by the local radio station. The concerto, which was the grand finale, was preceded by "Tales of the Vienna Woods," "My Curly-headed Baby," and "l'Amour, Toujours l'Amour."

Dr. Edward Cornell, who performed the operation, told John Walters, our New York correspondent. "It was no stunt. The radio station co-operated with us because we wanted to discover if music would ease the pain by imparting partial hypnosis. It was a great success. The mother enjoyed the music immensely. She weighs 7st. and baby, a boy, weighs 5lb. 2oz."

HARRY WON'T STOP FIGHTING

THEY'RE tough, mighty tough, in the Western Desert.

This is the story of Harry, one of our tank commanders, told by Major H. Barker, Royal Tank Regiment, in London yesterday:

Harry—a former test pilot—jumped from a sick bed to be in a desert drive against the Italians. When his tank was hit by a shell he was severely injured, but carried on.

At Bardia, Harry was in the thick of the fighting. A piece of shrapnel pierced his cheek as he popped his head out of his tank, but he was at it again as soon as a strip of sticking plaster had been put over the wound.

With his colonel, Harry set out on foot, at Tobruk, ignoring heavy fire, to an anti-tank ditch, where he watched tanks go into action.

LET ENGINE RUN—FINED

For wasting petrol by leaving his lorry engine running for two minutes, Thomas Waters, of Bridge-street, Witney, Oxfordshire, was fined 5s. at Witney yesterday.

RADIO JAMMING WAR GOES ON

Calais radio was heavily jammed when the German war communique was read in English last night.

It was almost impossible to hear. There was a drone like bagpipes, with a military band in the background.

The foreign voice on the B.B.C. Forces programme started to interfere with the 9 p.m. news bulletin when Big Ben was heard.

The voice was stronger than usual, but the "humour" was even poorer than on previous nights. The interruptions consisted mostly of "That's a lie" and "Says the B.B.C."

After five minutes the voice was silent.

SINGAPORE'S SPOTTERS

Singapore is raising an Observer Corps, composed of men and women, to spot hostile planes.

PLEASE KEEP MILK CHOCOLATE FOR THE CHILDREN

Milk is so good for the youngsters — so is chocolate. They get both in delicious Cadburys Milk Chocolate. But—made before milk rationing came in—supplies are very limited. So if you see it on sale, please leave it for the children—or, if you buy any, see that the children have it.

ISSUED BY

Cadburys
from Bournville

THE FACTORY IN A GARDEN

Stalin's plan to split rule

If Moscow falls Stalin plans to split the Russian Government into three, say German circles in Istanbul.

First would be known as the Central Government, headed by Stalin, and based probably on Samara, east of Moscow, on the Volga.

Second would operate from Tiflis, in the Caucasus, working closely with the British there.

Third would be one left in occupied Russia, working underground, organising and encouraging sabotage and guerrilla warfare.—British United Press

SUBSIDY FOR BAKERS

For thirteen weeks from October 20 bread bakers will be able to claim a special subsidy of 2s. to 4s. on each sack of flour used to make bread sold at or under the controlled maximum price of twopence a lb., stated the Ministry of Food last night.

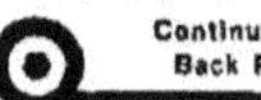

Daily Mirror

OCT. 21

No. 11,813
ONE PENNY
Registered at the G.P.O. as a Newspaper.

MOSCOW TROOPS SMASH GERMAN TANK ATTACKS

EARLY today the Russian official communique revealed that German troops made several fierce attacks with large tank formations on the Moscow front.

"Our troops repulsed the German attacks," the communique said.

"In the directions of Orel (south of Moscow) and Briansk (south-west of Moscow) our troops inflicted effective blows on the enemy.

"During the day of October 20 fighting continued along the entire front.

"Particularly stubborn battles took place in the directions of Mojaisk, Malo-Yaroslavets and Taganrog."

Taganrog is on the southern front, about fifty miles from the important oil port of Rostov.

German pressure continues to be heavy. Russian strategy in preventing a definite break through consists of hard-hitting local counter-attacks along the whole front from Kalinin to Orel.

Mojaisk, sixty-five miles west of Moscow, is now the farthermost point reached by the Germans, the line running through Mojaisk north and south.

Strongest Russian attacks are being pressed home around Kalinin, north-west of Moscow, which forms the northernmost arm of the German pincers movement. Kalinin is not yet in Russian hands.

Fairly heavy losses were inflicted on German forces around the city.

Tanks, supplies and motorised infantry were wiped out by Russian attacks, while in another sector of the same front, the

◼ **Continued on Back Page**

"Hold on, Moscow!"

Leningrad broadcast to Moscow last night.

"This is Leningrad speaking to our brothers in great Moscow," the announcer said. "Now the enemy is facing your city as he was facing Leningrad a short while ago. We smashed him back. All that was left of him were piles of dead and his mangled tanks.

"Hold on, Moscow, mother city of the Russian people. As we got rid of the German vermin, you shall be rid of them, too.

"In brotherly affection we fight our battles and we will go on until victory is ours. Our country will be rebuilt and we shall find peace and constructive progress after this war. New life and new greatness waits us.

"Death to Fascism. Greetings to our brotherly Moscow."

● Rome radio last night denied stories circulating in Italy—and attributed to British propagandists — that Hitler had ordered the capture of Moscow "by Monday."

And Breslau declared: "No responsible German will predict when Moscow will fall."

GROUPS OF RAIDERS BOMB MERSEYSIDE

Eight or nine raiders flew over a Merseyside town at about half-hourly intervals last night and dropped bombs which did some damage. Casualties were not heavy.

Bombs were also dropped in an East Coast area last night.

Shot Nazi curfew reprisal

FIRST reprisal for the shooting of the Nazi police commandant at Nantes, Lieutenant-Colonel Friedrich K. Holtz, is a 6 p.m. curfew throughout Occupied France, which began last night.

The killing has been followed by the quick arrest of new hostages, many of whom, it is expected, will be executed.

The assailants fired six shots at the Commander—the highest Nazi officer yet assassinated in France—as he crossed the Place St. Pierre in the black-out.

The German authorities say that the assassination was the outcome of Communist terrorism which has broken out again after a calm during the last three weeks.

Actually it is an indication of the rising tide of revolt against the German occupation.

Trailed to Square

Both assailants appear to have made good their escape, says British United Press.

Holtz was field commander of the Nantes area (which confers powers far exceeding those usually held by a lieutenant-colonel).

Two bullets entered the back of Holtz's neck, killing him instantly.

German patrols immediately rounded up scores of people on the quays and streets, despite the 11.30 p.m. curfew.

Police believe the assassination was carefully planned.

Strike threat by bus girls

Sixty Exeter bus conductresses have given notice that they will cease work at the end of the week if the Corporation insist on appointing a former conductress as supervisor.

No progress was made yesterday in negotiations between representatives of the women and officials of the Corporation.

CHRISTMAS PUDDING FOR THE SERVICES

In addition to their ordinary rations on Christmas Day, men in the Services will each get an egg, pork wherever possible, Christmas pudding and mince pies.

This has been arranged to counteract the shortage of food gifts—due to rationing—from relatives.

N.A.A.F.I. will make the puddings and pies.

PIT DEATH TOLL SIX

Doncaster pit explosion death-roll is now six. The injured man, Leonard Crane, has died in hospital from burns.

Shot love cheat: RAF man cleared

AN R.A.F. officer was acquitted yesterday of the murder of a man, shot during a struggle in a West End flat, whose influence had ruined the lives of beautiful women in the capitals of Europe.

Flying Officer Edward Alexander Reay Landon, 34, married, was found not guilty at the Old Bailey of the murder of Frantisek Mandaus, one-time wealthy Czech opera singer and film producer, and was discharged.

Landon denied in cross-examination that Mandaus "stole his girl," Miss Joan Coveny.

He admitted she had been his mistress since she was 19.

Landon described last Friday a struggle at the flat. He said that when he went there with Joan's sister, Kathleen, to get confirmation of a statement that Joan had been kept there against her will, Mandaus rushed at him and snatched his (Landon's) revolver. The revolver went off.

Yesterday Landon said that Joan told him that Mandaus had stripped and beaten her and locked her in the flat.

No Evil Intent

He had no evil intention when he took the revolver to the flat.

Mr. Justice Tucker: What happened is that the revolver went off somehow or other and killed Mandaus. That is a fact, is it not?—Yes.

Mandaus was married three times. His third wife was a Czech beauty queen.

Such was his power over women that after they had divorced him they were friendly towards him.

Penniless or wealthy, he attracted the company of beautiful women. He was known to have as many as twelve appointments with women in a day.

SPANISH GUEST OF DUKE OF GLOUCESTER

The Infante Alfonso de Orleans, a general of the Spanish Air Force, accompanied by an aide-de-camp, yesterday crossed the frontier to Gibraltar where he was invited to luncheon by the Duke of Gloucester, says Associated Press.

It was stated in London yesterday that the visit of the Duke of Gloucester to Algeciras, Spain, was "a marked success."

NEW U.S. AIRCRAFT CARRIER

The 19,900-ton U.S. aircraft-carrier Hornet was commissioned at Norfolk, Virginia, yesterday, six months ahead of schedule. She has space for more than 100 aircraft.

ROAD FLEET RUN BY GOVT.

THE Ministry of War Transport and the road haulage industry are to co-operate in a triple plan to secure better use and control of goods road transport during the war.

The scheme announced last night by the Minister of War Transport consists of:—

(1) A Ministry organisation covering the country and controlling the movement of a fleet of vehicles.

(2) An organisation managed by the industry alongside the Ministry organisation. The industry organisation will allocate traffic passed to it by the Ministry organisation.

(3) A series of "defence lines" to meet emergencies. This will consist of vehicles belonging to carriers and others who agree to place them at the Ministry disposal at short notice.

Shot German was U-boat chief

Lieutenant Berard Berndt, twenty-five, German naval officer shot dead by Lake District Home Guards in a second escape attempt, was Commander of the U-boat recently captured by a Hudson coastal command aircraft.

The submarine, identified as the U570, was captured in the North Atlantic and brought into a British port, manned by men of the Royal Navy.

U.S. anger at attack on Kearny

NEW outbursts against the Nazi submarine attack on the U.S. destroyer Kearny were made in Washington when it was disclosed that eleven of the crew are missing and ten injured.

When Mr. Cordell Hull, Secretary of State, was asked if he would send a note of protest to Germany, he said U.S.A. did not often send diplomatic notes to international highwaymen.

In Washington last night it was being recalled that it was on the eve of America's entry into the Great War that the U.S.A. Navy lost its first man.

He was a gunner on the American ship Aztec, sunk on April 2, 1917. War was declared on April 6.

Wants Vote on War

A Bill to repeal the entire Neutrality Act was introduced into the Senate in Washington yesterday by three Republican Senators.

Aiming to delay the Bill Isolationist Senator Wheeler announced that he had attached a rider to the Bill to force the Senate to vote on a declaration of war.

If the rider is defeated it would mean the acknowledgment by the Administration that the American people is not ready for war.

FROM BRITAIN TO FIGHT IN RUSSIA

Polish officers and men trained in Britain are to go to Russia to form the basis of new Polish forces there.

In an order of the day to the Poles in Britain, General Sikorski, Polish Commander-in-Chief, states:—

"I am sure you will find yourselves worthy of the sacrifices of Polish soldiers in Russia. You will take with you the spirit of friendly co-operation characteristic of our collaboration with the British.

"We shall proceed on different roads to one common aim—the liberation of Poland."

THE GHOST LIES LOW

The Ghost Voice failed to interfere with last night's 9 o'clock news in the Forces programme.

Daily Mirror

OCT. 23

No. 11,815

ONE PENNY

Registered at the G.P.O. as a Newspaper.

HUNS FLING MASS OF 'CHUTISTS ON MOSCOW

HE PROPOSED AT THE PALACE

HITLER is flinging masses of parachute troops behind the Russian lines on the Moscow front, trying to beat the snow storms which are aiding the defenders to hold up his panzers.

The weather is so severe, said a German radio reporter last night, that on one part of the front snow ploughs had to be used.

Not only men, in Russian army and police uniforms, but light tanks, armoured cars and field guns are being landed behind the Moscow lines.

Pilot-Officer H. H. Kitchener, D.F.M., and Miss Ida Bloxham.

Miss Bloxham went with him to the Palace recently when he received the D.F.M. from the King. He walked to the other side of the room, to show her the medal, and then blurted out his proposal of marriage. Miss Bloxham said "Yes," almost beneath the eyes of the King.

WAR AGAINST YOUR COLD

THREE Government Ministries, helped by a well-known comedian and a cartoonist, are going to put the common cold germ on the spot.

A nation - wide campaign against this invisible "enemy" of our war effort has been started by the Ministry of Health, aided by the Ministries of Labour and Information.

Arthur Askey may feature in a film to show how to dodge the common cold.

H. M. Bateman, cartoonist, has designed posters to boost the Ministry of Health's slogan: "Coughs and sneezes spread diseases. Use your handkerchief and trap the germs."

No cure has been discovered for a cold, but the Ministry of Health believes that by following simple rules people can prevent it spreading.

Fresh air and exercise are the finest ways to dodge colds.

TWO RAIDERS DOWNED

Nazi bombers, starting up their "nuisance" raids again last night, were spread out over wider areas of England than for several weeks.

Two were destroyed.

One of them was shot down in flames near a West Midlands town.

Enemy aircraft were traced from coast to coast across the breadth of the country—from East Anglia to Merseyside.

But bombs dropped were few and far between. Damage was small and only a few casualties reported.

Little damage was reported on Merseyside and few slight casualties. The raiders left the area before midnight.

No U.S. shipments to Vladivostok

The Vladivostok route for Russian supplies from the U.S. is to be abandoned after Tuesday. Future shipments will go to Archangel.

The change is said to be due to the "constantly increasing volume of shipments, essential to Russia's defence."

Suggestions that the changes constituted a concession to Japan were discounted in Washington.—Exchange.

R.A.F. OVER FRENCH COAST LAST NIGHT

Brilliant flashes lit a stretch of the North French coastline last night when Nazi A.A. guns went into action soon after dark.

Searchlights swept the sky, and "flaming onions" were seen bursting in the clouds across the sea. Main activity appeared to be in Dunkirk and Calais areas.

Duchess's cheapest dress: £60

BEFORE leaving the Bahamas the Duchess of Windsor ordered in New York twelve dresses, reported the New York *World Telegram* yesterday.

When she visited a home for unmarried mothers she wore a plain black jersey costume. This cost £60 and was the cheapest of the twelve.

Another of the dresses, a simple-looking dinner gown of white crepe, embroidered with beads cost £165 says the newspaper.

Mair Bocher, the Duchess's dressmaker, denies this, however saying: "That dinner gown didn't cost more than £100."

Plane crash fires houses

An R.A.P. plane crashed in Gowan-avenue, Fulham, last night and the pilot was killed. Petrol from the tank set fire to a house.

Two occupants of the house, Mrs. Morgan and Mrs. Sullivan, escaped by a back door.

Mr. Claxton, of Edgarley-terrace Fulham, was severely cut while helping to save them, and was taken to hospital.

The fire spread to four other houses, but the flames were extinguished by fire watchers.

1 TANK PER 45 MINUTES

The American Car and Foundry Company have just delivered their 2,000th tank to the U.S. Army, and are now ready to turn out one 12-ton tank every forty-five minutes.

42 STONE OF ONE HOME GUARD

HERE is some of the biggest news of the war. Barney Worth, the whole 42st. of him, has joined the Home Guard!

The *Daily Mirror* told recently the story of Barney, of Severn Beach, near Bristol. He was turned down by the Army. The A.R.P. did not want him either.

They remarked that if he became a casualty it would take a crane and not a stretcher party to get him to a shelter.

But the Home Guard are not worrying about that.

They have solved the uniform problem by indenting for two greatcoats and employing a local tailor to sew them together.

So Mr. Worth, in his two-in-one greatcoat, and specially built gas mask, is now guarding the shores of the Bristol Channel against invasion.

The only trouble that is likely to arise is when he asks his wife to knit him a nice warm pullover.

Maybe if the Russians can hold out another couple of years she will get it finished in time.

"The Nazis are trying to break our resistance with incessant dive-bombing and tank attacks," said the newspaper *Pravda* yesterday. "They are throwing in reinforcements and parachutists on a large scale."

"But fierce Soviet resistance has slowed down the rate of the German advance as the battle of Moscow approaches its twenty-second day."

The German news agency is

Day and night their rifles are ready

"Life in Moscow looks a lot different now," said a Moscow radio announcer last night. "All men and women carry rifles on their shoulders day and night. Workers labour in the factories with their rifles on the benches beside them, and people sleep with their guns to hand."

preparing the people for disappointment. It declared yesterday: "Moscow will fall when Adolf Hitler finds it necessary." But the fall of Moscow is not decisive for the outcome of the war.

According to a U.S. Stockholm correspondent the battle has cost the Germans 40,000 men a day for twelve days.

Bitter fighting is going on along the whole front with fierce attacks and counter-attacks.

Evacuation of Taganrog in the south was admitted in the Russian midnight communique.

During the battle, it said the Germans lost 35,000 men.

A Berlin spokesman last night said that the advance in the Donetz Basin had been

Continued on Back Page

German officer shot in France—100 held

ANOTHER German officer—a major—has been assassinated in Occupied France.

He was shot in daylight on the Boulevard St. George, Bordeaux.

Immediately after the shooting the German authorities arrested 100 hostages.

The fifty French hostages seized following the murder of Lieutenant-Colonel Hotz in Nantes have already been shot. It was confirmed by officials in Berlin yesterday.

Another fifty would be shot they said, unless the colonel's murderers were found.

Three more Frenchmen have been shot for possessing arms.

Among the fifty hostages shot were Michel, a Paris Communist Deputy, four trade union secretaries and fourteen followers of De Gaulle, it was learned last night.

With these executions, the number of shot hostages has risen to 123.

Pétain broadcast an appeal yesterday to Frenchmen to stop terrorism.

"Find one culprit," he exclaimed, "and 100 Frenchmen are saved. I cry out to you about this in a broken voice. Don't let any more harm befall France."

British United Press and Associated Press.

PILOT ON RADIO WAS FINUCANE

THE voice you heard on the radio last night in "The World Goes By" programme telling you of his air battles was that of Flight-Lieutenant Paddy Finucane, 21-year-old Irish leader of an Australian Spitfire squadron.

The B.B.C. did not announce his name, and would not admit afterwards that the voice was that of Finucane, but only one pilot answers his description.

They declared in an announcement that the pilot was a triple D.F.C., had recently been awarded the D.S.O. and was 21 —and that must be Paddy.

Went from Hospital

Paddy nipped to the studio from hospital. He fractured a bone in his foot while jumping over a wall in the black-out.

In his broadcast this destroyer of twenty-four enemy planes said most of his victories had been over France.

"Before going off on a trip," he said, "I usually have a funny feeling in my tummy.

"The brain is working fast, and if the enemy is met it seems to work like a clockwork motor. You don't have time to feel anything but your nerves may be on edge - not from fear, but from excitement and intensity.

"I have come back from a sweep to find my shirt and tunic wet through with perspiration."

WHAT A PITY THEY FAILED

"It is seventeen years ago tonight since a gang of Jewish Communists tried to murder me in Lambeth"—Haw-Haw, in his talk from Breslau last night.

Farnes killed flying

Six-foot-four Kenneth Farnes, 30, England and Essex cricketer, has been killed in a flying accident.

A native of Romford, he first played for Essex in 1930, and has played in Test matches against Australia and South Africa.

Saw boy once, left him a legacy

Peter Maisey, 8, of Whitkirk, Leeds, has been left a legacy in the £15,120 will of Dr. Arthur Robinson of Ilkley, Yorks, who only saw him once.

The doctor, said Peter's widowed mother yesterday, took a great fancy to Peter The legacy will probably be used for his education.

Peter's father, a lieutenant in the West Yorks Regiment, and a second cousin of Dr. Robinson, died on service in June last year.

Smile all the while

Whatever the day brings we've got to keep smiling. So let's make our smiles worth while. Above all don't take chances with your teeth. Don't risk using tooth-pastes which employ abrasives to secure whiteness. They can't avoid injuring the thin coating of enamel which alone prevents decay. What about the paste you are using now? Grind a little between your front teeth. If there's the least trace of grittiness, change to Odol. All Dentists know Odol is absolutely safe, yet it makes and keeps your teeth like pearls.

Besides being perfect for natural teeth, Odol Tooth Powder cleans False Teeth and Plates beautifully. 7½d., New Size 10½d.

Keep the winning

Odol

Toothpaste 7½, 1/3, 1/10½
Solid Dentifrice, 7½
including Purchase Tax.

Smile!

Daily Mirror

OCT. 24

No. 11,916   ONE PENNY
Registered at the G.P.O. as a Newspaper.

NAZI UNITS 38 MILES FROM MOSCOW

Your war programme

1. Production Blitz. Britain is now to launch the biggest production drive of the war. We have machine tools, raw materials, factory buildings in surplus. It remains to recruit all available labour. Night shifts must be started everywhere.

2. Work—Then Fight. When this job is finished and stocks built up the men must leave the benches, and use the weapons.

3. All-in Defence. When invasion comes the WHOLE POPULATION will be involved, just as the whole population of Moscow is involved in the defence of that city.

This war programme was forecast by the Minister of Supply in the House of Lords yesterday.

He told of the aid we were giving to Russia and the importance Stalin placed on tanks.

"Stalin told us this war was being decided by tanks. He said it was a tank war. I asked about

Continued on Back Page

Colonel beat ATS revue ban

A COLONEL of the Cherry-pickers—pink-trousered Lieutenant-Colonel G. C. P. Paul, M.C., commands 3,000 men of a training regiment in the Salisbury Plain area.

But the A.T.S. under his operational command were not permitted to take part in his regimental revue although he acted in it himself.

They were withdrawn from the show at the eleventh hour by Chief Commander the Hon. Mrs. Gilmour, A.T.S., sister of the Duchess of Marlborough, who is their disciplinary "boss."

She alleged that because they had a 3in. "skin belt" the costumes they were asked to wear were indecent.

Colonel Paul disagreed. He refused to alter the costume. Instead, he sent his bandmaster to London to collect six actresses forty-eight hours before the opening performance. The show went on, but the A.T.S. were relegated to back-stage duties.

"The Funniest Skit"

Name of the revue was "Raspberries and Cream," devised and produced by Bandmaster Anthony Swift.

The Colonel himself played the medical officer of health in a sketch described as "the funniest skit in the show—and the bluest."

He also took the part of the Grand Duke in another sketch. Six of the A.T.S. girls were to be in the chorus. The colonel of the Cherrypickers lived up to his name.

He could pick 'em and he did. "They were all pretty young girls, well suited to the song and dance acts they were to do," the Colonel told the *Daily Mirror*.

"We timed the rehearsals for their benefit and waited till after they had served dinner in the officers' mess.

Thought Costumes Normal

"Often we rehearsed about midnight. On Friday night the blow fell. Mrs. Gilmour went round to the dressing room and saw the costumes for the chorus. She said the girls were not to appear in them.

"We had had all the costumes. I thought they were normal for any stage show.

"I should never have taken part in the revue myself if I had considered for one moment that there was anything wrong either in the sketches or the dresses.

A *Daily Mirror* reporter saw the costumes.

They consisted of full pink silk "shorts" and green satin bodices with long sleeves. About three inches of skin would have shown between bodice and shorts.

LEAVE WITH HUSBANDS

Women in hosiery factories are to get leave for half the period of ordinary leave of their husbands in the Forces and for the whole period of embarkation leave.

STALIN, as chief of the Supreme Military Council, reorganised the defence of Moscow yesterday as the German High Command claimed that their forces had broken through the capital's outer defences from the west and south-west and were within thirty-eight miles of the heart of Moscow.

The chief move by Stalin was sensational. He appointed General Gregory Zhukov, Vice-Commissar for Defence, Chief of the Soviet General Staff, and Commander of the Outer Defences of Moscow, in place of Marshal Timoshenko as Commander of the Western Front, which includes the Moscow region.

Zhukov began his career as a private in 1915. His gallantry and courage are widely known.

Signor ("Woe! Woe!") Ansaldo broadcasting last night from Rome, said the Kremlin has been mined. This shows that Stalin has decided to leave Moscow in ruins before he will flee.

Despite bad weather, the German High Command said their advanced units were within thirty-eight miles of Moscow. Broadcasting this, Berlin radio threatened civilian defenders.

"The workers of Moscow have been called up for the defence of Moscow. We once more warn the Soviet Government. The fate of

Continued on Back Page

5 AIR ACES FOR U.S.A.

Five of Britain's air aces, including a V.C., all with special experience in bombers and fighters, will be attached for a short time to the U.S. Army Air Corps.

The officers are: Group-Captain H. Broadhurst, D.S.O., D.F.C., A.F.C.; Wing-Commander J. N. H. Whitworth, D.S.O., D.F.C.; Wing-Commander A. G. Malan D.S.O., D.F.C.; Wing-Commander H. I. Edwards, V.C., D.F.C.; Wing-Commander R. R. S. Tuck, D.S.O., D.F.C.

The U.S. Army Air Corps has official observers in this country.

Hertzog plumps for the Nazis

General Hertzog declared his support for Nazism at a congress of the Afrikander Party held in Johannesburg yesterday.

Nazism, he said, was not exclusively the product of any particular country or people.

An immediate result of this declaration is expected to be General Hertzog's break with his lifelong political associate Havenga and the break-up of the Afrikander Party, of which Hertzog is leader.

H.G. ALLOWANCES

"I am reviewing the matter of the subsistence allowance to Home Guards in the light of recent decisions in regard to fire-watching," said the Financial Secretary to the War Office yesterday.

"BRITISH TROOP-SHIP SUNK"

German High Command communique yesterday claimed that U-boats sank four merchant ships of a total of 32,000 tons, including the British troop transport Aurania, of 14,000 tons, sailing in a strongly-protected and fast-moving convoy in the Atlantic.

Gaylord, of Fertile, is father at 82

Mr. H. L. Gaylord, 82, lawyer, of Fertile, Minnesota, became the father of his nineteenth child yesterday.

Mr. Gaylord delivered the baby himself as he has delivered thirteen others.

DUTCH WATERS CLOSED

Navigation will be stopped in Dutch East Indies waters between October 28 and 30, says Vichy radio.

German threat of mass reprisals

TO the fifty French hostages already shot in a mass reprisal for the killing of a German officer, another 150 victims may be added before Monday.

While fifty hostages waited behind a military cordon at Nantes, liable to execution if the slayers of Lieutenant-Colonel Hotz were not discovered, by midnight last night, General Stuelpnagel, German Army of Occupation commander, ordered another fifty to be shot for the slaying of a German officer at Bordeaux on October 21.

He threatened that still another fifty would be executed if those responsible for the latter killing were not caught by midnight on Sunday.

A last-minute appeal to the people of France was broadcast over Paris radio last night inviting the murderers of Hotz to come forward in order to save the lives of the fifty hostages to be shot at midnight.

French police at Nantes last night helped the Germans to conduct a systematic comb-out.

The town was surrounded by Nazi troops, who were called in to cordon the area.

General de Gaulle asked French people, in a broadcast last night, not to kill Germans as, for the time being, it was easy for the Nazis to retaliate.

R.A.F. HIT NAZI 'DROMES

R.A.F. fighters yesterday attacked an aerodrome near Calais, Blenheims, with fighter escort, bombed Lannion aerodrome. None of our aircraft is missing.

'HUSH' POST FOR KING'S COUSIN

Lord Louis Mountbatten, second cousin to the King, is returning to England to take up a surprise appointment after only two months as commander of the 23,000-ton aircraft-carrier Illustrious.

Lord Louis flew to America last August when the Illustrious was being repaired there after being damaged in an attack in the Mediterranean.

At the time it was announced that the Illustrious "would re-enter the fight against Germany under the command of Lord Louis Mountbatten." But now it will be commanded by Captain A. G. Talbot.

Lord Louis' new post—a high one—is a close secret.

BETTER PUBLIC MORALS

The standard of public morals reflected in public behaviour is on the upward trend and better than in the last war, Mr. George Tomlinson, secretary of the Public Morality Council, said yesterday. He added that the cinema was the most moral public entertainment.

Daily Mirror

OCT. 25

No. 11,817   ONE PENNY
Registered at the G.P.O. as a Newspaper.

Louisa Chandler.

The demon Poles do it again! 7—0

THE "Polish Demons"—all-Polish Spitfire wing—shot seven German fighters out of the sky yesterday without loss to themselves in battle at even odds over France.

The enemy planes were shot down almost at the rate of one a minute. One after another they plunged to earth in flames or pieces.

Not one Pole followed them. It was all over in ten minutes.

It was a battle seen by no one except the combatants, because of a cloud blanket below. To the French people on the ground the only visible evidence of the fight they could hear raging above was the procession of German fighters screeching down.

The Germans had the advantage of height and dived down on the Poles as they flew from the Channel.

Big Attack on France

"We beat them up so thoroughly because our machines were better than theirs," said one of the Polish squadron leaders. "They dived on us from a height, it is true, but that saved us the trouble of going to look for them."

Earlier in the day two Czech sergeant pilots attacked and drove off in a crippled condition a Junkers 88 bomber which approached the East Coast.

Last night, after R.A.F. planes had swept out over the French coast there was the heaviest bombardment for some time.

Destroyer sunk by U-boat

DESTROYER H.M.S. Broadwater (Lieutenant - Commander W. M. L. Astwood, R.N.) has been torpedoed and sunk while on escort duty in the North Atlantic.

On the previous day she had attacked and probably destroyed a U-boat.

The Broadwater is the second to be sunk of the fifty American destroyers handed over to Britain by the United States.

One of the officers lost is Lieutenant John S. Parker, R.N.V.R., of Boston, U.S.A. He is believed to be the first American citizen serving in the Royal Navy to lose his life.

NEW GERMAN FIGHTER

Germany has, according to "The Aeroplane," a new fighter. It is the Focke-Wulf 190, a radial-engined aeroplane armed more heavily than any German fighter yet opposed to the R.A.F. It has been reported by our fighters as "very fast."

It is estimated that it can operate at 40,000ft.

Italian cruiser torpedoed

AN Italian armed merchant cruiser of the Citta di Genova class has been torpedoed by one of our submarines in the Central Mediterranean.

After being hit by a torpedo the cruiser stopped and it was seen that a large hole had been blown in her side. It is probable that she sank.

The Citta di Genova class are of about 5,300 tons.

During August and September enemy ships sunk and probably sunk by British submarines and naval planes in the Mediterranean averaged almost one a day.

The number known to be sunk was thirty-eight. Those probably sunk totalled twenty-one. In addition twelve other ships were hit.

CLASH IN FAR EAST LIKELY

—Knox says

"A COLLISION in the Far East is virtually inevitable," Colonel Frank Knox, U.S. Secretary of the Navy, warned yesterday.

In an article in The Army and Navy Journal, published today, he said:

"The Orient is like a vast powder keg, potentially ready to explode with a roar.

"Only a miracle seemingly can prevent the collapse of Russia's organised military strength — and the democracies everywhere are praying that this miracle will occur."

Tank production for the U.S. Army is to be doubled at once, President Roosevelt announced in Washington last night.

Plans call for many thousands of tanks and equipment.

MET OLD LOVE, STOPS WEDDING

THIRTY-SIX hours before she was to be married a girl met by chance a former sweetheart. Memories of their old romance stirred. She abandoned her wedding plans.

Last night the bridegroom standing among the wedding presents he is returning, told the Daily Mirror the story.

Ronald Worley, 25, airgunner, of Rosemead, New House-lane, Salfords, near Redhill, was to have married Louisa Chandler, 22, Redhill, at St. Matthew's Church.

Instead on his wedding day he walked unnoticed past the church where over 100 local people had gathered to see the ceremony.

"I have known Louisa since childhood," said Worley.

"We were very happy. We had no tiffs. On Monday morning I saw her and took her a rose as usual.

"On Monday night when I met her she said, 'It's off.'"

She had met Tim Moody, a former sweetheart to whom she had been engaged. He is a Metropolitan police-constable, whose parents live locally. Once before she had bought a wedding dress to marry him. Now she is going to marry him.

"We had invited 100 guests.

"Now I have 150 presents to return. Eaton, the Surrey cricketer, was to have been my best man."

Your paper means bullets

NEARLY twenty tons of paper is dropped every week about the streets of London in bus and tram tickets.

They could be made into shells to be dropped on the Germans.

Roadsweepers were busy in the Strand yesterday. Within two hours hundreds of bus tickets littered one side alone.

Even with their thinner tickets London Transport issue nearly 1,000 tons of tickets a year — roughly 1,885,000,000

Since the war began only 190 tons of tickets have been salvaged.

The call for waste paper is vital. The greatest effort is needed. All you have to do is to place your ticket in the box provided on all vehicles.

London has salvaged 695 tons of paper from litter baskets. Weight of tickets sold each week by Manchester transport services is 2 tons 12 cwts. Of this 11 cwts. is salvaged.

Shirt tails to help war

Here is the tale of the tail of a shirt—your shirt, perhaps, sir—and how it can help the war effort.

Laundries, men's outfitters and stores are telling their customers that there is no need to discard old shirts with frayed cuffs and collars.

They can be renovated, made as good as new, for only a few shillings—and without surrender of coupons.

The secret lies in the tail. New collars, cuffs and other worn parts can be cut out of the lower part of the shirt and perfectly matched.

Cost of a new collar is usually 2s. 9d. or 3s. New cuffs vary from 1s. 9d. to 2s. 3d. a pair.

A firm of London shirtmakers who in pre-war days specialised in making "bespoke" shirts are now renovating thousands of shirts a week.

If every man in Britain were to have two shirts renovated instead of buying two, something like 145,600,000 yards of cloth would be saved.

Our secret is stolen

The theft of two suitcases full of "vital secrets," which would disclose details of the production of aerial cannon in Britain and the United States was reported to the New York police yesterday, cables John Walters.

Crammed with blue prints and documents, the suitcases were stolen from a car belonging to Mr. W. A. Futter.

Futter, a financier, recently returned to New York from Britain.

... authorities sealed the ... when I left England. He s... because they wanted to ... they were not opened until safely in the United States.

PRICE OF IMPORTED EGGS TO BE REDUCED

The price of imported eggs, except those from Eire, is to be reduced to 2½d. each, regardless of weight, as from Monday next.

Further supplies of cooking eggs at a price of 2d. each—an increase of ½d.—are to be issued.

STALIN ORDERS MOSCOW H.G. TO FRONT

STALIN last night ordered the Workers' Battalions—the Moscow Home Guard—into the front line as German forces were being checked at vital points on the approaches to the capital.

In the key towns of Mojaisk and Malo Yaroslavets, Russian tank divisions were reported to be holding the panzer attacks.

Moscow radio said: "New armies, some from Siberia, are pouring in."

One-half of Kalinin on the north wing is in the hands of the Russians and the other is held by the Germans.

Berlin radio told of the ever-increasing bitterness of the fighting, with Russians "infesting" the forests and fighting on both sides of the streets.

Unconfirmed Reports

There were completely unconfirmed Berlin reports that announced German units were in the "suburbs" of Moscow.

But Lozovsky, head of the Soviet Press Bureau, declared that the nearest point the Nazi main forces had reached was sixty miles from the city.

Fighting is going on in the Orel sector, but the new and main German thrust seems to be developing at Kalinin, where street fighting rages with the Russians defending every house.

"The Germans have lost several hundred thousand men already in the new battle for Moscow and the fighting is growing fiercer every minute," M. Lozovsky said.

"We can resist for several years longer. It remains to be seen how much longer the Germans can stand the war."

German losses in the offensive on Moscow started three weeks ago are estimated by the Russians at 300,000.

The latest Russian communique stated:

"During October our troops were engaged in battles in the direction of Taganrog.

Continued on Back Page

NEW ARMIES FOR SOVIET

Stalin and the National Defence Council will appoint a successor to Marshal Voroshilov in the Leningrad sector at a later date.

Voroshilov and Marshal Budenny have been entrusted by Stalin with organising new Russian Armies while Marshal Timoshenko has taken over the command of the Southern Front, which includes the Don Basin area and the Crimea.

General Gregory Zhukov, former Russian Chief of Staff, is now in supreme command in the battle for Moscow, while General Antiniev commands the garrison inside the city

NAZI RAIDER IS BROUGHT DOWN

An enemy bomber was destroyed soon after dark last night, when raiders were operating over the North and South Wales, Merseyside and East Anglia areas.

High-explosive bombs dropped on a town in the south-west of England damaged property.

WRINKLES IN YOUR KNEES, MADAME

SHAPELY legs are to be rarer, madame. Wrinkles at knee and ankle will be patriotic. Stocks of fully-fashioned hosiery are used up.

Skilled workers are going into munitions, which means that it will soon be impossible to buy fully-fashioned stockings.

To take their place will be Government utility stockings, knitted without even a seam at the back. They will be sold at about 3s. a pair.

INDIANS' OWN HOSPITAL

Special foods are being brought from India for Indian Army patients in a West Country hospital.

Was a Secretary— now a Nurse

SHE'S at everyone's beck and call, every minute of the long hospital day. It's a big new tax on her nerves and her physical endurance. Like all 'raw' wartime nurses, somehow and from somewhere she has just got to find the necessary stamina for her new life.

On the Home Front, battles are being won every day — big little victories over tiredness, irritability, nervous strain. Nature's own tonic, sound natural sleep (whenever you can get it) is the best thing ever for your new wartime lives. A warming cup of Bourn-vita, still at the old peacetime price, will help you to get your essential ration of body-and-mind-restoring SLEEP. Bourn-vita is a light food-drink with special nerve-soothing properties that bring sleep very quickly.

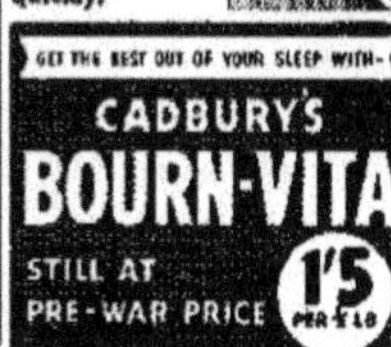

Daily Mirror

OCT. 28

No. 11,819   ONE PENNY
Registered at the G.P.O. as a Newspaper.

MOSCOW : SOVIET ATTACKS AT ALL KEY POINTS

Firing has begun
—Roosevelt

Women will run two fire stations

TWO fire stations staffed entirely by women will be in service in Scotland by Christmas.

Eighty women began training in Glasgow yesterday.

They will be the first all-women stations in Britain.

The experiment may be tested in England.

The Home Secretary is allowing Regional commanders to decide whether local conditions permit the training of women.

Engines in time will be operated entirely by women. They will be taught how to erect fire escapes, connect hose and generally perform duties usually done by men.

No Privileges

Training of the Glasgow women will last four weeks. They will wear slacks.

They will have no special privileges.

So many women aged from 20 to 40 have volunteered that only eighty can be trained at present.

These women's brigades will release men for duties at other stations.

RED TAPE KILLED SOLDIER'S WIFE

"The combination of a little ill-health and a great deal of bother over filling up forms overwhelmed her, and she decided that this was the only way out," said the coroner at an inquest at Romford (Essex) yesterday on Mary Elizabeth Allington, 38, of Brooklands-road, Romford, who was found gassed.

Her husband, a soldier, said his wife worried over the signing of forms for his supplementary allowance. One witness said she believed there were eleven or twelve papers to sign.

A verdict that Mrs. Allington killed herself while the balance of her mind was disturbed was recorded.

No ships for child evacuees

Although Canada wants to receive more children from Britain, the scheme has had to be turned down owing to the shipping situation.

The Parliamentary Under-Secretary for the Dominions revealed this yesterday.

All the Dominions are anxious to use the Children's Overseas Reception Scheme to take orphans of Servicemen after the war, he added.

Coxswain Blogg, 65, winner of three lifeboat V.C.s, who went yesterday to aid in the rescue of forty-four shipwrecked seamen eight hours after himself narrowly escaping drowning.

Escaped, back to save 44

TOUGH Harry Blogg, triple "Lifeboat V.C." and holder of the George Cross, coxswain of the Cromer boat, left his bed before dawn yesterday, eight hours after narrowly escaping drowning, put to sea and helped to rescue forty-four ship-wrecked seamen.

He and five of his crew had to abandon the attempt on Sunday, when they were washed overboard. One, Signalman Walter Allen died.

Blogg was so weak from exposure that he had to be undressed and put to bed.

The other men recovered in their homes and wanted to resume their mercy mission immediately, but the doctors made them wait.

Mountainous Seas

Twelve of the shipwrecked crew were taken off by the Cromer lifeboat, and the Gorleston boat, which had made unavailing rescue bids after the Cromer men were forced to give up, brought thirty-two to Great Yarmouth.

Robert Hayward, 38, of Battersea, S.W., one of the crew rescued by the Gorleston lifeboat, told the *Daily Mirror*:—

"We ran aground on a sand-

Continued on Back Page

HE WANTED TO BE WITH TWIN BROTHER

Twins, Samuel and George Vincent, of Great Yarmouth, had never been separated until George joined the Grenadier Guards and Samuel the R.A.F.

Yesterday Samuel, charged with being an absentee, was alleged to have said, when asked why he was at home, "because my brother is on leave." He was remanded for escort.

R.A.F. SHOOT DOWN 7 NAZIS, LOSE 11

Seven German planes were destroyed during R.A.F. activities yesterday.

British fighters attacked ships, barges and targets on land during a sweep over Northern France and the Belgian coast.

Two float planes on the sea were destroyed and three enemy fighters were destroyed in combat.

Blenheim aircraft, with a fighter escort, attacked a convoy off the Dutch coast. From all these operations two Blenheims and nine of our fighters are missing.

Later, two enemy bombers were shot down into the sea off the East Coast of England.

Five members of a bomber crew reported missing after Sunday night's raid on Germany have been rescued from the sea and landed in this country.

YUGOSLAV MARRIAGE BAN

A Yugoslav decree published yesterday makes marriage with a non-Aryan punishable by six months' imprisonment and loss of civic rights. Civil Servants are, in addition, threatened with dismissal.—Associated Press

THE Russians, having halted all German advances towards Moscow, are now counter-attacking in all directions on that front.

This news was flashed from the capital last night soon after General Zhukov, Russian Commander-in-Chief on the Western Front, had issued a dramatic "backs to the wall" appeal to Moscow's defenders as the city heard heavy artillery fire for the first time.

Soviet parachute troops are playing a big part in the counter-attacks.

South of Moscow, the Russians crossed the River Nara and drove the Germans out of a village.

Soviet troops, trapped near a town, broke through and rejoined the main armies after twelve days' fighting. Their artillery and equipment was intact.

Parachutists in Action

Fighting is most savage in the direction of Malo Yaroslavets and Mojaisk, Kharkhov and Tagranog, last night's Soviet communique stated.

One of the most vital stands made by the Russians is at Kalinin.

If the Germans broke through there they could make pincer thrusts at Leningrad or Moscow.

Crack Soviet parachutists held the Germans for seven hours until reinforcements arrived on one river near Moscow.

The Russians crushed two battalions of German motorised infantry as well as tanks and lorries.

"Not a Step Back !"

At one place where the Germans broke through the Soviet front line, a parachute group drove them back.

General Zhukov's order of the day to Moscow stated:—

"Not a step back ! This was the order given to us defenders of Moscow by the Government. We should not lose a minute in trying to stop the enemy.

"All cowards who leave the battlefield, disobeying the orders of commanders, should be mercilessly exterminated."

60,000 could help Russia

Sixty thousand Indian troops in Iraq and Iran can be sent to reinforce the Red Army if the Germans menace Baku and the Caspian.

That is the opinion of neutral military observers at Teheran.

Wavell has reinforcements for the Soviet Caucasus Army on about the same scale as the expedition sent to Greece, they say.

"The Caucasus is our pigeon —we should be more interested in the defence of that area than the Russians," said a British military spokesman.— Associated Press.

GRAB RAID IN GAS CAR

A Ford V8 car in which four smash-and-grab raiders at Lewisham made a successful getaway yesterday had a gasbag on top. The raiders hammered in a jeweller's window in Lewisham High-road and stole three trays of rings.

PRESIDENT ROOSEVELT asserted last night that "shooting has started," that "America has been attacked," and that the nation stood ready to face its newest and greatest challenger.

"We have wished to avoid shooting. But shooting has started, and history has recorded who fired the first shot."

Continued on Back Page

UNDIES GIRLS AGED 20-25 CALLED UP

GIRLS of 20-25 who make women's underwear are to be called up. Girls affected are those in the light clothing industry who were 20 and not above 25 on the date of their registration.

Special consideration is to be given to key workers.

The light clothing industry covers children's clothes, millinery, caps and hats, "women's clothing excluding outer wear" —and nothing in the tailoring category.

Important call-up consultations are taking place between the Government and industry, with the object of releasing even more women.

Big production and manpower changes soon

The Minister of Labour is likely to make an important statement on production, particularly man and woman power, when he presides at a meeting in London today of the joint consultative committee of the British Employers' Confederation and the General Council of the T.U.C.

He may indicate what further calls will be made on industry and the nation to meet the requirements, not only of Britain, but of Russia. Speedy action is expected.

Extension of Hours ?

A vast speed-up of production by the extension of working hours and introduction of week-end work in the factories may be discussed.

A further revision of the basis of the schedule of reserved occupations is foreshadowed, and women who have registered for war work either with the Forces or the factories will be interviewed without delay.

Two prosecutions in the provinces of women who have failed to obey the instructions of the national service officer are pending.

REPAIRERS OF BRITISH SHIPS GO ON STRIKE

The Industrial Union of Marine Shipbuilding Workers yesterday called a strike of 6,000 of its members at the Robins Dry Dock and Repair Company's Brooklyn (U.S.) yard which is repairing damaged British merchantmen.

The strike was called to back the union's demand for an increase in wages.

Add OXO to your vegetable water and you have a delicious soup — almost a meal in itself. This extra nourishment and goodness makes a welcome addition to war time meals. See how the family will enjoy its rich beefy flavour.

Still 1d. each — 6d. packet of 6

OXO MAKES IT BEEFY

Daily Mirror

NOV. 7

No. 11,828 — ONE PENNY
Registered at the G.P.O. as a Newspaper.

WE MUST HAVE A SECOND FRONT

↓ SAYS ↓

Deferred 25's must join army

DEFERRED calling-up of men under 25 (when they register) 's to be cancelled. Reservations for these men, except those in a special scheme—for example, agriculture and mining—are to be cancelled, too

There are two "cancelling dates" — December 1, 1941, and January 1, 1942.

These men are affected on December 1:—

Men aged 19 at the date of registration, in occupations reserved at age 21.

Men, 19 and 20 at registration, reserved at 23.

Men 19 to 21 at registration, reserved at 25 and over.

Cancellations on January 1, 1942, affect:

Men 20 at registration, reserved at 21.

Men 21 and 22 at registration, reserved at 23.

Men, 22 to 24 at registration, reserved at 25 and over.

Individual employers will be told of employees affected, and the "cancellation" date.

So many women are coming into war work that the reserve age of 18 for men fabric hands (aircraft, except balloon) is to be raised to 25 on January 1, 1942.

The released men will have their medical examinations this month or in December.

1,200 hours sabotaged

TWELVE hundred precious hours of production were wasted at an aircraft works near London last night.

As a protest against the dismissal of three of their fellow workers, 600 men and women downed tools two hours before the usual stopping time.

This is not the way to settle a grievance. There are other ways . . . which do not hamper the war effort. Twelve hundred hours is equivalent to fifty days. And a man can do a lot of work in that time

"There was no justification for their action," a works official told the Daily Mirror.

"The three men were 'released through the proper channels. They will be placed somewhere else in a day or two."

Milk cut is now 15 p.c.

Milk sales are to be cut by 10 per cent. from next Sunday to ensure that there is no shortage of supplies for priority classes.

This additional cut means that sales will be reduced by a total of 15 per cent. on the basis of the sales of the week ended October 25.

The cut is necessary to ensure that supplies to children, adolescents, schools, hospitals, invalids and expectant mothers are maintained.

U.S. join in world defence
—Roosevelt

AMERICANS insist on their right to join in the defence of the world against the Axis," declare President Roosevelt yesterday

He was addressing delegates to the International Labour Organisation Conference in the White House.

"We must furnish arms to Britain, Russia and China, and we must do it now—to-day," he declared.

"Germany has imported about 2,000,000 foreign civilian labourers. They have changed occupied areas into great slave areas for Nazi rulers.

"BERLIN IS THE PRINCIPAL SLAVE MARKET OF THE WORLD.

"American workers are under no illusions as to the fate awaiting them, and their free labour organisations, if Hitler wins.

He spoke of the "limited sacrifices" of Americans in the war, and added: "We have not, like the heroic people of Britain, had to withstand a deluge of death from the skies.

Chinese Sacrifices

"Nor can we even grasp the full extent of the sacrifices that the people of China are making in their struggle for freedom from aggression. We have, in amazement, witnessed the Russians oppose the Nazi war machine. . . .

"Most heroic of all, however, has been the struggle of the common men and women of Europe, from Norway to Greece, against the brutal force which, however powerful, will forever be inadequate to crush the fight for freedom.

"As far as we in the United States are concerned, that struggle shall not be in vain."

FIGHTERS' CHANNEL SWEEP

Our fighters continued offensive patrols over the Channel and Occupied territory yesterday. Barges and gun positions in the Dunkirk area were attacked. Three enemy fighters were destroyed in combat; three of our fighters are missing.

A SECOND front in Europe must definitely appear in the near future," Stalin declared last night. He added that he hoped one would be established.

Lack of it was the chief factor operating against the Red Army. The other factor was shortage of tanks and planes.

But tanks and planes, together with valuable raw materials, were coming from Britain and the U.S.

Russia had entered into a great coalition with Britain and the United States. This made defeat of Hitler's Germany absolutely certain.

Addressing the Moscow Soviet in connection with the twenty-fourth anniversary of the October Revolution, Stalin declared:

"Our Red Army, Navy and Air Force have already filled the rivers with the enemy's blood, but the enemy does not stop throwing fresh reserves to the front to achieve his aim before winter sets in

Why Hess Came to Britain

"We have lost 350,000 men killed, 378,000 missing, and 1,020,000 wounded. During the same period the enemy has lost in killed, wounded and prisoners over 4,500,000.

"There is no doubt that after four months of war the enemy's strength, which was certainly over-estimated, is falling, while our reserves are coming in increasing numbers.

"The enemy planned to finish us in one or one and a half months, and to reach the Ural Mountains in an even shorter period. This crazy plan has completely failed.

The Germans expected that a general coalition against the U.S.S.R. would be created with the participation of the United States, and that our country would be isolated.

"THEY HOPED, TOO, THAT GREAT BRITAIN WOULD JOIN THIS COALITION, AND THAT WAS THE REASON WHY HESS WAS SENT TO ENGLAND—TO TRY TO PERSUADE THE BRITISH POLITICIANS TO JOIN THE COALITION AGAINST THE U.S.S.R.

"However, Hess did not succeed in his task. On the contrary, a mighty coalition was created. Instead of isolation, new allies joined the Soviet Union.

"Another German hope was that the Soviet regime would crack

Continued on Back Page

SEBASTOPOL UNDER FIRE, NAZIS CLAIM

SEBASTOPOL, Russian naval base in the Crimea, is under fire from German artillery, Berlin claimed last night.

The claim followed the earlier admission that the German forces were at the outer defences and twenty miles from the city.

The position in the Crimea is admittedly serious, particularly as Sebastopol is the base of the Black Sea Fleet, but it is known that the Russian positions there are strongly fortified and well supplied.

The Russian midnight communiqué reported fighting on all fronts, and said that yesterday thirty-four planes were destroyed near Moscow.

Moscow Thrust Held

On the Moscow front, the weight of the German offensive remains centred in the Tula sector, south of the capital.

Combined with this attack, fierce thrusts are still being made over the arc-like front around Mojaisk, Kalinin and Volokolamsk.

Little news is available of the fighting in the Ukraine, but it is known that the Russians are still holding Rostov.

Further west, Berlin claimed today that Russian forces in the area between Voroshilovgrad, seventy-five miles north-west of Rostov, and the Donetz River had been forced back.

The fighting round Leningrad still centres on the German front to the west of the city, where Russian counter-attacks show no sign of diminishing.

£250,000,000 AID FROM U.S.

President Roosevelt last night authorised Lease-Lend aid to the Soviet Union amounting to £250,000,000.

There will be no interest payable, and Russia will not start repayment till five years after the end of the war.

The announcement came shortly after Stalin, in his speech in Moscow, had spoken of the great and growing assistance from Britain and the United States.

THAMES GUNS IN ACTION

Anti - aircraft guns were active in one area of the Thames Estuary last night. Firing was sharp for about ten minutes. Bombs fell in East Anglia and S.E. England. Damage was slight.

SEND MORE AIRGRAPHS

Make more use of the airgraph letters system is the advice of the Director of Army Postal Services after a 17,000-mile tour of the Middle East. Double the present number of 33,000 daily can be taken.

Daily Mirror

NOV. 8

No. 11,829   ONE PENNY
Registered at the G.P.O. as a Newspaper.

ENEMY ADMITS MOSCOW PUSH IS HELD

Soldier gets Fate's blitz

A SOLDIER has come home from Tobruk. He was laden with gifts for his family. But he found that his wife is in prison, his home is sold up, and his four children are in Barnstaple public assistance institution.

He is Sergeant William A. Wheelan. Last year, in the Middle East, he received a cable from his wife asking his consent to the children —Patrick, 9; Jean, 7; John, 5; and Hilary, 3— going to Canada. He said yes.

Later, he read that a ship going to Canada with children had been sunk. He suffered agonies of uncertainty. Finally, as he had no news, he hoped for the best.

But more bitter blows were in store for this man in the Libyan desert.

Then—Divorce Cable

His wife cabled again—asking for a divorce.

He was unable to obtain compassionate leave. No answers came to his cables home.

Then he got leave. But it was cancelled when he was suddenly sent to Tobruk.

Two days before he finally left for home he got another cable —about the children.

Frantically he cabled the police.

He arrived home at Weston-super-Mare to find he had no home. His wife was in prison for harbouring a deserter and neglecting her children.

Sergeant Wheelan has just visited his children in the institution. He had meant to tell them stories of Tobruk, to take them souvenirs of his Libyan campaign.

But when he saw them he had no heart to give them anything but a few sweets and odds and ends. He could scarcely speak to them.

A.T.S. suicide over salute

A N M.P.'s daughter in the A.T.S. failed to salute a woman officer. She was reprimanded and apologised.

Then she went out, climbed 40ft. up an electricity pylon—and killed herself.

A verdict of Suicide while her mind was unbalanced was recorded at a Guildford inquest yesterday on Miss Mary Clement Davies, 24.

Corporal Edith Hawkins, A.T.S., said that during an inspection, Miss Davies spoke to Miss Steel, an officer. Miss Davies failed to salute, so she checked her, and Miss Davies said she would apologise.

"She appeared just a wee bit snappy," said Corporal Hawkins.

Later the corporal went to Miss Davies' room. She flew into a "wee bit of temper," and the corporal reported to Miss Steel that Miss Davies would not come.

Second Subaltern Carmen Misbet-Steel said that when Miss Davies asked if she might go out, instead of playing the piano at a concert she gave Miss Davies permission.

"The Way She Spoke"

Miss Davies did not salute, and she had a conversation with Corporal Hawkins about the way Miss Davies spoke to her.

"I went to Miss Davies's room," she continued, "to check her for having failed to salute, and also for not carrying out instructions of Corporal Hawkins, who had given her orders to come back to me. Miss Davies then apolo-

Continued on Back Page

BOMBS ON N.E. COAST

Bombs were dropped by enemy planes on the north-east coast last night. Two houses were demolished in a coastal village. Three people were killed and several others injured. Ground defences were in action.

EVEN IF IT COSTS U.S. BILLIONS...

A MERICA is ready to spend "fifteen, or twenty-five, or forty, or seventy-five billion dollars" to aid in suppressing Hitler.

[75 billion dollars is about 19 thousand million pounds.]

Mr. Cordell Hull, U.S. Secretary of State, makes this statement on a report of his interviews with the Finnish Minister in Washington.

He told M. Procope that Russia was willing to make territorial concessions to Finland if peace could be arranged.

The question for Finland was whether she would be content to regain territory, and halt; or whether to go on, become a vassal of Hitler—and lose.

Helsinki radio last night denied any statement that Finland intended to end hostilities against Russia.

Then Berlin radio said it was "confirmed" that there was a "certain termination of operations" in the Karelian.

'Tugboat Annie's' tug is helping war

Remember "Tugboat Annie"? Remember Marie Dressler and Wallace Beery wise-cracking in that old tug which was sunk in the famous film?

That tug was worth just about enough to raise her from the bottom after the film producers had finished with her. She was bought by the British from America, and now, renamed Sabine, she has a tough naval crew who take her out into the North Sea.

Her job is to do the "dirty work" of the Navy. She brings back into port those ships which have been so badly mined, torpedoed or bombed that they cannot reach port under their own steam.

Her great feat was to bring in half a tanker. The tanker had been broken in two by a torpedo and the after-part sank.

Yesterday the First Lord of the Admiralty met the crew at Immingham and congratulated them on their valuable work.

Hurricanes carry bombs

H URRICANES have been equipped to carry bombs, the Air Ministry announced last night.

This will increase the power of the R.A.F. fighting force in low-level attacks on shipping and ground targets.

These fighter-bombers have already proved their worth in attacks in Northern France.

Their bombs are fitted with delayed-action fuses to enable the aircraft to get clear before the explosion.

Hurricanes carrying bombs took part yesterday in a successful low-level attack on a factory and gun positions in France. Hits were obtained with bombs on the factory building and a number of fires broke out.

T HE Germans admit that their latest offensive against Moscow is making no progress.

Their military spokesman last night declared that it was the weather, not the Russians, who were responsible for the hold-up.

He denied that any fresh offensive against Moscow was in progress and asserted that they could afford to wait for more suitable weather.

The Russians, however, say that the offensive has been going on for four days without making any headway.

Terrific storms of sleet and snow are raging, and the cold is intense and is getting worse.

A Stockholm version of the German military spokesman's statement is that the Germans have not started a Moscow offensive, but are "merely continuing military operations according to plan."

The Germans are hammering their heaviest blows on the flanks. Northwest of the capital, at Kalinin, where they are trying to cross the Volga, the murderous pace of the fighting has been maintained for three weeks.

On the southern flank at Tula, Soviet soldiers and workers alike are fighting for the life of this important strategic city.

Despite the vastness of the Moscow front and the intensity of the struggle there, German pressure has not showed any slackening on most of the other fronts. There is heavy fighting east of Kharkov, on the approaches to Rostov, and in the Crimea.

Infantry Break Through

The latest German communiqué says that in the Crimea, German and Rumanian troops are successfully continuing the pursuit, despite the difficult mountain country and stubborn fights with enemy rearguards.

It claims that in the central sector (Moscow front) infantry divisions broke through strongly-fortified enemy positions and captured many prisoners and guns.

NAZIS' GOD— HITLER

From JOHN WALTERS

New York, Friday.

O N every German altar will be nothing but a copy of "Mein Kampf" when the Nazis have crushed Christianity and established their "pure Aryan national church."

A secret German Government document containing this and other revelations which was mentioned by President Roosevelt in his October 27 speech was today printed in full in "Life" magazine. Here are extracts from the document which was drawn up by Alfred Rosenberg:

"The National Church has no pastors, chaplains or priests, but only National Reich orators

"It demands immediate cessation of the publishing and dissemination of the Bible in Germany. The National Church is conscious that 'Mein Kampf' is the greatest of all documents

"The National Church will

Continued on Back Page

EX-M.O.I. CHIEF DEAD

Mr. Frank Pick, former chief of London Transport and Director-General, Ministry of Information, died suddenly last night at his London home.

He would have been 63 on November 23.

AUSSIES MAY BE IN CAUCASUS FIGHT SOON

Major-General Albert Pewtrell, Commander of the Australian First Division, is quoted in Canberra newspapers as saying that Australian troops might soon be fighting with the Russians in the Caucasus.—British United Press.

GERMAN RADIO SILENCE

All German stations went off the air last night—even Breslau, which has hitherto transmitted during the heaviest raids.

Typist now says, 'Fares, please'

L IKE the bus girls, nearly all of us are leading more exhausting lives, tackling stiffer jobs, and finding that it takes more than peacetime energy to see us through a hard, exacting wartime day.

On the Home Front, battles are being won every day — big little victories over tiredness, irritability, nervous strain. Nature's own tonic, sound, natural sleep (whenever you can get it) is the best thing ever for your new wartime lives. A warming cup of Bourn-vita, still at the old peacetime price, will help you to get your essential ration of body-and-mind-restoring SLEEP. Bourn-vita is a night food-drink with special nerve-soothing properties that bring sleep very quickly.

GET THE BEST OUT OF YOUR SLEEP WITH—

CADBURY'S BOURN-VITA

STILL AT PRE-WAR PRICE   1/5 PER LB.

They were all optimists—

C HURCHILL (in a northeastern town): "We have passed through the darkest and most perilous period of this struggle and are once more masters of our own destiny.

✦ ✦ ✦

"The Russians are struggling and battling vigorously, with results which are particularly significant.

"On the other side of the Atlantic our kith and kin are struggling to see that we get all we need, and we find ourselves in goodly company.

"We are moving forward and looking forward, however long the road.

✦ ✦ ✦

"All will be well for the world. There will be a crown of honour to those who have endured and have never failed. History will accord it to them for having set an example to the whole human race."

S TALIN (addressing a military review in Moscow Red Square): "Germany is bleeding to death. . . . Another six months—a year, perhaps—and Germany will burst under the weight of her crimes.

"The enemy calculated that after the first blow our army would be dispersed, and our country would be forced to her knees, but the enemy badly miscalculated.

"The enemy is not as strong as certain terror-stricken weak intellectuals picture him. The devil is not as terrible as he is painted.

"Who can deny that our Army has more than once put the much lauded German troops to panicky flight?"

"The German Fascist invaders are facing disaster.

"The spirit of revolt is gaining possession, not only of the nations of Europe who fell under the yoke of the German invader, but of the German people themselves, who see no end to war."

B ENESH, President of Czechoslovakia (at Glasgow University): "I do not think Germany will endure another winter of war.

"I believe now that Hitlerism is doomed, and that the end may be accelerated if the people of Britain and their Allies will make a supreme effort now.

"We must know clearly what we are to do if we are to prevent Germany's lack of education from seeking violent expression in a war every ten or twenty years.

"We must uproot every vestige of the Nazi theory—otherwise we shall still be confronted with the German military machine.

"The German Army, though it will support Hitler as long as possible, will get rid of Hitler when it has decided that a German peace, and the preservation of her present conquest, can be purchased at the price of sacrificing Hitler and his régime."

D E GAULLE (in London): "The tide of victory is on the point of turning. The price of victory is currency all can provide — overwhelming mechanised force.

"The rhythm of Germany's colossal attacks has slowed down."

except

G OEBBELS (in a surprisingly serious article in Das Reich): "Only if Germany accomplishes final victory will it be possible to gain everything. But if Germany loses, more than everything will be lost.

"Every German must now give his all. If he complains of hardships, he will always be able to find another German who is suffering still more.

"The fate of the German people is hard and bitter."

Daily Mirror

NOV. 10

No. 11,830   ♦   ONE PENNY
Registered at the G.P.O. as a Newspaper.

TOMORROW is the twenty-first Poppy Day. Forty million poppies will be on sale. For the twenty-first time Britons are asked to remember the war-maimed, the blind and the dead.

This year more than ever the answer to the appeal should be generous, for the responsibilities of the Haig Fund have been enormously increased by the present fight for freedom.

Poppy day

YOU can help by:—
Paying generously for your poppy;
Offering your services as a seller;
Displaying posters;
Sending donations.

The organisers are determined to beat last year's record of £595,000 and ask for YOUR generous co-operation.

★

In a broadcast appeal from India last night, General Wavell said: " It is our most dangerous hour, and yet our greatest hour. To some of those 'who fought and saved us in 'he last war it must have seemed at one time as if their victory had been wasted.

" Today they know, and the world knows, that the old spirit of our people was only sleeping in the years of peace; that it needed but the challenge of the wild beast to call it forth in even sterner mood to meet a sterner danger."

★

Remembrance Sunday was observed by special services in London yesterday, and an Empire Field of Remembrance was opened at Westminster Abbey.

The King and Queen, with the Princesses, attended a service for troops in a country church.

Girl lost both arms, says "many worse off"

COLONEL S. W. Ashwanden, D.S.O., chairman of the British Legion, told this story yesterday.

A few weeks ago he visited a Ministry of Pensions Hospital in the north.

" In one ward," he said, " four of five women there had lost a leg. The other, a girl, 22, had lost both arms. I talked with her and after a while she looked up at me, tears streaming down her cheeks, and said, ' Many are much worse off than we are.' "

The colonel paused, and then added quietly: " Her sister was one of the four without a leg. Her father has a leg off and her mother is dead—the result of one bomb. Can we beat that for courage ? "

FINNS' "NO" TO U.S. PEACE DEMAND

Helsinki radio stated last night:

" The United States has exerted pressure on the Finnish Government to end the war with Russia.

" The Finnish Government will answer the American demand shortly, and its answer will be in the negative."

KNEE PADS FOR F.A.P.

A pair of knee pads is to be issued to each first-aid post to save the stockings of women members, who say their stockings wear out quickly after kneeling to attend casualties.

NAVY SINKS 11 ITALIAN SHIPS

A SMALL force of British warships yesterday wiped out two convoys of ten enemy supply ships and inflicted severe loss on the escorting Italian warships which were superior both in numbers and in armament.

Not one British warship was damaged. Not one British sailor was hurt.

Once again the Italian Navy refused to fight and left the ships they were supposed to protect to their fate.

Two British six-inch cruisers, Aurora and Penelope, and two destroyers, Lance and Lively, were sent to smash the convoys, which were escorted by two powerful Italian eight-inch cruisers of the Trento class and several destroyers.

Despite the disparity of force, Captain W. G. Agnew,

ITALY LOSES HALF HER DESTROYERS

Italy had sixty-one destroyers at the start of the war. We have sunk thirty of these—so far.

of the Aurora, who led the action, attacked.

This was what he did to the Italians:—

Nine of the ten supply ships were set on fire and sunk.

The tenth, a 10,000-ton laden tanker, burnt for ten hours. She is a total loss.

One Italian destroyer was sunk.

Thus the Italians lost eleven ships—WITHOUT A FIGHT.

At least one other Italian destroyer was seriously damaged.

Continued on Back Page

BLIND MAN MADE SHERIFF

FIVE children, all under 16 will watch a father who has never seen them, made Sheriff of Hull today.

Led by his wife, Mr. Godfrey Robinson will go into the Guildhall and leave it as the King's direct representative in Hull.

But he will never see the magnificent robes of office, nor the pomp of the ceremony. Mr. Robinson was blinded serving with the Royal Artillery in Belgium during the last war.

For twenty years the new Sheriff has worn a neat bandage round his eyes.

He is chairman of the Hull and East Riding Institute for the Blind and chairman of the Industries Committee of the National Institute for the Blind.

Anglo-U.S. plan shock for Japs

VHEN the Japanese mission to Washington 'ives with its so-called ultimatum to Roosevelt, its members will be confronted with joint Anglo-U.S. plans for action in the Far East.

Plans for combined Anglo-American use of bases in the Pacifi: in the event of a crisis are understood to have been considered.

War in 3 Weeks

" The United States will be at war with Japan in two or three weeks, or the entire matter will be settled," said Mr. Martin Dies, head of the committee which investigates un-American activities.

" There is a belief in Washington," he continued, " that the United States Navy will be engaged actively in war within ninety days, and that there will be a clamour for an American expeditionary force within eight months to a year."

Japan appeared yesterday to be concentrating her main forces in Indo-China in territory within reach of Thailand and Malaya.

Britons have been advised by the British Consul at Amoy to leave Fukien and Kulangsu as soon as possible, according to a Japanese report.

U.S. workers demand war

New York representatives of C.I.O., America's most powerful labour organisation, have defied its Isolationist leader, John L. Lewis, by demanding American intervention in the war.

In a statement disclosing the stand they will make at their Detroit congress on November 17, these New York representatives say:—

" It is no longer sensible, while our Navy battles in the Atlantic, to qualify our statement with such phrases as " short of war' or ' by peaceful means.' War has come to us. We must meet and fight it."

HUNS CLAIM BIG GAINS IN CRIMEA

GERMANY yesterday claimed the capture of Yalta, coastal pleasure resort and former playground of the Tsars, in the South-East Crimea, thirty-eight miles due east of Sebastopol. If this is true Sebastopol is cut off from the rest of the Crimea, and nearly all the south-eastern coast in under German control.

No mention of fighting on the other Russian fronts was made in the German communique.

The German drive towards Rostov-on-Don has made no progress, although the Germans are launching strong local thrusts with tanks to find a weak point in the Russian line between Taganrog and Voroshilovgrad, about 100 miles north-west of Rostov.

Claims by Hungary that her troops broke through the Russian lines at Voroshilovgrad were not confirmed in Moscow.

At several points on the Moscow front, which the German reports of recent fighting have not even mentioned, the Russians are engaged in fierce local counter-attacks "hich they admit have been "successful since the recapture of two villages near Volokolamsk, seventy-five miles north-west of the capital.

Street fighting is still going

Continued on Back Page

R.A.F. bash Germany's arms towns

THE R.A.F.'s mightiest thirty-six hours' offensive of the war came to a climax on Saturday night with fierce blows at the heart of the Nazi arms industry in Essen and other Ruhr towns.

The attack followed terrific day and night raids on Hitler's Western Front, in which between 600 and 800 bombers and fighters took part.

Bombers' crews saw violent explosions and watched large fires spring up which lit the sky for many miles on the return journey.

Eight of our bombers are missing from these attacks, making forty-five lost over the week-end.

Factories on Fire

R.A.F. bombers raided Brindisi for three and a half hours early on Saturday morning, and in the moonlight started many fires.

Objectives included railway marshalling yards and an aircraft factory. One pilot stated that he saw twenty fires growing in size as he left.

R.A.F. LOST 91 PLANES

R.A.F. losses from the bombing of Germany and occupied territory from November 2 to 9 were eighty-one aircraft.

In the Middle East our losses were ten aircraft.

Axis losses over the same period were eighteen aircraft, but a false impression is given by a mere comparison of losses.

S.E. COAST TOWN RAIDED LAST NIGHT

Several enemy aircraft made a sharp attack on a South-East Coast town last night.

High explosives and incendiaries damaged a number of houses and caused fires. Most of the incendiaries landed on open ground, where they were quickly extinguished. No one was killed and only a few people slightly injured.

"DON'T HAVE CHILDREN"

" Red Vienna," the secret radio station of the Austrian Socialists, yesterday appealed to Austrian women not to have children as long as the war lasts.

Brabazon query to Premier

SPEAKING at a meeting of the Amalgamated Engineers' Union at Southend last night, Jack Tanner, referring to the incident of the T.U.C. when he made his revelation about Colonel Moore-Brabazon, said: " I wonder if the Prime Minister's conscience on this point is as clear as mine."

Pointing out that maximum production had not been reached in this country he went on:

" We are not going to get the men to apply their full energy to their machines and secure maximum production while industry remains in private hands.

Still Private

Profit-makers still dominate the factory in industry today.

" I am tired of hearing the Government urging more sacrifices from the workers. What have employers given up in the interests of the country ?

Alluding to the speech of Lord Beaverbrook on Saturday, he said it was high time that some of these appeals were directed to the employers.

[" *The incident* " referred to by Mr. Jack Tanner is that when Lieutenant - Colonel Moore-Brabazon was alleged by Mr. Tanner to have said that he hoped the Russians and Germans would exterminate each other.]

U.S. OBSERVER IN SYRIA

Major Max Gooler, of the United States Staff of Observers in Cairo, has arrived at Beirut, Syria.

Daily Mirror

NOV. 15

No. 11,835   ONE PENNY
Registered at the G.P.O. as a Newspaper.

12-HOUR BATTLE FAILED TO SAVE ARK ROYAL

Rescuer was his girl's brother

ON the battlefield a wounded soldier hung helplessly over the shoulder of another man. Private Clifford Rollings struggled through shellfire and bursting bombs carrying his human load.

Hiding in shell holes and bushes, he kept the wounded man alive while he dodged the enemy. But just as he was about to make a last dash to safety he too collapsed and both men were captured.

First Meeting

The wounded man was Private James Ripley. Neither knew each other. It was their first meeting.

At the hospital in a German prison camp Rollings visited Ripley as he lay in bed. The wounded man gripped his hand and thanked him for saving his life.

"That's all right, chum. Forget it," said Rollings. "By the way what's your name and where do you come from?"

"My name is Ripley and I come from Brighton. Look down in that locker and you will see a picture of my girl. And she's the prettiest girl in Brighton."

"That's My Sister"

As Rollings was about to tell the wounded man that he also came from Brighton he picked up the photograph and shouted: "My God, that's my sister."

Yesterday, in Birmingham, Mrs. Rubena Rollings and her sister-in-law, Miss Nancy Rollings, 20, joined the A.T.S. together as thanksgiving for the safety and friendship of the two men.

Miss Nancy Rollings.

Japs call rejects

JAPAN is extending conscription to bring men previously rejected as unfit into the Services.

This development was announced as Mr. Kurusu, special envoy, reached San Francisco on his way to Washington to discuss a settlement of the Far East tension.

The Japanese Government has asked for another £288,000,000 for military purposes, and is reported to have sent two crack regiments to Hainan Island, off the coast of China.

Meanwhile Roosevelt has ordered the withdrawal of U.S. Marines from China.—British United Press.

TINNED FOOD PLAN— FORTNIGHT'S DELAY

YOU won't be able to buy sardines, baked beans or corned beef next week after all.

The points ration scheme for canned food, due to start on Monday, has been postponed until December 1.

Announcing the news yesterday, the Food Minister confessed that the delay had been largely caused by the over-optimism of himself and his advisers in believing that stocks could be got to the shops in time.

"We imposed a gigantic task on ourselves, on the food trade and on the transport organisations—all hampered by shortage of labour," he said.

"And we found it impossible to get the eighty million pounds of food involved distributed to a quarter-million retailers in the fortnight we allowed ourselves."

Half Rations

He revealed that while a number of shops—mainly multiple and chain stores—had received their full quota, thousands of others, including most of the small traders, were still short.

While I hate letting the public down, I received so many representations from the trade asking for delay that I decided to postpone the scheme," said the Minister.

From December 1-14 only eight-points coupons instead of sixteen will be valid. The remaining eight will be automatically cancelled.

Canned Fish Prices

New maximum prices for canned fish, to operate, presumably, from December 1, are:—

Salmon, grade 1, 8½d. per ½lb. to 1s. 10½d. lb.; grade 2, 7d. to 1s. 5½d.; grade 3, 5d. to 1s.

Herrings, pilchards and mackerel, 5d. per 5oz. or 6oz. tin to 10d. lb. Pilchard fillets, 8½d. lb. Small pilchards, 5d. to 5½d. per ½lb.

Crayfish, 7½d. per ½lb., 1s. 0½d. per ½lb. Cod, haddock, catfish, cod roes and fish balls, 1s. 6d. lb., 2s. 8d. 2lb.

Kipper snacks, 7d.

Struggle for Kerch

WHILE still stubbornly holding the enemy at the outer defences of Kerch—bridgehead from the Crimea to the Caucasus—the Russian "Commando" troops are playing havoc with the enemy flanks along the coast.

These shock troops are making frequent landings on the coast, shattering enemy communications and gun positions.

The German High Command communique says Kerch is now being shelled by artillery and is being heavily bombed.

One German spokesman said yesterday that the Kerch Straits were "an even better rehearsal ground for the crossing of the English Channel than Crete."

20 Villages Retaken

On the Moscow front, the Russians report successes on both flanks—at Tula, to the south-west, and at Kalinin, to the north-west.

Tass agency says that in the past twenty-four hours the Germans have been driven out of twenty villages in the Kalinin sector.

Berlin reports on the Moscow front say the Russians "are fighting desperately. They are constantly bringing up reserves who occupy superbly - built camouflaged positions."

In the Donetz area there is still fighting with no change in the position. In the north, the Russians have made gains around Murmansk, and they still hold the initiative at Leningrad, admitted Berlin radio last night.

BRITAIN'S famous aircraft carrier Ark Royal struggled along for nearly twelve hours with a gaping hole amidships after she was torpedoed.

The captain, senior officers and engineering staff, who had remained on board, fought all that time to bring her to Gibraltar.

But at 4.30 a.m. yesterday Captain L. E. H. Maund sadly realised that his ship could not be saved, and gave the order "abandon ship." Two hours later the majestic Ark Royal plunged to her grave.

"Just before she sank she had a list to starboard of 35 degrees," said an officer of a destroyer which stood by to the end. "We realised she was finished. She toppled over like a tired child. Her stern reared up for a moment, and then gently she slid beneath the waves."

An Exchange Telegraph Company special correspondent writes:

"I was in my cabin washing before going into tea when a torpedo hit us amidships on the starboard side. There was a sudden shuddering crash, the lights went out and I was flung against the wall.

"For fully a minute the ship shuddered like a harp string, and I knew we had been torpedoed. Grabbing a lifebelt I ran out along the passage-way in the dim light.

"I saw the officers and ratings filing up the ladder leading to the upper deck. Often I have heard of the coolness of Navy men in a crisis, and these men were as calm as though they were going down the gangway at Gibraltar.

"Damned hard luck on the old lady, sir," said a rating to an officer.

Down came the officer's hand with a friendly pat on the sailor's shoulder.

When I arrived on the quarter-deck I found a score of officers pumping up their lifebelts. The Ark was listing alarmingly to starboard and the white waves flowing past were ominously stained with dark brown oil. The fuel in the engines was still driving us forward but every minute the deck slant increased till it was difficult to stand upright.

"Abandon Ship!"

Suddenly the vibration of the engines beneath our feet died away, re-started for a moment and then stopped. We glanced at one another, and then through the loudspeaker above us came the words: "Everybody to the port side." Almost before we could move came the voice again: "Prepare to abandon ship."

"We reached the boat stations on the weather deck and found that it was impossible, owing to the heavy list, to launch the motor-boats. Crowding the decks were hundreds of the ship's crew, some in overalls and some in underwear.

Ropes began to snake down from the flight deck, and cork rafts splashed into the sea. Then we saw a destroyer pulling alongside.

An officer ordered the men to form up four deep and, although for ought they knew the ship might have heeled over and gone down any moment, they obeyed instantly. Soon the destroyer came close under our rails. Ropes leaped up from

Continued on Back Page

From RAF to £10 a week

"DAILY MIRROR" SPECIAL NEWS

SKILLED R.A.F. men are to be released to work in aircraft factories — at civilian pay of about £10 a week. Worked out by the Air Ministry and the Ministry of Labour, the scheme will boost production profitably, for instead of having to train men, the factories will have expert engineers, whose first and last love is aircraft engines.

Certain branches of the R.A.F., notably aero-engine fitting trades, have been asked for volunteers for periods up to six months, and officials are sorting out the applicants.

There will be no shortage of willing men—for while an R.A.F. fitter may receive as little as 28s. a week, his opposite number in a factory is taking home £10 and more weekly.

Can Be Spared

There is to be no compulsion. The main conditions are that volunteers must be willing to go wherever the Ministry of Labour requires them, and that the approval of their Commanding Officers must first be obtained.

"This is the best news for a long time," said the works chief of an aircraft factory to the Daily Mirror. "One good man is worth his weight in gold at present, and these airmen know their jobs from A to Z. We'll

Continued on Back Page

Monckton is at Baku

IT was stated officially this morning that the plane in which Sir Walter Monckton, Middle East Press chief, left Kuibishev landed safely on Thursday—at Baku, Russian oil port.

Accompanying Sir Walter were M. Litvinov, Soviet Ambassador to the U.S., and his wife and child, Mr. Laurence Steinhardt, U.S. Ambassador to Russia, and Mr. Quentin Reynolds, radio commentator.

The plane had been reported overdue. Cairo stated authoritatively yesterday that the plane had landed at Pahlevi, Iran.

This was, however, doubted last night by the Soviet Embassy at Teheran.

U.S. TRANSFER A LINER TO BRITAIN

The U.S. liner George Washington was transferred to Britain on September 26, it was announced in Washington yesterday.

The 23,788-ton vessel was used as a transport in the last war, and carried the Wilson Peace Conference. The ship was seized from her German owners in 1917.

MUST HAVE 18B, OR—

The Minister of Home Security, defending Defence Regulation 18 B yesterday, said that if his powers were unduly limited, with the result that he could not do his job, he would say to the Commons and the country, "Let somebody else do it."

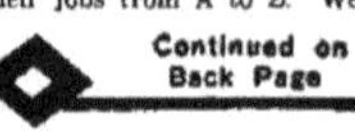

Continued on Back Page

Daily Mirror

NOV. 17

No. 11,836   ONE PENNY
Registered at the G.P.O. as a Newspaper.

Yesterday began the **22nd WEEK** of the war in Russia.

BLIZZARD SWEEPS CRIMEA IN 11-DAY BATTLE

Japs make war threat to U.S.A.

Mr. Cordell Hull, U.S. Secretary of State, and Mr. Kurusu, special Japanese messenger.

"The views of the two countries have generally been made clear through conversations which have now lasted for more than six months," said Mr. Togo.

"Consequently I believe it must be evident to the United States Government that, viewed even from a technical angle, there is no necessity for spending much time on negotiations.

"The Japanese Government are directing their best efforts to the successful conclusion of the negotiations, but there is naturally a limit to our conciliatory attitude.

"Should an occasion arise such as might menace the very existence of our Empire, or compromise the prestige of Japan as a great Power, it goes without saying that Japan must face it with a firm and resolute attitude."

"Fighting Chance of Peace"

Mr. Togo said Great Britain and the United States had established encircling positions against Japan by inducing Australia, the Netherlands East Indies and the Chungking regime to join in.

The Japanese Prime Minister, General Tojo, also made a speech in which he implied that Japan would risk war with Britain and America in her determination to press on with her greater East Asia expansion programme.

Kurusu will be met today by very solemn Cordell Hull, who will tell him there can be no American friendship with Japan unless she abandons Axis ties, and expresses willingness to withdraw her forces from China and Indo-China.

Canadians Sent To Far East.—Page 8.

'I WAS SACKED' SAYS KEYES

Admiral of the Fleet Sir Roger Keyes revealed yesterday that he had been sacked from his job as chief of the Commandos, Britain's new shock troops—secret work on which he has been engaged for the past fifteen months.

Sir Roger authorised a statement that he did not relinquish his appointment—which included the responsibility for organising and training the special Service troops known as Commandos, also the command of this Force.

The statement adds, "These responsibilities, however, were withdrawn a month ago."

JACK JONES GRAVELY ILL

Mr. Jack Jones, who figured in many Commons scenes as M.P. for Silvertown (E.), is critically ill at Leigh-on-Sea, where he has lived since he resigned owing to ill-health.

Tramped 50 miles barefoot

DRAGGED through the waves by his parachute after a jump for life over the Mediterranean, a young Canadian flying officer fought to free himself—then found that his rubber dinghy would not work.

He struggled out of his heavy flying kit, swam for seven hours, spent a night on a rocky island, walked fifty miles barefoot on the North Africa coast clad only in underpants and went sixty hours without water.

When he reached a British camp he was arrested until his identity was proved.

"It was tantalising," he said, "to walk on the beach in clear water and yet be unable to drink it."

BLITZ—ON RECORDS

ONLY bombs were lacking in a stupendous ear-splitting air-raid on New York, from which inhabitants are now recovering.

The sound of humming planes and explosions roared from loud speakers, cables John Walters, *Daily Mirror* New York correspondent. There were 55,000 wardens and 17,000 auxiliary firemen, fleets of ambulances and mobile kitchens.

This great test to discover how New York would behave while being bombed, started while Mayor La Guardia and thousands of his wardens and auxiliary firemen gathered in Union Square.

Suddenly the sirens started and with them amplified gramophone records of the 1940 London blitz. Some wardens twirled small rattles.

Normandie "Hit"

Then flares were dropped and fireworks went bang - bang. A.R.P. workers threw sand on the flames. Auxiliary firemen mounted ladders to "save" people from bombed buildings while professional firemen criticised their technique.

The awful news was broken to La Guardia that the liner Normandie had been bombed. Followed by a procession of reporters, wardens and firemen, he sped to the docks. They got there in time. The Normandie was announced saved.

"People who sneer at these demonstrations will be the first to cry for help in case of actual attack," said the Mayor.

But a good time was had by all—thanks to the absence of bombs.

On practice he downed a Nazi

On a special practice flight, a few miles off the north-east coast yesterday a D.F.C. squadron leader Spitfire pilot shot down a Ju. 88.

It was the second bomber shot down yesterday and the fourth during the week-end.

Criticism of Govt. essential

says Minister's M.P.-secretary

"**C**RITICISM of the war's conduct is essential," declared Mr. Wilfrid Roberts, M.P., holder of the Government post of Parliamentary Private Secretary to the Air Minister, at Carlisle on Saturday.

"My experience throughout this war has been that criticism in the House of Commons has never been that the Government were going too fast or taking on too much," he said.

"It has always been that not enough was being done, that there was a lack of organisation or bad organisation, and that more ought to be done.

"Yet the Prime Minister, although welcoming debates in the House of Commons, shows a certain sensitiveness about criticism. I think that is a mistake."

Mr. Roberts believes that while the Navy and Air Force must play an immense part it will rest ultimately with the Army to win the war.

"The Army will not be able to win the war by remaining in England"

★

In the face of inefficiency and muddle he did not believe in sitting back, folding one's arms and saying: "This is the sort of thing one can expect in a war."

The public should take an intelligent interest in suggesting how things might be done better.

"We in the House of Commons have not been slow to recognise the successes of the Government, and I think it is clearly desirable that all of us, if we are to contribute our maximum effort to this war, should take a lively interest in pointing out its mistakes."

Rome has got the blues

FROM DAVID WALKER

LISBON, Sunday.

THE Italians' low morale, described to me by arrivals by air from Italy, is not due so much to the Mediterranean losses as to food and material conditions.

The weather is very cold, but no heating will be allowed before December 15

Rome Alerts during British raids on Naples cause the population almost to panic. Food difficulties are increasing due to the necessity of sending everything possible to Libya, much of which is sunk.

The last annihilated convoy contained almost the entire vegetable stock of Greece, which was confiscated for this purpose.

Many large clothing stores are closed, as the promised coupons have not been issued.

Germans taunt Italian troops in Greece—David Walker article on page 2.

SIKORSKY AT TOBRUK

It was officially announced in Cairo yesterday that General Sikorsky, the Polish Premier and Commander - in - Chief, visited the Polish forces at Tobruk

---

BATTLE

ONE of the fiercest battles of the Russian war is being fought in snowstorms in the Crimea where, after repeated mass attacks for eleven days, the Germans have made some advance. The Germans have paid dearly for these gains.

Guerrilla forces are harassing the enemy, using snowstorms and darkness as cover for swooping on weak spots in the supply lines.

Many units of the Soviet Regular Army are fighting bitterly behind the German lines. The losses they have inflicted on the enemy have slowed up the Nazi push considerably.

Kerch, key port on the strait leading to the Sea of Azov, is the centre of the most violent fighting in the Crimea, M. Lozovsky, Soviet Press Chief, stated in Kuibishev, the second Soviet capital, last night.

"German infantry fought their way into the streets of Kerch, and are now over-

Continued on Back Page

Million wives to work

ONE million wives are urgently needed to do war jobs or work which will release younger women for work of national importance.

The Minister of Labour, announcing this yesterday, said, "I want to get these married women, either full time or part time, that is half a day, in many of our munition works.

"If not in munition work, I want the married women to help in the distributive trades, in offices and in commercial undertakings.

"I want employers to utilise them on part time if not on full time work to release younger mobile women to fill shells and make munitions.

"I must get these thousands of women into this terrific job."

"Sex Nonsense"

He repudiated responsibility for "this silly sex nonsense" in a reference to problems of man and woman power.

"I approach the problem on terms of equality of men and women alike," he said. "Women are intelligent beings and should be treated as such."

Direction and compulsion might have to be carried out to a far greater length than the British people had ever known before to win the war.

He could not leave a single citizen, man or woman, not doing a job they ought to be doing.

That would he expressed in steps he would be taking shortly, the first of which would be to get rid of the age reservation and have individual reservation.

"Inconveniences will have to be suffered," he added. "I have to ask the younger women to leave home."

Desert army is "The Eighth"

The British Army in the Western Desert is to be called the Eighth Army.

The Western Desert force was one of two armies formed from the Army of the Nile. The other is stationed in Palestine and Syria.

Both are under the supreme command of General Sir Claude Auchinleck, Commander - in - Chief, Middle East.

U.S. STRIKE TALKS FAIL

THE threatened strike by 53,000 U.S. coal miners is on.

Talks to avert the deadlock having collapsed last night, workers in the "captive" mines will not report for work today.

When, at midnight on Saturday, the 53,000 miners stopped work, it was made known that if their demand for a "closed shop" was not met, nearly half a million other miners would strike.

"You all know the terms of our contract," said Mr. John L. Lewis, president of the C.I.O. United Mine Workers, to reporters. "The conferences are terminated. No conclusions reached. We will make separate reports to the President tomorrow. The executives can only make agreement on an open shop basis."

Unqualified support for the efforts of the miners to obtain a closed shop was expressed in a resolution passed in Detroit by the Executive Committee of the Congress of Industrial Organisation.

Daily Mirror

NOV. 20

No. 11,839 — ONE PENNY
Registered at the G.P.O. as a Newspaper.

RUSSIANS SMASH BIG ATTACK ON ROSTOV

A GERMAN attempt to capture Rostov-on-Don, northern gateway to the Caucasus, by a surprise flank attack has ended in complete failure, Moscow announced last night.

Trapped in a pocket twenty-five miles north-east of Rostov, the Germans suffered a heavy defeat, losing thousands of men, 113 tanks—half the number they used—273 lorries and many guns.

General Kleist, commanding the German troops, flung two tank divisions, a mechanised division and an S.S. division into the attack.

His tanks—outnumbering the Russians by six to one—pierced the first and second Soviet defence lines. But the Russian infantry, concealed in deep dugouts, held their ground.

From all sides Soviet artillery poured in a withering fire. The tanks were caught in camouflaged pits, and mines blew off their caterpillar treads.

His Plans Upset

The first day's fighting upset Kleist's plans, which depended on a quick break-through. The Germans wheeled in all directions in an effort to find a weak spot, but everywhere they were thrust back.

Then Soviet planes went into action, carrying out hundreds of low-flying attacks on the German tanks, mechanised columns and artillery.

The Germans are hoping to attack the Caucasus, with its rich oilfields, in a pincer movement. The left arm of the pincers is trying to reach Rostov, while the right arm is hoping to make a sea-borne attack across the Straits from Kerch, Crimean port.

But the Russians are still holding out at Kerch, despite German High Command claims to have captured the town last week, M. Lozovsky, Soviet information chief, announced yesterday.

Apart from these sectors, the most important activity is on the wings of the Moscow front—at Kalinin and Tula—where the Germans are believed to be aiming at splitting the Russian Armies.

Russian reports say that at Kalinin, a new German attempt to smash through has been repulsed after three days' heavy fighting.

In the Tula sector, after massing forces for a week, the Ger-

Continued on Back Page

POLISH CROSS FOR STEAMER'S CAPTAIN

The Polish President has conferred the Cross of Valour with diploma on Captain Duncan Darroch, of the Scotland to Ireland steamer Royal Scotsman, and Second Officer W. R. Pitkeathly.

The Royal Scotsman took part in the evacuation of the Polish forces from France in July, 1940, and the awards are given in recognition of the gallant conduct of the captain, officers, engineers and crew.

Six of the Harvey kiddies, bombed twice out of their Canning Town homes, who were buried for three hours under debris on Tuesday night in the village to which they had been evacuated. Only the baby and their grandmother were hurt.

"O.K." village counts its dead

This column is a reminder to every town and every little village that, though the sirens have been silent lately, TONIGHT MAY BE THE NIGHT OF THE RAID.

Like you, the people of the village in the following story were beginning to feel themselves safe. They had given up using their shelters, were beginning to think of civil defence as dull routine.

Then the siren. And the bomb.

Sensation in Jap parliament

A sensation has been caused in the Japanese Parliament by the resignation of a member following a speech which was banned for publication by the Government. It was described as "improper for this session."

The member, named Miyazawa, was turned over to the disciplinary committee of the House and his resignation accepted by a unanimous vote, says Associated Press.

Apparently in sympathy with Miyazawa, nineteen other members have resigned from the pro-Fascist organisation called the "Throne Rule Assistance Group."

Senator Pepper, member of the Senate Foreign Relations Committee, declared yesterday: "If war is the price of resisting aggression than war will come."

MOST of a village in the south-east of England was wiped out on Tuesday night. Grocers have lost their shops, butcher and baker are looking for new premises.

Mrs. Stone, a newcomer to the village of fewer than 1,500 people was looking after her seven grandchildren, all under twelve—Tommy, Terence, Rose, Mary, Kathleen, Michael and Eileen Harvey—in their home on the high road.

The first bomb covered them in debris—the second one buried them. They all lay there until Army demolition squads and A.R.P. workers dug them out three hours later.

They had been bombed twice from their homes in Canning Town, and had evacuated to this quiet village hoping for safety. Only Michael and the grandmother were injured.

"We're going to our new homes tomorrow," said Mrs.

Continued on Back Page

"JOIN UNION" STRIKE APPEAL BY ROOSEVELT

President Roosevelt yesterday wrote to John L. Lewis, leader of the miners on strike, urging that the main issue be submitted to arbitration. This issue is the demand for a "closed shop"—the closing of the mines to all men not members of the union.

He also endorses a suggestion that the 5 per cent. outside the union should join it "to share the burdens as well as the benefits of trade unionism," and that the owners should give an assurance that they are not opposed to trade unionism.

Another 56,000 men joined the strike yesterday, but Mr. Roosevelt is reported to have said that he will not order the Army to take over the mines until the Congress of Industrial Organisation's convention ends this week-end.—British United Press.

EARL OF LEICESTER DIES

The Earl of Leicester died yesterday at his home, Holkham Hall, Norfolk, aged 93. The new peer is Viscount Coke, of Lymington, Hants.

Weygand sacked to Axis order

STATEMENTS in New York that General Weygand had been dismissed by Vichy from his post in North Africa could not be confirmed in London yesterday, but were believed to be extremely likely.

There has been growing suspicion of Weygand in Berlin, particularly since his declaration that he would defend North Africa against any attack. He would have been dismissed before now but for the fear that he would turn his armies against the Germans.

Weygand is now in Vichy. Whether even Darlan would dare to arrest such a popular figure is doubtful.

U.S. Supplies May Stop

Vichy officials refused to make any comment last night. Admiral William Leahy, American Ambassador, called on Marshal Petain to ask for information.

The United States, it was learned in Washington, has decided to withhold its decision on the French plea for food for Unoccupied France and French prisoners of war, pending definite information.

American supplies of kerosene, tea, sugar, and other essentials to North Africa may be suspended.

Admiral Platon, a protege of Admiral Darlan, is on his way to North Africa, says a New York source.

Pilot's "No" led to death

The pilot of a South African plane, carrying a British brigadier as passenger, refused a weather report just before he set off on a flight.

The plane met bad weather and crashed in the mountains. The pilot and the brigadier were killed.

This was revealed at the inquest at Harrismith yesterday on the pilot, Lieutenant Thompson, and his passenger, Brigadier H. G. Eady, a member of the British Military Mission to South Africa.

ONLY SMOKE INDOORS—OR BE FINED

NO smoking in the open in the black-out. It is definitely illegal.

Point was raised at Aberdare, Glamorgan, yesterday when Herbert Mundy, 30, member of Birmingham Fire Service, was fined 10s. for showing a light from a cigarette during an Alert.

He said he had never been instructed that it was dangerous; that he had seen people smoking during raids, and firemen smoking on duty.

Cigarettes were not specifically mentioned in the regulations, stated the magistrates' clerk, Mr. W. G. Protheroe, but it was not permissible to show any light in a black-out, never mind an Alert.

Confirmation from the Ministry of Home Security, who told the Daily Mirror: "Strictly speaking, it is an offence, but prosecution is left to the discretion of the local authority."

PENNY A HEAD A WEEK MORE FOR BREAD

Mr. George Griffiths (Soc., Hemsworth) complained in the House of Commons yesterday that recent replies by the Ministry of Food to questions on the price of flour for home baking were considered unsatisfactory throughout the country.

The Parliamentary Secretary to the Ministry of Food replied that the increase worked out at only a penny per head per week, and it was still cheaper to bake at home

---

Daily Mirror

NOV. 22

No. 11,841 ONE PENNY
Registered at the G.P.O. as a Newspaper.

Russian ships in Britain

HUNS LOSE HALF TANK FORCE IN LIBYA TRAP

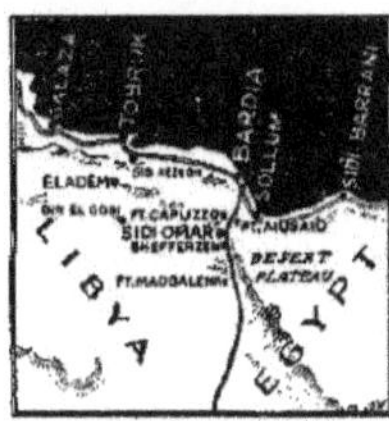

Three Russian girls were members of a crew of the first convoy of Soviet ships to reach Britain since the German attack on Russia. The ships brought timber to us.

One of the girls, Eydokia Tavine, is the leader of the workers' committee in the ship. She is 24 and comes from Kiev. Another, Kyra Corelhia, said she was happy in the ship and was well treated by all the crew. She had to help with the cooking and keep things clean. Her brothers, she said, were fighting the Germans.

The ships will turn round as soon as possible and take back to Russia vital supplies of arms.

GENERAL ROMMEL, GERMAN COMMANDER IN LIBYA, HAD LAST NIGHT LOST HALF HIS TANK FORCE IN THE GREAT DESERT BATTLE WHICH REACHED ITS CLIMAX WHEN THE BRITISH PANZERS DROVE THE ENEMY INTO A TRIANGULAR TRAP BETWEEN TOBRUK AND THE EGYPTIAN FRONTIER.

A Cairo military spokesman officially announced this at midnight and estimated that the German tank losses were three times greater than those of General Cunningham's Army.

Repeatedly Rommel hurled his panzers at the British Forces in attempts to break through, but each time the enemy was beaten back with heavy losses.

The initial British drive into Libya cut the main German armoured forces in two—the larger being in the Gambut-Capuzzo area near the border, and the smaller south of Tobruk.

Furious fighting raged forty-five miles west of Fort Capuzzo, where three separate German attacks were beaten back with "substantially heavier tank losses" than the British.

The battle is "going extremely well for the British forces," the Cairo military spokesman said.

"If the battle is won, that means the relief of Tobruk."

Earlier an official British communique announced the destruction of 130 Nazi tanks in two battles yesterday —one at Sidi Rezegh, 10 miles south-east of Tobruk's outer defences, and the other further east.

The Germans also lost 33 armoured cars.

Tanks Lightning Dash Over Desert

The Sidi Rezegh battle followed a lightning two-day dash by British armoured troops across the Western Desert.

After losing seventy tanks the Germans withdrew, leaving hundreds of prisoners in British hands.

The Germans were taken completely by surprise. As one officer put it, "We caught them with their trousers off."

The Germans had their own weapons and strategy turned against them. Masses of tanks made their own favourite encircling movement against them.

The position of the defenders of the fortified lines from Halfaya Pass to the south is desperate.

Their supply lines were cut by the advance close to Tobruk.

They are being hammered by strong containing forces in front and bombarded by the Navy on the flank.

"Now or never" was the time for the Italian Navy to come to their rescue. But they have remained in port.

In an action before the big battle two Territorial Yeomanry regiments reported that they had destroyed fifty-seven tanks.

Last night's Middle East communique stated:—

"The battle in Cyrenaica was joined in earnest yesterday afternoon.

"Following their rapid advance on two previous days our armoured forces on November 20 engaged German tanks in strength in the vicinity of Sidi Rezegh.

"After losing seventy tanks and thirty-three armoured cars the German forces withdrew leaving several hundred prisoners in our hands.

"Between this area and in Omar, a further British armoured formation came

Continued on Back Page

Big Nazi drive to encircle Tula

THE Russians are mobilising all their available forces in an effort to defeat a great German effort to encircle Tula.

Fierce fighting has continued in this sector for three days, the Nazis continuing to throw in new reserves.

During the three days, fifty Nazi tanks were destroyed in this sector, Moscow radio said last night, but the Germans continued to attack to the south-east of Tula, where a serious situation had arisen.

Russian counter-attacks drove the enemy out of the points they had captured.

A description of British tanks driven up to the front to go into battle was given by Red Star.

The newspaper described how the "N" tank unit, several miles long, moved up, and added:—

"In it there are particularly heavy tanks. These are powerful English tanks powered by Diesel motors.

"English instructors were pleased with the quick way our men learned the principles of construction and control of these machines.

"Our men particularly appreciate the high quality of the instruments and guns.

"Great interest was also aroused by armoured cars which have guns able to fire at both air and land targets."—Associated Press.

HITLER TO MEET PETAIN

New York reports last night said Hitler and Petain would meet in the near future, and that some new form of collaboration would result.

This will be the first result of the removal of Weygand from his post in North Africa.

The Independent French Agency says that Weygand was sacked because he opposed a German demand for the use of the French naval base at Bizerta.

BACK TO WORK

Completely recovered from his chill the Minister of Labour left the Stockton-on-Tees nursing home yesterday and returned to London—very well and ready for work.

REINFORCEMENTS AT SIERRA LEONE—NAZIS

German radio messages picked up in New York claim the arrival of big British reinforcements at Sierra Leone.

"According to the latest reports from Lisbon, six more British warships have anchored at Freetown," the reports said.

"Twenty British bombers, complete with ground personnel, are also said to have been landed at Freetown."

SHORT HAIR FOR WOMEN

THE Ministry of Health want women to wear their hair short.

"It is not necessary to go 'all shaven and shorn,' but the 'page-boy' bob and the thick, bunched clusters of curls reaching to the shoulders are definitely out of favour.

Reason is that hair is a great spreader of infection, which is much reduced if hair is kept short and frequently brushed and combed through.

The outbreak of typhus in parts of Spain and Northern France is causing some concern. There is always the possibility that it might attack this country.

"Typhus has certainly been mentioned to us as one reason for encouraging women to have their hair cut close to the head," the leader of a hairdressing organisation told the Daily Mirror. "There are, of course, other reasons.

"It is convenient for factory work and it is easier to keep clean."

Hellfire Pass attack

HALFAYA (Hellfire) Pass, defended by Germans, was last night being attacked by a famous Scottish regiment in the great Western Desert battle.

In the Sidi Omar area British and Indian troops were encircling Italian infantry concentrations.

South African and New Zealand infantry were also playing an important part in the successful operations.

Behind our armoured columns came the artillery, and overhead there roared, in flight after flight, British bombers and fighters, protecting the ground forces and bombing and gunning the enemy.

Axis air activity so far has been of the slightest, thanks to the R.A.F.'s "umbrella."

Black columns of smoke are shooting up from the horizon where the artillery is laying down a heavy barrage.

Terrific Beating

Forty-five Italian tanks were destroyed as one column of the British armoured forces ran into them at Bir el Guba, some thirty miles south of Tobruk.

Another report, however, puts the number of Italian tanks knocked out at almost 60.

The Italians west of Fort Capuzzo took a terrific beating at the hands of British cruiser tanks.

Tanks of a famous Yeomanry regiment accounted for 11 of the Italian tanks.

A Hussar regiment's armoured cars knocked out one of the biggest German eight-wheeled armoured cars and sent back prisoners.—Associated Press.

FLYING TO ALGIERS

M. Bergeret, Vichy Air Minister, and Francois Valentin, Leader of the French Legion, left Vichy by plane yesterday for Algiers.

Daily Mirror

NOV. 24

No. 11,842   ONE PENNY
Registered at the G.P.O. as a Newspaper.

WE SPLIT NAZIS, TAKE 15,000: THEY RUSH MORE BY PLANE

We smash two more Axis ferry convoys

TWO more Axis convoys, making a desperate bid to get supplies to Libya, have been smashed in the Mediterranean, it was revealed last night.

In the first, announced by the Admiralty, a cruiser was torpedoed by a British submarine, and a destroyer and two supply ships were torpedoed from the air. All four ships were probably sunk.

The second convoy, mentioned in an R.A.F. Cairo communique, was escorted by one cruiser and five destroyers.

It was attacked on Friday night by R.A.F. and naval aircraft.

One torpedo scored a direct hit on the cruiser causing a large flash and clouds of black smoke. One large merchant vessel was probably hit, and sticks of bombs straddled other ships.

In a raid on Argostoli Harbour, Greece, on Saturday, our aircraft bombed a naval vessel which was left with a heavy list, and patrol vessels were machine-gunned.

May Be Vital Blow

These successes are further shattering blows to the Axis Libya ferry—vital supply route for the enemy forces fighting in North Africa.

This new bid to run the gauntlet to Libya with supplies for their hard-pressed forces indicates the seriousness of the threat to the Axis African divisions. The effort has failed. The Navy has struck a blow that may prove decisive.

This is the third report of a big Mediterranean success in just over a fortnight.

On Sunday, November 9, the Navy wiped out two Axis convoys. They sank ten supply ships and four destroyers.

Three days later it was announced that British submarines had sunk four troopships on the way to Libya and two sailing ships and had damaged two armed merchant cruiser escorts and two more supply ships.

The number of Axis troops drowned on this occasion could not be estimated.

Raiders down in flames

Two German raiders were destroyed over this country last night.

Crowds cheered when one machine raced over the outskirts of a town like a huge blazing cigar and finally nose-dived.

As the machine crashed there was a terrific roar of exploding bombs.

A wounded German who baled out was arrested by George Giles, 17, a Home Guard.

The German shouted: "Help, kamerad—blood," as he pointed to two wounds.

A small number of enemy planes were reported over the Thames Estuary, the South Wales coast and the West and South-West of England.

THE NAVY GOT A PUNCTURE!

On November 9—you may remember—the Navy wiped out two Axis convoys in the Mediterranean. They sank ten supply ships and four Italian destroyers, and damaged a fifth.

Now, if you carefully examine the picture below you will see the damage the British Navy suffered in this engagement—a slight puncture in the funnel of one destroyer !

KILLED AS HE HIT SHIP

THE captain of a Dutch plane was killed yesterday just as one of his bombs hit a German supply ship off the coast of Norway.

There was an explosion forward of the ship's bridge, and smoke rapidly enveloped the ship. But a shell from an escorting ship exploded beneath the cockpit, and the pilot slumped forward.

The Hudson, which had dived to 200ft. to the attack, was about to hit the sea when the observer, leaning over the pilot's body, was able to straighten out the plane and put it into a gradual climb.

Observer Took Over

Then the rest of the crew came forward and lifted the captain from his seat.

And the observer, though he had flown a Hudson only once before, on a training circuit, brought the plane safely home.

The plane, one of the Dutch Naval Air Service, was looking for Nazi supply ships.

The supply ship which was attacked was heavily laden and had a powerful escort. One of the escorting ships was swept with the Hudson's guns before the pilot was killed.

WISHFUL THINKING

One of the strategems of the Soviet Army was to drop on the German lines at Kalinin twelve parachutists who were young and beautiful girls to seduce German soldiers, said an imaginative broadcaster on Rome radio last night.

Russians hit back in Donetz

MOSCOW reports that the Russians at one point in Donetz Basin have advanced twenty-two miles in two days.

Miners from the Don pits helped the Red Army to storm mountain heights and drove back the Germans, while Stormovik dive-bombers dealt terrific blows at German reinforcements.

The German claim to have captured Rostov-on-Don was officially denied yesterday. The Germans have broken in and violent fighting is going on in the streets.

Nazis Claim Advance

Claims that the Germans had crossed the Don and were advancing southwards were made in unofficial quarters in Berlin last night.

The Russian midnight communique mentions the Rostov, Kalinin, Volokolamsk, Tula areas as centres of fierce fighting.

German successes at Volokolamsk and Mojaisk, in the centre of the Moscow front and at another point to the south, were admitted yesterday by the Russians.

The position at Volokolamsk remains serious after a fierce battle which raged all day.

A German attempt to by-pass a town and cut the main road

Continued on Back Page

NAZIS BEGIN TO STERILISE CZECHS

The Nazis have begun a campaign of sterilisation in Czechoslovakia.

Himmler, during a recent visit to Prague, ordered mass sterilisations among the population, and set up a special Gestapo department to deal with them.

MORE BY PLANE

ENEMY forces enclosed by our tank ring—stretching in a wide sweep from the Egyptian frontier to Tobruk—have been split up into five groups. Cut off from their bases, the petrol supply is becoming a problem. Germans refuse to share fuel with the Italians.

We have already taken nearly 15,000 prisoners, including 8,000 Italians captured by an Indian division at Sidi Omar.

German troop reinforcements are arriving at Libyan bases in large numbers in heavily-laden giant Ju52 transports and towed gliders. Italians are rushing bombers and fighter planes.

The Nazis are flying to North Africa all available craft from Crete, Greece, Italy and even Germany.

It is considered that they may be withdrawing one or two squadrons from the Russian front.

Air Vice-Marshal Coningham, in command of the R.A.F. desert force, said yesterday: "We seem to have struck a panic note. They are rushing petrol, anti-tank guns and other vital supplies in big transport planes, some pulling two heavily-laden gliders.'

Tobruk Joined In

Our great triangular net of tanks seems to have been completed by the joining up at Sidi Rezegh of the Tobruk armoured sortie with our forces which swept westwards from Egypt.

Rommel is trying desperately to break out of the steel ring at this junction just south of Tobruk. As he had planned an attack himself on Egypt, it can be assumed that his reserves were nearby, and are now in the British net.

It is possible that in darkness or even in daylight a few Nazis may escape, but there is no doubt in official circles that most will be caught.

The splitting-up process in the big triangle has left one German group completely isolated in the heavily fortified Sollum-Halfaya area.

Loophole Closed

The one loophole was closed on Saturday with the capture of Bardia. New Zealanders cut the water pipe to Sollum, which has no independent water supply.

The huge petrol and ammunition dumps around

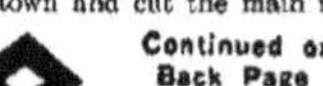

Continued on Back Page

PORTUGUESE IS A.A. BOSS

All the anti-aircraft defences of Moscow, and possibly of the entire North Russian front, are under the command of a young Portuguese officer named Anta, cables David Walker.

He fought against Franco in the Spanish civil war and escaped later to Paris, where Communists helped him to get to Moscow.

Since the outbreak of the Russian campaign this young Portuguese has been able to improve the Soviet air defence methods to such a degree that he was promoted at the age of 34 to command the A.A. defences of the vital Moscow area.

Inside the big triangular net, Tobruk—El Gobi—Halfaya, our forces are isolating German tank groups. (1) Halfaya and Sollum, heavily fortified, have had the only water supply cut off; (2) Gambut, airport and big fuel dump threatened by New Zealand troops; (3) El Gobi, another supply centre; (4) Tobruk, where the main tank battle is raging at Sidi Rezegh; (5) Unplaced group in centre of the triangle.

Our troops march into Bardia again

BRITISH troops entered Bardia again—but it was abandoned by the enemy this time—on Saturday night.

This advance base of Rommel's was occupied by New Zealanders advancing from captured Fort Capuzzo.

"The centre of gravity of the main tank battle," says yesterday's Cairo communique, "now appears to be about Sidi Rezegh [on the south-eastern perimeter of Tobruk.]

"Throughout Saturday night the battle continued without cessation. It is continuing this (Sunday) morning.

"Meanwhile, New Zealand forces, in the face of exceptional climatic difficulties, continued their advance

German Prisoners

"Rapidly capturing Sidi Aziz and Fort Capuzzo, these forces pushed on westward round the Trigh-Capuzzo road.

"Continuing their advance against opposition, the British Forces from Tobruk have again captured many hundreds of prisoners, of which fifty per cent. are German.

"Continuous air support was given by our air forces

AND THE R.A.F., TOO?

Leading statesmen representing Powers allied "against Bolshevism" will meet in Berlin today, the Germans announced last night.—Associated Press.

Daily Mirror

NOV. 25

No. 11,843   ONE PENNY
Registered at the G.P.O. as a Newspaper.

Map shows battle area, where infantry, mingling with the tanks, are clashing hand to hand.

INFANTRY FIGHTS HAND TO HAND IN DESERT

BIG BATTLES IN MOSCOW APPROACHES

FIERCE battles were last night being fought in towns near Moscow.

For twenty-four hours fighting went on non-stop at an unnamed town (believed to be Klin fifty miles north-west of the capital).

In this area Russian troops annihilated about two enemy battalions.

All the enemy attacks were repelled.

Under the pressure of German attacks, Russian troops later retired to new defence lines.

The Germans occupied two villages which cost them two infantry battalions, sixty to seventy lorries and fifteen tanks.

In the Mojaisk direction, all enemy attempts to advance failed.

By the end of the day Commander Yefremov's unit occupied a village, while Commander Golubev's unit continued holding their line.

40 Divisions Used

In the battle for Moscow, Von Bock is using forty divisions.

The capture of Solnechnaya Goya—a town forty miles north-west of Moscow—was claimed yesterday by the German High Command.

The Germans are throwing more tanks, planes and infantry into the battle for Tula, 100 miles south of Moscow.

Bitter street fighting is still taking place at Rostov.

WOMAN GETS POST ON FIRE COUNCIL

Mrs. B. W. Cuthbert, senior in the Women Staff Officers Fire Service Department, has been made an additional member of the Fire Service Council of England and Wales, of which the Home Secretary is chairman.

The wife of a naval officer, she joined the Women's Auxiliary Fire Service in July, 1938, and went through the big London raids, being made group commander in January, 1940.

FOOTBALLERS IN TURKEY

Ankara radio reported that a team of British footballers arrived at Istanbul yesterday. They are to play four matches against Turkish teams.

Five members of the team are internationals.

BRITISH and German infantry last night fought with bayonets and tommy guns among the tanks in the great battle raging in the Sidi Rezegh area.

New Zealand, South African and British regiments fought the enemy in the open. They had no trenches, only the natural cover the country afforded.

Grim hand - to - hand struggles occurred as British and German infantrymen closed.

A British column captured the Italian garrison at Gialo, the Rome communique said.

This is an oasis 135 miles south of Benghazi. It is the most southerly point at which fighting has yet been reported.

"The infantry battle is going hell for leather," the Cairo military spokesman said last night.

Petrol Dumps Taken

General Rommel drew off infantry from positions around Tobruk and sent them to reinforce those fighting Empire troops among the tanks.

The battle between the tanks continued with the same ferocity.

New Zealand forces captured Gambut, important enemy supply centre halfway between Tobruk and Bardia.

This will handicap the Germans, who must now rely on Derna and Gazala for supplies.

Great dumps of petrol and ammunition were captured.

German supply lines from Derna and Gazala are being incessantly bombed by the R.A.F.

The Germans fought with reckless courage, fury and desperation in a gigantic attempt to escape from their trap.

They counter-attacked with

Continued on Back Page

Tobruk "Aussies" had been relieved

Most of the Australians comprising the Tobruk garrison were recently withdrawn secretly by the Royal Navy and relieved by a force of Britons, Poles and Indians, the Australian News and Information Bureau reported last night in a dispatch to New York from Melbourne.—Associated Press.

Thames town raid, 1 down

DURING a sharp raid over the Thames Estuary last night bombs wrecked houses on the outskirts of a town. A number of people were injured. One raider was destroyed.

A man, his face gashed from chin to temple, refused first aid as he wandered among the ruins looking for his wife. He found eventually that she had been taken to hospital.

Rescue Work on Leave

Most of the people in the area were evacuated to rest centres for the night as their houses have been rendered uninhabitable.

R.A.F. men and soldiers on leave in the area formed a volunteer rescue party.

Grin from Ark Royal

The spirit that made Ark Royal feared by her enemies. More smiles like this on page 5.

U.S. to guard Dutch mines, aid de Gaulle

TWO sensational moves were made by Roosevelt last night to deal with the menace of Japan and Hitler.

1. It was announced that the U.S. is to send an Army contingent to help the Dutch protect their bauxite mines in Dutch Guiana, whence the U.S. draws more than 60 per cent. of her supply for aluminium manufacture.

2. America for the first time openly lined up against the Vichy puppet Government by authorising Lease-Lend aid to the forces of de Gaulle.

Immediately after the announcement of the U.S. aid to the Dutch, Roosevelt called the representatives of Britain, Australia, China and the Netherlands to a conference with Cordell Hull, U.S. Secretary of State.

Kurusu, leader of the Japanese mission to Washington, was also invited to the meeting, it is reported.

A new turn in the U.S.-Japanese conversations is said to have made such a meeting advisable.

Earlier it had been revealed that the Japanese Foreign Office had sent an urgent new communication to its U.S. mission which the official Tokio news agency said did not give ground for optimism.

Threat to Colony

Washington reports said last night that American troops are occupying Dutch Guiana because of grave developments in the neighbouring territory of French Guiana, where Nazi influence is becoming increasingly strong.

Numbers of influential Frenchmen in French Guiana are known to be strongly pro-Axis, and it is feared that they might place the colony under full Nazi control.

This might, it is feared, result in Nazi raids into Dutch Guiana. The Nazis had, it is believed, planned to gain a strong foothold on the American continent through French Guiana.

Japan to Sign New Anti-Soviet Declaration.—Page 4.

Soldiers wear light armour

SOLDIERS wearing light armour plating over their battle-dress are undergoing dusk-to-dawn training in conditions that reproduce 1941 warfare as closely as possible.

I watched an attack by a platoon on a machine-gun post (writes a reporter). Supporting Bren gun and mortar fire was laid on the flanks and over the heads of the riflemen to within a few seconds of the final assault.

The bullets were real.

MOSCOW SAYS "CHEERIO"

Moscow radio has always ended all its broadcasts with the slogan, "Workers of all countries unite."

As from last night, however, the last words in every transmission in English will be, "Cheerio, from Radio Centre,

Bus girls accused

Twenty-four bus drivers and conductresses were charged at Glasgow yesterday in connection with the recent transport strike.

It was alleged that they took part in a strike in connection with a trade dispute which had not been reported to the Ministry.

They pleaded not guilty, and their trial was fixed for next month.

Daily Mirror

NOV. 28

No. 11,846   ✦   ONE PENNY

Registered at the G.P.O. as a Newspaper.

FIRST ROUND WON BY LINK-UP WITH TOBRUK FORCE

JAP ATTACK ON THAILAND EXPECTED

MR. ROOSEVELT has made up his mind. His terms for peace in the Pacific are not likely to be accepted by Tokio.

Washington expects the Japanese to launch an attack on Thailand and the Burma Road in a few days.

This was the delicate position in the Far East last night, when it was revealed that all the time the Japanese special envoys have been talking in Washington, Japan has been massing troops to the north and south of Indo-China.

The Japanese News Agency was pessimistic yesterday.

"Little room for prolonging the conversations" was the general tone, with the explanation: "Americans and their Allies are adopting a strong stand against Japan."

Reports reaching authoritative Washington quarters indicated that Japan had been rapidly strengthening her forces in French Indo-China within the past week.

And Aviation Petrol

The reports mentioned not only large troop transports into Northern and Southern Indo-China, but also large shipments of war materials of all kinds, including aviation petrol.

President Roosevelt, Mr. Cordell Hull, Secretary of State; Admiral Nomura, the Japanese Ambassador, and Mr. Kurusu, the special Japanese emissary, met at the White House yesterday. — Associated Press, Exchange and British United Press.

Conscription for all, from 18 to 50, is coming soon

EVERY man and woman in this country between the ages of 18 and 50 will, within a fortnight, be liable for military service.

Every person outside these ages will be liable for any national service for which they are considered by the authorities to be suitable.

The House of Commons, in fact, is to be asked to approve of national all-in conscription for everybody.

This, writes the *Daily Mirror* political correspondent, is the secret behind the motion tabled in the House of Commons yesterday in the names of the Prime Minister, the Lord Privy Seal and the Ministers for Air, Health and Labour.

They ask the House to approve:

"That for the purpose of securing the maximum national effort in the conduct of the war and in production the obligation for national service should be extended to include the reserves of man and woman-power still available, and that the necessary legislation be brought in forthwith."

The Bill will be presented at the next sitting of the House of Commons, and will be rushed through in the shortest time possible.

The Prime Minister will deal with the whole situation when he opens the two-day debate on man-power. The Minister of Labour will wind up the debate.

Some in Industry

Though the calling-up age for men will be raised to 50, it is expected that men over 41 will be placed in Civil Defence units, such as the Fire Service, and possibly the Home Guard, as well as taken for production in the factories.

Of the women, those at the lower age will go almost automatically into the Services, and those at the higher ages to the factories, Land Army, and Civil Defence Services.

Within the ranks of the women's Services there will be a call for volunteers for "combatant service," such as a limited number do at present.

RESERVED MEN IN COMB-OUT

A DRASTIC review of the cases of men whose call-up has been deferred—with particular attention to the under-25's—is to take place with the change in the system of reservation, it was revealed last night.

Employers, it is understood, will have to make out a good case for the retention of men who are de-reserved by the raising of the ages.

The T.U.C. also considers that the employee should have a right to apply for deferment.

The T.U.C. wishes to be satisfied that the employees will have a square deal, and that there will be no victimisation of men whom the employer might not wish for reasons of his own to retain.

Clerical Work

The Amalgamated Engineering Union, which covers men engaged on key work in munitions, has strongly criticised the individual reservation proposal, and pointed out that it might cause serious difficulties in maintaining vital output.

The raising of the age of men liable for call-up will not necessarily imply that they will be called upon for general service.

It is considered that there is a certain amount of sedentary and clerical work which might be done by men of 40 to 50, releasing younger men for the front line.

18B: Admiral wants writ

The recent 18B judgment of the Law Lords will be discussed in the High Court today when application for habeas corpus writs, adjourned pending the House of Lords' decision, come before the Lord Chief Justice and Justices Humphreys and Wrottesley.

The applicants include Admiral Sir Barry Edward Domvile and Captain G. H. L. F. Pitt-Rivers, who were detained under Defence Regulations 18B.

Sandwiching the Passengers

The Railway Executive Committee announced last night that from Monday, December 8, restaurant cars will be withdrawn from certain trains on all four of the main lines.

Restaurant cars in about fifty trains will be affected, according to a list issued by the railway companies.

Ordinary coaches will take their place to carry extra passengers due to fewer trains.

U.S. plans Red Sea docks, rail

THE U.S. Lend-Lease administration was last night reported to be "in process of arranging" extensive building of warehouses, docks, railway sidings, and aeroplane landing facilities in the Red Sea area.

Work was progressing, officials said, under the immediate direction of the United States military mission to the Middle East, headed by Brigadier-General Maxwell.

Another military mission, assigned the task of expediting shipments to Russia through Persia and Irak, is reported to be undertaking extensive improvements in terminal facilities at Basra and Bandar Shah.

Continued on Back Page

Salvage is a must job now

Collection of salvage, by a new order, is now compulsory for local authorities.

Rags are included in the materials which must be salvaged. The public are asked to co-operate by keeping them separate from other waste.

RUMANIAN SHIP SUNK

The 2,369-ton Rumanian passenger liner Regele Carol has been torpedoed and sunk in the Black Sea, according to reports in Istanbul shipping circles.

WITH the link-up yesterday between the forces from Tobruk and the main armies, the first round in Britain's drive to crush Rommel's panzer army in Libya is won, though heavy fighting is yet to come, said a British military spokesman last night.

New Zealand forces operating with British tank formations battled through via Bardia and Gambut to recapture Sidi Rezegh—centre of the new big battle—and occupy Bir El Hamed after stiff fighting on Wednesday night.

Meanwhile, the Tobruk forces had fought their way to Ed Duda and there yesterday the link-up was made, says the British Middle East communique.

A British United Press correspondent describes how the forces joined hands, and how they first manœuvred to fight till they recognised each other.

"As the New Zealanders, with British tanks in front, rolled over the desert they spotted other tanks ahead in battle formation.

"Identification was difficult because of the distance separating them, and both sides manœuvred warily for some time. Then they recognised each other. And thus, for the first time in eight months, the men of Tobruk had broken through the ring of Axis troops surrounding them."

If the junction with the Tobruk garrison is maintained and the breach in the enemy besieging ring is widened, Tobruk will be used as a base to save long lines of communications across the desert.

Jockeying for Position

There are still pockets of enemy resistance along the channel opened by the forces which struck out from Tobruk. While this resistance remains Tobruk cannot be said to have been completely relieved.

Although a new big battle has begun in the area of Sidi Rezegh there is still no news of a clash between the main armoured formations.

Both ours and the enemy's had been regrouped and reinforced after their terrific encounters throughout last week.

It is believed that they are now manœuvring to get at one another, with each side

Continued on Back Page

"We must hold on"— Moscow

"**Y**OU must hold. It is now the moment to make a supreme effort. The situation is increasingly difficult, but we must, and can, stand the strain."

This was Moscow radio's message to citizens last night, as the German menace from the north-west and the south drew relentlessly nearer the city.

"The main task is to stop the enemy at the approaches to Moscow." went on the announcer.

"These battles must be won by you at all costs. Don't console yourself with the fact that the Germans are advancing at a slower pace than in September, or October.

"We have to defend every yard of our soil. These days are decisive for Moscow."

Nazis Claim Klin

The capture of Klin, sixty miles north-west of half-encircled Moscow was claimed by a Berlin spokesman last night.

The capture of fourteen towns "in the rear of the Russian fortifications," was announced by the German news agency.

Izvestia, Russian newspaper, said the grave situation near Volokolamsk had been aggravated.

South of Moscow, the German push seems to be spreading eastwards towards Ryazan, 100 miles south-east of the city.

Rostov, in the far south, continues to be a bright spot for the Russians, whose counter-attack has gained another thirty miles and inflicted 10,000 casualties on the Nazis. German reinforcements are on the way to this front.

M.P. ALLEGES SHOP CALL-UP DODGE

Allegations that certain chain stores were placing girls of calling-up age in their food and refreshment departments, where they are secure against being called up, and transferring these girls to other departments to replace those called up, were made in the Commons yesterday by Mr. De La Bere (Con., Evesham).

He was told that the Minister of Labour is not aware of the existence of the practice.

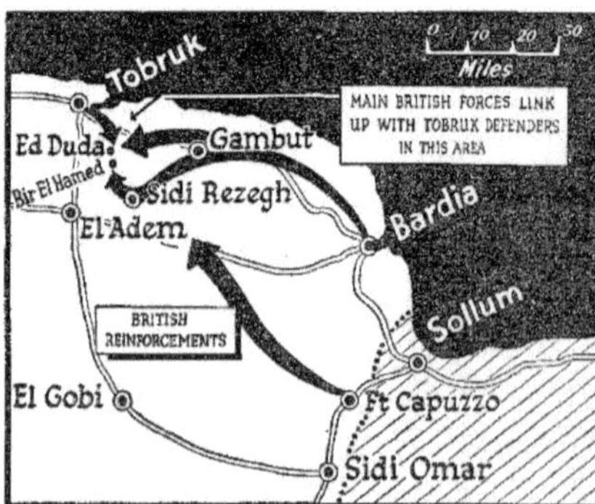

The arrows indicate the direction of the main British thrusts.

FRY'S for good chocolate

Especially—

TRY FOR FRY'S—and if you get some, remember the children need it most!

Daily Mirror

No. 11,854 — ONE PENNY
Registered at the G P O as a Newspaper

DEC 8

JAPANESE BOMB U.S. NAVAL BASES IN THE PACIFIC

2 tank fights open in Libya

BRITISH and enemy panzer forces last night began to fight it out in Libya. Two battles are now raging there. General Rommel, who had the chance of escaping with his tanks to the west, is instead making strong attempts to smash our supremacy

The tank battles were started with head-on clashes south of Tobruk It was officially stated in Cairo that forty-eight tanks, mostly Italian, were destroyed in the last three days.

As the new desert tank clash began German dive-bombers were sent to attack our forces. The R.A.F. smashed up this raid, destroying twenty Axis planes and damaging twenty others.

Troops danced like Dervishes around eleven blazing enemy planes on the ground.

The Fleet Air Arm followed this up by a night attack, lasting one hour, on big enemy mechanical transport in the desert beyond Sidi Rezegh.

Very few Germans are left between Tobruk and the Egyptian frontier where British mobile forces are mopping up.

This was stated in last night's Cairo communique which said

Battle in Moonlight

"During the last twenty-four hours there has been considerable activity in the area between El Adem and Bir el Gobi, which is due south of Tobruk

"In an action four miles east of Bir el Gobi, an enemy column of about 100 vehicles and two tanks was engaged by South African troops, one tank being knocked out, the transport dispersed and the column forced to withdraw

"Two other actions in this general area were still in progress when the latest reports reached Cairo. Fighting had continued in the moonlight.

"Further north again armoured forces of both sides were reported to have joined battle about midday on December 6.

"Reports of the progress of this engagement are not yet at hand.

"During these engagements in the Bir el Gobi area our air forces scored direct hits on the enemy forces while they were refuelling.

"South - east of Tobruk British patrols penetrated several miles south of El Duda without opposition.

"A little further east, in the Sidi Rezegh area, South African

Continued on Back Page

SIR MONTAGU BUTLER SERIOUSLY INJURED

While watching A.R.P. exercises early yesterday Sir Montagu Butler, 68, Mayor of Cambridge and Master of Pembroke College, was knocked down by a motor ambulance

He received a head injury and was taken to hospital in the ambulance which knocked him down. His condition is stated to be critical. He is the father of the President of the Board of Education.

A King's bride

The girl who has married King Leopold of Belgium—Mlle. Mary Leila Baels. She will take the title, not of Queen, but of the Princess of Rethey.

Below is Mlle. Baels with the royal children, and her father (in uniform). This picture was taken a considerable time ago; and even then Mlle. Baels was a close friend of the King and his children. (See story on page 4.)

Why Halifax didn't turn up

WHEN M. Litvinov, new Russian Ambassador to the United States, arrived in Washington by air yesterday he was met, not by Lord Halifax, but by the British Embassy's second secretary Sir Anthony Rumbold.

I understand (cables John Walters from New York) it had originally been planned for the British Minister Sir Ronald Campbell, to greet Litvinov and his English-born wife. The unexpected early arrival of the plane prevented this.

There was considerable comment in Washington on the failure of Lord Halifax to meet Litvinov personally at the airport, but some experts in diplomatic etiquette argued that this would have been incorrect.

Litvinov received a cordial letter from Lord Halifax on his arrival, and the two expect to have a long conference within the next few days.

His arrival is heralded as a new link in U.S.-Russian relations.

Litvinov stepped from the plane in a Russian wool jacket and wool shirt without tie.

In reply to questions about incident at Teheran involving his failure to get a seat aboard a British plane, he said, "I would rather forget the unpleasantness."

He said that in Washington he hoped to work in closest cooperation with Roosevelt and Cordell Hull.

JAPAN last night started the war in the Pacific by bombing the United States naval and air bases at Manila, in the Philippines, the Hawaiian base at Pearl Harbour and naval and military objectives on the chief island of Oahu.

President Roosevelt told America of Japan's attacks without declaring war in an announcement from the White House It was made while the two Japanese diplomats Kurusu and Nomura were carrying on the farce of negotiating for a "peaceful settlement" with Secretary of State Cordell Hull at the State Department

Several Japanese planes were shot down in attacks on Oahu and Pearl Harbour.

NAVAL ENGAGEMENTS ARE NOW IN PROGRESS OFF HONOLULU.

The White House later announced that an Army transport carrying lumber had been torpedoed 1,300 miles west of San Francisco.

PRESIDENT ROOSEVELT ORDERED THE ARMY AND NAVY TO CARRY OUT UNDISCLOSED ORDERS PREPARED FOR THE DEFENCE OF THE UNITED STATES.

The U.S. Navy sent out an urgent call to all officers on leave to report immediately to the naval districts in which they were situated.

Japan is believed to have used aircraft carriers to attack the

Within one hour

Speaking at the Mansion House, London, on November 10 Mr Churchill warned Japan.

"We do not know whether the efforts of the United States to preserve peace in the Pacific will be successful.

"BUT IF THEY FAIL, I TAKE THIS OCCASION TO SAY—AND IT IS MY DUTY TO SAY — THAT SHOULD THE UNITED STATES BECOME INVOLVED IN WAR WITH JAPAN, THE BRITISH DECLARATION WILL FOLLOW WITHIN THE HOUR."

Philippine and Hawaiian bases, which are more than 400 miles apart

Anti-aircraft guns went into action at Pearl Harbour, leaving clouds of smoke over the Navy yard.

Heavy smoke was seen rising from Hickman Field, in the Pearl Harbour area apparently from fires. One witness said that fires had been started on Ford Island.

About 150 planes took part in the attack on Hawaii.

Continued on Back Page

GERMANS RETREAT ON 3 FRONTS

WHILE Russian pursuit of Von Kleist's panzer columns continued yesterday beyond Taganrog, German forces were compelled to retreat on two Moscow fronts.

An indication of the strength of the Moscow defences, which not even the fiercest artillery barrage could overcome, was given in an unusually frank German broadcast last night.

"Our artillery has fired tons of steel for days, but no artillery can possibly smash the system of trenches and the many dug-in tanks, which form powerful pill-boxes, from every one of which the Soviets maintain a terrific fire." the broadcaster declared

"Only the utmost ruthlessness and no consideration for life can enable us to advance. We can only attack and attack again and take every trench and every position by fierce, man-to-man fighting"

Terrific Soviet Blows

Under the weight of terrific Russian counter-attacks, the Nazis have fallen back from the vital Mojsisk highway

The Germans are also retreating in the Volokolamsk area, and a dangerous German break through on the northern part of the Maloyaroslavets sector has been stopped.

In the Kalinin and Narofominsk sectors the Germans have been driven back at several points. At Tikhvin (120 miles east of Leningrad) Nazi forces are threatened with encirclement.

Berlin claimed last night that Nazi forces in the Donetz had checked the Russian offensive and had themselves taken the offensive.

£200 TAKEN FROM WAR SAVINGS STALL

While attendants were standing at a war savings stall in Kidderminster market more than £200 was stolen from a cashbox beneath the stall

The police have recovered nearly all the money from boys who are alleged to have crept beneath the stall and taken the notes.

THE FINISHING POST

The last war ended in France —this war must end in Germany.—The Air Minister at Newcastle.

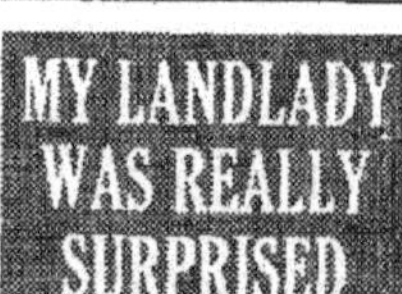

at the Quick Change in us!

I Am Never Without A Bottle Of YEAST-VITE

Dear Sirs. Blackpool, Nov 8th, 1941.

My husband and I had a very bad attack of the 'Flu. I said to my landlady. "*If you will please give me my handbag you will find some Yeast-Vite tablets That is our standby always.*"

We took two tablets three times a day and in two days we were both out of danger and my landlady was really surprised to see the quick change in us and my strong faith in your most marvellous tonic tablets.

I am never without a bottle of Yeast-Vite. I always recommend them whenever there is any sickness. I keep telling people about them and can't praise them too highly They are a blessing to everyone in poor health.

I gave my neighbours a sample to try and they bought some Yeast-Vite, as they were suffering from asthma for years and had never tried Yeast-Vite before. Well, they were amazed at the quick relief.

(Sgd) Mrs. W B.

Yeast-Vite Tonic Tablets bring quick relief from Headaches, Nerves, Lassitude, Depression, Insomnia, Rheumatism, Indigestion, etc. Sold everywhere at 1/4, 3/3, & 5/4, including purchase tax.

Daily Mirror

DEC 9

No. 11,855   ✦   ONE PENNY
Registered at the G.P.O. as a Newspaper.

WE MOP UP JAPS IN MALAY BEACH ATTACK

Casualties in Hawaii are 3,000

AMERICAN casualties in Hawaii are expected to number 3,000—about half of them fatal, it was stated at the White House in Washington last night.

It was admitted that "serious damage" had been caused to the American forces there.

President Roosevelt has revealed that heavy losses have been sustained by the U.S. Navy. There were also large losses among army units in Oahu Island, on which Honolulu stands.

Guam, the U.S. naval base in the Pacific east of the Philippines, is virtually destroyed. Tokio claims that Japanese vessels surrounded the base, which is on fire.

Tokio claimed last night that a U.S. aircraft-carrier and two battleships had been sunk, two more battleships damaged and four heavy cruisers hit.

The aircraft-carrier, they said, was sunk by a submarine off Honolulu.

Mr. Early, Roosevelt's secretary, admitted the loss of one battleship, the Oklahoma. The other battleship, West Virginia, had not been sunk, he said.

He added that a U.S. destroyer had been blown up and several smaller ships sunk. A large number of hangars in Hawaii had been destroyed.

Asked whether there was any official information why Japan was able to get inside the outer defences of the Hawaiian group, Mr. Early said that ex-

Continued on Back Page

U.S. pledges revenge

Threats of terrible revenge America will deal out to Japan are given prominence in U.S. newspapers, wires John Walters.

Raymond Clapper, in his widely circulated column, wrote, "Japan will die by the sword. Japan will be blasted, bombed, burned, starved. Her people will suffer ghastly tortures."

William Randolph Hearst, who, until the Japs attacked, was a leading Isolationist, wrote in the *New York Journal American*:

"Before the war is over we will have burned up all the paper houses in Japan and sunk most of their scrap iron battleships."

The *New York Daily News*, which a week ago coined the slogan, "Let's appease Japan," is equally threatening.

PROUD TO STAND WITH U.S.

The Labour Party is proud to think that Great Britain stands alongside the people and Government of the United States in the momentous struggle to which they are called, says a statement issued yesterday at a special meeting of the Labour Party Executive Committee.

U.S. & Britain declare war

Roosevelt given war vote

TWO hours after Roosevelt's request, the U.S. Congress last night voted declaration of war against Japan.

In the Senate the voting was eighty-two in favour, with none against, and in the House of Representatives 388 in favour, with one against.

The one objector was the Republican Pacifist representative, Mrs. Jeannette Rankin.

Grave Danger

Roosevelt, in his speech to Congress—relayed in Britain by the B.B.C.—said that "very many American lives had been lost," and that their people, territory, and interests were in grave danger.

December 7, the President said, was "a date which will live in infamy."

The U.S. had been suddenly and deliberately attacked by naval and air forces of Japan while at peace with that nation, and while conducting negotiations for the maintenance of peace in the Pacific.

The Japanese Government had deliberately sought to deceive the U.S. by false statements and expressions of hope for continued peace.

"In Grave Danger"

Japan had undertaken a surprise offensive extending throughout the Pacific area. The facts spoke for themselves. The people of the U.S. well understood the implications of these facts to the very life and safety of the nation.

"I believe that I interpret the will of the Congress and of the people when I assert that we will not only defend ourselves to the uttermost, but will make it very certain that this form of treachery will never again endanger it," said Mr. Roosevelt.

"There is no blinking at the fact that our people, our territory, and our interests are in grave danger."

BLACKED OUT

Thailand's Defence Ministry yesterday ordered a black-out after capitulation to Japan.

Churchill: 'I did not wait'

ANNOUNCEMENT by the Premier in the Commons yesterday that Britain had declared war on Japan was followed by a demand from M.P.s for greater efforts at home to make up for U.S. war equipment that may be delayed or diverted.

Mr. Churchill said he had talked with President Roosevelt on the Atlantic telephone, with a view to arranging the time of their respective declarations. He went on:

In view of the fact that Japan had invaded British territory in Malaya, I did not think it necessary to wait for a declaration by Congress.

We Were Ready

Japanese began a landing in British territory in Northern Malaya at 6 a.m. (local time) yesterday and they were immediately engaged by our forces, which were ready. (Cheers.)

I sent a message yesterday to the ruler of Thailand telling him that we would regard an invasion of his country as an attack on ourselves. I also sent a message to General Chiang Kai Shek assuring him that henceforward we would face the common foe together.

Mr. Lees-Smith (Keighley), in an appeal for further production activity, said equipment from the United States might be delayed and, to some extent, diverted. Another detrimental consequence was the effect on our shipping, for America would not be able to give the same assistance.

Berlin silent about new war

Germany, whose commitments under the Axis Pact oblige her to go to the assistance of Japan if she is "attacked," has so far officially referred to the Asiatic hostilities as "clashes."

Berlin radio made no comment when broadcasting the news of the new war

---

But the Battle for Burma—and the Burma road to China—was made easier for Tokio by Thai's capitulation after five and a half hours' fighting. They agreed to allow a free passage for Japanese troops across Thailand.

More Japanese troops have been landed from destroyers and transports at Patani, in Thailand, just north of the Malaya border.

An attack on British North Borneo has been repulsed; and the British islands of Nauru—which has a wireless station—and Ocean, in the Samoa group, have been attacked.

Moonlight Bombing

Hong Kong was bombed twice yesterday. Singapore was bombed again. Penang, on the western coast of Malay, was raided. The British Concessions at Tientsin has been taken over by Japanese troops.

The first full story of how our troops mopped up the Japanese invaders of north-east Malaya was told in a communiqué issued in Singapore last night.

We were ready. The day before the attack one of our planes had spotted approaching Japanese warships and transports. One of the ships opened fire on our plane, giving the game away.

About 1.30 a.m. yesterday ships approached the Kelantin River, north of Kota Bahru,

Continued on Back Page

China at war with Germany

China has declared war on Japan, Germany and Italy.

Other countries that have so far declared war on Japan and will fight with Britain and the United States are:—

Canada, Royal Netherlands Government, Czech Government in London, Nicaragua, Costa Rica, and the Republics of Honduras and Haiti.

By a Cabinet decision yesterday, Egypt severed diplomatic relations with Japan.

ARMY CASUALTIES

Of seven officers in today's War Office casualty list, which contains 126 names, one was previously reported missing, now reported killed, one died of wounds, one is wounded, and four have died.

Japan's three-pronged attack on the Malay peninsular is shown in this map. Singora and Patani are in Thailand, which capitulated after five and a half hours' fighting, but at Kota Bharu our forces repulsed one landing, then heavily machine-gunned the second, while our aircraft bombed the transports into retreat. Japs who filtered into the swamps have been mopped up.

Dodgers in U.S. may be rounded up

British conscription dodgers in U.S. may be compelled to return home now America is in the war.

The British Embassy in Washington is expecting orders from London for the compulsory registration of all British subjects in the United States with a view to conscription, cables John Walters, the *Daily Mirror* representative in America.

Now that the United States has become a fighting ally of Britain she will, it is understood, allow the British authorities to hunt down all slackers in the United States, a list of whom has been compiled, and compel them to return home.

Under the new conscription measures this will apply to women as well as to men.

As America also has conscription U.S. subjects in Britain, presumably, will be similarly affected.

Hong Kong's big defences

Hong Kong could withstand a complete blockade for at least nine months.

It is protected by big guns against assault from the sea, and the defence-in-depth plan has been adopted against land attack.

Last reinforcements to arrive were a large batch of Canadians. They will be the first men of the Dominion to see big battle operations in this war.

All British women and children have been evacuated.

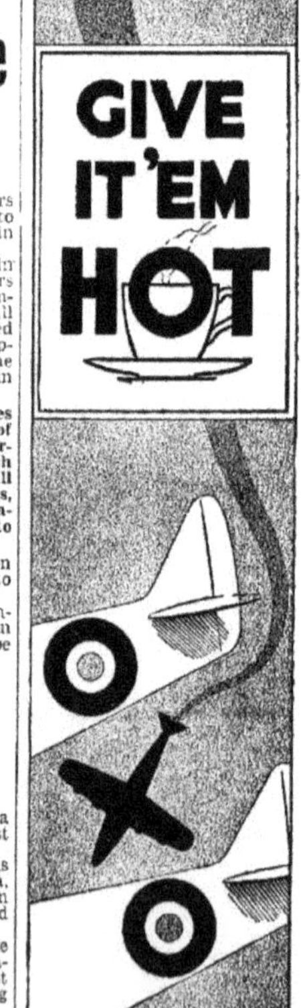

BRITISH FORCES HAVE MOPPED UP JAPANESE INVADERS IN THE JUNGLE SWAMPS OF NORTH-EAST MALAYA AFTER THE JAPANESE TRANSPORTS STEAMED AWAY AT FULL SPEED UNDER OUR HEAVY BOMBING.

Daily Mirror

No. 11,856   ONE PENNY
Registered at the G.P.O. as a Newspaper.

SINGAPORE NAVAL BATTLE, TOKIO BOMBED REPORTS

A NAVAL BATTLE WAS REPORTED LAST NIGHT TO BE RAGING OFF SINGAPORE.

Twenty-five Japanese troopships were spotted by our planes yesterday in the Gulf of Siam, creeping down the east Thailand coast from Indo-China bases.

These forces presumably are to be landed in Southern Thailand for a land attack over the border—for the Japs' main objective still is the seizure of Malaya and the Singapore naval base.

The cities of Tokio and Kobe, and Formosa Island have been bombed, according to both Vichy radio and the U.S. Columbia broadcasting system, though the news is not yet confirmed.

Rome radio quoted a Tokio claim that the U.S.A. aircraft carrier Lexington, which carries ninety planes, had been torpedoed and sunk.

Chinese offensives are in progress at several points against the Japs, who claim to have launched an attack on the Burma Road from Northern Thailand.

Japanese trying to cross Hong Kong's mainland frontier have been halted by our artillery fire, it is announced officially.

The border was manned by British troops at 5.30 a.m. yesterday and we started the demolition of roads and bridges.

Berlin adds that two Japanese divisions are attacking Hong Kong.

U.S. Gets Plane Carrier

In America's fight against Japan, Washington announced last night that U.S. naval forces had sunk six Japanese submarines and an aircraft carrier.

Japan claims 300 U.S. planes shot down over the Philippines and Hawaii.

Mr. Early, secretary to Mr. Roosevelt, admitted last night that the American losses at Pearl Harbour base were heavier than the 1,300 casualties at first reported.

General McArthur declared that in Manila that the Japs had "considerable air losses" in their attack on the Philippines.

Rome radio said last night

Japs did use gas, say doctors

Doctors have confirmed the use of Lewisite (blister) gas by the Japanese, the National Broadcasting Company of America reported yesterday.

Britain had informed Japan she intends to abide by the Geneva decision outlawing gas and had asked assurances Japan would do the same.

All U.S. was fooled in big A.R.P. test

IN the greatest A.R.P. test in history, the U.S. authorities yesterday hoaxed the whole of America, cables John Walters from New York.

But they did it so that the test would be a genuine one—a "dress rehearsal" one public safety official called it. "We had to fool the public to make it as thorough as possible," he said.

When the alarm was sounded in New York and other cities, it was reported that "hostile planes" were two hours distant from New York.

Then these things happened:

Two hundred and eighty army planes immediately took off from Mitchell Field, Long Island, chief air base for the defence of New York.

Rifles, gas masks and steel helmets were issued to 7,500 men on the field, while ambulances and fire-fighting equipment were rolled out, too.

All flights from the big La Guardia airport were cancelled.

Radio Off Air

Wireless stations were ordered off the air.

All New York school children were marched home. Coastguards were ordered to patrol the waterfront to deal with incendiary bombs.

All the 14,000 men on the day shift at the Bethlehem Steel Company's shipyard at Quincy, Massachusetts, which is working on defence orders, were sent home at 1.10 p.m.

Plane Carrier Report

A million inhabitants of San Francisco and neighbouring towns were warned last night to be prepared for enemy air raids, as reports persisted that a Japanese aircraft carrier might be 600 miles off the coast.

Thirty enemy planes approaching the coast, it was reported, were intercepted and fled out to sea, apparently back to the carrier.

Planes and naval craft were scouring the ocean for the carrier all day.

GIRLS TO MAN FIRE ENGINES

By BILL GREIG

WOMEN in the Civil Defence services are to have much greater scope, for it has been decided that they replace men.

Opportunity will be given them to drive fire engines and similar vehicles, and even to man the lighter type of pumps.

For this the young and fittest of the volunteers under the new scheme will be chosen.

I understand that "a gentleman's agreement" has been arrived at between the various departments under which all full-time defence workers over 41 are to be reserved.

Pending the provision of substitutes, the younger women will also remain, but those who are mobile will be moved later as required.

The number of immobile women is put as high as six million, but a fair proportion of these will be available for at least part-time work.

No fewer than 4,950,451 people registered for fire guard duty in September. A high proportion applied on various grounds for exemption. Those who did not apply totalled 1,213,303.

Mexican troop moves through U.S.

The United States has authorised Mexico to move troops through U.S. territory to reinforce the defence of lower California.

The movement of a considerable body of troops is expected to begin today.—Reuter.

RAID INJURY COMPENSATION

Supported by a large number of M.P.s of all parties, Mrs. Tate and Dr. Summerskill last night tabled an amendment to the National Service Bill that women injured by enemy action receive the same rate of compensation as men.

It is believed that although the amendment may not be accepted at this stage the Government will agree to review the whole matter at an early date. Debate—page 5.

★Raid-Jap plan for the U.S.

Note the lines drawn on the map between Manila and Vladivostok. Litvinoff, Russian Ambassador to the U.S., has suggested that if the U.S. formally declared war on Germany, U.S. could have air bases at Vladivostok, says our New York correspondent.

A glance at the map shows that in such conditions U.S. bombers could fly from the Philippines over Japan and bomb it, go on to Vladivostok, refuel there, and re-bomb, drop more bombs on Japan and fly on to the Philippines again. A kind of shuttle bombing service on Japan.

Rommel tries to re-group

BRITISH forces in Libya are still pushing to the west following the linking of forces from Tobruk and Sidi Rezegh.

London information late yesterday said that Rommel's panzers are trying to withdraw further west in Libya in an attempt to form a line behind which to regroup.

Axis forces, however, are still concentrated at El Adem, south of Tobruk, and so long as they remain there they cannot be said to have retired west of the Tobruk-Bir el Gobi line.

British forces now have complete freedom of manoeuvre between Tobruk and Sollum.

To the west of Tobruk the mobile columns continue to harass bodies of the enemy, while at Tobruk itself, a point a few miles west of El Duda has been taken and consolidated.

An attempted advance in this area by 2,000 enemy infantry supported by a few tanks was met by our artillery.

Woe, woe— by Sheehan

A sensational statement, which bears little resemblance to the news received throughout the day, was made by Mr. Vincent Sheehan, U.S. journalist and author of "Personal History," at Philadelphia yesterday.

He asserted that the United States has lost more ships by Japan's attacks than Britain has lost in the whole of the war.

"The United States will have the greatest humiliation in its history when it learns of the staggering number of Pacific Fleet battleships lost during the first thirty-six hours of the Japanese attack," he declared.

"We have lost all our Pacific possessions except Hawaii and the Philippines."

"Foreign" sky men in France

SWEEPING measures to stop attacks on Nazi officers in France were suddenly announced by Vichy last night.

The chief decree is death for parachutists, who were alleged to be one of the causes responsible for the attacks.

A statement from Admiral Darlan's office listed the "foreign parachutists" as "gangsters of the former Spanish Cheka, Jews and Communists."

Vichy radio added the phrase "organised by British agents." A guarded account was given of an attack on Madame Laval "by a bandit."

In the last three days 1,850 arrests have been made in France, making a total of 12,850 in six weeks.

U.S. DEFINES ALL AXIS AS "ENEMIES"

PRESIDENT ROOSEVELT has placed all Germans, Italians and Japanese in America in the category of "enemy aliens."

President Roosevelt said that in the case of the Japanese an invasion had been perpetrated on U.S. territory by Japan, and in the case of the Germans and the Italians, an invasion or predatory incursion was threatened.

His proclamation said that enemy aliens must "preserve peace towards America and refrain from crimes against the public, and actual hostility or giving aid to the enemy."

Nazi Declaration Soon

The arrest of 400 Germans and Italians designated "dangerous aliens" was begun by G men in America yesterday. Nine hundred Japs are detained under a previous proclamation.

"We naturally expect Germany to declare war on the U.S.," a Japanese spokesman in Tokio said last night.

NO GIFTS BY GERMANS

Appealing to the German people not to give Christmas presents, the Berlin announcer said last night: "This is a little sacrifice to ask when our soldiers are freezing on the Eastern Front."

HEALTHY GAINS for YOUR BABY

Deep, peaceful, unbroken sleep is vital to infant growth. Fretful, sleepless, those weekly ounces of gain do not appear on the scales. Mother, take care! Look to baby's digestion.

The minute you see baby feverish, constipated, suffering with wind, just give a little 'Milk of Magnesia' brand antacid. Soon comes pleasant relief. 'Milk of Magnesia' safely and surely sweetens the sour little stomach, regulates the tiny bowels, soothes and calms baby. And with sourness and sickness gone, with bowel movements regular, you are overjoyed to see restful, healthy sleep again. Baby makes those steady gains in weight, that are the delight of every Mother. Doctors and Nurses everywhere recommend 'Milk of Magnesia' as a safe, ideal antacid and gentle laxative for babies. Be careful, Mother, remember to ask for 'MILK of Magnesia,' which is the registered trade mark of Phillips' preparation of Magnesia. Prices, 1/5 and 2/10 (including Purchase Tax). You can get it everywhere.—(Advt.)

Japanese, Finns and Rumanians passing through London yesterday on the way to internment as enemy aliens. War was an unpleasant surprise to them.

Daily Mirror

DEC 11

No. 11,857   ONE PENNY

Registered at the G.P.O. as a Newspaper.

BRITISH TROOPS FORM NEW LINE AFTER HEAVY MALAY BATTLE

Soviet 2-front drive on Huns

WHILE the Russian war has been over-shadowed by the Pacific fighting, the Soviet forces have been gaining fresh successes.

Latest Russian victory is the recapture of Yeleta, 118 miles south-east of Tula.

This was announced in a special Moscow war communique last night, which added that the Nazis left behind 12,000 dead and large quantities of war material, including tanks.

The special communique followed a Soviet Information Bureau statement that, "on a number of sectors on the Moscow and Donetz fronts, Russian units moved forward and took a number of populated places."

Moscow radio reported that in the Kalinin sector seven villages had been retaken by the Red Army.

Ten thousand Germans were killed in the battle of Tikhvin. No prisoners were taken.

According to a New York broadcast last night, German armies in Russia are retiring to a depth of a hundred miles all along the front.

A Nazi military spokesman acknowledged that it was "possible" that the Russians had recaptured Tikhvin, because the Germans had withdrawn to bet-

"HITLER WANTS PEACE WITH RUSSIA"

Hitler would be ready to conclude peace with Russia if Moscow would agree to it, M. Lozovsky, Soviet spokesman, declared in a broadcast last night.

"The Hitler gang have just launched several peace kites," he said. "Hitler seems to be even inclined to quit big parts of Russia.

"There is no question, however, of Russia being prepared to make peace with Germany."

ter defence positions for the winter.

What were described as the spearheads of the German massed armies had now withdrawn from many regions of Russia, he said.

"Germany has no strategic ambitions this winter," the spokesman added.

More than 15,000 Germans have been annihilated during thirty days of the defence of Sebastopol, according to Red Star.

According to a high Rumanian source, Germany has asked Rumania to rush 500,000 men to the Russian front immediately as a consequence of the Rostov defeat.

REICHSTAG TO HEAR HITLER DECISION TODAY

FOLLOWING the sudden return to Berlin of Hitler, the German radio announced early today that the Reichstag will meet at 2 p.m. (B.S.T.) today.

Hitler will make a speech and a Government statement is expected.

Ankara reports stated that a joint German-Italian declaration of war on the United States was imminent.

The New York Times correspondent in Ankara suggested that Vichy France might range herself with the Axis Powers.

Darlan met Ciano, the Italian Foreign Minister, at Turin yesterday. According to Berne reports Darlan promised Italy warships.

Italy was said, in return, to have renounced territorial claims on France.

Boy, 15, cited in divorce

A FIFTEEN YEAR - OLD evacuee, James Hastings, was cited through his guardian as co-respondent in an undefended divorce case at Manchester Assizes, when a decree nisi was granted to Joe Fisher, a munitions foreman, on the ground of his 32-year-old wife's adultery.

The boy was said to have been evacuated from Salford to Fisher's house at Lancaster at the beginning of the war.

Fisher's case was that he and his wife had not lived together since August, 1939, and that Mrs. Fisher had written to him admitting misconduct with Hastings in October, 1939.

On her wedding morning, in 1934, Mrs. Fisher received a silver teapot which had been awarded to her in a "happiest bride" competition.

MINES IN NEW YORK HARBOUR

U.S. Navy Department announced late last night that the approaches to New York harbour have been mined.—British United Press.

Jap attack on Hong Kong fails

The Japanese attacking Hong Kong have suffered a reverse and a Japanese patrol has been wiped out.

"Our land forces have halted a Japanese attack, although fighting is continuing," stated a communique in Hong Kong yesterday.

Chinese forces in Kwangtung Province are attacking Canton from east and west, thus relieving the Japanese pressure on Hong Kong, according to a dispatch to a Chinese language newspaper.

BRITISH troops, fiercely resisting the Japanese drive on Singapore, were last night reorganising south of Kota Bahru, where the important airfield seems to have fallen into the Japs' hands after heavy fighting. Elsewhere in Malaya our frontier is unbroken.

BIG NAVAL BATTLE.—U.S. and Japanese Fleets are fighting off Hawaii. Berlin said the battle was the "biggest in naval history." Two British warships, Prince of Wales and Repulse, have been sunk off Singapore.

PHILIPPINES. — An American communique early today admitted that strong Japanese forces have landed on the island of Luzon, supported by big naval forces.

GUNS HIT HARD IN MALAY

BRITISH artillery inflicted severe losses on the Japanese in the fighting in Malay, Chungking radio reported last night.

The communique indicated that the aerodrome at Kota Bahru had been taken by the Japanese. It read:

"After acquitting themselves splendidly British troops have reorganised south of Kota Bahru and are now in excellent spirits after heavy fighting over a wide area.

"Our casualties are comparatively light. Elsewhere our frontier remains unbroken."

The communique said that in the Kedah area (fronting the Thai border) a Punjabi motorised unit destroyed seven enemy tanks.

Reinforcements

The situation at Kuantan—200 miles north of Singapore—remained unchanged since the morning communique, which reported the landing of Japanese troops and the attack of British land and air forces.

Naval and air reinforcements have arrived from the Dutch East Indies.

Dutch men o' war are already operating with Britain's Eastern Fleet in the China Seas.

Japan claimed that Japanese Marines landed at several points in the Gulf of Siam.

In Southern Thailand, said Tokio, Japanese troops are engaged with British troops.

Japanese troops are also claimed to be advancing from Southern Thailand in the direction of Singapore.

U.S. ADMIRAL KILLED DURING JAP ATTACK

Rear-Admiral Isaac C. Kidd, of the U.S. Navy, was killed at Pearl Harbour, Hawaii, during the Japanese attack on Sunday.

Admiral Kidd was flag secretary and aide on the staff of Admiral Kimmel, Pacific Fleet Commander-in-Chief. He was commanding a battleship division when killed.—Associated Press.

Are Japanese using a new sea weapon?

BRITISH naval experts are mystified by the sinking of the Prince of Wales.

The mystery will not be cleared up until full reports have been received from the Far East, but there was much speculation in London last night as to whether the Japanese had stolen a march on the navies of the world in constructing an aerial torpedo far bigger than anything now in use.

The possibility that the attack was made by a suicide squadron of bomber pilots, who blew themselves and their planes up against the ships, is not ruled out in London.

How the Prince of Wales and Repulse went down—page 5.

C-in-C was aboard Prince of Wales

The new C-in-C., Eastern Fleet, Rear-Admiral Sir Tom Phillips—Tom Thumb they call him because of his 5ft. 4in.—was on the Prince of Wales when she put to sea.

Patrols have been sent out to search for survivors from the Prince of Wales and Repulse.

The "loss of many brave sailors and highly - trained officers" was referred to by Mr. Duff Cooper in a broadcast from Singapore last night.

Rear-Admiral Phillips.

U.S. wants USSR bases

AMERICA is awaiting clarification from Moscow of the role to be played by Russia in the Anglo-U.S. war with Japan (cables John Walters from New York).

It is regarded as a matter of great urgency that Russia permits U.S.A. to establish air bases at Vladivostok.

With the use of such bases America could inflict severe damage on Japan.

But British United Press reported from Kuibishev last night that there is no evidence yet to justify an anticipation that Russia will abandon her policy to Japan—neutrality based on the Russo-Japanese Pact.

BIG JAP LANDING ON LUZON

STRONG Japanese forces have succeeded in landing on the west coast of Luzon, the island in the Philippines on which Manila is situated.

This was admitted in a communique issued by the United States War Department early today.

The communique said the landings were supported by heavy Japanese naval forces.

All day yesterday Japanese air forces made intermittent attacks on American military and naval installations on Luzon Island.

Particularly heavy assaults were made on the naval base at Cavite.

The War Department said that the initial Japanese attacks against the west coast of Luzon were repulsed with apparent heavy enemy losses.

The communique added that no action had been reported in the Hawaiian Islands since the initial attack on Sunday.

As the battle for the Philippines began to develop on a large scale, two waves of Japanese bombers raided Manila, the capital.

Military establishments, including Nichols Air Depot and Fort McKinley and the Nielson

Continued on Back Page

JAPS OCCUPY GUAM AND WAKE ISLANDS

GUAM and Wake Islands, two of America's most important "stepping stones" in the Pacific, were occupied yesterday by the Japanese.

Midway Island, 1,400 miles west of Honolulu, is being shelled.

This news came after President Roosevelt, in his speech early yesterday, had uttered this warning:—"Reports from Guam, Wake and Midway Islands are still confused, but we must be prepared for the announcement that all these three outposts have been seized."

The attacks on the Hawaiian Islands, Guam, The Philippines, Wake Island, and Singapore started simultaneously, the Japanese communique said, and Guam was occupied at noon (2 a.m. B.S.T.) yesterday.

The loss of Guam, which is 1,200 miles east of Manila, is a serious blow to the U.S. as this defence outpost lies in the heart of the Japanese mandated islands.—British United Press and Associated Press

Daily Mirror

DEC 12

No. 11,858

ONE PENNY

Registered at the G.P.O. as a Newspaper.

5 JAP WARSHIPS SUNK BY U.S. NAVY BOMBERS

AMERICAN naval bombers yesterday showed the Japanese that their warships can be destroyed from the air by sinking five of her naval vessels in the Pacific.

This was Japan's first big naval loss of the war —a battleship, a cruiser, a destroyer and two other naval units.

The 29,000 - ton battleship Hiranuma caught fire when bombed ten miles north-east of Northern Luzon in the Philippines. She sank later.

The cruiser and destroyer were sunk off Wake Island. These successes, National Broadcasting Company stated, were announced by the U.S. War Department, which also told of how Japanese attempt to capture Wake Island had been checked.

Four separate attacks were repulsed by the defending U.S. forces in the last forty-eight hours.

More Japanese attacks are expected.

Strong Japanese forces continued yesterday to try to establish themselves on the northern coast of Luzon.

"Driven Back to Coast"

Determined resistance confined this action to an attack in the vicinity of Aparri.

Manila, the capital, said the invaders had been driven back to the sea coast in this area.

Air activity continued in the vicinity of Manila, with intermittent attacks on the airfield at Cavite and Nichols Air Field.

Mr. Stimson, War Secretary said that Aparri was a small landing place shut off from the main part of the island by mountains, and added that if the Japanese attempt to transport an army through the mountain passes it will be a slow job.

He said that losses in planes

■ **Continued on Back Page**

SOVIET AT SIDE OF AMERICA

—Litvinov

M. LITVINOV, Soviet Ambassador to Washington, said last night that Russia was fighting side by side with U.S.A. in aid of the common cause.

He added, however, that he could not define his Government's attitude towards the American-Japanese war.

The Ambassador made his statement after he had been received by Mr. Cordell Hull, U.S. Secretary of State. Previously he had gone to see Mr. Roosevelt and Mr. Harry Hopkins.

Aid Pledge Renewed

He also had an interview with Lord Halifax.

Mr. Hull told his Press conference that he had no doubt that the Soviet Union would do its "full part in standing side by side with all liberty-loving people against the common menace."

Mr. Hull reiterated the U.S. pledge of continued aid for the Soviet Union.

Mr. Cordell Hull's statement was apparently intended to end reports that Russia might not extend full co-operation.

89—NEVER HAD A BATH

Ellen Haworth, 89, of Salesbury, near Blackburn, was said at a Blackburn inquest yesterday to have never had a bath. Verdict: Death from senility accelerated by gross neglect.

U.S. to call up 10,000,000— war on Axis

AMERICA last night announced vast plans to mobilise the nation's man and woman power a few hours after Congress had unanimously voted for declaring war on Germany and Italy.

Brigadier - General Louis Hershey, Director of Selective Service, stated that—

10,000,000 men will be called up

20,000,000 women will do war work

Hershey (cables John Walters from New York) said that of the 40,000,000 men in the United States, 12,500,000 could be called up if needed.

The immediate aim is to raise an army of 4,000,000.

Plans are being pushed for the black-out of New York, and on the east coast A.A. guns are being manned.

Sea approaches to Chesapeake Bay have been mined, and radio stations in the

Col. Knox in Honolulu

Colonel Knox, U.S. Secretary of the Navy, has arrived in Honolulu, which was subjected to heavy attacks by Japanese planes.

States of Washington and Oregon have been ordered to close.

A.R.P. services are being re-organised, and people are rushing to the shops to buy black-out materials, candles, torches and batteries.

Congress, having declared war on Germany and Italy, unanimously approved the sending of U.S. conscripts and national guards (territorials) abroad.

It is believed in Washington that America will send troops to Martinique, French Guiana and elsewhere.

President Roosevelt, in a message to Congress asking for declaration of war on Germany and Italy, referred to the fact that the Axis Powers had, a few hours before, told America that they were at war with her.

"The long known and long expected has thus taken place," he said. "The forces endeavouring to enslave the entire world now are moving toward this hemisphere."

mden attacked in daylight

Aircraft of Bomber Command again operated in daylight yesterday. Targets attacked included a dock near mden and an aerodrome in Holland.

All the planes returned.

WHY NO AIR SUPPORT OF SUNK SHIPS?

BY OUR POLITICAL CORRESPONDENT

THE Prince of Wales and the Repulse had no protection by our aircraft when the Japanese planes roared down from the clouds.

Our shore based planes, placed there for just such an emergency were unable to give the support it had been hoped because the Japanese land forces were at that moment attacking their aerodrome.

M.P.s listened aghast while questions drew this information from the Prime Minister in the House of Commons yesterday

"Keyes, Keyes" Cry

It was Sir Roger Keyes who lit the spark which for a moment seemed likely to cause an explosion. Immediately the Prime Minister sat down after reviewing the war situation for an hour (see report in page 2) but saying little on the point on which the House was most wanted information, a dozen M.P.s leaped to their feet.

But the cries from all sides of "Keyes, Keyes," showed that there was only one man they wanted to hear.

First he attempted to ask if the Prince of Wales was as well protected against underwater attack as the Bismarck, but was ruled out of order

■ **Continued on Back Page**

DOCTORS ASK BONUS

The Ministry of Health is to be asked for a war bonus for insurance doctors, who say that the present basic capitation fee, including next January's increase, is inadequate.

The extension of medical benefit to those earning £420 a year will result in a capitation fee increase from 9s. 2d. to 9s. 9d., whereas in 1922 the fee was 11s. 2d.

Spanish border is closed

SPAIN last night closed her frontier with France, according to Swiss reports quoted by British United Press.

Over the border, in Unoccupied France, there was a wave of arrests.

A hundred people were seized in Toulon.

At Nice, 3,600 were questioned and many arrested.

At the same time, Vichy radio said that 2,000 people, presumably in Occupied France, had been arrested "for not observing the curfew imposed by the German authorities."

Australians bomb Jap base

Australian bombers, based on the Dutch East Indies, have raided the Japanese air base on the Island of Pobra, between Celebes and Palau, south-east of the Philippines, said last night's Dutch East Indies Army communique.

One aircraft is missing.—Associated Press.

Sub.'s first V.C

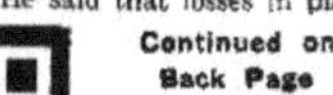

Ian, bonny two-year-old son of the submarine V.C.— Lieut. - Commander M. D. Wanklyn.

Royal baby's blue room

Preparations have been made for the arrival of the Duchess of Gloucester's baby within the next fortnight.

Upholsterers are painting and decorating two of the mullion-windowed bedrooms in a colour scheme of blue and white.

These will be the day and night nurseries. They will be the only bright colours in the severe stone-grey and brown colour scheme of the mixed Tudor and modern manor in which the baby will be born.

Blue indicates the wish that the baby will be an heir.

WILL WE ASK RUSSIA TO FIGHT JAPAN?

Mr. D L Lipson (Ind., Cheltenham) will ask the Prime Minister if the Government proposes to ask for war on Japan, following the precedent set up when the Soviet asked Britain to declare war on Finland, Rumania and Hungary.

V.C.—but mother in tears

THE widowed mother of Lieutenant - Commander Malcolm David Wanklyn, D.S.O., commander of H.M. Submarine Upholder, wept when she heard yesterday that he had won the V.C.

"Isn't that wonderful?" she cried, at her Kensington, W., flat. "He told me in a letter that he had been recommended for a decoration, but I never expected this."

This is the first V.C. won by a submarine commander in this war and seventh to go to the Navy

In relentless attacks he has hit at least thirteen enemy ships, including a U-boat, a cruiser, destroyers, transports, tankers and supply ships.

While on patrol off the coast of Sicily last May Lieutenant-Commander Wanklyn sighted a south-bound enemy troop convoy strongly escorted by destroyers.

Sank Troopship

Just as he was about to fire one of the enemy destroyers suddenly appeared out of the darkness at high speed, and he only just avoided being rammed.

Then he fired torpedoes which sank a large troopship.

The enemy destroyers then dropped thirty-seven depth charges near Upholder, but he brought her safe back to harbour.

Lieutenant - Commander Wanklyn, who was born in India, was married in Malta just over three years ago

ONE DELIVERY ONLY

Only one delivery of letters and parcels will be made on Christmas Day in England, Wales and Northern Ireland.

Pain after Meals

Is your stomach still struggling with your last meal? You're gasping with wind and doubled up with indigestion. Why? Because your stomach is always too acid. It sours every mouthful. It turns meat into leather. You can stop these agonising attacks this very day by taking 'Milk of Magnesia' Tablets. They relieve acidity at once. No matter what you eat, your stomach makes easy work of digesting it. No sour repeating, no heartburn no flatulence, not a twinge of your old agony.

What about your next meal? Are you going to submit to torture when 'Milk of Magnesia' Tablets will save you? Make that meal the test. Get a box of the Tablets now and have them in readiness. You'll be thankful you tried them. Neat flat boxes for the pocket, 7d. and 1/1½d. Also family sizes, 2/3 and 3/11½d. (Including Purchase Tax) Obtainable everywhere.

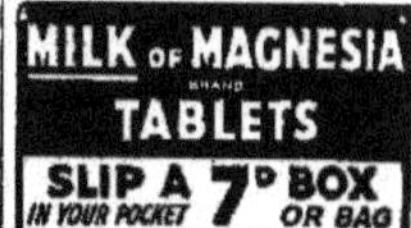

'Milk of Magnesia' is the trade mark of Phillips' preparation of Magnesia

Admiral Tom's last message—see page 5

Daily Mirror

DEC 15

No. 11,860   ONE PENNY

Registered at the G.P.O. as a Newspaper.

The Yellow Dwarfs won't like this!

"HI-HO, HI-HO, WE'RE OFF FOR TOKIO,

"TO BOMB EACH JAP RIGHT OFF THE MAP, HI-HO, HI-HO."

This is the war song of defiance composed by New York City's school-children, cables the "Daily Mirror" New York correspondent.

It is sung to the tune of "Hi-Ho," from the Disney film, "Snow White and the Seven Dwarfs."

JAPS PUSH ON HONG KONG, BURMA, MALAYA

TAGANROG CUT OFF

TAGANROG, into which Soviet troops drove the Germans after chasing them sixty miles from Rostov, is surrounded.

This announcement by the Russians last night followed a German admission that their Eastern Front forces are almost everywhere on the defensive.

From two other fronts—Moscow and Leningrad — came news of successes as the Soviet forces followed up their offensive which saved Moscow and the Caucasus.

The Soviet leader, General Godorov, revealed last night that a blazing barrier of hay, straw and other material about eight feet high checked the German drive on Moscow long enough for a counter-attack to be started.

At that time the Nazis were only twenty miles from Moscow, two spearheads having advanced on the flanks of the Mohisk highway to Goluitsino, south-west of the capital, and Svenigorodo, to the north-west.

After the Russians had erected their blazing barrier tank reinforcements arrived and routed the Germans.

Moscow Clean-up

The position on the main fronts now is:—

Moscow.—The Red Army, sweeping the Nazis in front of it, is clearing the approaches to Moscow with lightning thrusts.

Latest places to fall in this sector are Livyny and Yesrenov, in the Velets area, Uzlovaia, south-east of Tula; Dubna, west of Tula, and Verkhove, north-east of Livyny.

Moscow radio claimed last night that in the direction of Orel Soviet troops had made big advances.

German men and materials are being hurriedly evacuated from the most northern sector of the Kalinin front. The Germans are carrying away members of the Russian civilian population in their retreat.

Donetz.—Russians are pressing on without giving the Germans any respite.

They advanced so quickly that the Nazis did not have time to take their prisoners with them.

Leningrad.—The Russians have killed 400 Germans and occupied another point. A considerable amount of booty was captured

Allied war council is expected

A HINT that a Supreme War Council of the Allies is to be formed soon was given by Sir Keith Murdoch, former Australian Director-General of Information, in last night's B.B.C. postscript.

Speaking of America's entry into the war, Sir Keith said: "No doubt the vital Supreme War Council will soon be set up for the great war plan of victory."

Britain's war effort was "very great, thorough and brave" and it felt short anywhere of being a total effort, then it was not the fault of the people. The people were putting their whole lives into the business.

There is strong support by M.P.s for a suggestion that an Allied War Council should be set up immediately, writes the Daily Mirror Political Correspondent.

M.P.'s Question

Mr. Edgar Granville (Nat. Lib. Eve) is to ask the Prime Minister:—

Whether, in view of the fact that most of the world is now involved in the war, and that four-fifths of the population support our cause, he will consider taking steps to create an Allied War Council to include the representatives of Great Britain, Russia and the United States for the purpose of obtaining on all matters affecting production, propaganda, and the "world scale strategy" called for by President Roosevelt.

If the Prime Minister's answer is not considered satisfactory, an attempt may be made to secure a debate.

A "brains trust" of British, American and Russian scientists is being planned.

CHINA MISSION FOR MOSCOW

China Foreign Minister will go to Moscow very soon on a special mission, states the Swiss radio.

Leave Army for factory

Some men who did skilled jobs before the war are being released from the Army to make arms and munitions.

National Registration Officers now receive ex-soldiers who say they have been sent back to their old job and ask for civilian identity cards.

New code numbers exist in the National Register for these men who have to re-register when they leave the Army.

(Man-power Thefts Muddle War Drive—page 1.)

INTERNED — 'FIRST CLASS'

Nearly all British, United States and other Allied nationals in Bangkok, Thailand's capital, have been interned in a first-class hotel, says Axis radio.

Arrows on the large map show the directions from which the Chinese are attacking to relieve Japanese pressure on Hong Kong. Map inset is an enlargement showing the area of the Hong Kong Settlement, shown in black circle on the larger map. Senchuah is believed to be held by Chinese, who are advancing on the railway to Kowloon, now claimed by Japanese, which is the gateway to the fortified island of Hong Kong itself.

4 JAP TROOPSHIPS SUNK

A MERICAN bombers have sunk four Japanese troopships and damaged three others, a U.S. communique from Manila (Philippines) announced last night.

Japanese submarines are operating in Hawaiian waters and "vigorous attacks" are being made against them, said a Washington statement.

The Washington communique added:—

"There have been two additional bombing attacks on Wake Island. The first was light, but the second was undertaken in great force.

"Two enemy bombers were shot down. Damage was inconsequential.

"Marines on Wake Island continue to resist."

Japan has probably captured Guam, said a U.S. Navy Department statement.

Japanese air activity continues in the Philippines.

The total Japanese air losses from all causes during the first week of the war with U.S.A. are not less than forty.

Probably many others were lost

Japanese Army headquarters in Tokio reported yesterday that twelve planes were seen off Takao, Formosa.

It was claimed that the planes turned away without approaching the city.

13 men held drome

H EROISM of a rearguard of twelve Indian soldiers led by a British officer, Lieutenant Close, enabled the main body defending Khota Baru Aerodrome, Malaya to escape from superior Japanese forces.

The story, pieced together by a group of sepoys who were among the last to leave Khota Baru, came from Singapore yesterday.

Soon after midnight on December 8, Japanese troops reached the aerodrome, supported by aircraft, attacking it with bombs, machine-gun fire and hand grenades.

Destroyed Everything

Our forces decided to withdraw, destroying everything worth while in the aerodrome, leaving behind Lieutenant Close and his twelve sepoys.

Fighting gallantly under heavy pressure on land and in the air and with everything around them burning, they kept the Japs at bay long enough for all the remaining defenders to get free of the enemy.

Nothing has been heard since of Lieutenant Close, although some of the rearguard escaped and told of his bravery.

ANOTHER DEFEAT

Switzerland beat Germany by 3—1 in an international football match yesterday, said a Swiss broadcast.

London has a practice "Alert"

London's brief "Alert"— the first in the capital since November 1—early yesterday evening was a practice warning.

It was one of the shortest "Alerts" of the war, lasting only four minutes. Few people had time to get in their shelters before the "All clear" sounded.

NAZIS' PUPPETS IN WAR

Bulgaria, Rumania, Hungary, and the Axis puppet States of Croatia and Slovakia have declared war on the United States. Bulgaria, Croatia and Slovakia also declared war on Great Britain.

J APANESE forces were last night launching offensives against three points of the British Empire—Burma, Hong Kong and Malaya. The size of the attacks on Burma and Hong Kong are not yet known, but a big battle is raging in the jungle around Kedah, North-West Malaya.

Latest news from these Far East battle fronts is:—

HONG KONG

Tokio radio said that Japanese land and air units started a "general offensive" at dawn yesterday.

As city itself was being shelled by artillery British artillery opened up and shelled the Japanese gun positions

The Governor, Major-General E. F. Norton, refused to surrender in response to a demand by the Japanese commander.

General Norton, D.S.O., M.C., was leader of the Mount Everest expedition in 1924, which reached a height of 28,100ft.

Chang Kai Shek's forces are attacking north and north-west of Canton in an attempt to ease Japanese pressure on Hong Kong.

Chinese troops are reported to have occupied Senchuah, and to be pushing along the Canton-Kowloon railway

BURMA

"A slight penetration into Burma from Thailand by Japanese forces has taken place in the Point Victoria region," said an authorised London statement.

"Details of the entry into Burma are lacking, but it is believed to have been made by a force landed on the other side of the Peninsula some days ago."

Heavy air raids on Victoria were made by the Japanese.

MALAYA

British and Indian troops are fiercely resisting large-scale attacks in the north-western extremity of Malaya, where the Japanese have landed considerable reinforcements.

"Stubborn fighting continues

Continued on Back Page

DUTCH NAVY BAG EIGHT SHIPS

More successes by Dutch submarines in Malayan waters have been reported. N.B.C. (New York) stated:—

The Dutch submarine which was previously reported to have sunk four Japanese troop transports has scored another success by torpedoing two more Japanese troop transport ships and damaging four others.

An enemy oil tanker and a supply ship were sunk by other Dutch submarines, the latest Singapore communique stated.

'All with you' —Churchill

The Prime Minister sent this telegram to the Governor and defenders of Hong Kong yesterday:—

"We are all watching day by day your stubborn defence of the port and fortress of Hong Kong. You guard a link famous in world civilisation between the Far East and Europe. We are sure that the defence against barbarous and unprovoked attack will add a glorious page to British annals.

"All our hearts are with you in your ordeal. Every day of your resistance brings nearer our certain victory."

When Home on My Last Leave My Wife Heard Nothing But

'Yeast-Vite, Yeast-Vite, Yeast-Vite'

—— R.A.F. Station. Nov. 17th, 1941.

Dear Sirs,—Boy, oh boy, am I a new man thanks to Yeast-Vite!

When home on my last leave my wife heard nothing but "Yeast-Vite, Yeast-Vite, Yeast-Vite." But believe me I hope I shall never be without a bottle of them. I can recommend them to anyone for a genuine pick-me-up.

After having a very serious operation a few weeks ago I was terribly depressed, nervy and run-down, also sleepless. I started taking Yeast-Vite tablets and thanks to them I feel five years younger now than I did before I decided to try them.

You are at liberty to use this letter.

(Sgd.) E. W.

Burton-on-Trent, Nov. 11th, 1941.

Dear Sirs,

I have a patient recuperating from pneumonia, so I gave her a course of Yeast-Vite tablets and they have been a wonderful tonic.

(Sgd.) F.G.R., S.R.N.

Yeast-Vite Tonic Tablets being a relief from Headaches, Nerves, etc.,
Depression, Insomnia, Rheumatism, Indigestion, etc. Sold everywhere at 1/-,
3/3, & 5/4, including purchase tax.

Daily Mirror

DEC 17

No. 11,862   ONE PENNY
Registered at the G.P.O. as a Newspaper.

RETREAT FROM MOSCOW NOW A GERMAN ROUT

Allies plan war council: Hustle in 3 countries

BY OUR POLITICAL CORRESPONDENT

PLANS for the formation of an Allied Supreme War Council were being hurried forward in three countries last night.

Discussions with the British Diplomatic and Service representatives are taking place in both Moscow and Washington.

This can be revealed following the statement of the Lord Privy Seal in the Commons yesterday that all necessary steps are being taken to concert the military plans of the major allied Powers.

The Prime Minister and the Cabinet are understood to be in hourly contact with the principal Allied Governments.

Proceeding Favourably

First official news of the progress of negotiations may be given in the Government answer this week to Mr. Edgar Granville's question asking whether a Council to co-ordinate Allied production and strategy would be set up.

When the full story of these negotiations is known it will rank as one of the most dramatic episodes of the war.

Mr. Roosevelt said last night, according to British United Press: "Conversations designed to co-ordinate the Allied military effort are proceeding favourably."

Nova Scotia (Canada) radio reported last night that preliminary steps have been taken to conclude a military alliance between Britain, America and the Soviet Union.

THE German retreat from Moscow has become a rout. Recapture by the Russians of Kalinin, key point on the Moscow-Leningrad railway, from which the Huns launched repeated onslaughts against the capital, was announced early today.

Kalinin is 103 miles north-west of Moscow and fifty miles from Klin, captured twenty-four hours earlier.

The Ninth German Army, under General Strauss, was heavily defeated and six divisions were destroyed.

Remnants of these divisions are now retreating westwards.

The German panzer units which attacked so fiercely are now retreating with, in many cases, horse-drawn sleighs which they stole from peasants, replacing their shattered armoured vehicles.

Like wild beasts they are possessed by one desire—self-preservation.

The special communique adds that in the fighting for Kalinin, troops under Lieutenant-General Maslenikov and Major-General Yushkevich particularly distinguished themselves.

A great amount of booty was brought in. The enemy is being pursued and destroyed by Russian troops.

Many Towns Taken

The Russian communique also said that in several sectors of the Moscow and Donetz fronts Russian troops occupied towns and villages among them being Vysokoie (125 miles north-west of Moscow), Volovo (73 miles south of Tula) and Novopetrovsk.

The Russian counter-offensive now extends from the Sea of Azov to the sub-Arctic region—over 1,000 miles.

The Finnish High Command last night reported that the Russians had begun a general offensive in the Ostra sector, around the southern end of Lake Anega.

As this attack continues Moscow radio broadcast last night a "kill-every-Nazi" call to the Red Army.

The announcer declared: "Remember the enemy crimes. Do not spare them. Do not let one German slip through your hands alive. Help us to avenge the deaths and torture of our wives and children."

How Klin Fell

A Soviet military spokesman claimed the disintegration of the Finnish Army, which could no longer be regarded as a protecting flank for the Germans.

Soviet troops smashed through the German lines to recapture Klin (fifty miles north-west of Moscow) from opposite ends, stated Moscow radio last night. Enemy troops are being hotly pursued.

On the Tula front Russian forces penetrated into the rear of the enemy, and cavalry, commanded by General Belov, supported by artillery, are continuing the advance. A Nazi column was wiped out in this area.

D.S.O. FOR DESERT AIRMAN

Lieutenant-Commander J. W. S. Corbett, R.N., Fleet Air Arm, who, says the London Gazette, has been awarded the D.S.O., has been unceasingly active in attacking concentrations of enemy transport, ammunition dumps and other targets in the Western Desert. His squadron has particularly distinguished itself.

JAPAN'S WARSHIPS SHELL U.S. ISLANDS

JAPANESE warships, being sought by the U.S. Fleet, have been shelling U.S. islands in the Hawaiian area, announced Washington last night, "within the past twenty-four hours."

Naval operations are continuing against the enemy, it was added.

The two islands named are Johnston, a naval base between Pearl Harbour and Wake Island, and Maui, where the shipping centre of Kahului was bombarded by a submarine. Damage in both islands was slight.

Wake Island, much-battered U.S. air base west of Hawaii, has had more air raids but is holding. So is Midway Island, another air base.

Tokio issued a statement that the occupation of Guam was completed on December 12 with the capture of 350 Americans, including the Governor, Mr George McMillan.

In the Philippines, ground fighting is only of a local character, and air attacks have been of no consequence. Four Japanese fighter planes have been shot down.

★ ★ ★

New York got a report from Honolulu last night that radio communication with Wake Island had been made.

Asked what they needed most, American sailors on Wake Island replied: "Send us some more Japs."

Tokio claim to land tanks in Malaya drive

FOR the first time since war broke out in the Pacific, no British communique was issued in Singapore yesterday, and no official comment was offered on the fighting in Malaya.

A large number of tanks have been landed by the Japanese on the east coast of Malaya, said a Japanese spokesman at Shanghai last night. They will soon intervene in the fighting there, he added.

While he stressed the difficulties of tanks in the jungle, he

Continued on Back Page

Two-man subs. came 100 miles

MIDGET, two-man submarines were launched from a Japanese submarine "mother ship" which approached within about 100 miles of the Hawaiian island of Oahu on December 12.

This was revealed by the U.S. Navy last night.

The U.S. Navy has captured one of these midget submarines, which are manned by one officer and a rating. They have a 200-mile cruising range, and can be launched over the side of a larger vessel.

"There are indications that the personnel operating these submarines will go to any extreme, however desperate, even to self-destruction, to carry out their objective," a Navy Department official said.

PARIS BOMB ON GESTAPO

Three attacks on Germans were made in Paris yesterday.

A bomb exploded in a German military police mess. No further details are given.

A bomb was also thrown in the headquarters of the Gestapo in the Paris suburb of Villejuif and six people died. A German soldier—believed to be a lieutenant—was killed.

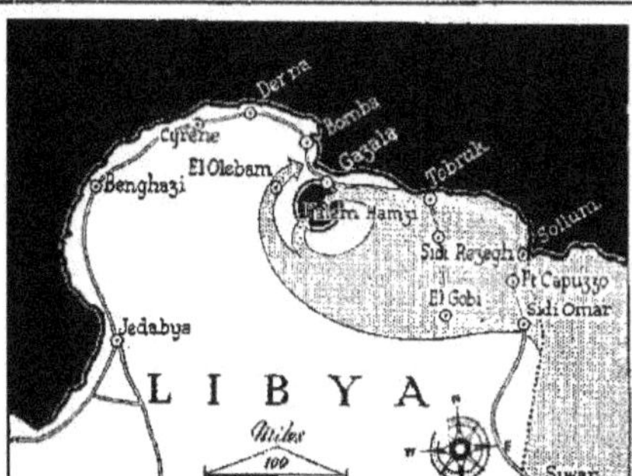

The position of the main battle in Libya is shown in this map, the shaded part of which is the area we hold. We have penetrated the German (black circle) main positions in a pincer movement, our southern sweep of these two concentrating on Halem Hamzi, where Rommel has all his reserve tanks. Our wider sweep to El Olebam, cutting the Axis supplies for the big battle, is shown by the left-hand arrow

We take Rommel reserves in rear

THREE fierce battles are raging amid dust-storms in Libya.

The main battle is near Gazala. German infantry, strongly entrenched, are staging desperate counter-attacks on our troops, who have penetrated their positions and keep steadily pressing forward.

All available German dive-bombers have been thrown into these attempts to save a vast quantity of supplies, but the R.A.F. have dealt with the Nazi planes.

Severe fighting broke out round Hamel Hamzi, fifteen miles to the south. Rommel had concentrated all his remaining tanks here, when our south-west sweep took these reserves—the remnant of a German panzer division and three Italian divisions—in the rear.

Indian troops penetrated the Axis positions.

Hard-pressed Rommel suddenly became aware of the third battle—a result of our great strategical sweep to El Olebam thirty miles to the west, not only trapping the enemy's reserves and supplies for the big battle, but threatening Derna.

Infantry Masses

A great number of German and Italian infantry supporting the tanks and armoured vehicles were flung into two counter-attacks, but our men threw them back and pressed on.

On Monday New Zealanders captured many machine-guns and 11,000 prisoners at little cost.

Polish troops took 200

Continued on Back Page

TOY PRICES CONTROLLED

TOY prices will be regulated from today, says a Board of Trade announcement.

This will knock the bottom out of the black market, in which toys bought at a low price in London were being sold to evacuees in country towns at three and four times their value.

Small dolls, bought for 5s., were being sold at £1.

Other articles for which prices are regulated today are: Motorcycles and parts; cooking, heating and other appliances and apparatus for personal or domestic use; boot polishes, floor polishes; trunks, women's handbags, suitcases and shopping baskets.

RITCHIE IS PROMOTED

Major-General (temporary) N. M. Ritchie, whose appointment as commander of the 8th Army in Libya in place of General Cunningham was announced by Mr. Churchill a week ago, is granted the acting rank of Lieutenant-General.

Smile all the while

Whatever the day brings we've got to keep smiling. So let's make our smiles worth while. Above all don't take chances with your teeth. Don't risk using tooth-pastes which employ abrasives to secure whiteness. They can't avoid injuring the thin coating of enamel which alone prevents decay. What about the paste you are using now? Grind a little between your front teeth. If there's the least trace of grittiness change to Odol. All Dentists know Odol is absolutely safe, yet it makes and keeps your teeth like pearls.

Besides being perfect for natural teeth, Odol Tooth Powder cleans False Teeth and Plates beautifully. Tube, ⅓ bn.

Daily Mirror

DEC 22

No. 11,866 — ONE PENNY
Registered at the G.P.O. as a Newspaper.

HITLER ADMITS A FULL STOP, TAKES OVER ALL COMMAND

HITLER has sacked the beaten von Brauchitsch, called off any further offensive in Russia till the spring, promised better defences of the western coast—and taken over supreme personal command of all German forces.

Last night he issued a "Backs to the wall" appeal to all Nazi soldiers in an effort to raise their morale.

In this personal plea he admits many difficulties, states that they are on the defensive, promises new weapons, and points to Japan's Pacific invasions as a timely help.

That all is not well within the German Army is shown in his reminder that he was wounded twice in the war of 1914-18, and there are no difficulties of the rank and file that he does not understand.

Here is this strange appeal of the Fuehrer:—

"The battle for the liberty of our people is now approaching its culminating and turning point.

Hell Tokio.

"The German Reich, Italy and the nations allied to us have had the fortune to find in Japan, who is a world Power, a new friend and comrade in arms.

"With the lightning destruction of the American Pacific Fleet, and the British forces at Singapore, with the occupation of numerous British and American bases in Western Asia by the Japanese forces, the present war is now entering upon a new and favourable stage for us.

"The armies in the East, after their immortal victories without parallel in world history against the most dangerous enemy of all time, must now, owing to the sudden onset of winter, be brought into a stationary front.

"It is their task, up to the coming of spring, to hold and defend with like fanaticism what they have hitherto conquered with immeasurable heroism and heavy sacrifices.

"Fresh units will be formed, and above all new and better weapons will be issued as they were last winter.

"The defence of the front in the West will be strength-

■ Continued on Back Page

Women's fur coats for German troops

The German radio regularly interrupted its programme last night to make special appeals for warm clothing for the troops on the Eastern front, following Goebbels's broadcast requests.

The announcer claimed that Goebbels's appeal had brought an overwhelming response, and gave listeners tips on how to make up warm clothing from scraps of wool and cloth.

"Minor alterations can make women's fur coats suitable for soldiers at the front," he said.

DUCHESS, BABY, DOING WELL

The Duchess of Gloucester and her baby son continue to make satisfactory progress. It was stated last night.

MALAYA: JAPS GAIN GROUND

BRITISH forces in north-eastern Malaya have withdrawn forty-five miles. The Japanese claim the whole of the north-western province of Wellesley.

Both sides now expect the guerrilla warfare to develop into a pitched battle across the widest part of the peninsula.

In the Philippines, the centre of the battle has shifted to Mindanao, the southern island, where says a U.S. communique, the position is "obscure."

Rome radio claimed last night that Japanese troops had made a landing in New Guinea, "which is of great strategic importance." (New Guinea, 69,700 square miles, under Australian mandate, lies to the north of the Australian continent.

(The southernmost point of New Guinea is only about 100 miles from the most northern point of Queensland.)

MALAYA

OUR Kelantan (north-eastern Malaya) withdrawal was announced officially in Singapore last night.

We had lost the aerodrome of Khota Bharu some days ago, and the vulnerability of our communications made a retirement advisable.

Our forces are now at Kualakrai, forty-five miles down the Central Malayan railway to Singapore.

"The withdrawal," says the announcement, "involved a series of co-ordinated night movements which resulted in bringing out the greater part of the British forces and the majority of stores and equipment despite attempted enemy interference."

This news, together with the loss of Penang on the west, has made the whole island of Singapore alive to the possibility of attack from any direction.

PHILIPPINES

JAPANESE appear to be striving to increase their forces invading the Philippines at several points, said the U.S. War Department last night.

Saigon radio states that heavy fighting is taking place.

A submarine lurking close to Northern California attacked the U.S tanker Emidio without warning, and left the 6,912-ton vessel sinking. It was sunk in Washington last night.

The captain and twenty-nine members of the crew have arrived at Blunt's Lightship, off California. Five of the crew are missing.

ROOSEVELT GREETS STALIN

Roosevelt has sent a telegram of birthday congratulations to Stalin, who was 62 yesterday.

When the Daily Mirror asked the Foreign Office and Mr. Churchill's secretary last night whether Mr. Churchill had sent a birthday message to Stalin, the reply was: "We have nothing to say about it."

The B.B.C. broadcast yesterday a special concert of Russian music from a Midland town in honour of Stalin's birthday.

Trick to save his own skin

General opinion in diplomatic circles last night was that Hitler's announcement was a cunningly designed move to throw the whole blame for the defeats on Field-Marshal Von Brauchitsch.

Hitler is thus, for the time being, allowed to retain his reputation and preserve the legend that he is the man who cannot make a mistake.

Hong Kong battle on racecourse

BITTER fighting and organised resistance was still continuing at Hong Kong at midday yesterday, says a radio message from the colony.

The Japanese say that the severest land encounter was near Happy Valley Racecourse (opposite Kowloon), and that direct hits were scored by Japanese planes on British gunboats in Deep Water Bay, on the other side of the island. One gunboat was sunk it was claimed.

Tokio also claimed that strong Japanese forces had occupied heights in spite of a fierce British barrage.

Despite their confident pronouncements about Hong Kong, the Japanese Cabinet Information Board yesterday issued a special notice advising people to refrain from excessive jubilation "when" the fall of Hong Kong is announced.

King's Message

Chinese forces are pushing forward near Shumchun, about seventeen miles from the Kowloon frontier. They are attacking Japanese positions ten miles beyond that town.

The King has sent the following message to Sir Mark Young, Governor of Hong Kong:—

"The thoughts of all at home are with you, and the people of Hong Kong, in your ordeal. I congratulate all ranks of the Fighting Services on their courageous resistance in the face of heavy odds, and I send my best wishes to you and all in the island. — George R.I."

It was announced yesterday that the Governor sent this message to all Forces on Friday after the Japanese had landed on the island:—

"The eyes of the Empire are on you. Be strong, be resolute, and do your duty."

MORE ATTACKS ON CAVITE AND WAKE

Japanese planes have again bombed Cavite and made two more attacks on Wake Island, a U.S. Navy communique announced in Washington.— British United Press.

Bag 10,000 Axis men in Libya chase

IN spite of severe dust storms in Libya, the British and Allied forces are still pursuing the Axis troops at full speed everywhere.

Ten thousand prisoners—6,000 Italians, 4,000 Germans—already have been numbered and registered, but many more are being rounded up.

The bulk of the German armoured forces seem to be in the Benghazi-Soluk area, while the remnants of the Italian infantry are north-east of Benghazi in a disorganised state.

Rommel's Dilemma

Rommel has the alternative of making a stand at Benghazi, it was stated in London yesterday, or retreating to the west towards Tripoli.

Our patrols are now more than sixty miles beyond Derna, which the Axis evacuated.

When British and Indian troops entered Derna they found sixty British wounded left behind in the Italian hospital, it was revealed yesterday.

The men said the Italians had made a hurried withdrawal, leaving only a few gendarmes.

ITALIAN VICTORY CLAIM

Rome claimed a "naval victory" yesterday, reporting that a British destroyer was sunk and several warships damaged in action with the Italian Fleet in the Gulf of Sirte (Libya).

MORE TOWNS CAPTURED BY RUSSIANS

RUSSIAN forces, relentlessly rolling back from Moscow the Nazi panzer divisions, last night claimed the capture of three more towns which puts back in Russian hands the direct rail line between Leningrad and Moscow.

The Russian war communique stated that Kadibna, in the Tula sector, Budogosk, south-west of Tikhvin, and Grusino were taken yesterday and vast quantities of arms and ammunition seized.

Moscow radio stated that Plavsk, key base and rail junction on the Tula-Orel highway, from where reserves were drawn by the Germans for onslaughts on the capital, has been occupied by Soviet troops.

Stalin, who celebrated his 62nd birthday yesterday, can look with satisfaction on the achievements of his army, which has recaptured 1,500 cities, towns and villages within the last twenty-five days.

Volkhov Battle

The Nazis, thrown back forty-five miles from Tikhvin, where they tried to entrench, are fighting stubbornly at a number of points, particularly in the Volkhov area.

The Nazis are retreating south and south-west, while Russians, under General Vlasov, who reoccupied Volokolamsk are pursuing the enemy.

Four Nazi divisions were routed when Volokolamsk fell.

In an effort to improve the impression created at home by reverses on all other sectors the Nazis have launched an offensive against Sebastopol.

German efforts to break through the defences were repulsed.

RAIDERS DRIVEN OFF

A.A. guns in the Thames Estuary opened up with a barrage early last night and drove off Nazi raiders.

The activity was comparatively brief and there were no reports of any bombs.

"Bully" in your ration

CORNED beef will form part of your meat ration from today week.

As from next Monday, the meat ration will remain at 1s. 2d. worth a week—but butchers will receive one-seventh of their allowance as canned corned beef.

Customers, therefore, must not expect to have more than 1s. worth of butcher's meat per adult ration book and half that amount for each child's ration book.

The balance will be made up from canned corned beef, which is not included in the points rationing scheme.

The Ministry of Food says this step has been taken to conserve meat stocks in cold store.

Daily Mirror

No. 11,867 — **ONE PENNY**

Registered at the G.P.O. as a Newspaper.

100,000 JAPANESE TROOPS LAND IN PHILIPPINES

Two Leningrad forces join up

TWO Russian forces south-east of Leningrad have joined up.

The forces are those under General Fedyuninsky, which have captured Volbokalo, fifty miles south-east of Leningrad, and General Meretskov, which re-occupied Tikhvin, fifty-miles west of Volbokalo.

General Fedyuninsky's troops, said Leningrad radio, have destroyed the 11th and 291st German Infantry Divisions and also two regiments of the 264th Division.

"The enemy is being cut off from Volkhov" (sixty-five miles south-west of Tikhvin), it was added.

The Russian night communique said that on several sectors of the Western, Kalinin, Leningrad and South-Western fronts Russian troops continued to advance and occupied a number of populated places after violent battles.

While the Russian advance goes on, there are indications that German resistance on the Moscow front is stiffening.

Following the recapture of Volokolamsk, west of Moscow, German rearguards, in prepared positions, are contesting every inch of ground.

One Day—100 Villages

But the Russians are confident. "The Battle of Moscow has been won." declares the capital's radio.

South-west of Tula, on the southern end of the Moscow front, the Russians are also meeting strong rearguard resistance from fortified positions.

In Marshal Timoshenko's ceaseless drive to clear the Nazis from Donetz basin. 100 villages have been recaptured.

On the south-western front, Major Popov's troops liberated another 100 villages in one day

VOROSHILOV FACES JAPS?

Marshal Voroshilov has been appointed Commander-in-Chief of the Russian Army in the Far East, says Berlin.

HITLER SACKS ANOTHER

HITLER has sacked another of his Army chiefs —Field-Marshal von Bock, Commander on the Moscow front.

The Germans say he is so "ill that he is unable to maintain his command."

"No successor to Von Bock has been mentioned." The Berlin correspondent of a Stockholm newspaper reported this news yesterday.

Reports of this fresh sacking came shortly after Hitler had bade personal farewell to Field Marshal von Brauchitsch.

"It is now apparent that Brauchitsch's dismissal was definite, and that he will not be entrusted with any new duties in the leadership of the German Army," says the Berlin correspondent of the Stockholm newspaper *Aftonbladet.*

News of Brauchitsch's dismissal, he says, came as a bolt from the blue to Berliners.

MARTINIQUE PACT WITH U.S.

Mr. Cordell Hull, U.S. Secretary of State, said yesterday that agreement had been reached with the French authorities of Martinique, assuring the neutralisation of that strategic Caribbean island.

Mr. Hull told his Press conference that the status quo would continue, which was interpreted to mean that the islands were in accord with American precautionary measures to prevent Axis seizure.

'JAPAN EXPECTS AXIS HELP'

N.B.C. (New York) radio quoted the Japanese newspaper *Nichi Nichi Shimbun* as stating that Japan expects help from the Axis partners if the Japanese operations in the Far East are to be carried out successfully.

THE biggest sea-borne invasion of all time was staged by the Japanese in the Philippines yesterday.

They landed an expeditionary force of between 80,000 and 100,000 men at different parts of Luzon, an island almost the size of England.

Fierce fighting is raging, the defenders consisting of well-equipped American and Filipino troops under the command of Major-General Wainwright, who knows the territory well.

Eighty transports conveyed the vast invasion force. Warships and air squadrons covered the landing operations.

Ohio radio reported last night that many of the Japanese transports have been sunk.

American heavy guns are also said to have sunk some enemy destroyers.

The invaders' main landing point was Lingayen Gulf, on the west of Luzon, 150 miles north of Manila.

Many Barges Used

A large number of 150-man barges entered the gulf and landed near Agoo.

At one point where the Japanese tried to land forces under the guns of their destroyers, they were driven off by American heavy batteries, which repulsed a large fleet of Japanese ships.

A big land, sea and air battle is thought to be imminent. The U.S. Asiatic Fleet, which has been operating in Philippine waters, is believed to be intact and ready to contest any major operations.

An announcement from General MacArthur's headquarters at Manila said that the Japanese after landing in the Lingayen Gulf, were pushing their attack.

Later it was stated that defenders were holding their own in heavy fighting.

The Supreme Test

During the landings, Japanese warplanes bombed Nichols Field, near Manila, while a second group attacked Cavite, south of Manila.

Disquieting news from Manila indicates that the Japanese have been able to develop substantial airfields at three beachheads in Luzon Island.

Washington, which estimated the Japanese invasion force at a minimum of 80,000 saw in this a bid by Japan for a knock-out blow at the very defences of the Archipelago.

"The supreme test has come," it was stated.

The massing of a huge fleet of eighty transports and supply ships meant only one thing to Washington—that Japan is in great haste to crush General MacArthur's resistance in the Philippines regardless of cost.

Our tanks in Russia surprised the Huns

A large number of Valentine and Waltzing Matilda tanks have been taking part in the Russian push

This was revealed by the Ministry of Supply last night.

The presence of British tanks came as a surprise to the Germans, who did not believe that the promises made to Stalin would be so quickly fulfilled.

AID FOR THE FREED

The committee of the Communist Party of the Moscow district have decided on measures to give aid to the civilian population in territory freed from Nazi occupation

---

Luzon Island, biggest of the Philippine group, contains 40,000 square miles; England 50,000. Lingayen Gulf, main Japanese landing point, is seen on the west coast.

Hong Kong: "We fight to the finish"

SIR MARK YOUNG, Governor of Hong Kong, will hold out until the end and until he is taken prisoner.

This was announced yesterday by the British Embassy in Chungking, which is in hourly contact by radio with Hong Kong.

A counter-attack threw back the Japs from Wongneichung Gap, a key point, on Friday, says a message from the Governor.

A further message received from the Governor stated that the enemy had been very active all Sunday but was being held.

The Japanese Fleet has joined in the attack, according to one dispatch, which claims that all the environs of Hong Kong have been mastered by naval guns.

British warships which have been anchored off Hong Kong have been completely encircled, and are being progressively destroyed, it said.

MALAYA

Last night's communique stated: "Nothing to report from the Northern Front."

Air activity over Kuala Lumpur (Central Malaya) is believed to have resulted in three enemy planes being brought down. We lost three fighters.

During offensive air patrols over the northern areas, bombers destroyed six Japanese planes.

In Perak our forces are now thirty miles south of the border of Wellesley Province. They have inflicted heavy losses on Japanese trying to cross the Perak River on rafts.

Fighting at Kuala Kangsar, thirty miles south of Lenggong, where a Japanese attack was countered on Saturday, was reported in yesterday's midday communique from Singapore.

It said that our troops continue to hold the position.

Dutch co-operation in the defence of Malaya was referred to in the Dutch East Indies communique, which said that aircraft of the Dutch East Indies Army have taken part in operations over Malaya.

BURMA

Aerodromes in Eastern Thailand which the Japanese are using for attacks on Burma have been raided for the first time by the R.A.F., who from tree-top height machine-gunned and destroyed a number of enemy machines on the ground and also destroyed a petrol dump. All our machines returned.

SARAWAK

British troops are still holding out, and are inflicting heavy losses on the Japanese, says Batavia (Dutch East Indies) radio.

F.D.R.'S WAR PLAN TALKS WITH ALLIES

IN conference with Soviet, Chinese and Dutch Ambassadors, President Roosevelt yesterday took preliminary steps in "joint planning for unity of action" by countries fighting the Axis.

The President had arranged separate talks with M. Litvinoff, Soviet Ambassador, M. Hu-Shih, Chinese Ambassador, and M. Loudon, Netherlands Minister. He saw Lord Halifax, British Ambassador, on Sunday.

M. Litvinoff spent half an hour with the President at the White House. He left without making any comment.

White House officials said the conferences were in accord with the announcement that Britain and the United States had taken steps towards the co-ordination of the war effort, and that joint planning for unity of action would be extended to Russia, China, the Netherlands and other Governments in the common cause.— Associated Press.

Berlin claims British aircraft carrier sunk

A British aircraft-carrier has been sunk, a special German High Command communique yesterday claimed, The message stated :—

"A U-boat operating in the Atlantic under the command of Captain Bigalk has torpedoed a British aircraft-carrier.

"The ship has sunk."

HEALTHY GAINS *for*

YOUR BABY

Deep, peaceful, unbroken sleep is vital to infant growth. When baby is cross, fretful, sleepless, those weekly ounces of gain do not appear on the scales. Mother, take care! Look to baby's digestion.

The minute you see baby feverish, constipated, suffering with wind, just give a little 'Milk of Magnesia' brand antacid. Soon comes pleasant relief. 'Milk of Magnesia' safely and surely sweetens the sour little stomach, regulates the tiny bowels, soothes and calms baby. And with sourness and sickness gone, with bowel movements regular you are overjoyed to see restful, healthy sleep again. Baby makes those steady gains in weight that are the delight of every Mother. Doctors and Nurses everywhere recommend 'Milk of Magnesia' as a safe, ideal antacid and gentle laxative for babies Be careful, Mother, remember to ask for 'MILK of Magnesia,' which is the registered trade mark of Phillips' preparation of Magnesia. Prices, 1/5 and 2/10 *(including Purchase Tax).* You can get it everywhere.—(Advt.)

Daily Mirror

DEC 29

No. 11,870   ONE PENNY

Registered at the G.P.O. as a Newspaper.

Our troops raid Norway

A COMBINED force of the Navy, Army and R.A.F. carried out a raid on the Norwegian coast on Saturday, mainly against enemy shipping.

"The operation was entirely successful in all respects and all our ships returned fit for immediate service," said an Admiralty communique last night.

The Admiralty described the operation as a "small-scale raid."

There have been a number of British expeditions against German occupied territory, but this is the first time it has been officially announced that the three Services collaborated.

Earlier the German news agency announced that British warships landed shock troops on various parts of the Norwegian coast.

The raids, it was stated took place "on small islands and peninsulas" remote from the central point of the coastal defences.

"After intervention by German aircraft and coastal patrols, the enemy withdrew his shock troops to the ships," the agency added.

Claim Destroyer Sunk

Yesterday's German communique also referred to these attacks.

"On December 27, British naval forces attempted to raid two remote points on the Norwegian coast.

"After short, fierce fighting with local defence units of the German Army and Navy, the British landing party was driven off and withdrew to its ships.

"German bombers sank one destroyer and damaged a cruiser and another destroyer out of the fleeing naval formation. Ten enemy bombers were also shot down."

Eden

Stalin

Molotov

Nye

EDEN PLANS WAR MOVES WITH STALIN IN MOSCOW

VITAL war talks in Moscow between Mr. Anthony Eden, British Foreign Minister, and Comrades Stalin and Molotov, were announced yesterday while the conferences between Mr. Churchill and Mr. Roosevelt continued in Washington.

Mr. Eden, who was accompanied by Lieutenant-General Nye, new ex-ranker vice-chief of the British Imperial Staff, also met high military representatives of General Chiang Kai Shek. [Brussels radio, quoting a Japanese newspaper, stated that Mr. Eden arrived yesterday in Chunking, to meet Chiang Kai Shek.]

Thus in the two capitals, 5,000 miles apart, leaders of the four great anti-Axis Powers reached agreement on plans which will have decisive effects in the world war.

The Moscow conference was planned before the Japanese attack on the United States.

Mr. Eden left London for Moscow before Japan entered the war.

"Both parties," stated an Anglo-Soviet communique issued last night, "are convinced that the Moscow conversations constitute a new important forward step towards closer collaboration between the U.S.S.R and Great Britain."

Views were exchanged on post-war organisations of peace and security.

"These provided much important and useful material which will facilitate a future elaboration of concrete proposals on this subject." the communique said.

"Utter Defeat of Huns"

"The conversations, which took place in a friendly atmosphere, showed identity of views of both parties on all questions relating to the conduct of the war and especially with regard to the necessity for the utter defeat of Hitlerite Germany and the adoption thereafter of measures to render completely impossible any repetition of German aggression in future."

The Soviet Ambassador in

 Continued on Back Page

DUTCH ISLE INVADED BY AIR

JAPANESE paratroops were dropped yesterday near Medan, on the northeast coast of Sumatra, Dutch East Indies, and a battle is raging outside the town.

The attack was made under cover of a raid by seventeen bombers on Medan Aerodrome.

A more stabilised line in Northern Malaya is apparent from the latest reports reaching Singapore.

British advanced units, backed by artillery, beat off a Japanese attack with "severe loss" on a railway point ten miles north of Ipoh.

Fifteen miles south-west of Ipoh, the British dispersed Japanese patrols near Blanja, strategic ferry crossing on the Peruk River.

Shot Out of Trees

After an enemy bicycle vanguard had been permitted to pass the British position, the defenders opened up, annihilating the main force of Japanese.

In a desperate effort to escape the withering fire, some Japanese climbed trees, where they were methodically picked off by British snipers.

One jungle pigmy tribe is reported to be attacking the Japanese with blow guns and poisoned arrows.

Local hunters are being used to build animal traps, which have sharp spikes under the camouflage.

Japanese raids on Rangoon, Burma capital, have caused more than 600 casualties.

The occupation of Hong Kong has been completed, according to Japanese Imperial Headquarters.

Jap cruiser in flames

Australian planes sighted a small Japanese cruiser off the Peninsula of Minahassa, on the Island of Celebes, East Indies, and scored direct hits.

The stern of the cruiser was seen in flames, reported the Netherlands news agency, Aneta yesterday.

One Japanese transport was sunk and another damaged by U.S. bombers off Davao, stated yesterday's U.S. communique from Manila.

HITLER SPEECHES ARE JUST PADDING

"For what else are Hitler's speeches good except to pad the frozen bodies of German soldiers?" asks Moscow radio, declaring that old newspapers are being sent to the Russian front as "underclothing."

German radio announces that everybody possessing skis is to hand them over, except men in military training or people of mountain areas.

BRAUCHITSCH DENIAL

It was denied in Dublin yesterday that Field-Marshal von Brauchitsch was on the plane which landed in Waterville, Co. Kerry, on Friday.

Manila lit up—Japs rain bombs

WHILE Manila, the Philippine capital, was lit up to emphasise the American declaration that it was an open city, Japanese planes again raided the city last night.

Heavy damage was done to the University, a newspaper office and an ironworks, said a direct broadcast from Manila, picked up by the Daily Mirror radio station.

Following their attempted justification for the previous savage bombing of Manila, the Japanese broadcast an impudent demand to the Philippine President.

They stated that they would recognise Manila as an open city if the Philippine Army co-operates with the Japanese and ceases all resistance.

Japanese forces have made two landings on the west coast of Luzon Island, about forty miles from Manila, says the German radio.

Apparently referring to the same attack. Rome says that 16,000 Japanese have gained a foothold, and that the island of Alabal has been occupied.

The towns of Tarlal, seventy miles from Manila, on the railway to Lingayen, and Santa Lucia, on the north-west coast of Luzon, are claimed by the Japanese.

Darlan at naval base

Admiral Darlan, Vichy Deputy Premier and Navy Minister, has been spending several days secretly at his home in Toulon, the Mediterranean naval base.

General Nogues, Resident-General for French Morocco, arrived there yesterday from Vichy, after conferences with Petain, says the German Official News Agency.

STRONG FORCES IN DAY RAID ON FRANCE

There was considerable aerial activity over the Channel yesterday afternoon, with strong forces of fighters and bombers flying towards the French coast. No sound of aerial combat could be heard on this side.

The Ministry of Home Security said last night there had been nothing to report over this country during daylight yesterday.

Huns plan big-scale gas war

"I AM afraid the Germans are preparing for the use of poison gas on a big scale."

This warning was given yesterday by Mr. G. H. Earle, U.S. Minister in Sofia, Bulgaria, when he arrived in Istanbul.

He said there was some evidence that the Germans were planning the utter destruction of everything in any Allied or occupied countries they were forced to leave "in the biggest piece of vandalism in history."

He warned that not too much faith should be placed in the possibility of a collapse within Germany.

"With Hitler in command, Germany can no longer be depended on to do the militarily logical thing," said Mr. Earle. "She will strike out wherever the easiest and most spectacular victories can be expected."—Associated Press.

ISLANDS: ALLIED TALKS

There will be talks between General de Gaulle and the interested Allied Governments on the diplomatic questions involved in the occupation of St. Pierre and Miquelon, the islands off Newfoundland, by the Free French, it was officially stated yesterday.

Our troops are now on Soviet soil

British troops from India are now on Russian territory.

Revealing this, Sir Gerald Campbell, British Information Officer at Washington, said it was reported that they were the same troops that played a prominent part in the British occupation of Iran and Iraq. They are in the Caucasus.

Dispatch of troops to Southern Russia may be an intelligent anticipation of Hitler's next big jump.

Many believe this will be an attempt to thrust through Turkey to the Caucasus and Iran, and so imperil the safety of India.

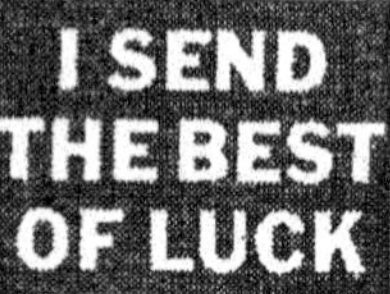

I Have Recommended

YEAST-VITE

To All My Friends When Feeling Below Par

Holbrook, Nov. 11th, 1941.

Dear Sirs,—I have been taking Yeast-Vite tablets and cannot speak too highly of them.

Before taking them I was suffering from indigestion, headaches, also various other aches and pains due to middle age. I now feel quite different and would not be without these valuable tablets.

Wishing you every success in the sale of your wonderful tonic, for which I send the best of luck—I have recommended these tablets to all my friends when feeling below par.

(Sgd.) Miss H. S.

Burton-on-Trent, Nov. 11th, 1941.

Dear Sirs,

I have a patient recuperating from pneumonia; so I gave her a course of Yeast-Vite tablets and they have been a splendid tonic.

(Sgd.) F. G. R., S.R.N.

Yeast-Vite Tonic Tablets bring quick relief from Headaches, Nerves, Lassitude, Depression, Insomnia, Rheumatism, Indigestion, etc. Sold everywhere at 7d., 1/4; 3/3 & 5/4, including purchase tax.

Hundreds of cooks are training

TWO hundred women are to be trained as cooks every six weeks under a new Ministry of Labour scheme. Trainees must be over thirty.

The scheme has been started because of a possible shortage of cooks for service or factory canteens.

Women with or without experience of catering, not suitable for other work of national importance, are asked to volunteer at their local Labour Exchanges.

"The first four weeks of their six weeks' training will be at a domestic school or college," a Ministry of Labour official said yesterday.

"The last two weeks will consist of practical training at a working canteen."

The wage for the first month of training will be 33s. a week with free mid-day meals.

For the last two weeks they will get 38s. a week with no free meals.

If women live more than two miles from the training centres, the Ministry will pay their travelling expenses, find billets, pay lodging allowances and fares for those who have to leave home to take up training.